The Integration of the Mediterranean Neighbours into the EU Internal Market

The Integration of the Mediterranean Neighbours into the EU Internal Market

by

Karolien Pieters

T.M.C.Asser press

ISBN 978-90-6704-313-7

SUMMARY OF CONTENTS

FOREWORD

In Antiquity, the Mediterranean world was a common space of classical civilization. The Romans referred to the Mediterranean Sea as *mare nostrum,* or 'our sea'. In their minds, it did not so much geographically separate the northern and southern shores, but rather bound people and cultures together. It would not have struck them as remarkable that the greatest book inspired by the Sac of Rome in 410 was written by a bishop from the present-day Algeria, St. Augustine.

Today, the gentle waves of the Mediterranean Sea no longer roll on the shores of one civilization. Centuries of divergent historic evolutions have resulted in a clearer conceptual demarcation of Europe on the northern shore and Africa on the southern one, with Asia starting at the eastern and northern shore. In the minds of some people, the Sea has even become a border – protection for some, an obstacle for others.

However, the geographical proximity is obviously still there. That is why it is important to stress the special relationship which continues to exist between the countries on the northern shore – the large majority of which is now member of the European Union – with the countries on the southern and eastern shores, culturally, commercially and politically.

This special relationship has always been acknowledged by the European Union and its forerunners. The EEC Treaty of 1957 signed in Rome (*ancora*!) already mentioned the importance of a relationship between the six founding Member States and the Mediterranean area. Closer ties were formalised with the Barcelona Process in 1995 and with the European Neighbourhood Policy in 2004. In recent years, the EU has taken measures to stimulate the Euro-Med relationship that led to the creation of the Union for the Mediterranean during the Paris Summit in July 2008.

The Euro-Med relationship has evolved rapidly over the last twenty years. While many important steps towards developing stronger ties have been taken, in particular in the area of trade, there is still a long road ahead in improving cooperation between the two flanks of the Mediterranean Sea. The political and economic differences between the two sides are considerable – and, in many respects, unfortunately so. However, the EU and the Mediterranean countries face important common challenges. To address those challenges, including illegal immigration and the financial crisis, both sides have stepped up their efforts to strengthen cooperation.

This study by Ms. Karolien Pieters focuses on one specific and crucial component of the developing Euro-Med relationship. It deals with the evolving participation of the Mediterranean neighbours in the EU internal market for goods, services, capital and persons. While the protection of the integrity of this internal market is vital for the Union, it is prepared to allow Mediterranean countries to participate in it. The free movement of goods should improve economic stability in the Mediterranean region, the free movement of capital ought to attract European investors to the region and the facilitation of the movement of persons might increase employment opportunities.

The crucial idea behind this book is that the EU could contribute to the development of an economically stable Mediterranean area by giving the Mediterranean partners a stake in the EU's internal market. Strengthened trade and economic ties should lead to an increase in employment and investment opportunities on both sides of the Mediterranean. Moreover, focusing on economic issues and improving commercial cooperation could help to bring forward the establishment of peace and security in the region. Strengthened trade and economic ties could also contribute to resolving old conflicts such as the Israeli-Palestinian conflict, which continue to threaten regional stability. Tensions in the region cannot be used as an excuse to slow down this cooperation. Conversely, this focus should trigger the development of stronger bonds across the Mediterranean. The Union would benefit considerably from stability and prosperity at its southern border, not least in terms of access to a potentially very important market.

The book discusses the unique nature of the EU internal market. It analyses each step towards a closer integration of the Mediterranean neighbours into the internal market and examines the results. It provides a comprehensive and detailed assessment of instruments used jointly by the EU and the Mediterranean countries to attain their integration goal.

While this integration process is far from complete, important steps have already been taken, for example in the field of the integration of the internal market for goods. In other areas, such as integration into the internal market for services, more work remains to be done. Mediterranean partners which are willing to benefit from participation in the EU internal market are required to take important further steps that will contribute to a fluent exchange of goods, services, capital and persons. Those steps will ultimately serve the purpose of freedom and prosperity.

A full integration of the Mediterranean countries in the EU internal market is currently not on the cards. There are too many political and economic obstacles for this to be a short-term policy objective. However, as Ms Pieters' study shows, the remarkable and significant steps toward economic integration which have been taken have proven to benefit people on both sides of the *Mare Nostrum*.

July 2010

Herman Van Rompuy
President of the European Counil

ACKNOWLEDGMENTS

I wish to express my sincerest gratitude to Professor Ramses Wessel of the University of Twente for his able guidance and constructive suggestions which helped me in completing this book.

I dedicate this book to Frederick and our daughters Amélie and Alexia.

The Hague, July 2010

TABLE OF CONTENTS

Chapter III
Multilateral instruments for integration of the Mediterranean countries into the EU internal market under the EMP and ENP 58

LIST OF TABLES

LIST OF ABBREVIATIONS

AA	Association Agreement
ACAA	Agreement of Conformity Assessment and Acceptance
AMU	Arab Maghreb Union
AP	Action Plan
CAP	Common Agricultural Policy
CARDS	Community Assistance for Reconstruction, Development and Stability in the Balkans
CCP	Common Commercial Policy
CEN	Comité Européen de Normalisation (European Committee for Standardisation)
CENELEC	Comité Européen de Normalisation Electrotechnique (European Committee for Electrotechnical Standardisation)
CFSP	Common Foreign and Security Policy
CS	Common Strategy
CSDP	Common Security and Defence Policy
DFTA	Deep Free Trade Agreement
EC	European Community
ECA	Egyptian Competition Authority
ECJ	European Court of Justice
ECOSOC	European Economic and Social Committee
ECU	European Currency Unit
EEA	European Economic Area
EEC	European Economic Community
EFTA	European Free Trade Area
EIB	European Investment Bank
EMDB	Euro-Mediterranean Development Bank
EMEA	Euro-Mediterranean Economic Area
EMP	Euro-Mediterranean Partnership
EMPA	European Mediterranean Parliamentary Assembly
ENP	European Neighbourhood Policy
ENPI	European Neighbourhood and Partnership Instrument
EP	European Parliament
ESDP	European Security and Defence Policy
ESP	European Strategic Partnership
ESS	European Security Strategy
ETSI	European Telecommunications Standardisation Institute
EU	European Union
FEMIP	Facility for Euro-Mediterranean Investment and Partnership

FEMISE	Forum Euro-Méediterranéen des Instituts de Sciences Economiques
FTA	Free Trade Agreement
GAERC	General Affairs and External Relations Council
GAFTA	Greater Arab Free Trade Area
GATS	General Agreement on Trade in Services
GATT	General Agreement on Tariffs and Trade
GCC	Gulf Cooperation Council
GDP	Gross Domestic Product
GLP	Good Laboratory Practices
GMP	Global Mediterranean Policy
ILO	International Labour Organisation
IMF	International Monetary Fund
JHA	Justice and Home Affairs
MFN	Most Favoured Nation
MNMC	Mediterranean Non-Member Country
MP	Member of Parliament
MRA	Mutual Recognition Agreement
NIP	National Indicative Programme
NIS	National Institute for Statistics
NMP	New Mediterranean Policy
NPP	New Partnership Perspective
OECD	Organisation for Economic and Cooperation Development
OSCE	Organisation for Security and Cooperation
PA	Palestinian Authority
PHARE	Poland and Hungary: Assistance for Restructuring their Economies
PJC	Police and Justice Cooperation
PLO	Palestine Liberation Organisation
PMA	Palestinian Monetary Authority
SEA	Single European Act
SPS	Sanitary and Phyto-Sanitary Products
TEU	Treaty of the European Union
TFEU	Treaty on the Functioning of the European Union
TRIPs	Trade-Related aspects of Intellectual Property rights
UM	Union for the Mediterranean region
UN	United Nations
UNESCWA	United Nations Economic and Social Commission for Western Asia
UNRWA	United Nations Relief and Works Agency
WMD	Weapons of Mass Destruction
WTO	World Trade Organisation

Chapter I
General introduction

1. The Mediterranean countries and the EU internal market

The Mediterranean countries and Europe have a long-standing relationship, with mutual interests and interdependence. Long before the European Economic Community (EEC) existed, Europe and the Mediterranean region had close links dating back to the days of the Roman Empire, when the *Mare Nostrum* was one functional and administrative unit. In the 19th and early 20th centuries, European countries were interested in the Mediterranean countries due to their position at the crossroads of three continents, where much world trade was conducted.[1] This interest resulted in the colonialisation of many Mediterranean countries by some European countries: Algeria, Tunisia and Syria were occupied by France; Egypt, Cyprus, Gibraltar, Malta and Palestine by Britain, and Libya by Italy.

Besides these historical links, the Mediterranean region and Europe are economically linked. The Mediterranean countries have always been economically and financially interested in Europe. Europe is a source of technical and financial support and a good relationship with Europe is of the highest importance for their prospects of economic development. The Mediterranean region has been interested in gaining benefits from the European integration process since its inception in 1957. Since the formal realisation of the European Union (EU) internal market in 1993, the Mediterranean countries have wished to integrate into the EU internal market of goods, services, capital and persons for many reasons. They wish to integrate into the EU internal market for goods because they have relatively small markets. As a result, their export is the key element for economic development. The EU is the main trading partner for almost 50% of imports and exports in the region. Agriculture remains an important sector in many of the Mediterranean countries and the main outlet market for these agricultural products is the EU. The Mediterranean countries also want a stake in the EU internal market of services. Liberalisation of trade in services produces substantial welfare gains, and services account for some 60% of Gross Domestic Product (GDP) in the Mediterranean countries. The Mediterranean countries are also interested in increasing the movement of capital from and towards the EU to attract more foreign investment to their region. For all Mediterranean partners it is also extremely important that Mediter-

[1] R.H. Ginsberg, 'The European Community and the Mediterranean', in J. Lodge, ed., *Institutions and Policies of the European Community* (London, Frances Pinter 1994) pp. 154-160.

ranean nationals are able to integrate into the EU internal market for persons.[2] The EU already employs the majority of their migrant workers.

For Europe, the Mediterranean countries have always been economically important since they are large suppliers of natural resources, such as gas and petroleum, to the European market.[3] The Mediterranean countries have also become an essential outlet for European exports. Therefore, the EU wants to develop economic stability in the Mediterranean region since this would create attractive export possibilities for the EU. Many of the Mediterranean countries have started a process to open their economy under the impulse of the EU. Tunisia, for example, launched efforts towards promoting a growth strategy based on exports and investments as early as in 1986. Syria, on the contrary, has shown little interest in developing a competitive private sector and integration into international trade. An economic reform orientation became more perceptible with the installation of the new Syrian President, Bashar Al-Assad, in 2000. Recently, the EU has been greatly interested in increasing migratory flows from the Mediterranean countries, seeing that it will soon be confronted with a decline in its working population because of the European demographic evolution. In Europe, the birth rate is low and there are more elderly people. Between 2010 and 2030, the EU could lose 20.8 million workers. This will be detrimental to the European economy and will result in a loss of European competitiveness. An increase in migratory flows from the Mediterranean countries could mitigate these economic problems.[4] The Mediterranean area has always been important for Europe for reasons of security and strategy as well. The EU is interested in providing peace on its southern flanks. A stable and secure Mediterranean region is in the best interest of Europe, but so far the situation in the region has remained unstable and sometimes even volatile. Conflicts in the Mediterranean region have direct consequences for political and social stability in the EU. Instability in the Mediterranean region will, for example, lead to mass migration, fundamentalist extremism, terrorism, drugs and organised crime, which is harmful to both the area itself and to the EU. The EU also fears the spill-over effect of national and interregional conflicts in the Mediterranean region, the main security threat of which is the Israeli-Palestinian conflict.[5] Libya's international isolation and its refusal to join the Euro-Mediterranean Partnership (EMP) is an important weakness in the security relations between the Mediterra-

---

[2] The Commission has defined 'integration' as a two-way process based on mutual rights and corresponding obligations of legally resident third-country nationals and the host society which provides for full participation of the immigrant, see the Communication of the Commission of 3 June 2003 on immigration, integration and employment, COM (2003) 336 final, pp. 17-18.

[3] T. Sadeh, 'The Economic Desirability of the Middle Eastern Monetary Cooperation', 20 *The World Economy* (1997) pp. 809-827.

[4] Communication from the Commission of 16 March 2005, Green Paper 'Confronting Demographic Change: A New Solidarity between the Generations', COM (2005) 94 final, p. 4; 'Femise Report on the Euro-Mediterranean Partnership 2006. Analysis and Proposals of the Euro-Mediterranean Forum of Economic Institutes', by coordinators S. Radwan and J.-L. Reiffers, September 2006, pp. 50-51.

[5] For more information, see R. Aliboni, 'The Geopolitical Implications of the European Neighbourhood Policy', 10 *European Foreign Affairs Review (EFAR)* (2005) pp. 1-16.

nean region and the EU. However, Libya has expressed its desire to join the EMP, but no agreements have been concluded yet. The EU interest also has a strategic dimension. The Mediterranean area includes some militarily and commercially important strategic points such as the Suez Canal and the Straits of Gibraltar.[6]

This high level of Euro-Mediterranean interdependence and mutual interests resulted in some Euro-Mediterranean integration efforts in the past. The EEC was willing to confer the Mediterranean countries some small benefits of its common market and responded to requests of the Mediterranean countries by taking little steps of limited economic significance. In the early 1960s, the EEC started concluding trade agreements with almost all Mediterranean countries. These agreements were negotiated at different stages in the evolution of the European integration process and consequently resulted in many different agreements with the Mediterranean countries. The EU is the world's leading and most open trading power, moreover in 1987, Jacques Delors argued that it must go further on the road to helping developing countries even when this road would be difficult and raise many questions:[7]

> 'How are we to explain to our farmers that they must adapt to a world situation in which the excess of supply over demand is structural in character, if other agricultural powers are not making the same effort? (...) How are we to state effectively the case for better relations between the North and South if we haggle endlessly over a few tens of millions of ECU in trade advantages or aids for countries suffering the direst poverty? One thing we have got to realise is this. There will be no tangible progress in European integration if the Community does not speak clearly to the outside world, with strength, courage and magnanimity. In fact, this is an aspect of Community life which is all too often neglected or even ignored. Let there be no mistake about it, the Community will prove its mettle, also, in the way it resists, now and in the future, the wrong kind of pressure, but yields to those in real need.'

After the formal completion of the EU internal market on 1 January 1993, its external dimension gained importance. The EU had time to focus on the countries behind the borders of its internal market. To the south of Europe, this resulted in the famous Barcelona Process of 1995. The Euro-Mediterranean integration process was sped up as EU was confronted with the globalisation process.[8] The world trading system was not longer the preserve of the OECD countries; China,

---

[6] F.J. Raya, 'A Review of the Barcelona Conference and a Summary of Policy Objectives', in C. Cosgrove-Sacks and G. Scappucci, eds., *The EU and Developing Countries: The Challenges of Globalization* (Great Britain, Macmillan Press Ltd. 1999) pp. 193-205.

[7] 'The Single Act: A New Frontier for Europe', COM (87) 100 final, p. 10.

[8] According to the definition of the UNESCWA, economic globalisation is the reduction of barriers between national borders in order to facilitate the flow of goods, capital, services and labour. The first important globalisation process took place in the 19th century. This century was characterised by a period of rapid international trade growth and investments among imperial powers and their colonies as well as the US. This first globalisation process declined at the start of World War I in 1914 and collapsed at the end of the 1920s due to the Great Depression. The globalisation process faced by the EU is the second globalisation process, which started after World War II and was reinforced, around 2000, with rising trade powers such as China.

Brazil, Russia and India also played an important role in world trade.[9] The EU needed to redesign the external dimension of the EU internal market to be able to compete in a changing world. The EU wanted to export its internal market rules, since the main problem it faced was constituted by the high barriers against EU export in world trade.[10] The EU wanted to obtain better access to foreign markets: fewer non-tariff barriers to European exports and investment, fewer export taxes and less restriction on access to resources such as energy and primary raw materials. It moreover wanted to further strengthen the presence of European companies in third countries through permanent establishment and to further liberalise trade in services through the protection of competition and intellectual property rights. In 1997, the Commission drafted an Action Plan for the EU internal market, in which the Commission also focused on the approximation of systems and rules in the Euro-Mediterranean area.[11] In 1999, the Commission called the final strategic objective of the EU internal market 'the exploitation of the internal market in a changing world.' The internal market principles in trade agreements with the Mediterranean countries acquired greater importance.[12] In 2003, the EU offered the Mediterranean countries 'a stake in the EU internal market' under the ENP: the Mediterranean countries not only obtained benefits from the EU integration process, but were offered integration into the EU internal market.

In conclusion, it can be stated that the Mediterranean countries have been interested in gaining benefits from the European integration process and its common market already since its inception. The EU has been eager to export its EU internal market rules to the Mediterranean countries since it has been confronted with a more globalised world with new trading powers. To what extent this Euro-Med integration process has been successful has not yet been analysed and will be the subject of this book.

2. A successful EU integration process

In Rome in 1957, France, Germany, Italy and the Benelux countries signed the EEC Treaty. One of the aims of this Treaty was to achieve integration between

[9] The OECD is the Organisation for Economic and Cooperation and Development established in 1961 in Paris and has 30 members: Australia, Austria, Belgium, Canada, Czech Republic, Denmark, Finland, France, Germany, Greece, Hungary, Iceland, Ireland, Italy, Japan, Korea, Luxembourg, Mexico, the Netherlands, New Zealand, Norway, Poland, Portugal, Slovak Republic, Spain, Sweden, Switzerland, Turkey, the United Kingdom and the United States.

[10] Commission Staff Working Document of 4 October 2006, Annex to the Communication from the Commission to the Council, the European Parliament, the European Economic and Social Committee and the Committee of the Regions, 'Global Europe: Competing the World', COM (2006) 1230, and the Communication from the Commission to the European Parliament, the Council, the European Economic and Social Committee and the Committee of the Regions of 18 April 2007, 'Global Europe: A Stronger Partnership to Deliver Market Access for European Exporters', COM (2007) 183 final.

[11] Communication from the Commission to the European Council and the Council of 6 May 1997, 'Draft Action Plan for a Single Market', COM (1997) 184 final, p. 13.

[12] Communication from the Commission to the European Parliament and the Commission of 24 November 1999, 'The Strategy for Europe's Internal Market', COM (1999) 624 final, pp. 18-20.

these six countries with a view to economic growth. The EEC Treaty provided for integration through the establishment of a common market, a customs union and common policies. Article 2 of the EEC Treaty specified that: 'The Community shall have as its task, by establishing a common market and progressively approximating the economic policies of Member States, to promote throughout the Community a harmonious development of economic activities, a continuous and balanced expansion, an increase in stability, an accelerated raising of the standard of living and closer relations between the states belonging to it.' This common market had to be founded on four freedoms, namely the free movement of goods, services, capital and persons and be progressively established during a transitional period of 12 years.

The EEC did not succeed in establishing the common market by the end of the transitional period on 31 December 1969 due to political sensitivities in creating a right of establishment and technical problems relating to the realisation of the free movement of capital. The accession of new Member States (Denmark, Ireland and the United Kingdom) in 1973 and the recession were also detrimental to the realisation of the common market.[13] In the early 1980s, progress towards a common market was almost brought to a halt due to inflexible national authorities and the inability to reach unanimous decisions to work towards unification of the markets. This led to an unsatisfactory economic and social situation in Europe and too much discontent among business people since free trade between the Member States was lacking. In 1982, the European Council in Copenhagen convinced the Commission that efforts should be made to strengthen and reinforce the common market.[14]

Therefore, on 14 June 1985, the Commission published a comprehensive White Paper in which it presented its ideas for the completion of the internal market by the year 1992 to the European Council.[15] This White Paper was not intended to cover every possible integration issue of the economies of the Member States. It focused on measures which were directly necessary to achieve a single integrated market embracing 320 million people by 1992.[16] The Commission wished to create a single integrated internal market free of restrictions on the movement of goods; to abolish obstacles to the free movement of persons, services and capital; to institute a system ensuring that competition in the common market was not distorted; and to achieve approximation of laws as required for the proper functioning of the common market.[17] To meet the deadline of 1992, it was necessary that decisions be taken by a majority vote in the EEC Council of Ministers instead of by unanimity. In 1986, the EEC adopted the Single European Act (SEA) which made it possible for certain necessary decisions to be taken by a majority vote in the Council.[18] The goal was to remove remaining barriers between Member States and increase

[13] K. Lenaerts and P. Van Nuffel, *Europees Recht in Hoofdlijnen* (Antwerpen/Apeldoorn, Maklu 2003), no. 133-134.

[14] *Bull.* EC. 12-1982, point. 1.2.3.

[15] 'Completing the Internal Market', White Paper from the Commission to the European Council (Milan, 28-29 June 1985), COM (85) 310 final, 14 June 1985.

[16] Recital 17 of the White Paper.

[17] Recital 4 of the White Paper.

[18] Single Act of 28 February 1986, *OJ* 1987 L 169.

harmonisation through a qualified majority vote. The SEA gave new impetus to European integration and to the formal completion of the internal market. Article 8A clearly defined the objective of the SEA, i.e., to progressively establish the internal market over a period expiring on 31 December 1992. The internal market was defined as 'an area without internal frontiers in which the free movement of goods, persons, services and capital is ensured in accordance with the provisions of this Treaty.' The SEA provided for a successful transformation of the common market into a single or internal market on 1 January 1993, founded on the free movement of goods, services, capital and persons. The internal market did not replace the common market. The internal market only focuses on the free movement of goods, services, capital and persons and can be considered as the core part of the common market which involves a broader range of policies such as competition issues, transport, agricultural policy etc.

3. The basic principles of the EU internal market

In the Treaty on the Functioning of the European Union (TFEU), the EU internal market is defined as an area without internal frontiers in which the free movement of goods, services, capital and persons is ensured, in accordance with the relevant provisions of the treaties.[19] These four freedoms are discussed below in order to be able to explain the integration of the Mediterranean countries in the EU internal market later on.

3.1 The free movement of goods

The free movement of goods between the Member States is one of the cornerstones of the EU internal market. The principle of free movement of goods is laid down in the TFEU, mainly in Articles 34, 35 and 36. Articles 34 and 35 prohibit quantitative restrictions on imports, exports or goods in transit and all measures having equivalent effect between the Member States. The ECJ clarified the concept of 'quantitative restrictions and measures having equivalent effect' in its famous *Dassonville* case: 'all trading rules enacted by Member States which are capable of hindering, directly or indirectly, actually or potentially, intra-Community trade are to be considered as measures having an effect equivalent to quantitative restrictions.'[20]

However, restrictions on the free movement of goods are possible. Article 36 provides for limited exceptions and stipulates that Member States may restrict the free movement of goods in exceptional cases. Restrictions may be justified on grounds of public morality, public policy or public security, the protection of health and life of humans, animals or plants, or the protection of industrial and commercial property, as well as other mandatory requirements recognised by the

[19] Art. 26 TFEU.

[20] Case 8/74, *Procureur du Roi* v *Benoît and Gustave Dassonville* [1974] *ECR* 837.

ECJ. Such prohibitions must not, however, amount to arbitrary discrimination or a disguised restriction on trade between Member States.

The free movement of goods entails the risks of allowing products on the national market of a Member State. These risks differ by product sector: allowing pharmaceuticals, for example, presents higher risks than allowing pasta. In order to minimise risks, the EU introduced harmonisation legislation containing technical regulations, in particular for high-risk products. Lower-risk sectors have not, in general, been the subject of legislation at European level. Trade in this 'non-harmonised' sector relies on the 'mutual recognition' principle. The 'mutual recognition' principle emerged from the *Cassis de Dijon* case of the ECJ:[21] EU Member States must allow all products from other Member States to their territory if these have been lawfully produced in the exporting Member State. The implementation of this principle was hampered by several problems. The European Parliament and the Council therefore adopted Regulation (EC) No 764/2008.[22] This Regulation aims to strengthen the functioning of the internal market by improving the free movement of goods. It defines the rights and obligations of, on the one hand, national authorities and, on the other hand, enterprises wishing to sell in a Member State products lawfully marketed in another Member State, when the competent authorities intend to take restrictive measures about the product such as the prohibition of the placing on the market of that product or type of product or the modification or additional testing of that product or type of product before it can be placed or kept on the market. The Regulation is in force since 13 May 2009.

The free movement of goods rules and the competition rules in the TFEU present complementary roles in creating an EU internal market in goods. Competition rules encourage companies to provide consumers with goods and services and push down prices. The EU competition rules can be found in Articles 101-102 TFEU: Article 101 prohibits agreements between two or more firms which restrict competition, such as a cartel between competitors which may involve price-fixing or market sharing. Article 102 prohibits the abuse of a dominant position by firms. The Commission is empowered by the TFEU to apply these prohibition rules and enjoys a number of investigative powers to that end (e.g., inspection in business and non-business premises, written requests for information, etc). It may also impose fines on undertakings that violate EU competition rules. Since 1 May 2004, all national competition authorities are also empowered to apply fully the provisions of the TFEU in order to ensure that competition is not distorted or restricted. National courts may also apply these prohibitions so as to protect the individual rights conferred on citizens by the TFEU.[23]

---

21 Case 120/78, *Rewe-Zentral AG* v *Bundesmonopolverwaltung für Branntwein* [1979] *ECR* 649.

22 Regulation (EC) No 764/2008 of the European Parliament and of the Council of 9 July 2008 laying down procedures relating to the application of certain national technical rules to products lawfully marketed in another Member State and repealing Decision No 3052/95/EC, *OJ* L 218/21.

23 Council Regulation (EC) No 1/2003 of 16 December 2002 on the implementation of the rules on competition laid down in Arts. 81 and 82 of the Treaty, *OJ* L 2003 1/1.

3.2 The free movement of services and the right of establishment

The free movement of services and the right of establishment are also essential to the functioning of the EU internal market. Trade in services has become larger than trade in goods. Technological processes and the liberalisation of policies have facilitated trade in services, including those that were untradeable a few decades ago. Services trade has become the engine of world growth.[24] It accounts for between 60 and 70% of economic activity in the EU. The freedom to provide cross-border services is set out in Articles 56 and 57 of the TFEU and enables an economic operator providing services in one Member State to offer services on a temporary basis in another Member State without having to be established there. Services are defined as 'normally provided for remuneration, in so far as they are not governed by the provisions relating to freedom of movement for goods, capital and persons.'

The free movement of services includes the freedom for a service provider and receiver to travel in order to provide/receive services as well as the right not to travel to provide/receive services (for example, involving internet and telephone). The freedom of establishment is laid down in Article 49 of the TFEU and enables an economic operator (whether a person or a company) to carry on an economic activity in a stable and permanent way in one or more Member States. For natural persons, Article 49 provides the right to take up and pursue activities as self-employed persons under the conditions laid down for its own nationals by the law of the country where such establishment is effected. For legal persons, Article 49 includes the right for legal persons to set up and manage companies or firms, and the abolishment of restrictions on the setting-up of agencies, branches or subsidiaries by nationals of any Member State in the territory of another Member State. National regulations of a Member State which refuse to recognise professional qualifications of a particular authority of another EU Member State, obstruct these fundamental freedoms. These obstacles have been overcome by EU rules which guarantee the mutual recognition of professional qualifications between EU Member States. EU Directive 2005/36/EC, which entered into force on 20 October 2007, covers all recognition rules (except for those applicable to lawyers, activities in the field of toxic substances and commercial agents).[25] Member States may only maintain limited restrictions where these are justified by overriding reasons of general interest, for instance, on grounds of public policy, public security or public health, and where they are proportionate. The Services Directive, in force since 28 December 2006, aims to create a legal framework for a wide variety of services ensuring the quick dismantling of remaining barriers, so that both service providers and service recipients benefit more easily from the fundamental freedoms guaran-

[24] G. Hufbauer and S. Stephenson, 'Services Trade: Past Liberalization and Future Challenges', 10/3 *Journal of International Economic Law* (2007) p. 605.

[25] Directive 2005/36/EC of the European Parliament and the Council of 7 September 2005 on the recognition of professional qualifications, *OJ* L 255/22.

teed in Articles 49 and 56 of the Treaty.[26] The Directive takes a selective approach, which takes into account the distinctive features of each type of service.

3.3 The free movement of capital

As regards the free movement of capital in the EU internal market, Article 63 of the TFEU provides the following:

> 'All restrictions on capital movements and payments, both between Member States and between Member States and third countries, are prohibited.'

Directive 88/361/EEC of 24 June 1988 completed the full liberalisation of the freedom of capital movements between the Member States.[27] Full liberalisation of capital movements between Member States has been effective since 1 July 1990.[28] Natural and legal persons enjoy free movement of capital in the EU internal market. Natural persons can carry out operations abroad, such as opening bank accounts, buying shares in foreign companies and purchasing real estate and legal persons can invest in and own other European companies and take an active part in their management. The introduction of the euro has made such capital movements easier.

There are exceptions to the free movement of capital between the Member States. Restrictions between Member States can be found in Article 65 TFEU. Member States can take restrictive measures to prevent major tax evasion and to monitor suspicious transactions, such as the movement of criminal funds or money laundering, and measures which are justified on grounds of public policy or public security. These measures may not constitute a means of arbitrary discrimination or a disguised restriction on the free movement of capital and payments.

3.4 The free movement of persons

The original EC Treaty did not provide for the freedom of movement for all persons: to qualify as a person, the individual had to be a national of a Member State and had to be engaged in an economic activity as a worker (now: Arts. 45-48 TFEU), as a self-employed person (now: Arts. 49-54 TFEU) or as a provider or receiver of services (now: Arts. 56-62 TFEU). Exceptions to the free movement of persons were possible on grounds of public policy, public security and public health and on the ground of employment in the public sector. Since there was no free movement for economically non-active persons within the EU, the EU adopted secondary legislation, for example, through Directive 2004/38/EC on the right to

[26] Directive 2006/123/EC of the European Parliament and the Council of 12 December 2006 on services in the internal market, *OJ* L 376/36.

[27] *OJ* L 178 of 8 July 1988.

[28] For Spain, Greece, Ireland and Portugal there was an extension until 31 December 1992.

move and reside freely within the EU for economically non-active nationals of a Member State, such as students enrolled in vocational training, retired persons and other non-active persons. During the discussions between the EC members at Maastricht at the end of 1991, the concept of 'European citizenship' was launched: every national of an EU Member State received the status of citizen of the EU with specific rights and obligations.

The free movement of persons is based on the principle of non-discrimination on the ground of nationality: migrants enjoy the same treatment as nationals in a comparable situation.[29]

3.4.1 *Free movement of self-employed persons*

Free movement of self-employed persons, service providers and recipients of services is provided under Community law by Directive 2004/38/EC of 29 April 2004 on the right of citizens of the Union and their family members to move and reside freely within the territory of the EU Member States. This Directive ensures the free movement of those who wish to establish themselves in another EU Member State to work as self-employed persons or to provide or receive services there on a temporary basis.

3.4.2 *Free movement of workers*

Freedom of movement for economically active workers (Arts. 45-48) is further regulated in secondary EU legislation: Regulation No 1612/68 on the free movement of workers,[30] Regulation 1251/70 on the right to remain in the territory of a Member State after having been employed in that state and Directive 2004/38/EC on the right of workers and their family members to move and reside freely within the territory of the Member States.[31] Regulation 1612/68 facilitates the movement of workers in the EU and integration into the Union: (1) any national of a Member State has the right to take up an activity as an employed person and to pursue such activity in another Member State; (2) a migrant worker may not be treated differently from national workers in respect of any conditions of employment and work, in particular as regards remuneration, dismissal, and should he become unemployed, reinstatement or re-employment; (3) a migrant worker may not be treated differently from national workers in respect of social and tax advantages. The coordination mechanism for national social security systems, developed on the basis of Regulation 1408/71 of 14 June 1971, is intended not to harmonise but simply to coordinate national social security systems; (4) the migrant should benefit from the same social advantages as national workers. This includes benefits, whether or not linked to a contract of employment, which are granted by virtue of the mere fact of their residence on the national territory and are suitable to facilitate

[29] C. Barnard, *The Substantive Law of the EU: The Four Freedoms* (Oxford, Oxford University Press 2004) p. 231.

[30] *OJ* 1968 Spec. Edn. I-475.

[31] *OJ* L 204 of 4 August 2007, p. 28.

their mobility within the EU. Examples are language rights, death benefits, and the right to be accompanied by unmarried companions; and (5) migrants have access to vocational schools and retraining centres under the same conditions as national workers.

Regulation 1251/70 lays down the right of workers to remain in a Member State after having been employed there, under certain conditions. In three situations, workers have the right to remain in a Member State: (1) retirement, (2) incapacity to work and (3) if they are frontier workers. Family members are entitled to stay in the host Member State in two situations, under certain conditions: (1) the worker is entitled to remain there, or (2) the worker dies during his working life.

3.4.3 *Free movement of economically non-active persons*

Economically non-active persons only have rights to reside and move freely within the Member States under Article 21(1) of the TFEU.[32] Article 21 stipulates the following:

> '1. Every citizen of the Union shall have the right to move and reside freely within the territory of the Member States, subject to the limitations and conditions laid down in this Treaty and by the measures adopted to give it effect.'

These rights have been implemented by Directive No 2004/38/EC, which applies to all citizens of the EU and their family members.

4. Failure of the Mediterranean integration process

While European integration was developing, the Mediterranean countries were plagued by violent conflicts and economic and political instability. Attempts at regional integration between the Mediterranean countries went back to the pre-independence period, but nearly always failed. Recent integration attempts occurred in 1989 when the Treaty founding the Arab Maghreb Union (AMU) was signed by Algeria, Libya, Mauretania, Morocco and Tunisia. The AMU agreement, however, has never been successfully applied. Another attempt was the 1998 Greater Arab Free Trade Area (GAFTA) of the Arab League. All parties to the GAFTA will gradually establish a free trade area which is limited to trade in goods. Trade in services as well as investments are excluded from the scope of the GAFTA, which greatly reduces its positive impact. As a result, non-tariff measures will remain important barriers to integration unless reforms are undertaken.[33] The end result of the many efforts to achieve some kind of Mediterranean integration has been deplorable. On 25 February 2004, a free trade agreement was concluded between

[32] Barnard, *supra* n. 29, p. 232.

[33] A. Galal and B. Hoekman, 'Between Hope and Reality: An Overview of Arab Economic Integration', in A. Galal and B. Hoekman, eds., *Arab Economic Integration: Between Hope and Reality* (Washington D.C., Brookings Institution Press 2003) p. 5.

Jordan, Egypt, Morocco and Tunisia. This agreement, known as the Agadir Declaration, can be considered as the first small step towards economic and social integration in the Mediterranean area.

There are many reasons why the Mediterranean countries never succeeded in establishing regional forms of integration, one of which being the fact that the Mediterranean area is still subject to political instability. Political reforms in the Mediterranean region have fallen behind political reforms in other regions of the world.[34] Classical integration theorists argue that the absence of complementarities between the Mediterranean countries, especially between the five North African countries, is another reason for the failure of Mediterranean integration. They have little to sell to one another and are often in fierce competition with each other.[35] The main reasons for the integration failure are the many atrocious conflicts in the Mediterranean world. Only few Mediterranean countries, such as Tunisia and Jordan, are free of international political or military conflict and remain relatively stable. At present, no Mediterranean country can be regarded as a military threat to Europe, but nearly every Mediterranean country has been involved in some form of military or political conflict with one or more of its neighbours since 1945.[36] Jordan and Tunisia are the only Mediterranean countries that are not involved in neighbouring conflicts but, on the contrary, are trying to enhance interregional cooperation. Jordan, for example, has signed an economic and trade cooperation agreement and a scientific cooperation agreement with Israel. In Tunisia, the political situation is stable, but human rights organisations criticise the failure to respect the rule of law and fundamental freedoms, including the freedom of association and of expression.[37]

The conflict between Israel and the Palestinian Authority (PA) remains the most volatile in the Mediterranean region. The West Bank and Gaza Strip are Israeli-occupied territories with current status subject to the Israeli-Palestinian Interim Agreement.[38] Syria maintained 14,000 troops in Lebanon after the country's civil

---

[34] R. Pace, 'Democracy, Economic Development and Regional Stability in the Mediterranean Region', in P. Xuereb, ed., *Euro-Med Integration and the 'Ring of Friends': The Mediterranean's European Challenge*, Vol. IV (Malta, University of Malta, European Documentation and Research Centre 2003) pp. 101-134.

[35] B. Chourou, 'Arab Regional Integration As a Perquisite for a Successful Euro-Mediterranean Partnership', 8/2-3 *Mediterranean Politics* (2003) pp. 195 and 204-205.

[36] See Common Strategy 2000/458/CFSP of the European Council of 19 June 2000 on the Mediterranean region, *OJ* 2000 L 183/5.

[37] On 29 September 2005, the European Parliament adopted a resolution on Tunisia in which it welcomed the significant economic and social progress made in Tunisia, but expressed its concern with the lack of progress on projects related to human rights, women's issues, health and justice; the final edition is available at http://www.europarl.eu.int, under reference P6_TA(2005)0368.

[38] After decades of living under Israeli occupation, a Palestinian uprising (Intifada 1987-1992) against Israeli rule brought about peace negotiations which led to the Oslo peace agreements. Palestinian cities, villages came under the authority of a self-governing Palestinian Authority (PA). In reality, however, the area remained under Israeli occupation with full Israeli military control. A second uprising (Al-Aqsa Intifada) began after the provocative visit of Israel's right-wing Likud Party Minister, Ariel Sharon, on 28 September 2000 to Jerusalem's Temple Mount, where the Al-Aqsa Mosque is located, the third holiest shrine of Islam. The Second Intifada is characterised by numerous Palestinian suicide bombings in Israeli residential areas. Israel has responded to these suicide missions by

war (1975-1990). In September 2004, the UN Security Council adopted a resolution in which the UN called for the withdrawal of all foreign forces from Lebanon and for free and fair elections in Lebanon without foreign interference. Syria only pulled out its troops in reaction to the killing of former Prime Minister Rafik Hariri on 14 February 2005 and subsequent international pressure. The ensuing political turmoil led to the organisation of free elections in Lebanon, which were won by an anti-Syrian coalition led by Sa'ad Hariri, son of Rafik Hariri. Syria has also been at conflict with Israel ever since the latter occupied the Golan Heights in the Six-Day War of 1967. Southern Lebanon was occupied by Israel for several years. Israeli forces withdrew from Southern Lebanon in May 2000. The Muslim militant group Hezbollah is still engaged in a conflict with Israel along the Israeli-Lebanese border, concentrated mainly at the Israeli-occupied Shebaa Farms. A priority issue in Lebanon is the resettlement of 387,000 UNRWA[39]-registered Palestinian refugees, most of whom fled to Lebanon as a result of the 1948 Arab-Israel war. Egypt carefully monitors the Sinai, the border with Israel and the Gaza Strip, and has increased its surveillance drastically since the attack on Taba and other Egyptian resorts in 2004. Yet again bombings struck the Egyptian resort of Sharm-el-Sheikh on 23 July 2005.[40] Libya, the only Mediterranean country without formal relations with the EU, claims more than 32,000 sq km in South-Eastern Algeria. Algeria's border with Morocco remains a problem to bilateral relations as each country has accused the other of harbouring militants and arms smuggling. Algeria has also suffered from internal conflicts, such as the *coup d'état* in 1992.

Regional integration between the Mediterranean countries would be in the best interest of the Mediterranean area itself since it would bring economic stability, peace and prosperity. But contrary to the successful EU integration process, the attempts at integration between the Mediterranean countries have failed. The free movement of goods, services, capital and persons between the Mediterranean countries is far from being realised.

5. Central question

The EU internal market is not merely a European internal process, but has a strong external dimension. The EU integration process did not stop in 1993 when the EU

---

setting up checkpoints, carrying out mass arrests of Palestinians and building the notorious West Bank Wall. As of April 2006, the length of the West Bank Wall as approved by the Israeli government is 703 kilometers. In response to the bombings and rocket attacks in the Gaza Strip, Israel withdrew its civilians and military presence from the Gaza Strip in 2005, but retained control over Gaza's airspace, maritime access and borders. Since the death of Yasser Arafat, the political wing of the Islamic Resistance Movement, Hamas, created in 1987 by Sheikh Ahmed Yassin, has won many local elections in Gaza. These election victories led to a Palestinian civil war between Hamas and the Palestinian National Liberation Movement, Fatah, the largest faction of the Palestine Liberation Organisation (PLO), created by Yasser Arafat who, after his death, was succeeded by the current Palestinian President, Mahmoud Abbas.

[39] United Nations Relief and Works Agency for Palestine Refugees in the Near East.

[40] A group citing ties to Al Qaeda issued a claim on an Islamic website.

internal market was formally realised, but the external dimension of the EU internal market became more and more significant. The EU wants to transfer the principles of its internal market to third countries such as the Mediterranean countries as it wants to get easier access to foreign markets in a globalised world. The Mediterranean countries, on their part, want to integrate into the EU internal market to reap the benefits of this successful integration process.

It has however never been established to what extent the Mediterranean countries are integrated into the European internal market of the four freedoms. A global overview will be presented of the extent of integration of the Mediterranean countries into the European internal market of goods, services, capital and person. It has also never been examined to what extent the EU exported its own European internal market principles to the Mediterranean countries to obtain this integration goal. Therefore it will be analysed to what extent the Euro-Med movement of goods, services, persons and capital is based upon the EU internal market principles itself. This comparison will be made separately for each of the four domains that form the EU internal market.[41]

The central question of this book is therefore as follows: 'To what extent did the Mediterranean countries integrate into the European internal market of four freedoms and to what extent did the EU internal market principles contribute to this Euro-Med integration process.' These questions will be answered in Chapter VI and Chapter VII of this book.

6. Body of knowledge

Since its inception in 1957, the European integration process has inspired many authors and integration theorists. The EU internal market itself has been the subject of many studies. The Commission has evaluated the EU internal market and commissioned several studies on this subject.[42] Economists have also thoroughly examined the economic effects of the EU internal market.

The EU's external relations have been the subject of important books (*External Relations of the European Union* by P. Eeckhout, *EU International Relations Law* by Koutrakos, *External Relations Law of the European Community* by Holdgaard and *Bilateral Agreements Concluded by the EC* by Marc Maresceau). The EU's external relations regime is studied by academics such as Ramses Wessel.[43]

---

[41] Cf., *infra* Ch. VI.

[42] For example, the study carried out by F. Ilzkovitz, A. Dierx, V. Kovacs and N. Sousa, 'Steps towards a Deeper Economic Integration: The Internal Market in the 21st Century', Economic Paper, 2007, European Commission, Brussels, 90 pp.

[43] R. Wessel, 'The Inside Looking Out: Consistency and Delimitation in EU External Relations', 37 *CMLR* (2000), pp. 1135-1171; R. Wessel, 'Revisiting the International Legal Status of the EU', 5 *EFAR* (2000) pp. 207-537; R. Wessel, 'Fragmentation in the Governance of EU External Relations: Legal Institutional Dilemmas and the New Constitution for Europe', in J. de Zwaan, J. Jans and F. Nelissen, eds., *The European Union: An Ongoing Process of Integration - Liber Amicorum Alfred E. Kellermann* (The Hague, T.M.C. Asser Press 2004) pp. 123-140; A. Ott and R. Wessel, 'The EU's External Relations Regime: Multilevel Complexity in an Expanding Union', in S. Blockmans and

The relationship between Europe and the Mediterranean area has aroused the interest of many authors. Several books and a large number of articles and working papers are available concerning the Euro-Mediterranean relations in general and many other related topics: these include research papers prepared by the EU, studies commissioned by the EU, studies by research institutions, think-tanks, individual academics and scholars, and so on. A great deal of literature has been produced about the Mediterranean area in general and each country in particular. The economic, political and social situation of the Mediterranean world and its individual countries has been analysed. The reasons for the failure of Arab and Mediterranean integration attempts have also been examined by some authors. Political points of view about the Mediterranean area and its relationship with the EU can be found in the journal *Mediterranean Politics* edited by Richard Gillespie. This is the main academic journal focusing on the politics, international relations and political economy of the Mediterranean area and its relations with Europe. The socio-economic organisation Femise also reports regularly on the social-economic effects of the Euro-Mediterranean relationship.[44] In the past, many articles in journals and some books were published concerning the Euro-Mediterranean Partnership and, more recently, about the European Neighbourhood Policy. Some authors are regular contributors to articles about the European Mediterranean Partnership (EMP) or the European Neighbourhood Policy (ENP), such as Raffaella Del Sarto, Tobias Schumacher, Sharon Pardo, Lior Zemer and Stephen Calleya.[45] Books about the implications of the ENP have been edited by authors such as Steven Blockmans, Adam Łazowski and Peter Xuereb. Marc Maresceau and Erwan Lannon have also published about the implications of the ENP and the effect of the EU enlargement on the Mediterranean area.[46] Many Israeli authors, such as Alfred Tovias, Guy Harpaz, Lior Herman, Mosche Hirsch, Efraim Inbar and Tal Sadeh Reich and others have focused mainly on the implications of the Euro-Mediterranean challenge for Israel.[47] Maghreb and Mashreq authors have also been interested in the Euro-Mediterranean relationship, such as Fadi Hakura

A. Łazowski, eds., *The European Union and its Neighbours: A Legal Appraisal of the EU's Policies of Stabilisation, Partnership and Integration* (The Hague, T.M.C. Asser Press 2006) pp. 1-41.

[44] Femise is a Euro-Mediterranean network gathering more than 71 independent economic institutes and conducting socio-economic analyses of the Euro-Mediterranean Partnership. 'Femise Report on the Euro-Mediterranean Partnership 2006. Analysis and Proposals of the Euro-Mediterranean Forum of Economic Institutes', by coordinators S. Radwan and J.-L. Reiffers, September 2006.

[45] R. Del Sarto and T. Schumacher, 'From EMP to ENP: What's at Stake with the European Neighbourhood Policy towards the Southern Mediterranean?', 10/1 *EFAR* (2005) pp. 17-38; S. Pardo and L. Zemer, 'Towards a New Euro-Mediterranean Neighbourhood Space', 10/1 *EFAR* (2005) pp. 39-77.

[46] E. Lannon and P. van Elsuwege, 'The EU's Emerging Neighbourhood Policy and Its Potential Impact on the Euro-Mediterranean Partnership', in Xuereb, ed., *supra* n. 34, pp. 21-84; M. Maresceau and E. Lannon, *The EU's Enlargement and Mediterranean Strategies: A Comparative Analysis* (Basingstoke, Palgrave 2001); in Blockmans and Łazowski, eds., *supra* n. 43.

[47] A. Tovias, 'Israeli Policy Perspectives on the Euro-Mediterranean Partnership in the Context of EU Enlargement', 8/2-3 *Mediterranean Politics* (2003) pp. 214-232; G. Harpaz, 'Enhanced Relations between the European Union and the State of Israel under the European Neighbourhood Policy: Some Legal and Economic Implications', 31/4 *Legal Issues of Economic Integration* (2004) p. 257; L. Herman, 'An Action Plan or a Plan for Action: Israel and the European Neighbourhood Policy', 1/3 *Mediterranean Politics* (2006) pp. 371-394.

with his book on the EU Mediterranean & Gulf Trade Agreements. A well-known Palestinian writer interested in Euro-Mediterranean relations is Bichara Khader. Other authors, such as Stelios Stavridis, Justin Hutchence, Marisa Cremona, Christophe Hillion and Sven Biscop have studied the Common Foreign and Security Policy (CFSP) of the EU in relation to the Mediterranean area.[48] Other authors have examined the Euro-Mediterranean democratisation process, such as Michael Emerson and Richard Youngs.[49]

A limited number of authors have focused on the process of integration of the Mediterranean countries into the EU internal market of goods, services, capital and persons. Only a small number of economists have examined the economic results of the integration of the Mediterranean countries into the EU internal market. Daniel Miller-Jentsch has researched the economic effects of deeper integration and trade in services in the Euro-Mediterranean region for the World Bank and the Commission.[50] Jakubiak put down interesting ideas in his book *Countries Bordering the EU and Enhanced Economic Integration* which is a social and economic research about the integration issue.[51]

None of the above-mentioned publications has examined the subject of this book, i.e., the extent of integration of the Mediterranean countries into the EU internal market as regards the liberalisation of the movement of goods, services, capital as well as persons.

This book will not focus on the European integration process, or on the Arab or Mediterranean integration process, but on the process of vertical integration of the Mediterranean countries into the EU internal market of goods, services, capital and persons and its outcome, regarding which literature is not yet available.

7. Structure of the book

This book is structured along seven chapters. Chapter II, which follows this general introduction in Chapter I, will present and explain the main Euro-Med policies and the different levels of integration. This clarification is necessary to better understand the subsequent chapters of this book. The Euro-Mediterranean relations are dealt with on the basis of different Euro-Med policies. Chapter II will clarify which Euro-Med policies intend to stimulate the Euro-Med integration

---

48 M. Cremona and C. Hillion, 'L'Union fait la force? Potential and Limitations of the European Neighbourhood Policy As an Integrated EU Foreign and Security Policy', EUI Working Paper LAW No. 2006/39; S. Biscop, 'The EU and Euro-Mediterranean Security: A New Departure?', in N. Casarini and C. Musu, eds., *European Foreign Policy in an Evolving International System. The Road towards Convergence* (Palgrave Macmillan 2007).

49 M. Emerson, *Democratisation in the European Neighbourhood* (Brussels, Centre for European Policy Studies 2006) and R. Youngs, *The European Union and the Promotion of Democracy* (Oxford, Oxford University Press 2002).

50 Office of the Publisher of the World Bank, Washington D.C., 'Deeper Integration and Trade in Services in the Euro-Mediterranean Region. Southern Dimensions of the European Neighbourhood Policy', by D. Miller-Jentsch for the World Bank and the European Commission.

51 M. Jakubiak, et al., *Countries Bordering the EU and Enhanced Economic Integration* (Warsaw, Centre for Social and Economic Research 2006).

process and, more specifically, which Euro-Med policies aim at the integration of the Mediterranean countries into the EU internal market. Therefore, the goals of each Euro-Med policy will be examined. Chapter II will also present the multilateral and bilateral instruments which the Euro-Med policies have produced to achieve their goals. These multilateral and bilateral instruments will be thoroughly examined in the next chapters. Chapter II will also focus on the concept of 'integration' itself as it is necessary to clarify what is meant by this term to have a better understanding of the Euro-Med integration process. Finally, Chapter II will explain the difference between the Euro-Med policies and the EU's Mediterranean policy.

The different *multilateral* and *bilateral* instruments that the EU and the Mediterranean countries have used for their vertical integration process will be discussed in Chapters III, IV and V.

Chapter III will look at all *multilateral* instruments that the EU and the Mediterranean countries use for the integration of the Mediterranean countries into the EU internal market. These are, for example, the Euro-Med Conferences of Ministers of Foreign Affairs and the Euro-Med Parliamentary Assembly. Some Mediterranean countries also gather in the meetings of the World Trade Organisation (WTO). The conclusions of these WTO meetings will not be considered in this book since not all Mediterranean countries are a member of this organisation. Chapter III will consider whether and to what extent these multilateral instruments have resulted in the integration of the Mediterranean countries into the EU internal market.

Chapter IV will examine the *bilateral* instruments under the Euro-Mediterranean Policy (EMP) for the integration of the Mediterranean countries into the EU internal market. These are the instruments which have been generated under the EMP since 1995. The main bilateral EMP instruments are the Euro-Med Association Agreements (Euro-Med AAs). Chapter IV, section 1 gives an overview of the Euro-Med AAs and their legal basis. The EU and its Member States have concluded Euro-Med AAs with Morocco, Algeria, Tunisia, Egypt, Lebanon, Jordan and Israel, and a Euro-Med Interim AA with the Palestinians. The Euro-Med AA with Syria is still in the process of ratification.

The Euro-Med AAs include important legally binding provisions that deal with the liberalisation of the movement of goods, services, capital and persons. These provisions are studied in section 2 of Chapter IV. The 'goods provision' relates to the trade in industrial and agricultural goods between the EU and the Mediterranean countries. Other provisions, such as the competition provisions and rules of origin, have a significant impact on the movement of goods between the EU and the Mediterranean countries. Furthermore, there is a 'services provision,' which will be evaluated together with the 'establishment rights' provision. The 'capital provision' and the 'movement of persons' provision will be analysed. Chapter IV will discuss whether and to what extent these bilateral EMP instruments have resulted in the integration of the Mediterranean countries into the EU internal market.

Chapter V will deal with the *ENP bilateral* instruments for the Mediterranean integration into the EU internal market. These are the instruments that have been created in the framework of the European Neighbourhood Policy (ENP) since 2002. The main ENP instruments that have an impact on the liberalisation of the movement of goods, services and capital and the movement of persons are the ENP Action Plans. These Action Plans are designed to upgrade the existing bilateral relations between the EU and its neighbouring countries, including the Mediterranean countries, by giving them a stake in the EU internal market. The ENP Progress Reports that indicate if the Mediterranean countries have achieved their goals as set out in the ENP Action Plans, will also be analysed. Chapter V will discuss whether and to what extent these bilateral ENP instruments have resulted in the integration of the Mediterranean countries into the EU internal market.

Chapter VI will present an overview of the extent of integration of the Mediterranean countries into the EU internal market of goods, services, capital and persons. Chapter VII will analyse the extents of which the EU exported its own EU internal market principles to the Mediterranean countries. Chapter VIII will entail some conclusions.

8. Territorial scope of the book

The term Mediterranean comes from the Latin word *Mediterraneus*, which means 'in the middle of the earth' (*medius* means 'middle' and *terra* 'earth'). The Romans called the Mediterranean Sea *Mare Nostrum* since it was their sea and no other country could claim it. Today, the territorial waters of the Mediterranean Sea belong to all bordering countries. The Eastern and Southern Mediterranean countries are those of the Maghreb (Morocco, Algeria, Libya and Tunisia), the Mashreq (Egypt, Lebanon, Jordan, Syria and the Palestinian Authority) and Israel. The Northern Mediterranean includes Malta, Cyprus and Turkey.

The Mediterranean countries in this book are those of the Maghreb (Morocco, Algeria, Libya and Tunisia), the Mashreq (Egypt, Lebanon, Jordan, Syria and the Palestinian Authority) and Israel. The Northern Mediterranean countries (Malta, Cyprus and Turkey) occupy a special position in this book. Malta and Cyprus are only considered Mediterranean countries until their membership of the EU as of 1 May 2004. Turkey does not fall within the territorial scope of this book since it has the special position of candidate country of the EU.

The Mediterranean area can be divided into three different groups in terms of production: the Mediterranean agricultural group (Tunisia, Morocco, Egypt, Lebanon, Syria and the West Bank & Gaza Strip), the manufacturing countries (Israel and Jordan) and the oil producers (Algeria, Libya, Saudi Arabia, Iran, Iraq, Kuwait, United Arab Emirates and Qatar). The Gulf States (Saudi Arabia, Iran, Iraq, Kuwait, United Arab Emirates and Qatar) are not part of the Mediterranean countries in this book since they fall within the scope of other European policies.[52]

[52] The EU has relations with the Gulf Cooperation Council (GCC) of which Bahrain, Kuwait, Oman, Qatar, Saudi Arabia and the United Arab Emirates (UAE) are members. In addition, the EU has bilateral relations with Iran, Iraq and Yemen.

Table I: Facts and figures regarding the Mediterranean countries (April 2009)

	Area (sq km)	**Population (mln)**	**Independence**	**Regime**	**Head of State**
Morocco	446,550	32.7	2 March 1956	Monarchy	King Mohammed II
Algeria	2,381,740	32.5	5 July 1962	Republic	President Bouteflika
Tunisia	163,610	10.1	20 March 1956	Republic	President Ben Ali
Libya	1,759,540	5.76	24 December 1951	Republic	Colonel Al-Qaddafi
Egypt	1,001,450	77.5	22 February 1922	Republic	President Mubarak
Jordan	92,300	5.75	25 May 1946	Monarchy	King Abdallah II
Syria	185,180	18.4	17 April 1946	Republic	President Al-Assad
Lebanon	10,400	3.8	22 November 1943	Republic	President Suleiman
Israel	20,770	7.22	14 May 1948	Parliamentary democracy	President Peres
West Bank & Gaza Strip	West Bank: 5,860 Gaza Strip: 360	West Bank:[53] 2,535,927 Gaza Strip: 1,482,405[54]			President Abbas

The most important international region that geographically neighbours the Mediterranean region is Europe.[55] The EU comprises 27 Member States. Germany, France, Italy and the Benelux countries have been members from the very beginning. Denmark, Ireland and the United Kingdom (UK) joined the six founding countries in 1973. Greece acceded in 1981, followed by Portugal and Spain in 1986. Austria, Finland and Sweden joined in 1995. On 1 May 2004, the biggest enlargement took place with 10 countries: Czech Republic, Estonia, Cyprus, Latvia, Lithuania, Hungary, Malta, Poland, Slovenia and Slovakia. Two more countries, i.e., Bulgaria and Romania, joined the EU on 1 January 2007. The EFTA (European Free Trade Association) countries Iceland, Liechtenstein, Norway and Switzerland do not fall within the scope of this book since they are no Member States of the EU.

[53] There are also some 267,163 Israeli settlers in the West Bank and more than 200,000 Israeli settlers in East Jerusalem.

[54] According to UNRWA, there were also 993,818 Palestinian refugees in 2006.

[55] S.C. Calleya, 'Political and Economic Perceptions in the Euro-Mediterranean Area', *The South-east European Yearbook: 1997-1998* (Athens, EILIAMEP 1998) pp. 147-148.

Chapter II

The multilateral *versus* the unilateral dimension of the Euro-Med relationship and the impact on the Euro-Med integration

Since the beginning of the European integration process in 1957, the six Member States have been interested in playing a crucial role in the development of the Mediterranean countries. The EEC Treaty of Rome of 1957 provided for the establishment of a particular relationship with non-European countries that had a special relation with the six Member States. These non-European countries were mainly former French colonies in North Africa. Article 131 of the EEC Treaty defined as follows:

> 'The Member States hereby agree to bring into association with the Community the non-European countries and territories which have special relations with Belgium, France, Italy and the Netherlands. These countries and territories, hereinafter referred to as "the countries and territories," are listed in Annex IV to this Treaty.'

This provision of the EEC Treaty formed the legal basis for a close relationship or association between the EEC and the Mediterranean countries. The close relationship has resulted in many policies towards the Mediterranean region. On the one side, there are the multilateral policies, which means that both parties, the EU as well as the Mediterranean countries, are involved in the Euro-Mediterranean decision-making process (hereafter referred to as the 'Euro-Med policies'), and on the other side there are the unilateral policies under which only the EU (and not the Mediterranean countries) is involved in the Euro-Mediterranean decision-making process. This book will first analyse the integration of the Mediterranean countries into the EU internal market through the multilateral policies (see 1.); subsequently, the unilateral dimension of the Euro-Mediterranean relationship will be discussed (see 2.). In the other chapters of this book, only the multilateral dimension of the integration of the Mediterranean countries into the EU internal market will be analysed, i.e., both parties must be involved in the Euro-Mediterranean integration process. This book will not study in detail the unilateral dimension of the Euro-Mediterranean relationship. A further thorough examination of the impact of the EU's unilateral Mediterranean policy and the EU financial aid on the integration of the Mediterranean countries into the EU internal market requires further research, which falls outside the scope of this book. Such further research will have to focus on an extensive array of EU documents and will have to generate other criteria.

1. The multilateral dimension of the Euro-Med relationship: the Euro-Med policies

This chapter will only discuss the Euro-Med policies that are relevant in the context of this book: these are the past and present policies that have contributed to the integration of the Mediterranean countries into the EU internal market of goods, services, capital and persons (or into the EEC common market before 1993).[56] It will do so in chronological order. Regarding each Euro-Mediterranean policy, the following will be set out: (1) the establishment of the Euro-Mediterranean policy (2) the goals as regards the integration of the Mediterranean countries into the EU internal market (or into the EEC common market before 1993). The different Euro-Mediterranean policies have had various goals, such as the establishment of political relations, economic and financial cooperation, cultural exchanges between Europe and the Mediterranean region, human rights education, conflict resolution in the Euro-Mediterranean cooperation context, etc. In this overview only goals relating to the Euro-Mediterranean liberalisation of the movement of goods, services, capital and persons will be considered; (3) the instruments used by the Mediterranean countries and the EU to achieve these goals. The Euro-

[56] Before examining the main Euro-Mediterranean policies as regards the movement of persons, it is interesting to explain the main immigration flows into the EU. In 2004, Breem and Thierry examined the immigration flows from the Mediterranean countries into the old EU Member States and presented their results at a conference on international migration in Europe in Rome in November 2004. Their paper 'Immigration in Europe and Development Levels of the Source Countries: What Are the Associations?' is available at: http://www.irpps.cnr.it. Breem and Thierry came to the following conclusions: Germany, Austria and Luxembourg receive migrants from the countries of Eastern Europe, notably former Yugoslavia. Germany and Austria are moreover historically receiving countries for Turkish citizens. Belgium and the Netherlands receive Moroccans and Turks. Sweden, Denmark and Finland attract two types of flows of asylum seekers: from developing countries (Iran, Iraq and Somalia) and from former Yugoslavia. Despite their common geographical position on the Mediterranean coast, the southern European countries receive very different types of immigrants. Greece mainly receives citizens from neighbouring countries (Bulgaria and Egypt), as well as Russians. Spain mainly receives Moroccan immigrants. Italy receives Moroccans as well as citizens from black Africa. Portugal keeps attracting immigrants from its former colonial empire, i.e., citizens from Cape Verde, Brazil and Angola. The United Kingdom and France also illustrate the diversity of the migratory situations in the EU. The main source of French immigration is North Africa (Morocco and Algeria). Migrants to the United Kingdom mainly come from Australia, New Zealand and the United States. The migratory situation is the result of the following factors: the role of migrations resulting from the remaining ties with former colonial empires, the position in relation to the EU's external borders, the effect of migration policies (control or *laissez-faire)* and the needs of the economy (skilled/unskilled workers). Ireland, as a relatively poor peripheral EU Member State with limited employment opportunities and no traditional colonial ties, has not attracted major immigration flows. Migration trends in Central and Eastern Europe have been strongly influenced by historical events such as the break-up of the Soviet Union or the accessions to the EU in 2004. The break-up of the Soviet Union and the fall of the Iron Curtain led to increased migration from Central and Eastern European countries to Western Europe. At present, there are increasing flows of temporary workers from the new EU Member States to other countries in Europe. In 2002, for instance, over 90% of labour migration to Germany came from Eastern Europe, particularly Poland. There is also a rising number of Polish workers in the United Kingdom. Austria and Germany are the two EU Member States that are likely to experience the largest inflows of migrants resulting from the lifting of restrictions on migration from the new EU Member States.

Mediterranean policies have generated many interesting integration instruments, such as multilateral and bilateral instruments which the EU and the Mediterranean countries have used to achieve integration of the Mediterranean countries into the EU internal market. These instruments will be analysed in the subsequent chapters of this book;[57] and (4) the level of integration which the Euro-Mediterranean policies aim to achieve. Some Euro-Mediterranean policies have contributed more than others to the Euro-Mediterranean integration process. Though there are many different levels of integration, integration issues have been divided into four categories by economists and international organisations, such as the WTO. The weakest level of economic integration is countries granting preferential tariffs to each other, resulting in the conclusion of a 'preferential agreement.' The second level is the establishment of a 'free trade area' through the abolishment of tariff as well as non-tariff barriers to trade between parties. Level three is the establishment of a 'customs union.' Finally, the highest level involves the establishment of an 'internal market,' which is characterised by full participation in the movement of goods, services, labour and capital, and can be defined as a customs union supplemented by an agreement to allow factors of production, including financial capital, human resources, technology, etc., to move freely across all boundaries within the internal market.[58] The establishment of a Euro-Med internal market goes much further than that of a Euro-Med free trade area. Creating a Euro-Med free trade area does not necessarily lead to the establishment of a Euro-Med internal market. Nevertheless, the experience of creating a Euro-Med free trade area shows many benefits which can be used in creating an internal market. 'Participation in the EU internal market' is a form of economic integration situated between the establishment of a customs union and that of an internal market.

It is important to point out that contrary to the integration of goods, services and capital, the integration of persons into the EU internal market has a human dimension. It is a twofold process: Euro-Mediterranean instruments can provide for the legal integration of Mediterranean persons into the EU's internal market. Consequently, the successfulness of the integration of Mediterranean persons into the EU internal market can be compared with the movement of persons within the EU internal market itself. However, the local community and the immigrants themselves play an important role: they are all responsible for the success of the actual integration into the EU.[59] In 2003, the Commission and the EU Member States agreed that the successful integration of Mediterranean persons consisted of different elements.[60] These elements can be summarised as follows: (1) immi-

---

[57] See Chapters III, IV and V.

[58] A. Tovias, *Options for Mashrek-Israeli Regionalism in the Context of the Euro-Mediterranean Partnership*, CEPS Paper No. 67 (Centre for European Policy Studies, Brussels 1997) pp. 8-9, and E. Kleiman, 'The Economic Provisions of the Agreement between Israel and the PLO', 28 *Israel Law Review* (1994) pp. 352-355.

[59] In the Netherlands, the key factor for successful integration is being self-supporting. The United Kingdom and Austria highlight that becoming a citizen is significant and indicates successful integration.

[60] Communication from the Commission to the Council, the European Parliament, the European Economic and Social Committee and the Committee of the Regions on immigration, integration and employment, COM (2003) 336 final.

grants must respect the fundamental values of a democratic society; (2) immigrants have the right to maintain their own cultural identity; (3) the Union confers rights comparable to those of EU citizens as well as corresponding obligations, and (4) immigrants must be able to actively participate in all aspects of life on an equal footing (economic, social, cultural, political and civil).

1.1 The Global Mediterranean Policy (GMP)

1.1.1 *The establishment of the GMP*

Immediately after the launch of the European integration process in 1957, the EEC began developing relations with Israel in 1958.[61] At Israel's request, the first trade agreement was concluded with the EEC in 1964.[62] This agreement was of a non-preferential nature and offered Israel a reduction in custom taxes on certain products.[63] However, the trade agreement was of minor economic importance. After long negotiations, it was agreed that a preferential trade agreement would be concluded between Israel and the EEC based on Article 133 EC Treaty (Art. 207 TFEU), on the condition that each Arab country would be able to conclude a similar preferential trade agreement with the EEC as well.[64] In 1970, a first preferential trade agreement was concluded between Israel and the EEC. The agreement had to create a free trade area between both parties. Israel succeeded in negotiating important concessions from the EEC: a tax reduction of 50% was applied to more than 85% of Israeli products exported to the EEC. Israel accepted the principle of reciprocity of tariff concessions on European imports. The agreement also stipulated that negotiations about a new agreement involving the gradual abolishment of trade restrictions between Israel and the EEC could begin 18 months after the

---

[61] There are several reasons which explain the rapprochement between Israel and Europe. First, Israel has always been politically and economically isolated in the Middle East. Second, there was a high demand for Israeli products in Europe, and Israeli traders could easily export their goods to Europe because of Israel's proximity to Europe. Third, many Israeli have roots in Europe, which explains the similar social, cultural and historical ties and the same living standard of Israelis and Europeans. Fourth, the Arab countries' economic boycott of Israel, in force since 1949, instigated Israel to develop trade relations with Europe as soon as possible.

[62] In 1960, at a conference with the President of the European Commission, Walter Hallstein, Prime Minister David Ben Gurion of Israel expressed Israel's wish to become *an associated member* of the EEC; see also R. Pomfret, 'Main Economic Trends in EC-Israel Economic Relations Since the Creation of the Common Market', in I. Greilsammer and J. Weiler, eds., *Europe and Israel: Troubled Neighbours* (Berlin, Walter de Gruyter, for the European University Institute 1988) p. 57; S. Terracini, 'The History of the Israel-EEC Agreement', in A. Rabello, ed., *Essays on European Law and Israel* (Jerusalem, The Harry and Michael Sacher Institute for Legislative Research and Comparative Law 1996) pp. 1063-1064; P. Malanczuk, 'The Legal Framework of the Economic Relations between Israel and the European Union', in A. Kellermann, K. Siehr and T. Einhorn, eds., *Israel among the Nations: International and Comparative Perspectives on Israel's 50th Anniversary* (The Hague, Kluwer Law International 1998) pp. 263-265.

[63] Art. I GATT.

[64] This condition was included for fear of Arab reprisals, such as the stopping of oil export to Western Europe and terrorist attacks on European soil.

expiry of the Israel-EEC trade agreement of 1970.[65] Not long after this 1970 Israel-EEC agreement had been concluded, the EEC changed its general approach to the Mediterranean area. It began to work on a more global policy towards the Mediterranean region. The first general EEC policy for the region was the Global Mediterranean Policy (GMP) in 1972, involving all Mediterranean countries, except Libya, and covering the period from 1976 to 1990.[66]

1.1.2 *The integration goals of the GMP*

The central pillar of the GMP was free access of manufactured goods from the Mediterranean countries to the European market, combined with a more coherent approach towards the Mediterranean area.

1.1.3 *The integration instruments of the GMP*

The new approach resulted in the need for a review of the Israel-EEC Agreement of 1970.[67] The Rossi Report of 1971 to the European Parliament also concluded that the agreement was unsatisfactory. Israel wished to conclude the reviewed agreement on the basis of Article 310 EC Treaty (now Art. 217 TFEU), but did not succeed in this. The trade agreement was again concluded on the basis of Article 133 EC Treaty (now Art. 207 TFEU).[68] The new agreement, called Cooperation Agreement,[69] was approved in Brussels on 11 May 1975[70] and entered into force

---

[65] F. Noureddine and J. Quatremer, *The New Euro-Mediterranean Economic Area* (Brussels, Club de Bruxelles 1996) pp. 92-93.

[66] *Bull. EEC* 10-1972, points 151 and 152. The EC adopted the global Mediterranean policy at a Conference in Paris in 1972, which should lead to the general economic development of the Mediterranean region. The EC used the term 'global' because it intended to pursue a uniform policy towards all Mediterranean countries, i.e., Albania, Algeria, Cyprus, Egypt, Greece, Israel, Jordan, Lebanon, Libya, Malta, Morocco, Portugal, Spain, Syria, Tunisia, Turkey and Yugoslavia. Some of these countries acceded to the EU, and in 1994 the PA was added to the list; A. Galper, 'Restructuring Rules of Origin in the U.S.-Israel Free Trade Agreement: Does the EC-Israel Association Agreement Offer an Effective Model?', 19/5 *Fordham International Law Journal* (1996) pp. 2072-2073.

[67] 'Les accords méditerranéens de la CEE au début de 1986', *Agence Europe* (1986) pp. 138-139, and A. Shlaim and G.N. Yannopoulos, eds., *The EEC and the Mediterranean Countries* (Cambridge, Cambridge University Press 1976) pp. 1-10.

[68] There was no parallelism between the economic and political situations of Israel and the EC at the time the preferential free trade agreement was concluded in 1975. The conclusion of the 1975 free trade agreement led to economic successes for both parties while the political relationship between them declined rapidly, see I. Greilsammer, *Israel et l'Europe: Une histoire des relations entre la Communauté européenne et l'Etat d'Israel* (Lausanne, Fondation Jean Monnet pour l' Europe et Centre de recherches européennes 1981) pp. 101-102.

[69] Agreement between the European Economic Community and the State of Israel, *OJ* 1975 L 136/3.

[70] The declaration of Minister Igal Allon of Israel demonstrates the importance of the agreement: 'The European Community is by far our main international trading partner. In the future we hope to become a full association with the EC. The today signed free trade agreement is not only economically important, but will play an important political role in the region. This agreement with the EC will serve as a good example of cooperation in our region.' See Greilsammer, *supra* n. 68, pp. 102-103.

on 1 July 1977.[71] In line with the new GMP, talks with the Maghreb states were held, resulting in a series of cooperation agreements with Morocco, Algeria and Tunisia in 1976. These agreements provided for free access to the EEC market for industrial goods and preferential treatment for agricultural products. They also included 'labour benefits': these provisions aimed to improve the standard of living of immigrant workers in Europe, to legalise family reunification and to give immigrants social rights equal to those of Europeans. Similar agreements were signed with the Mashreq countries in 1977 (Egypt, Jordan, Lebanon and Syria). The PA was not offered a cooperation agreement. The EC Council Regulation of 26 October 1986 on imports from the Occupied Territories stated that privileges had been granted to the Mediterranean countries but not to the Occupied Territories.[72] The Regulation stipulated that an end should be put to this situation. As a result, free access to industrial goods and 40 to 80% reductions in import duties on fruit and vegetables were granted. According to Lannon, this EC Regulation had two important consequences: at an economic level, the Occupied Territories were included in the Euro-Mediterranean relationship, and at a political level, it resulted in the recognition by the EU of a Palestinian autonomous entity.[73] However, this EU concession to the Palestinians led to years of bitter recriminations between Israel on one side and the Palestinians and Europeans on the other. The Israeli government limited Palestinian exports, labeled Palestinian products as 'made in Israel' and obliged Palestinian exporters to use the Israeli airport and harbours.[74]

1.1.4 *Level of Euro-Mediterranean integration*

At the time of the conclusion of the EEC-Mediterranean cooperation agreements, the European integration process was still taking shape. The Mediterranean countries could not benefit from the four freedoms of the EU internal market because the internal market was still far from being established. The GMP aimed at countries granting preferential tariffs to each other, resulting in the conclusion of preferential agreements between some Mediterranean countries and the EEC. The conclusion of a preferential agreement is considered the weakest level of economic

---

[71] At the time the agreement was signed, the *per capita* income in Israel was higher than that in Austria, Italy and England and approached that of Belgium, the Netherlands and Finland; see Y. Shachmurove, 'The Integration of the Israeli Economy into the EEC: Recent Trends and a Forecast', in Greilsammer, *supra* n. 62, p. 76.

[72] Council Regulation (EEC) No 3363/86 of 27 October 1986 on the tariff arrangements applicable to imports into the Community of products originating in the occupied territories, *OJ* 1986 L 306/103; Commission Regulation (EEC) No 4129/86 of 23 December 1986 on the definition of the concept of 'originating products' and methods of administrative cooperation applicable to imports into the Community of products originating in the Occupied Territories, *OJ* 1986 L 381/1, and Commission Regulation (EEC) No 2774/88 of 7 September 1988 amending Regulation (EEC) No 809/88 on the definition of the concept of 'originating products' and methods of administrative cooperation applicable to imports into the Community of products originating in the Occupied Territories, *OJ* 1988 L 249/5.

[73] E. Lannon, 'L'accord d'association intérimaire Communauté européenne-OLP: l'institutionnalisation progressive des relations euro-palestiniennes', *Revue des Affaires Européennes* (1997) p. 171.

[74] The Wye Memorandum of 23 October 1998 underlines the importance of a Palestinian harbour.

integration. The preferential cooperation agreements only resulted in free movement of industrial goods and preferential access of agricultural products from the Mediterranean countries to Europe. It is remarkable that at this early stage of Euro-Mediterranean cooperation, social cooperation was already provided for in the cooperation agreements, which included interesting provisions to improve the standard of living of immigrant workers in Europe, to legalise family reunification and to give immigrants social rights equal to those of Europeans.

1.2 The New Mediterranean Policy (NMP)

1.2.1 *The establishment of the NMP*

The impact of the GMP was quite modest due to a crisis in the European textile industry, the enlargement of the EEC with Spain and Portugal in 1986 and the lack of regional Mediterranean integration. The 1986 enlargement of the EEC to include Spain and Portugal had negative consequences for the Maghreb countries since the export patterns of these countries, on the one hand, and those of Spain and Portugal, on the other, were quite similar (fruits and vegetables). As a result, the Maghreb countries suffered a significant decline in their export of fruits and vegetables to the European market, since Spain and Portugal became the main suppliers of these products in the EU. Morocco's application to join the EEC in 1987 illustrates the Arab frustration. The EEC subsequently took a more Mediterranean turn. The New Mediterranean Policy (NMP) was launched in 1992.

1.2.2 *The integration goals of the NMP*

The NMP aimed at increasing the amount of development aid and extending trade preferences.[75] By offering these economic benefits, the EU hoped that the Mediterranean countries would be too involved in the growing regional prosperity to jeopardise peace. For example, by balancing trade-and-aid benefits between Israel and the Mashreq countries, the EU believed that a form of peaceful coexistence would develop between these states as a step towards political conciliation.[76] But the NMP did not bring the expected economic growth and development to the Mediterranean region either. It did, however, mark two important changes in the European approach to its southern neighbours. Firstly, the EU's economically-oriented cooperation with the Mediterranean countries started to give way to a more political approach; in other words, the NMP began to stress the importance of the region's social and economic development as a condition for the security of the EU Member States in the broadest sense. Secondly, the NMP placed greater emphasis on regional cooperation between the Mediterranean countries. The Commission emphasised that regional economic cooperation was a powerful tool in reducing the level of conflict, making peace irreversible and encouraging the people of the region to learn to live in peace.

---

[75] General Report 1992, No. 829 referring back to General Report 1990, Nos. 718-719.

[76] Ginsberg, *supra* n. 1, p. 162.

1.2.3 *The integration instruments used by the NMP*

The Commission proposed new instruments besides the already existing cooperation agreements. These new tools were of a technical and financial nature: the EEC would provide for technical assistance, balance of payments support and investment financing to the Mediterranean countries.

1.2.4 *Level of Euro-Mediterranean integration*

At the time of the NMP, the EU internal market was almost a reality. The NMP did not aim at integration of the Mediterranean countries into the EU internal market, but focused on Mediterranean regional integration. Under the NMP, in 1992 and 1993, the Commission made some proposals for the improvement of Mediterranean regional integration. In April 1992, it proposed a new framework that would gradually lead to a Euro-Maghreb partnership and the creation of a Mediterranean free trade area.[77] The Euro-Maghreb partnership involved the establishment of a free trade area between Europe and the Maghreb countries only (Algeria, Morocco and Tunisia). The Commission stated that, in addition to the economic cooperation between Europe and the Maghreb, the partnership should cover other forms of cooperation such as culture, social matters including migration, movement of persons and education. Negotiations were started, but the problems in the EU-Libya relations and the crisis in Algeria prevented this initiative from becoming successful. In 1993, the Commission, under the supervision of Commissioner Manual Marin, stimulated the establishment of a Mediterranean regional free trade area. By means of a Communication, the Commission thus laid the basis for a so-called 'Middle Eastern Economic Area,' implying freedom of movement of goods, services, capital and labour between the Mediterranean countries.[78] Commissioner Marin stated the following:

> 'One of the most urgent priorities for virtually all the countries of the Middle East, in particular the countries of the Mashreq and Israel is to encourage trade and foster an optimal division of labour between them. The present level of trade in goods and services between the Mashreq countries themselves and between them and Israel is minimal (less than two billion dollars per year, of which about 80% concerns Israeli-Palestinian trade). This situation is due essentially to the political obstacles, high levels of protectionism and inadequate transport links. With centres like Beirut, Amman, Tel Aviv, no more than 150 km from each other, the low level of trade between themselves is a costly "economic absurdity." Peace could bring about change, but as the Egypt/Israel experience since 1981 demonstrates, peace in itself is not a sufficient stimulus for intra-

[77] Communication from the Commission to the Council and the European Parliament of 30 April 1992, 'The Future of Relations between the Community and the Maghreb Countries', SEC (92) 401 final; R. Weltner-Puig, *Common Foreign and Security Policy in the EU and the Mediterranean Region*, Working Paper for the Universidad de Valencia (2001).

[78] Communication of the Commission to the Council and the European Parliament of 3 September 1993 on the future relations and cooperation between the Community and the Middle East, COM (93) 375 final.

> regional trade. The prospect of a free trade area encompassing some 120 million people by 2020 would make the region far more attractive for private investors. A free trade area between the Mashreq countries and Israel seems to inspire more fear than hope among the potential partners, especially the least developed ones. Therefore, the free trade area will have to be asymmetrical, Israel bringing down its protection immediately or in a much shorter transitional period (say 3-5 years) than the less developed Mediterranean countries (10-12 years). By opening up the Mediterranean markets between themselves and with Europe, the tiny economies of the Middle East will be in a better position, to raise the level of efficiency of their economies and therefore to attract more European investment and technical know-how ensuring the reduction of the prosperity gap between Europe and the Middle East.'[79]

It is not so strange that Mediterranean regional integration was emphasised at the time of the formal creation of the EU internal market. The Commission probably believed it was a good time to convince the Mediterranean countries to create also a 'Middle Eastern Economic Area,' implying freedom of movement of goods, services, capital and labour after the example of the newly established EU internal market. History, however, has already shown that this was an unrealistic and unrealisable project and, also this time, the Commission proposal failed. It is remarkable that the Commission proposed free movement of persons between the Mediterranean countries considering the political tensions and military conflicts between these countries.

1.3. The Euro-Mediterranean Partnership (EMP)

1.3.1 *The establishment of the EMP*

The formal completion of the EU internal market on 1 January 1993 and the creation of the World Trade Organisation (WTO) on 1 January 1995 led to the general belief that Europe once again needed a new economic strategy towards the Mediterranean region. In 1994, the Commission again proposed a new policy on the Mediterranean region.[80] Its Communication proposed an ambitious programme, building on existing economic and political relations between the Mediterranean countries and the EU. According to this programme, further strengthening of the relations between the Mediterranean countries and the EU should be achieved through the progressive establishment of a Euro-Mediterranean Economic Area (EMEA), a comprehensive political dialogue and EU-financed activities.[81] This Commission proposal led to a Euro-Mediterranean Conference in Barcelona in 1995, where the Barcelona Declaration was adopted, inaugurating the still existing

---

[79] COM (93) 375 final, Annex 1, p. 1.

[80] Communication of the Commission to the Council and the European Parliament of 19 October 1994, 'Strengthening the Euro-Mediterranean Policy: Establishing a Euro-Mediterranean Partnership', COM (94) 427 final.

[81] F.S. Hakura, 'The Euro-Mediterranean Policy: The Implications of the Barcelona Declaration', 34 *Common Market Law Review (CMLR)* (1997) pp. 337-366.

Euro-Mediterranean Partnership.[82] The Barcelona Conference took place on 27-28 November 1995 and included the fifteen EU Member States and twelve Mediterranean countries.[83] Under the EMP, the Mediterranean region stretches from Morocco in the Maghreb to Syria in the Mashreq including Israel.[84] The EMP presently covers Morocco, Algeria, Tunisia, Egypt, Jordan, Israel, Syria, Lebanon and the PA and all Member States of the EU. Albania and Mauritania joined in early November 2007. Turkey is not an EMP country as its relations with the EU are covered by the accession process. Libya has observer status.

1.3.2 *The integration goals of the EMP*

The Barcelona Declaration, with a work programme in annex, defines the goals of the EMP in the form of a triple partnership: (i) a political and security partnership aimed at establishing a common area of peace and stability; (ii) an economic and financial partnership aimed at creating an area of shared prosperity through the establishment of a free trade area of goods, services and capital; and (iii) a social and cultural partnership aimed at developing a better understanding between cultures and an exchange between civil societies.[85] The second chapter of the EMP is important in this context: economic prosperity and development of the Mediterranean world will be established through a free trade area of goods, services, including the right of establishment, and capital. As regards the movement of goods and services, including the right of establishment, the Barcelona Declaration states the following:

> 'The free-trade area will be established through the new Euro-Med Agreements and free-trade agreements between partners of the EU. The parties have set 2010 as the target date for the gradual establishment of this area which will cover most trade with due observance of the obligations resulting from the WTO. With a view to developing gradual free trade in this area: tariff and non-tariff barriers to trade in manufactured products will be progressively eliminated in accordance with timetables to be negotiated between the partners; taking as a starting point traditional trade flows, and as far as the various agricultural policies allow and with due respect to the results achieved within the GATT negotiations, trade in agricultural products will be progressively liberalised through reciprocal preferential access among the parties; trade in services including

[82] *Bull. EU* 11-1995, point 1.3.166; for a critical assessment of the progress the EU has been making in implementing the Barcelona Process, see C.M. Salama, 'The Euro-Mediterranean Partnership: Political and Economic Aspects', in P. Herrmann and A. Tausch, eds., *Dar Al-Islam: The Mediterranean, the World System and the Wider Europe* (New York, Nova Science Publishers 2005) pp. 57-84.

[83] Algeria, Cyprus, Egypt, Israel, Jordan, Lebanon, Malta, Morocco, Syria, Tunisia, Turkey and the West Bank and Gaza Strip.

[84] J. Marks, 'High Hopes and Low Motives: The New Euro-Mediterranean Partnership Initiative', 1 *Mediterranean Politics* (1996) p. 1.

[85] For an assessment of the EMP, see F. Attina, 'The Euro-Mediterranean Partnership Assessed: The Realist and Liberal Views', 8 *European Foreign Affairs Review (EFA Rev.)* (2003) pp. 181-199; and E. Philippart, 'The Euro-Mediterranean Partnership: A Critical Evaluation of an Ambitious Scheme', 8 *EFA Rev.* (2003) pp. 201-220.

> right of establishment will be progressively liberalised having due regard to the GATS agreement.'

As for the movement of capital, the Barcelona Declaration provides for reinforced cooperation and progressive elimination of obstacles to investment:

> '[They] acknowledge that economic development must be supported both by internal savings, the basis of investment, and by direct foreign investment. They stress the importance of creating an environment conducive to investment, in particular by the progressive elimination of obstacles to such investment which could lead to the transfer of technology and increase production and exports.'

The movement of persons as such is not mentioned as one of the goals of the EMP. However, the third chapter of the EMP puts migration on the agenda:

> 'Given the importance of the issue of migration for Euro-Mediterranean relations, meetings will be encouraged in order to make proposals concerning migration flows and pressures. These meetings will take account of experience acquired (...) particularly as regards improving the living conditions of migrants legally established in the Union. (...) Fighting terrorism will have to be a priority for all the parties. To that end, officials will meet periodically with the aim of strengthening cooperation among police, judicial and other authorities. In this context, consideration will be given, in particular, to stepping up exchanges of information and improving extradition procedures. (...) Officials will meet periodically to discuss practical measures which can be taken to improve cooperation among police, judicial, customs, administrative and other authorities in order to combat, in particular, drug trafficking and organised crime, including smuggling. All these meetings will be organised with due regard for the need for a differentiated approach that takes into account the diversity of the situation in each country. (...) Officials will meet periodically to discuss practical measures which can be taken to improve cooperation among police, judicial, customs, administrative and other authorities in order to combat illegal immigration.'

The EMP aims to stimulate the Euro-Med liberalisation of the movement of goods, services and capital. The movement of persons between the Mediterranean countries and the EU is a matter of (il)legal migration management.

1.3.3 *The integration instruments of the EMP*

The EMP has produced a set of instruments that should contribute to the achievement of the abovementioned goals. It has generated multilateral instruments, such as the Euro-Mediterranean Conference of Ministers of Foreign Affairs (Euro-Med Conference) and the Euro-Mediterranean Committee for the Barcelona Process (Euro-Med Committee). The Euro-Med Committee consists of the EU Troika and a representative from each of the Mediterranean partners. The Committee mainly discusses the agenda and work programme of the EMP. The different activities listed in the work programme are followed up by *ad hoc* sectoral meetings of ministers, senior officials and experts. Multilateral debates were also held in the framework of the Euro-Mediterranean Parliamentary Forum. The Euro-Mediterranean Parliamentary Forum for parliamentarians, which was set up in 1998, declared in 2002 that it should become a Parliamentary Assembly. This proposal was accepted at the 6th Euro-Med Conference in Naples on 2-3 December 2003 and resulted in the creation of the European Mediterranean Parliamentary Assembly (EMPA), which meets at least once a year to deliberate on developments of the EMP. Three committees, focusing on politics and security, economic and financial affairs, and culture, carry out the preparatory work for the plenary sessions.

Besides this multilateral framework, the Mediterranean countries and the EU also use bilateral instruments: the Euro-Mediterranean Association Agreements (AAs).[86] These AAs should serve as a tool for reforming the economic systems of the Mediterranean countries and aim to create a Euro-Med free trade area by 2010.[87] The establishment of a Euro-Med free trade area entails not only bilateral vertical trade liberalisation with Europe but also horizontal trade liberalisation between the Mediterranean countries themselves.[88] Therefore, the conclusion of bilateral AAs between the Mediterranean countries and the EU in order to create a free trade area by 2010 is not sufficient. Free trade agreements between the Mediterranean countries themselves are required as well. The Barcelona Declaration strongly supports the regional integration of Mediterranean economies as this may lead to peace and stability in the region. The idea behind this is that regional economic integration should prohibit future wars in the Mediterranean region. The obvious example here is the creation of the EEC as a way to discourage conflict between France and Germany after World War II. Since 1995, a number of actions have been taken to intensify the EMP's horizontal dimension, but only a limited number of free trade agreements have been signed between Mediterranean countries.

1.3.4 *Level of Euro-Mediterranean integration*

The EMP aims to set up a free trade area of goods, services and capital by the year 2010 through the abolishment of tariff as well as non-tariff barriers between the Mediterranean countries and the EU and between the Mediterranean countries themselves.[89] The establishment of a free trade area through the abolishment of tariff as well as non-tariff barriers to trade between parties is a form of economic

---

[86] For a legal overview of the Euro-Med AAs, see *infra* Ch. IV.

[87] According to Art. XXIV.8(b) GATT, a free trade area shall be understood to mean a group of two or more customs territories in which the duties and other restrictive regulations of commerce are eliminated on substantially all the trade between the constituent territories in products originating in such territories, except – where necessary – those permitted under Arts. XI, XII, XIII, XIV, XV and XX.

[88] Barcelona Declaration, adopted at the Euro-Mediterranean Conference of 27-28 November 1995, available at: http://europa.eu.int/comm/external_relations/euromed/bd.htm#5. In addition, all AAs stress the importance of regional cooperation. Art. 50 AA Algeria, for example, stipulates the following: 'In order to maximise the impact of this Agreement *vis-à-vis* the development of the Euro-Mediterranean partnership and within the countries of the Maghreb, the Parties shall foster all activities which have a regional impact or involve third countries (…).'

[89] The European Parliament is of the opinion that the date of 2010 will have to be reconsidered seeing the problems and backlog which the Euro-Med Partnership is facing; see the Resolution of the

integration that goes further than the preferential agreement but is considered as the second weakest form of economic integration after the preferential agreement. This free trade area takes the form of a triangle: 'Mediterranean country – Mediterranean country – EU' and not 'Mediterranean country – Mediterranean country – Member State – Member State' since all EU Member States are fully integrated in one internal market. The EMP free trade area is characterised by a vertical dimension, that is, the abolishment of tariff as well as non-tariff barriers between the Mediterranean countries and the EU, and a horizontal integration dimension, that is, regional integration between the Mediterranean countries through the abolishment of tariff and non-tariff barriers. So far, horizontal integration has been the main stumbling block in creating a Euro-Mediterranean free trade area. Horizontal integration between the Mediterranean countries would have many advantages since a network of commercial links between individuals and corporations from the Arab states and Israel would set a higher 'price' for any party considering the possibility of renewed conflict.[90]

All former Euro-Med policies referred to the (free) movement of persons. Contrary to these previous Euro-Med policies, the Euro-Med movement of persons was not an initial goal of the EMP of 1995 and definitely not a part of the Euro-Med free trade area. The EMP does not refer to the movement of persons between the Mediterranean countries themselves, nor between the Mediterranean countries and the EU. The free movement of persons issue was reduced to (il)legal migration management in the Barcelona Declaration of 1995. However, 10 years later, the Ministers of Foreign Affairs of the EU Member States and the Mediterranean countries decided to add a fourth chapter to the Barcelona Declaration regarding a human dimension of the EMP, involving social integration of migrants, migration and movement of persons. It can be questioned if the fact that this fourth chapter was added in 2005 means that the EMP offers the Mediterranean countries a stake in the EU internal market of persons or that it is time to put the discussion about (il)legal migration prominently on the agenda because of the increase in migration across the Mediterranean sea to the EU.

1.4 The European Neighbourhood Policy (ENP)

1.4.1 *The establishment of the ENP*

The EU enlargement to the East in May 2004 and the 'EU waiting room' position of Turkey incited the EU to reassess its relations with its southern and eastern

European Parliament of 15 March 2007 on the construction of the Euro-Mediterranean free trade zone (2006/2173(INI)) p. 3.

[90] M. Hirsch, *Asymmetric Factor Endowments, Progressive Rules of Origin and Commercial Cooperation in the Middle East*, Working Paper 13/98 for the Hebrew University of Jerusalem (1998) p. 16.

neighbours that would not be joining the EU in the near future.[91] Accordingly, the new European Neighbourhood Policy (ENP) was launched in 2002.[92] The ENP does not aim to replace the existing framework of the EMP, but intends to supplement and revitalise it.[93] Under the EMP, the Mediterranean region stretches from Morocco, along the Mediterranean coast, to Syria,[94] but the new geopolitical vision under the ENP consists in creating a 'ring of friends' of the EU, ranging from Morocco to Ukraine. The European Parliament considers the scope of the ENP as a complex geopolitical area which, for historical and cultural reasons and because of its geographical proximity, may be defined as a 'pan-European and Mediterranean region.'[95] In Europe, the ENP covers Ukraine, Belarus and Moldova. In June 2004, the Council decided to include Armenia, Azerbaijan and Georgia.[96] In the Mediterranean region, the ENP covers the same Mediterranean countries as those in the EMP framework.[97]

1.4.2 *The integration goals of the ENP*

The Commission stressed that the ENP would offer goals different from those available to European countries under Article 49 TEU.[98] According to this Article, only European states may apply to become a member of the EU. This means that accession is ruled out for the non-European Mediterranean countries.[99] Therefore, the ENP wanted to offer the non-European Mediterranean countries interesting alternatives, such as a stake in the EU internal market. Wessel and Ott state that, contrary to the EU enlargement process, the conditionality regarding the neigh-

---

[91] Del Sarto and Schumacher, *supra* n. 45, pp. 17-38. The enlargement of the EU is the proximate motivation for the ENP, but the European Security Strategy document points out that it is in the European interest that countries on our borders are well-governed, see also Aliboni, *supra* n. 5, pp. 1-16. The Mediterranean countries that fall within the scope of the ENP are Morocco, Algeria, Jordan, Egypt, Tunisia, Lebanon, Syria, Israel and the West Bank and Gaza Strip. Libya is not a member of the ENP, but was invited to become a full member of the EMP. It did not accept membership, particularly because of disagreement over the position of Israel and the PA, and has at present observer status with regard to the Barcelona Process. Libya has recently announced that it has begun working towards full entry into the EMP.

[92] Communication from the Commission to the Council and the European Parliament of 11 March 2003, 'Wider Europe – Neighbourhood: A Framework for Relations with our Eastern and Southern Neighbours', COM (2003) 104 final; Communication from the Commission, 'European Neighbourhood Policy – Strategy Paper' (12 May 2004), COM (2004) 373 final.

[93] Conclusions for the 7th Euro-Mediterranean Conference of Ministers of Foreign Affairs, Luxembourg, 30-31 May 2005, p. 15.

[94] The EMP covers Morocco, Algeria, Tunisia, Egypt, Jordan, Israel, Syria, Lebanon and the PA.

[95] European Parliament, Report on 'Wider Europe – Neighbourhood: A Framework for Relations with our Eastern and Southern Neighbours' (also called the Napoletano Report), COM (2003) 104.

[96] Communication from the Commission, 'European Neighbourhood Policy – Strategy Paper', COM (2004) 373 final. For Morocco, however, which already applied for EU membership in 1986, there is still no prospect of EU membership.

[97] With the exception of Cyprus, Malta and Turkey, since Cyprus and Malta became a member of the EU in May 2004 and Turkey has started negotiations to become a member.

[98] COM (2004) 373 final, p. 3.

[99] COM (2003) 104 final, p. 5.

bouring countries is not built around accession, but around extension of the EU internal market *acquis* to the neighbouring countries in the long term.[100] In 2003, the Commission issued a Communication on a Wider Europe, in which the Mediterranean countries were offered the prospect of a stake in the EU's internal market and further integration and liberalisation to promote the free movement of goods, services, capital and persons.[101] In this Communication, the Commission declared the following:

> 'In return for concrete progress demonstrating shared values and effective implementation of political, economic and institutional reforms, including in aligning legislation with the acquis, the EU's neighbourhood should benefit from the prospect of closer economic integration with the EU. To this end, Russia, the countries of the Western NIS and the Southern Mediterranean should be offered the prospect of a stake in the EU's Internal Market and further integration and liberalisation to promote the free movement of persons, goods, services and capital (four freedoms).'[102]

The economic benefits of getting a stake in the EU internal market are expected to be substantial: the reduction of tariff and non-tariff barriers to trade should bring about efficiency gains and improve welfare through increased market integration. The Mediterranean countries will be brought closer to the EU economic model, particularly through the planned extension of the internal market. Unlike under previous Euro-Med policies, the EU promised, for the first time, conditionality-based integration: the prospect of getting a stake in the EU internal market will be provided in return for concrete progress by the Mediterranean countries, which will have to demonstrate shared values and effective implementation of political, economic and institutional reforms, including alignment of legislation with the EU *acquis*. In 2004, the Commission issued a Strategy Paper in which it reaffirmed the prospect for the Mediterranean countries of getting a stake in the EU internal market, again based upon conditionality. However, this time, the Commission limited the territorial scope of integration: the Commission provides for a stake in the EU internal market, but only for the more advanced countries:[103]

> 'The implementation of the ENP itself brings with it the perspective of moving beyond cooperation to a significant degree of integration, as set out in the March 2003 communication, including through a stake for partner countries in the EU's Internal Market. (...) When the monitoring process demonstrates significant progress in attaining the priorities which have been set, these incentives can be reviewed, with a view to taking further steps along the path to greater integration with the internal market and other key EU policies. The process is a dynamic one, with the Action Plans constituting an important first step (...) It also offers neighbouring countries the prospect of a stake in the EU Internal Market based on legislative and regulatory approximation, the participation in a number of EU programmes and improved interconnection and physical links with the

[100] A. Ott and R. Wessel, 'The EU's External Relations Regime: Multilevel Complexity in an Expanding Union', in Blockmans and Łazowski, eds., *supra* n. 43, pp. 1-41 at p. 32.

[101] COM (2003) 104 final.

[102] Ibid., p. 4.

[103] COM (2004) 373 final.

> EU (...) Cooperation should promote regional economic integration between neighbouring countries or between countries willing to co-operate more closely on economic issues in view of the completion of the Euro-Mediterranean free trade area and the progressive participation of the more advanced countries in the EU internal market.'

In a next Strategy Paper of December 2006, the Commission stated that the ENP should also include 'behind the border' issues. Addressing 'behind the border' issues means progressively achieving comprehensive convergence in other areas, such as technical norms and standards, sanitary and phytosanitary rules, competition policy, enterprise competitiveness, innovation and industrial policy, research cooperation, intellectual property rights, trade facilitation customs measures and administrative capacity in the area of rules of origin, good governance in the tax area, company law, public procurement and financial services. Most remarkable is that the Commission changed its integration goal from 'getting a stake in the EU internal market of goods, services, capital and persons' to the 'conclusion of a new generation of free trade agreements (FTAs)' which should cover all goods and services with all Mediterranean countries. The Commission only referred to the movement of persons as a highly important issue, but the prospect of participation of the Mediterranean countries in the internal market of persons was left out.[104] The Commission stated the following:[105]

> 'The ENP should go beyond free trade in goods and services and should also include "behind the border" issues: this means addressing non-tariff barriers and progressively achieving comprehensive convergence in trade and regulatory areas. FTAs covering essentially industrial goods were already concluded with Mediterranean partners in the past and negotiations have recently been launched to expand their agricultural and fisheries coverage and include services and establishment. Over time, the implementation of the ENP Action Plans, particularly on regulatory areas, will prepare the ground for the conclusion of a new generation of "deep and comprehensive free trade agreements (FTAs)" with all ENP partners, like the one which the EU intends to negotiate with Ukraine. A deep and comprehensive FTA should cover substantially all trade in goods and services between the EU and ENP partners including those products of particular importance for our partners and should include strong legally-binding provisions on trade and economic regulatory issues. Existing Mediterranean FTAs should be expanded accordingly, to other regulatory areas. Results of trade sustainability impact assessments will be integrated into this process.'

---

104 'Even from the earliest days of the European Community, the ability of the citizens of our Member States to travel within the Community, on business, for educational purposes, or on holiday, has been vital in promoting internal trade and investment, in building mutual awareness and encouraging economic, social and cultural contacts. Mobility of persons is of the utmost importance also for all ENP partners. The Union cannot fully deliver on many aspects of the European Neighbourhood Policy if the ability to undertake legitimate short-term travel is as constrained as it is currently. Yet our existing visa policies and practices often impose real difficulties and obstacles to legitimate travel. Long queues in front of EU consulates are a highly visible sign of the barriers to entry into the Union.' See Communication of the Commission to the Council and the European Parliament of 4 December 2006 on strengthening the ENP, COM (2006) 726.

105 COM (2006) 726. On 15 November 2007, the European Parliament adopted a report on the 2006 Communication (P6_TA (2007)0538).

In its Communication of 5 December 2007 called 'A Strong European Neighbourhood Policy,' the Commission again no longer mentioned the prospect of the Mediterranean countries' participation in the EU internal market. As regards the movement of persons, no stake in the EU internal market was mentioned, only the importance for people to move and interact with each other was emphasised. The Commission again proposed measures towards further economic integration, such as tailor-made free trade agreements:[106]

> 'Tailor-made deep and comprehensive free trade agreements (DFTAs), including measures to reduce non-tariff barriers through regulatory convergence, are the keys to increased economic integration with ENP partners. A DFTA should cover substantially all trade in goods and services between the EC and the ENP partner as well as strong legally-binding provisions on the implementation of trade and economic regulatory issues.'

1.4.3 *The integration instruments of the ENP*

According to the Commission, the integration of the Mediterranean countries into the EU internal market is a dynamic process, with the ENP Action Plans constituting an important first step towards integration. The ENP includes individual Action Plans which help to promote democracy, good governance, the rule of law and human rights and to provide support for economic innovation in the ENP countries. These plans have been built on the existing Euro-Med AAs and provide an agenda for working with the EU for the next three to five years. Contrary to the Euro-Med AAs, the ENP Action Plans do not include legally binding provisions. Before starting to work on these individual Action Plans, the Commission had prepared Country Reports which were used to identify priorities for each country.[107] In the course of 2004, the Commission held exploratory talks with some Mediterranean countries, namely Jordan, the Palestinian Authority, Israel, Morocco, Tunisia, Egypt and Lebanon, in close coordination with the Member States. On the basis of these Country Reports, the Commission drafted individual Action Plans. The Commission sent the draft Action Plans to the European Parliament, as well as to the European Economic and Social Committee (ECOSOC) and the Committee of the Regions for their information. Once the Commission had approved the Action Plans, they were endorsed by the respective Association Councils. The first ENP Action Plans with the Mediterranean countries, namely Israel, Jordan, Morocco,

---

[106] COM (2007) 774 final.

[107] Commission Staff Working Paper 'European Neighbourhood Policy' Country Report Jordan (COM (2004) 373 final, Brussels, 12 May 2004), SEC (2004) 569; *idem* Country Report the Palestinian Authority of the West Bank and Gaza Strip (COM (2004) 373 final), Brussels 12 May 2004, SEC (2004) 565; *idem* Country Report Israel (COM (2004) 373 final), Brussels 12 May 2004, SEC (2004) 568; *idem* Country Report Morocco (COM (2004) 373 final), Brussels, 12 May 2004, SEC (2004) 569; *idem* Country Report Tunisia (COM (2004) 373 final), Brussels, 12 May 2004, SEC (2004) 570; *idem* Country Report Egypt (COM (2005) 72 final), Brussels, 2 March 2005, SEC (2005) 72 final; *idem* Country Report Lebanon (COM (2005) 72 final), Brussels, 2 March 2005, SEC (2005) 289/3.

Tunisia and the West Bank and Gaza Strip, were approved by the Commission on 9 December 2004.[108] The ENP Action Plan with Lebanon was adopted on 19 January 2007.[109] For each Mediterranean country, the Action Plan is specifically designed to identify the specific interests of the country concerned. By means of these Action Plans the EU is offering the Mediterranean countries involved the possibility to join certain EU programmes and to get a stake in the EU internal market. The Action Plans should be implemented in the Mediterranean countries by the Association Councils, Committees and Subcommittees set up in the framework of each AA. The Commission draws up periodic Progress Reports and specifies areas that need further effort. For these reports, the Commission invites the Mediterranean countries to provide information and also draws on the expertise of other organisations, such as the Council of Europe, the OSCE, UN bodies and international financial institutions. At the end of 2006, the Commission published a first set of country-specific Progress Reports on the implementation of the first Action Plans. The first Progress Reports intended for the Mediterranean area were those regarding Israel, Jordan, the PA, Tunisia and Morocco.[110] These first Progress Reports, together with a detailed technical Assessment Report on Sectoral Issues, resulted in an Overall Assessment Report of the ENP.[111] This Overall Assessment Report was the first evaluation of the ENP since its inception and provided a basis for suggestions for improving the ENP. The suggestions themselves were presented in the essential Strategy Paper of the Commission of 4 December 2006.[112]

---

[108] Communication from the Commission to the Council of 9 December 2004 on the Commission proposals for Action Plans under the European Neighbourhood Policy, COM (2004) 795 final;

[109] Communication from the Commission to the Council of 5 July 2006 on the position to be adopted by the European Community and its Member States within the Association Council established by the Euro-Mediterranean Agreement establishing an association between the European Community and its Member States, of the one part, and the Republic of Lebanon, of the other part, with regard to the adoption of a Recommendation on the implementation of the EU-Lebanon Action Plan, COM (2006) 365 final.

[110] Commission Staff Working Document Accompanying the Communication from the Commission to the Council and the European Parliament on strengthening the European Neighbourhood Policy, ENP Progress Report Israel (COM (2006) 726 final), Brussels, 29 November 2006, SEC (2006) 1507/2; ENP Progress Report Jordan (COM (2006) 726 final), Brussels, 4 December 2006, SEC (2006) 1508/2; ENP Progress Report PA (COM (2006) 726 final), Brussels, 4 December 2006, SEC (2006) 1509/2; ENP Progress Report Tunisia (COM (2006) 726 final), Brussels, 4 December 2006, SEC (2006) 1510; ENP Progress Report Morocco (COM (2006) 726 final), Brussels, 4 December 2006, SEC (2006) 1511/2.

[111] Commission Staff Working Document Accompanying the Communication from the Commission to the Council and the European Parliament on strengthening the European Neighbourhood Policy, Sectoral Progress Report (COM (2006) 726 final), Brussels, 4 December 2006, SEC (2006) 1512/2, and Commission Staff Working Document Accompanying the Communication from the Commission to the Council and the European Parliament on strengthening the European Neighbourhood Policy, Overall Assessment (COM (2006) 726 final), Brussels, 4 December 2006, SEC (2006) 1504/2.

[112] Communication of 4 December 2006 from the Commission to the Council and the European Parliament on strengthening the European Neighbourhood Policy, COM (2006) 726 final.

1.4.4 *Level of Euro-Mediterranean integration*

The ENP addresses the four freedoms that lie at the basis of the EU internal market. Under the ENP, the EU has promised to give the Mediterranean countries a stake in the EU internal market of goods, services, capital and persons. Participation in the EU internal market is a form of economic integration in between the establishment of a customs union and that of an internal market. Moreover, the ENP Action Plans aim to offer the Mediterranean countries and the EU a significant measure of 'economic integration' through gradual integration into the EU internal market.[113] This implies that the ENP countries will be able to benefit from the four freedoms of the EU (free movement of goods, services, labour and capital). However, since the end of 2006, the Commission has declared that the key to the economic integration of the Mediterranean countries into the EU are Deep Free Trade Agreements (DFTAs) that will cover all trade in goods and services. It is unclear why the movement of persons and capital has not been mentioned again. The ENP, contrary to the EMP, initially included a more ambitious outlook for the ENP neighbours, and thus also the Mediterranean countries, i.e., to get a stake in the EU's internal market. However, this ambitious outlook of the ENP is still vague, unclear and variable in time. The ENP tends to shift back to a form of Euro-Mediterranean integration that is the establishment of a Euro-Med free trade area, which was already the objective of earlier Euro-Med policies.

1.5 **The Barcelona Process: the Union for the Mediterranean (UM)**

1.5.1 *The establishment of the UM*

In 2008, the French Presidency of the EU launched the idea of a Union for the Mediterranean region (UM).[114] The French President, Mr Sarkozy, received opposition from the other EU Member States and the Commission. This UM would completely overlap with the already existing policies and the EU Member States around the Mediterranean Sea would play too dominant a role. The UM encompasses all EU Member States, the Commission, the members and observers of the EMP (Mauritania, Morocco, Algeria, Tunisia, Libya, Egypt, Jordan, PA, Israel, Lebanon, Syria, Turkey and Albania) and the other Mediterranean coastal states (Croatia, Bosnia and Herzegovina, Montenegro and Monaco).

---

[113] See Introduction to all ENP Action Plans. The ENP's objective is to move beyond cooperation to a significant degree of economic integration, including through a stake in the EU's internal market.

[114] The Commission issued a Communication discussed at the European Council meeting in June 2008. On the basis of this discussion, the Ministers could further adopt the agreed position of the EU put forward at the inaugural meeting of the 'Mediterranean Union' in Paris on 13 July 2008. See Commission Communication to the European Parliament and the Council of 20 May 2008, 'Barcelona Process: Union for the Mediterranean', COM (2008) 319 final.

1.5.2 *The integration goals of the UM*

The UM includes three main goals which should give a new impulse to the EMP in at least three ways: (1) upgrading the political level of the EU's relationship with its Mediterranean partners, (2) providing more co-ownership to the multilateral relations, and (3) making these relations more concrete and visible through additional regional and sub-regional projects, relevant for the citizens of the region. The UM also mentions other objectives, which are not among the UM's three main goals:[115] it also defines the integration goal of the EMP, which is the establishment of a Euro-Med free trade area by 2010, and aims at enhancing the flow of exchanges among the people of the whole region. It remains to been seen whether this emphasis on the movement of people underlines the commitment to facilitate legal movement of individuals or whether it will just involve an orderly management of (il)legal migration.[116] Regarding the Euro-Med free trade area, the UM states the following:[117]

> 'The EU remains the main partner of Mediterranean countries both in trade of goods and services. Significant progress has been made towards the establishment of a Euro-Mediterranean free-trade area by 2010. Progressive free trade with the EU has favoured exports and investment, but services, and to a lesser extent agriculture, accounting for two-thirds of the GDP, are only now being included in the Euro-Mediterranean Free Trade Area. Slow but steady advances have been made in South-South economic integration which remains below potential. There have been improvements in macro-economic stability, inflation down significantly over 10 years, while human development indicators show improvements in health conditions and overall life expectancy. However, it is also true that further and faster reforms are needed if the EU's Mediterranean partners are to reap the potential benefits of globalisation and free trade with the EU and regional integration. Economic reforms, gradual free trade of industrial products with the EU, and improvements in economic governance, have not been enough to attract the domestic and foreign investment needed to boost standards of living in the region. Growth has been good but insufficient. Reforms have been encouraging but short of initial expectations. Free trade with the EU has favoured exports and investment. The combined effect of these shortcomings has been a slower than expected process. As a consequence of the insufficient growth and continued demographic expansion the prosperity gap between the EU and most Mediterranean countries has increased and there has been no real economic convergence. The formula of trade plus investment plus cooperation is as pertinent as it was in 1995. While there is more that the EU can do to promote trade, investment and co-operation in the region, the greatest need is for the countries of the region to take up these opportunities as part of their domestic economic policies.'

---

[115] COM (2008) 319 final, no. 19.

[116] Joint Declaration of the Paris Summit for the Mediterranean of 13 July 2008, no. 12.

[117] *Ibid.*, no. 11.

1.5.3 *The integration instruments of the UM*

The UM is not clear about the instruments that it will use to achieve its goals. It will probably use the instruments provided for under the EMP. The UM stipulates that co-ownership of the multilateral relations between the EU and the Mediterranean countries is important. The EMP and its instruments should be owned not only by the EU but by all Mediterranean countries.

1.5.4 *Level of Euro-Mediterranean integration*

The UM stipulates that the establishment of a Euro-Med free trade area, as defined under the EMP, is its ultimate, vertical Euro-Med integration goal. It is worth mentioning that the UM pays significantly less attention to the establishment of a Euro-Med free trade area compared to the UM's other aims. The UM also offers the Mediterranean countries facilitation of the legal movement of persons. It remains to be seen whether the support for the legal movement of persons will really give the Mediterranean countries a stake in the EU internal market of persons or whether it will merely involve a debate about the management of (il)legal migration and a people-to-people exchange issue, where only educated persons from the Mediterranean countries are offered the possibility to cross the Mediterranean Sea to enter the EU. It will probably be the latter seeing that the same French President who launched the UM, Mr Sarkozy, has been calling for an EU Pact on Immigration and Asylum since spring 2007. This Pact organises (il)legal immigration but takes into account the priorities, needs and reception capacities determined by each Member State. Member States have to define their priorities and needs, taking into account the Union's *acquis*. Moreover, they should attract highly qualified workers and take new measures to further facilitate the reception of students and researchers and their movement within the EU. It seems that the UM will indeed give the Mediterranean countries a stake in the EU internal market of persons, but only for certain persons, whom the EU can choose and based on the needs of the labour market in the Member States. It is obvious that the Mediterranean countries will not be satisfied with this new EU approach. It is a good example of how one Member State can influence the whole discourse of the liberalisation of the movement of persons between the Mediterranean countries and the EU.

1.6 **Sub-conclusion**

The EMP offers the Mediterranean countries a Euro-Med free trade area of goods, services and capital by 2010. According to economists and international organisations, the establishment of a free trade area is the second weakest form of integration. The ENP offers the Mediterranean countries a stake in the EU internal market of goods, services, capital and persons. Participation in the EU internal market is a form of integration that lies between the establishment of a customs union and the creation of an internal market, which is the strongest form of integration. In 2003, however, it was decided, under the ENP, to apply the 'carrot-and-stick' principle:

the strong integration form should be based upon the conditionality of progress in the Mediterranean countries. This conditionality will be fulfilled if the Mediterranean countries demonstrate that they share values with the EU, effectively implement political, economic and institutional reforms and align their legislation with the EU *acquis*. Suddenly, the ENP became selective, offering this strong integration only to the more advanced Mediterranean countries. It was decided, without motivation, to alter the ENP's Euro-Med integration goal: it no longer offers a stake in the EU internal market, but deep free trade agreements will be concluded with the Mediterranean countries. Without reasonable grounds, the ENP switched from a strong form of integration to the second weakest level of integration, i.e., the establishment of a Euro-Med free trade area. This change of the ENP will affect not only the level of integration of Mediterranean goods, services and capital into the EU, but also and mainly the integration of Mediterranean persons into the EU internal market, since the latter type of integration disappears from the plan. The ENP still applies the 'carrot-and-stick' principle: the ENP maintains the same stick (the Mediterranean countries still have to share values with the EU, effectively implement political, economic and institutional reforms and align their legislation with the EU *acquis*), but offers another, less tasty, carrot. It is obvious that the Mediterranean countries are not satisfied with this new approach. The most recent Euro-Med policy, the UM, focuses on the establishment of a free trade area by 2010. It remains to be seen how this Euro-Med policy will evolve in the future.

At present, there are 2 Euro-Med policies: the European Neighbourhood Policy (ENP) and the Barcelona Process: the Union for the Mediterranean (UM) that replaces the Euro-Med Partnership (EMP). This replacement however raises questions: the UM encompasses Mauritania, Morocco, Algeria, Tunisia, Libya, Egypt, Jordan, PA, Israel, Lebanon, Syria, Turkey, Albania, Croatia, Bosnia and Herzegovina, Montenegro and Monaco. The territorial scope of the UM is much broader than the territorial scope of the EMP. Do the new countries Croatia, Bosnia and Herzegovina inherit the whole Barcelona *Acquis*? Negotiations with Turkey did not resort under the scope of the EMP; so what is the intention of having Turkey as a member of the UM? There are also questions about the material scope of the replacement: the EMP is built around three important chapters, to which a fourth one was added in 2005. These chapters include all intentions for which the EMP has been established and have served as the main framework for all negotiations and Euro-Med Association Agreements. These chapters seem to have disappeared under the UM and have been replaced by other priorities, such as the institutional aspects, political dialogue and a conditionality based on environmental efforts and harmonisation. For these reasons, it is hard to put that the UM replaces the EMP.

2. The unilateral dimension of the Euro-Mediterranean relationship

Besides the multilateral dimension of the Euro-Med relationship, there is also a unilateral dimension, whereby only the EU is involved in the decision-making process. This chapter will briefly describe the EU's Mediterranean policy in order to clarify what is meant by the unilateral dimension of the Euro-Mediterranean relationship, since the multilateral and bilateral dimension, on the one hand, and the unilateral dimension, on the other, are often mixed up, thus leading to confusion. This chapter will also briefly highlight the aspect of EU financial aid to the Mediterranean countries and make a short analysis of the impact of the unilateral EU policies on the integration of the Mediterranean countries into the EU internal market.

2.1 The EU's Mediterranean Policy

The Euro-Mediterranean policies mentioned above, such as the EMP, the ENP and the UM, are not the same as the EU's Mediterranean Policy.[118] Only EU institutions are involved in the decision-making process regarding the EU's Mediterranean Policy. The Commission and the European Parliament decide on matters covered by the TFEU. which involve the Mediterranean region. These matters towards the Mediterranean area are for example the Common Agricultural Policy (CAP), the Common Commercial Policy (CCP) and visas, asylum and immigration. For example, as regards visas, asylum and immigration, the EU sometimes maintains an open-door policy where immigrants are concerned, but regularly switches to a closed-door policy. The Common Foreign and Security Policy (CFSP) and the Common Security and Defence Policy (CSDP), are based on the TEU and are dealt with mostly by the External Relations Council and the European Council. Below, the EU's legislative framework as regards the CAP, CCP and immigration will be discussed, as well as two important EU Mediterranean policies under the CFSP and the ECDP regarding the Mediterranean area.

2.1.1 *The Common Agricultural Policy and its impact on the Mediterranean countries*

The Common Agricultural Policy (CAP) is outlined in favour of European producers. Sensitive agricultural products, such as beans, peas, olives, citrus fruit, peaches and natural honey, are often excluded from the full liberalisation schedule. These products will only progressively be given greater access to the EU internal market, which is a direct result of the EU's CAP. The EU also regulates the protection of European producers of textile and clothing products. As regards these industrial products, the EU provides for full liberalisation towards the Mediterranean countries over a transitional period. The CAP thus has a direct effect on the integration of the Mediterranean countries into the EU internal market of agricultural products. After negotiations with the Mediterranean countries, these restrictive CAP

[118] E. Lannon and P. Van Elsuwege, 'The EU's Northern Dimension and the EMP-ENP: Institutional Frameworks and Decision-making Processes Compared', in P. Xuereb, ed., *The European Union and the Mediterranean. The Mediterranean's European Challenge*, Vol. V (Malta, EDRC 2004) pp. 3-71.

measures towards the Mediterranean countries were included in the different Euro-Med AAs and their Annexes.[119]

2.1.2 *The Common Commercial Policy and its impact on the Mediterranean countries*

The Common Commercial Policy (CCP) organises the commercial relations of the EU Member States with third countries including the Mediterranean ones. The CCP contains instruments of trade defence and market access intended to protect the EU internal market of goods and services. A few examples are presented below.

Council Regulation 3285/94 of 22 December 1994 applies to imports of products originating in third countries and lays down common rules for these imports into the EU, taking into account that these products can be freely imported into the EU.[120] The Regulation provides for surveillance and safeguard measures against imports from third countries to protect the interests of European producers. Surveillance measures are taken against products from third countries, such as the Mediterranean ones, if the import of a certain product into the EU threatens to cause injury to the European producers of like or competing products. Safeguard measures are taken when products from third countries are imported into the EU in such greatly increased quantities and/or on such terms or conditions as to cause, or threaten to cause, serious injury to European producers. Another Council Regulation, of 22 December 1995, protects dumped imports from countries not members of the EU.[121] A product is considered to be dumped if its export price to the EU is less than the comparable price for a similar product established in the ordinary course of trade within the exporting country. Finally, Council Regulation 2026/97 of 6 October 1997 protects against subsidised imports from countries not members of the EU.[122] This Regulation provides for the imposition of countervailing duties for the purpose of offsetting any subsidy granted, directly or indirectly, for the manufacture, production, export or transport of any product from a third country whose release for free movement in the EU causes injury.

It is obvious that these CCP measures restrict the integration of the Mediterranean countries into the EU internal market. Most of them form part the Euro-Med AAs, after they were negotiated with the Mediterranean partners.[123]

---

[119] The Euro-Med AAs and their Annexes will be discussed in Chapter IV.

[120] Council Regulation (EC) No 3285/94 of 22 December 1994 on the common rules for imports and repealing Regulation (EC) No 518/94, *OJ* L 349 of 31 December 1994, pp. 53-70.

[121] Council Regulation (EC) No 384/96 of 22 December 1995 on protection against dumped imports from countries not EC members, *OJ* L 56 of 6 March 1996.

[122] Council Regulation (EC) No 2026/97 of 6 October 1997 on protection against subsidised imports from countries not EC members, *OJ* L 288 of 21 October 1997, pp. 1-33.

[123] See Chapter IV.

2.1.3 *The EU's legislative framework regarding immigration issues and its impact on the Mediterranean countries*

The EU has granted all immigrant workers who legally reside and work in Europe rights under the European legislative framework.[124] The main European legal instruments for Mediterranean workers are Directive 2003/86/EC on family reunification and Directive 2003/109/EC concerning the long-term resident status.[125] In June 2003, the European Council of Thessaloniki stressed the need for further exploration of legal means for third-country nationals to migrate to the EU, taking into account the reception capacity of the Member States. The Council invited the Commission to present an Annual Report on Migration and Integration in Europe mapping EU-wide migration data, immigration and integration policies and practices.[126] Based on the results of this Report, the Council and the European Parliament adopted Directive 2004/38/EC of 29 April 2004 on the right of citizens of the Union and their family members to move and reside freely within the territory of the Member States.[127] The Commission also adopted a new proposal for a Regulation on cross-border traffic by nationals of third countries who live in border areas and regularly travel for legitimate reasons to a Member State without constituting a threat to security.[128] The proposal provides for the possibility of issuing a special visa to nationals of third countries subject to visa requirements who reside in border areas for the specific purposes of local border traffic.[129] The visa's terri-

[124] Mediterranean workers in Europe can never invoke Art. 54 ECT as they are not European nationals.

[125] *OJ* 2003 L 251/12 and *OJ* 2004 L 16/44 respectively.

[126] Presidency Conclusions of the European Council in Thessaloniki on 19-20 June 2005, available at: http://ue.eu.int/ueDocs/cms_Data/docs/pressData/fr/ec/85324.pdf.

[127] European Parliament and Council Directive 2004/38/EC of 29 April 2004 on the right of citizens of the Union and their family members to move and reside freely within the territory of the Member States amending Regulation (EEC) No 1612/68 and repealing Directives 64/221/EEC, 68/360/EEC, 72/194/EEC, 73/148/EEC, 75/34/EEC, 75/35/EEC, 90/364/EEC, 90/365/EEC and 93/96/EEC, *OJ* 2004 L 158/77.

[128] Proposal for a Council Regulation on the establishment of a regime of local border traffic at the external land borders of the Member States, COM (2003) 502 final. The Commission also proposed the establishment of an agency at the external borders, see Proposal for a Council Regulation establishing a European Agency for the Management of Operational Cooperation at the External Borders, COM (2003) 687 final. The Agency will facilitate the application of Community measures concerning the management of the EU's external borders by coordinating Member States' actions in the implementation of those measures. To that end, the Agency will provide the necessary technical support and expertise. The proposal was adopted through Council Regulation (EC) No 2007/2004 of 26 October 2004 establishing a European Agency for the Management of Operational Cooperation at the External Borders of the Member States of the European Union, *OJ* L 2004 349/1. On 26 April 2005, the Council decided that the Agency should have its seat in Warsaw. At the G5 meeting in Evian on 4 July 2005, the Ministers of the Interior recognised the importance of the European Border Agency in the coordinated EU fight against illegal immigration.

[129] Art. 3(b) of the Proposal defines a 'border area' as an area which, as the crow flies, does not extend more than 50 kilometres from the frontier. Art. 3(c) of the Proposal explains local border traffic as regular crossing of the external land border of a Member State by persons lawfully resident in the border area of a neighbouring country in order to stay in the border area of that Member State for a limited period of time provided for in the Regulation.

torial validity will be limited to the border area of the Member State. The French Presidency of the EU proposed the EU Pact on Immigration and Asylum, which is an example of such closed-door policy: increase in EU border controls, a system of biometric visas and a policy based on the reception of migrants according to EU preferences.

In the field of social security, Council Regulation No 1408/71 of 14 June 1971 forms the basis of the coordination of the social security schemes of the different Member States.[130] This Regulation, however, only applied to *certain* third-country nationals. Therefore, it was necessary to provide for the application of Regulation No 1408/71 to third-country nationals legally resident in the Union who were not covered by the provisions of this Regulation on grounds of their nationality and who satisfied all the conditions provided for in this Regulation. Council Regulation No 859/2003 of 14 May 2003 made this possible and extended the scope of Regulation No 1408/71.[131] Hence, Regulation No 1408/71 is now applicable to nationals of third countries who are not already covered by those provisions solely on the ground of their nationality, as well as to members of their families and to their survivors, provided they are legally resident in the territory of a Member State and are in a situation which is not confined in all respects within a single Member State.[132]

2.1.4 *The EU Common Strategy towards the Mediterranean area*

The EU reaffirmed the EMP and its Barcelona Declaration of 1995 in its Common Strategy (CS) towards the Mediterranean Region of 19 June 2000, which was adopted at the Feira European Council.[133] It covered all the relations of the EU with all its partners in the Barcelona Process, as well as Libya.

---

[130] Council Regulation (EEC) No 1408/71 of 14 June 1971on the application of social security schemes to employed persons and their families moving within the Community, *OJ* L 149 of 5 July 1971, p. 2 (original reference) and *OJ* L 230 of 22 August 1983, p. 8 (1983 updated reprint). Its implementation measures are provided for in Council Regulation (EEC) No 574/72 of 21 March 1972, laying down the procedure for implementing Regulation (EEC) No 1408/71, *OJ* 1992 L 74.

[131] Council Regulation (EC) No 859/2003 of 14 May 2003 extending the provisions of Regulation (EEC) No 1408/71 and Regulation (EEC) No 574/72 to nationals of third countries who are not already covered by those provisions solely on the ground of their nationality, *OJ* 2003 L 124/1.

[132] The European Parliament and the Council adopted Regulation (EC) No 883/2004 of the European Parliament and of the Council of 29 April 2004 on the coordination of social security systems, *OJ* 2004 L 166. This new Regulation will repeal Regulation No 1408/71 from the date on which its implementing regulation comes into force, scheduled for the end of 2009. However, Regulation No 1408/71 will remain in force and its legal effects remain valid for the purposes of Council Regulation No 859/2003 for nationals of third countries who are not already covered by those provisions solely on the ground of their nationality.

[133] Common Strategy 2000/458/CFSP of the European Council of 19 June 2000 on the Mediterranean region, *OJ* 2000 L 183/5. The application of the Common Strategy, for an initial period of four years, was prolonged for 18 months until 23 January 2006 by Decision 2004/763/CFSP of the European Council of 5 November 2004 amending Common Strategy 2000/458/CFSP on the Mediterranean region in order to extend the period of its application, *OJ* 2004 L 337/72, until 23 January 2006. No new decisions have been adopted to extend the Common Strategy's period of application, so it must be assumed that it has been silently replaced by the ENP.

2.1.4.1 Integration goals

According to the CS, the EU had the following goals regarding the Mediterranean region: (1) to make significant and measurable progress towards achieving the objectives of the Barcelona Declaration and its subsequent *acquis*, i.e., to establish a common area of peace and stability through a political and security partnership, to create an area of shared prosperity through an economic and financial partnership and to establish a partnership in social, cultural and human affairs; (2) to promote the core values embraced by the EU and its Member States; (3) to encourage and assist Mediterranean partners with the process of achieving free trade with the EU and among themselves in the terms of the Barcelona Declaration, economic transition and attracting increased investment to the region; (4) to strengthen cooperation in the field of justice and home affairs, as outlined by the Tampere European Council, and (5) to pursue the dialogue between cultures and civilisations in order to fight intolerance, racism and xenophobia.

2.1.4.2 Integration instruments

Part IV of the CS mentioned all the instruments and means for implementing the CS. The CS would be implemented by the EU institutions, but the Member States themselves would also contribute to the objectives of the CS by making use of all their relevant instruments and means.

2.1.4.3 Level of Euro-Mediterranean integration

The CS intended to establish a Euro-Mediterranean free trade area with a horizontal and vertical integration dimension. A free trade area is considered to be the second weakest form of economic integration after the preferential agreement. According to the European Parliament, the CS confined the free trade area to the free movement of goods and capital only. It excluded the free movement of services and persons from the partnership. The European Parliament was very critical of the CS. It regretted the fact that it had not been involved in the drafting of the document and that it was not given a role in it. Moreover, the instruments and means for achieving the free trade area were vague and the European Parliament criticised the absence of a budgetary framework for financing the CS.[134] Contrary to the opinion of the EP, the scope of this CS was very broad: it being a CFSP instrument, one would expect to find in it only the EMP's political and security aspects, but it went further than that: the CS also covered economic and social measures. These economic elements were included since economic stability in the Mediterranean region was considered a *conditio sine qua non* for political stability and security in the region. The EU should actively work on economic measures such as the progressive liberalisation of trade in all areas relevant to the Mediterranean coun-

[134] Committee on Foreign Affairs, Human Rights, Common Security and Defence Policy, Report on the Common Strategy of the EU on the Mediterranean Region, 22 January 2001; Salama, *supra* n. 82.

tries; to support measures to increase the attractiveness of the region to investors, particularly through the creation of a larger market, encouraging the alignment of policies relating to the EU single market, improving the regulatory framework, ensuring fair and equitable treatment of investors and raising awareness in the EU of investment opportunities in the region; to support efforts by Mediterranean partners to increase horizontal trade, particularly through horizontal trade agreements and the progressive harmonisation of rules of origin; to assist Mediterranean Partners in strengthening their capacity to formulate appropriate trade policies and to participate actively in trade negotiations; to encourage the liberalisation of current account payments with a view to full liberalisation of capital movements as soon as possible. It should also promote the euro as the contract and settlement currency for Mediterranean trade; develop a common approach to ensure the integration into society of Mediterranean partners' nationals who have been lawfully resident in a Member State for a certain period of time and hold a long-term residence permit, aiming at approximating their legal status in that Member State to that enjoyed by EU citizens; and exchange information and statistics with the Mediterranean partners on migration flows.

2.1.5 *European Strategic Partnership*

2.1.5.1 From a European Security Strategy towards a European Strategic Partnership

In 2003, the EU presented a European Security Strategy (ESS), the first ever comprehensive strategic vision of the Member States, as the CFSP was lacking strategic clarity.[135] The ESS was mainly drafted in response to the attack on the World Trade Centre on 11 September 2001, but also with a view to the approaching enlargement of the EU in May 2004. The enlargement of the EU was expected to increase security in Europe, but would also bring the EU closer to troubled areas. The ESS therefore aimed to promote a ring of well-governed countries to the east of the EU and on the borders of the Mediterranean. In the ESS, the EU sums up the new global threats that Europe faces, some emerging from the Mediterranean region: (1) Europe is both a target and base for terrorism linked to violent religious regimes; (2) proliferation of weapons of mass destruction (WMD) is potentially the greatest threat to EU security. The possibility of a WMD arms race is growing, especially in the Middle East. Advances in the biological sciences may increase the potency of biological weapons in the coming years, and there is also a serious possibility of chemical or radiological attacks; (3) regional conflicts, such as in the Middle East, impact directly and indirectly on European interests; (4) state failure, such as the collapse of state institutions in Somalia and Liberia, just to the south of the Mediterranean, is an alarming phenomenon that adds to regional instability; and (5) Europe is also a prime target for organised crime, such as cross-border trafficking in drugs, women, illegal migrants and weapons. In Part II, the ESS

[135] *Bull. EU* 12-2003, points 1.32.83 and 84.

mentions three actions that the EU should take to defend its security. Firstly, it should address these threats and, for example, continue taking measures to tighten export controls and deal with illegal shipments and illicit procurement. Secondly, the EU should build security in its neighbourhood. The resolution of the Arab-Israeli conflict, for example, is a strategic priority for Europe. The EU must also continue its engagement with the Mediterranean countries through more effective economic, security and cultural cooperation, since the Mediterranean area continues to experience serious problems of economic stagnation, social unrest and unresolved conflicts. Thirdly, the EU must establish an international order based on effective multilateralism. In this context, the EU requests countries that have placed themselves outside the bounds of international society and have sought isolation, such as Libya, to join the international community. In 2003, the EU Member States requested a strengthening of the partnership between the EU and the Arab world. A press release, entitled 'Reinforcing the partnership between the EU and the Arab World,' was issued by Javier Solana, Chris Patten and Romano Prodi in December 2003.[136] After intensive consultations with the regional partners, a European Strategic Partnership (ESP) with the Mediterranean and the Middle East was adopted by the EU Council on 18 June 2004.[137] This Strategy complements the EMP and the ENP. The ESP focuses on countries in North Africa and the Middle East, including the GCC,[138] Yemen, Iraq and Iran.[139] The EU has contractual relations with the GCC and Yemen, whereas there is no contractual framework with Iran and Iraq.

2.1.5.2 Integration goals

The ESP sets out different goals of the Euro-Mediterranean relationship. It promotes: (1) political reform, good governance, democracy and human rights; (ii) trade and economic cooperation, economic liberalisation and people-to-people contacts; and (iii) conflict prevention and resolution in the Mediterranean and the Middle East as well as measures to combat terrorism, proliferation of weapons of mass destruction and illegal immigration. The second goal – trade and economic cooperation, economic liberalisation and people-to-people contacts – is relevant in this context. The ESP will stimulate trade and economic cooperation, economic liberalisation and people-to-people contacts by continuing trade liberalisation in the EMP context with further liberalisation of agriculture and services and the full incorporation of regional cumulation of origin and promote the approximation of the regulatory frameworks with those of the EU, notably through the ENP Action Plans. In the field of migration, the EU aims to promote a comprehensive approach towards migration and the social integration of legally residing migrants and to

[136] 'Reinforcing the partnership between the EU and the Arab World', CFSP 791, Press Release No. 15945/03, Brussels, 9 December 2003.

[137] EU Strategic Partnership with the Mediterranean and the Middle East, June 2004, available at: http://ec.europa.eu/external_relations/euromed/index_en.htm.

[138] Saudi Arabia, Kuwait, Bahrain, Qatar, United Arab Emirates and Oman.

[139] Aliboni, *supra* n. 5, pp. 10-12.

extend to all partners the dialogue and cooperation on migration which has already started with some Mediterranean partners.

2.1.5.3 Integration instruments

The ESP calls for instruments different to the EMP instruments since it addresses the countries of the GCC, Iran, Iraq and Yemen. Most Mediterranean countries, in particular the Maghreb countries, are not eager to share their EU relations with the GCC and Iran. A similar EMP approach towards these countries, using the EMP instruments, might be too premature for the Arab Mediterranean countries. The ESP takes into account the differentiation requirements of individual countries in the region – it is not a 'one size fits all' approach. Existing instruments between the EU and the countries of the Mediterranean and the Middle East reflect the complexity and diversity of the EU's partners and their situations. There is no single framework for partnership. With the Mediterranean countries, the EU has a partnership which covers political and security dialogue, economic relations – including the creation of a free trade area – and social and cultural relations. The Cooperation Agreement with the GCC covers a number of areas of economic cooperation, followed up by negotiations for a free trade agreement. There is already a Trade and Cooperation Agreement with Yemen. At present, there are no formal relations with Iraq. With Iran, negotiations for a Trade Cooperation Agreement are pending.

2.1.5.4 Level of Euro-Mediterranean integration

In its relations with the EMP, the EU will continue trade with further liberalisation of agriculture and services and the full incorporation of regional cumulation of origin. In general, it will continue to promote achievement of the Euro-Med free trade area by the target date of 2010. In an annex to the ESP, the EU refers to the already existing frameworks, and states that the creation of a free trade area with the conclusion of Association Agreements is an important aspect of the EMP and that relations with the Mediterranean countries will be further enhanced within the ENP which has the objective of giving Mediterranean partners a stake in the EU four freedoms.[140] The ESP refers to the participation of the Mediterranean countries in the EU internal market, but sets itself the Euro-Mediterranean integration goal: the achievement of a free trade area by 2010.

2.2 Financial aid of the EU to the Mediterranean countries

Financial aid of the EU to the Mediterranean countries is also a unilateral and autonomous EU matter as it is legally based on financial regulations adopted by the Council of the EU, unlike the financial protocols which are contractual agreements annexed to bilateral Euro-Med agreements.[141]

---

[140] See Annex to the EU Strategic Partnership with the Mediterranean and the Middle East.

[141] See Lannon en Van Elsuwege, *supra* n. 118, p. 59.

2.2.1 *Financial aid of the EU to the Mediterranean countries under the EMP*

The MEDA[142] Programme, created in 1995, was the main financial instrument of the EMP. Under the MEDA programme, a broad range of programmes has been developed covering all aspects of the EMP. The MEDA programme has supported economic transition, a better socio-economic balance and regional integration. The MEDA Regulation of 1996 formed the legal basis of the MEDA programme, and is usually called MEDA I.[143] The MEDA I Regulation of 1996 was amended in 2000 and was then called MEDA II.[144] Through the MEDA I and MEDA II programmes, funding support recently amounted to over €800 million per year. Based on Strategy Papers covering the period 2000-2006, three-year national indicative programmes (NIPs) (Algeria, Egypt, Jordan, Lebanon, Morocco, Syria and Tunisia) were drawn up. MEDA funding was subject to the programming in these NIPs. Morocco was the leading beneficiary of EU financial assistance among the Mediterranean countries.[145] Tunisia and Egypt were also major beneficiaries of EU financial aid.[146] Algeria, however, was a marginal beneficiary of community assistance.[147] Jordan is considered an excellent performer in terms of use of MEDA funds, with up to 70% of commitments disbursed. Between 1996-2002, Lebanon received €150 million and an additional grant of €80 million for specific actions such as reintegration of displaced persons and the fight against drugs. Following the withdrawal of Israel from Southern Lebanon in 2000, another €4 million was granted as well as €9.2 million for further rehabilitation projects in the southern region. For Syria, the use of MEDA funds was important in order to provide policy advice and institutional capacity building to facilitate necessary legislation and reforms.[148] Libya has not been granted financial benefits under the MEDA programme as it is not yet a member of the EMP.

In addition, the European Investment Bank (EIB) has played an important role in providing assistance to the Mediterranean countries since the mid-70s. Its lending activities have been expanding continuously and currently involve around

142 MEDA comes from the French word 'Mesure's d'accompagnent.'

143 The MEDA Regulation forms the legal basis that enables the EU to provide financial and technical assistance to the Mediterranean countries with a view to realising the objectives of the EMP, Council Regulation (EC) No 1488/96 of 23 July 1996 on financial and technical measures to accompany (MEDA) the reform of economic and social structures in the framework of the Euro-Mediterranean partnership, *OJ* L 189 of 30 July 1996, amended by Council Regulation (EC) No 780/98 of 7 April 1998, *OJ* 1998 L 113.

144 Council Regulation (EC) No 2698/2000 of 27 November 2000, *OJ* 2000 L 311/1.

145 For more information, see M. Boussetta, *Processus de Barcelone et Partenariat euro-méditerranéen: le cas du Maroc avec l'Union européenne*, Working Paper No. 0110, available at: http://www.erf.org.eg/uploadpath/pdf/0110.pdf.

146 Tunisia was granted €686 million between the end of 1995 and 2003; between 1995 and 2003, major programmes in Egype were funded: Social Fund for Development (€155 million), Basic Education Programme (€100 million), Industrial Modernisation Programme (€250 million) and Health Sector Programme (€110 million).

147 Algeria was granted €304.2 million between the end of 1995 and 2003.

148 EIB Facility for Euro-Mediterranean Investment and Partnership (FEMIP): Progress Report on the Implementation of FEMIP and Prospects for the Business Plan, 27 March 2003.

€2 billion per year. In 2002, at a meeting of the Ministers of Finance of the 15 Member States and the 12 Mediterranean countries in Barcelona, a new financing instrument was created. The EIB would grant loans to the Mediterranean countries through the 'Facility for Euro-Mediterranean Investment and Partnership' (FEMIP). In November 2003, the Ecofin Council agreed to review the FEMIP mandate before the end of 2006. The Mediterranean countries have recently underlined the importance of creating a 'Euro-Mediterranean Development Bank' (EMDB). The possibility of establishing a EMDB should be carefully considered in the light of the FEMIP experience and taking into account the overall review of the EIB's external mandates.[149] On 10 December 2007, the Association Council adopted a decision providing EU macro-financial assistance to Lebanon. The assistance is exceptional and for a limited period, and supports Lebanon's fiscal consolidation effort aimed at reducing public debt to a sustainable level through implementation of its economic reform programme.[150]

At first sight, the EU's financial allocation to the Mediterranean countries seems to have increased between 1995 and the present year. When comparing the financial allocation for MEDA I (1995-1999) and MEDA II (2000-2006), Philippart reached the opposite conclusion. According to the financial presentation of the EU, it looked as if under MEDA I, €685 million had been allocated against €764 million under MEDA II. This financial presentation did not take into account that 1995 was only a marginal year for MEDA, since the programme officially started mid-November 1995. One should therefore take 1996-1999 as a more accurate basis of comparison, whereby the annual allocation for this period amounted to €812.8 million. MEDA II represented a financial decline and will most probably prove to be insufficient after the entry into force of all the AAs.[151]

2.2.2 *Financial aid of the EU to the Mediterranean countries under the ENP*

Under the umbrella of the ENP, the Commission proposed budgetary means other than those under the EMP.[152] Until 2007, MEDA had been the main financial assis-

[149] The Commission submitted an assessment in 2006 in this respect, in consultation with the EIB, see the Communication of the Commission to the Council and the European Parliament: 10th Anniversary of the Euro-Mediterranean Partnership: A work programme to meet the challenges of the next five years.

[150] Decision 2007/860/EC (*OJ* L 337, 21.12.2007).

[151] Philippart, *supra* n. 85, pp. 210-211. For a further evaluation of the MEDA programmes: Evaluation Report of Economic Cooperation between the European Commission and Mediterranean countries (countries under consideration in this study are Algeria, Egypt, Jordan, Lebanon, Morocco, Syria and Tunisia) November 2003, available at: http://europa.eu.int/comm/europeaid/evaluation/program/medrep.htm; E. Philippart, 'The MEDA Programme: Evaluation of the New Design of EU Assistance to the Mediterranean', in F. Attina and S. Stavridis, eds., *The Barcelona Process and Euro-Mediterranean Issues from Stuttgart to Marseille* (Milano, Giuffrè 2001) pp. 121-169.

[152] Proposal of the Commission for a Regulation of the European Parliament and of the Council laying down general provisions establishing a European Neighbourhood and Partnership Instrument, COM (2004) 628 final; Communication from the Commission to the Council and the European Parliament, 'Building our common future – Policy challenged and budgetary means of the Enlarged Union 2007-2013', COM (2004) 101 final/2.

Table II: Overview payments under Meda I+II

MEDA I+II (1995-2003)	
Country	Payments (mio)
Morocco	€ 412.9
Tunisia	€ 411.7
Egypt	€ 366.6
Jordan	€ 300.4
Lebanon	€ 63.7
Algeria	€ 62.8
Syria	€ 20.8
Israel	
PA	
TOTAL	€ 1638.9

tance instrument for the Mediterranean countries. MEDA provided support for the ENP in general and for the implementation of the Actions Plans in particular. Starting from 2007, another financial instrument has been operational, namely the European Neighbourhood and Partnership Instrument (ENPI), which focuses in particular on supporting the implementation.[153] The ENPI supports cross-border cooperation as well as regional cooperation projects involving both EU Member States and all ENP partner countries, including the Mediterranean countries. Over the period 2007-2013, the Commission intends to set aside an amount of €300m for a Governance Facility. This Governance Facility will provide additional assistance (on top of the normal country allocations) to support the work of the partner countries that have made most progress in implementing their Action Plans.[154]

Since the ENP reaches out not only to the Mediterranean countries but also to the other ENP partner states, potential benefits have to be allocated to a large number of countries which all have enormous capital demands. The Commission has stated that the ENP's aim is 'to share the benefits of the EU's 2004 enlargement with the neighbouring countries in strengthening stability, security and well-being.' Under the ENP, the Commission granted €955 million for the period 2004-2006: €700 million under the INTERREG programme, €45 million under MEDA, €75 million under TACIS, €90 million under PHARE and €45 million under CARDS.[155] As a result, the Mediterranean countries are put in the same basket with other countries, notwithstanding their highly different political, cultural and historical backgrounds. It is possible that the Mediterranean countries will

[153] Regulation (EC) No 1638/2006 of 24 October 2006 laying down general provisions establishing a European Neighbourhood and Partnership Instrument, *OJ* 2006 L 310/1.

[154] Communication from the Commission to the Council and the European Parliament on strengthening the European Neighbourhood Policy, Brussels, 4 December 2006, COM (2006) 726 final, p. 12.

[155] COM (2004) 373 final, p. 24.

suffer financially considering the territorial overstretch of the ENP.[156] Lannon and Van Elsuwege fear that the concentration of the EU's financial and economic aid towards the EU's eastern periphery will be at the expense of the southern periphery, since the new financial initiatives under the ENP have already been developed at the expense of the EMP.[157]

Financial assistance to the various Mediterranean countries under the ENPI takes account of the specific needs of each Mediterranean country and varies greatly from country to country. Since 2007, financial assistance to Lebanon, for example, has mainly been provided through the ENPI. Due to the fact that Lebanon's socio-economic development has been much affected by the 2006 hostilities, the EU has developed a twofold strategy: financial aid is aimed at the reconstruction needs arising from the military destruction and focuses on the priorities in the ENP Action Plan. The National Indicative Programme 2007-10 (NIP) states that the EU will offer Lebanon €187 million. Financial assistance to Israel, for example, reveals Israel's status as a developed economy. The NIP only allocated €8 million to support the implementation of *acquis*-related activities in Israel. The PA, on the other hand, is allocated a huge amount of financial assistance under the ENP. In 2007, the EU provided €550 million to the Palestinians, intended for emergency assistance and humanitarian aid in the areas of food aid, emergency job creation, health, psycho-social support, water and sanitation. The EU has also increased its contribution to the UNRWA's General Fund to €66 million in order to address the needs of the Palestinian refugees. There is also money for the private sector, for the judiciary, for the Central Elections Commission and for the Palestine Monetary Authority. Financial aid for Egypt is focused on the key priorities of the ENP Action Plan: political reform, competitiveness and productivity of the economy, and socio-economic sustainability of the development process. In the 2007-2010 NIP, a total of €558 million is allocated to support these three priorities.

3. Conclusion

It is obvious that the integration of the Mediterranean countries into the EU internal market of goods, services, capital and persons has played a significant role throughout the different Euro-Mediterranean policies. All Euro-Med policies include elements that contribute to the integration of the Mediterranean countries into the EU internal market. Since the beginning of the European integration process, the Mediterranean countries have been offered small economic benefits of the EEC common market. In 1995, the Euro-Mediterranean relations received a boost from the establishment of the Euro- Mediterranean Partnership (EMP). At present, the Euro-Mediterranean relations are dealt with through several Euro-Mediterranean policies that have contributed to the Euro-Med integration process: the Euro-Mediterranean Partnership (EMP) since 1995, the European Neighbour-

[156] Del Sarto and Schumacher, *supra* n. 45, pp. 30-33.

[157] E. Lannon and P. Van Elsuwege, 'The EU's Emerging Neighbourhood Policy and Its Potential Impact on the Euro-Mediterranean Partnership', in Xuereb, *supra* n. 34, pp. 60-61.

hood Policy (ENP) since 2002, and the Union for the Mediterranean (UM) since 2008. The initial policies (Global Mediterranean Policy and New Mediterranean Policy) were replaced by the EMP.

Most Euro-Mediterranean policies have set as their goal the establishment of a Euro-Med free trade area through the free movement of goods, services and capital. The EMP's goal is the realisation of a Euro-Med free trade area by the year 2010. It is only since the EU has been confronted with new trading powers, such as China and Russia, that it has been eager to transport all its internal market principles of free movement of goods, services, capital and persons to the Mediterranean countries. It was the ENP, in 2003, that offered the Mediterranean countries, for the first time, 'a stake in the EU internal market of goods, services, capital and persons.' This Euro-Med policy proposed a stronger form of Euro-Mediterranean integration and set as its ultimate goal the participation of the Mediterranean countries in the EU internal market. Contrary to earlier Euro-Med policies, the ENP included the movement of persons in the Euro-Mediterranean integration process. A few years later, however, the ENP altered its integration goal into the establishment of a Euro-Med free trade area. The most recent Euro-Med policy, the UM, brings confusion. The UM is supposed to revitalise the EMP, but contains no new measures to speed up the development of the Euro-Med free trade area. The establishment of the Euro-Med free trade area seems to be of minor importance compared to the other aims of the UM.[158]

Over the last decennia, all Euro-Med policies have produced interesting multilateral and bilateral instruments, such as the Euro-Med Conferences of Ministers of Foreign Affairs, the Euro-Med AAs under the EMP and the ENP Action Plans. These instruments should be able to realise the abovementioned goals set by the different Euro-Med policies. But it is a reality that none of the Euro-Med policies have achieved their Euro-Med integration goals despite the many instruments at their disposal. The EU and the Mediterranean countries do not seem to be able to achieve their goals, do not always clearly define their ambitions and are not afraid to alter their goals. This book analyses what the different instruments have achieved so far. Where do the Mediterranean countries stand in the Euro-Med integration process as regards the four freedoms of the internal market? The next chapters will analyse the instruments that the EU and the Mediterranean countries have used in stimulating the Euro-Mediterranean integration process in order to establish to what extent the Mediterranean countries have so far integrated into the EU internal market of goods, services, capital and persons.

The unilateral measures taken by the EU in the field of the EU's Mediterranean Policy do not fall within the material scope of this book. However, it must be pointed out that the EU's Mediterranean Policy certainly has an effect on the integration of the Mediterranean countries into the EU internal market. The EU measures in the framework of the CFSP are in favour of establishing a Euro-Med free trade area; the European Security Strategy (ESS) refers to the participation of the Mediterranean countries in the EU internal market. The reason for this policy

[158] COM (2008) 319 final, pp. 4-5.

is that economic stability is a *conditio sine qua non* for political and military stability in the Mediterranean area. The EU's Mediterranean Policy in the framework of the movement of persons between the Mediterranean countries and the EU is, contrary to the CFSP, often restrictive as regards the integration of Mediterranean persons into the EU. The Euro-Med liberalisation of the movement of persons has often been limited under pressure from individual EU Member States. The Common Commercial Policy (CCP) and the Common Agricultural Policy (CAP) of the EU aim to protect the EU internal market itself. Therefore, these EU policies often hinder further integration of the Mediterranean countries into the EU internal market. For example, sensitive agricultural products from the Mediterranean countries are not allowed into EU territory. Finally, financial aid, unilaterally determined by the EU, has a positive effect on the integration of the Mediterranean countries into the EU. It is another question whether the amount of financial aid to the Mediterranean countries is sufficient.

Chapter III

Multilateral instruments for integration of the Mediterranean countries into the EU internal market under the EMP and ENP

The EU and the Mediterranean countries use a range of multilateral instruments to establish a closer relationship in the field of movement of goods, services, capital and persons. In practice, these multilateral instruments implement the 'policies' discussed in the previous chapter, which are the Euro-Mediterranean Policy (EMP), the European Neighbourhood Policy (ENP) and the Union for the Mediterranean (UM). These multilateral instruments are, amongst others, meant to establish step by step a better integration of the Mediterranean countries into the EU internal market.

The Ministers of Foreign Affairs have gathered many times, in the framework of the EMP, in Euro-Mediterranean Conferences, discussing, amongst others, the Euro-Med liberalisation of goods, services, capital and sometimes persons.[159] The Ministers realised that certain issues, such as trade, financial affairs and migration, require more specific knowledge. In 2000, the Ministers of Foreign Affairs decided to take the discussion to a more specialised level. As a result, specialised Ministers have gathered in several sectoral Euro-Med Conferences such as the sectoral Euro-Med Conference on Trade and the sectoral Euro-Med Conference on Migration. These Conferences have addressed all four freedoms of the EU internal market. Another multilateral instrument of Euro-Med integration which the EU and the Mediterranean countries set up was the Euro-Mediterranean Parliamentary Forum, later replaced by the Euro-Mediterranean Parliamentary Assembly (EMPA). Then there are the conferences of experts, where economic experts provide information on economic integration issues at the Euro-Mediterranean Conferences on Economic Transition.[160] Under the ENP umbrella only one Conference has been organised.[161]

The WTO is also an important multilateral forum for EU trade negotiations, but it only involves some Mediterranean countries. WTO members are: Morocco since 1 January 1995, Tunisia since 29 March 1995, Israel since 21 April 1995, Egypt since 30 June 1995 and Jordan since 11 April 2000. Algeria, Lebanon, Libya and Syria are not yet WTO members. Algeria applied in 1987, Lebanon in 1999, Libya in December 2001 and Syria applied three times: in October 2001, January 2004 and September 2005. The PA has no official relations with the WTO. Since not all

---

159 Cf., *infra* 1. The Euro-Med Conferences of Ministers of Foreign Affairs.

160 Cf., *infra* 4. Expert Conferences on the Euro-Med integration process.

161 Cf., *infra* 5. The first Conference under the ENP umbrella.

Mediterranean countries are WTO members, the specific trade negotiations in the framework of the WTO will not be discussed here.

The multilateral instruments are used as a forum for political discussions, cultural cooperation issues and much more. However, the instruments will only be analysed in terms of their contribution to the integration of the Mediterranean countries into the EU internal market. It is the first time they are studied in detail.

The conclusions of each Conference together with the corresponding preparatory documents will be presented and examined. This examination will give a good insight into the evolution of the integration of the Mediterranean countries into the EU internal market under the different multilateral instruments. After this analysis, conclusions will be drawn as to whether these instruments have contributed to the free movement of goods, services, capital and persons between the EU and the Mediterranean countries, and, if so, to what extent they have contributed to the establishment of the four freedoms between the EU and the Mediterranean countries.

1. The Euro-Med Conferences of Ministers of Foreign Affairs

The first multilateral instrument established by the EU and the Mediterranean countries for the liberalisation of goods, services, capital and persons is the so-called 'Euro-Med Conference.' A Euro-Med Conference is a meeting of the Ministers of Foreign Affairs of the EU Member States and of the relevant Mediterranean countries (Algeria, Cyprus, Egypt, Israel, Jordan, Lebanon, Malta, Morocco, Syria, Tunisia, Turkey and the West Bank & Gaza Strip).[162] So far, nine such Conferences have been held under the EMP umbrella (Barcelona, 27 and 28 November 1995; Malta, 15 and 16 April 1997; Stuttgart, 15 and 16 April 1999; Marseille, 15 and 16 November 2000; Valencia, 27 and 28 April 2002; Naples, 2 and 3 December 2003; Luxembourg, 30 and 31 May 2005; Tampere, 27 and 28 November 2006; and Lisbon, 5 and 6 November 2007).[163]

The foundation of these Euro-Med Conferences was laid at the meeting of the European Council in Corfu in June 1994, where the importance of close links between the EU and its Mediterranean partners was stressed. In addition, the European Council expressed its will to develop these relations further so that the Mediterranean area would become an area of peace, security, stability and well-being. To that end, the Council of the EU requested the Commission to submit guidelines to strengthen the Euro-Med policy. In response to this request, the Commission issued the Communication on the Strengthening of the Mediterranean Policy of the EU 'Establishing a Euro-Mediterranean Partnership,' of 19 October 1994.[164] In

[162] Cyprus and Malta changed sides after their entry into the EU in 2004 and Turkey no longer took part in the Euro-Med Conferences because of its special status as an EU candidate country.

[163] There were also a number of *ad-hoc* Euro-Mediterranean Conferences (Palermo, 3-4 June 1998; Crete, 26-27 May 2003; and Barcelona, 27-28 November 2005) and Euro-Mediterranean Mid-Term Conferences (Dublin, 5-6 May 2004, and The Hague, 29-30 November 2004).

[164] COM (94) 427 final; in 1994, the Commission called the Euro-Med free trade area MEFTA.

this document the Commission stated that Europe and the Mediterranean countries should establish a vast Euro-Med free trade area to be completed by around 2010.[165] Without such a free trade area, economic disorder and destabilisation in the Mediterranean would become uncontrollable in the coming years.[166] The free trade area should provide for reciprocal trade in all manufactured products, for preferential and reciprocal access for agricultural products of interest to both parties and for free trade among the Mediterranean countries.[167] Ultimately, the Euro-Med free trade area should constitute the biggest free trade area in the world, covering 600-800 million people. Besides the establishment of a Euro-Med free trade area, the Mediterranean countries and the EU should engage in many other areas of cooperation. This cooperation should lead to the establishment of a Euro-Mediterranean Partnership (EMP). The European Council in Corfu further suggested the possibility of convening a conference between the Mediterranean countries and the EU in order to strengthen the EU policy in the Mediterranean region:

> 'The European Council stresses the value for all Mediterranean partners of jointly examining political, economic and social problems to which solutions may be more effectively sought in the context of regional cooperation. The European Council has given a mandate to the Council to evaluate, together with the Commission, the global policy of the European Union in the Mediterranean region and possible initiatives to strengthen this policy in the short and medium term, bearing in mind the possibility of convening a conference attended by the European Union and its Mediterranean partners.'[168]

The Council of the EU reacted positively to this suggestion and decided to hold a first Euro-Med Conference in Barcelona in 1995.[169] There would follow many

[165] The European Parliament agreed to the establishment of a Euro-Med free trade area (*Bull. EU* 11-1995, 1.4.57) and the Committee of the Regions declared that it would also follow the global approach of the Commission (*Bull. EU* 6-1995, 1.12, 1.13 and 1.49).

[166] The Commission is of the opinion that the line of action proposed in the Communication of 19 October 1994, which is set out in detail in an additional Communication of 8 March 2005, is indispensable if the EU wants to help the Mediterranean basin. The Commission issued additional documents in order to establish a free trade area, such as the Communication from the Commission to the Council and the European Parliament of 8 March 1995 'Strengthening the Mediterranean Policy of the European Union: Proposals for Implementing a Euro-Mediterranean Partnership', COM (95) 72 final. These documents constituted a useful framework for the Barcelona Conference in 1995.

[167] Example of a regional integration agreement: the Gaza-Jericho Agreement of 4 May 1994, in its Annex IV called 'Protocol on Economic Relations between the Government of Israel and the PLO', deals with the economic ties between Israel and the PA, including issues such as import/export, monetary policy, taxation, and the Palestinian work force employed in Israel. In the preamble, Israel and the PLO state that the economic domain is one of the cornerstones in their mutual relations with a view to enhancing their interest in the achievement of a just, lasting and comprehensive peace. This example shows that regional integration agreements are not always successful.

[168] European Council in Corfu, 24-25 June 1994, 'Conclusions of the Presidency', *Bull. EU* 6-1994, pp. 7-23.

[169] The European Council in Cannes agreed to this decision of the Council of the EU, see *Bull. EU* 6-1995, 1.12, 1.13 and 1.49, and see Annex V to the Conclusions of the European Council in Essen on 9-10 December 1994, no. 10: 'The Council of the EU recommends that the European Council agrees that the European Union should convoke in the second half of 1995 a Euro-Mediterranean Ministerial Conference. All Mediterranean countries concerned should be invited to that Conference. The

more Euro-Med Conferences, each time carefully prepared by the Commission. This chapter will also examine all preparatory Commission documents. It is the first time that these documents are analysed. The analysis will give a good idea of the influence of the Commission's opinion on the outcome of the Euro-Med Conferences.

1.1 Launch of the idea of a Euro-Med free trade area of goods, services and capital

The Conference in Barcelona in 1995 established the Euro-Mediterranean Partnership (EMP) of the EU and the Mediterranean countries (Algeria, Cyprus, Egypt, Israel, Jordan, Lebanon, Malta, Morocco, Syria, Tunisia, Turkey and the PA). The members of the Conference agreed that the EMP should be established through the conclusion of a series of Association Agreements between the EU and the Mediterranean countries.[170] These Association Agreements should accelerate the trade liberalisation process.[171] The Conference resulted in the so-called 'Barcelona Declaration,' which lays down the ground rules of the EMP.[172] It was the EU Council that gave political legitimisation for this Declaration about the EMP.[173] The Barcelona Declaration is a political declaration and contains no legally binding provisions.[174] It consists of 3 chapters:

The first chapter, 'Political and Security Partnership: Establishing a Common Area of Peace and Stability,' contains an ambitious summing-up of fundamental principles, such as respect for human rights and fundamental freedoms, development of the rule of law and democracy in political systems, etc. The second chapter,

---

Conference, which will require intensive preparation in cooperation with the countries concerned, should allow an in-depth discussion of future Euro-Mediterranean relations, addressing all relevant political, economic, social and cultural issues. The Conference should reach agreement on a series of economic and political guidelines for Euro-Mediterranean cooperation into the next century. The Conference will establish a permanent and regular dialogue on all subjects of common interest.'

[170] There are also bilateral sectoral agreements between the EC and the Mediterranean partners, such as the agreements on scientific and technical cooperation between the EC and Israel, *OJ* 1996 L 209 of 19 August 1996; two agreements on procurement by telecommunications operators and on government procurement between the EC and Israel, *OJ* 1997 L 202 of 30 July 1997; agreement on mutual recognition of OECD principles of good laboratory practice (GLP) and compliance monitoring programmes between the EC and Israel, *OJ* 1999 L 263/6 of 9 October 1999, etc.; see also G. Steinberg, 'Science and Politics: The Links between Israel and the European Community', in I. Greilsammer and J. Weiler, eds., *Europe and Israel: Troubled Neighbours* (Berlin, Walter de Gruyter 1988) pp. 340-345, and M. Maresceau, 'Bilateral agreements Concluded by the European Community', 309 *Recueil des Cours* (2004) pp. 125-451.

[171] *Bull. EU* II-1995, 2.3.1, pp. 153-159.

[172] At the Euro-Med Conference in Stuttgart in 1999, Minister Joschka Fischer called the Barcelona Declaration the *Magna Carta* of the EMP.

[173] See 'EU Council report for the European Council in Essen concerning the future Mediterranean policy' in Annex V to the Conclusions of the European Council in Essen on 9-10 December 1994, no. 10: 'The Conference should reach agreement on a series of economic and political guidelines for Euro-Mediterranean cooperation into the next century. The Conference will establish a permanent and regular dialogue on all subjects of common interest.'

[174] Lannon and Van Elsuwege, *supra* n. 118, pp. 35-36.

and in this context the most important one, is 'Economic and Financial Partnership: Creating an Area of Shared Prosperity.' The fear of marginalisation due to trade globalisation has resulted in the will of the Mediterranean partners to participate in the process of economic integration in the EU and the rest of the world. According to the Barcelona Declaration, the economic and financial partnership is based on three aspects: firstly, the progressive establishment of free trade; secondly, the implementation of appropriate economic cooperation and concerted actions in the relevant areas, which should lead to direct foreign investment, regional cooperation and industrial modernisation by providing a favourable environment and regulatory framework; and thirdly, a substantial increase in the EU's financial assistance to its Mediterranean partners. The third chapter of the Barcelona Declaration is called 'Partnership in Social, Cultural and Human Affairs: Developing Human Resources, Promoting Understanding between Cultures and Exchanges between Civil Societies.' Topics such as social development, health, culture, education, migration, drugs, terrorism and organised crime were put on the agenda for future discussion. Possible solutions to conflicts in the Middle East and the Maghreb countries were not included in the Declaration because of their complexity.[175] A Work Programme was annexed to the Declaration, consisting of practical measures to facilitate the establishment of the Euro-Med free trade area.[176] These measures are: a) harmonisation of rules and procedures in the customs field with a view to the progressive introduction of cumulation of origin; b) finding *ad hoc* solutions in particular cases; c) harmonisation of standards, including meetings arranged by the European Standards Organisations; d) elimination of technical barriers to trade in agricultural products and adoption of relevant measures related to plant health and veterinary rules as well as other legislation on foodstuffs; e) cooperation among statistics organisations with a view to providing reliable data on a harmonised basis; and f) possibilities for regional and subregional cooperation.

An interesting point is that for the first time the Euro-Mediterranean relations were split up into three important chapters. The most significant chapter in this context is the second or the economic and financial chapter, which stipulates that the Mediterranean countries and the EU will establish a Euro-Med free trade area of goods, services and capital by 2010. It is remarkable that the Work Programme annexed to the Barcelona Declaration already contained an extensive set of practical integration measures. At present, the Mediterranean countries are still applying these measures. Contrary to previous Euro-Med policies, the liberalisation of the movement of persons between the Mediterranean countries and the EU was not included in the Barcelona Declaration. Ten years later, however, the Ministers of Foreign Affairs would decide to add a fourth chapter to the Barcelona Declaration,

---

[175] S. Keukeleire, *Het Buitenlands Beleid van de Europese Unie* (Antwerp, Kluwer 1998) p. 385.

[176] The different levels of economic development of the Mediterranean partners are the main obstacle to the establishment of a free trade area. Private investment in the Mediterranean countries and economic cooperation are absolutely necessary if the Mediterranean partners and the EU want to reap the fruits of their mutual economic integration efforts, see E. Lannon, 'La Déclaration interministérielle de Barcelone, acte fondateur du Partenariat euro-méditerranéen', 398 *Revue du Marché Commun et de l'Union Européenne* (1996) pp. 362-363.

focusing on the liberalisation of the movement of persons between the Mediterranean countries and the EU.[177]

1.2 Greater harmonisation with the EU's internal market

In its Communication of 19 February 1997 the Commission stated that it would propose guidelines for the Conclusions of the second Euro-Med Conference of Ministers of Foreign Affairs, in Malta.[178] It pointed out that the Euro-Med free trade area was not an end in itself, but a means of improving competitiveness and integrating the Mediterranean partners into international trade. In this Communication the Commission emphasised the problem of the unequal stages of development of the different Mediterranean countries. Therefore, the Commission argued that progress towards free trade should be gradual and that the Association Agreements must take full account of the specific characteristics of each of the Mediterranean partners.[179] The Commission also outlined four goals to be attained in order to create a joint economic area: (1) greater harmonisation and greater compatibility with the EU's internal market; (2) greater harmonisation of policies; (3) preparing the Mediterranean partners for the transformations in the EU[180] to enable them to change their economic policies accordingly; and (4) strengthening the links among the Mediterranean partners.

Taking into account this Commission Communication, the Ministers of Foreign Affairs gathered at the Euro-Med Conference in Malta agreed to give new drive to the establishment of a Euro-Med free trade area, with 2010 as the target date. The Euro-Med free trade area aims at mutual liberalisation of trade in industrial goods, limited mutual liberalisation of agricultural products and free trade among the Mediterranean countries. The establishment of this free trade area must be in accordance with Article XXIV 5-8 GATT.[181] The Ministers promised to work

---

[177] Cf., *infra* 1.7 The human dimension of the Euro-Med integration: will the Euro-Med movement of persons appear on the agenda?

[178] Communication from the Commission to the Council and the European Parliament of 19 February 1997, 'Progress Report on the Euro-Mediterranean Partnership and Preparations for the Second Conference of Foreign Affairs Ministers', COM (97) 68 final, pp. 2-3.

[179] S. Calleya, 'Political and Economic Perceptions in the Euro-Mediterranean Area', in T. Veremis en D. Triantahyllou, eds., *The Southeast European Yearbook 1997-98* (Athens, the Hellenic Foundation for European and Foreign Policy 1998) pp. 156-157. S. Calleya is of the opinion that free trade will result in an increase in trade between the EU and the Mediterranean area and between the Mediterranean countries themselves. An increase in exports to the Mediterranean countries will lead to a negative balance of payments of these countries.

[180] The transformation of the EU was due to the enlargement to the east of the EU, the introduction of the euro and the setting-up of the European Central Bank.

[181] According to Art. XXIV 5-8 GATT, a free trade area has to be established according to a plan and schedule for the formation of such a free trade area within a reasonable length of time. At the Uruguay Round, it was concluded that a *reasonable length of time* meant that the free trade area must be established within a maximum of 10 years. Countries may exceed this term on the condition that they indicate special circumstances. The Euro-Med free trade area, which must be established by 2010, exceeds this notion of reasonable length of time. The EU and the Mediterranean countries will have to indicate special conditions to justify exceeding the period of 10 years. A justification could be the solid devotion to further integration. According to Art. XXIV 8(b) GATT, a free trade area means a group

harder on the negotiations and ratification of the Euro-Med Association Agreements, these being among the essential elements of the free trade area. They agreed to increase intra-regional and sub-regional cooperation, which is another fundamental element of the free trade area. The Ministers aim at gradual implementation of all three chapters of the Barcelona Declaration and the Work Programme. All Ministers of Foreign Affairs have ensured that measures will be taken to enable greater harmonisation and greater compatibility with the EU's internal market.

Unlike the previous Euro-Med Conference, this Conference resulted in Conclusions of the Presidency and not in a Declaration.[182] These Conclusions do not contain legally binding provisions.[183] At this Conference, two important principles were introduced: (1) the principle of harmonisation: the Mediterranean countries should try to harmonise their rules and regulations with the EU's internal market; and (2) the principle of gradualism: the EU must gradually implement the EMP. According to the Commission, gradual implementation of the EMP means a slow but steady implementation of the EMP taking into account the specific characteristics of the different Mediterranean countries. The influence of the Commission's opinion on the outcome of this Euro-Med Conference was obvious, since these two principles had been proposed by the Commission.

1.3 Criteria to become a Mediterranean partner of the EU

The third Euro-Med Conference in Stuttgart in April 1999 was preceded by an interim Euro-Med Ministerial Meeting in Palermo in June 1998. At the Palermo meeting, the Ministers examined the economic and financial chapter of the Barcelona Declaration. They recognised this chapter as the engine of the EMP since the provisions in it will minimise as much as possible the current economic disparities among the Mediterranean countries and the EU. This economic approach requires the establishment of a free trade area, reforms towards economic transition, the development of industrial and agricultural cooperation and actions to encourage private investment of European undertakings.

The Commission submitted guidelines for the Conclusions of the Stuttgart Conference in a Working Document on 17 March 1999.[184] In this document,

---

of two or more customs territories in which the duties and other restrictive regulations of commerce are eliminated *with respect to substantially all the trade* between the constituent territories in products originating in such territories. The AAs provide for full liberalisation of industrial products but only for limited and gradual liberalisation of agricultural goods. The question arises whether the Euro-Med free trade area comprises substantially all trade when agricultural products still remain subject to customs duties. The EU answers this question in the affirmative, stating that it has made a political commitment to also liberalise all trade in agricultural goods in the future. However, there are authors who believe that the limited liberalisation of agricultural products in the AAs is in contradiction with the obligations arising from the GATT. See J. McMahon, 'The Euro-Mediterranean Partnership: Making the Same Mistakes Again?', 6(2) *Irish Journal of European Law* (1997) pp. 217-218.

[182] Only the first Euro-Med Conference in Barcelona resulted in a Declaration.

[183] Only the Association Council, the Association Committee and the Association Subcommittees can issue legally binding decisions, cf., *infra* Ch. IV.

[184] Commission Working Document of 17 March 1999 to prepare the 3rd Euro-Mediterranean Conference of Foreign Ministers, SEC (1999) 424 final.

the Commission recommends a working method that should be used during the Euro-Med Conferences. The Ministers of Foreign Affairs have to avoid prepared speeches and long negotiating sessions, basing themselves on a text setting out agreed conclusions. Ministers should only exchange views in a direct way. They should also try to avoid discussions on financial amounts, which are matters of EU competence.

At the Conference in Stuttgart in April 1999, the Ministers of Foreign Affairs declared that further liberalisation of trade was necessary. They also committed themselves to completing the network of Association Agreements and encouraged the conclusion of free trade agreements among the Mediterranean partners. They called for all necessary measures to be taken to ensure a system with identical rules of origin which will open the way to full cumulation throughout the Euro-Mediterranean area as soon as possible. Full cumulation means that all enterprises should be able to produce their goods in the EU or in the various Mediterranean countries.[185] The Ministers agreed that Libya, which participated in the Euro-Med Conference as a guest of the Presidency, would become a full member of the EMP as soon as the UN Security Council sanctions had been lifted and Libya had accepted the entire Barcelona *acquis*.[186]

Little progress was made in the field of economic and trade issues at the Conference in Stuttgart. The Conference was mainly a confirmation of economic issues that had been discussed at earlier Euro-Med Conferences. The Commission prepared the Conclusions of the Euro-Med Conference in a Working Document and added that long negotiations and speeches should be avoided during the Conference. Furthermore, the Commission noted that the Mediterranean countries should abstain from commenting on the financial side of the EMP, the financial aspect being an EU competence. It seems that at this Conference only the EU side had a say and that the Mediterranean partners could not contribute in a constructive manner. The Conference seemed to have a unilateral dimension. It created conditions which countries should meet in order to become a Mediterranean partner of the EU.[187] Libya has to accept the whole Barcelona *acquis* if it wants to become a member of the EMP. This can be compared with the 'Copenhagen criteria,' which were agreed at the European Council in Copenhagen on 21-22 June 1993. In conclusion it can be stated that this Euro-Med Conference made only small steps forward as regards the integration of the Mediterranean countries into the EU internal market but that it did result in important criteria for countries to become a member of the EMP. These conditions still apply.

1.4 Deeper Euro-Med integration of goods, services and capital needed

In 2000, it became obvious that welfare gains related to the Euro-Mediterranean economic development had failed to emerge and European investments in

[185] Full cumulation is applicable in the European Economic Area.
[186] Conclusions of the Presidency of the Euro-Med Conference in Stuttgart, no. 37.
[187] Lannon and Van Elsuwege, *supra* n. 118, p. 38.

the Mediterranean region had not increased either.[188] The Commission admitted this failure for the first time in its Communication of 6 September 2000, which prepared the 4th Euro-Mediterranean Conference in Marseille. This document was called 'Reinvigorating the Barcelona Process.'[189] The Commission stated that the global and comprehensive approach, agreed at the Barcelona Conference of 1995, should be maintained since it was the only approach capable of avoiding the stagnation of the past. Furthermore, the Commission considered that the Mediterranean countries and the EU should draw lessons from the first five years of the EMP. The Commission made specific proposals in a number of problematic areas and took steps aimed at further integration of the Mediterranean countries into the EU internal market.

In short, the main reinvigorating measures of the Commission were the following: (1) first, a detailed examination of steps that should lead to free trade agreements covering all sectors should be carried out.[190] (2) Second, the Commission noted that in relation to trade in services there were significant barriers to market access in the Mediterranean countries. This prevented service suppliers from taking full advantage of the opportunities available and also reduced foreign investment. Therefore, liberalisation of market access and improved regulation of trade in services should form an important dimension of the economic development of the Mediterranean partners. (3) Third, the European experience of establishing an internal market should be used to identify an appropriate regulatory framework for a Euro-Med free trade area. The Commission already issued a Communication on the EMP and the EU internal market in 1998.[191] It proposed that a timetable should be defined by 2002 for single-market type harmonisation measures of priority sectors such as rules of origin, customs matters, norms and standards and intellectual property protection. The implementation of this harmonisation programme, which would cover both convergence with the EU and intra-Mediterranean harmonisation, would take place as of 2004.

At the Euro-Med Conference in Marseille, the Ministers of Foreign Affairs submitted guidelines for the future in order to make the EMP a more efficient and credible preferential economic instrument.[192] The Ministers emphasised the prin-

---

[188] T. Schumacher, *The Survival of the Fittest: the First Five Years of Euro-Mediterranean Economic Relations,* EUI Working Paper RCSAS No. 2004/13, p. 14.

[189] Communication from the Commission to the Council and European Parliament of 6 September 2000 to prepare the 4th meeting of the Euro-Mediterranean Foreign Ministers, 'Reinvigorating the Barcelona Process', COM (2000) 497 final.

[190] The different steps that should lead to a Euro-Med free trade agreement were set out at the 6th sectoral Conference of Ministers of Trade on 21 October 2007 in Lisbon.

[191] Communication of the Commission of 23 September 1998 on the Euro-Mediterranean Partnership and the Single Market, COM (1998) 538 final.

[192] The Conference in Marseille in 2000 was held under great political tension. See *Voice of Palestine* of 11 November 2000: Nabil Sha'th, PA Minister of Planning and International Cooperation: 'We will attend the Euro-Mediterranean Conference, which will be held in Marseille next week 15th-16th November, but upon our own conditions. We agreed with the Arab brothers who are participating in the Conference that we will attend in spite of Israel's participation.' *AFP News Agency* of 13 November 2000: 'French Foreign Affairs Minister Hubert Vedrine on Monday 13th November insisted on the holding of the European-Mediterranean conference in Marseille despite the situation of pessimism

ciple of free movement of goods and services in the Euro-Mediterranean area; they also urged for new measures to be taken aimed at greater liberalisation of agricultural trade; they stressed the importance of the conclusion of free trade agreements amongst the Mediterranean countries which had signed Euro-Med AAs with the EU, within five years;[193] they insisted on the introduction of diagonal cumulation between countries with identical rules of origin and on the adoption of harmonisation measures in priority sectors. At the institutional level, the Ministers of Foreign Affairs proposed taking the discussions on the economic and trade chapter of the EMP to a higher level through regular meetings of senior officials of the ministries responsible for such matters.

In conclusion, it can be stated that significant reinvigorating measures were taken by the Euro-Med Ministers of Foreign Affairs in Marseille. Not only free movement of goods was considered to be important, but free movement of services appeared on the agenda of a Euro-Med Conference for the first time. It was again the Commission which pointed out the necessity of putting the emphasis on the Euro-Med liberalisation of the movement of services. The need for a regulatory framework in the Euro-Med area through the harmonisation of rules and regulations was reaffirmed and considered to be of top priority. The discussion about the Mediterranean integration of goods, services and capital into the EU internal market was taken to a more specialised level. Since then, the Euro-Med Conferences have taken place not only at the level of Ministers of Foreign Affairs but also at that of sectoral Ministers, government experts and representatives of civil society.[194]

1.5 Impact of the attacks of 11 September 2001 on the Euro-Med integration

Following the attacks of 11 September 2001, the Commission drafted an extensive document to prepare the meeting of the Euro-Med Ministers of Foreign Affairs in Valencia in 2002.[195] This document consisted of 15 recommendations to the Minis-

concerning the peace process.' *United Press International* of 15 November 2000: 'Syria and Lebanon said Tuesday they would boycott the Euro-Mediterranean Conference that starts in Marseille because of Israeli participation and what is called an unclear European position over the violence in the Middle East. A Syrian source told United Press International that Foreign Minister Farouk Sharaa would not participate in the Marseille meeting for a number of reasons but mainly because of the explosive situation in Palestine and the unclear European position vis-à-vis the situation.' *AFP News Agency* of 13 November 2000: 'Libya officially announced today that it would boycott the EU-Mediterranean Conference to be held in Marseille on 15th-16th November and called on the Arab countries not to participate in it. Libya will not attend the ministerial meeting, Mr. Hasuna Shayush, a senior official in the Libyan Foreign Ministry, told AFP, asserting that the meeting was aimed at integrating Israel into the Mediterranean.'

[193] It must be noted that such free trade agreements, except for the Agadir Agreement, have so far not been concluded.

[194] Cf., *infra* 2. Sectoral Euro-Med Conferences of specialised Ministers.

[195] Communication from the Commission to the Council and the European Parliament to prepare the meeting of Euro-Mediterranean Ministers of Foreign Affairs, Valencia, 22-23 April 2002, SEC (2002) 159 final.

ters and expressed the need for the Euro-Mediterranean partners to deepen their mutual relations and create a zone of peace and prosperity through the integration of goods, services and capital. The events of 11 September 2001 had an obvious impact on the Commission and the Euro-Mediterranean partners.[196] The tension in the Middle East was also peaking.

In its Communication, the Commission again stressed the importance of creating a free trade area with the Mediterranean partners not only for goods but also for services. Liberalisation of trade in agricultural products should be reciprocal instead of one-sided.[197] The Commission added that a free trade area could only be fully developed if it were accompanied by supporting measures such as the harmonisation of standards, technical regulations and (phyto)sanitary requirements. Harmonisation in these areas and other areas to be contemplated could pave the way for the creation of a Euro-Mediterranean internal market. The forthcoming Euro-Med Conference should put forward proposals with a view to introducing appropriate reforms for the gradual development of a Euro-Mediterranean internal market.

This Communication of the Commission and its 15 recommendations led the Euro-Med Ministers of Foreign Affairs to draft an Action Plan[198] on 23 April 2004 at the 5th Euro-Med Conference held on 22 and 23 April 2003 in Valencia.[199] In this Action Plan, important actions were proposed in relation to the political and security partnership, but also as regards the economic partnership. As for the economic chapter, the Action Plan welcomed the Agadir process, which created a free trade area between Morocco, Tunisia, Egypt and Jordan. The Action Plan emphasised the development of free trade in services and the prospects of a Euro-Mediterranean internal market through harmonisation of policies and regulations.[200] It also supported the creation of a Working Group on Trade Measures Relevant for Regional Integration and the participation of the Mediterranean partners in the pan-European system of rules of origin. The Ministers also agreed to reinforce the parliamentary dimension of the EMP and recommended establishing a Euro-Mediterranean Parliamentary Assembly (EMPA).

It is significant that the attacks of 11 September 2001 had a considerable impact on the Euro-Med integration process: the improvement of the economic situation in the Mediterranean region through further integration into the EU internal market

[196] See also M. Cebeci, 'EU Foreign Policy after September 11 and the Significance of the Mediterranean', in Xuereb, ed., *supra* n. 34, pp. 197-213.

[197] Recommendations 8 and 9.

[198] Also called the Valencia Action Plan.

[199] The Conference in Valencia brought together the Ministers of Foreign Affairs of the 15 Member States of the EU and of Algeria, the PA, Cyprus, Egypt, Israel, Jordan, Malta, Morocco, Tunisia and Turkey. Libya and Syria refused to take part. Also present were Mr Solana, High Representative for the CFSP and Secretary-General of the Council, Commissioner Patten, and, as special guests, representatives from Libya, the Arab League, Mauritania and the Arab Maghreb Union.

[200] The Euro-Med Conference in Valencia was preceded by an interim Euro-Med Ministerial Meeting in Brussels on the 5-6 October 2001. The Ministers of Foreign Affairs decided to convene after the 11 September attacks in an *ad hoc* ministerial meeting to condemn these terrorist actions. At this meeting, the Ministers already urged for the creation of a Euro-Med internal market.

was considered to be a *conditio sine qua non* for peace and prosperity in the Mediterranean region. The EU and its Mediterranean partners realised that, first and foremost, the economic chapter should be reinforced. Therefore, it was announced that the EU and its Mediterranean partners should prepare to create a 'Euro-Med internal market.'

1.6 Preparation of the extension of the Euro-Med free trade area to include ten new Member States

In 2003, it became obvious that the Mediterranean partners had failed to build the South-South dimension of the Euro-Med free trade area. The Agadir Agreement between Egypt, Jordan, Morocco and Tunisia was the only promising initiative regarding South-South free trade.

On 15 October 2003, the Commission issued a Communication to prepare the 6th Euro-Med Foreign Affairs Conference.[201] The Commission advised the Euro-Med Ministers of Foreign Affairs to take new steps to deepen and extend the Euro-Med free trade area.

It recommended the following actions: (1) The Commission prioritised regional and multilateral integration. Other Mediterranean partners should join the Agadir Agreement, implying the signature and implementation of genuine free trade agreements between Mediterranean countries as soon as possible, in order to complete a Euro-Med free trade area by 2010. The other Mediterranean partners should also be encouraged to respond positively to Turkey's attempts to conclude free trade agreements with them. (2) A higher level of progressive reciprocal liberalisation of trade in agricultural products should be attained in order to complete the Euro-Med free trade area. All Association Agreements already included provisions for further liberalisation of trade in agriculture and fishery. Additional protocols on further agricultural liberalisation were concluded with Tunisia and Israel and discussions with Morocco were well advanced. In the Agreement with Lebanon, a more open approach on agricultural liberalisation was based on a negative list of restricted products instead of on a positive list of totally or partially liberalised items. (3) The Commission stated that the movement of services should be further liberalised. In their provisions on services, Association Agreements vary greatly. Some include provisions on the right of establishment and commercial presence (Jordan and Algeria). Others contain *rendez-vous* clauses for further liberalisation of services (Morocco, Tunisia, Lebanon and Jordan). (4) Further actions should be carried out

---

[201] Communication from the Commission to the Council and the European Parliament to prepare the 6th Meeting of Euro-Mediterranean Ministers of Foreign Affairs in Naples on 2-3 December 2003 (Barcelona VI), COM (2003) 610 final. At the time of this Communication, AAs had been signed between the EC and 11 of the 12 Mediterranean partners. Two of these 11 (Cyprus and Malta) were EU acceding countries, and with Turkey, a candidate country, a customs union agreement had been concluded. With Tunisia, Israel, Morocco, Jordan and the PA, agreements were in force. Lebanon had signed an interim Association Agreement and Egypt would do so soon. Algeria had refused to sign an interim agreement. With Syria, negotiations for an Association Agreement were ongoing. The end date of the transition periods for tariff dismantling varies from 2008 (Tunisia) to 2014 (Lebanon). For Egypt and Algeria, the transition period will go beyond 2014.

as regards the approximation of legislation. Trade liberalisation depends on the convergence of technical regulations and regulatory provisions relating to the free movement of goods.

In conclusion, it can be stated that the Commission advised the Ministers of Foreign Affairs to agree on the necessary steps to be taken to complete the free trade area: increased reciprocal liberalisation of trade in agriculture and services, further approximation of legislation and the entry into force of the Agadir Agreement. These elements had to be in place by the time the new Member States would join the EU on 1 May 2004.[202]

The 6th Euro-Med Conference of Ministers of Foreign Affairs in Naples in 2003 took place during a period of stagnation in the Middle East peace process. The Second Intifada had erupted, resulting in multiple suicide attacks on Israeli territory and renewed occupation of the West Bank & Gaza Strip by the Israeli authorities. There was more tension in the Mediterranean region because of the crisis in Iraq and terrorist attacks in Istanbul, Saudi Arabia and Morocco. Furthermore, the Mediterranean countries faced other severe challenges over the years to come: strong pressure in the labour market, the need for deeper structural reforms, and insufficient integration into world trade and investment flows. These challenges and the instability in the Mediterranean region led the Ministers of Foreign Affairs to call for stronger commitments of the Mediterranean countries and the EU at the Conference: (1) Mediterranean countries should substantially reform their political system and economy. In return, the ENP[203] offers the Mediterranean countries gradual integration into the enlarged EU internal market and the possibility of eventually achieving the EU's four fundamental freedoms: free movement of goods, services, capital and people. In order to arrive at integration into the EU internal market, the Mediterranean countries should start regulatory and legislative approximation.[204] (2) The Ministers of Foreign Affairs established the Euro-Mediterranean Parliamentary Assembly. This newly created EMPA was included in the framework of the EMP process.[205] The text on the setting-up, election and functioning of the EMPA is attached as an annex to the Conclusions of the Presidency of this Euro-Med Conference.[206] (3) The Protocol on rules of origin to all agreements should be replaced by the pan-Euro-Mediterranean Protocol. Trade liberalisation in services should be reviewed. The Framework Protocol on Services common to all Mediterranean countries will serve as a basic document for all Mediterranean countries. (4) For the first time, the importance of migration appeared on the agenda since it was stated that migration could be a positive factor for the socio-economic growth of the whole region. There should be a dialogue on migration, legal migration and illegal migration should be regulated in readmission

[202] COM (2003) 610 final, p. 11, Recommendation 6.

[203] The European Neighbourhood Policy (ENP) was developed in 2004, but was first outlined in a Commission Communication called 'Wider Europe' in March 2003, COM (2003) 104 final.

[204] This Euro-Med Conference was the last one before the enlargement of the EU in 2004.

[205] The EMPA has 240 members, 120 from the Mediterranean countries and 120 from Europe (75 members of national parliaments and 45 members of the European Parliament).

[206] Cf., *infra* 3, The Parliamentary Dimension of the Euro-Med integration process: Attention for Citizens.

agreements, and the movement of legal persons and social integration of migrants should be facilitated.

It was expressly stated that the explosive situation in the Mediterranean region underlined the urgent need for the EU to support political and economic reform in the Mediterranean region. Therefore, this Conference led to many economic measures that would speed up the formation of the Euro-Med free trade area. Many were even more far-reaching than those suggested by the Commission. It was again the instability in the Mediterranean basin that pushed the EU to take further integration measures.

Also interesting is the fact that it was the last time the fifteen Member States convened before the EU enlargement in 2004, i.e., without the ten new members of the EU. Consequently, the fifteen discussed all matters relevant to the Mediterranean region before the ten new Member States shifted the emphasis to cooperation with their neighbours to the east of the EU in the framework of the ENP. The ENP gives the Mediterranean countries a stake in the EU internal market of goods, services, capital and persons, which is a more ambitious offer than the level of integration provided by the EMP. In 2004, two Euro-Med policies existed alongside each other, the EMP and the ENP. Both offered the Mediterranean countries a different level of integration into the EU. This is particularly relevant as regards the Euro-Med liberalisation of the movement of persons, which only appears on the ENP agenda.

1.7 The human dimension of the Euro-Med integration: will the Euro-Med movement of persons appear on the agenda?

The Luxemburg Conference was the first Euro-Med Conference that took place after the enlargement of the EU with ten new Member States on 1 May 2004.[207] For the first time, the Ministers of Foreign Affairs of the ten new Member States attended the Euro-Med Conference.[208] All participants in the Conference had to take account of the ENP, since 2004 was the year in which it was developed. At the Luxemburg Conference on 30 and 31 May 2005, the 25 Ministers of Foreign Affairs drafted an extensive overview of the past ten years of Euro-Mediterranean relations. For the future, it was decided in consensus to embark on a new chapter of Euro-Mediterranean integration by starting negotiations on the liberalisation of trade in services and a discussion on the right of establishment on a voluntary basis. The road map for the liberalisation of services and the right of establishment and for trade liberalisation in agricultural, processed agricultural and fishery products should be adopted. This road map provides for constant liberalisation with a selected number of exceptions and timetables for gradual implementa-

[207] However, a Euro-Med Mid-Term Meeting of Ministers of Foreign Affairs was held on 4 and 5 May 2004 in Dublin where the Foreign Affairs Ministers from the enlarged EU met with their Mediterranean counterparts. There was also a Euro-Med Meeting of Ministers of Foreign Affairs in The Hague on 29-30 November 2004 to prepare the 10th anniversary of the EMP.

[208] Cyprus and Malta already participated in the EMP, but attended the Euro-Med Conferences on the Mediterranean side.

tion. Accompanying measures providing for the structural, institutional, legal and administrative support necessary to ease access to export markets should be considered. Migration was considered to be a central element of the Euro-Mediterranean relations, which resulted in the decision to take the migration issue to a more specialised platform, namely specific meetings of relevant senior officials.[209]

This seventh Euro-Med Conference of Ministers of Foreign Affairs in Luxemburg prepared the way for the Barcelona Summit to be held on 27 and 28 November 2005 celebrating the 10th anniversary of the EMP. The Commission drafted a Communication which included an extensive five-year Work Programme to be presented at the Summit.[210]

First, the Commission stated that liberalisation of agricultural and fishery products was one of the main challenges of the next five years. Therefore, a road map and timetable should be agreed for trade liberalisation in agricultural, processed agricultural and fishery products. The road map should provide for a high degree of liberalisation with a very limited number of exceptions.

Second, the Commission proposed a new approach concerning the liberalisation of trade in services and the right of establishment. The EU and its Mediterranean partners would enter a new chapter of integration by engaging negotiations not on the traditional 'hub and spoke' model, which had been followed since 1995, but on a 'voluntary participation' model. This new approach would consist of opening up negotiations to all Mediterranean partners willing to enter into such a regional agreement.[211] The results of the bilateral talks with the willing Mediterranean partners would be transparent and would be made known to the other (willing and non-willing) Mediterranean countries on the basis of the principle of non-discrimination embedded in the so-called regional Most Favoured Nation (MFN) clause. This regional MFN clause would ensure that all Mediterranean partners would be guaranteed to get the best offer made by the EU in any sector to any country. In return, the Mediterranean countries would open their sectors to each other as well as to the EU. The EU and the Mediterranean countries should therefore agree to negotiate on the liberalisation and integration of trade in services and the right of establishment.

Third, the Commission stressed the importance of approximation of technical legislation. Approximation of technical legislation in the area of standards and conformity assessment is considered to be important for the integration of the economies. This approximation will lead to easier and cheaper market access through the reduction of costs related to duplicative testing and certification. The harmonisation of economic legislation already started on the basis of the Work Programme adopted at the Euro-Med Trade Ministerial Conference in Palermo

[209] Cf., *infra* 2. Sectoral Euro-Med Conference on Migration.

[210] Communication of the Commission to the Council and the European Parliament of 12 April 2005 'Tenth Anniversary of the Euro-Mediterranean Partnership: A work programme to meet the challenges of the next five years', COM (2005) 139 final.

[211] This approach mirrors the Framework Protocol on Services, which was adopted by the Ministers of Trade in Istanbul in July 2004 and which served as a template in further negotiations.

in 2003.[212] This Work Programme contains a number of important steps towards harmonisation and/or mutual recognition of trade-related standards across the Euro-Mediterranean region. The EU and its Mediterranean partners should jointly improve actual approximation, regulatory and infrastructure upgrading. Once the approximation is accomplished and equivalent legislation is in place, Agreements on Conformity Assessment and Acceptance (ACAAs) of industrial products can be negotiated. The Commission views these ACAAs for industrial products as regulatory 'trade corridors' to the benefit of economic integration.

Fourth, the Mediterranean countries should conclude free trade agreements between themselves and existing ones should be upgraded into genuine free trade agreements in order to achieve the objective of a wide Euro-Med free trade area by 2010. These free trade agreements should also implement the pan-Euro-Med cumulation of origin. The pan-Euro-Med cumulation of origin is expected to bring considerable benefit to the economic operators. In practice, it means that textiles woven in Syria can be made into mattresses in Israel, be finished in Jordan and subsequently be exported to the EU while these mattresses still benefit from preferential access to the EU.

At the Barcelona Summit in November 2005, Euro-Med Heads of State and Government agreed on a five-year Work Programme. Along with this Programme, a Code of Conduct to Counter Terrorism was agreed upon. A fourth chapter was added to the Barcelona Declaration, called 'Migration, Social Integration, Justice and Security.' This concerns the promotion of legal migration opportunities, the facilitation of legal movement of individuals, fair treatment and integration policies for legal migrants and reduction of the level of illegal immigration.

An interesting point is that the 25 EU Ministers and the Ministers from the Mediterranean countries at the Luxemburg Euro-Med Conference came to agreed Conclusions. It was the first time since 1995 that Ministers succeeded in presenting Presidency Conclusions that were taken in consensus.[213] The Ministers of Foreign Affairs drafted an extensive overview of the work done since the initiation of the Barcelona Process in 1995 and drew up guidelines for the future. They introduced the principle of voluntary participation regarding the liberalisation of services and the right of establishment; they adopted a road map for liberalisation of services and right of establishment with a selected number of exceptions and timetables for gradual implementation. They moreover suggested that the issue of movement of people should be dealt with by a group of experts in the field. The ACAAs should lead to further integration of industrial products of the Mediterranean countries into the EU.

1.8 Euro-Med movement of persons reduced to migration management

On 25 October 2006, the Commission issued a Communication on the preparation of the Tampere Euro-Mediterranean Conference of Ministers of Foreign Affairs

[212] Cf., *infra* 2.2.3, Six Point Work Programme.

[213] Agreed Conclusions of the Presidency are not legally binding either.

called 'The Euro-Mediterranean Partnership: Time to Deliver.'[214] Firstly, the Commission was of the opinion that the partners should, first and foremost, focus on negotiations about the liberalisation of services and the right of establishment. General talks had started with seven Mediterranean partners (Egypt, Israel, Jordan, Lebanon, Morocco, PA and Tunisia). These talks should be followed by bilateral and more specific negotiations with these Mediterranean partners. Secondly, the partners should focus on negotiations about deeper agricultural liberalisation. Negotiations on progressive liberalisation of agricultural, processed agricultural and fishery products had already begun with a number of Mediterranean partners with a view to concluding agreements. Thirdly, a dispute settlement mechanism should be established. Negotiations had been launched with all Mediterranean partners to agree on the establishment of a dispute settlement mechanism in order to solve trade disputes. Finally, the partners should focus on regulatory convergence.[215] In sectors where legislation was harmonised at EU level, Mediterranean countries were encouraged to align their legislation, standards and conformity assessment procedures with the EU system with the objective of removing technical barriers to trade. Mediterranean countries would receive assistance in order to accelerate reforms and regulatory convergence. They would also get assistance to put in place the necessary quality infrastructure and legislation, with a view to concluding ACAAs.

At the Tampere Conference at the end of November 2006, the Ministers of Foreign Affairs stated that the achievement of a Euro-Med free trade area by 2010 in accordance with the provisions of the Association Agreements was still a priority. Therefore, the Ministers drafted a Work Programme for 2007 as regards the progressive liberalisation of trade in services and the right of establishment, the progressive liberalisation of trade in agricultural, processed agricultural and fishery products, with some exceptions, and the establishment of a dispute settlement mechanism. They also focused on timetables for gradual and asymmetrical implementation, taking into account the characteristics of the agricultural sector in the different countries. Regulatory convergence, with the emphasis on approximation of technical legislation, should be put into practice. As regards the movement of people, the Ministers underlined the need for a better management of migratory flows and for improved cooperation on all aspects of migration between all parties, legal and illegal migration, including the fight against trafficking in human beings. They also urged for negotiations to be held on different kinds of readmission agreements.

In conclusion, it can be stated that the Ministers put the issue of (il)legal migration more prominently on the agenda. The fourth chapter of the Barcelona Declaration added at the former Euro-Med Conference regarding the legal movement of persons has turned out to be only a discussion about legal and illegal migration.

---

[214] COM (2006) 620 final.

[215] The Commission also awaited the results of the Sustainable Impact Assessment (SIA) on the Euro-Med Free Trade Area, which were expected by the end of 2006. These results would be very important for further negotiations on trade liberalisation. All reports are available at: http://www.sia-trade.org.

Other than that, the Ministers reproduced the ideas of the Commission in their Work Programme for 2007.

1.9 Euro-Med liberalisation of the movement of services including the right of establishment

On 17 October 2007, the Commission issued a Communication on the preparation of the Lisbon Euro-Mediterranean Foreign Affairs Conference called 'The Euro-Mediterranean Partnership: Advancing Regional Cooperation to Support Peace, Progress and Inter-cultural Dialogue.'[216] At the Lisbon Conference, the Ministers of Foreign Affairs again reproduced the conclusions of the Commission. They referred to the significant progress made in the negotiations on services and the right of establishment. Most Mediterranean partners had shown interest in negotiations on services and the right of establishment. Therefore, the Commission would launch bilateral negotiations with a 'number of willing Mediterranean partners.'[217] These negotiations on bilateral services and investment would start in early 2008 and be concluded by 2010. Negotiations on trade liberalisation in agricultural, processed agricultural and fishery products were progressing between Egypt, Israel and Morocco. Tunisia would open negotiations before the end of 2007. Such negotiations were concluded between the Commission and Jordan in 2005 and resulted in a high level of mutual liberalisation. Discussions were also being held on bilateral agreements on mutual recognition and protection of geographical indications for agricultural products. European direct investments in the Euro-Med region increased and the Facility for Euro-Mediterranean Investment and Partnership (FEMIP) was an important contributor to this positive evolution.

1.10 The launch of a new Euro-Med policy: 'the Barcelona Process: Union for the Mediterranean'

The Ministers of Foreign Affairs gathered for the first time in the framework of the 'Barcelona Process: Union of the Mediterranean' in Marseille. In July 2008, the French Presidency of the EU organised a Conference about the Barcelona Process: Union for the Mediterranean (UM). The UM builds further on the initiatives taken under the EMP umbrella but puts the emphasis on issues such as sustainable deployment, energy, water management, environment and fight against pollution. The UM favours a co-presidency with a small secretariat with 2 directors, one from the EU and one from the Mediterranean countries. This should enhance the joint ownership of the Euro-Med process. However, stumbling blocks are just around the corner. The Commission declared that the Arab countries would never accept a possible Israeli Presidency. Driss remarked that the co-presidency of the UM would be pointless if it had no decision-making power, because in that case the

[216] COM (2007) 598 final and SEC (2007) 1309.

[217] This was agreed at the Lisbon Meeting of Trade Ministers on 21 October 2007.

only decision-making power would remain with the EU.[218] It is very doubtful that the UM will lead to improved integration of the Mediterranean countries into the EU internal market for goods, services, capital and persons.

Most remarkable is the fact that a third Euro-Med policy, the UM, was launched besides the EMP and the ENP. The integration aim of this Euro-Med policy is the establishment of an ambitious, deep Euro-Med free trade area. To reach this integration goal, the UM proposes different actions: (1) bilateral negotiations with Egypt, Morocco, Tunisia and Israel on the liberalisation of trade in services and the right of establishment, launched in 2008, should continue in 2009; (2) priority should be given to speeding up Agreements on Conformity Assessment and Acceptance (ACAAs); (3) bilateral negotiations on the establishment of a more efficient dispute settlement mechanism for the trade provisions of the AAs should continue; and (4) capacity building and institutional development in trade and trade-related matters should be reinforced.

1.11 Sub-conclusion

The Euro-Med Conferences have proven to be a vital instrument for Euro-Med integration because of the following reasons: (1) the Conferences function as the engine of the Euro-Med integration process since they gather to discuss the most significant topics regarding the Euro-Med liberalisation of the movement of goods, services, capital and persons. The outcome takes into account world events, such as the volatile situation in the Middle East, the attacks of 11 September 2001 and more recently, the global financial crisis; (2) the Conferences split up the Euro-Med relations into three chapters and later added a fourth chapter on the human dimension of the partnership; (3) the Conferences launch essential principles for the further Euro-Med integration process, such as the principle of harmonisation with EU norms, the principle of gradualism of the Euro-Med integration process and the principle of voluntary participation in integration negotiations, such as the negotiations on the liberalisation of services between the Mediterranean countries and the EU; and (4) the Conferences take vital decisions, for instance, to create specialised Euro-Med Conferences to attain further liberalisation of the Euro-Med movement of goods, services, capital and, ultimately, persons.

Although these Euro-Med Conferences constitute an important instrument for Euro-Med integration, they have not led to the material integration of the Mediterranean countries into the EU as such because of the following reasons: (1) none of the interesting proposals, decisions and conclusions adopted at these Conferences have ever been further developed by the Ministers of Foreign Affairs; (2) no proposals, decisions and conclusions have ever been implemented in practice by the Ministers of Foreign Affairs. What can be learned from the Euro-Med Conferences is that the Ministers of Foreign Affairs act as stimulators of the Euro-Med integration process, but that it is up to other Euro-Med multilateral instruments to

[218] A. Driss, *Putting the Mediterranean Union in Perspective: North-African Perspectives*, Euromesco Paper, June 2008, pp. 20-23.

develop the ideas of the Ministers of Foreign Affairs and to put them into practice. These multilateral instruments will be discussed below.[219]

In addition to the previous, it is noteworthy that most new ideas, initiatives, principles, etc., proposed by the Ministers of Foreign Affairs at the Euro-Med Conferences are in fact mostly the ideas of the Commission. It is therefore obvious that the Commission has an important impact on the outcome of the Euro-Med integration process; many ideas and proposals of the Commission have been reproduced in the Conclusions of the Euro-Med Conferences. Consequently, it can be stated that it is mainly the Commission (and, to a lesser extent, the Ministers of Foreign Affairs) which acts as the engine or stimulator of the Euro-Med integration process. In other words, the Commission has had a positive, constructive and stimulating influence on the Euro-Med integration process.

It must be noted that it is not only the Ministers of Foreign Affairs of the EU Member States but also the Ministers of Foreign Affairs of the Mediterranean countries who reproduce the ideas of the Commission. It can be questioned whether the Ministers of the Mediterranean countries are always willing to reproduce the ideas of the Commission and, subsequently, whether there is a possibility for better participation of the Ministers of Foreign Affairs of the Mediterranean countries in the Euro-Med integration process. It was the European Council in Corfu that declared that the Mediterranean countries must 'jointly' examine political, economic and social problems in the context of regional cooperation. 'Jointly' means that both sides, European and Mediterranean, must have a say in the decision-making process. In practice, however, the Euro-Med Conferences of Ministers of Foreign Affairs manifestly adopt the carefully prepared Commission proposals which only represent the European side. The one-sided character of the Euro-Med Conferences is also emphasised by the fact that all Euro-Med Conferences have taken place in EU countries and never in a Mediterranean country.

In reality, the Mediterranean countries do no more than follow the EMP from the sidelines and each Euro-Med Conference has confirmed this state of affairs. This has created an EMP imbalance in favour of the EU. Some speak of an almost imposed European leadership. The EU, however, cannot be blamed for its strong urge to take initiative or for the efficient economic cooperation between the Member States. The main problem is that the Mediterranean countries are still not able to act together, since they are characterised by too many divergences and never speak with one voice.

Therefore, the Mediterranean partners should create an independent Mediterranean institution in which all Mediterranean countries can, through independent experts and delegates, jointly examine problems and prepare documents and joint statements for the Euro-Med Conferences in order to counterbalance the weight of the EU. In addition, the Ministers of Foreign Affairs have admitted that the Euro-Med Conferences are mainly a one-sided process. They looked for a solution and found one in the creation of sectoral Euro-Med Conferences that should enhance joint ownership of the EMP. Furthermore, the French Presidency of the

---

[219] Cf., *infra* 2. Sectoral Euro-Med Conferences of specialised Ministers.

EU, responsible for the creation of the 'Barcelona Process: Union for the Mediterranean', decided to hold the Euro-Med Conferences also in cities in the Mediterranean region.

2. Sectoral Euro-Med Conferences of specialised Ministers

Discussions about the liberalisation of the movement of goods, services, capital and persons between the EU and the Mediterranean countries required more specialised knowledge. In 2000, at the Euro-Med Conference in Marseille, the Ministers of Foreign Affairs decided that the Euro-Med movement of *goods, services and capital* should be discussed in the framework of a more specialised platform. This resulted in the establishment of sectoral Euro-Med Conferences where specialised ministers such as Ministers of Trade or Ministers of Finance discuss specific topics. In fact, the specialised Euro-Med Conferences already existed before 2000, but only for the Ministers of Industry of the Mediterranean countries and the Member States. Discussions on Euro-Med movement of *persons* were transferred to a specific platform as a result of a decision of the Euro-Med Conference in Luxemburg in 2005. At the Euro-Med Conferences on Migration, the specialised Ministers are mainly those responsible for Home Affairs.

These Euro-Med Conferences take place between specialised Ministers and/or senior officials of the EU Member States and the relevant Mediterranean countries (Algeria, Cyprus, Egypt, Israel, Jordan, Lebanon, Malta, Morocco, Syria, Tunisia, Turkey and the PA). Only the sectoral Euro-Med Conferences that have contributed to the integration of the Mediterranean countries into the EU internal market will be discussed below.[220] There are also sectoral Euro-Med Conferences on Environment, Water, Information Society, Energy, Transport, Culture and Health, which will not be examined here.

2.1 The liberalisation of the Euro-Med movement of industrial products

The first sectoral Euro-Mediterranean Conference took place in Brussels in 1996 between the Ministers of Industry of the Mediterranean countries and the EU Member States. This Conference adopted a mechanism of meetings at ministerial level, to be held every two years, aimed at identifying the Euro-Med priorities of the industrial sector.[221] The 4th and 6th Euro-Med Conferences of Ministers of Industry require particular attention because of their contribution to the Mediterranean integration into the EU internal market. At the 4th sectoral Euro-Med Conference in Malaga in 2002, the Ministers of Industry remarked that Euro-Med industrial

---

[220] The sectoral Euro-Med Conferences will be discussed in chronological order of establishment.

[221] First Euro-Med Conference of Ministers of Industry in Brussels in May 1996; 2nd Euro-Med Conference of Ministers of Industry in Klagenfurt in October 1998; 3rd Euro-Med Conference of Ministers of Industry in Limassol in June 2000; 4th Euro-Med Conference of Ministers of Industry in Malaga in April 2002; 5th Euro-Med Conference of Ministers of Industry in Caserta in October 2004; Euro-Med Conference of Ministers of Industry in Rhodes on 21-22 September 2006.

cooperation would lead to more stability in the Middle East, which had been hit by the Second Intifada. The Ministers of Industry noted moreover that approximation of standards, technical regulations and conformity assessment systems of the Mediterranean countries with those of the EU was extremely important. Some areas are more in need of harmonisation with EU rules than others. Areas where Mediterranean partners have significant export interests are considered to be top priority for harmonisation. The EU should support the process of approximation by establishing the necessary infrastructure in the Mediterranean countries, such as accreditation bodies, testing laboratories, certification bodies, metrology laboratories, inspection agencies and other technical institutions. In their Conclusions, the Industry Ministers stated the following:

> 'The experience of the EU's Internal Market suggests that the harmonisation of the regulatory framework could constitute a key element in the establishment of a well functioning Euro-Med Free Trade Area. Particular attention should therefore be paid to the proper implementation of the Euro-Med market programme, which could lead to the identification of areas where harmonisation with EU rules could be viewed as particularly useful and addressed as matter of priority. Non-tariff barriers should progressively be abolished to take full advantage of the Free Trade Area. In this respect, a key element in the establishment of a large market for goods should be, among other possibilities, the approximation of Mediterranean partners' standards, technical regulations and conformity assessment systems with those in force in the EU.'[222]

In 2006, at the Euro-Med Industry Conference in Rhodes, and in 2008, at the Euro-Med Industry Conference in Nice, the Ministers reiterated the importance of the approximation of legislation in the fields of technical legislation, standards and conformity assessment procedures with the EU system. Approximation will remove barriers and facilitate the free movement of industrial goods in the Mediterranean region and the EU. By 2006, the Mediterranean countries had identified their priority areas for harmonisation and the approximation process had begun. This process should lead to Agreements on Conformity Assessment and Acceptance of Industrial Products (ACAAs) in sectors relevant to both parties. The Ministers also addressed the issue of non-harmonised areas, where the Mediterranean countries and the EU have to rely on the principle of mutual recognition. They insisted on transparent legislation and administration on both sides since the mutual recognition system is based on trust in each other's system. The EU asked the Mediterranean partners to identify problems related to the movement of goods in non-harmonised sectors.[223]

Very significant issues regarding the liberalisation of the movement of industrial products have been discussed: (1) harmonisation will first happen in areas where the Mediterranean countries have essential export interests; (2) the EU

---

[222] See Conclusions of the 4th Euro-Med Conference of Ministers of Industry in Malaga, 9-10 April 2002.

[223] See the Conclusions of the 6th Euro-Med Conference of Ministers of Industry, Rhodes, 31-22 September 2006 and the Conclusions of the 7th Euro-Med Conference of Ministers of Industry, Nice, 5-6 November 2008.

will provide for the necessary infrastructure to make harmonisation feasible; (3) harmonisation will lead to the conclusion of ACAAs which will function as trade corridors for industrial products. Crucial is the fact that the Ministers of Industry also pay attention to non-harmonised sectors, the principle of mutual recognition and any practical problems encountered. These sectoral Euro-Med Conferences will lead to binding documents, such as Mediterranean legislation that is in conformity with the relevant Union *acquis* and ACAAs.

2.2 The liberalisation of the Euro-Med movement of goods and services, including the right of establishment

The sectoral Euro-Med Conferences on Trade were established at the 4th Euro-Med Foreign Affairs Conference in Marseille in 2000, where it was decided to take the discussion on trade issues to a higher level.

2.2.1 *A new and practical approach to the Euro-Med integration process*

The first Euro-Med Conference of Ministers of Trade took place in Brussels on 29 May 2001.[224] The objective of this sectoral Conference was to reinvigorate the economic and financial chapter of the Euro-Med Declaration of 1995. At this first Conference, the Ministers of Trade stressed the importance of the WTO as the main forum for multilateral trade matters.[225] Therefore, the EU and the Mediterranean countries had to agree on an outline to prepare for the next WTO meeting in Qatar.[226] With a view to reinvigorating the trade chapter of the Barcelona Declaration, the Ministers took a more practical approach: they established the Working Group on Services, the Working Group for Approximation of Legislation and the Working Group on Rules of Origin.

2.2.2 *Need for easier access of goods*

The second Euro-Med Conference on Trade was held in Toledo on 19 March 2002. The Ministers of Trade stated that the pragmatic approach to the trade chapter seemed to be very rewarding. The Working Group on Rules of Origin completed its work successfully within a few months. As a result, the Ministers of Trade agreed to the participation of the Mediterranean countries in the system of pan-European cumulation of origin.[227] The other Working Groups, on Services and Approximation of Legislation, were asked to continue their research. The Ministers agreed on an ambitious Action Plan on Trade and Investment Facilitation.[228]

---

224 Five years after the sectoral Euro-Med Conference on Industry in 1996.

225 The following Arab and Mediterranean countries are members of the WTO: Morocco, Tunisia, Israel, Egypt and Jordan.

226 The 4th Ministerial Meeting of the WTO was held in Doha, Qatar, from 9 to 13 November 2001.

227 These pan-Euro-Mediterranean Protocols on rules of origin are annexed to the Euro-Med AAs. See also the Explanatory Note of the Commission concerning the pan-Euro-Mediterranean protocols on rules of origin of 21 January 2006, *OJ* 2006 C 16/2.

228 The Action Plan is annexed to the Conclusions of the Presidency of the Euro-Med Conference on Trade in Toledo.

The Action Plan should meet the real interests of the business communities, such as small and medium-sized enterprises (SMEs). The Action Plan contains measures to (1) simplify and harmonise customs and trade procedures, reducing the delay for goods clearance and reducing administrative costs for traders; (2) ensure that public policy objectives such as protecting health, safety and the environment are met: there is a need to ensure that mandatory technical regulations for assessing conformity with technical regulations and standards do not create unnecessary obstacles to trade; (3) foster investments flows; (4) ensure that intellectual property rights are adequately protected; and (5) improve technical assistance. In order to implement this Action Plan, the Ministers set up another Working Group, namely the Working Group on Trade Measures Relevant for Regional Integration.

2.2.3 *Major steps forward as regards the integration of the Mediterranean countries into the EU*

At the 3rd Euro-Med Conference in Palermo in July 2003, the Ministers of Trade endorsed the new Protocol on the pan-European system of cumulation of rules of origin.[229] This Protocol allows the extension of the pan-European system of cumulation of origin to the Mediterranean countries. The harmonisation of rules of origin in the Euro-Mediterranean area represents a major step forward since it will significantly facilitate trade in the Euro-Mediterranean region and contribute to the creation of a free trade area.

The Ministers reaffirmed the objective of liberalisation of trade in services between the EU and the Mediterranean countries. To this end, they agreed on establishing a non-binding Framework Protocol for the liberalisation of trade in services. This Framework Protocol was to explain the main principles of movement of services between the Mediterranean countries and the EU.[230] They instructed the Working Group on Services to draw up this Framework Protocol.

Furthermore, the Ministers launched a new initiative on the approximation of legislation in the field of standards, technical regulations and conformity assessment procedures. The initiative involved concluding Euro-Med agreements according to which certain products will enter the EU internal market freely without additional testing and certification.

Finally, the Euro-Med Ministers of Trade approved the Action Plan for the Free Movement of Industrial Products and instructed the Working Group on Trade Measures Relevant for Regional Integration to implement the Six Point Work Programme necessary to approximate legislation.[231] These six points are: 1) identification of priority sectors for which approximation is most needed; 2) acquain-

---

[229] The Working Group on Rules of Origin no longer needs to convene since it has completed its task. Future issues as regards rules of origin will be dealt with by the Pan-European Group of Experts.

[230] Conclusions of the Euro-Med Trade Ministerial Conference in Palermo on 7 July 2003, no. 4. The main principles are defined in the Annex to the report of the Working Group.

[231] *Ibid.*, no. 6.

tance with the applicable EU legislation and a gap analysis on the basis of existing legislation; 3) transposition of EU framework legislation and sectoral legislation in the Mediterranean countries; 4) creation or adaptation of existing institutions; 5) setting-up of necessary certification and conformity assessment bodies; and 6) identification of technical assistance needs.

2.2.4 *Emphasis on approximation of sectoral legislation by the Mediterranean countries*

A year later, on 21 July 2004, at the 4th Euro-Med Ministerial Conference in Istanbul, the Ministers of Trade acknowledged the substantial progress made in the Working Group on Trade Measures Relevant for Regional Integration.[232] A number of Mediterranean countries had identified their priority sectors and all had started becoming acquainted with the EU legislative approach. The Ministers prompted the Working Group to press ahead with the Six Point Work Programme, including actions to facilitate the approximation by the Mediterranean countries of the necessary framework and sectoral legislation for the priority sectors.

2.2.5 *Official launch of the negotiations on the Euro-Med liberalisation of services and the right of establishment*

The 5th Euro-Med Conference of Ministers of Trade took place in Marrakech on 24 March 2006. The Ministers officially opened the negotiations on the liberalisation of services and the right of establishment. The official launch of these negotiations took place in a special session held on the sidelines of the Conference between the EU Ministers and the Ministers of Trade of Morocco, Tunisia, Egypt, Jordan, Lebanon, Israel and the PA.[233] They agreed to follow a two-track approach as regards the organisation of the negotiations. First, negotiations on general provisions of interest to all participants on services and the right of establishment would be conducted collectively. A draft text containing these mutually agreed standard provisions had to be finalised by the end of 2007. Second, there would be a bilateral round of negotiations with the Mediterranean countries. These negotiations should take into account the specific commitments, schedules and individual characteristics of the Mediterranean partners. Furthermore, the Ministers of Trade emphasised that approximation of technical legislation, standards and conformity assessment procedures with the EU system should, in the end, result in free circulation of industrial products between the Mediterranean region and the EU. Last but not least, the Ministers agreed to launch negotiations on the establishment of an efficient dispute settlement mechanism specifically related to trade in goods and services.

---

[232] 4th Euro-Med Trade Ministerial Conference, Istanbul, 21 July 2004.

[233] See the Ministerial Declaration of Marrakech on the Launch of Euro-Mediterranean Negotiations on the Liberalisation of Trade in Services and the Right of Establishment of 24 March 2006. Algeria, Libya and Syria did not participate.

2.2.6 *Start of the negotiations on the Euro-Med liberalisation of services, including the right of establishment, with a first wave of Mediterranean countries*

The 6th sectoral Euro-Med Conference of the Ministers of Trade, which took place in Lisbon on 21 October 2007, is significant. The Ministers concluded that the Euro-Med free trade area, which should be in place by 2010, remained far from being established. Therefore, they proposed several actions to be taken by the Mediterranean countries and the EU in the short term. First, the Ministers decided that bilateral negotiations concerning the liberalisation of services and the right of establishment would start only with those Mediterranean partners that were ready and interested. These negotiations should be concluded as soon as possible before 2010 and lead to written agreements. Consequently, the EU should start negotiations with a first wave of Mediterranean countries with the aim of concluding binding agreements as regards the movement of services and the right of establishment. In addition, the EU should prepare the Mediterranean partners for the future implementation of legislation and standards in the field of movement of services and the right of establishment. Second, ongoing negotiations on further liberalisation of agricultural, processed agricultural and fishery products with Egypt, Israel and Morocco should be concluded as soon as possible.[234] The other Mediterranean countries and the EU should launch negotiations on the liberalisation of agricultural, processed agricultural and fishery products. Third, the Ministers stressed the importance of regional integration.[235] A network of free trade agreements in the Mediterranean region already existed, i.e., the Agadir Agreement between Morocco, Tunisia, Jordan and Egypt, the free trade agreement between Turkey and Egypt and the free trade agreement between Turkey and Syria.[236] This

[234] The negotiations are in accordance with the Rabat Euro-Med Road Map for Agriculture.

[235] A decade ago, Inbar stated that the Middle East was not at all ready for Mediterranean regionalism, unlike the European countries. Moreover, it was impossible for the Mediterranean countries to copy cooperation models of other regions, such as the Benelux, because of the special characteristics of the Mediterranean area (for example, future trading partners were former belligerents). Inbar, however, stated that some degree of institutionalisation between the Mediterranean countries was needed and the only way to achieve this was through a multilateral framework dealing with economic issues. Cooperation on economic issues was the most safe and plausible way of cooperation between the Mediterranean countries. If the economic experiment should fail, stated Inbar, there were no other safety nets. See E. Inbar, *An OEEC for the Middle East?,* Working Paper 5/97 for the Hebrew University of Jerusalem (1997) pp. 30-32. There were also more optimistic voices. Yoran was of the opinion that the world would see the Middle East as a new fascinating 'Middle Eastern Economy' with advanced technology and cheap labour, because of the opening of the European and United States' markets to the Mediterranean countries. All Mediterranean countries must therefore negotiate a new regional economic order with freedom of movement of people, goods, services and capital. In doing this, the Mediterranean countries must learn from the European example. See A. Yoran, 'A Peace-Time Economic Regime for the Middle East – Towards an MEU?', in A.M. Rabello, ed., *Essays on European and Israel Law* (Jerusalem, The Harry and Michael Sacher Institute for Legislative Research and Comparative Law 1996) pp. 1139-1140.

[236] The Agadir Agreement between Morocco, Tunisia, Jordan and Egypt was signed in Rabat on 25 February 2004, the free trade agreement between Turkey and Egypt was signed in December 2005 and the free trade agreement between Turkey and Syria in December 2004.

network, however, should be strengthened through more regional free trade agreements, better trade relations between the PA and Israel and the adoption of the Protocol on the Pan-Euro-Med system of cumulation of origin by more Mediterranean countries. Fourth, the Euro-Med institutional and legal framework should be reinforced through the establishment of a dispute settlement mechanism regarding which negotiations were already ongoing. Such a dispute settlement body will bring increased legal certainty for economic operators across the Mediterranean region. A first proposal for such a dispute settlement body was released by the EU Council on 14 July 2009 for Tunisia.[237] This proposal has resulted in a Council Decision of 3 November 2009 in which it is stated that the parties shall endeavour to resolve any difference regarding the interpretation and application of the provisions by entering into consultations in good faith with the aim of reaching a prompt, equitable, and mutually agreed solution (Art. 3). If consultations fail to produce a mutually agreed solution, the parties may, by mutual agreement, seek recourse to a mediator (Art. 4). Where the parties fail to resolve the dispute by consultations or mediation, the complaining party may request the establishment of an arbitration panel (Art. 5).

Besides these actions to be taken to reach a Euro-Med free trade area, the Ministers explained the characteristics of the Euro-Med free trade agreement: the free trade agreement should provide for significant and progressive liberalisation of trade in goods and services; it should include strong legally binding provisions on trade and economic regulatory areas; it should lead to a similar degree of market access while account should be taken of each party's situation and sensitivities; and it should result in a common regulatory basis. Subsequently, the Ministers clarified the different steps for the conclusion of a Euro-Med free trade agreement. First, ongoing negotiations will be concluded. Second, the preparation of the free trade agreement will start gradually: the initiation of a free trade agreement depends on the interest and readiness of the Mediterranean partners, but also on the support of the EU. Third, a preparatory process with a first wave of Mediterranean partners that are ready for this ambitious trade agenda will be launched. Fourth, during 2008, a Senior Officials Working Group would work on a road map of next steps in the field of trade till 2010 *and beyond*.[238] Its discussions should focus on how to enhance trade, in order to encourage industrial integration and European investments in the Mediterranean countries. The Group will consider further work on issues such as non-tariff barriers, intellectual property rights, competition,

[237] The mandate for these negotiations was given in Marrakech in 2006 and has led to the Proposal for a Council Decision on the conclusion of an Agreement in the form of a Protocol establishing a dispute settlement mechanism applicable to disputes under the trade provisions of the Euro-Mediterranean Agreement establishing an association between the EC and their Member States, of the one part, and the Republic of Tunisia, of the other part, COM (2009) 357 final. Council Decision of 10 November 2009 on the conclusion of an Agreement in the form of a Protocol establishing a dispute settlement mechanism applicable to disputes under the trade provisions of the Euro-Mediterranean Agreement establishing an association between the European Communities and their Member States, of the one part, and the Republic of Tunisia, of the other part, nyp, *OJ* 2010 L 40/75.

[238] For the first time, the Ministers used the word 'beyond' as they feared they would not achieve a Euro-Med free trade area by 2010.

public procurement, technical barriers to trade and improved consultation on trade measures having an impact on access to markets.

2.2.7 *Urgent need for deeper integration of the Mediterranean countries into the EU through fewer trade restrictions*

The 7th Euro-Med Trade Conference took place in Marseille on 2 July 2008. Bilateral negotiations about progressive, reciprocal and asymmetric liberalisation of trade in services and the right of establishment were launched with Egypt, Morocco, Tunisia and Israel in 2008. They should be concluded in the course of 2009. Ministers agreed that ongoing market access negotiations were not sufficient to bring the benefits of deep integration to the Mediterranean partners. Ministers shared the view that Euro-Med trade relations needed to address more deeply non-tariff barriers and 'behind the border' issues. The Working Group moreover looked at possible means of strengthening the Euro-Med trade partnership and made a distinction between ongoing and future actions. Priority should be given to ongoing negotiations and to the negotiations on the ACAA. Future actions should focus on South-South regional integration. This should also include efforts to facilitate Palestinian trade with other Euro-Med partners. The Group also suggested reinforcing some areas, which should lead to a deepening of trade relations under the current Euro-Med AAs, i.e., technical regulations on industrial products, standards and conformity assessment, sanitary and phytosanitary measures, intellectual property rights, competition policy, public procurement, trade facilitation, customs and rules of origin.

2.3 The liberalisation of the Euro-Med movement of agricultural products

In 2003, the EU was about to admit ten new Member States where agriculture constitutes an important segment of the economy. It was therefore opportune that the Mediterranean countries and the EU convened to discuss the liberalisation of trade in agricultural goods. The Mediterranean countries and the EU adopted a Work Programme aimed at improving the quality of agricultural products through better knowledge of EU legislation and legislation in the Mediterranean countries as regards designations of origin and geographical indications. The Ministers wanted to arrive at similar or identical standards for designations, protection and monitoring in order to ensure conformity with the TRIPs agreements. To that end, cooperation between the Mediterranean and the EU administrations should be enhanced in order to harmonise and align systems of rules, including plant-health and agri-food standards.

In conclusion, it can be stated that the Ministers of Agriculture insist on cooperation in the field of quality of agricultural goods, which will lead to the progressive implementation of a more consistent set of rules and standards. This coherent system will facilitate Mediterranean exports to the EU, though it should be pointed out that the EU is still protective as regards the import of Mediterranean agricultural products.

2.4 The liberalisation of the Euro-Med movement of capital

The Ministers of Economy and Finance of the Mediterranean countries and the EU met for the first time in Rabat in June 2005. In preparation for this meeting, the Commission submitted a paper for discussion entitled 'Economic Developments, Prospects and Challenges in the EU Mediterranean Partners.' The Ministers came to several conclusions, which were merely a reproduction of the discussion paper issued by the Commission.[239] The Ministers stated that the Barcelona Process failed to produce shared prosperity. Poverty and unemployment in the Mediterranean countries remained high and the income gap between the Mediterranean region and the EU had not been reduced. Therefore, the Ecofin Ministers emphasised four priority areas in order to achieve economic reforms in the Mediterranean region: (1) investment by European enterprises in the Mediterranean countries must be simplified, for example by eliminating unnecessary regulation and the administrative burden on European enterprises; (2) liberalisation of trade must continue and include movement of services, right of establishment, and movement of agricultural, processed agricultural and fishery products; (3) public institutions and governance systems must be improved and be made transparent; (4) countries with high debt ratios must accelerate fiscal consolidation to achieve economic stability. Besides these priority areas, regulatory and legislative convergence must be pursued on a selective basis depending on the development of each Mediterranean country. The Ministers recommended using the regulatory convergence experience of the new EU Member States.

The Ecofin Ministers of the Mediterranean countries and the EU met for a second time in Tunis in June 2006. This meeting was again prepared by the Commission, which drew up a background note.[240] The Commission concluded that progress had been made in the four priority areas but that further steps forward were certainly required. The Conclusions of the Ministers again reflected most of the ideas and conclusions of the Commission.

A third Euro-Med Ecofin Meeting was held in Porto in September 2007. This time, the meeting was prepared by a Senior Officials Group that met in Brussels on 27 June 2007. This Group had been set up to give new drive to the discussion on economic reforms as the Conclusions of the Euro-Med Ecofin Meetings were merely a reproduction of the work done by the Commission. Mediterranean countries had to be more involved in the debates. The Commission provided this Group with a background note with an overview of recent economic developments in the

[239] See the Conclusions of the Euro-Med Ecofin Ministerial Meeting in Rabat on 19-20 June 2005, available at: http://ec.europa.eu/external_relations/euromed/conf/.

[240] Commission Background Note for the Ecofin Meeting in Tunis on 25-26 June 2006 'Economic Reforms in the Mediterranean Region: An Overview of Progress in the Four Priority Areas Agreed by the Euro-Med Ecofin in Rabat', pp. 1-10.

Mediterranean countries, focusing on the four priorities.[241] The Ministers stated that by 2006 the Mediterranean countries had achieved considerable economic reforms by implementing the four priorities in their countries: the economy was growing, employment was rising, inflation had been subdued, European investments were growing and public debt had been reduced. The Mediterranean countries, however, still had high unemployment rates and therefore needed to continue the economic reform programme. The Mediterranean countries should focus on improving market access for small and medium-sized European enterprises through the liberalisation of banking services across the national borders. It should be made possible for European firms to get easy access to banks and financial services in the Mediterranean countries. The Commission drafted a paper on the establishment of a Euro-Med Network of Public Finance Experts to be discussed at the Senior Officials Meeting on 27 June 2007.[242] The Ecofin Ministers agreed on the creation of this Network of Public Finance Experts almost exactly as proposed by the Commission in its paper.[243] The 'Public Finance Reform' debate focused on the lifting of obstacles to the labour and capital market in the Mediterranean countries and the strengthening of the Mediterranean financial institutions. Strict labour regulations do not tempt European firms to invest in the Mediterranean countries and weak financial institutions do not give these European firms confidence. The Network of Public Finance Experts was set up to deal with these issues and bring together experience of national authorities of the Mediterranean countries and the EU. The 4th Euro-Med Ecofin Ministerial Meeting brought together the Euro-Med Ministers of Economy and Finance in Luxemburg on 7 October 2008.

In conclusion, it can be stated that the Euro-Med Ecofin Ministers have focused on improving the right of establishment of Europeans firms in the Mediterranean countries. The Ministers drafted a reform agenda with four priorities to be achieved by the Mediterranean countries. This agenda was mainly determined by the Commission. The Mediterranean countries have made a great deal of effort to fulfil the four priorities to make their countries more attractive to foreign investment. Europeans should be able to establish a business on the southern shores of the Mediterranean without encountering too many obstacles. The liberalisation of the movement of capital has also been placed on the agenda in order to make the establishment of a European firm less complicated. Not only capital movements should be liberalised, but financial institutions in the Mediterranean countries should be strengthened and be made more transparent as well in order to be able to resist exogenous financial shocks. European firms will not be attracted to invest in countries with a weak financial system, especially not after the US financial crisis also hit the EU in September 2008.

---

[241] Commission Background Note for the Senior Officials Group, 'Overview of Recent Economic Developments in the Mediterranean Countries with a Focus on the Four Priority Areas Agreed by the Euro-Med Ecofin in Rabat', pp. 1-18.

[242] Commission Paper, 'Euro-Mediterranean Network of Public Finance Experts: Issues and Options', pp. 1-9, only available at: http://ec.europa.eu/external_relations/euromed/conf/ecfin/2007/06_issues_paper_network.pdf.

[243] See Annex I to the Conclusions of the Euro-Med Ecofin Meeting of 15 September 2007.

For the larger part, it is the Commission which takes all the initiatives as regards the opening of the Mediterranean market to European investors. The Mediterranean countries can learn a lot from these Commission documents. For example, the initiative to create a Network of Public Finance Experts will greatly help the Mediterranean partners to build upon European finance experiences, such as that regarding the need for transparency and strong bank systems. These initiatives have, to some extent, already led to economic reforms in the Mediterranean region.

2.5 The liberalisation of the Euro-Med movement of persons

On 19 November 2007, the first Euro-Med Conference on migration was held in Algarve in Portugal, where Ministers of Home Affairs of the Mediterranean countries and the Member States met to discuss migration issues.[244] The Mediterranean countries and the EU had the intention of improving the legal movement of workers. The Ministers came to the conclusion that they needed an analysis of the possibilities to facilitate legal migration procedures for workers 'in demand.' This study should focus on different categories of legal workers and different forms of mobility such as circular and temporary migration. It is also expressively stated that mechanisms should be set up to facilitate the transfer of migrants' remittances to their home country. This will motivate legal migrants to transfer large sums of money to their home country and thus contribute to the development of their country of origin.

In conclusion, it can be stated that the Ministers of Home Affairs of the Mediterranean countries and the Member States support an increase in legal migration of a selective category of workers, namely workers in demand. For those workers, improved forms of legal movement should be developed alongside a mechanism for the transfer of their remittances. The increase in the movement of workers should go together with easier movement of capital, in principle from the EU to the Mediterranean countries.[245]

The Euro-Med Conference on Employment and Labour between Employment and Labour Ministers, Marrakech, 9 and 10 November 2008 was the first sectoral Euro-Med Conference that took place in the framework of the Union for the Mediterranean, under the co-presidencies of Egypt and France. The Ministers stressed the urgency of investment in employment and in human capital, since the Mediterranean countries are faced with rapidly growing working populations, while the EU will soon need a bigger labour force due to low birth rates

---

[244] Ministerial Conclusions of the Euro-Med Conference on Migration, available at: http://www.eu2007.pt/UE/vEN/Noticias_Documentos/20071119Conclusoeseuromed.htm.

[245] In July 2008, under the French Presidency, President Sarkozy and the EU Ministers of Home Affairs started drafting a European Pact on Immigration and Asylum, based on a policy of preference. The Pact asks the EU Member States to strengthen their border controls and to bring in biometric visas for all entrants by 2012. Member States and the Commission must implement policies for labour migration, with due regard to the Community preference and using the most appropriate resources, which take account of all the needs of the labour market of each Member State. This policy of Community preferences might lead to a random acceptance of migrants.

and an ageing population. Therefore, the Ministers committed themselves to a 'Euro-Med Framework of Actions on Employment, Employability and Decent Work' which should contribute to the development of a social dimension of the Euro-Mediterranean relationship. The key objectives of this Framework of Actions are as follows: 'more jobs, more human capital and more decent jobs.' In the Framework, the Ministers propose many actions to manage labour migration, taking into account the labour market needs of both sides of the Mediterranean. An interesting point is that the importance of decent jobs is emphasised. Decent jobs can be created by: (1) completing the ratification of the International Labour Organisation (ILO) conventions and ensuring their implementation; (2) ensuring full respect of rights at work, preventing segmentation of the labour market and fighting undeclared work; (3) developing effective social dialogue; (4) increasing the coverage and level of social protection; (5) improving health and safety measures in the work environment; and (6) implementing ILO Decent Work Country Programmes. In addition, the Ministers set up a Euro-Med Employment and Labour Working Group.

2.6 Sub-conclusion

The sectoral Conferences are a very significant instrument for the integration of the Mediterranean countries into the EU internal market. Contrary to the work of the Ministers of Foreign Affairs, the outcomes of the sectoral Euro-Med Conferences have been implemented in practice. The practical approach has taken shape through the establishment of many different Working Groups. The work of these Working Groups has been very rewarding and has been carefully followed up by the specialised Ministers. It would be advisable to also set up a Working Group that mainly deals with Euro-Med competition issues.

The most significant examples of further integration of the Mediterranean countries into the EU internal market through the sectoral Euro-Med Conferences can be summarised as follows: (1) participation of the Mediterranean countries in essential non-binding documents, such as the Six Point Work Programme and the Framework Protocol on Services; (2) inclusion of the Mediterranean countries in important legal documents, such as the Protocol on pan-European cumulation of origin; (3) the adoption of relevant EU *acquis* in Mediterranean legislation according to efficient methods defined at the sectoral Conferences; (4) the proposal for establishment of a dispute settlement body with legal power regarding trade issues between the Mediterranean countries and the EU; (5) the tackling of non-tariff barriers and 'behind the border' issues, which could lead to deeper Mediterranean integration into the EU internal market; (5) the start of negotiations with a first wave of Mediterranean countries; and (6) the establishment of a Euro-Med Network of Public Finance Experts to improve the Euro-Med liberalisation of capital.

There are some issues that need further development: (1) the Conferences have put the need for infrastructure in the Mediterranean countries on the agenda. Mediterranean countries need better laboratories, accreditation and certification bodies and other technical institutions in order to improve alignment with EU legislation. However, until now, the necessary infrastructure has not been established in the Mediterranean countries; and (2) the movement of persons and other (il) legal migration topics can sometimes be found in the Conclusions of the Euro-Med Conferences. The sectoral Conference on Migration in 2007, for instance, looked more closely at this problematic issue, but has not led to further material integration into the EU internal market.

The sectoral Euro-Med Conferences have also proved to be a better expression of joint ownership of the Euro-Mediterranean policies.

3. The parliamentary dimension of the Euro-Med integration process: attention for citizens

Another significant multilateral instrument relevant for the Mediterranean integration into the EU internal market is the Euro-Mediterranean Parliamentary Assembly (EMPA). The EMPA is the successor of the Euro-Mediterranean Parliamentary Forum established in November 1998.[246] Neither the EMPA nor the Forum has a legal basis in the EU Treaties. The EMPA has a political basis only, as it was established by the Euro-Med Conference in Naples on 3 December 2003. The first Plenary Session of the EMPA took place in Cairo from 12 to 15 March 2005. Delegations from the 35 parliaments of the Mediterranean countries and the Member States, on the one hand, and members of the European Parliament, on the other, attended the meeting.[247] The Members of Parliament (MPs) aimed at easier access of Mediterranean agricultural and industrial exports to the EU market. Above all, they aimed at deriving practical advantages from the four freedoms of the EU internal market for the Mediterranean partners.[248] The MPs adopted three Resolutions.[249] In the Resolution about the assessment of the Barcelona Process the MPs stated that the commercial chapter of this process was weak due to the stagnation of trade relations between the Mediterranean partners and to the major political problems in the Mediterranean region. The Barcelona Process failed to produce the expected benefits or to narrow the gap between the EU and the Mediterranean countries. Nevertheless, the MPs were convinced that the EMP could be improved. In the Resolution on economic and financial issues, the MPs stated that the Euro-Med

[246] The Euro-Mediterranean Parliamentary Forum held five plenary sessions: 1st Parliamentary Forum in Brussels, October 1998; 2nd Parliamentary Forum in Brussels, February 2001; 3rd Parliamentary Forum in Brussels, November 2001; 4th Parliamentary Forum in Bari, June 2003; and 5th Parliamentary Forum in Naples, December 2003.

[247] There were 120 MPs from the Mediterranean countries and 120 MPs from the EU (75 MPs from the national parliaments and 45 from the European Parliament).

[248] Final Declaration of 15 March 2005 regarding the first session of the EMPA, available at: http://www.europarl.europa.eu/intcoop/empa/plenary_sessions/cairo_2005/cairo_03_05_final_declaration_en.pdf.

[249] Resolution of the EMPA on the assessment of the Barcelona Process on the eve of its tenth anniversary, 15 March 2005; Resolution of the EMPA on economic and financial issues, social affairs and education, 15 March 2005; and Resolution of the EMPA on improving quality of life, exchanges between civil societies and culture, 15 March 2005, available at: http://www.europarl.europa.eu/intcoop/empa/assembly_documents/resolutions_committees_en.htm.

Association Agreements contributed to the legal certainty necessary for European investments in the Mediterranean region. The Resolution on improving quality of life, exchanges between civil societies and culture related to the movement of people. The MPs condemned the establishment of Initial Reception Centres in the Mediterranean countries for immigrants wanting to enter the EU.[250] The EU and its Member States must accept their part of responsibility as regards the reception and integration of immigrants from the Mediterranean countries, in particular, states should be more flexible and humane in the field of visa-granting procedures. The MPs supported a possible common Euro-Mediterranean strategy on legal immigration.[251]

The EMPA met again in 2005 in an Extraordinary Plenary Session in Rabat,[252] where the MPs issued three Resolutions.[253] In the Resolution on the future of the Barcelona Process, they asked the Commission and the EU Council to clarify the relationship between the EU institutions and the EMP institutions. They also called for a Permanent Secretariat to coordinate the EMP. In the Resolution on economic and financial issues, the MPs recommended that all negotiations about the liberalisation of goods and services should be held in the framework of the WTO. Mediterranean countries must not be forced to go beyond the concessions made in the framework of the WTO. The Resolution on improving quality of life, exchanges between civil societies and culture called for a genuine European immigration policy to be adopted as soon as possible. The EU should adopt all appropriate measures, including legislative measures, to accelerate the integration of migrants legally resident in the EU, which means the right of access to education, training, health care, accommodation, work and free legal assistance, with full respect of the nature of the migrants' civilisations.

The EMPA met in a second Plenary Session in Brussels in March 2006, where former European Parliament President Joseph Borrell stated:

> 'I am more convinced than ever that Europe's relations with the Muslim world will be the major challenge facing Europe in the years ahead since the Mediterranean region is on the one hand extremely dynamic and on the other hand becoming increasingly fragile.'[254]

---

250 The EU indicated the extent to which the EU's 'immediate environment' was regarded as a region of strategic interest by incorporating the Mediterranean policy in the first part of the ex-Constitutional Treaty (Title VIII, Art. 56). The MPs also supported the extension of the EMP to include new dimensions such as possible participation of the Mediterranean countries in the ESDP.

251 The Green Paper of the Commission on legal migration should lead to a common Euro-Mediterranean strategy about legal immigration.

252 Declaration of the Presidency addressed to the Tenth Anniversary Euro-Mediterranean Summit, Rabat, 21 November 2005.

253 Resolution of the EMPA on the future of the Barcelona Process, 21 November 2005; Resolution of the EMPA on economic and financial issues, social affairs and education, 21 November 2005; and Resolution of the EMPA on improving quality of life, exchanges between civil societies and culture, 21 November 2005.

254 See Final Declaration of the Presidency regarding the second session of the EMPA, Brussels, March 2006, available at: http://www.europarl.europa.eu/intcoop/empa/home/default_en.htm.

The MPs stated that more and more people supported the idea of a clash of civilisations between the Mediterranean and European people. Therefore, the MPs reiterated their Conclusions drawn at the Extraordinary Plenary Session in Rabat.

A third Plenary Session of the EMPA took place in Tunis on 16 and 17 March 2007. The members of the EMPA considered that the results achieved by the Barcelona Process did not comply with the objectives of this Process. They urged the Mediterranean countries and the EU to build a common Euro-Med agricultural policy truly integrating the two Mediterranean shores. They regarded migration as a key component of the globalisation processes.[255] In this session, four Recommendations were adopted.[256] While this Plenary Session was dominated by the Middle East conflict and the fight against terrorism, the MPs made recommendations in order to reduce the economic gap between the Mediterranean countries and the EU. The EU must respect the principles of 'asymmetry' and 'gradualism' of liberalisation in the run-up to the free trade area to be established by 2010, since over-precipitation of liberalisation results in negative effects. National governments make good efforts in establishing an integration policy but still have to remove obstacles for the immigrants to gain full access to education, social security systems and employment in the Member States. Migrants must be lawfully integrated into the labour market and legal immigrants must be offered voting rights and the right to stand for election in local elections. In its last Recommendation, the EMPA makes a comparative analysis of EU legislation and Mediterranean legislation as regards women's rights.

The EMPA met for a fourth time in Athens on 27-28 March 2008. This Plenary Session was also dominated by the situation in the Middle East.[257] In their Final Declaration, the MPs insisted on a strengthening of the conditions for Euro-Med free trade of goods, services and persons. The MPs also extensively discussed the movement of persons. Discrimination based on the geographical provenance of immigrants must be avoided. A simpler system for the management of legal immigration was needed. Full portability of pension rights also in countries of origin must be ensured. The MPs stated that women immigrants encountered problems in terms of 'ghettoisation,' limited access to public, social and health services, diffi-

[255] See Final Declaration of the Presidency regarding the third session of the EMPA, Tunis, 16-17 March 2007, available at: http://www.europarl.europa.eu/intcoop/empa/home/default_en.htm.

[256] Recommendation of the EMPA of 17 March 2007 on the implementation of the Code of Conduct on Countering Terrorism, the Middle East peace process and landmines; Recommendation of 17 March of the EMPA based on the proposals presented by the Rapporteurs Ms Jamila Madeira, Vice-Chairperson of the EMPA Economic Committee, on 'The Millennium Development Goals in the Euro-Mediterranean Area', and Mr Abderrahman Bouhrizi, on 'The Future of Investment between the Euro-Mediterranean Countries'; Recommendation of the EMPA of 17 March 2007 on improving quality of life, exchanges between civil societies and culture; and Recommendation of the EMPA of 17 March 2007 on women's rights in the Euro-Mediterranean countries.

[257] The MPs did not reach consensus on paragraph 33: 'Express deep concern at and condemns the Israeli aggression against the Palestinian territories in Gaza and the West Bank and the killing of children, women and the elderly and the destruction of the infrastructure, which has a negative effect on economic development and investment opportunities in the Palestinian territories'; see EMPA Recommendation of 27 March 2008 on behalf of the Economic and Financial Social Affairs and Education Committee of the Euro-Mediterranean Parliamentary Assembly, p. 8.

culties in accessing the labour market, low employment rates, and employment in temporary or low-paid jobs often without social and economic protection. Women immigrants must be able to fully enjoy secure legal and labour status in the host countries and must not suffer discrimination on the basis of gender or origin, in accordance with the Union's *acquis*. The MPs adopted three Recommendations,[258] in which, for the first time, they emphasised the need to liberalise the capital market and facilitate access to the financial sectors.[259]

The EMPA met in an Extraordinary Plenary Session in Jordan on 12-13 October 2008 under the Barcelona Process: Union for the Mediterranean. There, the EMPA expressed its will to see a legal basis created and a formal link established with the executive branch of the EMP. This new institutional structure for the EMPA as the legitimate parliamentary representation of a Union for the Mediterranean was launched under the French Presidency under President Sarkozy.

In conclusion, it can be said that the EMPA has put the issue of movement of persons, and specifically workers and women on the agenda. The EMPA seems a good expression of joint ownership of the EMP and contributes to democracy since it functions as a platform where MPs from both sides can express their opinions, and emphasises the liberalisation of the movement of people.[260] Nevertheless, the EMPA's resolutions and recommendations on the Euro-Med movement of persons have not led to any significant results in terms of the integration of the Mediterranean countries into the EU internal market. However, this might change in the future since the UM will provide the EMPA with a legal basis and an institutional relationship with the (sectoral) Euro-Med Conferences. These changes might give the EMPA more legal power.

4. Expert Conferences on the Euro-Med integration process

The Euro-Med Conferences on Economic Transition were established in 1997 under the EMP umbrella. They bring together economic experts from the World Bank, IMF, Femise[261] network and economic research institutes.[262] These experts

[258] Recommendation of the EMPA of 27 March 2008 on the situation in the Middle East, the Union for the Mediterranean, the evaluation of the action plans in the framework of the five-year programme, the implementation of the Code of Conduct on Countering Terrorism and parliamentary contribution to peace in the Middle East; Recommendation of the EMPA of 27 March 2007 on behalf of the Economic and Financial Social Affairs and Education Committee; and Recommendation of the EMPA of 27 March 2008 on women and immigration: the role and place of immigrant women in the framework of the Euro-Mediterranean partnership and on women and science.

[259] Recommendation of the EMPA of 27 March 2007 on behalf of the Economic and Financial Social Affairs and Education Committee, p. 6.

[260] The European Parliament sends delegates to the EMPA, who have an additional voice. This could create an imbalance between the Mediterranean and European side.

[261] Femise is an EU-funded network that brings together 71 independent economic institutes which analyse the socio-economic implications of the EMP, see http://www.femise.org.

[262] 6th Meeting of Government Experts on Economic Transition in Brussels, 18-19 June 2002; 7th Meeting of Experts on Economic Transition in Brussels, 23-24 April 2003; 8th Annual Conference on Economic Transition in Brussels, 10-11 June 2004; 9th Annual Conference on Economic Transition,

provide information on economic issues to be used by the Ministers of Foreign Affairs in order to prepare the economic topics of Euro-Med Conferences of Foreign Affairs. The work of the group of experts represents their independent views and not the opinions of the governments of the Member Sates and Mediterranean countries. Various economic topics relevant to the economic transformation process towards the establishment of a Euro-Med free trade area have been discussed at these annual Euro-Med Conferences on Economic Transition. An overview of all Conferences on Economic Transition can be found at the Euro-Med Economic Transition website, where the EU and the Mediterranean partners can post comments.[263] At the Economic Transition Conference in 2006, Mrs Anne Houtman, Director for Horizontal Policy Development at the Commission's Directorate General for Internal Market and Services, gave an interesting introduction, indicating the questions which the experts tried to solve at the Conference:

> 'The ENP opens new perspectives of moving beyond amongst them "The perspective of moving beyond cooperation to a significant degree of economic integration, including through a stake in EU's Internal Market, and the possibility to participate progressively in key aspects of EU policies and programmes." Given this background, is it possible for you as neighbours and ENP partners to get a "stake in the Internal Market" and what would that involve? Is it possible to get "EU membership" in only one or two selected areas, or are we obliged to go for the all-embracing model of the European Economic Area, EEA? The agreement covers all areas of the Internal Market giving these three countries the same rights and obligations as Member states.'

Another Economic Transition Conference took place in Brussels in 2008 and focused on financial and banking services. This Conference was attended by many Ministers of Finance and financial experts from all the Mediterranean countries and the Member States. All Ministers or experts from the different Mediterranean countries presented an overview of their financial system and the problems encountered. Mr Jean-Louis Reiffers, Chairman of Femise, made many critical remarks about the evolution of the financial system in the Mediterranean countries, which is unsatisfactory. For example, he is of the opinion that banks in the Mediterranean countries should be more competitive in order to reduce interest. Mr Tomas Dupla del Moral, Director at the Directorate-General for External Relations of the Commission concluded the Conference by stating that it was time to include the discussion on the movement of financial services in the negotiations on the liberalisation of the movement of services between the Mediterranean countries and the EU which have started with some Mediterranean countries.

These Euro-Med Conferences on Economic Transition give us a general impression of the financial, fiscal and economic situation in the Mediterranean countries but do not offer concrete solutions to the many problems that the Mediterranean countries are facing. Further material integration of the Mediterranean countries

---

11-12 April 2005; 10th Annual Conference on Economic Transition, called 'Giving the neighbours a stake in the EU internal market', 6-7 June 2006; 11th Annual Conference on Economic Transition, 18-19 June 2007; 12th Annual Conference on Economic Transition, 20-21 February 2008.

[263] http://ec.europa.eu/external_relations/euromed/etn/index_en.htm.

into the EU internal market requires more than merely a debate on financial and banking services.

5. The first Conference under the ENP umbrella

The Commission organised an ENP Conference in Brussels in September 2007 between the EU and ENP partner countries. The ENP is another form of cooperation between the Mediterranean countries and the EU, although more countries are involved, such as some Eastern neighbouring countries of the EU. The Conference provided an occasion for EU and Mediterranean governmental and non-governmental actors from civil society, business groups and academics to exchange views and ideas on the ENP.

In his opening speech, the EU Commissioner for External Relations and ENP, Benita Ferrero-Waldner, outlined the key areas where discussion was mostly needed, namely economic integration of the ENP countries into the EU, the movement of persons, energy and financial assistance. As regards the importance of the economic integration into the EU, the EU Commissioner was very clear:

> 'Our vision is of an economically integrated area which spans the whole of the EU and its closest European and Mediterranean partners. An area where goods, services and capital flow freely, opening up new possibilities and greater opportunities for us all. The chance to integrate into the EU's internal market is an immensely important opportunity, and an unprecedented offer from the EU. We want to lay the groundwork for the conclusion of deep and comprehensive free trade agreements. These should go beyond the level of tariffs and tackle "beyond the border" issues – as well as services and investment. We need to make sure that, whether it is construction products or toys, potatoes or pharmaceuticals, *all* products, – including those of most interest to our neighbours – really can enter our markets, without being stopped by phyto-sanitary, safety or quality standards. We are currently working out the most sensible approach. In particular, we need to make sure that such deep and comprehensive FTAs are introduced in the right way and at the right speed. The situation of every partner country is different, and for some a certain level of asymmetry may be needed.'

As regards the movement of persons between the EU and ENP countries, the EU Commissioner made an unambiguous statement:

> 'We know that mobility, the freedom for people to travel to the EU, is enormously important. So in "strengthening ENP" we want to do as much as we can to increase mobility. As my EU colleagues can testify, we have pushed our Member States hard on visa facilitation. We want simpler, cheaper and faster visa procedures for business, government, and educational travellers throughout our neighbourhood. (…) But most radically of all, the Commission has proposed a new system of Mobility Partnerships, which we hope we can pilot with ENP countries. The idea, as the name suggests, is to focus on the joint responsibility of all countries to tackle the challenges posed by migration. So it will cover both steps to combat illegal migration *and* more opportunities for legal migration from third countries to the EU. We ask for commitments on readmission and to promote productive employment and decent work. And we propose ways

> of facilitating access to our Member States' labour markets such as labour quotas, short stay visas, and practical instruments to match job offers with job seekers.'

Although this ENP Conference can be considered a good example of joint ownership of the Euro-Med integration process, it has not led to significant results relevant for the Mediterranean integration into the EU internal market.

6. Conclusions

6.1 The EMP Euro-Med Conferences

The EMP Euro-Med Conferences of Ministers of Foreign Affairs are the engine of the Euro-Mediterranean integration process. They have put forward new integration ideas, placing them in a global perspective, such as the establishment of a Euro-Med free trade area of goods, services and capital by 2010, together with a Work Programme containing practical measures (1995); greater harmonisation and compatibility of legislation of the Mediterranean countries with the EU internal market (1997); the possibility of Euro-Med integration only for countries that accept the entire Barcelona *acquis* (1999); a focus on Euro-Med free movement of services (2000); the creation of a Euro-Mediterranean internal market (2002); the Euro-Med liberalisation of movement of persons (2003); the fourth chapter of the Barcelona Declaration, on migration and social integration (2005); and the principle of voluntary participation and the road map for the Euro-Med liberalisation of services (2005).

The Ministers of Foreign Affairs are also able to react instantly to arising situations. For example, the attacks of 11 September 2001 triggered a prompt reaction from the Euro-Med Ministers of Foreign Affairs to speed up further integration efforts in order to establish a more stable Mediterranean region and decrease Islamic fundamentalism. The question is whether the Euro-Med Conferences will also be able to react to the global financial crisis, which began as a bank crisis. This bank crisis is becoming much larger and is also affecting the manufacturing industry. At present, the EU internal market itself is in danger on account of the protectionist attitude of some Member States. It is recommended that at the following Euro-Med Conferences the Euro-Med Ministers of Foreign Affairs should tackle this danger and try to protect the Mediterranean region from European protectionist tendencies.

The Euro-Med Conferences of Foreign Affairs have launched many interesting Euro-Med integration proposals and have responded quickly to changes in the global environment. They form an appropriate framework for further Euro-Mediterranean integration efforts as regards the four freedoms. However, they have not led to material integration of the Mediterranean countries into the EU internal market. The proposals made at the Euro-Med Conferences have never been further developed at these Conferences.

6.2 The EMP sectoral Euro-Med Conferences

The EMP sectoral Euro-Med Conferences have resulted in a significantly deeper integration of the Mediterranean countries into the EU internal market.

These sectoral Conferences have often resulted in important legal documents such as the Protocols on rules of origin, and in better approximation of the relevant legislation of the Mediterranean countries and EU legislation through the Six Point Working Programme for approximation. The Conferences moreover launched the negotiations regarding Euro-Med movement of services and implemented the proposals of the Ministers of Foreign Affairs by creating several Working Groups and establishing the Euro-Med Network of Public Finance Experts. The work carried out by these Working Groups and Experts has significantly led to better integration of the Mediterranean countries into the EU internal market of *goods, services and capital*. The sectoral Euro-Med Conferences have contributed to the material integration of the Mediterranean countries into the EU internal market, as well as to the free movement of goods, services and capital between the Mediterranean and Member States.

At the start of almost each Conference, the Ministers of Foreign Affairs mentioned that, despite their efforts, only minor progress was made as regards the Euro-Med liberalisation of the movement of goods, services and capital. In general, the extent of Euro-Med integration has not been satisfactory: the Euro-Med integration process has evolved steadily but very slowly. Only the sectoral Euro-Med Conferences have been able to speed up the integration of the Mediterranean countries into the EU internal market. Below, the Euro-Med integration results that they have realised will be set out.

The sectoral Euro-Med Conferences have contributed to the integration of the Mediterranean countries into the EU internal market of goods. The Euro-Med movement of goods was already ensured by the Euro-Med AAs.[264] The sectoral Conferences have taken the following measures aimed at further and better integration of the Mediterranean countries into the EU internal market of goods:

1) A Euro-Med Working Group on rules of origin was set up in 2001. This initiative has resulted in the application of pan-Euro-Med cumulation of rules of origin in the Euro-Med area. Pan-Euro-Med cumulation of origin allows countries to use originating products from another country in the manufacture of export products that will then also have originating, preferential status. This system is only intended for those countries that are linked by preferential trade agreements. In the Euro-Med area, it seems that only the Agadir Agreement[265] together with the four Euro-Med AAs which the members of the Agadir Agreement have concluded with the EU, are compatible with the pan-Euro-Med cumulation system. This means that products from one Agadir country can be exported to another Agadir country for additional processing without losing the preferential status under the relevant Euro-Med AA. Products of European origin can be processed in an Agadir coun-

[264] Cf., *infra* Ch. IV, 3.1.

[265] The Agadir Agreement was signed in Rabat on 25 February 2004 between Jordan, Tunisia, Egypt and Morocco.

try and be exported to Europe without losing their preferential status under the relevant Euro-Med AA.

2) The process of approximation of legislation regarding industrial products has been started up. As regards the approximation process aimed at improving the Euro-Med movement of industrial goods, there is an important distinction between industrial goods for which there is an EU harmonisation directive and those for which there are no such EU rules. In Europe, there are industrial products to which a European harmonisation directive applies, but there are also industrial products for which there is no such directive. Where there is no EU harmonisation, technical rules create obstacles to the free movement of goods between the EU Member States. Technical obstacles can be eliminated by applying the so-called mutual recognition principle. According to the principle of mutual recognition, all goods lawfully produced in one EU Member State can freely enter the market of another EU Member State, even if the product does not fully comply with the technical rules of the EU Member State of destination, unless the restrictions laid down by the EU Member State of destination are justified on the grounds specified in Article 36 TFEU, or on the basis of overriding requirements of general public importance recognised by the European Court of Justice, and are proportionate. It is estimated that about 28% of European trade is covered by the mutual recognition principle.[266]

The Mediterranean countries want to implement the European standards in EU harmonisation directives in their legislation, as this will lead to better access for Mediterranean goods to the European market. The Mediterranean countries have identified 'priority areas' for this harmonisation process and have started adopting certain relevant Union *acquis*. A question that arises is whether it is essential for the Mediterranean countries to implement all EU harmonisation directives. Since the Mediterranean countries have no prospect of accession to the EU, they are not obliged to implement all of them. It is recommended that they implement those directives which will lead to the economic development of the Mediterranean countries, namely those that cover the export of industrial goods that are most essential for the Mediterranean countries. Each Mediterranean country has to indicate which EU harmonisation directives it wants to implement. In the end, this approximation process should lead to the conclusion of Agreements on Conformity Assessment and Acceptance of Industrial Products (ACAAs), on which negotiations have been initiated with some Mediterranean countries within the sectoral Euro-Med Conferences.

At the sectoral Conferences, the Mediterranean countries and the EU started a discussion about the applicability of the principle of mutual recognition to the movement of industrial goods in non-harmonised EU areas between the Medi-

[266] Commission Staff Working Document Accompanying the Proposal for a Regulation of the European Parliament and of the Council laying down procedures relating to the application of certain national technical rules to products lawfully marketed in another Member State and repealing Decision 3052/95/EC: Executive summary of the impact assessment, SEC (2007) 113, p. 2; Proposal for a Regulation of the European Parliament and of the Council laying down procedures relating to the application of certain national technical rules to products lawfully marketed in another Member State and repealing Decision 3052/95/EC of 14 February 2007, COM (2007) 36 final.

terranean countries and the EU. Several problems have already been identified by the Mediterranean countries as regards the (future) application of the principle of mutual recognition between the EU and the Mediterranean countries. Radwan and Reiffers state that the Mediterranean countries and the EU can choose between three levels of mutual recognition: (i) a high level of mutual recognition, whereby all national regulations are considered equivalent; (ii) an average level, whereby countries recognise only institutions of certification of partner countries; and (iii) a low level, whereby certification of a partner country is recognised for certain goods only.[267] According to Jakubiak, one of the problems will be that the principle of mutual recognition requires a substantial amount of confidence in the other party, which will take time to develop in the Euro-Mediterranean relationship.[268]

3) Regarding the Euro-Med movement of agricultural products, negotiations on the Euro-Med liberalisation of agricultural, processed agricultural and fishery products were launched at the sectoral Euro-Med Conferences with Egypt, Israel, Tunisia and Morocco. This has resulted in further integration of Morocco, Tunisia, Egypt and Israel into the EU internal market of agricultural goods. Jordan, Lebanon and the PA did not start such negotiations and have made no further progress as regards the integration of agricultural goods into the EU internal market.

4) The sectoral Euro-Med Conferences have contributed to the Euro-Med liberalisation of services, including the right of establishment: the sectoral Conferences have started negotiations on the liberalisation of services including the right of establishment with the ready and interested Mediterranean partners. Negotiations on general provisions followed by bilateral negotiations have started with Egypt, Morocco, Tunisia and Israel. In the future, this should lead to services agreements, which are preferential economic agreements on the liberalisation of services and on the right of establishment with the EU in accordance with Article V of the GATS. As for the other Mediterranean countries, there has been no further integration into the EU internal market of agricultural goods.

5) The sectoral Euro-Med Conferences have promoted the facilitation of movement of capital from the EU to the Mediterranean countries, but has not yet resulted in concrete Euro-Med integration results. The Euro-Med Network of Public Finance Experts, created in 2008, focuses on the lifting of obstacles to the labour and capital market in the Mediterranean countries and on the strengthening of the Mediterranean financial institutions. This Network could contribute to the Euro-Med liberalisation of movement of capital.

Only the sectoral Euro-Med Conferences have resulted in concrete integration of the Mediterranean countries into the EU internal market of goods, services and capital. The sectoral Euro-Med Conferences have promoted the facilitation of movement of persons between the EU and the Mediterranean countries, but have not led to any concrete results in terms of better integration.

---

[267] S. Radwan and J.-L. Reiffers, *Femise Report on the Euro-Mediterranean Partnership 2006: Analysis and Proposals of the Euro-Mediterranean Forum of Economic Institutes* (France, Institut de la Méditerranée 2006) p. 33.

[268] Jakubiak, et al., *supra* n. 51, pp. 22-23.

6.3 The Euro-Med Parliamentary Assembly (EMPA)

The recommendations and resolutions of the Euro-Mediterranean Parliamentary Assembly (EMPA) have not led to significant results relevant for the Mediterranean integration into the EU internal market. The Euro-Med movement of persons has not improved either, despite the many discussions about this topic. The Barcelona Process, Union for the Mediterranean (UM), is aimed at providing the EMPA with a legal basis and establishing an institutional relationship with the (sectoral) Euro-Med Conferences. At present, there is no link between the EMPA and the Euro-Med Conferences. Changes to that effect might give the EMPA more legal power.

6.4 The Euro-Med Conferences on Economic Transition

These Conferences provide us with a general idea of the financial situation in the Mediterranean countries but do not lead to further material integration of the Mediterranean countries into the EU internal market. It is recommended that the Ministers include the discussion on the financial and banking services in the negotiations on the liberalisation of the Euro-Med movement of services which have already started with some Mediterranean partners.

6.5 The ENP Conference

Under the ENP, only one multilateral Conference was organised, which was merely a forum for debate and has not led to further Euro-Mediterranean integration as regards the four freedoms. All multilateral integration efforts take place in the framework of the EMP, except for this ENP Conference.

All in all, there is only one multilateral instrument that has achieved considerable further integration of the Mediterranean countries into the EU internal market, namely the sectoral Euro-Med Conferences and the Working Groups created by these Conferences. They have mostly focused on the liberalisation of Euro-Med movement of goods, services and capital. As a result of this conclusion, more Working groups should be established by the sectoral Euro-Med Conferences in the future, such as on competition issues. Recently, a Euro-Med Conference on migration was created as well. It remains to be seen whether this sectoral Conference on the Euro-Med liberalisation of the movement of persons will really address problems of labour movement or will be reduced to (il)legal migration border management and an exchange of students and highly skilled professionals.

Chapter IV

Bilateral EMP instruments for integration of the Mediterranean countries into the EU internal market

The conclusion of bilateral Euro-Med Association Agreements (AAs) between the EU, the Member States on the one hand and the Mediterranean partners on the other hand has been a crucial bilateral aspect of the realisation of the Euro-Mediterranean Partnership (EMP). The Euro-Med AAs are designed to lead to improved integration of the relevant Mediterranean countries into the EU internal market of goods, services and capital. The Jordanian AA, for example, stipulates that the AA aims at establishing the conditions for the progressive liberalisation of trade in goods, services and capital.[269] Some Euro-Med AAs also contain a number of liberal provisions regarding the movement of persons. This chapter will give an overview of all Euro-Med AAs, their legal basis in Article 217 TFEU (before: Art. 310 EC Treaty) and a detailed legal analysis of the main provisions concerning the movement of goods, services, capital and persons. It will also deal will the existing implementation measures in the form of decisions of the Euro-Med Association Councils. The decisions of the Euro-Med Association Councils are also an essential bilateral part of the realisation of the EMP. The Association Councils have to implement provisions of the Euro-Med AAs that do not have direct effect.

It will be investigated whether and to what extent these bilateral EMP instruments have led to Mediterranean integration into the EU as regards the distinct fields of goods, services, capital and also persons.

There are also bilateral sectoral Euro-Med Agreements, resulting from the need for closer cooperation in certain sectors as stipulated in the Euro-Med AAs. There are bilateral sectoral agreements for Israel: the EU/Israel Agreement on scientific and technical cooperation; the EU/Israel Agreement on procurement by telecommunications operators; the EU/Israel Agreement on government procurement; and the EU/Israel Agreement on mutual recognition of OECD principles of good laboratory practice.[270] There are also the EU/Jordan Agreement on certain aspects of air services, the EU/Lebanon Agreement on certain aspects of air

[269] Art. 1 Jordan AA.

[270] Agreement on scientific and technical cooperation between the European Community and the State of Israel, *OJ* L 220 of 25 August 2007, pp. 5-21 (according to the Israel/EC AA, Israel and EC will intensify scientific and technological cooperation); Agreement between the European Community and the State of Israel on procurement by telecommunications operators – Art. 1(6) side letters – Agreed minutes, *OJ* L 202 of 30 July 1997, pp. 74-84; Agreement between the European Community and the State of Israel on government procurement, *OJ* L 202 of 30 July1997, pp. 85-88; Agreement on mutual recognition of OECD principles of good laboratory practice (GLP) and compliance moni-

services and the EU/Egypt Agreement for scientific and technological cooperation.[271] These bilateral Agreements will not be studied because they only contain very detailed and technical regulations, such as certain aspects of air services or principles of good laboratory practice.

1. Overview of the current Euro-Med Association Agreements

1.1 What is an Association Agreement?

An Association Agreement (AA) is an agreement between the EU, its Member States and a third country that creates a framework for cooperation on areas such as trade, politics and culture. An AA has to be ratified not only by the EU but by all EU Member States and can therefore be considered as a so-called 'mixed' agreement. The AAs establish joint institutions for the effective functioning and implementation of the AA: the Association Council and the Association Committee. Some AAs function as an instrument of accession of the third country to the EU, while others have no accession perspective whatsoever. The Euro-Med AAs belong to the latter category: Euro-Med AAs are used to establish privileged links between the EU and a Mediterranean country covering a broad spectrum of EU policies.[272]

1.2 The Euro-Med Association Agreements

Before the landmark Summit in Barcelona in November 1995, the EC and its Member States had already signed a Euro-Med AA with Tunisia on 17 July 1995, which came into force on 1 March 1998 after being ratified by all 15 EU Member States. In the framework of the Barcelona process, the EU and its Member States signed an AA with Morocco on 26 February 1996, which entered into force on 1 March 2000, with Israel,[273] which entered into force on 1 June 2000, with Jordan on 24 November 1997, which entered into force on 1 May 2002, with Egypt on

toring programmes between the European Community and the State of Israel – Agreed Minutes, *OJ* L 263 of 9 October 1999, pp. 7-18.

[271] Agreement between the European Community and the Hashemite Kingdom of Jordan on certain aspects of air services, *OJ* L 68 of 12 March 2008, pp. 15-24; Agreement between the European Community and the Republic of Lebanon on certain aspects of air services *OJ* L 215 of 5 August 2006, pp. 17-25; Agreement for scientific and technological cooperation between the European Community and the Arab Republic of Egypt, *OJ* L 182 of 13 July 2005, pp. 12-19.

[272] P. Eeckhout, *The External Relations of the European Union: Legal and Constitutional Foundations* (Oxford, Oxford University Press 2005) p. 106.

[273] Before the enlargement of the EU to Spain in 1986, Israel's export to the EC was similar to that of Spain to the EU. When Spain entered the EU, Israel feared it would be one of the countries most affected by the enlargement of the EU considering that the EU was Israel's main trading partner and the similarity of its export to that of Spain. In addition, Israel had already encountered problems as regards the export of certain goods to the EU, such as high-tech and pharmaceutical products, software and diamonds. Israel was of the opinion that the creation of the EU internal market would increase its export problems regarding the EU and therefore wished to review its free trade agreement of 11 May

25 June 2001, which entered into force on 1 June 2004, with Algeria on 22 April 2002, which entered into force on 1 September 2005, and with Lebanon on 17 June 2002, which entered into force on 1 April 2006.[274] An Interim[275] Association Agreement on trade and trade-related matters between the EU and the PA has been in force since 1 July 1997.[276] Negotiations with Syria started in 1998. In 2002, after four years of negotiations, a compromise was reached on all topics except the provisions regarding the non-proliferation of weapons of mass destruction. This issue was again brought up during the negotiations in 2003. Finally, an agreement on the text for these provisions was reached in September 2004. At the end of 2004, the AA with Syria had been submitted to the political authorities on both sides for final approval and signature. At this moment, the EU Council still has to decide on signature.[277] Syria's relations with the EC are presently covered by their Cooperation Agreement of 18 July 1977.

2. The legal basis of a Euro-Med Association Agreement

2.1 Article 217 TFEU

The Euro-Med AAs concluded between the Mediterranean countries and the EU are based on Article 217 TFEU.[278] Article 217 TFEU enables the EU to 'conclude with one or more third countries (before the TFEU: States) or international organisations, agreements establishing an association involving reciprocal rights

1975 with the EU as soon as possible. See also A. Tovias, *Options for Mashrek-Israeli Regionalism in the Context of the Euro-Mediterranean Partnership*, CEPS Paper No. 67 (1997) pp. 17-18.

[274] The EU signed an Interim Agreement on trade and trade-related matters with Lebanon for early implementation of trade measures, which entered into force on 1 March 2003, *OJ* 2000 L 262/02.

[275] The interim aspect implies that only limited commitments could be made considering that the West Bank and the Gaza Strip were (and still are) not accepted as a 'state.'

[276] In 1995, the Commission issued a Communication regarding the future economic support from the EU to the West Bank and the Gaza Strip (Communication from the Commission to the Council and the European Parliament of 23 October 1995 on Future European Union Economic Assistance to the West Bank and the Gaza Strip, COM (95) 505 final). Despite the EU's efforts to ease the Middle East conflict, there were several serious bomb attacks in Israel in 1996 after Prime Minister Netanyahu had come to office. This led to the isolation of the West Bank and the Gaza Strip, and the EU's efforts to support the Palestinians financially and economically had no positive impact on the peace process. Since the EU was not capable of intermediating in the Middle East conflict, the US decided to exclude the EU from the important Washington Conference aimed at stimulating the peace process in 1996. In reaction to this exclusion, the EU met with PLO leader Yasser Arafat on the day of the Washington Conference in order to start negotiations on a Euro-Med Interim AA. The Commission also examined the competence of the PLO to conclude international agreements. According to the Israeli/PA Interim Agreement of 28 September 1995, the PLO has the competence to conclude international agreements in certain fields, including economic ones (Art. IX:5(b) Israel/PLO Interim Agreement concerning the West Bank and Gaza Strip). For more detailed information see S. Keukeleire, *Het Buitenlands Beleid van de Europese Unie* (Deventer, Kluwer 1998) pp. 397-398.

[277] COM (2008) 853 final.

[278] According to the Lisbon Treaty (Treaty of Lisbon amending the Treaty on European Union and the Treaty establishing the European Community, *OJ* 2007 C 306 of 17 December 2007, pp. 1-231), Art. 310 will become Art. 188M. The Lisbon Treaty has not yet been ratified.

and obligations, common action and special procedures.'[279] The content of this Article is not very clear as regards the drafting of the Euro-Med AAs. Keukeleire is of the opinion that the vague formulation of Article 217 leaves room for different provisions in the Euro-Med AAs depending on the political and economic aims of the EU and the third country.[280] According to Zapater, Article 310 EC Treaty (now Art. 217 TFEU) is not easily interpreted and it is difficult to reach conclusions about what kind of agreements can be concluded on this legal basis. Zapater, however, correctly believes that this type of agreement is a highly useful instrument for enabling a flexible relation between subjects of international law by creating the possibility to tighten their relationship.[281]

2.2 Analysis of the elements of Article 217 TFEU

2.2.1 *The concept of 'association'*

Although the legal basis for the conclusion of Euro-Med AAs is not very clear, the ECJ and various authors have tried to explain the different elements of Article 217 TFEU. In the *Demirel* case, the ECJ offered a definition of the concept of 'association.'[282] According to the ECJ, an association creates a special, privileged link between the EC and the Member States, on the one hand, and the non-member country, on the other, and the non-member country must, at least to a certain extent, 'take part in the Community system.' Eeckhout explained the meaning of the concept of 'taking part in the Community system.' According to him, the ECJ did not have in mind participation by the non-member country in the work of the EU and its institutions, since no Euro-Med AA provides for that. The reference to participation in the Community system is in all likelihood to be interpreted in material terms. It means that the system of the TFEU must in certain policy areas, such as the internal market or competition policy, be in some measure extended to the associated country.[283]

[279] The first AAs were concluded with states that would later seek accession to the EC: Greece in 1961, Turkey in 1963, Malta in 1970 and Cyprus in 1972. All four agreements entered into force in the year after they were signed and provided for the creation of a customs union with the EC. Even though only the first two agreements held out the prospect of accession for the associated states, AAs are a commonly used way of preparing for EU accession.

[280] Cf., *supra* n. 276, pp. 130-131.

[281] E. Zapater, *El Fundamento juridico de la actuacion exterior de las Comunidades Europeas en el ambito de la cooperacion energetica internacional* (Catalunya, Universidad Autonoma de Barcelona 2000) p. 389, cited by D. Miralles Sole, *An Instrumental Analysis of the European Union's Capability to Act in Conflict Response* (Catalunya, Grup Artyplan-Artympres 2004) p. 27.

[282] C-12/86 *Demirel* v *Stadt Schwäbisch Gmünd* [1987] *ECR* 3719, paras. 9-10.

[283] K. Lenaerts and E. De Smijter, 'The European Community's Treaty-Making Competence', 16 *Yearbook of European Law (YEL)* (1996) pp. 20-25 cited by Eeckhout, *supra* n. 272, p. 105.

2.2.2 *The concept of 'agreement'*

It is also important to know what kind of 'agreement' is meant by Article 217 TFEU. The agreement takes the form of a mixed agreement, i.e., concluded by both the EU and the Member States, on the one hand, and the associated Mediterranean country, on the other.[284] Moreover, the agreement is binding on the institutions of the EU, the Member States and the Mediterranean country.[285] It covers EU policies as a whole but also involves exclusive powers for Member States, arising from the more intergovernmental cooperation within the EU (the CFSP).[286] Whether the ECJ is allowed to interpret a mixed agreement between the EU and its Member States, on the one hand, and the Mediterranean country, on the other, has been the subject of several ECJ judgments and many opinions of Advocates-General to the ECJ. In de *Demirel* case, the ECJ declared that the ECJ could interpret the provisions of the mixed agreement that come within the powers of the EU, such as that regarding the freedom of workers in the AA, which is an EU competence. The ECJ is also competent to interpret provisions of the mixed agreement that come within the powers of the EU even if it is for the Member States to implement the provisions necessary to give effect in their territory to the provisions of the mixed agreement or the decisions to be adopted by the Association Council.[287] The ECJ implicitly puts limits on its interpretative jurisdiction: it has no jurisdiction to interpret provisions which come within the exclusive competence of the Member States.[288] Another difficulty concerning the interpretation of provisions of mixed agreements relates to the interpretation of provisions of an AA that fall under the scope of national law and EU law. It is settled case

[284] R. Leal-Arcas, 'The European Community and Mixed Agreements', 6 *EFA Rev.* (2001) pp. 483-513.

[285] Art. 300, para. 7 EC Treaty.

[286] The agreements cover trade in industrial and agricultural goods, trade in services and the right of establishment, payments and capital movements, competition, intellectual property rights, financial cooperation, economic cooperation, agriculture and investments, transportation, telecommunications and energy, science and technology, environment and tourism, statistics and the fight against illegal drugs.

[287] '9 (...). Since the agreement in question is an association agreement creating special, privileged links with a non-member country which must at least to a certain extent, take part in the Community system, Article 238 must necessarily empower the Community to guarantee commitments towards non-member countries in all the fields covered by the Treaty, since freedom of movement for workers is, by virtue of Article 48 of the EC Treaty, one of the fields covered by that Treaty, it follows that commitments regarding freedom of movement fall within the powers conferred on the Community by Article 238. Thus the question whether the Court has jurisdiction to rule on the interpretation of a provision of a mixed agreement containing a commitment which only the Member States could enter into the sphere of their own powers does not arise.'

'10 Furthermore, the jurisdiction of the Court cannot be called in question by virtue of the fact that in the field of freedom of movement of workers, as Community law now stands, it is for the Member States to lay down the rules which are necessary to give effect in their territory to the provisions of the Agreement or the decisions to be adopted by the Association Council.'

[288] M.T. Karayigit, 'Why and To What Extent a Common Interpretative Position for Mixed Agreements?' 11 *EFAR* (2006) pp. 445-469, at p. 449.

law that the ECJ can interpret these 'mixed' provisions in order to guarantee the uniformity of interpretation. In the *Dior* case, for example, the ECJ stated that it had jurisdiction to interpret a provision of an AA which could apply both to situations falling within the scope of national law and to those falling within that of EU law, in order to forestall future differences of interpretation.[289] A final problem concerns the interpretation of agreements concluded on the basis of Article 217 TFEU with a view to accession to the EU.[290] Many agreements concluded on the basis of Article 217 refer to the prospect of future membership of European states, but the Euro-Med AAs never embodied the idea of future accession to the EU. According to Article 49 EU Treaty, only European states may apply to become a member of the EU. States are considered to be European when they are established on European territory[291] and Morocco, Tunisia, Algeria, Egypt, Israel, Palestine, Lebanon, Syria, Jordan and Libya are not. One of the aims of accession agreements is the approximation of economic and legal systems in order to achieve 'full acceptance' by the associated country of the obligations of the EU Treaties. Full acceptance includes the fundamental freedoms required for the establishment of the common market. Therefore, it is necessary that all the subjects which are *a priori* to be covered by such acceptance are set out in the agreement in a EU perspective and that it is possible for the European courts to interpret them with a view to their uniform application. It can be stated that provisions of an agreement concluded with a view to accession to the EU are brought under the jurisdiction of the European courts.[292]

It is also crucial to determine which provisions of association agreements have direct effect.[293] In numerous judgments on the interpretation of international agreements, the ECJ has held that, to determine whether a provision in an international agreement has direct effect within the legal order of the Member States, it is necessary first to ascertain whether the content of that provision is clear, precise and unconditional and then to evaluate the content in the light of the aims

[289] Joined cases C-300/98 and C-392/98 *Dior and Others* [2000] *ECR* I-11307, paras. 35 et seq., C-53/96 *Hermès* [1998] *ECR* I-3603, paras. 28 and 29 and Opinion of Advocate General Trstenjak delivered on 11 November 2008, paras. 71-73 to C-62/05 P, *Nordspedizionieri di Danielis Livio & C. Snc in liquidazione, Livio Danielis and Domenico D'Alessandro* v *Commission of the European Communities*.

[290] Eeckhout, *supra* n. 272, p. 104.

[291] Turkey is considered to be a European state even when only 10 percent of the Turkish territory is on European soil. Morocco applied for European membership several times, but all requests were denied. Important Israeli authors, such as A. Tovias and political leaders like Nabil Sha'ath have raised the issue of Israeli membership in the EU.

[292] Opinion of Mr Advocate General Darmon delivered on 19 May 1987 in Case 12/86, *Meryem Demirel* v *Stadt Schwäbisch Gmünd* [1987] *ECR* 3719.

[293] Case 106/77 *Amministrazione delle Finanze dello Stato* v *Simmenthal S.p.A.* [1978] *ECR* 629, paras. 14-15. The ECJ held that direct applicability meant that rules of Community law must be fully and uniformly applied in all the Member States from the date of their entry into force and for so long as they continue in force. Therefore, these provisions are a direct source of rights and duties for all those affected thereby, whether Member States or individuals, who are parties to legal relationships under Community law.

and context of the agreement.[294] It is settled case-law that a provision of an agreement entered into by the EU with a non-member country must be regarded as being directly applicable when it may be concluded that the provision contains a clear, precise and unconditional obligation which is not subject, in its implementation or effects, to the adoption of any subsequent measure.[295] Provisions of the Euro-Med AAs that do not have direct effect need to be implemented by the Association Council. The Association Council issues binding bilateral decisions under the EMP.

2.2.3 *The concept of 'states'*

Another element of the former Article 310 EC Treaty that requires explanation is the concept of 'states.' Article 310 explicitly referred to the conclusion of agreements with 'states.' With the entry into force of the TFEU, the concept of 'states' is replaced by the concept 'third countries' in Article 217 TFEU. The West Bank and Gaza Strip are internationally still not considered as an independent state or a country. Therefore, it was not possible to use Article 310 EC Treaty in concluding an AA with the PA. The conclusion of an agreement with the PA on the basis of Article 310 EC Treaty could lead to the implicit recognition of the Palestinian State by the EC.[296] However, the PLO, representing the West Bank and the Gaza Strip, does have legal power to conclude certain international agreements, such as economic ones.[297] Consequently, the PLO concluded a Euro-Med Interim AA on trade and cooperation with the EC. This Interim AA has been based on Article 133 EC Treaty *juncto* Article 181 EC Treaty with a reference to Article 177 EC Treaty.[298] Article 133(3) EC Treaty stipulates that the conclusion of agreements,

---

[294] N. Munin. 'Should the High Court Intervene in the Economic Considerations of the Israel Government within the Framework of the Implementation of Israel's Regional Free Trade Agreements?', in A.M. Rabello, ed., *Essays on European Law in Israel* (Israel, Hebrew University of Jerusalem 1996) pp. 1078-1090; see judgments in 87/75 *Bresciani* [1976] *ECR* 129, para. 16; C-270/80 *Polydor* v *Harlequin* [1982] *ECR* 329, paras. 14 et seq.; C-17/81 *Pabst* [1982] *ECR* 1331, paras. 26 and 27; C-104/81 *Kupferberg* [1982] *ECR* 3641, paras. 11-14 and 23; C-12/86 *Demirel* [1987] *ECR* 3719, para. 14; C-192/89 *Sevince* [1990] *ECR* I-3461, para. 15; C-18/90 *Kziber* [1991] *ECR* I-199, para. 15; C-432/92 *Anastasiou* [1994] *ECR* I-3087.

[295] C-12/86 *Demirel* v *Stadt Schwäbisch Gmünd* [1987] *ECR* 3719, para. 14.

[296] E. Lannon, 'L'Accord d'Association Intérimaire Communauté Européenne-OLP: l'Institutionnalisation Progressive des Relations Euro-Palestiniennes', *Revue des Affaires Européennes* (1997) pp. 176-179; S. Melchor, *The 1997 Euro-Mediterranean Interim Association Agreement between the European Community and the Palestinian Liberation Organisation*, Working Paper for the College of Europe (Bruges, 1998) pp. 38-43; I. MacLeod, I. Hendry and S. Hyett, *The External Relations of the European Communities: A Manual of Law and Practice* (Oxford, Oxford University Press 1996) pp. 283-286.

[297] Art. IX:5(b) Israel-PLO Interim Agreement on the West Bank & the Gaza Strip.

[298] The EC has exclusive competence for the common trade policy as provided for in Art. 133 EC Treaty. Art. 181 EC Treaty was introduced with the Maastricht Treaty and provided a legal basis for agreements that included a development dimension. The PA Interim AA made development cooperation official and maintained trade and economic issues; see E. Zapater, *El Fundamento juridico de la actuacion exterior de las Comunidades Europeas en el ambito de la cooperacion energetica internacional* (Barcelona, Universidad Autonoma de Barcelona 2000) p. 357, cited by D. Miralles Sole, *An*

on the basis of Article 300(2) EC Treaty, with one or more states or international organisations, such as AAs, require unanimity of the Member States. By using Article 133 EC Treaty, the PA evaded the unanimity requirement. However, the consent of the European Parliament was still needed, since Article 300(3) EC Treaty stipulates that the EP's consent is needed not only for international agreements based on Article 310 EC Treaty but also for all other international agreements that establish an institutional framework.[299]

2.2.4 *Reciprocal rights and obligations*

Another concept in Article 217 TFEU consists of the 'reciprocal rights and obligations' of an AA. In the past, there have been certain AAs which the ECJ considered contrary to European law because of an imbalance of obligations between the EU and the associated states. These kinds of agreement were mostly development AAs, such as the Yaoundé Convention. This Convention provided for 'non-reciprocal' duty-free entry into the EU of goods from the ACP countries and was considered contrary to European law by the ECJ in the *Bresciani* case.[300] According to the ECJ, the Yaoundé Convention, based on a 'non-reciprocal' duty scheme, did not ensure equality in the obligations which the EU assumes with regard to the associated states. The reciprocal rights and obligations between the EU, the Member States and the associated states can be considered as a typical feature of an AA. All Euro-Med AAs are characterised by a balance between rights and obligations of the EU, its Member States and the Mediterranean countries.[301] The aim of the Euro-Med AAs is progressive 'mutual' liberalisation of

---

Instrumental Analysis of the European Union's Capability to Act in Conflict Response (Catalunya, Grup Artyplan-Artympres SA 2004) p. 26.

[299] Art. 310 ECT has become art. 217 TFEU; Art. 133 ECT has become Art. 207 TFEU; Art. 177 has become Art. 208 TFEU and Art. 181 has become Art. 211 TFEU.

[300] Case 87/75 *Conceria Daniele Bresciani* v *Amministrazione Italiana delle Finanze* [1976] *ECR* 129, paras. 19-23. The ECJ ruled as follows: '(...) As far as customs duties and charges having equivalent effect are concerned, Article 2(1) of the Convention provides as follows: "Goods originating in the Associated States shall, when imported into the Member States, benefit from the progressive abolition of customs duties and charges having an effect equivalent to such duties (...)." Article 3(2) of the Convention limits the obligation on the Associated States to abolish customs duties and charges having an effect equivalent to such duties by providing that "each Associated State may retain or introduce customs duties and charges having an effect equivalent to such duties which correspond to its development needs or its industrialization requirements or which are intended to contribute to its budget." Article 61 of the Convention provides that the EC and its Member States shall undertake the obligations in Articles 2, 5 and 11 even with respect to the Associated States which (...) may consider themselves not yet able to offer the EC the reciprocity provided for in Article 3(2) of the Convention. It is apparent from these provisions that the Convention was not concluded to ensure equality of obligations which the EC assumes with regard to the Associated States, but in order to promote their development (...).' Therefore, the ECJ ruled that 'whatever its designation and mode of application, a pecuniary charge which is unilaterally imposed on goods imported from Member States when they cross a frontier constitutes a charge having an effect equivalent to a customs duty (...).'

[301] There is, however, the infant industry clause to protect fragile sectors and to aid underdeveloped countries, such as the West Bank and the Gaza Strip.

goods, services and capital between the EU, its Member States and the Mediterranean countries.

2.2.5 *Common action*

The AA is also characterised by 'common action' as it should be possible for the EU, the Member States and the Mediterranean countries to take joint decisions in all fields covered by the AA.[302]

2.2.6 *Special procedures*

The concept of 'special procedures' in Article 217 TFEU refers to the importance of the institutionalisation of the Euro-Med relationship. The institutional element means that the association leads to the creation of several institutions, such as the Association Council, the Association Committee and the Parliamentary Assembly.[303] All AAs establish an Association Council and an Association Committee.[304] The Association Council consists of members of the EU Council, of the European Commission and of the government of the Mediterranean country. The Association Council tries to settle all disputes relating to the application or interpretation of the AA. The AAs provide for the establishment of an *ad hoc* dispute settlement body if the Association Council fails to settle the dispute. Each party may notify the other of the appointment of an arbiter.[305] The other party must then appoint another arbiter. The Association Council itself appoints a third arbiter. The arbiter's decision is taken by majority vote. The Association Council also examines any major issue arising from the AA and any other bilateral or international issue of interest, may decide to set up any working group necessary for the implementation of the AA[306] and may delegate all its power to the Association Committee. The Association Council takes decisions which are binding upon the parties and make appropriate recommendations.[307] The Association Committee consists of representatives of EU Member States and of the European Commission, on the one hand, and of representatives of the Mediterranean country, on the other. The Association Committee is responsible for the implementation of the AA. The

[302] H. Dominik and P. Dengler, *Accords d' Association*, Research Paper for the College of Europe (Bruges, 2004) p. 5.

[303] For a critical overview of the Euro-Med institutions, see S. Pardo and L. Zemer, 'Towards a New Euro-Mediterranean Neighbourhood Space', 10 *EFAR* (2005) pp. 39-77.

[304] The PA Interim AA provides for a Joint Committee and not for an Association Council and an Association Committee (Arts. 63 and 67 PA Interim AA).

[305] The EU and the Member States are one party to the dispute.

[306] See, for example, proposal for a Council Decision of 15 May 2005 on a Community position in the Association Council on the implementation of Art. 67 and Art. 80 of the Euro-Mediterranean Agreement establishing an association between the EC and their Member States, on one part, and the Arab Republic of Egypt, of the other part, COM (2005) 188 final. This proposal sets up a working group on migration, social and consular affairs and subcommittees attached to the Association Committee.

[307] The Council shall, for example, take appropriate measures to facilitate the cooperation and contacts between the European Parliament and the parliament of the Mediterranean country.

Committee also has the power to take decisions regarding the management of the AA as well as in those areas where the Association Council has delegated its powers. The decisions are binding upon the parties. The Association Council and the Association Committee meet on a regular basis and the technical subcommittees guarantee practical implementation.

2.3 Sub-conclusion

All Euro-Med AAs, except for the PA Interim AA, are based on Article 217 TFEU, which stipulates that the Union may conclude with one or more third countries or international organisations agreements establishing an association involving reciprocal rights and obligations, common action and special procedures. This legal basis has made it possible for the EU and the Mediterranean countries to establish associations by concluding international agreements. Association should not be confused with accession, as none of the Euro-Med AAs provide for accession of the Mediterranean countries to the EU. In other words, the goal of the Euro-Med AAs is not for the Mediterranean countries to fully accept the Union's *acquis* relating to the EU internal market. Their aim is to establish an association, which means that the EU only extends some policies, such as the EU internal market and competition policy, to the Mediterranean countries. The difference between accession and association also has an impact on the jurisdictional power of the ECJ. In cases of full acceptance or accession, it is possible for the ECJ to interpret all provisions of the international agreement. Euro-Med AAs, however do not fall under the full jurisdiction of the European courts. The ECJ may interpret provisions falling within EU competence, such as those relating to the freedom of workers in the Euro-Med AAs, as well as those coming under EU competence that require implementation measures, such as the competition provisions in the Euro-Med AAs. Provisions that come under EU and national competence will be interpreted by the ECJ for the purpose of establishing uniformity. The ECJ, however, is not competent to interpret provisions of the Euro-Med AAs that fall within exclusive national competence. Natural and legal persons can also rely on provisions of the Euro-Med AAs before the European courts and national courts, but only if these provisions have direct effect in the national legal order. A provision is considered to be directly applicable when it contains a clear, precise and unconditional obligation which is not subject, in its implementation or effects, to the adoption of any subsequent measure.

Furthermore, Article 217 TFEU stipulates that the association should involve reciprocal rights and obligations, common action and special procedures. This means that the association will be based on the principle of reciprocity of concessions between the EU and the Mediterranean countries. In most cases, the EU will open its markets sooner to entries from the Mediterranean countries. But the aim of the Euro-Med AAs is that the Mediterranean countries will follow the EU example and gradually open their borders to European entries. Unilateral abolishment of restrictive practices will not be accepted. Association means that the EU and the Mediterranean countries can take decisions jointly. Therefore, the

Euro-Med AAs provide for an institutional infrastructure according to which the EU and the Mediterranean countries can take cooperative decisions.

3. Legal analysis of the provisions regarding movement of goods, services, capital and persons in the Euro-Med Association Agreements

Provisions regarding the four movements, i.e., of goods, of services, of capital and of persons, are included in the Euro-Med AAs. There are also other important provisions in these AAs that have an impact on these movement provisions, for example, the provisions on competition law and the rules of origin. All these provisions will be presented, thoroughly analysed and illustrated by case law of the European Court of Justice (ECJ).

Some of these movement provisions require implementation measures of the Association Council or the Association Committee. Implementation measures of the Association Council or Committee have taken the form of binding decisions. At present, many decisions of the Association Council concern the setting-up of subcommittees to assist the Association Council and Committee. For example, on 18 June 2007, the EU Council adopted a decision concerning the EU position within the Association Council on the implementation of Articles 76 and 98 of the Algeria-EU AA. The decision establishes a working party on social matters and six subcommittees to assist the EU Council and the Association Committee in the implementation of the Euro-Med AA.[308] On 24 May 2007, the Council of the EU adopted a decision on the EU position in the Association Council regarding the implementation of Article 75 and Article 80 of the Lebanon-EU AA.[309] This decision provides for the establishment of 10 subcommittees to assist the Council and the Association Council in the implementation of the Euro-Med AA. Only the most relevant decisions of the Association Council or Committee will be examined, namely those that have contributed to the integration of the Mediterranean countries into the EU internal market of goods, services, capital and persons.

It will be investigated whether these provisions on the movement of goods, services, capital and persons and their implementation measures have led to better integration of the relevant Mediterranean countries into the EU internal market of goods, services, capital and persons.

---

[308] Proposal of the Commission of 11 April 2007 for a Council Decision concerning the Community position within the Association Council on the implementation of Arts. 76 and 98 of the Euro-Mediterranean Agreement establishing an Association between the European Community and its Member States, of the one part, and the People's Democratic Republic of Algeria, of the other part, COM (2007) 179 final.

[309] COM (2007) 64 and COM (2007) 84.

3.1 The 'goods provisions' in the Euro-Med Association Agreements

3.1.1 *Liberalisation of goods through the prohibition of customs duties and charges having equivalent effect*

All AAs ensure the movement of goods between the Mediterranean countries and the EU. The goods provisions of the AA apply to products imported and exported between the Mediterranean countries and the EU. The movement of goods between the EU and the Mediterranean countries should lead to the establishment of a Euro-Med free trade area in the future. The maximum period for the creation of the Euro-Med free trade area is different for each Mediterranean country and is set at 12 years after the entry into force of the Euro-Med AAs.[310] Only the Israel-EU AA does not provide for a final date for establishment of this free trade area. The date for the West Bank and the Gaza Strip was set at 2001.

Goods which are still in transit in Europe but are destined for a Mediterranean country fall within the scope of the TFEU and not within that of the Euro-Med AA. The *Rioglass* case serves as a good example in this respect.[311] In November 1997, Rioglass sold a consignment of windows and windscreens, produced in Spain, to Jann, a company registered in Poland. The goods were exported from Spain through France to Poland.[312] French customs officers carried out an inspection. They drew up a report of detention of the goods and a report of seizure of the goods on suspicion of infringement of trade mark. The ECJ was requested whether this measure of detention under customs control could have the same effect as a quantitative restriction. Therefore, the ECJ had to find out whether the EC Treaty or the international agreement was applicable considering the fact that the goods were destined for a third country. The ECJ ruled that goods in transit which are intended for a non-member country come within the scope of Articles 34 EC to 36 TFEU. The interpretation of Articles 34 and 36 TFEU does not apply in the context of the relations between the Mediterranean countries and the EU, since the TFEU and the Euro-Med AA do not serve the same purpose.[313]

The AAs make a distinction between trade in industrial products, on the one hand, and agricultural, fishery and processed agricultural products, on the other. Other economic provisions in the AAs related to the movement of goods are those concerning competition law,[314]state aid,[315]state monopolies,[316] public enter-

---

[310] PA: 2001; Tunisia: 2010; Morocco: 2012; Jordan: 2014; Egypt: 2016; Algeria: 2017 and Lebanon: 2018.

[311] C-115/02, *Administration des douanes et droit indirects* v *Rioglass SA and Transremar SL* [2003] *ECR* I-12705 and C-350/97 *Monsees* [1999] *ECR* I-2921.

[312] At the time, Poland was not a member of the EU.

[313] C-270/80 *Polydor Limited and RSO Records Inc.* v *Harlequin Records Shops Limited and Simons Records Limited* [1982] *ECR* 329, paras. 18-19.

[314] Cf., *infra* 3.2. An analysis of the competition law provisions in the Euro-Med Association Agreements.

[315] Art. 41 Algeria AA; Art. 36 Morocco AA; Art. 36 Tunisia AA; Art. 34 Egypt AA; Art. 36 Jordan AA and Art. 35 Lebanon AA.

[316] With regard to state monopolies, all AAs stipulate that the Member States and the Mediterranean country shall progressively adjust any state monopoly of a commercial character to ensure that

prises[317] and public procurement,[318] those related to intellectual, industrial and commercial property matters[319] and those regarding rules of origin.

3.1.1.1 Liberalisation of trade in industrial goods

The Algeria AA serves as an example for the movement of industrial goods.

> Art. 8 AA: Products originating in Algeria shall be imported into the Community free of customs duties and charges having equivalent effect.
> Art. 9, para. 1 AA: Customs duties and charges having equivalent effect applicable on import into Algeria of products originating in the Community listed in Annex 2 shall be abolished upon the entry into force of this Agreement. Art. 9, para. 2 AA: Customs duties and charges having equivalent effect applicable on import into Algeria of products originating in the Community shall be progressively abolished in accordance with the following timetable: (…). Art. 9, para. 3 AA: Customs duties and charges having equivalent effect applicable on import into Algeria of products originating in the Community other than those listed in Annexes 2 and 3 shall be progressively abolished in accordance with the following timetable: (…).

The movement of industrial products between a Mediterranean country and the EU is as follows: goods originating in a Mediterranean country which are imported into the EU are completely free of 'customs duties' and 'charges having equivalent effect.' Goods originating in the EU which are imported into a Mediterranean country are still subject to 'customs duties' and 'charges having equivalent effect,' but the duties and charges will be progressively abolished according to the timetables in the Annexes to the AA.

The free trade area in industrial goods between Europe and the Mediterranean countries is of an asymmetrical nature. This means that the European markets will be opened more rapidly to traders from the Mediterranean countries than the Mediterranean markets to European traders. Imports into the EU are free of all customs duties and equivalent charges upon entry into force of the AAs. The Mediterranean countries will gradually abolish customs duties on an industrial basis in accordance with a timetable, which is different for each category of product. Some products will enter the Mediterranean countries without customs duties

---

by the end of the fifth year following the entry into force of the agreement, no discrimination regarding the conditions under which goods are procured and marketed exists between nationals of the Member States and the Mediterranean country.

[317] With regard to public enterprises and enterprises which have been granted special or exclusive rights, the Association Council ensures that no measure which disturbs trade between the EU and the Mediterranean country in a manner which runs counter to the interests of the parties is adopted or maintained.

[318] All AAs state that the parties shall set as their objective a reciprocal and gradual liberalisation of public procurement contracts. The Algerian AA also stipulates that parties shall adopt appropriate measures to ensure the protection of personal data in order to eliminate barriers to the free movement of such data between parties (Art. 45 Algeria AA).

[319] All AAs state that the parties shall provide suitable and effective protection of intellectual, industrial and commercial property, in line with the highest international standards.

upon entry into force of the AA; others will enter the Mediterranean countries without customs duties only several years after the entry into force of the AA and some will only be completely free of charges at the moment the free trade zone is established.

In 2007, the ECJ ruled on an interesting case in which the notions 'customs duties' and 'charges having equivalent effect' are explained. In *Commission* v *Italian Republic*, the Commission claimed that Italy had failed to fulfil its obligations under Articles 23, 25, 26 and 207 TFEU as well as Articles 4 and 9 of the Algeria Cooperation Agreement.[320] The breach concerned the imposition of an environmental tax, provided for in Sicilian law, on the import of an industrial product, namely methane gas. The Commission submitted that the imposition of the tax on gas affected the trans-Mediterranean pipeline owned by an Algerian company. The pipeline distributes gas in Italy and transports gas from Italian soil to other Member States. The Commission argued that it was settled case law that the imposition of new charges or measures having equivalent effect on goods imported directly from non-member countries was prohibited. Article 9(1) of the Algeria Cooperation Agreement provides that products originating in Algeria shall be imported into the EU free of customs duties and charges having equivalent effect. The scope of the prohibition of customs duties and charges having equivalent effect is identical to that in the context of intra-EU trade.[321] Furthermore, the Commission stated that the introduction of the environmental tax distorted the equalisation of customs charges imposed at the EU's external frontiers on goods imported from third countries, potentially causing deflection of trade with those countries and distortion in the free movement of goods or in conditions of competition between Member States. The Commission also stated that the concept of a 'charge having equivalent effect to a customs duty' is an objective legal EU concept, which has to be interpreted without taking into account the aim of the custom duty.[322]

Advocate-General Léger stated that the term 'charge having equivalent effect to a customs duty' in Article 9 of the Cooperation Agreement must be understood as any *pecuniary charge, whatever its designation and mode of application, which is imposed unilaterally on goods by reason of the fact that they cross a frontier, and which is not a customs duty in the strict sense, even though such pecuniary charge is not levied for the benefit of the state.*[323] The interpretation of the concept 'customs duty or a charge having equivalent effect' as regards products originating from a Mediterranean country must be the same as the interpreta-

[320] C-173/05 *Commission* v *Italian Republic* [2007] *ECR* I-04917 and Opinion of Advocate-General Léger delivered on 5 October 2006.

[321] C-125/94, *Aprile Srl, in liquidation* v *Amministrazione delle Finanze dello Stato* [1995] *ECR* I-2919, paras. 32-42.

[322] Joined cases C-485/93 and C-486/93, *Maria Simitzi* v *Dimos Kos* [1995] *ECR* I-2655, para. 14. The ECJ held that customs duties were prohibited, independently of any consideration of the purpose for which they were introduced and the destination of the revenue.

[323] For the concept of 'charge having equivalent effect,' see joined cases 37 and 38/73, *Sociaal Fonds voor de Diamantarbeiders* v *Indiamex NV et Association de fait De Belder* [1973] *ECR* 01609, paras. 15-18.

tion upheld by the ECJ regarding intra-EU trade. In order to determine whether the tax on gas has the constituent elements of a charge having equivalent effect to a customs duty, it has to be established whether that tax is imposed on goods and whether those goods are taxed by reason of their crossing a frontier. The Advocate-General was of the opinion that the constituent elements of the definition of a charge having an equivalent effect were present.

The ECJ confirmed that there was no reason to interpret the prohibition of charges having an effect equivalent to customs duties differently depending on whether the trade concerned is conducted within the EU or with non-member countries under agreements such as the Cooperation Agreement.[324] Therefore, the ECJ found that the tax introduced by Sicilian Law was a fiscal charge levied on goods imported from a non-member country, namely Algerian methane gas. Such a tax on goods imported from Algeria is contrary to both Articles 23 and 133 EC Treaty (now Arts. 31 and 207 TFEU) and Article 9 of the Cooperation Agreement. The ECJ also noted that the tax on Algerian gas which was imported into Italy and subsequently exported to other Member States was likely to affect intra-EU trade. Therefore, the ECJ determined that, by introducing an environmental tax on methane gas from Algeria, Italy breached Articles 23, 25 and 133 EC-Treaty (now Arts. 31, 38 and 207 TFEU) and Article 9 of the Cooperation Agreement.

In conclusion, it can be stated that the Euro-Med AAs ensure the 'free' movement of industrial goods from the Mediterranean countries to the EC. The EC can expect a fully liberalised export of industrial goods to the Mediterranean countries, preferably by 2010, the year of the creation of the Euro-Med free trade area. The maximum period for the creation of the Euro-Med free trade area, however, is 12 years after the entry into force of the individual Euro-Med Association Agreements. Until then, European exports to the Mediterranean countries are submitted to customs duties and measures having equivalent effect.

3.1.1.2 Liberalisation of trade in agricultural, fishery and processed agricultural products

The EU and all Mediterranean countries have stated that they shall progressively establish a greater liberalisation of their trade in agricultural, fishery and processed agricultural products. The Moroccan AA serves as an example in this respect:

> Art. 15 AA: The provisions of this chapter shall apply to the products originating in the Community and Morocco listed in Annex II to the Treaty establishing the European Community. Art. 16 AA: The Community and Morocco shall gradually implement greater liberalisation of their reciprocal trade in agricultural and fishery products. Art. 17 AA, para.1: Agricultural and fishery products originating in Morocco shall benefit on import into the Community from the provisions set out in Protocols 1 and 2 respectively. Art. 17 AA, para. 2: Agricultural products originating in the Community

[324] See *Aprile*, *supra* n. 321, para. 39.

> shall benefit on import into Morocco from the provisions set out in Protocol 3. Art 18 AA, para. 1: From 1 January 2000, the Community and Morocco shall assess the situation with a view to determining the liberalisation measures to be applied by the Community and Morocco with effect from 1 January 2001 in accordance with the objective set out in Art. 16 AA, para. 2: Without prejudice to the provisions of paragraph 1 and taking account of the patterns of trade in agricultural products between the Parties and the particular sensitivity of such products, the Community and Morocco will examine on a regular basis in the Association Council, product by product and on a reciprocal basis, the possibilities of granting each other further concessions.

The Mediterranean countries liberalise trade in agricultural products, fishery products and industrial products with an agricultural component according to agreed schedules in the relevant Mediterranean country. The prohibition of customs duties and measures having equivalent effect does not apply to agricultural products, fishery products and industrial products with an agricultural element. These products remain subject to customs charges and quotas.[325] The Mediterranean countries and the EU will examine on a regular basis in the Association Council, product by product and on a reciprocal basis, the possibilities of granting each other further concessions. Case law as regards the prohibition of customs duties and charges having equivalent effect cannot be applied to the movement of agricultural products, fishery products and industrial products with an agricultural component, since these products remain subject to customs charges.

In conclusion, it can be stated that at present there is no 'free' movement of agricultural products, fishery products and industrial products with an agricultural component between the Mediterranean countries and the EU. Customs duties and measures having equivalent effect remain, but should be progressively abolished in order to create a Euro-Med free trade area.

3.1.2 *The liberalisation of trade in goods through the prohibition of quantitative restrictions and equivalent measures*

All AAs have a similar provision concerning the prohibition of quantitative restrictions and equivalent measures which are common to industrial products, on the one hand, and to agricultural, fishery and processed agricultural products on the other. The Jordan AA serves as an example in this respect:

> Art. 18 AA: (i) no new quantitative restrictions on imports and measures having equivalent effect shall be introduced in trade between the EC and Jordan; (ii) quantitative restrictions on imports and measures having equivalent effect on trade between the EC and Jordan shall be abolished upon entry into force of this Agreement and (iii) the EC and Jordan shall not apply to exports between themselves either customs duties

---

[325] The Communication of the Commission on its new neighbourhood policy in an enlarged Europe also points out that there is still room to deepen the Euro-Med AAs in the domain of trade in agricultural products.

or charges having equivalent effect, or quantitative restrictions or measures having equivalent effect.

The prohibition concerning quantitative restrictions and equivalent measures only applies to fully liberalised goods, namely industrial goods. Other goods, such as agricultural products, fishery products and industrial products with an agricultural element, which remain subject to charges, can still be subject to quantitative restrictions or measures having the same effect.

This prohibition deals with direct or indirect obstacles to trade between the EU and the Mediterranean country. 'Direct' restrictions concern quotas or other bans related to the quantity of trade in industrial goods between the EU and the Mediterranean country. 'Indirect restrictions' or 'measures having the same effect as quantitative restrictions' are less clear and thus more controversial. The indirect restrictions do not deal with numerical limits in relation to trade in goods, but result from conflicting technical and regulatory standards between the Mediterranean country and the EU. For example, if Lebanon were to apply an electrical standard for hair dryers different from the EU one, a German manufacturer of hair dryers who wants to sell his goods in Lebanon would have to meet both the European and the Lebanese standard. However, a local Lebanese manufacturer would only have to meet the local standard, which would place the German manufacturer at a competitive disadvantage.[326]

The ECJ ruled that the provision regarding the unconditional abolition of certain restrictions, such as quantitative restrictions and measures having equivalent effect in the AA, cannot be interpreted in the same way as the similar provision in 34 TFEU.[327]

3.1.3 *Grounds for derogation from the 'movement of goods provision'*

All AAs contain an infant industry clause for industrial products.[328] This means that the Mediterranean countries may take exceptional measures which derogate from the general provisions on the liberalisation of industrial imports. The Mediterranean countries are allowed to increase or reintroduce customs duties under certain conditions. These conditions are the following: (1) the exceptional measures are intended for new and infant industries or sectors undergoing restructuring or facing serious difficulties, particularly where these difficulties entail major social problems; (2) these duties may not exceed 25 per cent of the value of the product; (3) an element of preference for products of EU origin must be contained; (4) the duties must be temporary; and (5) the duties cannot be intro-

[326] Example from F. Hakura, *EU Mediterranean and Gulf Trade Agreements* (Isle of Wight, Palladian Law Publishing Ltd 1999) p. 10.

[327] C-270/80 *Polydor Limited and RSO Records Inc.* v *Harlequin Records Shops Limited and Simons Records Limited* [1982] *ECR* 329.

[328] 'Anti-dumping and Safeguards in the Euro-Mediterranean AAs', study carried out in collaboration with UNCTAD Technical Cooperation Project on Trade Relations and Economic Cooperation in the Mediterranean Region (INT/93/A34), April 1998.

duced for a product if more than three years have elapsed since the elimination of all duties and quantitative restrictions or charges or measures having equivalent effect concerning that product. The inclusion of the infant industry clause is another example of the asymmetric nature of the liberalisation of industrial goods between the Mediterranean countries and the EU, since the provision cannot be invoked by the Member States.

Similar to what is stated in Article 36 TFEU,[329] the parties to the AAs may derogate from the principle of free movement of goods on the grounds of: (i) public morality, public policy or public security; (ii) the protection of life and health of humans, animals or plants; (iii) the protection of national treasures possessing artistic, historic or architectural value; (iv) the protection of intellectual, industrial or commercial property; (v) rules related to gold and silver; and (vi) the conservation of exhaustible natural resources.[330] The derogations, however, must not constitute a means of arbitrary discrimination or disguised restriction on trade between the parties. This signifies that the national measure which derogates from the free movement of goods must be the least restrictive on the free movement of goods. In other words, it means that the protected interest cannot be safeguarded by less restrictive measures.

This provision applies to industrial goods as well as to agricultural, fishery and agricultural processed products. The Algeria AA serves as an example in this respect:

> Art. 27 AA: Nothing in this Agreement shall preclude prohibitions or restrictions on imports, exports or goods in transit justified on grounds of public morality, public policy or public security, of the protection of health and life of humans, animals or plants, of the protection of national treasures possessing artistic, historic or archaeological value, of the protection of intellectual, industrial and commercial property or of regulations concerning gold and silver. Such prohibitions or restrictions shall not, however, constitute a means of arbitrary discrimination or a disguised restriction on trade between the Parties.

The Middle East and North Africa are regions with religious and cultural sensitivities. When the Mediterranean countries believe that religion or culture are undermined by certain trading activities, they are likely to impose trade restrictions, especially on the grounds of public morality and public policy, and are given wide liberty by the EU to do so.[331] An interesting European case is that

[329] According to settled case law, a mere similarity in the wording of a provision of the EC Treaty and an international agreement between the EC and a non-member country is not sufficient to give to the wording of that agreement the same meaning as it has in the EC Treaty, see *Polydor* case, paras. 14-21; Case 104/81 *Kupferberg* [1982] *ECR* 3641, paras. 29-31, and C-312/91 *Metalsa* [1993] *ECR* I-3751, paras. 11-20.

[330] Art. 27 Algeria AA; Art. 28 Morocco AA; Art. 28 Tunisia AA; Art. 26 Egypt AA; Art. 27 Jordan AA; Art. 27 Israel AA and Art. 27 Lebanon AA. The derogation regarding the conservation of the exhaustible natural resources is only provided for in the Lebanon AA (Art. 27 Lebanon AA).

[331] Hakura, *supra* n. 326, p. 12.

of *Omega Spielhallen* of 14 October 2004.[332] In this case, the ECJ ruled that a restriction on the free movement of goods between the Member States was possible to protect fundamental values laid down in the national German constitution. According to the ECJ, the concept of 'public policy' in the EU context must be interpreted strictly; public policy may be relied on only if there is a genuine and sufficiently serious threat to a fundamental interest of society.[333] If the same principle is also applied in the Euro-Med relationship, many goods will be prohibited from entering the Mediterranean region because of their strict national constitutions. However, it is accepted case law that the interpretation of similar articles in the TFEU and international agreements differs. The interpretation given by the ECJ to the derogation provision Article 36 TFEU is not necessarily valid for the derogation principles in the Euro-Med AAs. In the *Polydor* case, the ECJ ruled that a similarity of terms was not a sufficient reason for transposing ECJ case law to the provisions of the international agreement. The interpretation in the Euro-Med context is different; more restrictions are allowed in the Euro-Med context, since the Euro-Med does not aim at a unified market with the least possible restriction. So, does this mean that there need not be a genuine and sufficiently serious threat to a fundamental interest of the Mediterranean society? Another criterion has not yet been established.

In 1982, the ECJ ruled on the *Polydor* case as regards the derogation from the free movement of goods between a non-member country and the EU on the grounds of the protection of intellectual, industrial and commercial property. The *Polydor* case concerned the import into the EU of gramophone records from Portugal, where they had been purchased from the exclusive licensee for that country.[334] They were then sold in the UK without the consent of the copyright holder or his exclusive licensee in the UK. The question was whether their exclusion was justified under Article 23 of the EU-Portugal Agreement on the basis of protection of intellectual, industrial and commercial property. Article 23 was substantially identical to the derogation in Article 36 TFEU. The ECJ nevertheless gave a less restrictive interpretation to the provision in the EC-Portugal Agreement than to the similar provision in the EC Treaty.[335] It stated that the restriction on trade in goods was allowed in the EC-Portugal relationship on the grounds of the protection of industrial and commercial property where such restriction would not be possible within the EU. The TFEU tries to unite national markets into a single market reproducing as closely as possible the conditions of a domestic market with only limited restrictions. A comparison between the objectives and context of the agreement and those of the TFEU is thus of considerable importance in that regard.

As regards the movement of goods provisions, it can be deduced from the *Polydor* case that the interpretation of Article 36 TFEU does not apply in the

332 C-36/02 *Omega Spielhallen- und Automatenaufstellungs-GmbH* v *Oberburgermeisterin der Bundesstadt Bonn* [2004] *ECR* I-9609.

333 See also C-54/99, *Association Eglise de Scientologie de Paris* [2002] *ECR* I-1335.

334 Case 270/80 *Polydor and RSO* [1982] *ECR* 329, paras. 14-21.

335 *Polydor* case, paras. 19-20.

context of the relations between the Mediterranean countries and the EU, since the TFEU and the Euro-Med AA do not serve the same purpose. In general, this interpretation principle applies to all provisions of international agreements that are similar or even identical to the TFEU. According to the ECJ, a mere similarity in the wording of a provision of the TFEU and an international agreement between the EU and a non-member country is not sufficient to give to the wording of that agreement the same meaning as it has in the TFEU.[336]

In the *Cassis de Dijon* case about the rule of reason, the ECJ stated that other restrictions to the free movement of goods within the EU were also possible.[337] Restriction of free movement of goods is allowed, in anticipation of harmonisation of laws in particular fields at EU level, if a mandatory requirement or public interest needs to be satisfied such as the protection of public health, the protection of consumers, the protection of the environment, the protection of traffic safety, or the proper functioning of telecommunication services.[338] The national measure that restricts trade must be of a non-economic nature, applicable without any distinction at the national level as to imported products. The proportionality principle must be met. The rule of reason can only be applied in the Euro-Med relations in anticipation of harmonisation of particular fields if a mandatory requirement or public interest needs to be satisfied. The question is whether the Mediterranean countries and the EU aim at harmonisation of their laws.[339] The Mediterranean countries and the EU also aim at aligning their legislation in certain fields, such as areas where the Mediterranean countries have vital export interest to the EU.[340] It can be argued that the rule of reason also applies between the Mediterranean countries and the EU in anticipation of harmonisation of laws in particular fields. Parties may restrict free movement of goods if a mandatory requirement or public interest needs to be satisfied, but only in fields that are not harmonised.

3.1.4 *Sub-conclusion*

At present, industrial goods originating in a Mediterranean country which are imported into the EU are completely free of customs duties and charges having equivalent effect. The interpretation of the concept of customs duty or charges having equivalent effect as regards products originating in a Mediterranean country must be the same as the interpretation upheld by the ECJ regarding intra-EU trade. Goods originating in the EU and exported to a Mediterranean country will be progressively liberalised, which means that some industrial products from

---

336 Case 104/81 *Kupferberg* [1982] *ECR* 3641, paras. 29-31, and C-312/91 *Metalsa* [1993] *ECR* I-3751, paras. 11-20.

337 Case 120/78 *Rewe-Zentral AG* v *Bundesmonopolverwaltung für Branntwein* [1979] *ECR* 00649.

338 This list in not exhaustive.

339 The EU/Turkey Association Council, for example, established a list of EU instruments relating to the removal of technical barriers to trade and conditions governing their implementation by Turkey. See *OJ* 1997 L 191/1.

340 Cf., Ch. III, 2.1. The liberalisation of industrial products.

the EU and destined for the Mediterranean region are still subject to charges or measures having equivalent effect. The progressive liberalisation process should lead to total free movement in the future. Free movement of goods between the Mediterranean countries and the EU will then be guaranteed.

The prohibition concerning quantitative restrictions and equivalent measures only applies to fully liberalised goods, which at present only includes industrial goods. Other goods, such as agricultural products, fishery products and industrial products with an agricultural element, which are not entirely liberalised, can still be subject to quantitative restrictions or measures having the same effect. In the future, however, these goods will also be fully liberalised and the same prohibition will then apply to them. According to the ECJ, the provision about quantitative restrictions and measures having equivalent effect in the AA cannot be interpreted in the same way as the similar provision in the TFEU.

The derogation provision in the Euro-Med AAs and that in Article 36 TFEU are similar provisions. But here too, the ECJ ruled that they should not be interpreted in the same way. The interpretation of Article 36 TFEU does not apply in the context of the relations between the Mediterranean countries and the EU, because the TFEU and the Euro-Med AA do not serve the same purpose. The EU aims at an internal market where fewer restrictions are tolerated. The EU and the Mediterranean countries aim at a free trade area and not at a common market, which leaves more room for restrictions. The ECJ has stated that restrictions on trade in goods between a Mediterranean country and the EU may be justified in a situation where their justification would no be possible within the EU.

Most interesting is the conclusion that the deeper the Euro-Med integration becomes, the fewer restrictions will be tolerated. According to the ENP, the EU and the Mediterranean countries aim at a gradual participation of the Mediterranean countries in the EU internal market through the alignment of their legislations. This more advanced level of Euro-Med integration will accept only few restrictions. Since the Euro-Med policies have different integration goals, i.e., the EMP wants to attain a Euro-Med free trade area and the ENP a gradual participation in the EU internal market, it is advisable that the ECJ judges not only take into account the goals of Euro-Med integration as proposed by the different Euro-Med policies, but also look at the extent of Euro-Med integration in reality. This level of integration is different for each of the four freedoms of the EU internal market and is subject to annual changes.

3.2 An analysis of the competition law provisions in the Euro-Med Association Agreements

3.2.1 *Main competition law provisions*

The European competition rules need to be extended to the Mediterranean countries in order to establish a Euro-Med free trade area.[341] The AAs contain provisions similar to the cartel prohibition in Article 101(1) TFEU. The provisions banning the abuse of a dominant position by an undertaking in the AAs are also, to a large extent, drafted in a similar manner to Article 102 TFEU.[342] Consequently, the abuse by one or more undertakings of a dominant position affecting the whole or a substantial part of the territory of the associated parties is incompatible with the proper functioning of the Euro-Med AAs. Here too, it must be noted that the interpretation of provisions in the TFEU that are comparably, similarly or identically worded to provisions in the Euro-Med AA depends on the aim of each provision in its particular context. This means that the objectives and the context of the Euro-Med AA and those of the TFEU differ, and therefore interpretation will not be the same.[343] Article 36 of the Israel-EU AA serves as an example in this respect:

> Article 36
> 1. The following are incompatible with the proper functioning of the Agreement, in so far as they may affect trade between the Community and Israel:
> (i) all agreements between undertakings, decisions by associations of undertakings and concerted practices between undertakings which have as their object or effect the prevention, restriction or distortion of competition;
> (ii) abuse by one or more undertakings of a dominant position in the territories of the Community or Israel as a whole or in a substantial part thereof;
> (iii) any public aid which distorts or threatens to distort competition by favouring certain undertakings or the production of certain goods.

The Tunisia, Algeria, Morocco and Jordan AAs stipulate that any practice contrary to the cartel provision and the dominant position provision shall be assessed on the basis of the criteria arising from the application of the rules contained in

---

[341] For more information, see F.S. Hakura, 'The Extension of E.C. Competition Law to the Mediterranean Region', 19 *European Competition Law Review* (1998) pp. 204-210, at p. 205; D. Geradin and N. Petit, 'Competition Policy and the Euro-Mediterranean Partnership', 8 *EFA Rev.* (2003) pp. 153-180; D. Geradin and N. Petit, 'Competition Policy in the Southern Mediterranean Countries', 3 *Review of Networks Economics* (2004) pp. 65-82; and T. Einhorn, 'The Need for a Rule-Oriented Israeli-Palestinian Customs Union: The Role of International Trade Law and Domestic Law', 44/3 *Netherlands International Law Review* (1997) pp. 319-322. Einhorn deplores the lack of competition law provisions amongst the Mediterranean countries themselves. Infringements of competition rules between Mediterranean countries are subject to each other's legislation.

[342] Art. 41 Algeria AA; Art. 36 Morocco AA; Art. 36 Tunisia AA; Art. 34 Egypt AA; Art. 36 Jordan AA; Art. 35 Lebanon AA.

[343] See, for example, C-312/91 *Metalsa* paras. 9-13 [1993] *ECR* I-3751.

Articles 101 and 102 TFEU.[344] This means that the distorting practices will be determined in accordance with the decisions, notices and recommendations of the Commission and the decisions of the European Courts.[345] In applying these rules, the Commission and the ECJ will have to take into account the specific characteristics of the Mediterranean countries. When defining the relevant product or service market, for example, the substitutability aspect of products and services will not be the same as in the EU. The Lebanon, Egypt and Israel AAs contain no similar provision. Lebanese, Egyptian and Israeli judges will apply their respective national competition legislation. Infringement of a cartel prohibition and abuse of a dominant position will have different judicial consequences in the EU, on the one hand, and in Lebanon and Egypt, on the other, due to the lack of uniformity.

The AAs do not provide for an exemption procedure comparable to Article 101(3) TFEU.[346] The question is whether an unlawful cartel can be exempted on grounds provided for in the domestic legislation of the Mediterranean country. Furthermore, the question arises whether the national competition authorities are obliged also to examine all four conditions of Article 101(3) TFEU when they wish to exempt an agreement. All AAs state that the parties shall make their best endeavours to approximate their respective laws in order to facilitate the implementation of the AA. This 'best endeavours' clause contains no obligation for the Mediterranean country to adapt its legislation to EU law. This means that the Mediterranean country can apply its own competition legislation and that the domestic competition authorities of the Mediterranean countries are allowed to exempt anti-competitive agreements on the basis of other criteria than those provided for in Article 101(3) TFEU.[347]

[344] Art. 36 para. 2 Morocco AA; Art. 36 para. 2 Tunisia AA; Art. 53 para. 2 Jordan AA. In the case of Algeria, only the EC is committed to evaluating any practice contrary to Art. 41(1) on the basis of the criteria resulting from the rules contained in Arts. 81 and 82 of the Treaty establishing the European Community, including secondary legislation, see *OJ* 2005 L 265/227.

[345] This, for example, involves the claims for damages provided for in C-453/99 *Courage Ltd.* v *Bernard Crehan* [2001] *ECR* I-06297. The ECJ ruled that it followed from the automatic nullity provision in Art. 81(2) and the fact that Art. 81(1) had direct effect that any individual, even a party to a contract that was liable to restrict or distort competition within Art. 81(1), could rely before a national court on that breach of that provision. Since it was the duty of national courts effectively to protect rights conferred on individuals by Community law, such a party could in principle claim damages for loss caused to him by the contract. However, in the light of the general principle that a litigant should not benefit from his own unlawful conduct, Community law did not prevent national law from refusing relief to a party who was found to have borne significant responsibility for the distortion of competition. Matters that were to be taken into account for that purpose included whether one party to the contract was in a markedly stronger position than the other, and so, *inter alia*, was in a position to impose terms on the other.

[346] The AAs do not deal with mergers either. The Commission is likely to apply its merger control rules to operations carried out by undertakings from associated countries which have an impact on the EU market.

[347] Hakura, *supra* n. 326, pp. 206-207.

3.2.2 *Implementation by the Association Councils*

In order to implement the competition rules, the Association Council is empowered to adopt adequate decisions within five years from the entry into force of the Association Agreement. So far, only the EU-Morocco Association Council has adopted rules for the implementation of competition rules.[348] This Association Council decided that anti-competitive cases[349] should be dealt with by the national competition authorities. The competition authority of the EU is the Commission and the competition authority in Morocco is the Deputy Ministry for Economic and General Affairs and the Upgrading of the Economy.[350] The Commission and the Moroccan Deputy Ministry for Economic Affairs should deal with the anti-competitive cases on the basis of their respective competition laws.[351] For the EU, the competition rules are Articles 101 and 102 TFEU, Council Regulation No 4064/89 of 21 December 1989 on the control of concentrations between undertakings and related secondary legislation adopted by the EU. For Morocco, the competition rules consist of the Price Liberalisation and Free Competition Act of 5 June 2000 and related secondary legislation. If this decision of the Association Council, leading to the application of the national competition laws, serves as a precedent for all Mediterranean countries in the future, serious problems might arise caused by the non-existent or insufficient competition laws in the Mediterranean countries.[352]

The EU-Morocco Association Council established a Mechanism of Cooperation and Coordination between the competition authorities, i.e., the Commission and the Deputy Ministry for Economic Affairs. This Mechanism should not lead to harmonisation of each other's competition laws, but to cooperation and coordination as regards the application of these laws. This decision does not provide for legal protection of natural or legal persons as regards competition problems. The EU-Morocco Association Council established five methods of cooperation and coordination between the Competition Authorities. Firstly, the Competition Authorities are subject to a detailed notification duty. In several cases, they have to inform the other party of their enforcement activities.[353] There

[348] Decision No 1/2004 of the EU-Morocco Association Council of 19 April 2004 adopting the necessary rules for the implementation of the competition rules, *OJ* 2005 L 165/10-13.

[349] These are cases relating to practices contrary to Art. 36(1)(a) or (b) of the Morocco AA.

[350] The Competition Authority in Morocco is part of the Ministry for Economic Affairs and thus not an independent institution.

[351] See also the proposal for a Council Decision on a Community position in the Association Council on the implementation of Art. 36 of the Euro-Mediterranean Agreement establishing an association between the European Communities and their Member States, of the one part, and the Kingdom of Morocco, of the other part, COM (2003) 0365 final.

[352] D. Geradin and N. Petit, 'Competition Policy in the Southern Mediterranean Countries', 3/1 *Review of Network Economics* (2004) p. 74. Petit and Geradin state that while the Maghreb countries have enacted competition legislation under French influence, Jordan, Egypt and Lebanon show little progress in this field.

[353] According to the Association Council 'enforcement activities' mean any application of competition law by means of investigation or proceeding conducted by the Competition Authority which may result in penalties or remedies.

is a notification duty where (a) the notifying party considers these activities relevant to enforcement activities of the other party; (b) they may significantly affect important interests of the other party; (c) they relate to restrictions on competition which may directly and substantially affect the territory of the other party; (d) they involve anti-competitive activities carried out mainly in the territory of the other party; and (e) they condition or prohibit action in the territory of the other party. Secondly, the EU and Morocco will exchange information which will facilitate the effective application of their respective competition laws and promote a better understanding of their respective legal frameworks. Each Competition Authority maintains the confidentiality of any information provided. Thirdly, the respective Competition Authorities may express their willingness to coordinate enforcement activities with respect to a specific case.[354] This coordination does not prevent them from taking autonomous decisions. Fourthly, the Moroccan Competition Authority will request consultations with the Commission when important interests of Morocco are adversely affected due to the Commission's enforcement activities and *vice versa*. The requested Competition Authority should give full consideration to the views expressed by the requesting Competition Authority, in particular to any suggestions regarding alternative means of enforcement. Besides, if the Moroccan Competition Authority considers that one or more undertakings are or have been engaged in anti-competitive activities that are substantially and adversely affecting the interests of Morocco, it may request consultations with the Commission, and *vice versa*. The requested Competition Authority may take the appropriate remedial action in the light of the legislation in force. Finally, the EU and Morocco are open to technical cooperation in order to enable them to take advantage of their respective experience and to strengthen the implementation of their competition law and policies.

The EU embraces the 'principle of extraterritoriality' of EU competition law, which means that the EU can apply its competition rules outside the EU territory. Foreign companies that violate competition law whereby anti-competitive effects are noticeable on EU territory can be penalised before the European courts. For example, EU competition law can be applied to a price-fixing agreement between Israeli mobile telephony companies that hinders EU competition. A cartel based in Tunisia which artificially increases prices of textiles imported into the EU can be subjected to EU competition rules. The EU may decide to apply its competition laws to the participating companies and impose fines. So far, the EU has very often succeeded in bringing cases under this extended territoriality notion. The 'principle of extra-territoriality,' however, does not confer rights on Mediterranean natural and legal persons who notice competition law breaches on Mediterranean soil by European companies.[355]

---

[354] The competition authority will consider the effective results which coordination could produce, the additional information to be obtained, the reduction in costs for the competition authorities and the economic agents involved and the applicable deadlines under their respective legislation.

[355] D. Floudas, 'The Application Framework of European Competition Provisions', in D. Floudas, ed., *The Extraterritorial Application of EU Competition Law: A Contribution to the Study of EU Law in Russia* (Moscow, European Profiles – Business Tezaurus 2007) p. 30.

3.2.3 *Sub-conclusion*

The Euro-Med AAs contain a cartel prohibition similar to Article 101(1) TFEU and a prohibition on the abuse of a dominant position similar to Article 102 TFEU. None of the Euro-Med AAs entail a possibility for exemption of unlawful agreements, which means that each Mediterranean country and the EU will rely on its own exemption procedure, if existing, which will lead to a diversity of application of competition rules. Some Mediterranean countries have stipulated in their Euro-Med AAs that they will rely on European practices and rules as regards the interpretation of the cartel prohibition and the prohibition of abuse of a domination position, but others have included no such clause and rely on their own national practices and rules. This too will result in a diverse application of competition rules throughout the Mediterranean region.

The competition provisions in the AAs lack direct effect as they call for implementing measures and make no mention of their direct application. For most Mediterranean countries there are still no implementation measures and no guidance within the Euro-Med AAs, except for the Morocco one, as to what the implementing measures should consist of. Therefore, it can be concluded that under all AAs the protection afforded to individuals is very low or non-existent. The competition provisions in the Morocco AA are implemented by a decision of the EU-Morocco Association Council. This decision, however, contains no provisions that individuals or enterprises can rely on. In the relationship between the EU and Morocco legal protection as regards competition issues is not guaranteed either.

The extension of the EU competition rules to the Mediterranean countries is a *condition sine qua non* for the establishment of the Euro-Med free trade area, but they have to work in practice. At present, enforcement of the Euro-Med competition rules is weak and no Euro-Med competition cases or questions for a preliminary ruling have been brought before the ECJ for lack of direct effect, but European natural and legal persons might circumvent this by invoking the extraterritorial effect of EU competition law, which however cannot be relied upon by Mediterranean individuals or companies.[356]

3.3 **An analysis of the Euro-Med rules of origin**

3.3.1 *Introduction*

Rules of origin are created to determine the country where goods are made. They are specific provisions which allow authorities to establish the country of origin of a particular product. A certificate is issued to goods that comply with preferential origin rules. This means that only those certified goods can benefit from the

---

[356] A.E. Kellermann, 'The Rights of Non-Member State Nationals under the EU Association Agreement', 10/3 *European Journal of Law Reform* (2008) pp. 362-363.

preferential trade regime within the free trade area. Under the Euro-Med rules of origin only goods made in the Mediterranean country or the EU enjoy preferential treatment.

'Cumulation' is an important mechanism for the admission of non-originating materials. It allows producers to use non-originating materials from specified origins without losing the preferential status of the final product. Cumulation is generally applied to materials which do not originate in the preference-seeking country but in another country.

3.3.2 *Rules of origin: a tool for peace*

Establishing cumulation rules between belligerents in the Mediterranean area is of particular importance because economic cooperation may reduce the level of conflict and trigger the development of cooperation in other spheres.[357] But history has also shown that such reasoning is not always correct. Israel was involved in a trade dispute with the EU as regards the use of rules of origin. It labelled many goods originating or produced in the West Bank and Gaza Strip as 'made in Israel.' Already in 1997, the EU urged Israel to end this distortion of rules of origin.[358]

Brita, a company specialised in water purification systems, exported its goods to Germany and requested preferential treatment under the Israeli-EU AA. The German customs authority, however, had doubts as to the originating status of the goods. According to German customs, the goods did not originate in Israel, but in an area which is merely under Israeli control, namely the West Bank. When preferential treatment was refused by German customs, Brita appealed before the *Finanzgericht* in Hamburg. On 1 September 2008, the *Finanzgericht* submitted four questions for a preliminary ruling to the ECJ.[359] The

---

[357] M. Hirsch, *Asymmetric Factor Endowments, Progressive Rules of Origin and Commercial Cooperation in the Middle East*, Working Paper 13/98 for the Hebrew University of Jerusalem (1998) p. 16.

[358] Notice to Importers about imports from Israel into the Community, *OJ* C 338/10 (1997) p. 13; *OJ* C 328/6 (2001) and most recent version in *OJ* C 20/2 (2005); See also D. Stephnes, *The European Union and Israel: An Ambiguous Relationship*, paper for the College of Europe (Bruges, 1998) pp. 20-21.

[359] Case C-386/08: Reference for a preliminary ruling from the Finanzgericht Hamburg (Germany) lodged on 1 September 2008 – *Brita GmbH* v *Hauptzollamt Hamburg-Hafen*, *OJ* 2008 C 285/26. The four preliminary questions are the following: (1) Should the importer of goods which originate in the West Bank be granted the preferential treatment requested in any event in light of the fact that preferential treatment is provided under two agreements which come under consideration in the present case, namely the Israel-EC Euro-Med AA and the PA-EC Euro-Med Interim AA for goods originating in the territory of the State of Israel or in the West Bank, even if only a formal certificate of origin from Israel is submitted? (2) Is the customs authority of a Member State bound under the Israel-EC Euro-Med AA, *vis-à-vis* an importer who is requesting preferential treatment for goods which have been imported into Community territory, by a proof-of-origin certificate issued by the Israeli authority as long as the customs authority has no doubt as to the originating status of the goods other than that as to whether the goods originate in an area which is merely under Israeli control? (3) May the customs authority of the country of importation refuse automatically to grant preferential treatment for the following reason alone, namely that, pursuant to its request for verification, it was confirmed by the

German judge wants to know whether European imported goods originating in the West Bank but with a certificate of origin from Israel should always be granted preferential treatment because two Euro-Med AAs cover this situation, namely the Israel-EU AA and the PA-EU Interim AA. Secondly, the judge wants to know whether German customs are bound under the Israel-EU AA by the proof-of-origin certificate issued by Israel, even when German customs suspect that the goods originate in an Israeli-controlled area, namely the West Bank. Thirdly, the judge wishes to determine whether German customs may refuse to grant preferential treatment to goods considered to be of Israeli origin by the Israeli authorities because they were manufactured in an area which is subject to Israeli customs jurisdiction (namely the West Bank). In answering this question, the ECJ has to take into account that Israel refused to answer further requests from German customs as to the actual origin of the goods. Finally, the judge wishes to know if German customs may refuse to grant preferential treatment under the Israel-EU AA in the case where it has become clear that the goods truly originate in the West Bank. In answering this final question, it is important for the ECJ to take into account that no dispute settlement procedure has been carried out concerning the interpretation of the expression 'territory of the State of Israel' used in the Israel-EU AA. The expression 'territory of the State of Israel' might change in the event that it is scrutinised during a dispute settlement procedure. The answer of the ECJ in this political sensitive case is much awaited since the ECJ has been asked to interpret not merely a problem of EU law, but also a question of international law as regards the territory of the State of Israel.

Advocate-General Bot has delivered his Opinion in the *Brita* case and has proposed that the German authorities are not bound by the verification carried out by the Israeli authorities. Further, the Advocate-General is of the opinion that goods certified by the Israeli customs authorities as being of Israeli origin but which prove to originate in the occupied territories, more specifically the West Bank and the Gaza Strip, are not entitled to the preferential treatment under the EU/Israel AA or the EU/PLO Interim AA.

3.3.3 *The rules of origin in the Euro-Med Association Agreements*

The rules or origin are set out in Protocols annexed to the AAs. The Protocols to the AAs do not constitute a unified system of rules of origin. The AAs with

Israeli authorities (only) that the goods were manufactured in an area which is subject to Israeli customs jurisdiction and that they were for that reason of Israeli origin, and where the subsequent request by the customs authority of the country of importation for further specification by the Israeli authorities remained unanswered, in particular without the actual origin of the goods having to be taken into account? (4) May the customs authority refuse automatically to grant preferential treatment under the Israel-EC Euro-Med AA in the case where – as has become clear in the meantime – the goods originate in the West Bank, or should preferential treatment also be granted under the Israel-EC Euro-Med AA for goods originating in that area, in any event as long as no dispute settlement procedure has been carried out under Art. 33 of Protocol 4 to the Israel-EC Euro-Med AA concerning the interpretation of the expression 'territory of the State of Israel' used in the Israel-EC Euro-Med AA? See also Opinion of Advocate-General Bot of 29 October 2009 to Case C-386/08.

the Mashrek countries (Egypt, Jordan and Syria) allow for bilateral cumulation. Bilateral cumulation allows each party to use materials originating from the territory of the other party without violating the 'rules of origin.' As a consequence, both parties have the same materials. The Jordan AA, for example, provides for a system of 'bilateral cumulation of origin.' Preferential status is granted to: (i) goods which are wholly obtained in the EU or Jordan;[360] or (ii) goods obtained in the EU or Jordan incorporating materials which have not been wholly obtained there, provided that such materials have undergone sufficient working or processing in the EU or Jordan. The Protocol sets out what work or process is required to be carried out on non-originating materials in order for the product manufactured to obtain originating status.[361] Materials originating in the EU will thus be considered as originating in Jordan when incorporated into a product obtained in Jordan. Materials originating in Jordan are considered as originating in the EU when incorporated into a product obtained in the EU. A fabric can be produced in Belgium, dyed in Hungary and made into a dress in Jordan for export to Spain without any duty having to be paid. This possibility has brought about new trade and investment opportunities in Jordan, for regional and European business partners. In the relationship EU-Jordan, it creates an asymmetric system since Jordan has to rely more on materials from the EU than *vice versa*. This leads to higher transport costs for Jordan.[362]

The Maghreb countries (Algeria, Tunisia and Morocco) also operate under a system of bilateral cumulation, but full cumulation with the EU is also possible. The Tunisian AA serves as an example in this respect. The Tunisian AA includes a system of bilateral cumulation in Article 3 of the Protocol.[363] Furthermore, Article 5 also provides for a full cumulation system among the Maghreb coun-

[360] Products wholly obtained in the EC and Jordan are: (a) mineral products extracted from their soil or from their seabed; (b) vegetable products harvested there; (c) live animals born and raised there; (d) products from live animals raised there; (e) products obtained by hunting or fishing conducted there; (f) products of sea fishing and other products taken from the sea outside the territorial waters of the Community or Jordan by their vessels; (g) products made aboard their factory ships exclusively from products referred to in subparagraph (f); (h) used articles collected there fit only for the recovery of raw materials, including used tyres fit only for retreading; (i) waste and scrap resulting from manufacturing operations conducted there; (j) products extracted from marine soil or subsoil outside their territorial waters provided that they have sole rights to work that soil or subsoil; (k) goods produced there exclusively from the products specified in subparagraphs (a) to (j).

[361] Simple operations such as removal of dust, washing, painting, affixing labels, simple assembly of parts to constitute a complete product; slaughter of animals, ventilation or placing in salt during transport are examples of insufficient working or processing operations provided for in Art. 6 of the Jordan AA.

[362] M. Hirsch, *Asymmetric Factor Endowments, Progressive Rules of Origin and Commercial Cooperation in the Middle-East*, Working Paper 13/98 for the Hebrew University of Jerusalem (1998) pp. 3-8.

[363] Art. 3 Tunisian AA: 1. Notwithstanding Art. 2(1)(b), materials originating in Tunisia within the meaning of this Protocol shall be considered as materials originating in the Community and it shall not be necessary that such materials have undergone sufficient working or processing there, provided however that they have undergone working or processing going beyond that referred to in Art. 8 of this Protocol. 2. Notwithstanding Art. 2(2)(b), materials originating in the Community within the meaning of this Protocol shall be considered as materials originating in Tunisia and it shall not be necessary

tries: (i) working or processing carried out in Tunisia, Algeria or Morocco shall be considered as having been carried out in the EU when the products obtained undergo subsequent working or processing in the EU; (ii) working or processing carried out in the EU, Algeria or Morocco shall be considered as having been carried out in Tunisia when the products obtained undergo subsequent working or processing in Tunisia; and (iii) where the originating products are obtained in two or more of those Mediterranean countries or in the EU, they shall be considered as products originating in the Mediterranean country or the EU according to where the last working or processing took place. Under full cumulation, all the processing carried out in the Maghreb countries and the EU is assessed in deciding whether there has been subsequent working or processing activities. For example, a dress made in Tunisia from fabrics from Algeria gets preferential access to the EU, even if the yarns that constitute the fabrics come from China. The yarns underwent sufficient working processes in Tunisia and Algeria to get preferential status. The final product obtains Moroccan origin and can be exported to the EU. Full cumulation provides for deeper integration of the Maghreb countries into the EU.[364] The full cumulation granted to Algeria, Morocco and Tunisia remains an exception in the Mediterranean region.

3.3.4 *Further development of the Euro-Med rules of origin*

At the Euro-Med Conference on Trade in Toledo in 2002, the Ministers of Trade agreed to extend the system of diagonal cumulation, also called pan-European cumulation of origin, to the Mediterranean countries.[365] Diagonal cumulation allows for materials supplied by countries which are not parties to the AA to be counted as domestic. A less restrictive application of the rules of origin was indeed essential, as products contained materials originating from different countries due to the globalisation of the economy. The Mediterranean countries were allowed to enter the system of diagonal cumulation on the condition that they initiated negotiations among themselves to set up free trade areas and harmonised their rules of origin with those of the EU.

A Euro-Med Working Group developed a Protocol on 'pan-Euro-Mediterranean' rules of origin. This protocol was endorsed by the Euro-Med Trade Ministerial Meeting in Palermo on 7 July 2003. Accordingly, the EU had to replace the existing Protocols on rules of origin to the Euro-Med AAs by the pan-Euro-Mediterranean Protocol.[366] The system of diagonal cumulation is applicable between

---

that such materials have undergone working or processing there, provided however that they have undergone working or processing going beyond that referred to in Art. 8 of this Protocol.

[364] P. Brenton and H. Imagawa, 'Rules of Origin, Trade, and Customs', in L. De Wulf and J.B. Sokol, eds., *Customs Modernization Handbook* (Washington, The International Bank for Reconstruction and Development/The World Bank 2005) pp. 195-196.

[365] Diagonal cumulation is the system established in the agreements between the EU and EFTA countries.

[366] To establish the system of pan-Euro-Mediterranean cumulation, the Council of the EU approved, on 11 October 2005, a Commission proposal to amend protocols on rules of origin annexed to the various Euro-Med AAs.

the EU and Algeria, Egypt, Israel, Jordan, Lebanon, Morocco, Syria, Tunisia, the West Bank and Gaza Strip.[367] In the context of the pan-Euro-Mediterranean system, diagonal cumulation means that products which have obtained originating status in one of the 42 countries may be added to products originating in any other one of the 42 without losing their originating status within the pan-Euro-Mediterranean area. For example, the finished product will have Egyptian origin if Egypt produces an originating product using components that have EU origin.[368] Countries of the pan-Euro-Mediterranean area, however, can only cumulate originating status of goods if they have concluded free trade agreements amongst each other. A country of the pan-Euro-Mediterranean area which is not linked by free trade agreements with the others cannot claim benefits from the new system. For example, to make the change operational, the original protocol of the Jordan AA will have to be amended, and Jordan must conclude free trade agreements including harmonised rules of origin with other Mediterranean partners. To help in achieving the rules of origin required by the EU, the Agreement was signed between Jordan, Egypt, Tunisia and Morocco. The Agadir Agreement entered into force on 6 July 2006. Tunisia has signed a free trade agreement with Turkey, but pan-Euro-Mediterranean cumulation also requires that the rules of origin of the Tunisia Euro-Med AA be amended to be identical to the Turkish rules of origin. A complete network of free trade agreements amongst all pan-European countries is far from being realised. It can be stated that since only the Agadir Agreement has entered into force, the Euro-Med rules of origin have limited impact in the Euro-Med area. The EU, however, has decided that the diagonal cumulation system should be launched at the earliest possible date, i.e.,

[367] Decision of the EU-Algeria Association Council of 28 September 2005 amending Protocol 6 to the Euro-Mediterranean Agreement, concerning the definition of the concept of 'originating products' and methods of administrative cooperation: Common Guidelines, *OL* 9525/05; Decision of the EU-Egypt Association Council of 28 September 2005 amending Protocol 4 to the Euro-Mediterranean Agreement, concerning the definition of the concept of 'originating products' and methods of administrative cooperation: Common Guidelines, *OL* 9525/04; Decision No 2/2005 of the EU-Israel Association Council of 22 December 2005 amending Protocol 4 to the Euro-Mediterranean Agreement, concerning the definition of the concept of 'originating products' and methods of administrative cooperation, *OJ* (2005) L 20/1; Decision of the EU-Lebanon Cooperation Council amending Protocol 4 to the Interim Agreement, concerning the definition of the concept of 'originating products' and methods of administrative cooperation: Common Guidelines, *OL* 9517/05; Decision No 2/2005 of the EU-Morocco Association Council of 18 November 2005 amending Protocol 4 to the Euro-Mediterranean Agreement, concerning the definition of the concept of originating products and methods of administrative cooperation, *OJ* 2005 L 336/1; Decision of the EU-Tunisia Association Council of 28 September 2005 amending Protocol 4 to the Euro-Mediterranean Agreement, concerning the definition of the concept of 'originating products' and methods of administrative cooperation: Common Guidelines, *OL* 9518/05; Decision of the EC-PLO Joint Committee of 28 September 2005 amending Protocol 3 to the Euro-Mediterranean Interim Association Agreement, concerning the definition of the concept of 'originating products' and methods of administrative cooperation: Common Guidelines, *OL* 9515/05.

[368] A User's Handbook to the Rules of Preferential Origin used in trade between the European Community, other European Countries and the countries participating to the Euro-Mediterranean Partnership, pp. 12-16 available at: http://ec.europa.eu/taxation_customs/resources/documents/handbook_en.pdf.

before all pan-European countries have signed free trade agreements with each other.

3.3.5 *Sub-conclusion*

In conclusion, the Euro-Med rules of origin entail that only goods made in the Mediterranean countries or the EU benefit from preferential treatment and access to the Mediterranean countries or EU without taxes. A mechanism of flexibility was needed to allow certain non-originating materials in goods. This flexibility mechanism is called 'cumulation' and allows producers to use non-originating materials without losing the preferential status of the final product. The EU decided to expand the use of its diagonal cumulation system which it had developed with the pan-European countries (Bulgaria, Romania, Norway, Iceland, Switzerland and Turkey) to its Mediterranean partners. The system of diagonal cumulation applies between the EU and Algeria, Egypt, Israel, Jordan, Lebanon, Morocco, Syria, Tunisia, the West Bank and Gaza Strip. A basic condition for the application of pan-Euro-Mediterranean cumulation is the existence of free trade agreements with identical rules of origin between the countries of the pan-Euro-Mediterranean area. These countries can only cumulate originating status of goods if they have concluded free trade agreements amongst each other. While the EU has concluded the necessary free trade agreements with the Mediterranean, most of the Mediterranean countries have still to conclude free trade agreements with each other.

3.4 The 'services provision' and the 'right of establishment provision' in the Euro-Med Association Agreements

3.4.1 *General provisions*

All Euro-Med AAs, except for the PA-EU Interim AA, include services provisions.[369] A service within the scope of the Euro-Med AAs is an economic activity which is intangible and involves an element of commercial motivation, such as transport, advertising, construction, engineering, distribution, education and the transmission of television signals.[370] For instance, Euro-Mediterranean services apply to situations where a European professor offers his educational services in Tunisia; where a French construction company builds roads in Jordan; and where a Tunisian or Moroccan professional football player offers his professional services in the EU. It does not apply to state education and sports purely based on sporting interests, since these involve no economic element.[371] An economic

[369] On 23 June 2005, the Commission adopted a proposal to open negotiations on the liberalisation of services and investment with the Mediterranean countries. This marks an important step towards the creation of the free trade area between Europe and the Mediterranean.

[370] Films are considered as goods.

[371] Hakura, *supra* n. 326.

activity in the Euro-Med AA means an activity of an industrial, commercial or professional character.[372]

The provisions in the AAs with Morocco, Tunisia, Israel and Egypt differ from those in the AAs with Algeria, Lebanon and Jordan. Morocco, Tunisia, Israel and Egypt were members of the World Trade Organisation (WTO) at the time the AAs were drafted. These countries basically referred to the services provisions as provided for in the GATS (General Agreement on Trade in Services) in general and the MFN (Most Favoured Nation) treatment in particular.[373] The MFN treatment means that each WTO member shall accord immediately and unconditionally to services and service suppliers of any other WTO member, treatment no less favourable than it accords to like services and service suppliers of any other country.[374] This MFN treatment will not apply when WTO parties decide to conclude a 'preferential economic services agreement' as provided for in Article V of the GATS.[375] In the event of such an agreement, the partners to the agreement will grant each other preferential treatment.[376] Foreign countries will not all be treated on an equal footing. The Tunisian AA serves as an example in this respect:

> Article 30
> 1. At the outset, each of the Parties shall reaffirm its obligations under the GATS, particularly the obligation to grant reciprocal most-favoured-nation treatment in the service sectors covered by that obligation.
> 2. In accordance with the GATS, such treatment shall not apply to:
> (a) Advantages granted by either Party under the terms of an agreement of the type defined in Article V of the GATS or to measures taken on the basis of such an agreement;
> (b) Other advantages granted in accordance with the list of exemptions from most-favoured-nation treatment annexed by either Party to the GATS.

Jordan, Algeria and Lebanon were not a member of the WTO at the time the AAs were drafted.[377] Jordan, however, joined the WTO in April 2000.[378] These Mediterranean countries had to create a legal framework concerning the movement of services themselves. They included a different services provision in their AAs, since they could not simply refer to the GATS and the MFN treatment. Jordan and the EU will consider the possibility of concluding an economic integration agreement only after the Association Council has examined this issue.[379] Algeria and Lebanon drafted services provisions similar to those provided for in the

---

[372] Definitions are based on Art. 36 Algeria AA.

[373] Art. 32 Morocco AA; Art. 30 Tunisia AA; Art. 31 Israel AA and Art. 29 Egypt AA.

[374] Art. II(1) GATS.

[375] See, for example, Art. 30(2)(a) Tunisia AA.

[376] The 'preferential economic services agreement' must fulfil all conditions set out in Art. V of the GATS.

[377] At the time its Euro-Med AA was drafted, Syria was not a member of the WTO either.

[378] Jordan has been a member of the WTO since 11 April 2000.

[379] Art. 65 Jordan AA.

GATS and included the possibility of concluding an economic integration agreement on services. The Algerian AA serves as an example in this respect:[380]

> Article 30
> 1. The European Community and its Member States shall extend to Algeria the treatment which they are obliged to grant under Article II. I of the General Agreement on Trade in Services, hereinafter referred to as GATS.
> 2. The European Community and its Member States shall grant to Algerian service suppliers no less favourable treatment than that accorded to like service suppliers as specified in the schedule of specific commitments taken by the European Community and its Member States under the GATS to which it is annexed.
> 3. This treatment shall not apply to advantages accorded by either Party under the terms of an agreement of the type defined in Article V of the GATS or to measures taken on the basis of such an agreement and to other advantages granted in accordance with the list of most-favoured-nation exemptions annexed by the European Community and its Member States to the GATS.
> 4. Algeria shall grant no less favourable treatment to service suppliers of the European Community and its Member States than that specified in Articles 31 to 33.

3.4.2 *Further liberalisation of trade in services*

Most parties to the Euro-Med AAs wish to further liberalise trade in services. Some are more willing and ready than others. Liberalisation of trade in services can take place through four modes of supply, namely cross-border supply, consumption abroad, movement of natural persons and commercial presence.[381] The Euro-Med AAs include several provisions regarding the further liberalisation of trade in services.

3.4.2.1 Cross-border supply of services

Cross-border supplies of services involve services supplied by European service suppliers in a Mediterranean country without commercial presence or the presence of a natural person in the Mediterranean country. Morocco, Tunisia, Egypt and Israel will consider extending the scope of their Euro-Med AA to cover the liberalisation of the provision of services by a company to consumers of services of the other party.[382] The Egypt AA serves as an example:

> Article 30 Egypt AA
> 1. The Parties will consider extending the scope of the Agreement to include the right of establishment of companies of one Party in the territory of another Party and the liberalisation of the supply of services by companies of one Party to service consumers in another Party.

[380] Art. 30 Algeria AA and Art. 30 Lebanon AA.

[381] See Art. 1 GATS: the four modes of supply which constitute the definition of trade in services are cross-border supply, consumption abroad, commercial presence and presence of natural persons.

[382] Art. 31 Morocco AA; Art. 31 Tunisia AA; Art. 30 Egypt AA; and Art. 29 Israel AA.

The Association Council will broaden the scope of the AA to further liberalise the supply of services.[383] It will take measures to grant service suppliers the right to supply services under the same laws that apply to national suppliers. In doing this, the Association Council has to take into account all the relevant provisions of the GATS, especially those of Article V of the GATS.[384] For the time being, these countries will use the relevant provisions of the GATS.[385] So far, the Association Council has not taken any measures.

The provisions in the AAs with the WTO countries Morocco, Tunisia, Israel and Egypt differ from those in the AAs with Jordan, Algeria and Lebanon. The latter countries drafted their own provisions on cross-border supply of services. The Jordan AA only includes a 'best endeavours' clause as regards the supply of cross-border services.[386] Jordan and the EU will use their best endeavours to allow progressively the supply of services by European and Jordanian companies. Algeria grants treatment to European cross-border service suppliers no less favourable than that accorded to companies of any third country.[387] Lebanon only included a reference to the obligations under the GATS, which will take effect from the date of accession of Lebanon to the WTO. For the time being, Lebanon and the EU will refrain from taking measures which will render the conditions of supply of services more discriminatory than those existing on the date of entry into force of the Lebanese AA.[388]

---

[383] Art. 30 Egypt AA; Art. 31 Morocco AA; Art. 29 Israel AA; and Art. 31 Tunisia AA.

[384] Art. V GATS allows members to enter into an agreement liberalising trade in services, provided that the agreement has substantial sectoral coverage and provides for the elimination of substantially all discrimination in the sectors in paragraph (a) of Art. XVII of the GATS by prohibiting new discriminatory measures and eliminating existing ones.

[385] The GATS applies to the following: legal services, accounting, auditing and book-keeping, taxation, architecture, engineering, medical and dental services, veterinary services, midwives, nurses, physiotherapists and para-medical personnel, computer and related services, research and development, real estate, rental/leasing services, advertising, market research and public opinion polling services, management consulting services, maintenance and repair of equipment, building-cleaning services, photographic, packaging, printing, publishing, postal and courier services, telecommunication, audiovisual services, construction work for buildings, construction work for civil engineering, installation and assembly work, commission agents' services, wholesale trade services, retailing and franchising services, education, environmental services such as sewage services and sanitation, all insurance and insurance-related services, banking and other financial services, hospital and social services, tourism and travel such as hotels and restaurants (incl. catering), travel agencies and tour operators, tourist guides, recreational, cultural and sports services, entertainment services (including theatre, live bands and circus services), news agency services, libraries, archives, museums, sporting and other recreational services and transport.

[386] Art. 37 Jordan AA.

[387] Art. 31 Algeria AA.

[388] Art. 30 Lebanon AA: Treatment granted by either party to the other with respect to the rights of establishment and the supply of services shall be based on each party's commitments and other obligations under the GATS. This provision shall take effect from the date of the final accession of Lebanon to the WTO. The parties shall not, between the date of entry into force of this agreement and Lebanon's accession to the WTO, take any measures or actions which will render the conditions for the supply of services by the EC or Lebanese service suppliers more discriminatory than those existing on the date of entry into force of this Agreement.

None of the Euro-Med AAs includes a provision about the cross-border supply of services by individual persons. In other words, there is no right for natural persons to provide cross-border self-employed services. Service suppliers in the Euro-Med framework are always supposed to be legal persons; these are companies and their personnel implementing the service.

3.4.2.2 Consumption abroad

Consumption abroad is the freedom for European residents to purchase services in the territory of a Mediterranean country and *vice versa*. For example, it applies to situations where an Algerian patient goes to France to obtain medical services. The Euro-Med AAs do not include such provisions, but the WTO countries (Morocco, Tunisia, Israel and Egypt) can apply the GATS provisions regarding consumption abroad.

3.4.2.3 Temporary presence of natural persons

Temporary presence relates to persons of one country temporarily entering the territory of another country to supply a service (for example, accountants, doctors or teachers). This concept is narrowly related to the movement of persons. The WTO countries Morocco, Tunisia, Egypt and Israel refer to the GATS as regards the provision on temporary presence of natural persons until the Association Council will make recommendations for specific implementation provisions.

The Algeria and Jordan AAs include specific provisions about the temporary presence of natural persons in the territory of the other party.[389] A European or Algerian/Jordan company, established in the territory of the other party, is entitled to temporarily employ, *in accordance with the legislation in force in the host country of establishment*, employees who are key personnel and are employed exclusively by such companies, subsidiaries or branches. The residence and work permits of such employees only cover the period of employment. These natural persons must be intra-corporate transferees and can only be key personnel of a business.[390] An intra-corporate transferee is a natural person who is working within a company in the territory of one country and is temporarily transferred in the context of pursuit of economic activities in the territory of the other country. The company for which the transferee is working must be a legal person and the transferee must have been employed by it or have been partner in it (other than as a majority shareholder) for at least the 12 months immediately preceding the transfer. There are two kinds of key personnel. First, they are persons working in a *senior* position, who primarily direct the management of the business and have been given this task principally from the board of directors or stockholders of the business. This task also involves directing the establishment or a department or subdivision of the establishment and supervising the work of

[389] Art. 33 Algeria AA and Arts. 34, 35 and 36 Jordan AA.

[390] For the rights of these persons under the Euro-Med AA, see *infra* 3.6 about the movement of persons provision.

other supervisory, professional or managerial employees, and also includes the authority to recruit and dismiss or recommend recruiting, dismissing or other personnel actions. Second, key personnel are also *highly qualified persons* who have uncommon knowledge which is essential to the service of the company. Such knowledge can be specific technical knowledge, including membership of an accredited profession. A professional football player can be considered as key personnel because of his special qualities which are essential to the football club. Only the Jordan AA stipulates that the Association Council will take steps regarding the mutual recognition of qualifications in order to render the liberalisation of services easier.[391]

The supply of services between Lebanon and the EU will be based on their commitments under the GATS, but this provision will only take effect from the date of the final accession of Lebanon to the WTO. In the meantime, Lebanon will refrain from taking measures or actions which will render the conditions for the supply of services by the EU or Lebanese service suppliers more discriminatory than those existing on the date of entry into force of this AA.[392]

3.4.2.4 Commercial presence or right of establishment

The right of commercial presence means that European or Mediterranean companies have a right of establishment in the territory of the other party. The respective companies can take up economic activities by means of the setting-up of subsidiaries and branches in the Mediterranean country or in the EU. A subsidiary is a company which is controlled by the first company. A branch is a place of business not having legal personality which has the appearance of permanency, such as the extension of a parent body.

Morocco, Tunisia, Egypt and Israel, on the one hand and the EU, on the other, consider extending the scope of their Euro-Med AA to include the right of establishment of companies.[393] The Egypt-EU AA defines this as follows:

> Article 30 Egypt AA
> 1. The Parties will consider extending the scope of the Agreement to include the right of establishment of companies of one Party in the territory of another Party and the liberalisation of the supply of services by companies of one Party to service consumers in another Party.

Their Association Councils will make recommendations for implementation of this right of establishment. In anticipation of these recommendations, the WTO countries refer to the GATS provisions on commercial presence. So far, the Association Councils have not made any proposal regarding implementation of the right of establishment provisions in the Euro-Med AAs.

---

391 Art. 35 and 36 Jordan AA.
392 Art. 30 Lebanon AA.
393 Art. 31 Morocco AA; Art. 31 Tunisia AA; Art. 30 Egypt AA; and Art. 29 Israel AA.

Algeria, Lebanon, Jordan and Syria were not a member of the WTO, so these countries drafted their own right of establishment provision. The Jordan AA, for example, stipulates that the EU and its Member States shall grant for the establishment of Jordanian companies, its subsidiaries and its branches, a treatment no less favourable than that accorded to like companies, its subsidiaries and its branches, of any third country. Jordan shall grant for the establishment of European companies, subsidiaries and branches treatment no less favourable than that accorded to its own companies or to companies of any third country.[394] The agreement includes reservation lists where both Jordan and the EU sum up sectors that are not open to investment. The EU, for example, is not committed to granting the national treatment conditions to subsidiaries of Jordanian companies in the field of mining, fishing, real-estate purchase, audio-visual services including radio, telecommunications services including mobile and satellite services, agriculture and news agency services.[395] The Algeria AA contains similar provisions, but does not include reservation lists.[396] The Jordan and Algeria AAs also state that a company only has legal status in the European or Mediterranean territory if its economic activities relate to activities in the country of origin. For example, a company will only be considered as an Italian company if its operations have a 'real and continuous link' with the Italian economy.[397] If the Italian company only has its registered office in Italy and all its economic activities in Tunisia, the company will not be considered as an Italian company because its activities have no 'real and continuous link' with the Italian economy. The same applies, *vice versa*, to Mediterranean companies: if the Algerian company only has its registered office in Algeria and all its economic activities in Europe, the company will only be considered an Algerian company if its business has a 'real and continuous link' with the Algerian economy. Lebanon only included a reference to the obligations under the GATS which will take effect from the date of accession of Lebanon to the WTO. Treatment with respect to the right of establishment will then be based on commitments and other obligations under the GATS.[398]

None of the Euro-Med AAs provide for the right of natural persons to move for the purpose of self-employment. Only companies have the right to move and establish themselves in the territory of the other party in the Euro-Med framework.

[394] Art. 30 Jordan AA.

[395] See Annex V to the Jordan AA, *OJ* 2002 L 129/56.

[396] Arts. 30, 32 and 34 Algeria AA.

[397] A European company will be set up in accordance with the laws of Italy and will have its registered office, central administration or principal place of business in the territory of the EU.

[398] Art. 30 Lebanon AA.

3.4.3 *The liberalisation of financial services between the EU and the Mediterranean countries*

The Euro-Med AAs also include a provision relating to financial services cooperation. The aim of cooperation is to achieve tighter common rules and standards in areas such as in the case of Tunisia: (a) bolstering and restructuring Tunisia's financial sectors; and (b) improving accounting, auditing, supervision and regulation of financial services and financial monitoring in Tunisia.[399] Egypt and the EU also cooperate with a view to the rapprochement of their standards and rules to improve (a) the financial sector in Egypt and (b) accounting and supervisory and regulatory banking systems and other parts of the financial sector in Egypt.[400] Israel and the EU also cooperate, where appropriate through the conclusion of agreements, on the adoption of common rules and standards for accounting and for supervisory and regulatory systems of banking, insurance and other financial sectors.[401]

3.4.4 *Grounds for derogation from the 'services provision' and 'right of establishment provision' in the Euro-Med Association Agreements*

The Morocco, Tunisia, Egypt and Israel AAs do not entail specific derogations from the movement of services and the right of establishment, since it is the task of the Association Council to make all necessary recommendations, including provisions concerning the derogation from the movement of services and the right of establishment. So far, no recommendations have been made. In the meantime, these countries refer to the obligations under the GATS, i.e., also the derogation provisions under the GATS.

As regards the non-WTO countries, the Lebanon-EU AA does not provide for derogations from the movement of services and the right of establishment. The Jordan and Algerian AAs, however, offer several possibilities to derogate from the movement of services and the right of establishment. The Jordan AA includes a 'best endeavours' clause which stipulates that Jordan and the EU will use their best endeavours to avoid taking restricting measures which render the conditions for the establishment and operation of other companies more restrictive.[402] Derogations in the Jordan and Algeria AAs are the following: (1) The movement of services and the right of establishment can be limited on grounds of public policy, public security or public health.[403] (2) The provisions on the movement of services and the right of establishment do not apply to activities connected, even occasionally, with the exercise of official authority.[404] (3) The EU, on the one hand, and Jordan/Algeria, on the other, can take measures for prudential

399 Art. 53 Tunisia AA.

400 Art. 49 Egypt AA.

401 Art. 48 Israel AA, as well as Art. 50 Lebanon AA.

402 Art. 33 Jordan AA.

403 Art. 35 para. 1 Algeria AA and Art. 41 Jordan AA.

404 Art. 35 para. 2 Algeria AA and Art. 41 Jordan AA.

reasons which derogate from the movement of services or the right of establishment. These measures are taken, for example, to protect investors, depositors, policy holders or persons to whom a fiduciary duty is owed by a financial service supplier. They can also be taken to ensure the integrity and stability of the financial system. Where they derogate from the provisions of the AA, they will not be used as a means of avoiding the obligations under the AA.[405] The difference in treatment does not go beyond what is strictly necessary, as regards financial services, for prudential reasons.[406] Particular rules concern the establishment and operation in one party's territory of branches of companies of the other party. These measures must be justified by legal or technical differences between such branches as compared to branches of companies incorporated in a party's territory or, as regards financial services, for prudential reasons.[407]

The Jordan and Algerian AAs also stipulate that the movement of services and the right of establishment do not apply to air transport, inland waterways transport and maritime transport.[408]

3.4.5 *Sub-conclusion*

It can be stated that the WTO countries Morocco, Tunisia, Egypt and Israel in essence refer to their obligations under the GATS, until their Association Councils make specific recommendations as regards the liberalisation of services and the right of establishment. The Association Councils, however, have not issued any decisions as regards services and the right of establishment. This means that only the GATS obligations apply in the case of Morocco, Tunisia, Egypt and Israel. The provisions in the GATS have no direct effect, which means that the supplier of services cannot invoke a violation of the GATS provisions. The provisions concerning free movement of service in the TFEU are directly and immediately applicable. The individual citizen may directly invoke Art. 56 TFEU.

The non-WTO countries Algeria, Jordan and Lebanon drafted their own services and right of establishment provisions as well as many derogation possibilities, which make it all quite puzzling. There is no right to self-employment for individuals in the territory of the other country. But in the future, all Mediterranean countries and the EU wish to create some kind of preferential economic integration agreement as regards services and the right of establishment. These future agreements, on which negotiations have already begun with some Mediterranean countries, must include similar provisions on services and the right of establishment for all Mediterranean countries in order to ensure consistency of

405 Art. 46 Jordan AA and Art. 35 para. 4 Algeria AA.

406 Art. 35 para. 3 Algeria AA.

407 Art. 30 Jordan AA.

408 Art. 34 Algeria AA and Arts. 31 and 39 Jordan AA.

the legal framework.[409] However, it will be necessary to take into account the individual needs and different stages of development of the Mediterranean countries. These preferential economic agreements should therefore include specific provisions for each Mediterranean country.

It must be noted that Jordan has become a member of the WTO in 2000. For Jordan, the GATS provisions and the Euro-Med provisions apply. As regards the interaction between the relevant services provisions in the Jordan/EU AA and the GATS, Article 44 of the Jordan/EU AA stipulates that treatment granted by a party to the other shall, as from the day one month prior to the date of entry into force of the relevant obligations of the GATS, in respect of sectors or measures covered by the GATS, in no case be more favourable than that accorded by such first party under the provisions of the GATS and this in respect of each service sector, subsector and mode of supply.

3.5 The 'movement of capital provision' in the Euro-Med Association Agreements

3.5.1 *Limited capital movement versus full liberalisation of capital*

According to Article 63 of the TFEU, all restrictions on the movement of capital between Member States *and between Member States and third countries* are prohibited.[410] Only limited restrictions are possible under Articles 64, 66 and 75 TFEU.[411]

All Euro-Med AAs include movement of capital provisions.[412] Rules on movement of capital are intended to facilitate direct investments in the Mediterranean region. Therefore, all AAs provide for the free movement of capital as regards direct investments.[413] For example, all capital relating to direct investments in Moroccan companies can move freely and all the benefits from such investments can be liquidated and repatriated. All countries, except for Israel and Jordan, need to cooperate further to achieve full liberalisation of capital in

[409] Negotiations have started on the basis of the Istanbul Framework Protocol which serves as a framework for negotiations about the liberalisation of services between the Mediterranean countries and the EU. The Istanbul Protocol, however, does not provide a framework for negotiations on the right of establishment.

[410] Art. 63 TFEU (1) Within the framework of the provisions set out in this chapter, all restrictions on the movement of capital between Member States and between Member States and third countries shall be prohibited. (2) Within the framework of the provisions set out in this chapter, all restrictions on payments between Member States and between Member States and third countries shall be prohibited.

[411] Cf., *infra* 3.5.2 Grounds for derogation from the 'movement of capital provision' in the Euro-Med AAs.

[412] Arts. 48-52 Jordan AA; Arts. 31-33 Egypt AA; Arts. 31-34 Lebanon AA; Arts. 38-40 Algeria AA; Arts. 33-35 Morocco AA; Arts. 31-34 Tunisia AA; and Arts. 27-28 and 35 PA Interim AA.

[413] Art. 39 Algeria AA; Art. 34 Morocco AA; Art. 34 Tunisia AA; Art. 32 Egypt AA; Art. 49 Jordan AA; Art. 31 Israel AA; and Art. 28 PA Interim AA.

the future.[414] Israel and Jordan, on the one hand, and the EU, on the other, allow no restrictions on the movement of capital.[415] The movement of capital between Israel/Jordan and the EU is thus fully liberalised. Israel and the EU have already emphasised that the AA aims at the harmonious development of economic relations through the expansion of trade in goods and services and the free movement of capital.[416]

The Maghreb countries and Egypt undertake to authorise current payments for current transactions in a convertible currency, for example, the euro.[417] The other Mediterranean countries stipulate that all current payments connected with the movement of goods, persons, services and capital within the framework of the Euro-Med AA are free of restrictions.[418]

3.5.2 *Grounds for derogation from the 'movement of capital provision' in the Euro-Med Association Agreements*

The EU or the Mediterranean country may take restrictive measures regarding current payments when one or several Member States or a Mediterranean country face or risk facing serious difficulties concerning the balance of payments. These restrictions will be limited in time and may not go beyond what is strictly necessary to remedy the balance of payments situation.[419]

Only Israel and Jordan can take safeguard measures with regard to the movement of capital.[420] Where, in exceptional circumstances, movements of capital between Israel/Jordan and the EU cause, or threaten to cause, serious difficulties for the operation of exchange rate policy or monetary policy in Israel/Jordan or the EU, both parties may take safeguard measures with regard to movements of capital between Israel/Jordan and the EU for a period not exceeding six months if such measures are strictly necessary. The safeguard measures can only be taken in accordance with the GATS conditions and the conditions laid down by the International Monetary Fund. Article 66 TFEU stipulates that in exceptional circumstances, where movements of capital to or from third countries cause, or threaten to cause, serious difficulties for the operation of economic and monetary union, the EU Council, acting by a qualified majority on a proposal from the Commission and after consulting the ECB, may take safeguard measures with regard to third countries for a period not exceeding six months if such measures are strictly necessary.

Israel, Jordan and Lebanon can apply certain restrictions which existed between them and the EU on the date of entry into force of their respective AA in

---

414 Art. 39 para. 2 Algeria AA; Art. 34 para. 2 Morocco AA; Art. 34 para. 2 Tunisia AA; Art. 32 para. 2 Egypt AA; and Art. 28 para. 2 PA Interim AA.

415 Art. 31 Israel AA and Art. 31 Lebanon AA.

416 Art. 1 Israel AA.

417 Art. 33 Tunisia AA; Art. 38 Algeria AA; Art. 33 Morocco AA; and Art. 31 Egypt AA.

418 Art. 32 Israel AA; Art. 32 Lebanon AA; Art. 48 Jordan AA; and Art. 27 PA Interim AA.

419 Art. 40 Algeria AA; Art. 35 Morocco AA; Art. 35 Tunisia AA; Art. 33 Egypt AA; Art. 34 Lebanon AA; Art. 52 Jordan AA; Art. 26 Israel AA; and Art. 35 PA Interim AA.

420 Art. 34 Israel AA and Art. 51 Jordan AA.

regard of the movement of capital between them. These are the existing restrictions involving direct investment (including in real estate, establishment, the provision of financial services or the admission of securities to capital markets).[421] The TFEU itself provides for such restrictive measures for the EU in relation to third countries. Article 64 TFEU states that the provisions of Article 63 shall be without prejudice to the application to third countries of any restrictions which exist on 31 December 1993 under national or EU law adopted in respect of the movement of capital to or from third countries involving direct investment (including investment in real estate, establishment, the provision of financial services or the admission of securities to capital markets). Whilst endeavouring to achieve the objective of free movement of capital between Member States and third countries to the greatest extent possible, the EU Council may, acting by a qualified majority on a proposal from the Commission, adopt measures on the movement of capital to or from third countries involving direct investment (including investment in real estate, establishment, the provision of financial services or the admission of securities to capital markets). Unanimity will be required for measures which constitute a step back in EU law as regards the liberalisation of the movement of capital to or from third countries.

3.5.3 *Sub-conclusion*

All Euro-Med AAs provide for the free movement of capital as regards direct investments but have to work on further liberalisation in other sectors. Israel-EU and Jordan-EU have fully liberalised the movement of capital. Restrictive measures on current payments in the event of serious difficulties in the balance of payments of the Mediterranean country or the Member State are always possible. Safeguard measures can be taken by Israel and Jordan, on the one hand, and by the EU, on the other. Restrictions already existing before the entry into force of the Euro-Med AAs can still be applied in the relationship Israel-EU, Jordan-EU and Lebanon-EU.

3.6 The 'movement of persons' in the Euro-Med Association Agreements

3.6.1 *Right to non-discrimination based on nationality in the field of working conditions, remuneration and dismissal*

The Maghreb AAs contain a provision on non-discrimination between workers from Morocco, Algeria and Tunisia and European workers with regard to working conditions, remuneration and dismissal.[422] A difference is made between workers employed on a permanent basis and those employed on a temporary basis. Maghreb workers employed in the EU on a permanent basis will not be discriminated on the basis of nationality as regards working conditions, remu-

---

[421] Art. 33 Israel AA; Art. 33 Lebanon AA; and Art. 50 Jordan AA.

[422] Art. 52 Algeria AA; Art. 64 Tunisia AA; and Art. 64 Morocco AA. The Israeli AA contains no similar provision.

neration and dismissal. As regards working conditions, remuneration and dismissal, the Member States grant Maghreb workers the same treatment as their own nationals. The same applies to temporary workers with Maghreb nationality. Nor are temporary workers discriminated on the basis of nationality, but only as regards working conditions and remuneration. This non-discriminatory treatment does not apply in the case of dismissal of a temporary worker. The omission of the non-discriminatory treatment in the case of dismissal is unclear. Europeans who immigrate to Maghreb countries to work on a permanent or temporary basis will receive the same treatment. Article 64 of the Tunisia AA concerning the cooperation in social and cultural matters, for example, stipulates the following:

> '(1) The treatment accorded by each Member State to workers of Tunisian nationality employed in its territory shall be free from any discrimination based on nationality, as regards working conditions, remuneration and dismissal, relative to its own nationals;
> (2) All Tunisian workers allowed to undertake paid employment in the territory of a Member State on a temporary basis shall be covered by the provisions of paragraph 1 with regard to working conditions and remuneration;
> (3) Tunisia shall accord the same treatment to workers who are nationals of a Member State and employed in its territory.'

This non-discrimination provision in the field of working conditions, remuneration and dismissal is not included in the Egypt, Jordan, Israel and Lebanon AAs and the PA Interim AA. There is also interesting case law of the ECJ about non-discrimination on the basis of nationality in the field of working conditions, remuneration and dismissal. Two cases will be discussed below, namely the *El-Yassini* case and the *Gattoussi* case.[423]

In *El-Yassini*, the ECJ found that this non-discrimination provision had direct effect. The ECJ ruled as follows:

> 'The provision in the field of working conditions and remuneration establishes a clear and unconditional principle which is sufficiently practical that it can be applied by national courts and is therefore capable of directly governing the legal situation of individual(s).'

The ECJ also held that the principle of non-discrimination as regards working conditions or remuneration was to be interpreted as follows: a host Member State can in principle refuse to extend the residence permit of a Moroccan national whom it has authorised to enter its territory and take up gainful employment there, where the initial reason for the grant of his leave to stay no longer exists by the time that his residence permit expires. The situation would be different only if, in the absence of grounds relating to the protection of a legitimate national interest, such as public policy, public security or public health, that refusal were to affect the right actually to engage in employment conferred on the person con-

[423] C-416/96 *Nour Eddline El-Yassini* v *UK Secretary of State of the Home Department* [1999] *ECR* I-01209, paras. 30-32, and C-97/05 *Mohamed Gattoussi* v *Stadt Rüsselsheim* [2006] *ECR* I-11917.

cerned by a work permit duly granted by the competent national authorities for a period exceeding that of his residence permit. It is for the national court to determine whether that is the case.[424]

In the other ECJ case, Mr Mohamed Gattoussi, a Tunisian national, married a German citizen on 30 August 2002. Mr Gattoussi was issued a visa by the Germany Embassy in Tunis for family reunification. Later, on 24 September 2002, a residence permit for 3 years was granted to him by the German authorities. On 22 October 2002, the German authorities granted him a work permit of unlimited duration. In 2004, it became clear that Mrs and Mr Gattoussi had lived apart since 1 April 2004. Therefore, the German authorities shortened the validity period of his residence permit. The authorities required Mr Gattoussi to leave Germany without delay, failing which he would be deported to Tunisia. Mr Gattoussi relied on Article 64(1) of the Tunisia AA before the ECJ to contest this decision of the German authorities. The ECJ investigated whether Mr Gattoussi could rely on Article 64(1) of the Tunisia AA to contest the decision. The ECJ stated that it was necessary to examine whether Article 64(1) of the Tunisia AA had direct effect. The ECJ stated that this provision satisfied the requirements necessary for being accorded direct effect since the provision lays down a clear and precise obligation which is not subject, in its implementation or its effects, to the adoption of any subsequent measure. In other words, Article 64(1) could be invoked by Mr Gattoussi to defend his right to remain in Germany. Furthermore, the ECJ examined whether Article 64(1) of the Tunisia AA had any effect on the right to remain. According to the ECJ, Article 64(1) may have effects on the right of a Tunisian national to remain in the territory of a Member State in the case where that person has been permitted by that Member State to work there for a period extending beyond the period of validity of his permission to remain. The Member State curtailed the right to remain, but also restricted the right of employment, which extended beyond the period of validity of his permission to remain and which had been granted through the issue of a work permit. The ECJ examined whether this measure of the Member State concerning the right to remain of a Tunisian national was contradictory to Article 64(1) of the Tunisia AA as regards the right of employment. The ECJ stated that the Euro-Mediterranean AA was *not designed to secure any kind of freedom of movement for workers* and did not prohibit a Member State from taking measures concerning the right to remain of a Tunisian national whom it had previously authorised to enter its territory and to engage in gainful employment there. Consequently, it is possible for the Member State to oblige the person to terminate his employment before the end of the contractual term agreed with his employer, but only if this decision is justified on the grounds of protection of a legitimate national interest such as public policy, public security or public health. The concept of public policy, for example, presupposes the existence of a genuine and sufficiently serious threat to one of the fundamental interests of society. To defend his position, Mr Gattoussi could therefore rely on the lack of any ground of justification.

[424] C-416/96 *Nour Eddline El-Yassine*.

3.6.2 *Right to non-discrimination based on nationality in the field of social security*

The Maghreb AAs contain a non-discrimination provision regarding social security. Moroccan, Algerian and Tunisian workers benefit from treatment free from discrimination based on nationality in the field of social security. This non-discrimination provision also applies to family members who live in the Member State where the worker is employed. The Maghreb AAs accord *similar* treatment to nationals of a Member State who are employed in Maghreb countries and to the members of their families.[425]

In the *Hallouzi* case and the *Babahenini* case, the ECJ ruled that the principle of freedom from any discrimination based on nationality in the field of social security against Maghreb migrant workers and members of their family living with them in relation to nationals of the Member States in which they are or have been employed, meant that the persons referred to by that provision must be treated as if they were nationals of the Member States concerned. They may claim social security benefits under the same conditions as nationals of the host Member State without its being possible for the legislation of that Member State to impose upon those persons more or stricter conditions than those applicable to its nationals.[426]

Article 65(1) of the Tunisian AA concerning the cooperation in social and cultural matters, for example, stipulates as follows:

> (1) Subject to the provisions of the following paragraphs, workers of Tunisian nationality and any members of their families living with them shall enjoy, in the field of social security, treatment free from any discrimination based on nationality relative to nationals of the Member States in which they are employed. The concept of social security shall cover the branches of social security dealing with sickness and maternity benefits, invalidity, old-age and survivors' benefits, industrial accident and occupational disease benefits and death, unemployment and family benefits. These provisions shall not, however, cause the other coordination rules provided for in Community legislation based on Article 51 of the EC Treaty to apply, except under the conditions set out in Article 67 of this Agreement;
> (2) …
> (3) …
> (4) …
> (5) Tunisia shall accord to workers who are nationals of a Member State and employed in its territory, and to the members of their families, treatment similar to that specified in paragraphs 1, 3 and 4.

The other Euro-Med AAs do not contain a non-discrimination provision as regards social security. European workers legally employed in Israel, for exam-

---

[425] This non-discrimination provision in Art. 65(1) has been granted direct effect by the ECJ in Case C-18/90 *Kziber*.

[426] C-126/95 *A. Hallouzi-Choco* v *Bestuur van de Sociale Verzekeringsbank* [1996] *ECR* I-4807 and C-113/97 *Henia Babahenini* v *Belgian State* [1998] *ECR* I-183.

ple, are entitled to certain social security benefits. But are they not discriminated on the basis of nationality since the Israel AA contains no non-discrimination provision as regards social security matters? Since there is no non-discrimination provision in the Israel AA, the Israeli government could make the granting of social security benefits subject to nationality criteria. An example of Israeli legislation in the field of social security concerns old-age benefits. The Israeli law on old-age benefits[427] explains that an old-age pension is, by law, paid to residents of Israel who were born in Israel, or who immigrated to Israel for the first time prior to the age of 65. Women residents of Israel will be eligible for a pension if, in addition to the above stipulations, additional conditions are fulfilled.[428] It seems that European nationals, who temporarily work in Israel, struggle to obtain the same benefits as Israelis in Europe since Israeli legislation is bound to the principle of territoriality and does not interpret equality between men and women in the same way. The principle of equality between men and women is subject to even looser interpretation in the Maghreb countries.

There is also interesting case law of the ECJ about the non-discrimination provision on the basis of nationality in the field of social security, namely the *Kziber* case and the *Echouikh* case.[429]

Mrs Bahia Kziber, a Moroccan national, lived with her father, who had the same nationality and who had retired in Belgium after having been employed there. After finishing her studies, Mrs Kziber applied for unemployment benefits for school leavers, which were denied by the Belgian Office of Employment because of her Moroccan nationality. She appealed against this refusal on the basis of Article 41(1) of the Morocco-EU Cooperation Agreement regarding non-discrimination in the field of social security.[430]

The prohibition in Article 41(1) can be read as unconditional, clear and precise, which results in the application of the doctrine of direct effect of provisions of international agreements. Furthermore, the ECJ investigated whether the social security claims of Mrs Kziber fell within the material scope of Article 41(1). The ECJ declared that the concept of 'social security' contained in that Article had a meaning analogous to that in Article 4 of Regulation 1408/71, which mentions 'unemployment benefits' among the branches of social security. Finally, the ECJ investigated whether Mrs Kziber fell within the personal scope of Article 41(1). According to the Court, the concept of 'worker' encompasses both workers in active employment and those who have withdrawn from the

---

[427] Available at http://www.btl.gov.il/.

[428] They must fall into one of the following categories: 1) a single woman: an unmarried, divorced or widowed woman (except for a widow who receives a survivors' or dependants' pension and does not work outside her household); 2) a married woman who works outside her household (employed or self-employed), or a married woman whose husband is not insured with old-age and survivors' insurance (due to his age or because he is not a resident of Israel) even if the woman is not an employee and is not self-employed; and 3) an abandoned wife (a married woman whose husband has disappeared for 2 or more years or has been abroad without her consent for 2 or more years and does not pay her alimony) even if the woman is not an employee and is not self-employed.

[429] C-18/90 *Office National de l'Emploi* v *Bahia Kziber* [1991] *ECR* I-00199 and C-336/05 *Ameur Echouikh* v *Secrétaire d'Etat aux anciens combattants* [2006] *ECR* I-05223, paras. 39-41.

[430] The Morocco-EC Cooperation Agreement of 1976 has been replaced by the Morocco-EC AA.

employment market because of age or of a work accident. Mr Kziber was considered to be a worker in the sense of Article 41(1) and Mrs Kziber as his relative. The non-discrimination provision also applies to family members. All this led to the conclusion that the principle of freedom from discrimination based on nationality in the field of social security in Article 41(1) precludes a Member State from refusing to grant an unemployment benefit to a resident family member of a Moroccan worker on the ground that the person seeking work is a Moroccan national.[431]

The other ECJ case concerned Mr Ameur Echouikh, a Moroccan national, who was resident in France and served in the French army from 1949 to 1964. On 28 January 2002, he submitted a claim, under Article L. 252-2 of the French Code, for an armed services invalidity pension in respect of an illness contracted in Saigon in 1953 where he was for the purposes of his service in the French army. The French Minister of Defense rejected the claim since it fell within the scope of Article 71 of the Law of 26 December 1959 by which the French Republic ceased to confer any new rights under that law on nationals of non-member countries, such as Morocco.[432] Mr Echouikh, however, appealed against this decision and invoked the non-discrimination provision as regards social security in Article 65(1) of the Morocco AA.

The ECJ examined whether Mr Echouikh could invoke the non-discrimination provision in Article 65(1) of the Morocco AA. First, the Court stated that the prohibition of discrimination based on nationality in Article 65(1) of the Morocco AA had direct effect. Therefore, Mr Echouikh could invoke the non-discrimination provision as regards social security before the national court even though the Association Council had not adopted implementing measures. Secondly, the ECJ examined whether Mr Echouikh fell within the personal and material scope of the principle of non-discrimination. Regarding the personal scope, the ECJ checked whether Mr Echouikh was considered to be 'worker' within the meaning of the non-discrimination provision in the first subparagraph of Article 65(1) of the Morocco AA. According to the ECJ, the concept of 'worker' encompasses both active workers and those who have left the labour market after reaching the age required for receipt of an old-age pension or after becoming the victims of one of the risks creating entitlement to allowances under other branches of social security. Therefore, Mr Echouikh, a Moroccan national who undertook paid employment in France, must be regarded as a 'worker' within the meaning of the first subparagraph of Article 65(1) of the Morocco AA. As regards the material

---

[431] W. Alexander, 'Free Movement of Non-EC Nationals. A Review of the Case-Law of the Court of Justice', 3 *EJIL* (1992) p. 53, at pp. 62-63.

[432] Art. 71 of Law No 59-1454 of 26 December 1959, on the Finance Act for 1960 (JORF) of 27 December 1959, p. 12363) ('the law of 26 December 1959') is worded as follows: 'I – With effect from 1 January 1961, pensions, allowances and life annuities chargeable to the budget of the French State or public authorities for which nationals of countries or territories which were members of the French Union or of the Community or which were French protectorates or trust territories are eligible will be replaced for the duration of their entitlement, by annual allowances payable in francs, calculated on the basis of the tariffs in force in relation to such pensions and allowances at the date of conversion.'

scope of the non-discrimination provision, the ECJ examined whether an armed services invalidity pension belonged to the field of 'social security' within the meaning of that provision. The answer was positive since Article 65(1) expressly refers to invalidity benefits among the branches of social security.

The ECJ concluded that the French law was incompatible with Article 65(1) of the Morocco AA as it created inequality in the treatment of pensioners solely on the basis of their nationality.

3.6.3 *Right to social security allowances*

3.6.3.1 (In)direct effect of the social security provisions

The Maghreb AAs and the Israeli AA include provisions on social security allowances.[433] The aim of these provisions is that workers from Morocco, Tunisia, Algeria or Israel receive *certain* social security benefits provided under the legislation of the Member State(s) where they work. These provisions only apply to nationals residing or working legally in the territory of their host countries.[434]

The social security provisions provided for in Article 65(2) to (5) of the Tunisia AA require a decision of the Association Council in order for them to take effect.[435] The implementation measures adopted by the Association Council may not affect any rights or obligations arising from bilateral agreements between the Maghreb countries, Israel and the Member States where those agreements provide for more favourable treatment of nationals. The decision of the Association Council needs to be incorporated into a decision of the Council of the EU in order to have legal effect.[436] On 12 December 2007, the Commission launched a package of proposals which explain the Commission's position in the Association Council that will set the rules for implementation of the social security provisions in Morocco, Algeria, Tunisia and Israel, and Europe. These proposals are almost

[433] Arts. 68-71 Algeria AA; Arts. 65-68 Tunisia AA; and Arts. 65-68 Morocco AA. The social security field includes: (i) sickness and maternity benefits, invalidity, old-age and survivors' benefits, industrial accident and occupational disease benefits, and death, unemployment and family benefits; (ii) right of aggregation of periods of insurance, employment and residence completed in various Member States; (iii) family allowances for family members; and (iv) right to transfer pensions and other benefits. Under the Agreements, the Association Council has competences to adopt provisions pertaining to the implementation of the equal treatment principle in the social security field.

[434] Art. 69 Algeria AA.

[435] See Art. 67 Tunisia AA. Art. 65(1) of the Tunisia AA does not require implementation by the Association Council since it already has direct effect.

[436] Art. 300(2), para. 1 EC Treaty: 'Subject to the powers vested in the Commission in this field, the signing, which may be accompanied by a decision on provisional application before entry into force, and the conclusion of the agreements shall be decided on by the Council, acting by a qualified majority on a proposal from the Commission. The Council shall act unanimously when the agreement covers a field for which unanimity is required for the adoption of internal rules and for the agreements referred to in Article 310.' Art. 300(2), para. 2 EC Treaty: '(...) the same procedures shall apply (...) for the purpose of establishing the positions to be adopted on behalf of the Community in a body set up by an agreement' (in this case the Association Council) 'when that body is called upon to adopt decisions having legal effects.'

identical so as to facilitate the application of these provisions by the Member States' social security institutions.[437] The provisions adopted by the Association Council may not affect any rights or obligations arising from bilateral agreements linking the Mediterranean country and the Member States where those agreements provide for more favourable treatment of nationals of the Mediterranean country or of the Member States. So far, the Association Council has not yet taken an implementation decision. Consequently, social security provisions in the Euro-Med AAs lack direct effect.

The social security provisions in the Euro-Med AAs will be set out below with reference to the relevant parts of the Commission proposal of 12 December 2007 preparing the Association Council's decision in this respect.

3.6.3.2 The concept of 'social security' in the Euro-Med AAs

What does social security mean for a Mediterranean worker in Europe? According to Article 65 of the Tunisia AA, paragraph (1), sentence 2, the concept of social security covers the branches of social security dealing with sickness and maternity benefits, invalidity, old-age and survivors' benefits, industrial accident and occupational disease benefits and death, unemployment and family benefits.

However, in its proposal of 12 December 2007, the Commission severely limits the scope of the social security benefits. Sickness and maternity benefits, invalidity benefits for other reasons than accidents at work and occupational diseases,[438] death benefits and unemployment benefits are not included in the Commission proposal. In practice, individuals can only rely on the benefits which are included in the decision of the Association Council, proposed by the Commission, and not directly on the social security benefits as provided for in the Euro-Med AA as these lack direct effect. It must be noted that the Commission also

---

[437] Proposal for a Council Decision on the position to be taken by the Community within the Association Council created by the Euro-Mediterranean Agreement establishing an association between the European Communities and their Member States, of the one part, and the Republic of Tunisia, of the other part, with regard to the adoption of provisions on the co-ordination of the social security systems, COM (2007) 788 final; proposal for a Council Decision on the position to be taken by the Community within the Association Council created by the Euro-Mediterranean Agreement establishing an association between the European Communities and their Member States, of the one part, and the Kingdom of Morocco, of the other part, with regard to the adoption of provisions on the co-ordination of the social security systems, COM (2007) 0792 final; proposal for a Council Decision on the position to be taken by the Community within the Association Council created by the Euro-Mediterranean Agreement establishing an association between the European Community and its Member States, of the one part, and the People's Democratic Republic of Algeria, of the other part, with regard to the adoption of provisions on the co-ordination of the social security systems, COM (2007) 790 final; proposal for a Council Decision on the position to be taken by the Community within the Association Council created by the Euro-Mediterranean Agreement establishing an association between the European Communities and their Member States, of the one part, and the State of Israel, of the other part, with regard to the adoption of provisions on the co-ordination of the social security systems, COM (2007) 793 final.

[438] Except for the proposal of the Commission of 12 December 2007 for the EU-Israel Association Council, where the scope includes all invalidity benefits.

made a proposal in 2000 for the EU-Tunisia Association Council as regards the implementation of the social security provisions of the Tunisia AA.[439] According to that Commission proposal, Tunisian workers were entitled to sickness and maternity benefits, invalidity benefits, old-age benefits, survivor's benefits, benefits in respect of accidents at work and occupational diseases, death grants, unemployment benefits and family benefits.[440] In 2000, the Commission granted Tunisian workers the same social security benefits as provided for in the Euro-Med AA. This proposal, however, was replaced by a new Commission proposal regarding Tunisian workers, in which they are entitled to less socials security benefits. In conclusion, it can be stated that the Commission proposal of 12 December 2007 is more restrictive than the Maghreb AA. And what does social security mean for a European worker in a Mediterranean country, for example, Tunisia? The Commission proposal of 12 December 2007 preparing the Association Council's decision stipulates that a European worker will receive benefits within the meaning of Tunisian legislation, but does Tunisia have a properly functioning social security system and legislation? The Commission also clarifies that benefits are granted to a European worker in Israel under the legislation of Israel, but the same question is relevant regarding the Israeli legislation.

It is interesting to examine whether an Algerian plumber in France and an Italian plumber in France enjoy the same social security rights. First of all, Algerian workers in the EU can only be employed persons. Mediterranean workers do not have the right to work in the EU as self-employed persons and, consequently, there are no social security provisions governing their self-employment. The Algerian plumber must be an employed person. Furthermore, according to the Commission proposal of 12 December 2007, Algerian workers legally employed in a Member State are entitled to certain social security benefits, which include old-age benefits, survivors' pensions, benefits in respect of accidents at work and occupational diseases, invalidity benefits resulting from accidents at work and occupational diseases, and family benefits. Whether such benefits are granted depends on the legislation of the Member State in which the Algerian is working. The question arises whether Algerian nationals, working, for example, in France, are entitled to the same socials security benefits as Italians working in France. European nationals working in another Member State are entitled to social security benefits provided for by Council Regulation (EC) No 1408/71 of 14 June 1971 on the application of social security schemes to employed persons, to self-employed persons and to members of their families moving within the EU. Italian workers can be employed persons or self-employed persons. In either case, they will receive social benefits under the Regulation, which include sickness and maternity benefits, invalidity benefits, including those intended for the maintenance or improvement of earning capacity, old-age benefits, survivors' benefits, benefits in respect of accidents at work and occupational diseases, death

[439] COM (2000) 216 final.

[440] Art. 4 of this Commission proposal.

grants, unemployment benefits and family benefits.[441] Contrary to the case of Italian workers, the Commission proposal indicates that Algerian workers are not entitled to sickness and maternity benefits, invalidity benefits for the maintenance or improvement of earning capacity, death grants and unemployment benefits, but only to old-age or survivors' pensions, benefits in respect of accidents at work and occupation diseases, invalidity benefits resulting from accidents at work and occupational diseases.

The ECJ, however, has clarified the concept of social security several times. In doing so, the ECJ has extended the scope of the relevant Articles of the Euro-Med AAs, as will be illustrated below by two ECJ cases, namely the *Kziber* case and the *Alami* case.[442] In *Kziber*, the ECJ declared that the concept of 'social security' contained in Article 41(1) of the Morocco-EEC Cooperation Agreement had a meaning analogous to that in Article 4 of Regulation 1408/71, which mentions 'unemployment benefits' among the branches of social security.

In the *Alami* case, the ECJ held that the term 'social security' contained in Article 41(1) of the Euro-Med Agreement must be deemed to bear the same meaning as the identical term used in Council Regulation (EC) No 1408/71 of 14 June 1971 on the application of social security schemes to employed persons, to self-employed persons and to members of their families moving within the EU. The fact that Article 41(2) of the Euro-Med Agreement, unlike Regulation No 1408/71, does not mention unemployment benefits among the schemes to which the aggregation of insurance or employment periods applies cannot result in the exclusion from the concept of social security, within the meaning of the Agreement, of those unemployment benefits, which are traditionally regarded as a branch of social security. Consequently, benefits such as the supplement at issue in the main proceedings fall within the scope of Article 41(1) of the Agreement.

3.6.3.3 The meaning of 'similar treatment'

The Maghreb countries and Israel accord to European workers in their territory and to the members of their families, similar treatment. Paragraph (5) of Article 65 of the Tunisia AA stipulates that Tunisia will accord to workers who are nationals of a Member State and employed in its territory, and to the members of their families, treatment similar to that specified in paragraphs 1, 3 and 4. No Euro-Med AA, however, provides an explanation of the meaning of the word 'similar.' The Association Council has to implement the social security provisions and will have to determine what 'similar' means.[443]

---

441 *OJ* 1971 L 149 of 5 July 1971, p. 2, and the consolidated version *OJ* 1997 L 28 of 30 January 1997, p. 1, Art. 4.

442 Cf., *supra* n. 429 and C-23/02 of 12 February 2003 in C-23/02, *Office national de l'emploi* v *Mohamed Alami*, [2003] *ECR* I-01399, paras. 23-26.

443 According to Art. 67 Tunisia AA, the Association Council shall adopt provisions to implement the principles set out in Art. 65 Tunisia AA.

3.6.3.4 The aggregation of periods of insurance, employment or residence

According to paragraph (2) of Article 65 of the Tunisia AA, all periods of insurance, employment or residence completed by Maghreb or Israeli workers in the various Member States shall be added together for the purpose of pensions and annuities in respect of old-age, invalidity and survivors' benefits and family, sickness and maternity benefits and also for that of medical care for the workers and for members of their families resident in the EU. Article 65(5) of the Tunisia AA stipulates that Tunisia accords to workers who are nationals of a Member State and employed in its territory, and to the members of their families, treatment similar to that specified in paragraphs (1), (3) and (4), but does not mention paragraph (2). Consequently, there seems to be a difference in treatment between Mediterranean workers in Europe and European workers in the Maghreb countries or Israel. The Tunisia AA says nothing about the aggregation of periods for the purpose of pensions and annuities in the case of European workers in the Maghreb countries or Israel.

3.6.3.5 Allowances for family members

According to paragraph (3) of Article 65 of the Tunisia AA, the workers in question receive family allowances for members of their families who are resident in the EU. Tunisia accords to workers who are nationals of a Member State and employed in its territory, and to the members of their families, similar treatment.[444] The ECJ clarified the term 'member of the family' in the *El-Youssfi* case of 17 July 2007:[445]

> 'It should be made clear that the term "members of the family" refers not only to the worker's spouse and descendants but also to persons having a close family relationship with him such as his relatives in the ascending line, including those related to him by marriage.'[446]

The right of a Tunisian worker to family benefits is subject to the condition that his family members are legally resident with him in the Member State where he is employed. There is no entitlement to family benefits for family members who are resident in another state. According to the implementation measures, a Tunisian worker will receive family benefits within the meaning of Article 1(u) (i) of Regulation No 1408/71 on the application of security schemes to employed persons and their families moving within the EU. The proposed decision of the Association Council interprets the meaning of the word 'similar' and ensures that the provision on the granting of family benefits also applies by way of reciprocity

---

444 Art. 65(5) Tunisia AA.
445 C-276/06 *Mamate El Youssfi* v *Office National des Pensions (ONP)* [2007] *ECR* I-02851.
446 See, by analogy, the judgment in C-179/98 *Mesbah* [1999] *ECR* I-7955, para. 46.

to European workers legally employed in Tunisia and their family members legally resident in Tunisia.[447]

3.6.3.6 The transfer of pensions or annuities

Article 65 Tunisia AA, paragraph (4) stipulates the following:

> 'The workers in question shall be able to transfer freely to Tunisia, at the rates applied by virtue of the legislation of the debtor Member State or States, any pensions or annuities in respect of old age, survivor status, industrial accident or occupational disease, or of invalidity resulting from industrial accident or occupational disease, except in the case of special non-contributory benefits.'

According to paragraph (4) of Article 65 of the Tunisia AA, a Tunisian worker can freely transfer his social security allowances to Tunisia.[448] Tunisia accords to workers who are nationals of a Member State and employed in its territory, and to the members of their families, similar treatment.[449] The Commission proposal of 12 December 2007 preparing the Association Council's decision ensures that the provision on the export of benefits also applies, by way of reciprocity, to European workers legally employed in Tunisia and clarifies that the export of cash benefits is limited to certain benefits: for a Tunisian worker in a Member State these are old-age or survivors' pensions, benefits in respect of accidents at work and occupational diseases or of invalidity benefits resulting from accidents at work and occupational diseases, with the exception of special non-contributory cash benefits. For a European worker in Tunisia, these are the corresponding benefits provided under Tunisian legislation, with the exception of special non-contributory cash benefits.[450]

3.6.3.7 Cooperation mechanism between social security systems of the Member States and the relevant Mediterranean countries

Only the Maghreb AAs and the Israel AA contain limited provisions on coordination between the social security systems of the Member States and of the Mediterranean countries. The Commission proposal of 2007 for the Association Council's decision provides further details about this cooperation mechanism between the social security institutions of the Member States and the relevant Mediterranean countries. The Commission proposal for the Algeria Association Council, for example, stipulates that: social security institutions of the Member States and Algeria will communicate directly with one another and with the persons involved, the social security institutions of the Member States and Algeria will lend one another their good offices and act as though implementing their own legislation, the administrative assistance given by the social security institutions

[447] Art. 5 proposed Decision of the Association Council.

[448] Art. 65 Morocco AA (except in the case of special non-contributory benefits).

[449] Art. 65(5) Tunisia AA.

[450] See the 'waiving of residence' clause in Art. 4 of the proposed Decision of the Association Council.

will be free of charge, and the persons involved must inform the institutions of the Member State or Algeria as soon as possible of any change in their personal or family situation which affects their right to benefits.[451]

3.6.4 *Grounds for derogation from the 'movement of persons provision' in the Euro-Med Association Agreements*

The Euro-Med AAs do not provide for specific derogation provisions regarding the movement of persons. The reason behind this is that the Euro-Med AAs are not intended to establish free movement of persons. Therefore, no derogation provisions were considered necessary. However, in its case law, the ECJ has offered some possibilities as regards the derogation from the principle of movement of persons. According to the ECJ in *Gattoussi*, it is possible for the Member State to oblige the Mediterranean person to terminate his employment before the end of the contractual term agreed with his employer, if this decision is justified on grounds of protection of a legitimate national interest such as public policy, public security or public health.[452] The concept of public policy presupposes the existence of a genuine and sufficiently serious threat to one of the fundamental interests of society. In the *El-Yassini* case of 2 March 1999, the ECJ refers to grounds relating to the protection of a legitimate national interest, such as public policy, public security or public health, for a Member State to refuse to extend the residence permit of a Moroccan national whom it has authorised to enter its territory and to take up gainful employment there.[453]

3.6.5 *'Illegal immigration provisions' in the Euro-Med Association Agreements*

The EU and the Mediterranean countries also agreed to cooperate in the field of illegal immigration. Algeria, Egypt and Lebanon included provisions about immigration in their AAs.[454] These countries and the EU will exchange information on illegal immigration flows. They will readmit their nationals illegally present on the territory of the other party after the necessary identification formalities have been completed and will provide their nationals with the appropriate identity documents for this purpose. The Lebanon AA, for example, contains a chapter on cooperation for the prevention and control of illegal immigration. Article 6 of the Lebanon AA stipulates the following:

> 1. The Parties agree to cooperate in order to prevent and control illegal immigration. To this end: (a) each of the Member States agrees to readmit any of its nationals present on the territory of Lebanon, upon request by the latter and without further formalities once such persons have been positively identified as such, (b) Lebanon agrees

[451] Art. 7 Commission proposal of 12 December 2007.

[452] Cf., *supra* 3.6.1. Right to non-discrimination based on nationality in the field of working conditions, remuneration and dismissal.

[453] C-416/96 *Nour Eddline El-Yassine*.

[454] Arts. 83-84 Algeria AA; Arts. 68-70 Egypt AA; and Arts. 68-70 Lebanon AA.

> to readmit any of its nationals illegally present on the territory of a Member State, upon request by the latter and without further formalities once such persons have been positively identified as such. The Member States and Lebanon will also provide their nationals with appropriate identity documents for such purposes.
> 2. In respect of the Member States of the European Union, the obligation in this Article applies only in respect of those persons who are to be considered their nationals for Community purposes in accordance with the Treaty establishing the European Community.
> 3. In respect of Lebanon, the obligation in this Article applies only in respect to those persons who are considered Lebanese in accordance to the Lebanese legal system and all the relevant laws concerning citizenship.

These countries will also conclude bilateral agreements on combating illegal immigration and on readmission. Article 69 of the Lebanon AA, for example, describes what these bilateral agreements should cover:

> 1. After the entry into force of this Agreement, the Parties, at the request of any of them, shall negotiate and conclude bilateral agreements with each other, regulating specific obligations for the readmission of their nationals. These agreements shall also cover, if deemed necessary by any of the Parties, arrangements for the readmission of third country nationals. Such agreements will lay down details about categories of persons covered by these arrangements as well as the modalities of their readmission.
> 2. Adequate financial and technical assistance to implement these agreements may be provided to Lebanon.

The Association Council will examine the possibility of other forms of joint action for the prevention and control of illegal immigration, including ways of detecting forged documents.[455] The only explicit provision on maintaining the visa requirements within a simplified and expeditious procedure can be found in the Algerian AA.[456] Apart from these references, the AAs do not devote special attention to immigration issues.[457]

3.6.6 *Sub-conclusion*

In the Euro-Med AAs, the most restrictive provisions relate to the movement of persons. Fear of mass migration from the Mediterranean countries to Europe was

---

[455] Art. 70 Lebanon AA.

[456] Art. 83 Algeria AA: Desirous of facilitating the movement of persons between them, the parties shall ensure, in accordance with relevant Community and national legislation in force, that the formalities for the issue of visas are carefully applied and executed and shall agree to examine, within the limits of their powers, ways of simplifying and speeding up the issue of visas to persons contributing to the implementation of this Agreement. The Association Committee shall periodically examine the implementation of this Article.

[457] Tunisia, for example, is only engaged in a regular dialogue on immigration issues with the EU. With regard to illegal immigration, Art. 69(c) Tunisia AA stipulates that a dialogue between the parties shall cover all issues connected with illegal immigration and the conditions governing the return of individuals who are in breach of the legislation dealing with the right to stay and the right of establishment in their host countries.

one of the main reasons why these rights were limited.[458] Many Europeans view the Mediterranean region as a demographic time bomb. According to forecasts of the World Bank, the population of the Mediterranean countries, which stood at 209 million in 1992, will reach 304 million in 2010.[459] Furthermore, the wealth gap between the EU and the Mediterranean countries will increase from level one to ten to level one to twenty. As a consequence, immigration and drug trafficking into the EU will increase in the future.[460] The Commission refused several calls from the Mediterranean countries to ease migratory access.[461] Labour movement, however, has always been one of the key factors of economic development in the Mediterranean region because it improves the chronic unemployment in this region and is essential to compensate for the scarcity of unskilled labour in Europe.

The Maghreb AAs and the Israel AA contain liberal provisions as regards the movement of persons. The aim of these Euro-Med AAs is the gradual liberalisation of trade in goods, services and capital and the facilitation of human exchanges, particularly in the context of administrative procedures. The Algeria AA, for example, stipulates that Algeria and the EU are eager to facilitate the movement of persons between them. They will carefully apply and execute the formalities for the issue of visas and examine ways of simplifying and speeding up the issue of visas. The Association Committee will periodically examine the implementation of this provision.[462]

The Maghreb AAs contain two non-discrimination provisions. Firstly, there is one regarding working conditions, remuneration and dismissal. In the *El-Yassini* and *Gattoussi* cases, the ECJ found that this provision had direct effect. Secondly, the Maghreb AAs contain a non-discrimination provision in the field of social security. Moroccan, Algerian and Tunisian workers benefit from treatment free from discrimination based on nationality in the field of social security. This provision also applies to the family members who live in the Member State in

---

[458] For an overview of the impact of a new EU immigration policy on the EMP, see L. Hugelin, 'L'incidence d'une nouvelle politique communautaire de l'immigration sur le partenariat euro-méditerranéen', in Xuereb, *supra* n. 34, pp. 201-232.

[459] *Economic and Social Development in the Middle East and North Africa*, Discussion Paper Series 3, October 1992, available at: http://www.worldbank.org.

[460] The countries of southern Europe do not receive the same types of immigrants, despite their common geographical position on the Mediterranean coast where the pressure of African migration is felt. Greece mainly receives citizens from Egypt, Bulgaria and Russia. Spain receives mainly flows of Moroccans. Italy receives Albanians, Moroccans and citizens from black Africa and the Indies. Portugal keeps attracting immigrants from its former colonial empire (Cape Verde, Brazil and Angola). France and the UK, the two greatest colonial powers of the 20th century, receive citizens from Morocco, Algeria, Australia and New Zealand respectively. The role of national histories, namely the ties with former colonial powers, the position with regard to the EU's external borders, the different national migration policies and the needs of the national economy (skilled/unskilled workers) explain the national characteristics of migration. See Y. Breem and X. Thierry, 'Immigration in Europe and Development Levels of the Source Countries: What Are the Associations?', (2004) available at: http://www.irpps.cnr.it/ricmob/web_conf/download/thierry_paper.pdf.

[461] Communication on Proposals for Implementing the Euro-Mediterranean Policy of 8 march 1995, COM (1995) 72 final, pp. 1-18, at p. 6.

[462] Art. 83 Algeria AA.

which the worker is employed. Again the ECJ ruled, in the *Kziber* and *Echouik* cases, that the non-discrimination provision had direct effect. None of the other Euro-Med AAs provide for a non-discrimination provision in the field of working conditions, remuneration and dismissal, or in the field of social security.

Algerian, Tunisian, Moroccan and Israeli nationals who work and reside legally in Europe are conferred further social rights by their Euro-Med AAs. Only Maghreb nationals and Israelis legally working in Europe have social security rights under the AA. The Maghreb AAs and Israel indeed contain a number of further principles on the coordination of social security schemes. However, in order for these principles to take effect, these AAs also require that the Association Councils adopt measures to implement them. The Commission issued a few proposals in December 2007. These proposals intend to establish the position to be taken by the EU in the Association Council. Since the Association Council has taken no decision yet as regards the social security provisions in the Euro-Med AAs, they lack direct effect. The Maghreb countries and Israel accord to European workers in their territory and to the members of their families, similar treatment. In its proposals of December 2007, the Commission interpreted the word 'similar' as meaning 'reciprocal.' It should be noted that the Euro-Med AAs do not provide for a right of self-employment of Mediterranean workers or European workers in the territory of the other party, but only for rights for employed persons.

An Egyptian, Lebanese, Jordanian or Palestinian football player or plumber will not be able to rely on their respective Euro-Med AAs to invoke social rights. The Jordan, Lebanon and Egypt AA and the PA Interim Agreement contain no provisions that relate to the movement of workers. These AAs only establish a regular dialogue procedure on social matters.[463] The Egypt AA reaffirms the importance of fair treatment of workers legally residing and employed in the territory of a party and agrees to initiate talks on reciprocal bilateral agreements related to the working conditions and social security rights of Egyptian and Member States' workers.[464]

Contrary to all other Euro-Med instruments, the Euro-Med AA is the only instrument that clearly makes a distinction between Euro-Med movement of persons (labour) and management of (il)legal migration. All other instruments treat these issues as if they are one and the same problem.

[463] For example, Art. 72 Algeria AA: The parties shall conduct regular dialogue on any social matter which is of interest to them. Such dialogue shall be used to find ways to achieve progress in the field of movement of workers and equal treatment and social integration for Algerian and Community nationals residing legally in the territories of their host States. The dialogue shall cover, *inter alia*, all issues related to the living and working conditions of workers and their dependants; migration; illegal immigration and the conditions governing the return of individuals who are in breach of the legislation dealing with the right to stay and the right of establishment in the host State; schemes and programmes to encourage equal treatment between Algerian and Community nationals, mutual knowledge of cultures and civilisations, the furthering of tolerance and the removal of discrimination.

[464] Art. 62 Egypt AA.

4. Conclusion

All Euro-Med AAs, except for the PA Interim AA, are based on Article 217 of the TFEU. This legal basis allows the EU and the Mediterranean countries to establish an 'association' through the conclusion of an international agreement. The Euro-Mediterranean association should result in an extension of some EU policies, such as the EU internal market and competition policy, to the Mediterranean countries. The Mediterranean countries, on their part, are eager to take part in the EU internal market, which consists of four freedoms: the freedom of goods, services, capital and persons. Many provisions of the Euro-Med AAs reflect the four freedoms of the EU internal market and the supporting provisions. There are also provisions in the Euro-Med AAs that have an impact on the goods, services, capital and persons provisions, such as those on competition and rules of origin.

All Euro-Med AAs include comparable movement of goods provisions, in which a distinction is drawn between trade in industrial goods and in agricultural goods. At present, only industrial goods originating in a Mediterranean country which are imported into the EU are totally free of customs duties and charges having equivalent effect. European industrial goods exported to a Mediterranean country will be progressively liberalised. The progressive liberalisation process should lead to total free movement in the future. Free movement of goods between the Mediterranean countries and the EU will be guaranteed in the future. At present, agricultural products, fishery products and industrial products with an agricultural element are not fully liberalised. In the future, however, these goods will be totally liberalised as well. Derogation from the movement of goods is possible in the Euro-Med relations; moreover, the derogation provision in the Euro-Med AAs and in the TFEU is similar. According to the European Courts, however, the interpretation of the derogation provisions in the Euro-Med AAs and in the EC Treaty (now: TFEU) differs, since the Euro-Med AA and the European Treaty have different purposes: the EU and the Mediterranean countries do not constitute a Euro-Med internal market, which leaves more room for restrictions than in the EU internal market itself. However, the Mediterranean countries and the EU are involved in a gradual liberalisation process. This means that the deeper the Euro-Med integration becomes, the fewer restrictions will be tolerated.

In conclusion, it can be stated that at present there is only free movement of Mediterranean industrial goods to the EU. The asymmetrical but reciprocal liberalisation of industrial goods will lead to free movement of industrial goods in the future. The liberalisation of agricultural products, fishery products and industrial products with an agricultural element will also lead to free movement of agricultural goods in the future. The final liberalisation date for industrial and agricultural goods is the same. For Tunisia, for example, the date is the end of 2010; for Lebanon, the end of 2018. After these dates, no more customs duties/charges having equivalent effect or quantitative restrictions/equivalent measures will be tolerated.

The Euro-Med AAs provide for provisions on competition law and rules of origin. These provisions are linked to the goods provisions. For example, goods can only move freely when competition rules are respected by the producers of the goods. At present, these supporting provisions do not apply to the movement of services, but only to goods. The provisions on competition law and rules of origin in the Euro-Med AAs can only support the integration of the Mediterranean countries into the EU internal market of goods if they really work in practice. After the final liberalisation date, each Mediterranean country and the EU should have a properly functioning competition system. The competition provisions in the Euro-Med AAs require implementing measures, but at present only minor implementation measures have been taken by the Association Council. European natural and legal persons might circumvent this by invoking the extraterritorial effect of EU competition law, which cannot be relied upon by Mediterranean individuals or companies. It would be advantageous for the Mediterranean countries if the Association Council were to take action in this field. In order to create a Euro-Med free trade area of goods, uniform competition rules are needed throughout the Euro-Med area as well as a properly functioning enforcement system for these rules. Another essential feature of a Euro-Med free trade area concerns the Euro-Med rules of origin, which identify which goods are eligible for preferential treatment. The uniformity and enforcement of Euro-Med competition rules are far from being realised. The Euro-Med rules of origin also have limited impact in the Euro-Med area, as no free trade agreements between the Mediterranean countries have entered into force. Free movement of goods between the Mediterranean countries and the EU will be difficult to achieve if the implementation of essential provisions, such as those on competition rules, fails to occur.

Contradictory to the 'movement of goods' provisions, the Euro-Med AAs do not contain common 'movement of services' or 'right of establishment' provisions. As regards the liberalisation of services, the Euro-Med AAs should be divided into two categories: those of countries that are member of the WTO and those that are not. The WTO countries Morocco, Tunisia, Egypt and Israel apply the GATS obligations until their Association Councils make specific recommendations on the liberalisation of services and the right of establishment. At present, no decision of the Association Council as regards services and the right of establishment has been issued. According to the GATS, the obligation to allow free market access and ensure national treatment only applies if the service for which access to the market or national treatment is requested is included in a special list. Only then will the country be obliged to refrain from putting up barriers to market access or from imposing quantitative restrictions. In that case, the GATS guarantees freedom of services for individuals (self-employment) as well as legal persons. In conclusion, it can be stated that for Algeria, Tunisia, Egypt and Israel there will be limited free movement of services, namely if the service for which free market access to the EU is requested figures on a special list. It can also be concluded that the Association Council is not working properly as regards the movement of services; there are still no proposals for the implementation of the relevant provisions of the Euro-Med AAs.

The non-WTO countries Algeria, Jordan and Lebanon drafted their own services and right of establishment provisions. The Lebanon AA only stipulates that Lebanon will apply the GATS rules after it has become a member of the WTO in the future. Algeria and Jordan included some liberal provisions, such as the right of establishment of companies and their key personnel, but none of these countries provides for the right for individuals to self-employment in the territory of the other country. The free movement of services in the TFEU guarantees the freedom for the provider of services: he should be able to carry out his activities whenever he wants in another Member State for a limited period of time. Services mean activities carried out on a self-employed basis; this is as opposed to workers who perform their activities within a relationship of dependency. This means that there is only limited free movement of services in the Euro-Med AAs of the non-WTO countries: it is limited to supply of services by companies and their personnel.

In the future, all Mediterranean countries and the EU wish to create some kind of preferential economic integration agreement as regards services and the right of establishment. These future agreements must include similar provisions on services and the right of establishment for all Mediterranean countries in order to ensure the consistency of the legal framework. It will, however, be necessary to take into account the individual needs and different stages of development of the Mediterranean countries. Therefore, these preferential economic agreements should include specific provisions for each Mediterranean country.

The TFEU itself provides for free movement of capital between the EU and third countries, but the TFEU also provides for restrictions on this free movement. Free movement of capital between Israel and the EU and between Jordan and the EU is also guaranteed in the Euro-Med AAs. All other Euro-Med AAs provide for limited free movement of capital, i.e., only for direct investments. This limited free movement of capital is, in fact, in contradiction with the TFEU itself. In the future, these countries have to work on further liberalisation of capital with the EU in other sectors as well. The Mediterranean countries are of the opinion that they have not derived sufficient economic benefits from the EMP. Therefore, the Mediterranean countries hope to gain real economic under the more recent Euro-Med policy, namely the ENP.[465] The ENP should provide further drive to economic reforms in the Mediterranean countries by opening up the region to agricultural exports and investment in major infrastructure projects. The Mediterranean countries are indeed suffering from the protectionist character of the agricultural EU policy, but also from the restrictions imposed on trade in textiles. They also feel resentment towards the EU since the EU and its companies do not make direct investments in their country. These investments could stimulate economic reorganisation in the Mediterranean countries, which is necessary for the establishment of a free trade area. Erwan Lannon and Peter Van

[465] S. Biscop, *The European Security Strategy and the Neighbourhood Policy: A New Starting Point for a Euro-Mediterranean Security Partnership?*, Paper presented at the EUSA Ninth Biennial International Conference Austin, Texas, 31 March-2 April 2005, available at: http://aei.pitt.edu/archive/00002984/01/Paper_EUSA_ESS-EMP.txt.

Elsuwege call the lack of foreign direct investment in the Mediterranean countries one of the most important failures of the EMP and its AAs.[466]

Contrary to the 'movement of goods' provisions, there is no common 'movement of persons' provision in the Euro-Med AAs. A distinction has to be made between the Maghreb and the Mashrek Euro-Med AAs. The Maghreb AAs contain some liberal provisions as regards the movement of persons, such as non-discrimination provisions with regard to working conditions, remuneration and dismissal and a non-discrimination provision in the field of social security. Both non-discrimination provisions have direct effect. None of the other Euro-Med AAs include a non-discrimination provision in the field of working conditions, remuneration and dismissal, nor in the field of social security. The Maghreb AAs and the Israel AA include some social security rights. However, in order for these principles to take effect, the AAs also require that the Association Councils adopt measures to implement the principles on the coordination of social security systems. Since the Association Councils have not yet taken any decision regarding the social security provisions in the Euro-Med AAs, they lack direct effect. The Jordan, Lebanon and Egypt AAs and the PA Interim Agreement contain no provisions that relate to the movement of workers. There is no free movement of persons between the two shores of the Mediterranean, only limited rights arising from the Maghreb AAs en the Israel AA. The few rights that are provided in the Maghreb AAs have already resulted in quite some jurisprudence of the ECJ. This signifies that the movement of persons is a matter of great concern to people from the Mediterranean countries. However, also in this respect, the Association Councils have as yet failed to take any implementing measures.

[466] Lannon and Van Elsuwege, *supra* n. 118, at pp. 60-61.

Table III: Do the Euro-Med AAs provide for freedom of goods, services, capital and persons between the different Mediterranean countries and the EU?

	GOODS	SERVICES	CAPITAL	PERSONS
Morocco	YES,[467] by 2012 (at present, only free movement of industrial goods from Morocco to EU)	NO (the GATS apply)	YES, for direct investment	NO
Tunisia	YES, by 2010 (at present only free movement of industrial goods from Tunisia to EU)	NO (the GATS apply)	YES, for direct investment	NO
Algeria	YES, by 2017 (at present, only free movement of industrial goods from Algeria to EU)	NO, only for companies and their personnel	YES, for direct investment	NO
Egypt	YES, by 2016 (at present, only free movement of industrial goods from Egypt to EU)	NO (the GATS apply)	YES, for direct investment	NO
Israel	YES (at present, only free movement of industrial goods from Israel to EU)	NO (the GATS apply)	YES	NO
West Bank & Gaza Strip	YES by 2001 (but hindered in practice by Israeli blockades)	NO	YES, for direct investment	NO
Jordan	YES, by 2014 (at present, only free movement of industrial goods from Jordan to EU)	NO, only for companies and their personnel	YES	NO
Lebanon	YES, by 2018 (at present, only free movement of industrial goods from Lebanon to EU)	NO	YES, for direct investment	NO
Libya	/	/	/	/
Syria	/	/	/	/

467 All industrial products and 80% of agricultural products will be liberalised.

Chapter V

Bilateral ENP instruments for the integration of the Mediterranean countries into the EU internal market

The enlargement of the EU on 1 May 2004 brought a historical change to the EU in political, geographical and economic terms. It provided the opportunity to 'deepen' the relations between the enlarged EU and its new neighbouring countries to the East and South.[468] Before the enlargement, the EU and those countries were already associated, for example, to the South through the Euro-Med Association Agreements (AAs), extensively described above. After the enlargement, the EU decided to go beyond the existing association with these new neighbouring countries. To this end, the EU launched a new policy: the European Neighbourhood Policy (ENP). The Commission drafted Action Plans in the framework of the ENP, which offer the EU and its new neighbours a 'deepening of the political relationship' and *the prospect of a significant measure of 'economic integration' through gradual integration in the EU internal market.* Here, only the economic integration of the Mediterranean countries through the gradual integration into the EU internal market will be discussed.[469] The integration of the countries to the East into the EU internal market does not fall within the scope of this book.

This chapter will examine to what extent the Mediterranean countries have integrated into the four freedoms of the EU internal market by means of the ENP Action Plans. The ENP Action Plans include many Euro-Med integration intentions, which will be examined in this chapter. To measure the extent of integration of the Mediterranean countries into the EU internal market of goods, services, capital and persons through the ENP Action Plans, it is not sufficient to only analyse the Euro-Med integration intentions of the parties as provided for in these Action Plans. The extent of integration of the Mediterranean countries into the EU's internal market can only be measured by examining the different ENP Progress Reports. These Progress Reports explain to what extent the Mediterranean countries have achieved the integration intentions set out in the ENP Action Plans. It is the first time that these Progress Reports are scrutinised as regards

[468] Conclusions of the 7th Meeting of Experts on Economic Transition, 23-24 April 2003, based on the paper 'The Economic Impact of the EU Enlargement on the Mediterranean Partners', prepared by DG External Relations, available at: http://europa.eu.int/comm/external_relations/euromed/etn/7mtg/agenda.htm.

[469] The political deepening of the Euro-Med relationship does not fall within the scope of this book either. For an overview of this subject, see: M.E. Smith and M. Webber, 'Political Dialogue and Security in the European Neighbourhood: The Virtues and Limits of "New Partnership Perspectives"', in 13 *EFAR* (2008) pp. 73-95.

the integration of the Mediterranean countries into the EU internal market. The Progress Reports issued in April 2008 and April 2009 will be examined as regards all aspects of the internal market for the first time. About this issue, there is no literature available yet. This analysis gives a good impression of the evolution of the integration of the different Mediterranean countries into the EU internal market and the extent of integration at this moment in time.

First, the legal basis, a possible definition and an overview of the ENP Action Plans will be presented in this chapter.

Second, the focus will be on the 'New Partnership Perspectives' (NPPs) of the Mediterranean countries and the EU as regards liberalisation aimed at promoting the four freedoms of the EU internal market. These perspectives are called 'new' because the ENP Action Plans intend to go beyond the perspectives of the Euro-Mediterranean Partnership (EMP). This overview will present all new NPPs of the ENP and will analyse if they indeed aim at further integration in comparison with the EMP.

Third, all ENP Action Plans will be analysed and compared in terms of their priority issues. Each Action Plan has a different set of priorities in order to achieve the abovementioned NPPs. This analysis is necessary to establish which freedom (goods, services, capital or persons) is the most significant for the Mediterranean countries. Some Mediterranean countries might prefer further integration into the EU internal market of goods, while others might favour being more deeply integrated into the EU internal market of services.

Fourth, an analysis will be made of all the provisions of the ENP Action Plans that contribute to the achievement of their priority issues. This analysis will clarify the extent of integration that the Mediterranean countries and the EU wish to achieve as regards the integration into the four EU freedoms. In the case of each Mediterranean country it will be examined to what extent it is willing and allowed to integrate into the four freedoms of the EU internal market.

Finally, it will be established whether these integration intentions of the Mediterranean countries and the EU as formulated in the ENP Action Plans have been achieved in reality. This will be done through an analysis of the ENP Progress Reports for each Mediterranean country. This examination is necessary to find out to what extent the ENP Action Plans have contributed to the integration of the Mediterranean countries into the EU internal market.

1. The ENP Action Plans

The Commission started drafting bilateral ENP Action Plans at the end of 2004. They are called 'bilateral' since the Mediterranean countries were each individually consulted before the drafting of the Action Plans. The Commission drew up Action Plans for Israel and all the Mashreq countries (Jordan, Lebanon, the West Bank & Gaza Strip, and Egypt)[470] except Syria. The Action Plans for Jor-

[470] The Egyptian Action Plan emphasises Egypt's unique geographical position and strategic relations with the Arab and African countries. For that reason, this Action Plan includes some exceptional

dan, Lebanon, Egypt, the PA and Israel state that the EU and these countries are closer together than ever before and will, as near neighbours, enforce their political and economic interdependence. The EU also has Action Plans for two Maghreb countries: Morocco and Tunisia. There are no Action Plans for Algeria and Libya. Since Algeria has no Action Plan, the Commission will continue to work closely on the implementation of its Euro-Med AA. The Action Plans are the most important instrument of the ENP and have been developed in close consultation with the Mediterranean countries concerned. They differ for each Mediterranean country as they are based on the principle of differentiation. The ENP Action Plans' legal basis is Article 207 TFEU. They offer a means to strengthen the Euro-Mediterranean relations, which is distinct from the possibilities available to European countries under Article 49 EU Treaty.[471] The Action Plans do not contain legally binding provisions. They are political commitments that set out the boundaries of the EU's relations with the Mediterranean countries. They do not replace but build on the existing Euro-Mediterranean AAs.

The Action Plans are defined by the authors Smith and Webber as 'umbrella documents, collecting together existing initiatives developed under the Euro-Med Association Agreements, as well as more specific technical provisions that often predate or run outside of the ENP.'[472]

2. The 'New Partnership Perspectives' of the ENP Action Plans

The Action Plans include New Partnership Perspectives (NPPs) relating to several subject matters which are also covered by the Euro-Med AAs. Compared with the Euro-Med integration goals, these NPPs should be *new or deeper Euro-Med integration aims*. The NPPs regarding the movement of goods, services, capital and persons between the Mediterranean countries and the EU will be outlined below (2.1). Furthermore, it will be analysed whether these NPPs really go beyond the aims of the Euro-Med AAs (2.2).

2.1 The 'New Partnership Perspectives' in the field of Euro-Med movement of goods, services, capital and persons

Each Action Plan includes a first NPP of moving beyond the existing Euro-Med relationship to a significant degree of economic integration, through a stake in the EU's internal market, in return for economic reform in the Mediterranean countries in general and approximation with EU law specifically. The European support for the economic progress in the Mediterranean countries by offering the Mediterranean countries deeper integration into the four freedoms of the EU

aspects since it must also provide for cooperation on international issues, such as peace and stability in the Middle East.

[471] COM (2004) 795 final, p. 2.

[472] Smith and Webber, cf., *supra* n. 469 at p. 79.

internal market can be considered as a 'positive conditionality.'[473] This NPP also involves the participation of the relevant Mediterranean countries in EU policies and programmes. In addition, the Moroccan Action Plan includes an NPP which specifically relates to the movement of persons. This Action Plan supports a dialogue on visa issues between the EU and Morocco, including the examination of visa facilitation in compliance with the Union's *acquis*.

All Action Plans promote a second NPP, which is the opening of economies to each other and the reduction of trade barriers. This NPP should stimulate investment and growth in the relevant Mediterranean countries. To open economies and reduce trade barriers, all Action plans, except the Egyptian one, aim to approximate economic legislation. The Egyptian Action Plan provides for the continuous upgrading of economic legislation.

A third NPP, figuring in all Action Plans, is the approximation of Mediterranean legislation with EU norms and standards in certain areas through mechanisms such as TAIEX.

Finally, all Action Plans promote the NPP of deepening trade and economic relations through the liberalisation of the agricultural and services sector. The Israeli Action Plan also particularly encourages the extension of these relations to the service sector, particularly financial services.

Progress in meeting these NPPs should be evaluated in sub-committees established by the Euro-Med AAs. On the basis of the evaluation of the sub-committees, the EU and its Mediterranean partner review the content of the Action Plan and decide on its adaptation and renewal. After three years, the EU and its Mediterranean partner consider the possibility of new contractual links, which could take the form of a 'European Neighbourhood Agreement.'

In conclusion, it can be stated that Euro-Mediterranean integration under the ENP umbrella builds upon the existing Euro-Med AAs, but should offer new forms of integration resulting in deeper integration than the Euro-Med AAs. In short, deeper economic integration in the ENP framework will be achieved through 4 NPPs: (1) the Mediterranean countries will get a stake in the EU internal market; (2) approximation of the economic legislation of the Mediterranean countries and that of the EU; (3) approximation of Mediterranean legislation with

[473] The ENP has not only been developed to enhance the economic chapter of the Barcelona Declaration, but also aims to contribute to the political-military cooperation between the EU and the Mediterranean countries. Under the EMP, Mediterranean countries have been reluctant to take part in discussions on political and security matters. Progress has been made in strengthening dialogue and cooperation since the Council launched several proposals on 19 March 2003 to open up the European Security and Defence Policy (ESDP) to the Mediterranean countries. The Mediterranean countries, however, have remained extremely reluctant to engage in dialogue. Under the ENP, actual participation in ESDP as part of the EU's CFSP is mentioned in the Action Plans of Jordan, Morocco and Tunisia. The mutual dialogue on ESDP has been integrated into the EMP bodies since November 2004. Consequently, the Mediterranean countries seem to be willing to participate in political and security debates, also for fear of terrorism and because of the spill-over effect of the Iraqi conflict. See S. Biscop, 'Opening up the ESDP to the South: A Comprehensive and Cooperative Approach to Euro-Mediterranean Security', 34 *Security Dialogue* (2003) pp. 183-197.

EU norms and standards in certain areas; and (4) bringing the liberalisation of services and agricultural goods within the scope of the Euro-Med AAs.

2.2 Are the 'New Partnership Perspectives' new?

The Action Plans build upon the existing Euro-Med AAs but should offer new forms of integration resulting in deeper integration than the Euro-Med AAs. Smith and Webber studied the NPPs as regards the political dialogue and security in the ENP. Their conclusion is that the Action Plans do not entail new initiatives as regards political and security issues. According to them, the Action Plans are based on the already existing EU priorities set out at the beginning of the ENP and reflect the tense balance between the EU and its partners.[474] Below, it will be examined whether the Action Plans contain new initiatives as regards the Euro-Mediterranean liberalisation of goods, services, capital and persons.[475] Before examining this, it was to be expected that the answer would be contrary to the conclusions of Smith and Webber. Europe has never been very effective in influencing political events in the Mediterranean area, but it has been very successful in establishing excellent trade relations with all Mediterranean partners. It is the first time that the question of whether the NPPs regarding integration into the EU internal market are original is examined.

2.2.1 *The NPP of getting a stake in the EU internal market*

The fact that the Mediterranean countries will integrate into the EU also figures in the Euro-Med AAs. The Euro-Med integration process under the EMP, however, has been limited to the economic field: the Euro-Med AAs contribute to integrating the economies of the partner countries into a wider economy and lay down detailed provisions on the gradual establishment of a free trade are by 2010. The Tunisia, Morocco and Jordan AA refer, in their preamble, to the social and economic modernisation that they have undertaken with the objective of the full integration of their economies in the world economies. The Israel AA promotes a 'further integration of Israel's economy into the European economy.'[476] So, no stake in the EU internal market of persons is offered to the Mediterranean countries under the EMP umbrella, not even when a fourth chapter was added to the Barcelona Declaration, called 'Migration, Social Integration and Social Security.' This chapter will lead to a better controlled migration management based on a EU preference-based system of immigration, which means that only highly qualified and very necessary workers from the Mediterranean countries are allowed into the EU.

[474] Smith and Webber, cf., *supra* n. 469 at p. 80.

[475] See I. Greilsammer and J.H.H. Weiler, eds., *Europe and Israel: Troubled Neighbours* (Berlin, Walter de Gruyter 1998) p. 3.

[476] M. Maresceau, *Bilateral Agreements Concluded by the EC, Académie de droit international, Recueil des cours* (Leiden, Martinus Nijhoff Publishers 2006) pp. 388-389.

At first sight, it can be stated that the 'NPP of offering a stake into the EU internal market' is new since it goes further than the Euro-Med integration goal under the EMP umbrella, which is the establishment of a free trade area. However, in 2006, in a Strategy Paper of the Commission, the Commission does not offer anymore a stake into the four freedoms of the EU internal market, but it seems that the economic integration through the ENP Action Plans is reduced by this ENP Strategy Paper of 2006 to the establishment of a free trade area of goods and services. If the Commission maintains this lower level of economic integration, same as under the EMP, it can be concluded that the NPP offers no original Euro-Med integration perspective after all.[477]

Eeckhout has an interesting opinion about the term 'association.' He believes that 'association' as used in the Euro-Med AA means that the EC Treaty (now: TFEU) must, in some policy areas, such as the internal market, be extended to the associated country (in this case the Mediterranean country).[478] According to the ECJ, association as used in the Euro-Med AA means that the non-member country (in this case the Mediterranean country) must, at least to a certain extent, 'take part in the Community system.' The reference to taking part in the Community system must, according to Eeckhout, in all likelihood be interpreted in material terms, which means, in the case of the Euro-Med AAs, that the EC Treaty (now: TFEU) must be extended to the Mediterranean country in certain policy areas, such as the internal market or competition policy.[479] The term 'association' in the Euro-Med AAs refers, according to Eeckhout, to the extension of the EU internal market as a whole, i.e., of goods, services, capital and persons. The NPP of offering a stake in the EU internal market under the ENP is no different from offering association under the EMP AAs.

In conclusion, it can be stated that this NPP is no longer original after the ENP Strategy Paper of 2006 choose a lower level of Euro-Med economic integration.[480] In this Strategy Paper there are no more references to the four freedoms of the EU internal market.

2.2.2 *The NPP of approximation of economic legislation of the Mediterranean countries and that of the EU*

The second NPP is not innovative since the Euro-Med AAs also provide for approximation of legislation through the 'approximation clause' which is included in all Euro-Med AAs. The Maghreb AAs stipulate that Algeria, Tunisia and Morocco shall bring their legislation closer to that of the EU in areas covered by the Euro-Med AA.[481] The other Mediterranean countries shall use their best

---

477 COM (2006) 726 final.

478 See Ch. IV, 2.2.1. *supra*, The concept of association.

479 *Idem.*

480 COM (2006) 726 final.

481 Art. 52 Morocco AA, for example, stipulates: 'Cooperation shall be aimed at helping Morocco to bring its legislation closer to that of the Community in areas covered by this Agreement.'

endeavours to approximate their respective laws in order to facilitate the implementation of the Euro-Med AAs.[482]

2.2.3 *The NPP of approximation of Mediterranean legislation with EU norms and standards in certain areas*

It is obvious that this NNP is not new either, as all Euro-Med AAs state that the Mediterranean countries shall use EU rules in standardisation, metrology, quality control and conformity assessment.[483] The objective of this harmonisation is to promote trade by aligning standards and technical requirements, reducing costs related to duplicative testing and certification and thus facilitating market access. The Tunisia AA serves as an example in this respect:

> 'Cooperation in standardisation and conformity assessment
> The Parties shall cooperate in developing: (a) the use of EC rules in standardisation, metrology, quality control and conformity assessment; (b) the updating of the Tunisian conformity assessment and metrology bodies or laboratories, leading eventually to the conclusion of mutual recognition agreements for conformity assessment; and (c) the bodies responsible for intellectual, industrial and commercial property and for standardisation and quality in Tunisia.'[484]

Egypt wishes to take the same cooperation measures but emphasises the recognition of conformity, in particular as regards sanitary and phytosanitary standards for agricultural products and foodstuffs.[485] Lebanon also aims to take the same measures and conclude mutual recognition agreements as soon as the conditions for them are met.[486] Jordan wants to cooperate in the same way and in due time and to the extent feasible to conclude agreements of mutual recognition of conformity assessment.[487] The Israel AA aims at reducing differences in standardisation and conformity assessment, but does not include these specific cooperation measures. The PA Interim AA also aims at cooperation to narrow the gap in standards and certification of goods and will discuss mutual recognition arrangements where appropriate.[488] The Tunisia and Morocco AA add that the parties shall take appropriate steps to promote the use by them of EU technical rules and European standards for industrial and agri-food products and certification procedures.[489] The Israel AA also aims at concluding, where appropriate, agreements on mutual recognition in the field of conformity assessment.[490]

---

[482] Art. 48 Egypt AA, for example, stipulates: 'The Parties shall use their best endeavours to approximate respective laws in order to facilitate the implementation of this Agreement.'

[483] Art. 55 Algeria AA; Arts. 40 and 51 Morocco AA; Arts. 40 and 51 Tunisia AA; Art. 47 Egypt AA; Art. 48 Lebanon AA and Art. 68 Jordan AA.

[484] Art. 55 Algeria AA; Art. 51 Tunisia AA; and Art. 51 Morocco AA.

[485] Art. 47 Egypt AA.

[486] Art. 48 Lebanon AA.

[487] Art. 68 Jordan AA.

[488] Art. 40 PA Interim AA.

[489] Art. 40 Tunisia AA and Art. 40 Morocco AA.

[490] Art. 47 Israel AA.

Besides these provisions in the different Euro-Med AAs, a number of important steps towards eventual harmonisation and/or mutual recognition of trade-related standards across the Euro-Mediterranean region have been achieved under the EMP umbrella. The harmonisation of economic legislation has already started on the basis of the Work Programme adopted at the Euro-Med Trade Ministerial Conference of Palermo in July 2003. The Euro-Med Ministers instructed the existing Working Group on Trade Measures to start addressing the approximation of legislation in the field of standards, technical regulations and conformity assessment procedures.[491] At the 4th Euro-Med Trade Ministerial Conference in Istanbul in July 2004, the Ministers acknowledged the substantial progress made by the Working Group with regard to the approximation of legislation in the field of standards, technical regulations and conformity assessment procedures.[492] A number of Mediterranean countries have identified their priority sectors and all have started becoming acquainted with the EU legislative approach.[493] The adoption of EU standards is most needed in areas where exports to the EU are important. In May 2005, at the Luxemburg Euro-Med Conference, the Ministers of Foreign Affairs again stressed the importance of the approximation of technical legislation in the area of standards and conformity assessment, since this harbours significant potential in terms of trade facilitation, investment attraction and, eventually, integration of economies.[494]

Furthermore, in 1999 Israel concluded a Mutual Recognition Agreement (MRA) with the EU in the chemical sector. The MRA concerns mutual recognition of OECD principles of good laboratory practice and compliance monitoring programmes between the EU and Israel.[495]

It is clear that this NPP is not new both since all Euro-Med AAs include similar provisions and, moreover, many important steps towards harmonisation and mutual recognition of trade-related standards across the Euro-Mediterranean region have been achieved under the EMP.

However, it should be noted that there are still important shortcomings as regards the approximation of Mediterranean legislation with EU norms and stan-

---

[491] Conclusions of the Euro-Med Trade Ministerial Conference in Palermo on 7 July 2003, 64 *Euromed Report* (2003) para. 6. The Ministers instructed the Working Group to implement a six-point work programme that defines the steps required to approximate legislation in this field: (1) identification of priority sectors; (2) acquaintance with the applicable EC legislation and conducting a gap analysis on the basis of the existing legislation; (3) transposition of the necessary framework legislation and sectoral legislation; (4) creation/reformation of existing institutions; (5) setting up of necessary certification and conformity assessment bodies; and (6) identification of technical assistance needs and making the most of existing programmes.

[492] For an overview of the progress in the approximation of legislation in the field of standards, technical regulations and conformity assessment procedures, see Annexes A, B and C to the Report on the Approximation of Legislation of 15 July 2004, available at: http://europa.eu.int/comm/enterprise/enterprise_policy/ind_coop_programmes/med/doc/f1947_en.pdf.

[493] Conclusions of the 4th Euro-Med Trade Ministerial Conference in Istanbul on 21 July 2004, 81 *Euromed Report* (2004).

[494] Conclusions of the 7th Euro-Mediterranean Conference of the Ministers of Foreign Affairs, Luxembourg, 30-31 May, 90 *Euromed Report* (2005) para. 31.

[495] *OJ* 1999 L 263/10.

dards. It is regrettable that the ENP Action Plans do not focus on these important shortcomings, such as the installation of infrastructure for testing, certification and accreditation bodies to carry out the conformity assessments and harmonisation of technical regulations. The adoption of harmonised European standards in the Mediterranean countries does not in itself remove all technical barriers to exports to the EU. The Mediterranean countries need institutions, as well as an appropriate system of voluntary product testing and certification and the accreditation of independent testing and certification bodies. This is a necessary step to allow products for export to the EU to be tested for conformity with EU regulations by domestic certification bodies. Brenton and Manchin also give a few examples of deficiencies of the Euro-Med AAs which the ENP Action Plans could have filled. They argue that the Euro-Med AAs are constrained by a lack of ambition with regard to technical regulations and conformity assessment systems. First, all Euro-Med AAs aim reducing differences in standardisation and conformity assessment, yet none of them mentions how to achieve these objectives. Second, the Euro-Med AAs envisage mutual recognition agreements but only if it is 'appropriate' or 'as soon as the conditions for them are met.'[496] This, too, could have been clarified in the ENP Action Plans.

2.2.4 *The NPP of bringing the liberalisation of services and agricultural goods under the scope of the Euro-Med AAs*

The fourth NPP – bringing the liberalisation of services and agricultural goods within the scope of the Euro-Med AAs – does not contain original prospects either, since the Euro-Med AAs include several provisions regarding the further liberalisation of trade in services. Morocco, Tunisia, Egypt and Israel, for example, have agreed to consider extending the scope of their Euro-Med AA to cover the liberalisation of the provision of services.[497] The EU and all Mediterranean countries also state in their Euro-Med AA that they shall progressively establish a greater liberalisation of their trade in agricultural, fishery and processed agricultural products.

2.2.5 *Sub-conclusion*

Contrary to expectations, it can be concluded that as regards the Euro-Med liberalisation of goods, services, capital and persons the NPPs are based on the already existing EU priorities, which do not aim at deeper Euro-Med integration compared with the Euro-Med integration aims set out in the Euro-Med AAs.

---

[496] P. Brenton and M. Manchin, *Trade Policy Issues for the Euro-Med Partnership* (Brussels, CEPS 2003) p. 9.

[497] Art. 31 Morocco AA; Art. 31 Tunisia AA; Art. 30 Egypt AA, and Art. 29 Israel AA. For example, Art 30 Egypt AA states: '1. The Parties will consider extending the scope of the Agreement to include the right of establishment of companies of one Party in the territory of another Party and the liberalisation of the supply of services by companies of one Party to service consumers in another Party.'

3. The Action Plan 'priorities' regarding the Euro-Med movement of goods, services, capital and persons

The Action Plans are the result of bilateral negotiations between the EU and its Mediterranean partners. The Mediterranean partners were able to express their wishes while drafting the Action Plans. Consequently, each Mediterranean country has identified different priorities as regards the Euro-Med liberalisation of goods, services, capital and persons. Some prioritise further integration into the EU internal market of goods, others prefer to be more deeply integrated into the EU internal market of services, etc. All Action Plans contain a different set of priorities, all of which of equal importance. Below, the different priorities of each Mediterranean country will be presented.

This presentation is necessary to establish from which freedom(s) of the EU internal market (goods, services, capital and persons) the Mediterranean country prefers to benefit.

The Moroccan Action Plan emphasises the negotiation of an agreement on liberalising trade in services. In addition, Morocco wants to develop a climate favourable to foreign direct investment, growth and sustainable development. The Action Plan moreover stresses the importance of effective management of migration flows, including the signing of a readmission agreement with the EU and the facilitation of the movement of persons in accordance with the Union's *acquis*. Morocco also prioritises the integration of the Moroccan electricity market into the European electricity market pursuant to the Memorandum of Understanding of 2 December 2003 on the gradual integration of the electricity markets of the Maghreb countries into the EU's internal electricity market.

The Tunisian Action Plan focuses on cooperation on labour issues and social policy and the gradual approximation of Tunisian legislation to EU rules and regulations. In addition, Tunisia and the EU should facilitate trade in goods and services, including through the negotiation of free trade agreements. Another priority is the approximation of technical regulations, standards and conformity assessment procedures. Tunisia also prioritises the development of conditions favourable to foreign direct investment. Finally, the Action Plan emphasises the importance of the effective management of migration flows, including the possibility of concluding a readmission agreement with the EU and the facilitation of the movement of persons within existing structures in accordance with the Union's *acquis*.

The Egyptian Action Plan prioritises the increase of economic integration with the EU. For that reason, Egypt and the EU aim to take steps to gradually liberalise trade in services, the right of establishment and trade in agriculture, processed agricultural products and fishery, namely by upgrading the quality of Egypt's agricultural production through the improvement of sanitary and phytosanitary standards. The Action Plan mentions a second priority, which is the liberalisation of capital movement through the elimination of institutional, regulatory and administrative obstacles so as to attract increasing national and foreign investments. Third, Egypt should identify areas suitable for gradual regulatory upgrading and approximation with EU technical legislation, standards and conformity assessment procedures. Fourth, Egypt and the EU must strengthen cooperation on migration-related issues, including the effective joint management of migration flows, legal and illegal migration, readmission, facilitation of the legal movement of individuals, equal treatment and social integration for legal migrants, and asylum issues.

The Israeli Action Plan also emphasises economic integration with the EU. Therefore, Israel and the EU aim to take measures to liberalise trade in services, in particular financial services. The Action Plan explicitly states that the liberalisation of financial services takes place with a view to preparing Israel for 'participation' in the EU internal market. In addition, Israel and the EU should enhance the existing economic dialogue and identify areas relevant for regulatory approximation with EU legislation. Finally, they should strengthen cooperation on migration-related issues.

The Jordanian Action Plan's main concern is the enhancement of Jordan's export potential. To that end, Jordan and the EU should further liberalise trade in goods and agriculture, simplify customs legislation, improve industrial standards and modernise the sanitary and phytosanitary systems. Second, Jordan and the EU want to prepare for a progressive liberalisation of trade in services. Finally, they also underline the importance of migration and facilitation of movement of persons in conformity with the Union's *acquis*, whereby in particular the scope for visa facilitation for short stays should be examined.

The Lebanese Action Plan stresses the enhancement of Lebanon's export potential by further liberalisation of trade in goods and agriculture, improvement of industrial standards and modernisation of the sanitary and phytosanitary systems. In addition, Lebanon and the EU should prepare for progressive liberalisation of trade in services and the right of establishment. Finally, the Action Plan stresses the organisation of migratory flows and dialogue on visa issues.

The PA Action Plan gives priority to full implementation of the Interim Association Agreement given the current political situation in the West Bank and Gaza Strip, but sets no concrete priorities as regards the participation of the PA in the EU internal market. The instability in the Middle East, more specifically the ongoing Israeli-Palestinian conflict, resulted in a number of constraints and limitations in the PA Action Plan. The continuing occupation of the West Bank and Gaza Strip, including settlement activity and the closure policy, has led to restrictions to movement of goods, services, capital and persons between the West Bank and Gaza Strip and the EU. This conflict has affected the scope of possible actions under the PA Action Plan.[498] The limitations on the PA pending the creation of a Palestinian state were also taken into account when the PA Action Plan was drawn up. Contrary to the limited scope of actions provided for in the PA Action Plan, the Israeli Action Plan emphasises the special position of

[498] However, since the start of the EMP in 1995, the PA has been considered as a full partner of the EU. See Communication from the Commission to the European Parliament and Council on the future European Union Economic Assistance to the West Bank and the Gaza Strip, COM (95) 505 final, 23 October 1995, p. 6.

Israel.[499] The Israeli AP refers to the Essen Council in December 1994, where the European Council considered the following:[500]

> '(t)hat Israel, on account of its high level of economic development, should enjoy special status in its relations with the EU on the basis of reciprocity and common interest.'

In short, it can be stated that all Mediterranean countries are very ambitious. All Mediterranean countries, except the PA and Israel, prioritise the Euro-Med liberalisation of all four freedoms: goods, services, capital and persons. However, some relevant observations should be made:
(1) Morocco and Israel had already reached a high degree of liberalisation of goods. At the moment, Israel and Morocco therefore give priority to the liberalisation of services. They are prepared to negotiate an agreement on the liberalisation of trade in services.
(2) Egypt does not give priority to the liberalisation of trade in goods in general, but prioritises the improvement of its agricultural sector, that is, trade in agriculture, processed agricultural products and fishery. Therefore, the quality of Egypt's agricultural production has to be upgraded.
(3) For Israel, the liberalisation of the movement of persons is not a priority issue. Jordan, Morocco and Tunisia, however, opt for far-reaching measures as regards the movement of persons and wish to align their relevant legislation with the Union's *acquis*.
(4) An unfortunate situation has arisen for the PA: the Commission noted that it was not possible for the PA to set priorities in view of the conflict between Israel and the PA.
(5) Only the Israeli Action Plan explicitly emphasises the participation of Israel in the EU internal market. This confirms the advanced and special position of Israel among the other Mediterranean countries.

4. Provisions in the ENP Action Plans to stimulate the integration of the Mediterranean countries into the EU internal market

All Action Plans contain provisions with actions that the EU and its Mediterranean partner should take in order to achieve the abovementioned priorities.

---

[499] Israel's special status already became clear in the 70s. Israel's exports to the EEC have become less similar to those of the Mediterranean countries, but increasingly comparable to those of the developed countries. J. Silber and Z.M. Berrebi, 'The 1975 Free Trade Agreement and Its Impact on Israeli Exports to the EEC', in I. Greilsammer and J.H.H. Weiler, eds., *Europe and Israel: Troubled Neighbours* (Berlin, Walter de Gruyter 1998) p. 145, and R. Pomfret and B. Toren, *Israel and the European Common Market: An Appraisal of the 1975 Free Trade Agreement* (Tubingen, J.C.B Mohr 1980) pp. 23-25.

[500] Communication from the Commission, 'A Strong European Neighbourhood Policy', 5 December 2007, COM (2007) 774 final.

Table IV: Priorities of the different Mediterranean countries in the ENP Action Plans as regards the integration of the Mediterranean countries into the EU internal market (June 2009)

	GOODS	SERVICES	CAPITAL	PERSONS
Morocco		+ (agreement on services)	+	+
Tunisia	+	+ (agreement on services)	+	+
Algeria: no AP				
Egypt	+ (mainly agricultural products)	+	+	+
Israel		+	+	-
PA	-	-	-	-
Jordan	+	+	+	+
Lebanon	+	+	+	+
Libya: no AP				
Syria: no AP				

Below is an analysis of all provisions of the ENP Action Plans that contribute to the achievement of the priority issues. It has already become clear that the priorities of most Mediterranean countries are aimed at further integrating all four freedoms of the EU internal market. This analysis will clarify to what extent the Mediterranean countries and the EU wish to integrate in each of the four freedoms of the EU internal market, which is not the same as the extent of integration that the Mediterranean countries have achieved in reality. Only the ENP Progress Reports present an overview of the real achievements.

4.1 The 'movement of goods' provisions in the ENP Action Plans

All Action Plans include provisions on the 'movement of goods' between the Mediterranean countries and the EU. The movement of goods between the Mashreq countries and the EU and that between the Maghreb countries and the EU will be dealt with separately. The Mashreq and Maghreb Action Plans first consider the movement of agricultural and/or fishery products, then focus on the movement of industrial products and finally reflect on the movement of food products.

4.1.1 *The Mashreq Action Plans*

The Mashreq Action Plans propose further liberalisation of trade in *agricultural, processed agricultural and fishery products*. The Egyptian Action Plan also recommends increasing the quality of Egyptian agricultural products to improve Egypt's export capability. The Mashreq Action Plans advises facilitating market access for *industrial products* and continuing the implementation of the Palermo

Action Plan for the Free Movement of Industrial Products of 7 July 2003.[501] According to the Palermo Action Plan, the EU and its Mediterranean partners should start bilateral negotiations leading to Agreements on Conformity Assessment and Acceptance of Industrial Products (ACAAs).[502] The ACAAs should allow certain products to freely enter the European and Mediterranean markets, without further requirements. The Jordanian Action Plan explicitly states that Jordan will analyse its own legislation in order to remove discrimination against imported products and requests interested Jordanian private sector associations to comment on new Jordanian draft legislation. Furthermore, the Action Plans advise the Mashreq countries to harmonise the remaining national standards with European and international standards for industrial products. In addition, they should cooperate in the field of legislation on liability for defective products and general product safety, including market surveillance. Jordan wishes to strengthen the institutions in charge of standardisation, accreditation, conformity assessment, metrology and market surveillance. It also wants to integrate these institutions within European and international structures. The Israeli Action Plan goes further: Israel and the EU aim to develop cooperation on e-commerce issues.[503] Particular attention is to be given to the issue of digital signatures within the framework of Directive 99/93/EC on electronic signatures.[504] Contrary to the advanced provisions concerning the movement of industrial goods in the Israeli Action Plan, the PA Action Plan includes no provisions about the movement of industrial goods whatsoever.

All Action Plans specifically refer to the *movement of food products*, since the Mediterranean countries and Europe wish to increase food safety for their consumers. The EU and the Mediterranean partners aim at cooperating in the field of sanitary and phytosanitary issues and to explore possible areas of cooperation. In addition, Israel wishes to explore the possibility to increase convergence of (1) Israeli legislation with EU legislation on sanitary (live animals and animal products) and of phytosanitary issues (plant hygiene, plant variety and quality) and (2) food legislation in compliance with EU food safety principles. Israel also wants adapt Israeli legislation regarding foodstuff labelling. Jordan should draw up a list of measures for gradual legislative approximation towards the princi-

---

[501] The Palermo Action Plan for the Free Movement of Industrial Products was approved by the July 2003 Euro-Mediterranean Conference of Trade Ministers. Implementation of the Palermo Action Plan differs for each Mediterranean country, depending on the will of each Mediterranean partner to make progress, on its state of legislation, its alignment with EU legislation, its infrastructure and its technical assistance.

[502] The legal basis is Art. 207 TFEU.

[503] Directive 2000/31/EC of the European Parliament and of the Council of 8 June 2000 on certain legal aspects of information society services, in particular electronic commerce, in the Internal Market (*OJ* L 178, 17.7.2000, pp. 1-16) is the basic legal framework for electronic commerce in the European internal market. The Directive removes obstacles to cross-border online services in the EU. Online services are, for example, online newspapers, selling of books, financial services and travel services, advertising, professional services provided by lawyers, doctors and estate agents, and entertainment services.

[504] Directive 1999/93/EC of the European Parliament and of the Council of 13 December 1999 on a Community framework for electronic signatures, *OJ* L 013 of 19 January 2000, pp. 12-20.

ples of EU legislation: sanitary and phytosanitary, food and animal traceability and hygiene. Jordan wishes to increase convergence with EU food safety principles and general foodstuff labelling requirements and to examine potential for progressive abolition of pre-market approval systems for food products. The PA also wishes to enhance veterinary and phytosanitary standards in order to improve access to the EU market.

4.1.2 *The Maghreb Action Plans*

Tunisia, Morocco and the EU aim to further liberalise the movement of goods. Tunisia and Morocco should continue the liberalisation of *agricultural products and processed agricultural products* and initiate talks on the gradual liberalisation of fishery products. Concerning agricultural products, Morocco should ensure the introduction of a coherent agricultural policy with the aim of convergence towards the necessary conditions for establishment of a Morocco-EU free trade area.

Concerning the *movement of industrial goods*, Morocco and Tunisia have to facilitate market access for industrial products and bring their legislation on industrial products further into line with international and European rules and practices. In the short term, they want to pursue implementation of the Palermo Action Plan for the Free Movement of Industrial Products of 7 July 2003. This means approximation of legislation on standards, technical regulation and conformity assessment. To this end, they should identify priority sectors and analyse the applicable EU legislation, highlighting discrepancies with existing national legislation. Finally, they must strengthen the institutions responsible for standardisation, conformity assessment, metrology and market supervision and their incorporation into European and international structures. In the medium term, they will bring national standards into line with European and international standards for industrial products and abolish conflicting national standards. They should also adopt a programme for the harmonisation of conformity assessment legislation and procedures and implement the necessary framework and sectoral legislation. They are willing to negotiate an ACAA in sectors of common interest where the legislation is applied to the same standards as in the EU.

Concerning the *movement of food products*, Morocco and the EU want to exchange know-how and experience on upgrading food legislation. Furthermore, there should be progressive approximation to EU veterinary and phytosanitary rules. There should also be convergence towards progressive application of rules on food hygiene and food safety in agricultural and food production and on the labelling of food products. They have to regulate and ban the sale of certain substances, including phyto-pharmaceuticals, without creating unnecessary barriers to trade, and introduce schemes to monitor residues of pharmaceuticals in animals, products of animal origin, plant products, food products and animal feed. In addition, they must step up efforts to progressively eradicate rabies and other major animal diseases in Morocco, including foot-and-mouth disease and sheep pox, and establish a phytosanitary statute with regard to the organisms mentioned in Directive 2000/29/EC. They wish to examine the possibility of cooperation under the early warning system. Tunisia should gradually implement the EU animal and plant health rules relating to imports of live animals, products of animal origin, plants and plant products. Tunisia should ensure controls at production level, not just on the finished product. It must also progressively apply the EU's food safety rules for the production of agricultural and food products and for production level controls. The EU wants to help Tunisia to organise public campaigns to eradicate certain diseases or harmful organisms identified in the Union's *acquis* which are present in Tunisia. Morocco and Tunisia aim to develop a strategy on institution-building, including laboratories, as well as develop *instruments and organs* of trade facilitation.[505] They wish also take more steps to deal with animal diseases.

In the light of gradual future integration of Maghreb *energy markets* into the EU internal energy market, there should be a Maghreb electricity and gas market which is in line with the principles of the EU internal electricity and gas markets. To this end, the EU and Tunisia/Morocco should step up energy policy dialogue.

4.1.3 *Sub-conclusion*

At first sight, Tunisia and Morocco seem to have Action Plans similar to those of the Mashreq. All (except for the PA one) provide for the further liberalisation of agricultural products and industrial goods through the implementation of the Palermo Action Plan: the Mediterranean countries should facilitate European market access for industrial products, bring their legislation on industrial products further into line with international and European rules and practices and begin negotiations for ACAAs.

The Maghreb countries, however, had already reached a higher level of liberalisation of goods with the EU. Therefore, the Maghreb Action Plans include more detailed measures as to the movement of goods: the Maghreb countries aim to work towards an enhanced *quality* of products, a strengthening of *instruments and organs* of trade facilitation and the movement of *energy* products. This improved quality should be achieved through, for example, a ban on the sale of certain substances, including phytopharmaceuticals, through efforts to eradicate rabies and other major animal diseases, and through controls at production level.

In many places, the Israeli Action Plan reflects the special status of Israel in the ENP framework, which is in profound disparity with the PA Action Plan. The PA Action Plan only provides for the gradual liberalisation of trade in agricultural and fishery products. In the words of the PA Action Plan, 'the prevailing

[505] This involves (1) increasing support to the Committee for the Facilitation of Procedures (COFPRO), chaired by a representative of the private sector, and to the administrative bodies responsible for facilitation; (2) automating the workflow and decision-making processes of technical control agencies linked to the TTN (Tunisia Trade Net) system by means of 'back-office' re-engineering; (3) implementing an integrated risk management system at the level of each technical control agency; (4) implementing a digital database on current technical control regulations; and (5) building the capacity of the authorities responsible for information and enforcement of the legislation.

political situation in the West Bank and Gaza Strip, is the cause of this lack of proposed actions. The Commission states that the PA should develop competencies, required knowledge and skills for trade negotiations. The almost non-existing PA Action Plan reflects very well the role which the EU nowadays is willing to take in the Israeli-PA conflict. The Commission only mentions that Israel should work towards the facilitation of Palestinian trade, but does not state how Israel should facilitate Palestinian trade.

Table V: Actions for further integration of the Mediterranean countries into the EU internal market of goods (June 2009)

	Measures for further integration into the EU internal market of goods
Morocco	Agricultural goods: continuation of the liberalisation process Fishery products: start of the liberalisation process Industrial products: ACAAs + strengthening of institutions on conformity assessment Food products: alignment with EU legislation on food safety Energy products: integration of Morocco's energy market into the EU internal energy market + Enhanced quality of all goods through, for example, a ban on the sale of certain substances, including phytopharmaceuticals, and controls at production level, not only on the finished product
Tunisia	Agricultural goods: continuation of the liberalisation process Fishery products: start of the liberalisation process Industrial products: ACAAs + strengthening of institutions on conformity assessment Food products: alignment with EU legislation on food safety Energy products: integration of Tunisia's energy market into the EU internal energy market. + Enhanced quality of all goods through, for example, a ban on the sale of certain substances, including phyto-pharmaceuticals, and controls at production level, not only on the finished product
Algeria: no AP	
Egypt	Agricultural and fishery products: further liberalisation needed + increase in quality of agricultural products Industrial products: ACAAs + alignment with EU legislation on product liability Food products: alignment with the relevant EU legislation
Israel	Agricultural and fishery products: further liberalisation needed Industrial products: ACAAs + alignment with EU legislation on product liability + cooperation on e-commerce issues Food products: alignment with the relevant EU legislation
PA	Increase in food safety
Jordan	Agricultural and fishery products: further liberalisation needed Industrial products: ACAAs + alignment with EU legislation on product liability Food products: alignment with the relevant EU legislation
Lebanon	Agricultural and fishery products: further liberalisation needed Industrial products: ACAAs + alignment with EU legislation on product liability + strengthening of institutions on conformity assessment Food products: alignment with the relevant EU legislation
Libya: no AP	
Syria: no AP	

4.2 Competition, state aid and intellectual property rights

4.2.1 *Overview of the relevant provisions in all ENP Action Plans*

Competition rules prevent companies from raising barriers that reduce the benefits gained from the liberalisation of goods, services, capital and persons. With a view to homogeneity, the same competition rules should apply to all companies throughout the Euro-Med free trade area. The Euro-Med free trade area should provide for equal competition between the EU and the Mediterranean companies but also amongst Mediterranean companies. The Egyptian Action Plan states that the EU should adopt implementing rules on competition by 1 June 2009.[506] Egypt must also align its competition law with that of the EU and establish an independent and adequately-resourced competition authority. The Jordanian Action Plan stipulates that the Association Council should adopt a decision on implementing rules on competition. Jordan must develop competition legislation and an anti-trust control regime compatible with that of the EU. Lebanon wants to adopt and enforce draft competition law and establish an independent and adequately-resourced competition authority. The Israeli Action Plan contains no competition provisions, except for a few on state aid. The PA Action Plan contains no competition measures either. Morocco has to implement the decision of the Association Council on the competition rules implementing legislation.[507] It aims to develop its legislation in line with EU legislation. Moreover, it should build administrative capacity for the enforcement of competition law and identify possible cooperation measures (market analysis techniques, conduct of competition investigations, merger control, and dealing with disputes). In addition, Morocco should build a judicial enforcement mechanism compatible with the EU enforcement mechanisms.[508] This mechanism will ensure the right of appeal to independent courts against anti-trust decisions and ensure the specialised training of judges dealing with competition cases. Morocco aims to reinforce the administrative capacity and decision-making powers of its competition bodies.[509] Finally, Morocco wants to assess the implementation of the current Moroccan legislative framework, including the principles of non-discrimination, transparency and procedural fairness. Tunisia must develop legislation and a control mechanism compatible with those in the EU. It has to adopt a decision of

---

[506] Art. 34(2) of the Egypt AA states the following: 'The Association Council shall, within five years of the entry into force of the Agreement, adopt by decision the necessary rules for the implementation of paragraph 1. Until these rules are adopted, the provisions of Article 23 shall be applied as regards the implementation of paragraph 1(iii).'

[507] Art. 36(3) of the Morocco AA states the following: 'The Association Council shall, within five years of the entry into force of this Agreement, adopt the necessary rules for the implementation of paragraphs 1 and 2. Until these rules are adopted, the provisions of the Agreement on interpretation and application of Articles VI, XVI and XXIII of the General Agreement on Tariffs and Trade shall be applied as the rules for the implementation of paragraph 1(c) and related parts of paragraph 2.'

[508] Art. 36 AA.

[509] See Arts. 37-38 of the Morocco AA.

the Association Council on the implementing provisions of Article 36(3) of the Association Agreement.[510]

All Action Plans contain similar state aid provisions, except for the PA Action Plan, which does not contain such provisions. First, they stipulate that there should be a state aids control regime and legislation meeting the requirements of the Union's *acquis* for each sector that participates in the European internal market. There has to be a prohibition of state aid which distorts trade between the EU and the Mediterranean country, a system of prohibition and ex-ante control of state aid, and a procedure between the EU and the Mediterranean country to settle cases that distort competition. Second, they also agree on a uniform definition of state aid which is compatible with that of the EU and on the development of a national mechanism for collecting information on state aid.

Movement of goods and services also goes hand in hand with intellectual property rights. All Action Plans include similar provisions on intellectual property rights. First, they all, except for those of Israel and Egypt, aim to strengthen the level of protection in order to reach a level comparable with that of the EU. To this end, they wish to explore the possibility of applying key elements from the EU *acquis*. All Action Plans, except for the Israeli one, provide for the accession to the main international agreements – including the conventions provided for by the Association Agreement – and the application of international standards. Israel and Egypt wish to enhance the dialogue on intellectual property issues, including, for example, data protection and enhancement of enforcement through a dialogue with prosecutors.

4.2.2 *Sub-conclusion*

All Action Plans, except for those of Israel and the PA, include interesting competition measures which truly aim at a better Euro-Med liberalisation of goods through the strengthening of their competition rules. Israel already possesses a good functioning competition system in line with the European competition rules. First, the Action Plans provide for the alignment of their competition legislation with EU legislation. Second, they aim for the establishment of competition enforcement bodies. The Moroccan Action Plan contains the most advanced measures in this respect, as Morocco aims to establish an administrative and a judicial competition body as well as a national competition authority in line with the EU rules. Third, decisions taken by the Association Council concerning competition rules should be adopted.

The Action Plans contain comparable state aid provisions. The relevant Mediterranean countries should find a uniform definition of state aid, provide for state

[510] Art. 36(3) of the Tunisia AA states the following: 'The Association Council shall, within five years of the entry into force of this Agreement, adopt the necessary rules for the implementation of paragraphs 1 and 2. Until these rules are adopted, the provisions of the Agreement on interpretation and application of Articles VI, XVI and XXIII of the General Agreement on Tariffs and Trade shall be applied as the rules for the implementation of paragraph 1(c) and related parts of paragraph 2.'

aid legislation and create a state aid control mechanism in line with the Union's *acquis*. They also include similar provisions on intellectual property rights. Their aim is to reach a level of protection of intellectual property rights comparable to that of the EU.

Table VI: Actions for further integration of the Mediterranean countries into the EU internal market of goods through the improvement of the functioning of Euro-Med competition law (June 2009)

	Competition law measures for further integration into the EU internal market of goods
Morocco	• Assessment of the implementation of the current Moroccan legislative framework, including respect for the principles of non-discrimination, transparency and procedural fairness • Alignment of its competition legislation with EU legislation • Reinforcement of the competition enforcement body in line with EU rules • Adoption of decisions taken by the Association Council concerning competition rules
Tunisia	• Consolidation of the status of the Competition Council, in particular by guaranteeing its independence and ensuring adequate staffing levels and budgetary resources and by endowing it with appropriate powers, notably for decision making, enforcement, effective sanctions and own investigations • Ensuring the right of appeal to an independent court against decisions on anti-trust; • Adoption of decisions taken by the Association Council concerning competition rules • Assessment of the current Tunisian legislative framework and its implementation, in particular respect for the principles of non-discrimination, transparency and procedural fairness.
Algeria: no AP	
Egypt	• Alignment of their competition legislation with EU legislation • Establishment of a competition enforcement body • Adoption of implementing rules on competition (see Art. 34(2) Euro-Med AA), for which the deadline is five years after the entry into force of the Association Agreement (1/6/2009)
Israel	/
PA	/
Jordan	• Alignment of its competition legislation with EU legislation • Strengthening of the Competition Directorate of the Ministry of Industry and Trade and other concerned institutions • Adoption of decisions taken by the Association Council concerning competition rules
Lebanon	• Adoption and enforcement of the draft competition law • Establishment of a competition enforcement body
Libya: no AP	
Syria: no AP	

4.3 The provisions on the movement of services, including the right of establishment, in the ENP Action Plans

4.3.1 *The Euro-Med movement of services*

The majority of the Action Plans provide for the movement of services. There is, however, a profound discrepancy between them. Some Action Plans are still in an initial phase as regards the movement of services, while others already mention the conclusion of a Euro-Med Economic Agreement on Services. Below, an overview of the movement of services in the Action Plans will be given, starting with the Action Plan that does not mention the subject and ending with the Action Plan with the most advanced provisions in this field.

The PA Action Plan includes no provisions as regards the Euro-Med movement of services.[511] The Lebanese Action Plan refers to the development of a strategy to enhance the competitiveness of the Lebanese services sector, including regulatory and administrative simplification for Lebanese and EU sectors. The Egyptian Action Plan recommends facilitating the supply of services and removing identified barriers. The Jordanian Action Plan provides for a gradual abolition of restrictions on supply of services. The EU aims to support Jordan to prepare for future liberalisation of trade in services in selected sectors. Jordan wants to proceed with consultations with its private economic operators to identify sectors for potential cooperation and explore possibilities of facilitating the supply of services and removing identified barriers. Israel and the EU promote the opening of bilateral negotiations on liberalisation of services, in which regard account should be taken of the specific nature of the Israeli economy, the overall objectives set in the conclusions of the Euro-Med Ministerial Meetings and the objectives set in the draft Framework Protocol for Liberalisation of Services among Euro-Mediterranean partners,[512] particularly mutual recognition of professional services. Morocco wants a gradual liberalisation of trade in services between Morocco and the EU. Therefore, Moroccan legislation should be screened with a view to concluding an agreement on trade in services. The EU and Morocco aim to exchange experience and know-how on legislation with a view to convergence with the EU's regulatory framework. Concerning the movement of financial services, they wish to develop a regulatory framework for the supervision of financial markets converging towards the EU's. Tunisia aims to gradually eliminate restrictions on trade in services with the EU in a significant number of services and negotiate an agreement to liberalise trade in services in

[511] Nor does the PA-EC Interim AA contain any provisions about the movement of services and the right of establishment. All other Euro-Med AAs include such provisions.

[512] This Framework Protocol was adopted at a Euro-Med meeting held in Istanbul in July 2004. It is also known as the Istanbul Framework Protocol and is not *per se* an agreement creating rights and obligations between Euro-Med parties. It should be considered as a template which Ministers recommend using for possible negotiations on economic integration agreements between Euro-Med countries.

accordance with Article V GATS.[513] The EU and Tunisia should contribute to finalisation of the Framework Protocol for Liberalisation of Services in the Euro-Med services working party, launch bilateral negotiations on the conclusion of a free trade area in services, exchange experience and know-how regarding existing legislation in the EU, identify national priorities and draw up an appropriate schedule of negotiations in the service sector with the EU.

[513] Art. V of the GATS provides for economic integration agreements on services.
Art. V.1 states the following: 'This Agreement shall not prevent any of its Members from being a party to or entering into an agreement liberalizing trade in services between or among the parties to such an agreement, provided that such an agreement: (a) has substantial sectoral coverage (note: this condition is understood in terms of number of sectors, volume of trade affected and modes of supply. In order to meet this condition, agreements should not provide for the *a priori* exclusion of any mode of supply); (b) provides for the absence or elimination of substantially all discrimination, in the sense of Article XVII, between or among the parties, in the sectors covered under subparagraph (a), through: (i) elimination of existing discriminatory measures, and/or (ii) prohibition of new or more discriminatory measures, either at the entry into force of that agreement or on the basis of a reasonable time-frame, except for measures permitted under Articles XI, XII, XIV and XIV bis.
2. In evaluating whether the conditions under paragraph 1(b) are met, consideration may be given to the relationship of the agreement to a wider process of economic integration or trade liberalization among the countries concerned.
3. (a) Where developing countries are parties to an agreement of the type referred to in paragraph 1, flexibility shall be provided for regarding the conditions set out in paragraph 1, particularly with reference to subparagraph (b) thereof, in accordance with the level of development of the countries concerned, both overall and in individual sectors and subsectors; (b) Notwithstanding paragraph 6, in the case of an agreement of the type referred to in paragraph 1 involving only developing countries, more favourable treatment may be granted to juridical persons owned or controlled by natural persons of the parties to such an agreement.
4. Any agreement referred to in paragraph 1 shall be designed to facilitate trade between the parties to the agreement and shall not in respect of any Member outside the agreement raise the overall level of barriers to trade in services within the respective sectors or subsectors compared to the level applicable prior to such an agreement.
5. If, in the conclusion, enlargement or any significant modification of any agreement under paragraph 1, a Member intends to withdraw or modify a specific commitment inconsistently with the terms and conditions set out in its Schedule, it shall provide at least 90 days advance notice of such modification or withdrawal and the procedure set forth in paragraphs 2, 3 and 4 of Article XXI shall apply.
6. A service supplier of any other Member that is a juridical person constituted under the laws of a party to an agreement referred to in paragraph 1 shall be entitled to treatment granted under such agreement, provided that it engages in substantive business operations in the territory of the parties to such agreement.
7. (a) Members which are parties to any agreement referred to in paragraph 1 shall promptly notify any such agreement and any enlargement or any significant modification of that agreement to the Council for Trade in Services. They shall also make available to the Council such relevant information as may be requested by it. The Council may establish a working party to examine such an agreement or enlargement or modification of that agreement and to report to the Council on its consistency with this Article; (b) Members which are parties to any agreement referred to in paragraph 1 which is implemented on the basis of a time-frame shall report periodically to the Council for Trade in Services on its implementation. The Council may establish a working party to examine such reports if it deems such a working party necessary; (c) Based on the reports of the working parties referred to in subparagraphs (a) and (b), the Council may make recommendations to the parties as it deems appropriate.
8. A Member which is a party to any agreement referred to in paragraph 1 may not seek compensation for trade benefits that may accrue to any other Member from such agreement.'

4.3.2 *The Euro-Med right of establishment*

The PA Action Plan is the only one that does not include provisions on the right of establishment. The Egyptian Action Plan states that Egypt will liberalise the establishment of companies and foreign investment and progressively remove obstacles to establishment. Jordan and the EU aim to remove obstacles to the establishment and operation of companies. The Jordanian Action Plan describes in detail how this should be effectuated. Companies should be able to function in a suitable environment and reciprocal national treatment should be guaranteed for EU and Jordanian subsidiaries, companies or branches. The EU and Jordan should work towards convergence with key principles of international and EU rules and standards including the establishment of a public register of undertakings and a national gazette for the publication of company data and should ensure control of the incorporation of a company or the compatibility of certain acts in accordance with national laws and regulations. Lebanon wishes to review its national legislation with a view to identifying measures to facilitate the establishment of companies, including foreign-owned companies, and work towards the progressive removal of barriers to establishment. Israel and the EU promote greater freedom in the areas of establishment and foreign investment and therefore aim to widen the scope of their Euro-Med AA. The EU and Israel wish to carry out an assessment of the scope for legislative approximation with a view to inclusion of this sector in a free trade agreement and ultimately Israel's participation in the EU internal market for financial services.

The Moroccan Action Plan promotes a suitable environment for companies and the screening of Moroccan legislation on establishment so as to identify barriers to establishment with a view to widening the scope of the Euro-Med AA in relation to establishment. In addition, the scope of the Euro-Med AA should be extended to include companies' right of establishment in the territory of the other party.[514] Tunisia and the EU promote greater freedom in relation to establishment and foreign investment. Therefore, a comparative study must be made of Tunisian and EU legal systems regarding all aspects of company establishment, to identify in particular suggestions for improvements that would encourage foreign investment. There should also be a screening by Tunisia of national legislation so as to identify barriers to establishment. Tunisia and the EU wish to ensure that the conditions for establishment of companies are not more restrictive than when the Euro-Med AA was concluded and they want to widen the scope of the Euro-Med AA to include the right of establishment.

4.3.3 *Sub-conclusion*

All Action Plans, except for the PA one, provide for a kind of Euro-Med movement of services, but from these ENP Action Plans it can be seen that there are many differences between the Mediterranean countries as regards the Euro-Med

[514] This should happen on the basis of the review clause in Art. 31 AA.

Table VII: Actions for further integration of the Mediterranean countries into the EU internal market of services (June 2009)

	Measures for further integration into the EU internal market of services, including the right of establishment
Morocco	• Gradual liberalisation of trade in services between Morocco and the EU through screening of Moroccan legislation with a view to concluding an *Economic Agreement on the Liberalisation of Services* with the EU, by contributing to the finalisation of the Palermo Action Plan and by opening bilateral negotiations on services on the basis of Article 31 of the Euro-Med AA in accordance with Article V GATS. • Liberalisation of the right of establishment of companies (not persons) by continuing the screening of Moroccan legislation on establishment so as to identify barriers and by extending the scope of the Euro-Med AA to include companies' right of establishment.
Tunisia	• Gradual liberalisation of trade in services between Tunisia and the EU through screening of Tunisian legislation with a view to concluding an *Economic Agreement on the Liberalisation of Services* with the EU, by contributing to the finalisation of the Palermo Action Plan and by launching bilateral negotiations on services on the basis of Article 31 of the Euro-Med AA in accordance with Article V GATS. • Liberalisation of the right of establishment of companies (not persons) through a comparative study of Tunisian and EU legal systems regarding all aspects of company establishment and the screening by Tunisia of national legislation so as to identify barriers to establishment; ensuring that the conditions for establishment of companies are not more restrictive than when the Euro-Med was concluded and widening the scope of the Euro-Med AA to include the right of establishment.
Algeria: no AP	
Egypt	• Facilitating the supply of services according to the parties' commitments under GATS, including through the development of administrative structures and the removal of identified barriers; preparing for negotiations on the progressive liberalisation of trade in services and right of establishment; establishing a list of EU Member States' contact points on services to provide information to the Egyptian services suppliers/providers who seek to access the European market. • Liberalisation of the right of establishment of companies (not persons) through, for example, the progressive removal of obstacles to establishment and the adoption of key principles of international accounting standards.
Israel	• Promoting the opening of bilateral negotiations on liberalisation of services with Israel. This should be done by taking into account the specific nature of the Israeli economy, the overall objectives set in the conclusions of the Euro-Med Ministerial Meetings and the objectives set in the draft Framework Protocol for Liberalisation of Services among Euro-Mediterranean partners (known as 'the Istanbul Protocol'), notably mutual recognition of professional services. • Liberalisation of the right of establishment of companies (not persons) by widening the scope of the Euro-Med AA and creating a framework favourable to foreign direct investment covering all economic sectors. • Financial services: carrying out an assessment of the scope for legislative approximation with a view to the inclusion of this sector in a free trade area and ultimately Israel's participation in the EU internal market for financial services.
PA	/

Table VII: Cont.

	Measures for further integration into the EU internal market of services, including the right of establishment
Jordan	• Continuation of negotiations on services and establishment and facilitation of the supply of services including the development of the necessary administrative structures and the removal of identified barriers. • Liberalisation of the right of establishment of companies (not persons), through more detailed measures. (Reciprocal national treatment should be guaranteed for EU and Jordanian subsidiaries, companies or branches. The EU and Jordan should work towards convergence with key principles of international and EU rules and standards, including the establishment of a public register of undertakings and a national gazette for the publication of company data, and should ensure control of the incorporation of a company or the compatibility of certain acts in accordance with national laws and regulations).
Lebanon	• Continuation of negotiations on services and establishment and facilitation of the supply of services including the development of the necessary administrative structures and the removal of identified barriers. • Liberalisation of the right of establishment of companies (not persons) Lebanon wants to review its national legislation with a view to identifying measures to facilitate the establishment of companies, including foreign-owned companies, and work towards the progressive removal of barriers to establishment. • As regards financial services: enhancement of a regulatory framework for financial services and setting up of independent authorities to ensure effective supervision.
Libya: no AP	
Syria: no AP	

liberalisation of services. Tunisia and Morocco are the only Mediterranean countries that seem to be ready to conclude an Economic Agreement on the Liberalisation of Services with the EU in conformity with Article V of the GATS. Israel is the only Mediterranean country that is ready to be integrated into the EU internal market of financial services. The provisions relating to the Euro-Med liberalisation of services reflect very well the advanced status of Tunisia, Morocco and Israel in the Euro-Med integration process.

All Action Plans, except for that of the PA, aim to liberalise the right of establishment of companies. The Action Plans intend to remove existing barriers to establishment and to widen the scope of the Euro-Med AAs as regards the right of establishment. An interesting point is that in the Action Plans there is no intention either to bring persons within the scope of the right of establishment. Only companies will benefit from the Euro-Med right of establishment.

4.4 The 'movement of capital' provisions in the ENP Action Plans

The PA Action Plan contains no provisions regarding the movement of capital. The Egyptian Action Plan states that Egypt will improve its national regulatory framework for financial services.[515] Lebanon only aims to exchange experiences with the EU concerning liberalisation of capital movements. The Jordanian Action Plan proposes complete liberalisation of capital movements. To this end, Jordan should review its current legislation to assess the need for further liberalisation of movement of capital and to guarantee the free transaction movement of capital relating in particular to direct investment and the protection of foreign investment. The Moroccan and Tunisian Action Plans aim at full liberalisation of capital. Therefore, the conditions in Article 34 of their Euro-Med AA should be met.

It can be stated that Morocco, Tunisia, Israel and Jordan aim at full liberalisation of the movement of capital in the medium term, whereas Egypt and Lebanon only included insignificant provisions in their Action Plans on this subject.

Table VIII: Actions for further integration of the Mediterranean countries into the EU internal market of capital (June 2009)

	Measures for further integration into the EU internal market of capital
Morocco	Full liberalisation of capital in the medium term (by means of consultations on facilitating full liberalisation of capital once the necessary conditions of Article 34 Euro-Med AA are met).
Tunisia	Full liberalisation of capital in the medium term (by speeding up the implementation of Title IV of the Euro-Med AA.
Algeria: no AP	
Egypt	No intention regarding full liberalisation of capital (removal of obstacles to foreign investment)
Israel	Full liberalisation of capital through Israel's participation in the EU internal market for financial services.
PA	/
Jordan	Full liberalisation in the medium term after reviewing current legislation to assess the need for further liberalisation of capital.
Lebanon	No full liberalisation of capital (Egypt and the EU aim to assess the national regime for capital movements, exchange experiences concerning liberalisation of capital movements and ensure the protection of foreign investments)
Libya: no AP	
Syria: no AP	

[515] Williamson and Mahar distinguish six different dimensions of financial liberalisation: the elimination of credit controls, the deregulation of interest rates, free entry into the banking sector, bank autonomy (bankers decide who to employ, at what wage rate, where to open branches, etc.), privatisation of bank ownership, and liberalisation of international capital flows, see J. Williamson and M. Mahar, *A Survey of Financial Liberalization,* 1998 Princeton Essays in International Finance No. 211.

4.5 The 'movement of persons' provisions in the ENP Action Plans

4.5.1 *Overview of the relevant provisions*

The PA Action Plan has no provision relating to the Euro-Med movement of persons. Israel will only exchange information concerning migration and implement the social security provisions of its Euro-Med AA.[516]

Egypt and the EU wish to facilitate the legal movement of persons through better employment institutions and through information about employment opportunities for labour migrants in the EU. The EU ensures fair treatment of legal Egyptian migrants. Egypt and the EU also wish to negotiate readmission agreements[517] and develop a dialogue on various migration-related issues.[518] Visa-issuing procedures should be facilitated for certain agreed categories of persons in accordance with the Union's *acquis*.

Jordan and the EU aim to make the movement of persons easier. To this end, Jordan should simplify its national procedures in conformity with the Union's *acquis*. First and foremost, the Jordanian Action Plan aims at equal treatment of Jordanian and EU workers who are legally residing and working in the territory of the EU or Jordan and at coordination of social security schemes. There should also be cooperation in the field of (il)legal migration, readmission, visas and asylum.

Lebanon and the EU want to facilitate the movement of persons in conformity with the Union's *acquis*.[519] They should discuss legal migration issues such as admission policies, work on offer and skills available in Lebanon, employment opportunities and procedures in Europe. They wish to discuss the possibility of a readmission agreement between Lebanon and the EU and its Member States. The Action Plan mentions that Lebanon and the EU should consider the special circumstances of the Palestinian refugees in Lebanon.

In order to facilitate the movement of persons, particularly workers, Morocco aims to pursue full implementation of commitments under Articles 64-67 of the Euro-Med AA. It should also examine possibilities for facilitating the issue of visas in line with the Union's *acquis*. Morocco and the EU should improve cooperation with regard to the readmission of Moroccan nationals, stateless persons and nationals of third countries, which should lead to the conclusion of a readmission agreement with the EU. Morocco aims to promote migration through information campaigns for Moroccans about the positive aspects of migration

---

[516] Arts. 64 en 65 Israel AA.

[517] See Art. 69 Egypt AA.

[518] Such as legal migration, seasonal migration, status of Egyptian migrants and workers residing legally in Europe, brain drain, asylum, control of illegal migration.

[519] Lebanon wishes to participate in European programmes such as AENEAS. The AENEAS programme aimed at cooperation with third countries in order to support third countries' efforts in better managing migration flows. The Commission decided to replace the AENEAS programme by a new programme of cooperation with third countries on migration and asylum for the period 2007-2013. In January 2006, the Commission adopted a Communication presenting the objectives and priorities of this new programme.

(such as work opportunities, equal treatment, integration and family reunification), but also about the dangers of illegal migration. In the field of employment and social policy, the EU and Morocco should implement Articles 69 to 72 of the Euro-Med AA and align Moroccan legislation with EU standards and practices in the social and employment sectors. In January 2008, the Association Council adopted a decision on the coordination of social security systems.

Tunisia and the EU should fully implement Article 64 of the Euro-Med AA. This means: (a) the full application of the clause on equal treatment irrespective of nationality as regards working conditions, remuneration and dismissal; (b) freedom of movement, the right of establishment and professional mobility within the EU for workers and members of their families legally residing in the Member States in accordance with EU law; and (c) improvement of conditions for reuniting families as a factor in ensuring a balanced family life for immigrants and members of their families in accordance with EU law. Tunisia and the EU should also fully implement Articles 65 to 68 of the Euro-Med AA about equal treatment as regards nationality and social security. This means: (a) full application of the clause on non-discrimination in the area of social security for workers and members of their family via the coordination of social security schemes; (b) adoption of a decision in the Association Council concerning the implementation of Article 65 on the coordination of social security systems; and (c) implementation of the provisions on coordinating EU and Tunisian social security systems in accordance with Article 67 and continuation of the dialogue in the ad hoc working party on social security. In addition, Tunisia and the EU should set up a joint expert group on legal migration to Europe in which they discuss previous commitments made by Member States and suggest possible ways to facilitate legal migration. They also want to discuss the implementation of the common immigration policy, including the relevant EU legislative instruments. They should talk about the possibility of a readmission agreement with the EU. Finally, the visa issue procedures should be simplified in accordance with the Union's *acquis*.

4.5.2 *Sub-conclusion*

From the ENP Action Plans it can be deduced that Tunisia provides most measures to stimulate the integration of Tunisians into the EU internal market of persons. But also Morocco and Jordan aim at the equal treatment of Moroccan/Jordanian and European workers who are legally residing and working in the European territory or in Morocco/Jordan. The other Mediterranean countries only offer measures to manage (il)migration. Indeed, all Action Plans, except for the PA one, provide for measures regarding movement of persons under the Justice and Home Affairs (JHA) chapter. The Israeli Action Plan only refers to the exchange of information with the EU as regards the Euro-Israeli movement of persons. Egypt and Lebanon have included no measures for further integration into the EU internal market of persons. The PA Action Plan does not include movement of persons provisions either. Even if there were such provisions, they would not apply in practice since Israel obstructs the entrances and exits of the Palestinian territories. The Lebanon Action Plan states that Lebanon should be 'mindful' of the Palestinian refugee presence when liberalising the movement of persons. What is meant by 'mindful' is unclear. Should Lebanon grant the refugees the same movement rights as it grants to Lebanese nationals or should it maintain exceptions for the Palestinian refugees residing in Lebanon?

Table IX: Actions for further integration of the Mediterranean countries into the EU internal market of persons (June 2009)

	Measures for further integration into the EU internal market of persons
Morocco	Full implementation of commitments under Articles 64-67 Euro-Med AA. Under the JHA chapter: conclusion and implementation of a balanced readmission agreement with the EU; dialogue on visa issues; legislation in accordance with international principles and standards on asylum and refugees.
Tunisia	Tunisia and the EU should fully implement Articles 64 to 68 Euro-Med AA Under the JHA chapter: establishing a dialogue between Tunisia and the EU on visas and examining possibilities for facilitating visa issue procedures.
Algeria: no AP	
Egypt	Under the JHA chapter: Egypt aims to facilitate the movement of persons, for example, by simplifying visa issue procedures in accordance with the Union's *acquis*.
Israel	Israel and the EU should prepare for a decision of the Association Council concerning the implementation of the objectives in Articles 64-65 of the Euro-Med AA on the coordination of social security schemes. Under the JHA chapter: effective management of migration flows through exchange of information on (legal) migration and the integration of migrants: best practices, evaluation, joint studies; and cooperation to increase the effectiveness of measures designed to prevent or curb the flow of illegal immigration.
PA	/
Jordan	Jordan and the EU should facilitate the movement and integration of workers through equal treatment of Jordanian and EU workers and nationals who are legally residing and working in the territory of the EU or Jordan, elimination of discrimination, and coordination of social security schemes. Under the JHA chapter: discussion on migration issues (legal and illegal migration, readmission, visas, asylum).
Lebanon	Under the JHA-chapter: improving cooperation on the management of migratory flows; cooperating on facilitating the movement of persons in conformity with the EU *acquis*, in particular examining the scope for facilitating visa procedures for short stays for some categories of persons travelling to Europe or *vice versa*; and cooperating to improve the security of travel documents and visas in conformity with international standards.
Libya: no AP	
Syria: no AP	

5. INTEGRATION OF THE MEDITERRANEAN COUNTRIES INTO THE EU INTERNAL MARKET AS PER 1 JANUARY 2007 (ENP PROGRESS REPORTS APRIL 2008)

The integration into the EU internal market of goods, services, capital and persons will be analysed on the basis of the Progress Reports of 2008.

Jordan integrated further into the EU internal market of goods through negotiations on an ACAA and the adoption of harmonised standards for the priority sectors and the harmonisation of its sanitary and phytosanitary legislation with EU standards. Jordan did not integrate further into the EU internal market of services (including the right of establishment) since it did not join the first group of countries that started bilateral negotiations on services and the right of establishment in 2008. Jordan still lacked good policies for investment promotion and facilitation, export and enterprise developments and, as a result, did not further integrate into the EU internal market of capital. No further integration into the EU internal market of persons could be seen in the case of Jordan.

Lebanon integrated further into the EU internal market of goods through negotiations on an ACAA, the establishment of an ACAA committee in 2005 and the transposition of European standards into Lebanese law. For example, Lebanon prepared regulations on defective products liability and general product safety in conformity with relevant EU legislation, but little progress was made on sanitary and phytosanitary issues. Competition issues were further regulated. Lebanon also integrated further into the EU internal market of services (including the right of establishment): it started negotiations on the Framework Protocol for Liberalisation of Services and right of establishment. As regards the right of establishment, Lebanon is still trying to eliminate discriminatory elements between Lebanese and European companies. No further integration into the EU internal market of persons could be seen for Lebanon.

Israel further integrated into the EU internal market through negotiations on an ACAA; it created an infrastructure in the fields of standardisation, accreditation, conformity assessment and metrology; EU sectoral legislation was transposed in the priority sectors: i.e., pharmaceuticals legislation and standards in the areas of pressure equipment and medical devices. There was convergence with certain EU sanitary and phytosanitary rules and Israel became a member of the European standards bodies CEN and CENELEC. Israel integrated further into the EU internal market of services, including the right of establishment: Israel negotiated a free trade agreement on the liberalisation of services and establishment, and opened its markets more widely to European services providers. Israel tried to further liberalise the Euro-Mediterranean movements of capital, but major European investments were still lacking. As regards the movement of persons, Israel only granted permanent resident status to the children of European workers, but also adopted a strict deportation policy for illegal migrants: they are expelled immediately, regardless of their status.

The PA did not integrate further into the EU internal market. The movement of goods, services, capital is hindered by Israeli restrictions. Israel still falls short of 'facilitating Palestinian trade.' Its permanent restrictions on access and the movement of goods and persons have had a negative impact on the Palestinian economy. For the PA, all movement of labour/persons is hindered by Israeli restrictions. Israel is still doing little to facilitate Palestinian trade, which also has a negative effect on the movement of persons.

Egypt integrated further into the EU internal market of goods through: (1) a work programme towards an ACAA; (2) the transposition of relevant European standards in the priority sectors; (3) legislative approximation on essential safety requirements, accreditation, conformity assessment and market surveillance; (4) the alignment of the Egyptian system of drafting technical regulations on essential health and safety requirements with the EU drafting system; and (5) the establishment of an independent quality institute that will guarantee the quality of goods. Little progress was made as regards the setting up of infrastructure, such as institutions for standardisation, accreditation and conformity assessment. Egypt also became a member of the European standards body CEN. Progress was made in the area of competition policy. Egypt also integrated further into the EU internal market of services, including the right of establishment, since it joined the first group of negotiators. Egypt further liberalised capital movements through many measures, such as the reduction of the minimum starting capital. Egypt did not further integrate into the EU internal market of persons, but had already concluded migration agreements, including provisions on the economic and social rights of migrants.

6. Integration of the Mediterranean countries into the EU internal market as per 1 January 2008 (ENP Progress Reports April 2009)

6.1 Integration of Morocco into the EU internal market[520]

The following can be stated as regards the integration into the EU internal market of industrial goods: Morocco made slow progress in preparing for negotiations on an Agreement on Conformity Assessment and Acceptance of Industrial Products (ACAA). It identified its priority sectors for harmonisation: construction products, electrical appliances, toys, gas equipment and machinery. Some harmonisation progress was made in this field, but Morocco needs to set up an accreditation and normalisation institution to speed up the process of implementation of European standards in Moroccan legislation. Morocco also made some progress as regards competition issues, for example, by appointing a president and members

[520] Commission Staff Working Document Accompanying the Communication from the Commission to the European Parliament and the Council 'Progress Report Morocco' of 23 April 2009, SEC (2009) 520/2.

of the Moroccan Competition Council. As regards the integration into the EU internal market of agricultural products, negotiations on the liberalisation of trade in agriculture and fishery products continued. Morocco made important steps forward as regards food product safety. Concerning the integration into the EU internal market of services, bilateral negotiations on the liberalisation of services and right of establishment were launched in February 2008. Certain Moroccan acts improved the right of establishment of companies. No further liberalisation of capital was reported in 2008, and there was only some progress as regards migration management.

6.2 Integration of Tunisia into the EU internal market[521]

As regards the integration into the EU internal market of industrial goods, Tunisia progressed well in its preparations for an ACCA as well as in the adoption of European norms in the priority sectors, such as electrical equipment. Tunisia also made progress in the field of competition law. As for the integration into the EU internal market of agricultural products, negotiations were launched in 2008. Bilateral negotiations on the liberalisation of services and right of establishment were launched in March 2008. In the field of liberalisation of capital, Tunisia took prudent but important steps forwards, for example, as regards the law to protect investors and facilitation of the conditions for the establishment of companies. Tunisia only progressed in terms of migration management and took some bilateral steps with some Member States, such as the agreements on visa facilitation with France, signed in October 2008.

6.3 Integration of Egypt into the EU internal market[522]

Regarding the integration into the EU internal market of industrial goods, Egypt continued preparations for negotiations on an Agreement on Conformity Assessment and Acceptance of Industrial Products (ACAA). Selected priority sectors for harmonisation with EU rules and standards are construction products, electrical appliances, pressure equipment, medical devices, gas appliances and machinery. The adoption of EU standards in these priority sectors progressed well. Egypt also started upgrading quality infrastructure, but further progress is required. As for the integration into the EU internal market of agricultural products, Egypt and the EU signed a preliminary agreement on further liberalisation of bilateral trade in agricultural, processed agricultural products and fish and fishery products on 1 July 2008. The agreement provides for the dismantling of tariffs applied to the trade of agricultural, processed agricultural and fish and

---

[521] Commission Staff Working Document Accompanying the Communication from the Commission to the European Parliament and the Council 'Progress Report Tunisia' of 23 April 2009, SEC (2009) 521/2.

[522] Commission Staff Working Document Accompanying the Communication from the Commission to the European Parliament and the Council 'Progress Report Egypt' of 23 April 2009, SEC (2009) 523/2.

fishery products, leaving only a very limited number of sensitive products subject to certain protections on both sides. This new agreement amends the current provisions of the Egypt-EU AA for those products. Regarding sanitary and phytosanitary issues, Egypt took further steps to prepare a law on the agro-industry, which includes, *inter alia*, the establishment of a single food safety authority. The Egyptian competition authority (ECA) continued to pursue violations of competition rules. In October 2008, a new law establishing the system of economic courts entered into force. The new system aims to improve the predictability and rapidity of justice in areas such as intellectual property rights, competition, capital markets and banking. Bilateral negotiations on liberalisation of trade in services and the right of establishment were launched in 2008. Egypt made good progress in the liberalisation of capital. Many efforts were made to attract foreign investment. In order to improve the business climate, Egypt continued implementing a strategy for regulatory reform and administrative simplification of regulations and legislation related to economic activity. Egypt offers one-stop shop services to issue all licenses required for establishment and operations and to lessen the burden associated with company registration. Egypt simplified the procedures and reduced the time span for establishing a company (48 hours). Commercial registration fees were also reduced. There is also a department in charge of answering questions of investors. Corporate governance rules are being set down for insurance companies and mortgage lenders to promote greater transparency and stability. Regarding financial services, Egypt continued implementing the financial sector reform programme in line with international best practices. In 2008, the Central Bank of Egypt implemented the Basel II principles for effective banking supervision. Egypt plans to consolidate its various regulatory bodies for financial services into a unified financial supervision authority. A draft law was already prepared. In the area of migration, there was limited progress throughout 2008. Cooperation between the EU and Egypt on migration issues continued expanding steadily, particularly in the context of the Working Group on Migration, Social and Consular Affairs and the Subcommittee on Justice and Security, which met in June 2008 for the second time.

6.4 Integration of Israel into the EU internal market[523]

Israel made progress in implementing a large number of priorities of the ENP AP. However, a lack of progress could be seen regarding a certain number of commitments, for example, facilitating Palestinian trade. As regards the integration into the EU internal market of industrial goods, the EU and Israel launched negotiations on an Agreement on Conformity Assessment and Acceptance of Industrial Products (ACAA) in one of the priority sectors, namely Good Manufacturing Practice (GMP) for pharmaceuticals, in November 2008. The conformity of the Israeli Inspectorate with EU practices had been positively assessed

[523] Commission Staff Working Document Accompanying the Communication from the Commission to the European Parliament and the Council 'Progress Report Israel' of 23 April 2009, SEC (2009) 516/2.

by a European Commission expert mission in Israel in August 2008. With regard to competition policy, in the anti-trust field, the Israeli system is comparable to the systems in place in the EU Member Sates. Negotiations aimed at achieving greater EU-Israel reciprocal liberalisation of trade in agricultural, processed agricultural products and fish and fishery products were concluded in April 2008. In July 2008, Israel and the Commission initialled the preliminary agreement on further liberalisation of bilateral trade in agricultural, processed agricultural products and fish and fishery products. In February 2009, Israel adopted a new phytosanitary law for import of plants and plant products. Bilateral negotiations on liberalisation of services and establishment were launched in 2008. As for the liberalisation of capital, Israel adopted the International Financial Reporting Standards system in 2008. In December 2008, the Commission and Israel agreed to start a dialogue to get a better understanding of the Israeli system for oversight and regulation of the auditors' profession. The Companies Act of 1999 was amended in July 2008 to include provisions on independent directors. Furthermore, broader changes to that Act on corporate governance were initiated but not yet adopted in the course of 2008. In the field of financial services, preparations for a new law on the Bank of Israel are ongoing. The draft law includes provisions for the establishment of a monetary policy committee. Basel II principles for effective banking supervision are to be implemented as of January 2010. The Bank Fees Reform, in place since July 2008, enables customers to obtain all relevant information regarding fees charged by banks for their services. Finally, Israel proposed key amendments to its legislation on, *inter alia*, marketing and portfolio management, to the regulation and supervision of secondary markets as well as to the regulation of new financial instruments. No progress was reported as regards the integration into the EU internal market of persons.

6.5 Integration of Jordan into the EU internal market[524]

As regards integration into the EU internal market of industrial goods, tariff dismantling continued efficiently in accordance with the Jordan-EU AA. Tariff dismantling for products started in May 2008, based on two lists of products for which tariffs will be dismantled in two and seven years respectively (mostly textiles and furniture). Jordan continued preparations to negotiate an Agreement on Conformity Assessment and Acceptance of Industrial Products (ACAA). The adoption of harmonised standards and approximation to relevant EU directives for the priority sectors progressed (construction products, electrical appliances, pressure equipment, toys, measuring instruments and gas appliances). The review of competition law is still under preparation. It will transform the Competition Directorate in the Ministry of Industry and Trade into an independent competition commission established under the framework of the National Agenda. For the integration into the EU internal market of agricultural products, a draft law

[524] Commission Staff Working Document Accompanying the Communication from the Commission to the European Parliament and the Council 'Progress Report Jordan' of 23 April 2009, SEC (2009) 517/2.

on standards, metrology and product safety and a draft accreditation law were prepared but not yet adopted by Parliament. Jordan and the EU continued cooperation on the harmonisation of sanitary and phytosanitary rules with EU standards, particularly through two twinning projects. Jordan prepared a new food law, which aims at harmonisation with EU rules. It issued legislation regarding a national identification and farm registration system. Jordan continued to participate in workshops under the Commission's 'Better training for safer food' programme. Negotiations on the liberalisation of trade in services and right of establishment with the EU have not yet started. As regards the right of establishment, the required capital for establishing a company was reduced. Jordan is working on a draft regulation enabling 100% foreign ownership in transport services, insurance agent services, travel agencies and tour operator services. Concerning the liberalisation of capital, good progress was made in improving the business environment. As for the business climate, Jordan remains one of the better-performing Mediterranean countries. Amendments to the 1997 company law are being reviewed by Parliament. They aim at facilitating the establishment of companies and at attracting investments in a more flexible environment. Furthermore, Jordan is working on a corporate governance manual for companies. Jordan made progress in financial sector reforms. The Basel II principles for effective banking supervision have been applied from January 2008. No progress was reported as regards the integration into the EU internal market of persons.

6.6 Integration of Lebanon into the EU internal market[525]

As regards integration into the EU internal market of industrial goods, tariff dismantling is proceeding as foreseen in the Euro-Med AA. Lebanon made slow progress in preparing for negotiations on an Agreement on Conformity Assessment and Acceptance of Industrial Products (ACAA). The Lebanese ACAA National Committee continued to review progress in the transposition of European standards into Lebanese law in the selected priority sectors, which are construction products, electrical appliances and pressure equipment. The new draft of the competition law has still not been adopted. Negotiations on the liberalisation of trade in agriculture have not yet been launched. Lebanon announced its willingness to start discussions on the issue. Lebanon has taken part in the regional phase of the negotiations on the Framework Protocol for Liberalisation of Services and right of establishment, as indicated last year, but bilateral negotiations have not yet been launched. As for the liberalisation of Euro-Med capital, insufficient progress was made in improving the business climate. However, Lebanon continued to implement the 2007 administrative simplification programme which aims at establishing one-stop shops in post offices to arrange company registration and at developing easily accessible standard forms for business registration. This is still to be completed and extended to licensing procedures. Lebanon also

[525] Commission Staff Working Document Accompanying the Communication from the Commission to the European Parliament and the Council 'Progress Report Lebanon' of 23 April 2009, SEC (2009) 518/2.

worked on making its public register of companies available online. The draft budget law 2008 provides for the cancellation of import licence fees and the elimination of foreign branches fees. No progress was reported as regards the integration into the EU internal market of persons.

6.7 Integration of the PA into the EU internal market[526]

Further integration into the EU internal market of goods is impossible due to obstacles to trade and economic development in the occupied Palestinian territory. Palestinian exports to the EU decreased dramatically by 49.1%. No further progress as regards integration into the EU internal market of services was observed either. As for the Euro-PA liberalisation of capital, it should be noted that the Palestinian legal framework for business remains weak, which leads to uncertainty of the business climate. The process of starting up a company is burdensome due to the assembling of documentation for registration and the obtaining of permits and licences. The authorities continued their efforts to attract new investments via a major Palestinian Investment Conference where investment opportunities were discussed and partnerships forged between the Palestinian and international business communities, via the Israel-Palestinian Business Forum, which is the first organisation run jointly by Israelis and Palestinians to facilitate contacts, promote the founding of new businesses and support existing ones, and via an Israel-Palestinian Chamber of Commerce established by leading Israeli business people. In the field of financial services, the Palestine Monetary Authority (PMA) continued to perform well, regulating the Palestinian banking sector. In May 2008, the PMA launched the Credit Bureau, a credit registry which should make for better risk assessment and improve the quality of loans. No further progress was noted as regards integration into the EU internal market of persons.

7. The influence of the EU Member States on the Euro-Med liberalisation of persons

Under the ENP, the Commission offered to grant all ENP partner countries, including the Mediterranean ones, free movement of people as the cornerstone of a wider Europe. The European Parliament, in its Napoletano Report of 5 November 2003, welcomed this idea and expressed its belief that the ENP should include a policy to facilitate the free movement of people.[527]

---

[526] Commission Staff Working Document Accompanying the Communication from the Commission to the European Parliament and the Council 'Progress Report PA' of 23 April 2009, SEC (2009) 519/2.

[527] European Parliament, Report on 'Wider Europe – Neighbourhood: A Framework for Relations with our Eastern and Southern Neighbours' (also called the Napoletano Report), COM (2003) 104.

The ENP was often interfered with and contradicted by the EU's external immigration policy.[528] In its 2003 Communication on immigration, integration and employment, the Commission predicted that labour migration to the EU would become increasingly necessary to fill job and skill shortages. Some governments, however, fear an enormous increase of uncontrolled immigration once the free movement of persons regime is extended to the Mediterranean countries.[529] Other governments are concerned about the entry of Islamic terrorists. These concerns have evoked strong reservations in the EU about the proposal made under the ENP to extend the full EU *acquis*, including the free movement of persons, to the Mediterranean countries. This has had many implications amongst the leaders of the EU Member States. For example, on 1 October 2004, the Justice and Home Affairs Council of Ministers discussed the establishment of EU-financed camps in North Africa to control the inflow of potential immigrants.[530] The Justice and Home Affairs Council in Luxemburg on 3 June 2005 indicated the importance of cooperation with Libya on matters of migration. The Council urged the EU to engage, as soon as possible and on an *ad hoc* basis, in a discussion with Libya on the management of migratory flows between Africa and Europe.[531] In June 2005, the European Parliament condemned the setting up, in the Mediterranean countries, of 'preliminary reception centres' for immigrants heading for EU territory, which do not offer minimum guarantees to the people concerned in terms of fundamental rights.[532] On 4 July 2005, the G-5 Ministers of the Interior[533] met in Evian to set stricter immigration controls. The Ministers welcomed Italy's proposals on immigration by sea from Africa. Italy proposed to set up joint patrols in the Mediterranean; to cooperate in repatriation; to jointly analyse migration flows from sub-Saharan Africa; and to create joint investigation teams at departure point for immigrants. They also agreed to develop joint grouped flights for the repatriation of illegal immigrants.[534]

The EU policies as regards the movement of persons towards the Mediterranean region have often been contradictory. In its '2006 ENP Reinforcement Communication' of 4 December 2006, the Commission examined how visa procedures could be made less of an obstacle to legitimate travel from neighbour-

---

[528] Cf., *supra* Ch. II.

[529] Immigrants from the Mediterranean countries already established in the EU, however, should not fear increased competition from workers from the new Member States. No significant changes in the West European labour market are expected as a result of the EU's enlargement; see B. Khader, *Elargissement à l'Est et impact migratoire sur les pays arabes et méditerranéens*, report in preparation for the 7th meeting of Experts on Economic Transition, 23-24 April 2003, available at: http://europa.eu.int/comm/external_relations/euromed/etn/7mtg/kha.pdf, p. 19.

[530] Del Sarto and Schumacher, *supra* n. 45, pp. 30-31.

[531] Conclusions of the Council of Justice and Home Affairs, Luxembourg, 3 June 2005, available at: http://www.eu2005.lu/en/actualites/conseil/index.html.

[532] Resolution of the European Parliament on the links between legal and illegal migration and integration of migrants of 9 June 2005 (2004/2137/INI), *OJ* 2006 C 124E, pp. 535-542.

[533] UK, France, Italy, Spain and Germany.

[534] Conclusions of the G5 Meeting in Evian on 4 July 2005, available at: http://www.statewatch.org/news/2005/jul/03eu-g5-meeting.htm.

ing countries to the EU (and *vice versa*).[535] Visa facilitation agreements should be negotiated back-to-back with readmission agreements and should respond to the specific needs of the third country concerned. By way of illustration of what can be achieved, visa facilitation and readmission agreements were initialled on a readmission agreement with Morocco and have almost been concluded. The EU should be willing to enter into negotiations on readmission and visa facilitation with each country with an Action Plan in force. The Commission even proposed more far-reaching measures, such as the launching of negotiations between Member States on the creation of the Visa Information System and the creation of common visa-application centres, which could greatly facilitate the reception of visa applications in ENP countries.

The Commission issued another Communication on 16 May 2007 on circular migration and mobility partnerships between the EU and third countries.[536] This Communication is looking for developing new approaches to improve the legal movement of people between the EU and third countries. Following its Communication, the Commission proposed that a limited number of *Pilot Mobility Partnerships* should be negotiated with selected third countries, in particular ENP countries. Partnerships will require pilot countries to commit themselves to cooperating actively with the EU on the legal movement of persons.

The Commission proposed impressive developments in the area of free movement of persons in its Communication 'A Strong European Neighbourhood Policy' of 5 December 2007.[537] The Commission aimed again at visa facilitation regarding legitimate short-term travel, but also proposed long-term developments in the area of migration. The first long-term proposal concerns the opening up of the labour markets of the Member States on the condition that the opening of the labour market is to the mutual benefit of the sending and receiving countries. For that reason, the Commission urged the Council of the EU and the European Parliament to adopt its 2006 package on legislative proposals. This package aims at solving some outstanding problems in the delivery of Schengen visas. This should provide easier proof that a traveller is *bona fide*, improve access of visa applicants to consulates, ensure better consular presence in the region and provide for the establishment of Common Application Centres where needed. A second long-term proposal of the Commission is that Member States should use all existing opportunities to facilitate travel. The Regulation of 20 December 2006 about traffic at the external borders of the Member States allows Member States to conclude bilateral agreements with neighbouring third countries to improve people-to-people contacts in border areas. This Regulation

---

[535] Communication from the Commission, 'Strengthening the European Neighbourhood Policy', Brussels, 4 December 2006, COM (2006) 726 final, pp. 5-6.

[536] Communication from the Commission of 16 May 2007 to the European Parliament, the Council, the European Economic and Social Committee and the Committee of the Regions: On circular migration and mobility partnerships between the European Union and third countries, COM (2007) 248 final.

[537] Communication from the Commission: A Strong European Neighbourhood Policy, of 5 December 2007, COM (2007) 774 final, pp. 5-6.

is not used to full advantage by the Member States.[538] In addition, the Member States should make better use of the flexibilities provided for under the present Schengen *acquis*, which could contribute to smoother arrangements.[539]

Under the French Presidency, the Council of the EU proposed in July 2008 a 'European Pact of Immigration and Asylum.' This pact calls for stricter control of migratory flows, but has been criticised as being a *selective* immigration policy, since EU preferences play a role in the acceptance of immigrant. The EU Heads of State and Government formally endorsed this Pact on 15 October 2008.

8. Conclusion

As regards the content of the ENP Action Plans, they all except for the PA contain provisions to stimulate the further integration of the Mediterranean countries into the EU internal market of free movement of goods, services, capital and persons. The ENP Action Plans offer the Mediterranean countries *the prospect of a significant measure of 'economic integration' through gradual integration into the EU internal market.* In its 2003 Communication on a Wider Europe, the Commission offered the Mediterranean countries the prospect of a stake in the EU's internal market and further integration and liberalisation to promote the free movement of persons, goods, services and capital (four freedoms).[540] It is, however, significant that these so-called new aims as regards the integration of the Mediterranean countries into the EU internal market of good, services, capital and persons in the ENP Action Plans are not original after all. All ENP Action Plan intentions already existed under the EMP.

Participation in all four freedoms of the EU internal market is not possible overnight. To this end, each Mediterranean country has specified its own preferences/priorities to be realised through the ENP Action Plan as regards the four freedoms, taking into account its own level of integration into the EU internal market. It can thus be stated that each ENP Action Plan provides for different Integration Aims.

As regards the freedom of movement goods, all Mediterranean countries aim at further integration of industrial products into the EU and at bringing their legislation on industrial products further in line with international and European

[538] Regulation (EC) No 1931/2006 of the European Parliament and of the Council of 20 December 2006 laying down rules on local border traffic at the external land borders of the Member States and amending the provisions of the Schengen Convention, *OJ* 2006 L 405.

[539] The EU Council adopted provisions and measures, taken by the signatory states, which formed a genuine *acquis*, i.e., a body of law which could serve as a basis for further cooperation. A list of the elements which make up the Schengen *acquis* was adopted on 20 May 1999. See Council Decision 1999/435/EC of 20 May 1999 concerning the definition of the Schengen *acquis* for the purpose of determining, in conformity with the relevant provisions of the EC Treaty and the TEU, the legal basis for each of the provisions or decisions which constitute the acquis, *OJ* 1999 L 176 – Corrigendum: *OJ* 2000 L 9.

[540] Communication from the Commission, 'Wider Europe – Neighbourhood: A New Framework for Relations with our Eastern and Southern Neighbours', COM (2003) 104 final, p. 4.

rules and practices. Furthermore, all Mediterranean countries, except for the PA, propose launching negotiations on ACAAs. Tunisia, Morocco and Israel have already reached a higher level of liberalisation of goods with the EU than the other Mediterranean countries. Therefore, these countries have taken more detailed measures as regards the movement of goods: enhanced quality of goods, strengthening of instruments and organs of trade facilitation and movement of energy products. All Mediterranean countries, except for Israel and the PA, have taken interesting competition measures: alignment of their competition legislation with EU legislation, establishment of competition enforcement bodies and implementation of decisions taken by the Association Council concerning competition rules. The most advanced competition measures can be seen in Morocco.

As regards the freedom of movement of services, Tunisia and Morocco aim at establishing an Economic Agreement on the Liberalisation of Services with the EU in conformity with Article V of the GATS and all Action plans provide for the right of establishment of companies, but not for persons.

Concerning the freedom of movement of capital, Egypt and Lebanon have little intention to liberalise the movement of capital. Jordan, Israel, Morocco and Tunisia aim at full liberalisation of the movement of capital. Israel mentions full participation of Israel in the EU internal market of financial services.

As regards the freedom of movement of persons, all Action Plans provide for provisions relating to migration under the JHA chapter: simplification of visa issue procedures in accordance with the Union's *acquis*, negotiation of readmission agreements, dialogues concerning various migratory issues, etc. Only Tunisia, Morocco, Israel and Jordan try to facilitate the movement of persons with respect to equal treatment of legal migrants and nationals.

The extent of the integration of the Mediterranean countries into the EU internal market of goods, services, capital and persons through the ENP Action plan is measured by examining the ENP Progress Reports of 2008 and 2009. These reports explain in detail which Mediterranean country has achieved its ENP Action Plan Integration Aims. The extent of the integration of the Mediterranean countries is illustrated in the table below.

Table X: Integration into the EU internal market according to the ENP Progress Reports of April 2008 and April 2009. Provisions in bold are the ENP Integration Aims.

	GOODS	SERVICES, incl. establishment	CAPITAL	PERSONS
Morocco	**measures for further integration of goods (ACAAs and detailed measures)** **competition measures** 2007: Further integration (industrial and agricultural goods) 2008: Industrial goods: slow progress in preparing for negotiations on an ACAA + little harmonisation with EU rules in the priority sectors Agricultural goods: further negotiations on the liberalisation of trade in agricultural products	**- aim: agreement on the movement of services** **- aim: right of establishment of companies** 2007: Further integration (first-wave negotiating country) 2008: Further integration: negotiations on the liberalisation of trade in services and the right of establishment were launched	**intention: full liberalisation** 2007: Further liberalisation 2008: Minor progress as regards the liberalisation of capital	**measures for further integration** 2007: No further integration 2008: No further integration, only migration management
Tunisia	**measures for further integration of goods (ACAAs and detailed measures)** **competition measures** 2007: Further integration (industrial and agricultural goods) 2008: Industrial goods: good progress in preparing for negotiations on an ACAA + good harmonisation with EU rules in the priority sectors Agricultural goods: negotiations on the liberalisation of trade in agriculture were launched	**- aim: agreement on the movement of services aim** **- aim: right of establishment of companies** 2007: Further integration (first-wave negotiating country) 2008: Further integration: negotiations on the liberalisation of trade in services and the right of establishment were launched	**intention: full liberalisation** 2007: Further liberalisation 2008: Progress in the liberalisation of capital	**measures for further integration** 2007: No further integration 2008: No further integration, only migration management and visa facilitation agreement
Algeria: no AP				

Table X: Cont.

	GOODS	SERVICES, incl. establishment	CAPITAL	PERSONS
Egypt	**measures for further integration of goods through, for example, ACAAs** Competition measures 2007: Further integration (industrial and agricultural goods) Competition: progress 2008: Further integration (industrial and agricultural goods) Industrial goods: preparations for negotiations on an ACAA and good harmonisation with EU rules in the priority sectors Agricultural goods: Egypt and the EU signed a preliminary agreement on further liberalisation of bilateral trade in agricultural, processed agricultural and fish and fishery products	**aim: right of establishment of companies** 2007: Further integration (first-wave negotiating country) 2008: Further integration: negotiations on the liberalisation of trade in services and the right of establishment were launched	**intention: no full liberalisation** 2007: Further liberalisation efforts 2008: Many further liberalisation efforts	**No measures for further integration** 2007: No further integration 2008: No further integration, only dialogues
Israel	**measures for further integration of goods (ACAAs)** 2007: Further integration (industrial and agricultural goods) Lack of progress in 'facilitating Palestinian trade' Competition: no progress 2008: Further integration (industrial and agricultural goods) Industrial goods: launch of negotiations on an ACAA Agricultural goods: preliminary agreement on further liberalisation of bilateral trade in agricultural, processed agricultural and fish and fishery products Lack of progress in 'facilitating Palestinian trade' Competition: Israeli anti-trust system is comparable to the systems of the EU Member States!	**aim: right of establishment of companies** 2007: Further integration (first- wave negotiating country) 2008: Further integration: bilateral negotiations for the liberalisation of services and establishment were launched	**intention: full liberalisation** 2007: Further liberalisation, but no results in practice 2008: Many further liberalisation efforts with effective results	**Measures for social security** 2007: Further integration for children of European workers but also deportation policy regarding illegal immigrants 2008: No further integration

Table X: Cont.

	GOODS	SERVICES, incl. establishment	CAPITAL	PERSONS
PA	2007: No further integration 2008: No further integration	2007: No further integration 2008: No further integration	2007: No further liberalisation 2008: Further liberalisation efforts, but business climate remains weak.	2007: No further integration 2008: No further integration
Jordan	**measures for further integration of goods (ACAAs)** **competition measures** 2007: Further integration (industrial goods) Competition: no concrete results yet 2008: Industrial products: preparations to negotiate an ACAA; the adoption of harmonised standards and approximation to relevant EU directives for the priority sectors progressed Agricultural goods: no negotiations on the liberalisation of trade in agriculture	**Aim/measures: right of establishment of companies** 2007: No further integration (not in first wave) 2008: No negotiations on the liberalisation of trade in services and right of establishment with the EU	**intention: full liberalisation** 2007: No further liberalisation 2008: Good progress as regards liberalisation of capital. Jordan remains one of the better-performing Mediterranean countries in terms of attractiveness to foreign companies	**measures for further integration** 2007: No further integration 2008: No further integration
Lebanon	**measures for further integration of goods (ACAAs)** **competition measures** 2007: Further integration (ind. goods) Competition: progress 2008: Industrial goods: slow progress in preparing for negotiations on an ACAA + competition law still not adopted Agricultural goods: no negotiations on the liberalisation of trade in agriculture	**aim: right of establishment of companies** 2007: Further integration efforts (but not first-wave negotiating country) 2008: No negotiations on the liberalisation of trade in services and right of establishment with the EU	**intention: no full liberalisation** 2007: No further liberalisation 2008: Insufficient progress	**No measures for further integration** 2007: No further integration 2008: No further integration
Libya: no AP				
Syria: no AP				

Table X leads to several interesting conclusions about the Euro-Med integration process:

(1) This table clearly shows that Lebanon and the PA have not made any significant progress as regards further integration into the EU internal market. Lebanon has not realised its Integration Aims due to the fact that it was severely hit by the war that broke out in 2006 between the Israeli military and Hezbollah. It is highly possible that Lebanon will make good efforts in the near future to further integrate into the EU internal market since it is recovering well from the war. The PA integration into the EU internal market, however, is hindered by Israeli obstructions. Contrary to Lebanon, no significant integration results are expected in the near future as there is no imminent solution to the Israeli-PA conflict.
(2) This table indicates that the ENP Action Plans resulted in further integration of the Mediterranean countries into the EU internal market, mainly in the field of movement of goods. Tunisia, Egypt and Israel have done very well in achieving their Integration Aims, also as regards industrial and agricultural products. It is noteworthy that Israel has a competition system that is fully in line with the EU competition rules. Egypt, too, has made progress as regards the Euro-Med competition rules. On the other hand, it is regrettable that Israel is still hindering Palestinian trade. Egypt has also produced positive results, has been preparing for negotiations on an ACAA and signed a preliminary agreement on the liberalisation of agricultural products. Tunisia, as expected, has also achieved relevant integration results. Egypt is preparing for negotiations on an ACAA and for further liberalisation of agricultural goods. In addition, it is advancing significantly in its harmonisation efforts. Morocco and Jordan, however, are not advancing as expected. Morocco is slowly progressing in negotiations on an ACAA and has made little progress as regards harmonisation of its legislation with EU legislation in the priority sectors. Morocco has only advanced well as regards the liberalisation of agricultural products. Jordan, however, has further integrated into the EU market of industrial products by preparing for negotiations on an ACAA and adopting all relevant EU legislation, but has not made any progress as regards the liberalisation of agricultural products.
(3) Tunisia, Egypt, Israel and Jordan have further liberalised the Euro-Med movement of capital. Morocco has also made good efforts in this field, but not as many as expected. Egypt has progressed well as regards integration into the EU internal market, possibly due to an enhanced political will to further integrate into the EU.
(4) It is also striking that, despite the large amount of attention which all ENP Action Plans give to the movement of persons, the ENP Progress Reports of 2008 and particularly the ENP Progress Reports of 2009 note that no further integration in the EU internal market of persons has been established. The ENP plan to consider the movement of persons as a cornerstone of the Euro-Med relations has seemed to turn out to be idealistic in reality.
(5) Algeria has not further integrated into the EU internal market of goods, services, capital and persons as it has no ENP Action Plan, only a Euro-Med AA.

Chapter VI

The extent of integration of the Mediterranean countries into the EU internal market

After having analysed all bilateral and multilateral existing Euro-Med instruments in the previous chapters of this book, the following conclusions can be drawn as regard the extent of integration of the Mediterranean countries into the EU internal market of goods, services, capital and persons.

1. The extent of integration of the Mediterranean countries into the EU internal market of goods

As regards the integration of the Mediterranean countries into the EU internal market of goods, there is a very relevant distinction between trade in industrial goods, on the one hand, and movement of agricultural, fishery and processed agricultural goods, on the other.

1.1 The extent of integration into the EU internal market of industrial products

The Euro-Med AAs provide for an asymmetrical system of movement of industrial goods between the Mediterranean countries and the EU. This system entails, on the one hand, that industrial goods from Morocco, Tunisia, Algeria, Jordan, Lebanon, the PA, Egypt and Israel which are imported into Europe are completely free of customs duties and charges having equivalent effect. European industrial goods exported to the Mediterranean countries, on the other hand, are to be progressively liberated over a transitional period of 12 years upon entry into force of the Euro-Med AA. The progressive liberalisation process should lead to total free movement of European goods to the markets of Morocco, Tunisia, Algeria, Jordan, Lebanon, the PA, Egypt and Israel in the future. The final liberalisation date for industrial goods, for example, as regards Tunisia, is set at the end of 2010; and for Lebanon at the end of 2018. After these dates, customs duties/charges having equivalent effect or quantitative restrictions/equivalent measures will no longer be accepted where it concerns the import of European industrial products into the Mediterranean countries. Derogation from the movement of goods is possible. The European courts state that the interpretation of the derogation provisions in the Euro-Med AAs and in the EC Treaty (now: TFEU) differs, since the Euro-Med AA and the European Treaty have a different purpose: the EU and the Mediterranean countries do not constitute a Euro-Med internal market, which leaves more room for restrictions than in the EU internal market. The Mediterranean countries and the EU, however, are going through a gradual liberalisation process. This means that the deeper the Euro-Med integration becomes, the fewer restrictions will be tolerated.

The Mediterranean countries and the EU want to further facilitate the integration of industrial goods into the EU internal market by bringing their legislation on industrial goods in line with international and EU norms and practices. The Euro-Med AAs only stipulate that the Mediterranean countries should approximate their legislation to that of the EU in the areas covered by them. They do not explain how this approximation process should be initiated and developed. For example, in the case of the Maghreb countries, the Euro-Med AAs state that 'the cooperation shall be aimed at helping to bring the legislation closer to that of the Community.' In the case of Lebanon and Jordan, they stipulate that 'the Parties shall use their best endeavours to approximate their respective laws in order to facilitate the implementation of this Agreement.' The Euro-Med AAs only contain a small article on standards and conformity assessment of industrial goods between the Mediterranean countries and the EU. They do not stimulate the Mediterranean countries to become part of European specialised organisations for testing, certification and standardisation.

The sectoral Euro-Med Conferences and the ENP Action Plans have stimulated further integration of Morocco, Tunisia, Jordan, Lebanon, the PA, Egypt and Israel into the EU internal market of industrial goods. The Conferences initiated negotiations on Agreements on Conformity Assessment and Acceptance of Industrial Products (ACAAs). Morocco, Tunisia, Jordan, Lebanon, Egypt and Israel have made progress as regards further integration into the EU internal market of industrial goods through preparations for these agreements. The ACAAs should function as trade corridors for industrial goods between the Mediterranean countries and the EU. The ENP Action Plans include measures relating to the Euro-Med movement of industrial goods. Tunisia, Morocco and Israel have already reached a higher level of liberalisation of goods with the EU in comparison with the other Mediterranean countries. Therefore, the ENP Action Plans of these countries include more detailed measures as to the movement of industrial goods: enhanced quality of goods, a strengthening of instruments and organs for trade facilitation and the movement of energy products. According to the ENP Progress Reports, the Mediterranean countries have continued the approximation of their legislation with EU law in selected sectors and are gradually upgrading their administrative structures, but they still lack the necessary administrative, legal and technical capacity to manage and enforce the legislation. The PA has made no further progress as regards integration into the EU internal market of industrial goods and Israel has been indicated as the cause of this stagnating integration since it has failed to 'facilitate Palestinian trade.'

As regards the approximation process aimed at improving the Euro-Med movement of industrial goods, an important distinction should be made between industrial goods for which an EU harmonisation directive exists and those for which there are no EC harmonisation rules.

The Mediterranean countries want to implement European standards contained in EU harmonisation directives in their legislation, as this will lead to better access for Mediterranean goods to the European market. A question that arises is whether it is essential for the Mediterranean countries to implement all EU harmonisation directives. Since the Mediterranean countries have no prospect of accession to the EU, they are not obliged to implement all directives. It is recommended that they implement those that will lead to economic development of the Mediterranean countries, namely those that cover industrial goods which constitute a significant part of Mediterranean countries' export to the European market. Each Mediterranean country has to indicate which EU harmonisation directives it wants to implement. The Mediterranean countries have identified 'priority areas' for this harmonisation process and have started adopting some relevant EU *acquis*. In the end, this approximation process should lead to the conclusion of ACAAs, on which negotiations have been initiated with some Mediterranean countries within the sectoral Euro-Med Conferences.

In Europe, there are also goods regarding which no EU harmonisation directive applies. In the case of absence of EU harmonisation, technical rules create obstacles to the free movement of goods between the EU Member States. Technical obstacles can be eliminated by applying the so-called mutual recognition principle. According to the principle of mutual recognition, all goods lawfully produced in one EU Member State can freely enter the market of another EU Member State, even if the product does not fully comply with the technical rules of the EU Member State of destination, unless the restrictions laid down by the EU Member State of destination are justified on the grounds specified in Article 36 TFEU or on the basis of overriding requirements of general public importance recognised by the ECJ, and are proportionate.[541] The Mediterranean countries and the EU wish to apply the principle of mutual recognition to the movement of industrial goods in these non-harmonised EU areas. The Mediterranean countries have identified problems as regards the (future) application of the principle of mutual recognition between the EU and the Mediterranean countries. So far, only Israel signed a Mutual Recognition Agreement on Good Laboratory Practices (GLP) with the EU, which entered into force in May 2000. The Mediterranean countries and the EU can opt between 3 levels of mutual recognition: (i) a high level, whereby all national regulations are considered equivalent; (ii) an average level, whereby countries recognise only institutions of certification of partner countries; and (iii) a low level, whereby certification of a partner country is recognised for certain goods only.[542] According to Jakubiak, one of the problems will be that the principle of mutual recogni-

[541] Commission Staff Working Document – Accompanying Document to the Proposal for a Regulation of the European Parliament and of the Council laying down procedures relating to the application of certain national technical rules to products lawfully marketed in another Member State and repealing Decision 3052/95/EC: Executive summary of the impact assessment, SEC (2007) 113, p. 2; Proposal for a Regulation of the European Parliament and the Council laying down procedures relating to the application of certain national technical rules to products lawfully marketed in another Member State and repealing Decision 3052/95/EC of 14 February 2007, COM (2007) 36 final.

[542] S. Rawdan and J.-L. Reiffers, *FEMISE Report on the Euro-Mediterranean Partnership 2006: Analysis and Proposals of the Euro-Mediterranean Forum of Economic Institutes* (Marseille, Institut de la Méditerranée 2006) p. 33.

tion requires a substantial amount of confidence in the other party which will take time to develop in the Euro-Mediterranean relationship.[543]

1.2 The extent of integration of the Mediterranean countries into the EU internal market of agricultural, fishery and processed agricultural products

The Euro-Med AAs provide for gradual liberalisation of agricultural products, fishery products and industrial products with an agricultural element between the EU and Morocco, Tunisia, Algeria, Jordan, Lebanon, the PA, Egypt and Israel. Each Euro-Med AA includes a calendar for the progressive abolishment of customs duties and charges having equivalent effect for agricultural products, fishery products and industrial products with an agricultural element between the EU and the relevant Mediterranean country. The movement of these goods should be completely liberalised in 2010. The final liberalisation date for industrial and agricultural goods is the same. After these dates, customs duties/charges having equivalent effect or quantitative restrictions/equivalent measures will no longer be tolerated.

Measures for further integration of the Mediterranean countries into the EU internal market of agricultural goods are presented at the sectoral Euro-Med Conferences and in the ENP Action Plans. Egypt, Israel, Tunisia and Morocco have started negotiations, which are still ongoing, as regards the Euro-Med liberalisation of agricultural, processed agricultural and fishery products. This has resulted in further integration of Morocco, Tunisia, Egypt and Israel into the EU internal market of agricultural goods. Jordan, Lebanon and the PA have not started such negotiations and have made no further progress as regards integration into the EU internal market of agricultural goods.

Improved food safety and quality of food products would lead to more export of Mediterranean food products to Europe, but approximation to European sanitary and phytosanitary (SPS) standards is still lacking in the Mediterranean countries. The Mediterranean countries have made limited progress on SPS issues. Egypt has reinforced controls on potatoes, as a result of which the Commission allowed potato exports to the EU in the 2007/08 season under certain conditions. Some Mediterranean partners have taken measures to combat animal diseases such as avian influenza in Egypt or blue tongue in sheep in the Maghreb countries. The Jordan twinning project has helped to draft a first framework food law in the country and has contributed to equipping laboratories.[544] It is recommended that the Mediterranean countries should continue further alignment with European sanitary and phytosanitary (SPS) standards in the near future.

---

[543] Jakubiak, et al., *supra* n. 51, pp. 22-23.

[544] MEMO/07/548, available at: http://europa.eu/rapid/searchAction.do.

1.3. Euro-Mediterranean competition law linked to the Euro-Med movement of goods

Goods can only move freely between the Mediterranean countries and the EU when competition rules are respected by the producers of these goods. The Euro-Med AAs for Morocco, Tunisia, Algeria, Jordan, Lebanon, the PA, Egypt and Israel contain competition provisions that are similar to Articles 101 and 102 of the TFEU. The competition provisions in the Euro-Med AAs lack direct effect since they require implementing measures via decisions of the Euro-Med Association Councils and make no mention of their direct application. Only the EU-Morocco Association Council has taken implementation measures. Contrary to the exemption procedure provided for in Article 101(3) TFEU, there is no possibility of exemption of unlawful agreements in the Euro-Med relationship.

Since the relevant competition provisions in the Euro-Med AAs lack direct effect and implementation, it can be concluded that there is no protection in the field of competition law in the Mediterranean countries. In the EU, however, there is some kind of protection in this field since European natural and legal persons can rely upon the 'principle of the extra-territorial effect of EU competition law.' This means that European natural and legal persons can ask for the application of European competition rules in regard to competition violations occurring outside the EU territory: Mediterranean companies that violate competition law, whereby anti-competitive effects are noticeable on EU territory, can be penalised by the European courts. This principle cannot be relied upon by Mediterranean individuals or companies. It would be in the favour of the Mediterranean countries if the Euro-Med Association Council were to take action in the competition field.

Under the ENP umbrella, Morocco, Tunisia, Jordan, Lebanon and Egypt (not the PA) have provided interesting competition measures: (1) alignment of their competition legislation with EU legislation; (2) the establishment of competition enforcement bodies; and (3) the implementation of decisions taken by the Association Council concerning competition rules. Morocco included the most advanced competition measures in its ENP Action Plan. According to the ENP Progress Reports, however, only Tunisia, Lebanon and Egypt have made progress in the competition field, not Morocco and Jordan. Israel's ENP Action Plan contains no specific measures about how to improve its competition system, since Israel is the only Mediterranean country whose competition system is fully in line with that of the EU.

1.4. Euro-Mediterranean rules of origin

The Euro-Med rules of origin identify which goods are eligible for preferential treatment. At present, the Euro-Med AAs for Morocco, Tunisia, Algeria, Jordan, Lebanon, the PA, Egypt and Israel contain provisions on rules of origin, as well as annexes on the application of the pan-European system of cumulation of rules of origin in the Euro-Med area.

The rules of origin can only support the integration of the Mediterranean countries into the EU internal market of goods when they really work in practice. Currently, they seem to have little practical impact because the basic condition for the application of the rules of origin system, which is the conclusion of free trade agreements between the members of the system, has not been fulfilled.

2. The extent of integration of the Mediterranean countries into the EU internal market of services, including the right of establishment

There are no common rules on the Euro-Med movement of services or the right of establishment. The WTO countries – Morocco, Tunisia, Egypt, Jordan and Israel – apply the GATS obligations until their Association Councils make specific recommendations on the liberalisation of services and the right of establishment. So far, no Association Council has taken a decision about services or the right of establishment. According to the GATS, the obligation to allow free market access and ensure national treatment only applies if the service in question for which access to the market or national treatment is requested, is included in a special list. Only then will the country be obliged to refrain from putting up barriers to market access or from imposing quantitative restrictions. In that case, the GATS guarantees free movement of services for individuals (self-employment) as well as for legal persons. In conclusion, it can be stated that for Algeria, Tunisia, Egypt and Israel, there will be limited free movement of services, namely if the service for which free market access to the EU is requested is included in a special list; this means that free movement is limited to certain services.

The non-WTO countries Algeria and Lebanon drafted their own services and right of establishment provisions. Lebanon will apply the GATS rules after it has become a member of the WTO in the future. So, at present, nothing has happened yet regarding the movement of services between Lebanon and the EU. Algeria included the right of establishment of companies and their key personnel in the Euro-Med AA, but not the right of individuals to self-employment. There is only limited free movement of services between Algeria and the EU, i.e., limited to the supply of services by companies and their personnel.

At first sight, the ENP Action Plans aim at further integration into the EU internal market of services. The ENP Action Plans of Tunisia and Morocco provide for an Economic Agreement on the Liberalisation of Services with the EU in conformity with Article V of the GATS, and all Action Plans include the right of establishment of companies. However, the Euro-Med AAs already contain equivalent *rendez-vous* clauses providing for negotiations on trade in services, which should lead to Economic Agreements on the Liberalisation of Services in accordance with Article V of the GATS five years after the entry into force of these Agreements.[545] The Euro-Med AAs also contain the possibility to extend their scope to include the right of establishment. The ENP Action Plans aim to stimulate the liberalisation of services and the right of establishment, but do not entail innovative actions as regards the movement of services and the right of establishment. Moreover, the ENP Action Plans also exclude from their scope the right of individuals to self-employment.

The sectoral Euro-Med Conferences have also tried to stimulate the Euro-Med integration process. They started negotiations on the liberalisation of services and the right of establishment with the ready and interested Mediterranean partners. Negotiations on general provisions, followed by bilateral negotiations, have started with a first wave of negotiating countries: Egypt, Morocco, Tunisia and Israel. At a later stage, negotiations should also be launched with the other Mediterranean countries. It is recommended that this should be followed by a process of approximation of Mediterranean legislation to the EU internal market rules on services. In the future, the negotiations and the approximation process should lead to a preferential Economic Agreement on the Liberalisation of Services and the Right of Establishment with the EU in conformity with Article V of the GATS. These future agreements must include similar provisions on services and the right of establishment for all Mediterranean countries in order to ensure consistency of the legal framework. In the EU, the free movement of services is provided for not only in the TFEU, but also in an EU Directive on Services, which was adopted by the European Parliament and the Council in December 2006 and will have to be transposed by the EU Member States by the end of 2009.[546] The Mediterranean countries' first step will be alignment with the relevant provisions in the TFEU. A next step can be alignment with this new EU Directive on Services, which, however, will lead to a series of problems. It would be advisable for the Mediterranean countries to take account of the provisions in the EU Directive on Services to enhance mutual trust between the EU Member States. The trust problem will, in any event, also arise between the Mediterranean countries and the EU. The Directive includes, for example, measures to promote mutual assistance between Member States for enforcement purposes, harmonisation measures with respect to consumer protection and measures to promote the quality of services. It is very difficult for the EU Member States to reach agreement and, consequently, even more so for the Mediterranean partners and the EU. This is due to several reasons: (1) it is difficult for parties to assess what the liberalisation of services will bring in the future; (2) the liberalisation

[545] Sometimes, when EU leaders are discussing an important legal document, they cannot reach agreement on a particular issue. So they may decide to come back to this subject at a later date. Their decision is made official by putting it in writing and including it as a clause in the legal text they are discussing. This type of clause is known as a '*rendez-vous* clause.'

[546] Directive 2006/123/EC of the European Parliament and of the Council of 12 December 2006 on services in the internal market, *OJ* L 376, pp. 36-68. The services excluded from its scope are: financial services, telecommunications, transport, port services, temporary work agencies, healthcare services, audiovisual services, gambling, activities connected with the exercise of official authority, social services relating to social housing, childcare and support of families and persons in need, and private security services .

of services must always adapt to rapid developments in some service sectors, for example, telecommunications; and (3) there is a lack of trust in the quality of each others' services. Therefore, the EU Directive on services set up a system of rules that should increase mutual trust between the EU Member States. The EU Directive contains provisions for the fast removal of barriers to the movement of services, but also provides for a system that promotes quality of services, such as voluntary certification of cooperation activities between chambers of commerce. Recently, negotiations on the liberalisation of services and establishment have been started with Egypt, Morocco and Tunisia. It is recommended that the Mediterranean countries and the EU should first and foremost focus on a system that can enhance mutual trust in the quality of services offered, similar to the approach taken in the EU Directive on Services.[547]

In addition, it will be necessary to take into account the individual needs and different stages of development of the Mediterranean countries. These preferential economic agreements should therefore include specific provisions for each Mediterranean country. Israel, for example, is the only Mediterranean country whose ENP Action Plan states its intention to fully participate in the EU internal market of financial services. Israel will have to align its laws to the specific EU legislation regarding the movement of financial services.

Since, at present, the competition rules do not apply to the movement of services, it is recommended that the competition rules should apply to this field as well.

3. The extent of integration of the Mediterranean countries into the EU internal market of capital

3.1 European legislative framework

As regards the free movement of capital in the EU internal market, Article 63 of the TFEU states the following about free movement of capital between the Member States and third countries:

> 'All restrictions on capital movements and payments, both between Member States and between Member States and third countries, are prohibited.'

This means that the Mediterranean countries, being third countries, can benefit from the free movement of capital on legal grounds provided for in the TFEU itself. This is a significant provision when compared with the other freedoms of the EU internal market as provided for in the TFEU: the Treaty does not provide for free movement of goods, services and persons between the EU and third countries.

---

[547] See also S. Togan and J. Michalek, *The Role of the Services As the Factor of Integration of Euromed*, Research Paper for FEMISE (2007).

However, free movement of capital between the Member States and third countries (Mediterranean countries) is limited since the TFEU subjects these capital movements to a significant set of restrictions: (1) the EU may take restrictive measures regarding the movement of capital to or from third countries involving direct investment – including investment in real estate – establishment, the provision of financial services or the admission of securities to capital markets (Art. 64 TFEU); (2) the EU may restrict capital movements, in exceptional circumstances, to or from third countries that cause, or threaten to cause, serious difficulties for the operation of economic and monetary union (Art. 66 TFEU); and (3) the EU may also restrict capital movements to or from third countries in case of financial sanctions under the Common Foreign and Security Policy (CFSP) (Art. 75 TFEU): a Member State may, for serious political reasons and on grounds of urgency, take unilateral restrictive measures against a third country with regard to capital movements and payments.

In addition, Directive 88/361/EEC of 24 June 1988 for the implementation of Article 63 TFEU stipulates the following as regards the liberalisation of capital movements between Member States and third countries (Art. 7 of the Directive):

> '1. In their treatment of transfers in respect of movements of capital to or from third countries, the Member States shall endeavour to attain the same degree of liberalization as that which applies to operations with residents of other Member States, subject to the other provisions of this Directive.
>
> The provisions of the preceding subparagraph shall not prejudice the application to third countries of domestic rules or Community law, particularly any reciprocal conditions, concerning operations involving establishment, the provisions of financial services and the admission of securities to capital markets.
>
> 2. Where large-scale short-term capital movements to or from third countries seriously disturb the domestic or external monetary or financial situation of the Member States, or of a number of them, or cause serious strains in exchange relations within the Community or between the Community and third countries, Member States shall consult with one another on any measure to be taken to counteract such difficulties. This consultation shall take place within the Committee of Governors of the Central Banks and the Monetary Committee on the initiative of the Commission or of any Member State.'

It is noteworthy that the implementing Directive states that the Member States only have a 'best endeavours' obligation as regards the establishment of completely free movement of capital between the Member States and third countries. The requirement to use its 'best endeavours' is not an absolute obligation of result.[548] A 'best endeavours' clause should only be re-interpreted as an absolute obligation of result when membership of the EU is applied for or is pending.[549] Since for the Mediterranean countries membership of the EU is not an option,

[548] K. Pieters, 'The Mediterranean Countries (Morocco, Algeria, Tunisia, Libya, Egypt, Jordan, Syria and Lebanon)', in Blockmans and Łazowski, eds., *supra* n. 43, at p. 416.

[549] About the dynamic interpretation of the 'best endeavours' clause, see A. Łazowski and S. Yosifova, 'Bulgaria', in Blockmans and Łazowski, eds., *supra* n. 43, at p. 219.

this clause should be interpreted as it is, i.e., that 'best endeavours' are to be used without this implying an absolute responsibility in case of failure on the part of the EU Member States.

In conclusion, it can be stated that the free movement of capital between the EU and third countries as provided for in the TFEU is not as free as it seems at first sight, since the free movement of capital between the EU and the Mediterranean countries is subject to many restrictions and is formulated as a 'best endeavours' clause in the implementing Directive.

3.2 Movement of capital in the Euro-Med AAs and ENP Action Plans

The EU-Israel and EU-Jordan Euro-Med AAs provide for free movement of capital between the EU and Israel/Jordan. The Euro-Med AAs of all the other countries provide for free movement of capital but only for direct investments. In the future, they will have to work on further liberalisation of capital in other sectors.

One of the ENP's aims is to further liberalise the movement of capital between the EU and the Mediterranean countries. In their ENP Action Plans, Jordan, Israel, Morocco and Tunisia aim at full liberalisation of movement of capital. Egypt and Lebanon have little intention to liberalise movement of capital. The PA will try to improve the conditions for liberalising capital movement and attracting investors. According to the ENP Progress Reports of 2008, Jordan, Lebanon, Israel, Egypt and the PA did not make any progress as regards the liberalisation of capital, despite their intentions. Only Morocco and Tunisia achieved greater Euro-Med liberalisation of capital. However, the Progress Reports of 2009 mention good progress as regards the liberalisation of capital. Jordan remains one of the better performing Mediterranean countries in terms of attractiveness to foreign companies. Only between Lebanon and the EU does the liberalisation of capital remain insufficient.

A good development is that, in 2008, the sectoral Euro-Med Conference set up a Euro-Med Network of Public Finance Experts, which will focus on lifting obstacles to the labour and capital market in the Mediterranean countries and on strengthening their financial institutions. This Network could contribute to the Euro-Med liberalisation of capital since so far the ENP Action Plans and the sectoral Euro-Med Conferences have not succeeded in liberalising the movement of capital between the EU and the Mediterranean countries.

The TFEU states that all restrictions on the movement of capital between EU Member States and between EU Member States and third countries, in this case the Mediterranean countries, shall be prohibited. Restrictions are possible under Articles 64, 66 and 75 TFEU. All Euro-Med AAs provide for the free movement of capital for direct investments.[550] From a legal perspective, the Mediterranean countries have to a large extent integrated into the EU internal market of capital.

[550] Art. 39 Algeria AA; Art. 34 Morocco AA; Art. 34 Tunisia AA; Art. 32 Egypt AA; Art. 49 Jordan AA; Art. 31 Israel AA, and Art. 28 PA Interim AA.

4. The extent of integration of the Mediterranean countries into the EU internal market of persons

At present, there are still many constraints on the movement of Mediterranean persons in the EU; it is often the EU Member States that block the liberalisation of the Euro-Med movement of persons.

It is expected that the integration of Mediterranean workers into the EU labour market will have a positive effect on the economic situation of both the EU and the Mediterranean countries. Therefore, many multilateral instruments, such as the (sectoral) Euro-Med Conferences, the ENP Euro-Med Conference and the Euro-Mediterranean Parliamentary Assembly (EMPA), also promote the facilitation of movement of persons between the EU and the Mediterranean countries. But none of these instruments have led to concrete results in terms of further integration of the Mediterranean countries into the EU internal market of persons. The ENP Action Plans also contain measures aimed at further integration of the Mediterranean countries into the EU internal market of persons, such as facilitation of the movement of persons with respect to equal treatment of legal migrants and nationals. The ENP Progress Reports of 2008 and 2009, however, report no further integration whatsoever of the Mediterranean countries into the EU internal market of persons.

All in all, Moroccans, Tunisians and Algerians can rely on the non-discrimination provisions relating to working conditions, remuneration and dismissal and in the field of social security. They also have some social security rights, which require implementation by the Association Council for them to take effect. Israelis cannot rely on non-discrimination provisions, but do have some social security rights, which require implementation by their Association Council for them to take effect. Jordanians, Lebanese, Egyptians and Palestinians have no rights regarding the Euro-Med movement of persons.

5. Conclusion

Industrial goods from Morocco, Tunisia, Algeria, Jordan, Lebanon, the PA, Egypt and Israel which are imported into Europe are completely free of customs duties and charges having equivalent effect. European industrial goods exported to the Mediterranean countries, on the other hand, are to be progressively liberated over a transitional period of 12 years upon entry into force of the Euro-Med AA. Some Mediterranean countries, Morocco, Tunisia, Jordan, Lebanon, Egypt and Israel, have taken steps to facilitate the liberalisation process and have started negotiations on Agreements on Conformity Assessment and Acceptance of Industrial Products (ACAAs) which will be free trade corridors for industrial goods between the Mediterranean countries and the EU. To achieve good functioning ACAAs, the Mediterranean countries will approximate some of their legislation to EU legislation: a distinction should be made between industrial goods for which an EU harmonisation directive exists and those for which there are no EU harmonisation rules. For products for which a EU harmonisation regulation/directive exists, the Mediterranean countries want to implement European standards contained in EU harmonisation regulation/directive in their legislation. In the case of absence of EU harmonisation, technical rules create obstacles to the free movement of goods between the EU Member States. The Mediterranean countries and the EU also wish to apply the principle of mutual recognition to the movement of industrial goods in these non-harmonised EU areas.

Agricultural products, fishery products and industrial products with an agricultural element are subject to a gradual liberalisation programme between the EU on the one hand and Morocco, Tunisia, Algeria, Jordan, Lebanon, the PA, Egypt and Israel on the other hand. There should be free movement of agricultural products, fishery products and industrial products with an agricultural element by 2010. Egypt, Israel, Tunisia and Morocco took measures for further integration and have started negotiations, which are still ongoing, as regards the Euro-Med liberalisation of agricultural, processed agricultural and fishery products. The Euro-Med movement of goods should go along with a good-functioning Euro-Med competition mechanism and Euro-Med rules of origin. Competition provisions and rules of origin provisions are present but do not function properly.

The Euro-Med movement of services or the right of establishment is being negotiated at present. For the time being, the WTO countries – Morocco, Tunisia, Egypt, Jordan and Israel – apply the GATS obligations. The non-WTO countries Algeria and Lebanon drafted their own services and right of establishment provisions in the Euro-Med AAs. Lebanon will apply the GATS rules after it has become a member of the WTO in the future. The EU on the one hand and Egypt, Morocco, Tunisia and Israel on the other hand have started negotiations on the further liberalisation of services and the right of establishment. In the future, these negotiations, together with the approximation process in the field of services should lead to a preferential Economic Agreement on the Liberalisation of Services and the Right of Establishment with the EU in conformity with Article V of the GATS.

The Euro-Med free movement of capital is the only freedom that finds his legal basis in the TFEU. The TFEU provides for free movement of capital between the EU and third countries but also subjects this free movement of capital between the EU and the Mediterranean countries to many restrictions. The EU implementing directive of the relevant TFEU provisions formulate the Euro-Med free movement of capital merely as a 'best endeavours' clause. The Euro-Med free movement of capital is not as free as might seem at first sight. Jordan, Israel, Morocco and Tunisia aim at full liberalisation of movement of capital. Egypt and Lebanon have little intention to liberalise movement of capital. The PA will try to improve the conditions for liberalising capital movement and attracting investors. Only Morocco and Tunisia achieved greater Euro-Med liberalisation of capital in 2009.

There is no such thing as free movement of persons between the Mediterranean countries and the EU. There are no provisions about the free movement of person in the Euro-Med AAs, only limited rights are attributed to some Mediterranean persons. Also the ENP Actions Plans lack proper provisions about the Euro-Med movement of persons. This lack of free movement of persons is confirmed in the ENP Progress Reports which do not notify any free movement of persons, nor any form of progress towards free movement of persons between the Mediterranean countries and the EU.

Chapter VII

Exporting the EU internal market principles to the Mediterranean countries

In this chapter, it will be analysed to what extent the EU internal market principles contributed to integration of the Mediterranean countries in the EU internal market. Therefore, the EU internal market principles of movement of goods, services, capital and persons will be compared to the 'movement of goods, services, capital and persons' rules as applied in the Euro-Med relationship. A short overview of the EU internal market principles can be found in Chapter II of this book. The Euro-Med movement of goods, services, capital and persons rules were extensively examined in the previous chapters.

1. The EU and the Euro-Med 'movement of goods' rules compared

The integration of the Mediterranean goods into the EU will be compared with the principles of the fully liberalised EU internal market of goods.

1.1 Goods in the Euro-Med context and in the EU context

At the moment, the rules on the movement of goods between the Mediterranean countries and the EU are different for industrial products, on the one hand, and agricultural products, fishery products and industrial products with an agricultural element, on the other. The TFEU makes no distinction between industrial and agricultural goods. According to the ECJ, the free movement of goods within the EU applies to all products which can be valued in money and which are capable, as such, of forming the subject of commercial transactions. The rules of the common market, for example, apply to items possessing artistic or historic value subject only to the exceptions expressly provided by the Treaty.[551] When the trade in industrial products, agricultural products, fishery products and industrial products with an agricultural element is fully liberalised between the Mediterranean countries and the EU, the distinction between industrial and agricultural goods will disappear. At that moment, all goods will move freely and under the same rules between the Mediterranean countries and the EU, but they might still be subject to exceptions provided for in the TFEU or secondary legislation, for example, where it involves agricultural products or sensitive industrial goods.

[551] Judgment of the ECJ of 10 December 1968 in Case 7/68 *Commission* v *Italian Republic* [1968] *ECR* 423.

1.2 The concept of 'customs duties and charges having equivalent effect' compared

Article 30 of the TFEU states that all customs duties on imports and exports and charges having equivalent effect shall be prohibited between Member States. Regarding the movement of goods between the Mediterranean countries and the EU, the same rule applies, but only for industrial goods: goods originating in a Mediterranean country which are imported into the EU are also completely free of customs duties and charges having equivalent effect. However, the prohibition of customs duties and measures having equivalent effect does not apply to agricultural products, fishery products and industrial products with an agricultural element. These products remain subject to customs charges and quotas.[552] Another question that arises is whether what is meant by 'charges having equivalent effect' has the same meaning for trade within the EU as for trade between a Mediterranean country and the EU. According to the ECJ, a charge having equivalent effect levied on the EU movement of goods is 'any pecuniary charge, however small and whatever its designation and mode of application, which is imposed unilaterally on domestic or foreign goods by reason of the fact that they cross a frontier, and which is not a customs duty in the strict sense even if it is not imposed for the benefit of the state, is not discriminatory or protective in effect and if the product on which the charge is imposed is not in competition with any domestic product.'[553] According to Advocate-General Léger the expression 'charge having equivalent effect to a customs duty' in Article 9 of the Mediterranean Cooperation Agreement must be understood as any pecuniary charge, whatever its designation and mode of application, which is imposed unilaterally on goods by reason of the fact that they cross a frontier, and which is not a customs duty in the strict sense, even though such pecuniary charge is not levied for the benefit of the state.[554] So, the concept of charges having equivalent effect in intra-EU trade has the same meaning as in trade between a Mediterranean country and the EU.

1.3 The concept of 'quantitative restrictions and measures having equivalent effect' compared

The free movement of goods within the EU internal market is defined in Article 34 of the TFEU, which states that all quantitative restrictions on imports and all measures having equivalent effect shall be prohibited between Member States. The ECJ clarified the concept of 'quantitative restrictions and measures having equivalent effect' in the famous *Dassonville* case: 'All trading rules enacted by

---

[552] The Communication of the Commission on its New Neighbourhood Policy in an enlarged Europe also points out that there is still room to deepen the Euro-Med AAs in the domain of trade in agricultural products.

[553] Case 24/68 *Commission* v *Italy* [1969] *ECR* 193, para. 9.

[554] C-173/05 *Commission* v *Italian Republic* [2007] *ECR* I-04917 and Opinion of Advocate-General Léger delivered on 5 October 2006.

Member States which are capable of hindering, directly or indirectly, actually or potentially, intra-Community trade are to be considered as measures having an effect equivalent to quantitative restrictions.'[555] All Euro-Med AAs contain a similar provision on the prohibition of quantitative restrictions that only applies to completely liberalised, i.e., industrial, goods. Agricultural goods remain subject to restrictions. In the *Polydor* case, the ECJ stated that the provision for the unconditional abolition of certain restrictions, such as quantitative restrictions and measures having the equivalent effect in the AA, cannot be interpreted in the same way as the similar provision in Article 30 EC Treaty (renumbered as Art. 34 TFEU).[556] Indeed, the interpretation of the derogation provisions in the Euro-Med AAs and in the TFEU differs, since the Euro-Med AA and the TFEU have a different purpose: the EU and the Mediterranean countries do not constitute a Euro-Med internal market, which leaves more room for restrictions than in the EU internal market. The Mediterranean countries and the EU, however, are going through a gradual liberalisation process. This means that the deeper the Euro-Med integration becomes, the fewer restrictions will be tolerated. Besides, according to settled case law, a mere similarity in the wording of a provision of the TFEU and an international agreement between the EU and a non-member country is not sufficient to give the wording of that agreement the same meaning as in the TFEU.[557]

1.4 Derogations from the free movement of goods compared

Article 36 TFEU allows some restrictions on imports, exports or goods in transit justified on grounds of public morality, public policy or public security; the protection of health and life of humans, animals or plants; the protection of national treasures possessing artistic, historic or archaeological value; or the protection of industrial and commercial property. The Mediterranean countries and the EU may also derogate from the principle of free movement of goods for the same reasons, but more grounds were added: the protection of national treasures possessing architectural value, rules related to gold and silver, and the conservation of exhaustible natural resources.[558] Such prohibitions or restrictions should not, however, constitute a means of arbitrary discrimination or a disguised restriction on trade between parties. The ECJ has given a restrictive interpretation of these prohibitions, which are always of a non-economic nature.[559] The justification of a restrictive national measure on grounds of public morality, public policy or public security and also on grounds of protections of health and life

---

[555] Case 8/74 *Procureur du Roi* v *Benoît and Gustave Dassonville* [1974] *ECR* 837.

[556] C-270/80 *Polydor Limited and RSO Records Inc.* v *Harlequin Records Shops Limited and Simons Records Limited* [1982] *ECR* 329.

[557] *Polydor* case, paras. 14-21; Case 104/81 *Kupferberg* [1982] *ECR* 3641, paras. 29-31, and C-312/91 *Metalsa* [1993] *ECR* I-3751, paras. 11-20.

[558] Art. 27 Algeria AA; Art. 28 Morocco AA; Art. 28 Tunisia AA; Art. 26 Egypt AA; Art. 27 Jordan AA; Art. 27 Israel AA, and Art. 27 Lebanon AA. The derogation regarding the conservation of exhaustible natural resources is only provided for in the Lebanon AA (Art. 27).

[559] Case 7/61 *Commission* v *Italy* [1961] *ECR* 317 and Case 13/68 *Salgoil* [1968] *ECR* 453.

of humans, animals and plants might lead to interesting situations. Keeping the *Henn and Darby* case of the ECJ in mind, it is the Member State itself which may define the sense of morality which should pertain in the Member State.[560] The EU Member States might have a similar sense of morality, but the principles of morality, public policy and security and even the value of life and health might be very different in some Mediterranean countries. It is expected that the Mediterranean countries will define the principles in a stricter way and will prevent more European goods from entering their territory than *vice versa*. There might raise more problems when delimitating the concept 'protection of health and life of humans, animals and plants.' The derogation of 'public health' was examined in the *Sandoz* case of the ECJ.[561] In this case it is defined that the justification of a restrictive national measure on the grounds of the health exception must be based on scientific evidence. Further the ECJ stated that the restrictive national measure must be accepted in cases of absence of scientific evidence. The difficulty which might occur in the Euro-Med relationship is the 'recognition of scientific evidence.' Will the Europeans recognise scientific proof from the Mediterranean countries and *vice versa*?

The principle of proportionality applies in intra-community trade as well as in trade between the Mediterranean countries and the EU. The ECJ's doctrine in the *Polydor* case applies here as well: the less integrated, the more restrictions will be possible or the more advanced the level of Euro-Med integration, the fewer restrictions will be accepted. Since the Euro-Med policies have different integration aims, which have not yet been realised, it is advisable for the ECJ judges to not only take into account the goals of Euro-Med integration that are proposed by the different Euro-Med policies, but also look at the extent of Euro-Med integration in reality. This level of integration is different for each of the four freedoms of the EU internal market and is subject to changes each year.

As regards intra-EU trade in goods, in the *Cassis de Dijon* case about the rule of reason the ECJ stated that other restrictions to the free movement of goods within the EU were also possible.[562] The parties may restrict free movement of goods in anticipation of harmonisation of laws in particular fields at EU level, if a mandatory requirement or public interest needs to be satisfied such as the protection of public health, the protection of consumers, the protection of the environment, the protection of traffic safety, or the proper functioning of the telecommunication services.[563] The national measure that restricts trade must be of a non-economic nature, applicable without any distinction to national products as to imported products. The proportionality principle must be met. So far, the rule of reason has never been applied in the Euro-Med relationship. However, it can be argued that the rule of reason rule may also apply between the Mediter-

[560] Case 34/79 *Regina* v *Maurice Donald Henn and John Frederick Ernest Darby* [1979] *ECR* 3795.

[561] Case 174/82 *Officier van Justitie* v *Sandoz* [1983] *ECR* 2445.

[562] Case 120/78 *Rewe-Zentral AG* v *Bundesmonopolverwaltung für Branntwein* [1979] *ECR* 00649.

[563] This list is not exhaustive.

ranean countries and the EU in anticipation of harmonisation of laws. If so, the Mediterranean countries and the EU may restrict free movement of goods if a mandatory requirement or public interest needs to be satisfied, such as, for example, the protection of public health, the protection of consumers, the protection of the environment, the protection of traffic safety, or the proper functioning of the telecommunication services, but only in fields that have not been harmonised. It is the ECJ that will have to determine – on a case-by-case basis – whether or not there is a mandatory requirement. So far, the ECJ has not delivered any judgments about the possible application of the rule of reason in the trade circulation between the Mediterranean countries and the EU. An interesting conclusion is that the deeper the Euro-Med integration becomes, the fewer restrictions will be tolerated.

1.5 Direct effect?

Articles 34 and 36 of the TFEU as well as the relevant movement of goods provisions in the Euro-Med AAs have direct effect in the national legal orders. Nationals from the Member States and persons from the Mediterranean countries can rely on these provisions before their national courts.

1.6 Harmonisation of Mediterranean law with EU law

Article 36 of the TFEU and the rule of reason can no longer be applied when the national laws of the different EU Member States have been harmonised at European level.[564] Article 114 TFEU, however, provides some possibilities for restrictions by Member States after harmonisation at European level. These exceptions have not often been invoked.[565] Such an 'Article 114 TFEU' exception is not available under the Euro-Med relationship.

There is harmonisation at European level, but harmonisation is also in the making at Euro-Med level. The Mediterranean countries have implemented some interesting EU harmonisation directives, for example, those covering industrial goods which constitute a large part of Mediterranean countries' export to the European market. Ultimately, this approximation process should lead to the

---

[564] Case C-1/96 *The Queen* v *Minister of Agriculture, Fisheries and Food,* ex parte*: Compassion in World Farming Ltd* [1998] *ECR* I-1251. The ECJ made it clear that a Member State could not rely on the views or behaviour of a section of national public opinion in order unilaterally to challenge a harmonising measure (in this case a directive) adopted by the EC institutions.

[565] Art. 95, para. 4 EC Treaty: 'If, after the adoption by the Council or by the Commission of a harmonisation measure, a Member State deems it necessary to maintain national provisions on grounds of major needs referred to in Article 30, or relating to the protection of the environment or the working environment, it shall notify the Commission of these provisions as well as the grounds for maintaining them.' Art. 95, para. 5 EC Treaty: 'Moreover, without prejudice to paragraph 4, if, after the adoption by the Council or by the Commission of a harmonisation measure, a Member State deems it necessary to introduce national provisions based on new scientific evidence relating to the protection of the environment or the working environment on grounds of a problem specific to that Member State arising after the adoption of the harmonisation measure, it shall notify the Commission of the envisaged provisions as well as the grounds for introducing them.'

conclusion of ACAAs. These ACAAs will thus be an example of harmonisation at Euro-Med level. According to the existing EU rules, derogations from the free movement of goods will no longer be possible after the Mediterranean countries and the EU have concluded these ACAAs. They will moreover no longer be able to rely on the derogation provisions provided for in their Euro-Med AAs, similar to Article 36 TFEU, to invoke restrictions on the free movement of industrial goods.

1.7 Mutual recognition in non-harmonised areas

At European level, the Member States apply the principle of mutual recognition of goods in non-harmonised areas. The 'mutual recognition' principle emerged from the *Cassis de Dijon* case of the ECJ:[566] EU Member States must allow all products from other EU Member States to their territory if these have been lawfully produced in the exporting EU Member State. The implementation of this principle was hampered by several problems. The European Parliament and the Council therefore adopted Regulation (EC) No 764/2008,[567] which will apply from 13 May 2009. The Mediterranean countries and the EU are also considering applying the principle of mutual recognition to the movement of industrial goods in non-harmonised EU areas. It is recommended that the Mediterranean countries take account of this new Regulation in order to anticipate problems that may arise between them and the EU. Jakubiak correctly remarks that the principle of mutual recognition requires a substantial amount of confidence in the other party which will take time to develop in the Euro-Mediterranean relationship.[568]

It is recommended that the Mediterranean countries continue further alignment with European sanitary and phytosanitary (SPS) regulations. A better quality of Mediterranean food products would enhance European buyers' trust in these products and thus lead to better integration of Mediterranean food products into the EU. In my opinion, trust can be improved by setting up the necessary infrastructure in the Mediterranean countries: to improve the quality of goods all Mediterranean countries need an institute that deals with alignment with European SPS regulations. For the application of the mutual recognition principle all Mediterranean countries must have an institute that ensures and certifies the quality of products for which there are no harmonisation rules.

---

[566] Case 120/78 *Rewe-Zentral AG* v *Bundesmonopolverwaltung für Branntwein* [1979] *ECR* 649.

[567] Regulation (EC) No 764/2008 of the European Parliament and of the Council of 9 July 2008 laying down procedures relating to the application of certain national technical rules to products lawfully marketed in another Member State and repealing Decision No 3052/95/EC, *OJ* L 218/21.

[568] Jakubiak, et al., *supra* n. 51, pp. 22-23.

1.8 Competition rules and rules of origin

The Euro-Med competition rules are not successful in guiding the process of integration of Mediterranean goods into the EU. The integration of the Mediterranean countries into the EU internal market of goods will be difficult to achieve if implementation of essential provisions, such as the competition rules, fails to occur. The lack of competition rules is hindering the integration of the Mediterranean countries into the EU internal market of goods. After the final liberalisation date for goods, each Mediterranean country and the EU should have a well-functioning competition system and a proper system for enforcing these competition rules, but so far most ENP Action Plans have produced no significant results as regards the improvement of the Euro-Med competition system. Only Israel has a properly functioning competition system. Contrary to the EU rules, the Euro-Med competition rules only apply to the Euro-Med movement of goods and not to that of services.

Contrary to the situation in the EU internal market, the successful integration of goods is severely hampered by the lack of a properly functioning competition system and the inapplicability of the Euro-Med rules of origin. It would be advisable to set up a Working Group within the framework of the specialised Euro-Med Conferences that mainly deals with Euro-Med competition issues. This Group should address the issue of exemption of anti-competitive agreements in the Euro-Med relationship, because at the moment each Mediterranean country is allowed to exempt anti-competitive agreements on the basis of criteria other than those provided for in Article 101(3) TFEU. In addition, the Working Group should investigate whether it would also be possible for the Mediterranean countries to take action when agreements between European firms or abuses by European dominant undertakings harm the interests of competitors established in the Mediterranean countries. Another significant point is that the Euro-Med competition provisions do not apply to undertakings that provide services on the market, but only to the movement of goods. It is recommended that while negotiations are ongoing as regards the Euro-Med liberalisation of the movement of services, the application of the Euro-Med competition rules should also be taken into account. Besides, it would be to the advantage of the Mediterranean countries if the Euro-Med Association Councils were to take action in the competition field and implement the provisions of the Euro-Med AAs.

The Euro-Med rules of origin should also facilitate the integration of the Mediterranean countries into the EU internal market, but the main condition for the application of the rules of origin in the Euro-Med relationship has not been fulfilled, namely the conclusion of free trade agreements between all the countries involved. It can therefore be concluded that the Euro-Med rules of origin are not being successfully applied.

2. The EU and the Euro-Med 'movement of services, including the right of establishment' rules compared

The integration of services of the Mediterranean countries into the EU will be compared with the principles of the EU internal market of services.

2.1 What is the definition of services and establishment in the Euro-Med context and in the EU context?

In the EU, services are normally provided for remuneration, in so far as they are not governed by the provisions relating to freedom of movement of goods, capital and persons. They include activities of an industrial and commercial character, activities of craftsmen and activities of the professions. There is no definition of 'services' in the Euro-Med AAs or the ENP Action Plans.

The Euro-Med AAs however provide for a definition of 'establishment' as the right of EU or any Jordanian companies to take up economic activities by means of the setting up of subsidiaries and branches in Jordan or in the EU.[569] An 'economic activity' is an activity of an industrial, commercial and professional character.[570] The TFEU itself has no definition of the term 'establishment.'

2.2 The provision of free movement of services and the right of establishment compared

The free movement of services is guaranteed in the TFEU: the provider of services should be able to carry out his activities whenever he wants in another EU Member State for a limited period of time. Article 56 TFEU provides for the free movement of services in the EU; it prohibits restrictions on the freedom to provide services within the EU in respect of nationals of Member States who are established in a state of the EU other than that of the person for whom the services are intended. This provision has direct effect in the legal orders of the Member States. The non-discrimination provision in the field of the EU movement of services stipulates that the person providing a service may temporarily pursue his activity in the Member State where the service is provided, under the same conditions as are imposed by that state on its own nationals.[571] This provision also has direct effect. The right of establishment in the EU is laid down in Article 50 of the TFEU:

> '1. In order to attain freedom of establishment as regards a particular activity, the Council, acting in accordance with the procedure referred to in Article 251 and after consulting the Economic and Social Committee, shall act by means of directives.'

---

569 Art. 32 Jordan/EC AA.
570 *Idem.*
571 Art. 57 TFEU.

For the Mediterranean countries and the EU there is no similar provision on the free movement of services, including the right of establishment. Free movement of services and establishment is only guaranteed for the WTO countries (Morocco, Tunisia, Egypt, Jordan and Israel) but is limited to a certain range of services (see Table). For Algeria, there is free movement of services of companies.[572] The Euro-Med AAs do not include a non-discrimination provision regarding the Euro-Med movement of services. The WTO countries apply the Most-Favoured-Nation principle, which stipulates that each member accords immediately and unconditionally to services and service suppliers of any other member treatment no less favourable than that it accords to like services and service suppliers of any other country.

	Egypt	Jordan	Morocco	Tunisia	Israel
Business		x	x		x
Communications	x	x	x	x	x
Construction	x	x	x		
Distribution		x			
Education		x			
Environmental		x	x		x
Financial	x	x	x	x	x
Health/social		x			
Tourism	x	x	x	x	x
Recreation/sport		x			
Transport	x	x	x		

(Source: based on the Services Database of the WTO, available at: http://tsdb.wto.org/default.aspx, June 2009)

2.3 Services provided by legal or natural persons

Services within the EU context include activities carried out by companies and on a self-employed basis. Performing activities on a self-employed basis is different from performing activities in a relationship of dependency. Free movement of services for companies and on a self-employed basis is only guaranteed for the WTO countries but limited to a certain range of services. For the other Mediterranean countries, free movement of services is limited to companies (Algeria) or there is no free movement of services at all (Lebanon and the PA). A critical remark is in order regarding the ENP Action Plans, which are supposed to establish further integration of the Mediterranean countries into the EU internal market of services. The Action Plans take a step backwards by not including in their scope the right of individuals to self-employment. It is recommended that if the Mediterranean countries aim for strong alignment with the rules of the EU inter-

[572] Jordan became a WTO member in 2000.

nal market of services, they should negotiate incorporation of the right of individuals to self-employment (and not only of companies) into their future agreements.

2.4 The concept of 'prohibition or restrictions and all measures having equivalent effect' compared

The ECJ has clarified its *Dassonville* case law applicable to the EU free movement of services by stating that all trading rules enacted by Member States which are capable of hindering, directly or indirectly, actually or potentially, intra-EU trade of services are considered to be measures having an effect equivalent to quantitative restrictions and are not tolerated. In the Euro-Med relationship there is no such provision that prohibits restrictions and measures having an equivalent effect on the movement of services, since no free movement is guaranteed. The Euro-Med movement of services is still subject to many restrictions. For the WTO countries, however, the GATS determines whether or not restrictions are possible.

2.5 Derogations from the freedom of services compared

Some restrictions on the EU free movement of services are possible: the freedom of services does not apply to activities which in the Member State are connected, even occasionally, with the exercise of official authority (Art. 51 TFEU) and where there are grounds of public policy, public security or public health (Art. 52 TFEU).

In the Euro-Med relationship, the WTO countries are subject to the derogations as provided for in the GATS. Jordan is for services covered by the GATS subject to the derogations provided for in the GATS. For the other services the Jordan/EU AA applies. Article 41 of this Euro-Med AA provides for limitations on the free movement of services on the basis of public policy, public security or public health. Furthermore, this article defines that the freedom of services does not apply to activities which in Jordan or the EU are connected, even occasionally, with the exercise of official authority. The Algeria/EU AA provides for exactly the same derogations provisions (Art. 35 Algeria/EU AA). The Lebanon/EU AA foresees in a Euro-Med liberalisation only at the date of entry of Lebanon to the WTO. After entry to the GATS, Lebanon will be subject to the provisions as regards the movement of services and its derogations as provided for in the GATS. The PA/EU Interim Agreement entails no provision on the movement of services.

The ECJ also made it possible to restrict free movement of services on the grounds of the rule of reason within the EU. In the Euro-Med relationship, the rule of reason has never been applied.

2.6 Harmonised areas

The EU also created a legal framework via a Directive on Services in the internal market to harmonise certain services sectors between the Member States.[573] Not all sectors are covered by this Directive. The following services are excluded from the scope of the Directive: electronic communications; transport (urban transport, taxis, ambulances); financial services; audiovisual services; gambling; social services (housing, childcare, family support); taxation; public and private healthcare provided by professionals to patients; and pharmaceutical services.

There is no such legal framework between the Mediterranean countries and the EU. Harmonisation of certain services does not seem to be the goal of the Euro-Med liberalisation process, but the objective is the removal of the main tariff and non-tariff barriers that hinder the movement of services, depending on the state of economic development of the respective Mediterranean country and the desired degree of integration.[574]

2.7 Mutual recognition in non-harmonised areas

Mutual recognition can apply to the circulation of goods, but also to the movement of services in fields where technical legislation has not been harmonised. In this way, it contributes to economic integration. The ECJ formulated the principle of mutual recognition in the *Cassis de Dijon* case.[575] Jakubiak correctly remarks that the principle of mutual recognition requires a substantial amount of confidence in the other party which will take time to develop in the Euro-Mediterranean relationship.[576]

The EU guarantees the mutual recognition of professional qualifications between the different Member States via Directive 2005/36/EC covering all recognition rules (except for those applicable to lawyers, activities in the field of toxic substances and commercial agents).[577] There is no mutual recognition of professional qualifications between the Mediterranean countries and the EU.

3. The EU and the Euro-Med 'movement of capital' rules compared

The Euro-Med free movement of capital and payments is in the best interest of the Mediterranean countries since this freedom will lead to more foreign invest-

---

573 Directive 2006/123/EC of the European Parliament and of the Council of 12 December 2006 on services in the internal market, *OJ* L 376/36.

574 D. Müller-Jentsch, Deep integration and trade in services in the Euro-Mediterranean Region, World Bank/European Commission, p. 15.

575 C-120/78 *Rewe-Zentral AG* v *Bundesmonopolverwaltung für Branntwein* [1979] *ECR* 649.

576 Jakubiak, et al., *supra* n. 51, pp. 22-23.

577 Directive 2005/36/EC of the European Parliament and of the Council of 7 September 2005 on the recognition of professional qualifications, *OJ* L 255/22.

ment in these countries, which could stimulate their economic development. But do the EU internal market principles for the movement of capital apply in the Euro-Med integration process? The Euro-Med liberalisation process will be compared with the free movement of capital in the EU internal market itself.

3.1 Legal provisions

As mentioned above, the free movement of capital in the EU internal market is laid down in Article 63 and subsequent articles of the TFEU. Article 63 states the following about free movement of capital between the Member States and third countries:

> 'All restrictions on capital movements and payments, both between Member States and between Member States and third countries, are prohibited.'

This means that from a legal point of view, the Euro-Med liberalisation of capital is in accordance with the free movement of capital within the EU internal market. Moreover, the Euro-Med AAs and ENP Action Plans also provide for free movement of capital between the EU and the Mediterranean countries. It is the only freedom of the EU internal market which is made applicable between the EU and third countries in the TFEU itself.

3.2 Direct effect?

Article 56 of the EC Treaty (now renumbered as Art. 63 of the TFEU) was held to have direct effect in case *Sanz de Lera* of the ECJ.[578] This means that nationals from the Member States as well as nationals from the Mediterranean countries may rely on the 'free movement of capital provision' before the national courts.

3.3 Similar freedom?

Considering Article 63 of the TFEU, it is to be expected that the free movement of capital within the EU and the Euro-Med movement of capital and investment is identical. This is not so, since the other articles of the TFEU qualify Article 63 of the TFEU to non-member countries, *in casu* the Mediterranean countries.[579] Capital restrictions between the Member States and the Mediterranean countries which existed before 31 December 1993 may remain (Art. 64 TFEU). Article 64 TFEU and Article 7 of Directive 88/361/EEC of 24 June 1988 for the implementation of Article 63 TFEU stipulates further delimit the scope of the free movement of capital between the Mediterranean countries and the Member States by inserting a 'best endeavours' clause: the Member States and the EU Council shall

[578] C-163, 165, and 250/94 *Criminal Proceedings against Lucas Emilio Sanz de Lera* [1995] *ECR* I-4821.

[579] P. Craig and G. De Burca, *EU Law Text, Cases and Materials Fourth Edition* (Oxford, Oxford Univeristy Press 2008) p. 725.

try to attain the same degree of liberalisation as that which applies to operations with residents of other Member States. Art. 66 TFEU leaves the possibility for taking safeguard measures between the Member States and the Mediterranean countries.

3.4 Exporting case-law of the European Court of Justice (ECJ) to the Mediterranean countries

Since Article 63 and subsequent articles of the TFEU can be interpreted by the ECJ, it follows that the interpretation of the notion of free movement of capital between the EU and third countries in Article 63 and subsequent articles of the TFEU also applies in the EU-Med context. An example of such a judgment can be found in case *Staatssecretaris van Financiën* v *Orange European Smallcap Fund NV* of the ECJ of 20 May 2008.[580] The definition of a restriction covered by Article 64 TFEU given by the ECJ as 'being a restriction on the movement of capital involving direct investment in so far as it relates to investments of any kind undertaken by natural or legal persons and which serve to establish or maintain lasting and direct links between the persons providing the capital and the undertakings to which that capital is made available in order to carry out an economic activity' also applies in the Euro-Med context.

4. The EU and the Euro-Med 'movement of persons' rules compared

The Euro-Med movement of persons will be compared with the free movement of persons in the EU internal market.

4.1 Distinction between free movement of persons and (il)legal migration

The TFEU clearly makes a distinction between the free movement of persons and (il)legal migration issues. The freedom of movement for persons itself is divided into persons who are a national of a Member State and are engaged in an economic activity: (1) as a worker (Arts. 45-48); (2) as a self-employed person (Arts. 49-54) or (3) as a provider or receiver of services (Arts. 56-62). Exceptions to the free movement of persons are possible on grounds of public policy, public security and public health and on the ground of employment in the public sector.

In the Euro-Med context, this distinction between persons and immigrants is often neglected. The Euro-Med AA is the only instrument that clearly makes a distinction between the Euro-Med movement of persons (*in casu*: workers) and the management of (il)legal migration. All other instruments are not consistent about this issue: sometimes they deal with the Euro-Med movement of workers and migration management as if these are one and the same thing.

---

[580] C-194/06 *Staatssecretaris van Financiën* v *Orange European Smallcap Fund N.V.* [1998] *ECR* I-03747.

4.2 Free movement of self-employed persons compared

Free movement of self-employed persons, service providers and recipients of services is provided under EU law by Directive 2004/38/EC of 29 April 2004 on the right of EU citizens and their family members to move and reside freely within the territory of the EU Member States. The Euro-Med AAs and the ENP Actions Plans exclude the right of movement for self-employed persons from their scope. In other words, the EU rules on establishment for natural persons do not apply in the Euro-Med relationship.

4.3 Free movement of workers compared

This freedom is laid down in Article 45 of the TFEU, stating the following:

> '1. Freedom of movement for workers shall be secured within the Community.
> 2. Such freedom of movement shall entail the abolition of any discrimination based on nationality between workers of the Member States as regards employment, remuneration and other conditions of work and employment.
> 3. It shall entail the right, subject to limitations justified on grounds of public policy, public security or public health: (a) to accept offers of employment actually made; (b) to move freely within the territory of Member States for this purpose; (c) to stay in a Member State for the purpose of employment in accordance with the provisions governing the employment of nationals of that State laid down by law, regulation or administrative action; (d) to remain in the territory of a Member State after having been employed in that State, subject to conditions which shall be embodied in implementing regulations to be drawn up by the Commission.
> 4. The provisions of this article shall not apply to employment in the public service.'

Freedom of movement for economically active workers (Arts. 45-48) is further regulated in secondary EU legislation: Regulation No 1612/68 on the free movement of workers,[581] Regulation 1251/70 on the right to remain in the territory of a Member State after having been employed in that state and Directive 2004/38/EC on the right of workers and their family members to move and reside freely within the territory of the Member States.[582]

There are no common 'movement of workers' provisions in the Euro-Med AAs. Although a distinction should be made between the Maghreb and the Mashrek Euro-Med AAs. The Maghreb AAs contain some liberal provisions relating to the movement of workers, such as on non-discrimination as regards working conditions, remuneration and dismissal and in the field of social security. These non-discrimination provisions have direct effect. None of the other Euro-Med AAs provide for non-discrimination regarding working conditions, remuneration and dismissal or in the field of social security. The Maghreb AAs and the Israel AA include some social security rights. However, in order for these principles to take effect, the AAs also require that the Association Councils

---

[581] *OJ* 1968 Spec. Edn. I-475.
[582] *OJ* L 204 of 4 August 2007, p. 28.

adopt measures to implement the principles on the coordination of social security systems. Since no Association Council has yet taken a decision in relation to the social security provisions in the Euro-Med AAs, they lack direct effect. The Jordan, Lebanon and Egypt AAs and the PA Interim Agreement contain no provisions concerning the movement of workers. There is no free movement of persons between the two shores of the Mediterranean, only limited rights resulting from the Maghreb AAs and the Israel AA. The modest rights provided for in the Maghreb AAs, however, have already resulted in quite some jurisprudence of the ECJ.

Another interesting issue concerns the social security for workers. In the EU, Regulation 1408/71 of 14 June 1971 defines the coordination mechanism for national social security system in which all EU nationals can benefit from the same social advantages as national workers. Examples in this Regulation are language rights, death benefits, and the right to be accompanied by unmarried companions; and migrants have access to vocational schools and retraining centres under the same conditions as national workers. This Regulation served as the basis for the Coordination Mechanism for social security system which was only set up for Morocco.

4.4 Free movement of economically non-active persons compared

For a long time there was no free movement for economically non-active persons within the EU. To free the movement of economically non-active persons, the EU adopted secondary legislation, for example Directive 2004/38/EC on the right to move and reside freely within the EU for economically non-active nationals of a Member State, such as students enrolled in vocational training, retired persons and other non-active persons.

Economically non-active persons only have rights to reside and move freely within the Member States under Article 21(1) of the TFEU.[583] Article 21 stipulates the following:

> '1. Every citizen of the Union shall have the right to move and reside freely within the territory of the Member States, subject to the limitations and conditions laid down in this Treaty and by the measures adopted to give it effect.'

These rights have been implemented by Directive No 2004/38/EC, which applies to all citizens of the EU and their family members.

The free movement of economically non-active persons is non-existing in the Euro-Med relationship. Persons from Mediterranean countries, however, can benefit from the Directive No 2004/38/EC if they are classified as a family member of a EU national.

[583] Barnard, *supra* n. 29, p. 232.

4.5 The principle of non-discrimination

The free movement of persons in the EU is based on the principle of non-discrimination on the ground of nationality: migrants enjoy the same treatment as nationals in a comparable situation.[584] The Euro-Med AAs that entail some liberal provisons as regards the movement of workers are also grounded on the principle of non-discrimination as regards nationality.

5. Conclusion

5.1 Exporting the EU internal market principles in the field of goods

It may be concluded that the integration of the Mediterranean countries into the EU internal market of industrial goods has been successful and happens according to the main EU internal market principles. The Euro-Med liberalisation of agricultural products also takes place along these same principles. It is only a matter of time before the integration of Mediterranean agricultural goods into the EU internal market will be a success. So far, trade negotiations on agricultural and fishery products have finished with Egypt and Israel and are ongoing with Morocco and Tunisia. However, it can be expected that the EU will maintain some restrictive measures in order to protect its common market from the influx of Mediterranean agricultural products.

5.2 Exporting the EU internal market principles in the field of services

All in all, it can be concluded that Morocco, Tunisia, Egypt, Jordan and Israel have free access to the European market under the GATS rules. Free movement of services of the Mediterranean countries to the EU is only possible for listed services (see Table under 2.2, p. 231, *supra*). As indicated in this Table, Jordan has by far the most liberalised market access for services. Restrictions on market access for services and limitations on national treatment are possible under the GATS, and are specific for each country.

The integration of Egypt, Jordan, Morocco, Tunisia and Israel into the EU internal market of services and the right of establishment is successful, but only thanks to the GATS. These countries are not integrating on the basis of the EU internal market principles but according to the GATS principles. They have free market access to the EU where it concerns the services listed in the Table above. Restrictions on market access for services have been negotiated with each Mediterranean country individually. Consequently, restrictions on Euro-Med free movement of services differ from country to country.

For certain services there is still no integration into the EU internal market, but it should be pointed out that the EU internal market has also liberalised only

[584] C. Barnard, *The Substantive Law of the EU: The Four Freedoms* (Oxford, Oxford University Press 2004) p. 231.

very slowly and is still hampered by restrictions. In addition, the EU Directive on Services excludes many services from its scope: electronic communications; transport; financial services; audiovisual services; gambling; social services (housing, childcare, family support); taxation; public and private healthcare provided by professionals to patients; and pharmaceutical services.

The integration of Lebanon and the PA into the EU internal market has been unsuccessful because there is no free market access for services to the European market. For Algeria, there is free movement of services to the EU on the condition that the service is offered by legal persons.

The ENP Action Plans that aim at deeper integration of the Mediterranean countries into the EU internal market of services particularly emphasise the deeper integration into the EU of services offered by Mediterranean companies, but not of those offered by individuals on a self-employed basis. What does this mean for Egypt, Jordan, Morocco, Tunisia and Israel? The GATS already establishes market access for services provided by a service supplier through commercial presence or by a service supplier through presence of natural persons. Does this mean a step backwards for the WTO countries?

At Euro-Med level, it is up to the Euro-Med Association Councils to take a decision about the future development of the Euro-Med movement of services. At present, no such decision about services and the right of establishment has been issued.

5.3 Exporting the EU internal market principles in the field of capital

The TFEU gives the impression that it exports its free movement of capital principle to the Mediterranean countries. The main legal provision aimed at liberalising the movement of Euro-Med capital is indeed in place, but is further in the TFEU qualified by other TFEU articles. These articles allow much more restrictions as regards the Euro-Med movement of capital as compared to the movement of capital within the EU itself.

It must be noted that exporting the EU 'free movement of capital' without additional restrictions to the Mediterranean area would not bring the required solution to the Mediterranean countries. A full transposition of the EU free movement of capital would not produce real benefits for the Mediterranean countries. For them, the main problem is how to attract European investors to their market. European companies are not investing in the Mediterranean region because they do not trust the Mediterranean financial institutions and the currency. A fully liberalised Euro-Med movement of capital would not necessarily lead to more investment in the Mediterranean region. The success of the integration into the EU market of capital depends not only on the creation of sound legal provisions on the Euro-Med movement of capital, but foremost on the development of effective and secure national financial systems in the Mediterranean countries. The level of European investment in the Mediterranean region remains insufficient and this lack of foreign investment has been identified as one of the major shortcomings of the Euro-Mediterranean economic partnership. Most Mediterranean countries are starting to feel resentment towards the EU because the EU and its companies are not making direct investments in their region. But why are the Mediterranean countries not gaining real benefits from all the efforts to liberalise the Euro-Med movement of capital? It is the threat to security in the Mediterranean region that frightens investors. The success of Euro-Med movement of capital also depends on the security situation in the Middle East. In more stable regions, such as Tunisia, Morocco as well as Jordan, there is more foreign investment. More recently, the global financial crisis has shown that instability may lead to bankruptcy of financial institutions. European investors do not trust the Mediterranean financial institutions and the currency, because war can easily change the whole financial system.

Moreover, Mediterranean countries still have to work hard on making their investment procedure more transparent. European investment will increase if peace in the Mediterranean area is assured. Despite all legal efforts, it must be concluded that the Euro-Med liberalisation process has been unsuccessful until now.

If the Mediterranean countries want to draw real benefits from their participation in the EU internal market of capital, they and the EU should consider the following recommendations: (1) the Mediterranean region should build security in the region; (2) the Mediterranean countries should focus all their attention on the development of effective and secure national financial systems: an efficient and secure national financial system is a requirement for effective Euro-Mediterranean financial integration;[585] (3) the Mediterranean countries need a regulatory framework different from that of the EU: according to Jakubiak, they need not align all of their legislation to the EU financial *acquis* since (a) EU legislation is too complex and (b) the EU financial *acquis* itself is still developing and will change even more following the outbreak of the recent global financial crisis in 2008; (4) alignment of Mediterranean and EU legislation should start with the Mediterranean country that has the best developed financial system or with a group of Mediterranean countries that have a developed and trustworthy financial system and similar levels of economic development.

It is also recommended that the specialised ministers include the discussion on the financial and banking services in the negotiations on the liberalisation of the Euro-Med movement of services which have already started with some Mediterranean partners.

Finally, it is recommended that the Euro-Med Ministers of Foreign Affairs should try to protect the Mediterranean region from European protectionist tendencies. The global financial crisis that hit Europe in 2008 is already affecting the EU internal market itself. It is now under threat of protectionism of the Member States. The Euro-Med Ministers of Foreign Affairs should examine whether these protectionist tendencies within the EU affect the Euro-Mediterranean integration process.[586]

---

[585] Jakubiak, et al., *supra* n. 51, p. 44.

[586] 'Single-Market Blues', *The Economist*, 7-13 February 2009, p. 30.

5.4 Exporting the EU internal market principles in the field of persons

Only persons from the Maghreb countries have limited legal rights in Europe. It can be concluded that the integration of Mediterranean persons into the EU is not grounded on the EU internal market principles concerning the movement of persons.

Hoekman and Jakubiak recommend that the issue of Euro-Med labour mobility should be included in the negotiations on the liberalisation of Euro-Med trade in services because these issues are connected.[587] Negotiations on the Euro-Med movement of services have already started with some ready and interested Mediterranean countries. Later, similar negotiations will be initiated with the other Mediterranean countries. Jakubiak states the following:

> 'It should be possible to establish a predictable, harmonised and transparent system with the overall object of allowing the necessary mobility of service providers on a temporary basis without compromising immigration policy.'[588]

In addition, the Euro-Med Association Councils should start implementing the social security provisions in the Euro-Med AAs since they still lack direct effect.

---

[587] See B. Hoekman, *A Stake in the Internal Market: Trade in Services As a Partial Substitute for Migration?*, paper presented at the Euro-Mediterranean Economic Transition Conference, 6-7 June 2006.

[588] Jakubiak, et al., *supra* n. 51, p. 41.

Chapter VIII
Summary

1. European, Mediterranean and Euro-Med integration

The European integration process started with the EEC Treaty of Rome in 1957. The six members of the EEC declared their intention to create one common market which should be founded on the free movement of goods, services, capital and persons. The EU internal market was formally established on 31 December 1992. The Mediterranean countries, i.e., the Maghreb (Morocco, Algeria, Libya and Tunisia), the Mashreq (Egypt, Lebanon, Jordan, Syria and the Palestinian Authority) and Israel, have never been able to successfully integrate since they have always been troubled by many violent conflicts and economic and political instability. Any form of free movement of goods, services, capital and persons between these countries is far from being realised. Most Mediterranean countries have been wanting to integrate into the EEC since its inception in 1957 in order to reap the benefits of this promising European integration process. Since the formal establishment of the EU internal market on 31 December 1992, they have wanted to profit from the EU free movement of goods, services, capital and persons. The EU internal market is attractive for the Mediterranean countries since they want to export their industrial and agricultural goods to Europe, to trade in services and attract foreign investment to their region. Mediterranean nationals want to integrate into the EU internal market for persons. For Europe, the Mediterranean countries are economically very important as well since they are major suppliers of natural resources, such as gas and petroleum, to the European market and are an essential outlet for European exports. Security reasons also play a role as Europe wants to build a stable and secure Mediterranean region.

At the beginning of the European integration process, the Mediterranean countries were only offered small economic advantages of the EEC common market, amongst others, through the conclusion of Euro-Mediterranean Cooperation Agreements. But when the EU was confronted with newly emerging trading powers such as China and Russia in the 1990s, it insisted on integration of the Mediterranean countries into the EU internal market. The reason behind this was to give the EU easier access to the Mediterranean markets: a bigger trading area is necessary in a more globalised world.

This book focuses on the policy and legal aspects of this process of integration of the Mediterranean countries into the EU internal market of goods, services, capital and persons. It analyses all instruments used for integration by the Mediterranean countries and the EU, legally analyses all provisions relating to the liberalisation of goods, services, capital and persons of the Euro-Med Association Agreements, describes the state of play of integration of the Mediterranean countries into the EU internal market at present and makes a legal comparison between the EU internal market provisions and the Euro-Med internal market principles.

2. Tools for Euro-Med integration

2.1 The different Euro-Med policies and their integration goals

There are many different degrees of economic integration: the weakest level is countries granting each other preferential tariffs, resulting in the conclusion of a 'preferential agreement.' Second in line is the establishment of a 'free trade area' through the abolishment of tariff as well as non-tariff barriers to trade between parties. Third is the establishment of a 'customs union.' The highest level is the establishment of an 'internal market,' characterised by full participation in the movement of goods, services, labour and capital. The establishment of a Euro-Med internal market goes much further than that of a Euro-Med free trade area. 'Participation in the EU internal market' is a form of economic integration situated between a customs union an internal market.

Euro-Mediterranean relations are dealt with through the Barcelona Process: Union for the Mediterranean (UM) since 2008, which replaced the Euro-Mediterranean Partnership (EMP) established in 1995, and through the European Neighbourhood Policy (ENP) since 2002. These policies have contributed to the integration of the Mediterranean countries into the EU internal market. Some have contributed more than others to this process, but all contain elements of the Mediterranean countries' integration into the EU internal market.

The EMP set as a goal the establishment of a Euro-Med free trade area by 2010 through the free movement of goods, services and capital. The ENP proposed a stronger form of Euro-Mediterranean integration, its ultimate goal being participation of the Mediterranean countries in the EU internal market. It seems, however, that the Commission is changing its integration goal since the reference to the participation of the Mediterranean countries in the EU internal market has disappeared from recent Communications of the Commission. However the main ENP instruments, i.e., the ENP Action Plans, still mention their participation in the EU internal market of goods, services, capital and persons. The UM also offers the Mediterranean countries a Euro-Med free trade area by 2010 through the free movement of goods, services and capital.

None of these Euro-Med policies has reached its Euro-Med integration goal. This book tries to answer the question of what has been realised so far and thus examines the extent of integration of the Mediterranean countries into the EU internal market.

2.2 The concretisation of the Euro-Med policies: the Euro-Med instruments

This book answers the question to what extent the Mediterranean countries have integrated into the EU internal market by analysing all instruments which the EU and the Mediterranean countries have used to stimulate the Euro-Mediterranean integration process in the field of free movement of goods, services, capital and persons. Not all of these instruments have led to substantial Euro-Med integration.

At multilateral level, there are the Euro-Med Conferences of Ministers of Foreign Affairs under the EMP, the sectoral Euro-Med Conferences of specialised Ministers and experts under the EMP, the Euro-Mediterranean Parliamentary Assembly (EMPA) and one multilateral ENP Conference. The EMP Euro-Med Conferences of Ministers of Foreign Affairs are the engine of the Euro-Mediterranean integration process. They put new integration ideas in a global perspective and respond quickly to changes in the global environment, such as the terrorist attacks of 11 September 2001 and the global financial crisis which started in 2008. They have not resulted in material integration of the Mediterranean countries into the EU internal market as their Euro-Med integration proposals have never been further developed during these Conferences. Nor have the recommendations and resolutions of the EMPA led to significant results relevant for the Mediterranean integration into the EU internal market, even though on several occasions the EMPA emphasised the importance of the Euro-Med free movement of persons. The Barcelona Process: the Union for the Mediterranean (UM) aims to provide the EMPA with a legal basis and an institutional relationship with the (sectoral) Euro-Med Conferences, which might improve the legal power of the EMPA. Under the ENP, only one multilateral Conference was organised, which was merely a forum for debate and has not led to further Euro-Mediterranean integration as regards the four freedoms. Only the sectoral Euro-Med Conferences of specialised Ministers/experts have resulted in material integration of the Mediterranean countries into the EU internal market of *goods*, *services* and *capital*. These sectoral Conferences have often led to important legal documents, such as the Protocols on the application of the pan-Euro-Med rules of origin and to the successful approximation of relevant legislation of the Mediterranean countries to EU legislation. So far, however these sectoral Conferences have not resulted in material integration into the EU internal market of *persons* seeing that the first sectoral Euro-Med Conference on the movement of persons took place in 2007 and has not yet produced any significant Euro-Med integration results.

At bilateral level, there are the Euro-Med Association Agreements (AAs), under the EMP, for Morocco, Tunisia, Algeria, Jordan, Lebanon, the PA and Egypt, but not (yet) for Syria or Libya. All bilateral Euro-Med AAs reflect the four freedoms of the EU internal market. The movement of goods, services, capital and persons provisions in the Euro-Med AAs have been legally analysed in this book, as have the provisions that have an impact on the goods, services, capital and persons provisions, such as those on competition and rules of origin.

All provisions are legally binding on the EU, the Member States and the Mediterranean countries, and some require implementation by the Euro-Med Association Councils, which issue binding decisions. These Euro-Med AAs and their relevant provisions have resulted in material integration of the Mediterranean countries into the EU internal market of goods, services, capital and persons. The decisions of the Euro-Med Association Councils have also resulted in further integration of the Mediterranean countries, but they should have implemented more provisions of the Euro-Med AAs by now.

At bilateral level, there are also the ENP Action Plans for Morocco, Tunisia, Jordan, Lebanon, the PA, Egypt and Israel, but not for Algeria, Syria or Libya. All ENP Action Plans, except for the PA one, contain interesting provisions aimed at stimulating the further integration of the Mediterranean countries into the EU internal market. The Plans contain no legally binding provisions but only intentions which cannot be judicially enforced. To measure the extent of integration of the Mediterranean countries into the EU internal market of goods, services, capital and persons as a result of the ENP Action Plans, it is not sufficient to only analyse the parties' intentions as set out in these Plans; the state of integration can only be measured by examining the different ENP Progress Reports. These explain to what extent the Mediterranean countries have achieved the integration intentions set out in the ENP Action Plans. The Progress Reports indicate that the ENP Action Plans have resulted in further integration of the Mediterranean countries into the EU internal market, mainly in the field of movement of *goods* and for some Mediterranean countries also regarding the movement of *capital*. Algeria and Syria have no ENP Action Plan. It is becoming clear that Algeria is now getting behind the other Maghreb countries in the Euro-Med integration process. If Algeria wants to maintain the same Euro-Med integration pace as the other Maghreb countries, it is recommended that it should also draw up an ENP Action Plan. Another interesting point regarding the ENP Action Plans and the Euro-Med integration process is that the ENP Progress Reports of 2009 show that Egypt is moving forward fast in terms of Euro-Med integration compared with its integration results in the past. These recent Reports also indicate that Morocco is slowing down in the Euro-Med integration process. The reasons for these changes have to be sought at political level. Changes at political and governmental level in the Mediterranean countries can lead to better Euro-Med integration results because of the improved political will.

After analysing all multilateral and bilateral instruments which the Mediterranean countries and the EU have used, it may be concluded that the sectoral Euro-Med Conferences; the Euro-Med AAs for Morocco, Tunisia, Algeria, Jordan, Lebanon, the PA, Egypt and Israel; the decisions of the Euro-Med Association Councils of Morocco, Tunisia, Algeria, Jordan, Lebanon, the PA, Egypt and Israel; and the ENP Action Plans for Morocco, Tunisia, Jordan, Lebanon, the PA, Egypt and Israel have resulted in material integration of the Mediterranean countries into the EU internal market of *goods*, *services* and *capital*. As regards the integration of the Mediterranean countries into the EU internal market of *persons*, the instruments used under the EMP and ENP will not be able to achieve the set goals. The EU and its Member States will have to adapt their policies towards immigrants before we can speak of successfully integrated Mediterranean persons. Their integration into the EU internal market of persons requires more than legal provisions. Integration is a two-way process involving both immigrants and their local community: the legal possibility for a Mediterranean person to integrate into the EU may be provided for, but integration will only be successful after the conditions set out in the Communication of the Commission of 2003 have been met.[589] Successful integration of Mediterranean persons comprises different elements which can be summarised as follows: (1) immigrants have to respect the fundamental values of a democratic society; (2) immigrants have the right to maintain their own cultural identity; (3) the Union provides rights comparable to those of EU citizens and corresponding obligations; and (4) immigrants must be able to actively participate in all aspects of life on an equal footing. It will not be sufficient for the Mediterranean countries to adopt the relevant EU *acquis* for migrants: national authorities should also provide Mediterranean persons with the necessary education, healthcare, etc.

3. The state of play of integration of the Mediterranean countries into the EU internal market of goods, services, capital and persons

The *Euro-Med movement of goods* should be divided into the movement of 'industrial' goods and 'agricultural, fishery and processed agricultural' goods. The distinction between trade in industrial goods, on the one hand, and movement of agricultural, fishery and processed agricultural goods, on the other, leads to different conclusions regarding these products.

Industrial goods from Morocco, Tunisia, Algeria, Jordan, Lebanon, the PA, Egypt and Israel which are imported into Europe are completely free of customs duties and charges having equivalent effect. European industrial goods exported to the Mediterranean countries, on the other hand, are to be progressively liberalised over a transitional period of 12 years upon entry into force of the Euro-Med AA. The Mediterranean countries and the EU want to facilitate the integration of industrial goods into the EU internal market by bringing the Mediterranean countries' legislation on industrial goods in line with international and EU norms and practices. Therefore, some Mediterranean countries, i.e., Morocco, Tunisia, Jordan, Lebanon, Egypt and Israel, started negotiations on Agreements on Conformity Assessment and Acceptance of Industrial Products (ACAAs). The ACAAs should function as trade corridors for industrial goods between the Mediterranean countries and the EU. As regards the approximation process aimed at improving the Euro-Med movement of industrial goods, a distinction should be made between industrial goods for which an EU harmonisation direc-

[589] COM (2003) 336 final, Communication from the Commission to the Council, the European Parliament, the European Economic and Social Committee and the Committee of the Regions on immigration, integration and employment.

tive exists and those for which there are no EU harmonisation rules. For products for which an EU harmonisation regulation/directive exists, the Mediterranean countries want to implement the European standards contained in those regulations/directives in their legislation. However, in the EU there are also products regarding which no EU harmonisation regulation/directive applies. In the case of absence of EU harmonisation, technical rules create obstacles to the free movement of goods between the EU Member States. The Mediterranean countries and the EU also wish to apply the principle of mutual recognition to the movement of industrial goods in these non-harmonised EU areas. Agricultural products, fishery products and industrial products with an agricultural element are subject to a gradual liberalisation programme between the EU, on the one hand, and Morocco, Tunisia, Algeria, Jordan, Lebanon, the PA, Egypt and Israel, on the other. There should be free movement of these products by 2010. Egypt, Israel, Tunisia and Morocco have taken measures aimed at further integration and have started negotiations, which are still ongoing, as regards the Euro-Med liberalisation of agricultural, processed agricultural and fishery products. Jordan, Lebanon and the PA have not started such negotiations and have made no further progress as regards integration into the EU internal market of agricultural goods. The Euro-Med movement of goods should benefit from a properly functioning Euro-Med competition mechanism. For Morocco, Tunisia, Algeria, Jordan, Lebanon, the PA, Egypt and Israel there are competition provisions similar to Articles 101 and 102 of the TFEU, but it is unfortunate that all these provisions lack direct effect since they require implementing measures through decisions of the Euro-Med Association Councils. The rules of origin are intended to support the integration of the Mediterranean countries into the EU internal market of goods, but do not function in practice.

There are no common rules on the *Euro-Med movement of services or the right of establishment* in the Euro-Med context. The WTO countries – Morocco, Tunisia, Egypt, Jordan and Israel – apply the GATS obligations until their Association Councils make specific recommendations on the liberalisation of services and the right of establishment. The non-WTO countries Algeria and Lebanon have drafted their own services and right of establishment provisions. Lebanon will apply the GATS rules after it will have become a member of the WTO in the future. The EU, on the one hand, and Egypt, Morocco, Tunisia and Israel, on the other, have started negotiations on the further liberalisation of services and the right of establishment. In the future, these negotiations, together with the approximation process in the field of services, should lead to a preferential Economic Agreement on the Liberalisation of Services and the Right of Establishment with the EU in conformity with Article V of the GATS.

The *Euro-Med free movement of capital* is the only freedom that finds its legal basis in the TFEU. The TFEU provides for free movement of capital between the EU and third countries but also subjects it to many restrictions. The EU implementing directive for the relevant TFEU provisions formulates the Euro-Med free movement of capital merely as a 'best endeavours' clause. The Euro-Med free movement of capital is not as free as it might seem at first sight. Jordan, Israel,

Morocco and Tunisia aim at full liberalisation of movement of capital. Egypt and Lebanon have little intention to liberalise such movement. The PA will try to improve the conditions for liberalising capital movement and attracting investors. In 2009, only Morocco and Tunisia achieved greater Euro-Med liberalisation of capital.

There is no *Euro-Med free movement of persons*. There are no provisions regarding the free movement of persons in the Euro-Med AAs, only limited rights are given to some Mediterranean persons. The ENP Actions Plans also lack proper provisions on the Euro-Med movement of persons. This lack is confirmed in the ENP Progress Reports, which do not report any free movement of persons, nor any form of progress towards free movement of persons between the Mediterranean countries and the EU.

4. Exporting the EU internal market principles to the Mediterranean countries

After the comparison of the Euro-Med movement principles with the principles of the EU internal market itself, it might be concluded that the integration of the Mediterranean countries into the EU internal market of industrial goods happens according to the main EU internal market principles. The Euro-Med liberalisation of agricultural, fishery and processed agricultural goods also takes place along these same principles. It is only a matter of time before the integration of the Mediterranean into the EU internal market will be realised. At this moment, trade negotiations on agricultural and fishery products have finished with Egypt and Israel and are ongoing with Morocco and Tunisia. However, it can be expected that the EU will maintain some restrictive measures in order to protect its common market from the influx of Mediterranean agricultural products.

As regards the Euro-Med liberalisation of services, it can be concluded that the integration of Egypt, Jordan, Morocco, Tunisia and Israel into the EU internal market of services and the implementation of the right of establishment in these countries does not take place on the basis of the EU internal market principles but according to the GATS principles. Algeria, Lebanon and the PA have included their own services provisions in the Euro-Med AA. Only the provisions of the EU-Algeria AA are to some extent grounded on the EU internal market principles, meaning that this AA comprises provisions on the free movement of services of companies and applies the same derogations to services as the TFEU, that is to say, on the basis of public policy, public security or public health.

The legal basis of the Euro-Med movement of capital is to be found in the TFEU. Indeed, the TFEU applies its main free movement of capital provision to third countries, *in casu* the Mediterranean countries. This implies that the jurisprudence of the European Courts concerning this free movement of capital provision in the TFEU also applies in the Euro-Med context. The main legal provision aimed at liberalising the movement of Euro-Med capital thus corresponds with the EU free movement of capital itself, but is further qualified by other TFEU provisions. These subsequent provisions allow far more restrictions as regards the Euro-Med movement of capital which do not apply to the movement of capital within the EU itself.

As regards the movement of persons, it must be noted that there is no free movement of persons between the Mediterranean countries and the EU. Only persons from the Maghreb countries have limited legal rights in Europe which are similar to those for EU nationals. Therefore, it must be concluded that the EU has not transposed any EU internal market principle as regards the free movement of persons to the Mediterranean countries.

BIBLIOGRAPHY

A. Legislation

1. Euro-Mediterranean Legislation

Algeria

Euro-Mediterranean Agreement establishing an association between the European Communities and their Member States, of the one part, and the People's Democratic Republic of Algeria, of the other part, COM (2002) 157 final.

Egypt

Euro-Mediterranean Agreement establishing an association between the European Communities and their Member States, of the one part, and the Arab Republic of Egypt, of the other part, *OJ* 2004 L 304/39.

Agreement for scientific and technological cooperation between the European Community and the Arab Republic of Egypt, *OJ* 2005 L 182/12.

Israel

Euro-Mediterranean Association Agreement between the European Economic Community and the State of Israel, *OJ* 1975 L 136/3.

Agreements on scientific and technical cooperation between the European Community and Israel of 19 August 1996, *OJ* 1996 L 209/22.

Agreement between the European Community and the State of Israel on procurement by telecommunications operators of 30 July 1997, *OJ* 1997 L 202/74.

Agreement between the European Community and the State of Israel on government procurement of 30 July 1997, *OJ* 1997 L 202/85.

Agreement on mutual recognition of OECD principles of good laboratory practice (GLP) and compliance monitoring programmes between the EC and Israel of 9 October 1999, *OJ* 1999 L 263/6.

Agreement on scientific and technical cooperation between the European Community and the State of Israel of 16 July 2007, *OJ* 2007 L 220/5.

Notice to Importers about imports from Israel into the Community, *OJ* C 338/10 (1997) at p. 13; *OJ* C 328/6 (2001) and most recent version in *OJ* C 20/2 (2005).

Jordan

Euro-Mediterranean Agreement establishing an association between the European Communities and their Member States, of the one part, and the Hashemite Kingdom of Jordan, of the other part, *OJ* 2002 L 129/3.

Agreement between the European Community and the Hashemite Kingdom of Jordan on certain aspects of air services of 25 February 2008, *OJ* 2008 L 68/15.

Lebanon

Euro-Mediterranean Agreement establishing an association between the European Community and their Member States, of the one part, and the Republic of Lebanon, of the other part, COM (2002) 170 final.

Interim Agreement on trade and trade-related matters between the European Community, on the one part, and the Republic of Lebanon, on the other part, *OJ* 2002 L 262/2.

Agreement between the European Community and the Republic of Lebanon on certain aspects of air services *OJ* 2006 L 215/17.

Libya

Common Position 1999/261/CFSP of 16 April 1999 defined by the Council on the basis of Article J.2 of the Treaty on European Union concerning Libya, *OJ* 1999 L 103/1.

Council Common Position 2004/698/CFSP of 14 October 2004 concerning the lifting of restrictive measures against Libya, *OJ* 2004 L 317/0040.

Council Regulation (EC) No 1786/2004 of 14 October 2004 repealing Regulation (EC) No 3274/93 preventing the supply of certain goods and services to Libya, *OJ* 2004 L 317/7.

Morocco

Euro-Mediterranean Agreement establishing an association between the European Communities and their Member States, of the one part, and the Kingdom of Morocco, of the other part, *OJ* 2000 L 70/2.

Decision No 1/2004 of the EU-Morocco Association Council of 19 April 2004 adopting the necessary rules for the implementation of the competition rules, *OJ* 2005 L 165/10.

Palestinian Authority

Euro-Mediterranean Interim Association Agreement on trade and cooperation between the European Community, of the one part, and the Palestine Liberation Organization (PLO) for the benefit of the Palestinian Authority of the West Bank and the Gaza Strip, of the other part, *OJ* 1997 L 187/3.

Tunisia

Euro-Mediterranean Agreement establishing an association between the European Communities and their Member States, of the one part, and the Republic of Tunisia, of the other part, *OJ* 1998 L 97/2.

Syria

Euro-Mediterranean Association Agreement, Negotiations concluded, Council to decide on signature.

2. EU Legislation

Treaties

Single Act of 28 February 1986, *OJ* 1987 L 169.

Treaty establishing the European Economic Community.

Treaty on European Union of 24 December 2002 (consolidated text), *OJ* C 325.

Treaty establishing the European Community of 24 December 2002 (consolidated text) *OJ* C 325.

Treaty of Lisbon of 13 December 2007 (consolidated text), *OJ* C 83.
Consolidated versions of the Treaty on European Union and the Treaty on the Functioning of the European Union, *OJ* C 115 of 9 May 2008.

Directives

Directive 1999/93/EC of 13 December 1999 on a Community framework for electronic signatures, *OJ* 2000 L 013/12.
Directive 2000/31/EC of 8 June 2000 on certain legal aspects of information society services, in particular electronic commerce, in the Internal Market, *OJ* 2000 L 178/1.
Directive 2004/38/EC of 29 April 2004 on the right of citizens of the Union and their family members to move and reside freely within the territory of the Member States amending Regulation (EEC) No 1612/68 and repealing Directives 64/221/EEC, 68/360/EEC, 72/194/EEC, 73/148/EEC, 75/34/EEC, 75/35/EEC, 90/364/EEC, 90/365/EEC and 93/96/EEC, *OJ* 2004 L 158/77.
Directive 2005/36/EC of 7 September 2005 on the recognition of professional qualifications, *OJ* L 255/22.
Directive 2006/123/EC of 12 December 2006 on services in the internal market, *OJ* L 376/36.

Regulations

Regulation (EEC) No 1408/71 of 14 June 1971 on the application of social security schemes to employed persons and their families moving within the Community, *OJ* L 149/2 (original reference) and *OJ* 1983 L 230/8.
Regulation (EEC) No 574/72 of 21 March 1972, laying down the procedure for implementing Regulation (EEC) No 1408/71, *OJ* 1992 L 74.
Regulation (EEC) No 3363/86 of 27 October 1986 on the tariff arrangements applicable to imports into the Community of products originating in the occupied territories, *OJ* 1986 L 306/103.
Regulation (EEC) No 4129/86 of 23 December 1986 on the definition of the concept of 'originating products' and methods of administrative cooperation applicable to imports into the Community of products originating in the Occupied Territories, *OJ* 1986 L 381/1.
Regulation (EEC) No 2774/88 of 7 September 1988 amending Regulation (EEC) No 809/88 on the definition of the concept of 'originating products' and methods of administrative cooperation applicable to imports into the Community of products originating in the Occupied Territories, *OJ* 1988 L 249/5.
Regulation (EC) No 3285/94 of 22 December 1994 on the common rules for imports and repealing Regulation (EC) No 518/94, *OJ* L 349/53.
Regulation (EC) No 384/96 of 22 December 1995 on protection against dumped imports from countries not EC members, *OJ* 1996 L 56.
Regulation (EC) No 1488/96 of 23 July 1996 on financial and technical measures to accompany (MEDA) the reform of economic and social structures in the framework of the Euro-Mediterranean partnership, *OJ* L 189, amended by Council Regulation (EC) No 780/98 of 7 April 1998, *OJ* 1998 L 113.
Regulation (EC) No 2026/97 of 6 October 1997 on protection against subsidised imports from countries not EC members, *OJ* 1997 L 288/1.
Regulation (EC) No 2698/2000 of 27 November 2000 amending Regulation (EC) No 1488/96 on financial and technical measures to accompany (MEDA) the reform of economic and social structures in the framework of the Euro-Mediterranean partnership *OJ* 2000 L 311/1.
Regulation (EC) No 1/2003 of 16 December 2002 on the implementation of the rules on competition laid down in Articles 101 and 102 of the Treaty, *OJ* 2003 L 1/1.

Regulation (EC) No 859/2003 of 14 May 2003 extending the provisions of Regulation (EEC) No 1408/71 and Regulation (EEC) No 574/72 to nationals of third countries who are not already covered by those provisions solely on the ground of their nationality, *OJ* 2003 L 124/1.

Regulation (EC) No 883/2004 of the European Parliament and of the Council of 29 April 2004 on the coordination of social security systems, *OJ* 2004 L 166.

Regulation (EC) No 2007/2004 of 26 October 2004 establishing a European Agency for the Management of Operational Cooperation at the External Borders of the Member States of the European Union, *OJ* L 2004 349/1.

Regulation (EC) No 1638/2006 of 24 October 2006 laying down general provisions establishing a European Neighbourhood and Partnership Instrument, *OJ* 2006 L 310/1.

Regulation (EC) No 1931/2006 of the European Parliament and of the Council of 20 December 2006 laying down rules on local border traffic at the external land borders of the Member States and amending the provisions of the Schengen Convention, *OJ* 2006 L 405.

Regulation (EC) No 764/2008 of the European Parliament and of the Council of 9 July 2008 laying down procedures relating to the application of certain national technical rules to products lawfully marketed in another Member State and repealing Decision No 3052/95/EC, *OJ* 2008 L 218/21.

3. CFSP documents

Common Strategy 2000/458/CFSP of the European Council of 19 June 2000 on the Mediterranean region, *OJ* 2000 L 183/5.

Decision 2004/763/CFSP of the European Council of 5 November 2004 amending Common Strategy 2000/458/CFSP on the Mediterranean region in order to extend the period of its application, *OJ* 2004 L 337/72.

4. International Agreements

General Agreement on Tariffs and Trade (GATT)

General Agreement on Trade in Services (GATS)

B. Jurisprudence

Case 7/61 *Commission* v *Italy* [1961] *ECR* 317.

Case 7/68 *Commission* v *Italian Republic* [1968] *ECR* 423.

Case 13/68 *Salgoil* [1968] *ECR* 453.

Case 24/68 *Commission* v *Italy* [1969] *ECR* 193.

Cases 37 and 38/73 *Sociaal Fonds voor de Diamantarbeiders* v *Indiamex NV et Association de fait De Belder* [1973] *ECR* 1609.

Case 8/74 *Procureur du Roi* v *Benoît and Gustave Dassonville* [1974] *ECR* 837.

Case 87/75 *Conceria Daniele Bresciani* v *Amministrazione Italiana delle Finanze* [1976] *ECR* 129.

Case 106/77 *Amministrazione delle Finanze dello Stato* v *Simmenthal S.p.A.* [1978] *ECR* 629.

Case 120/78 *Rewe-Zentral AG* v *Bundesmonopolverwaltung für Branntwein* [1979] *ECR* 649.

Case 34/79 *Regina v Maurice Donald Henn and John Frederick Ernest Darby* [1979] *ECR* 3795.

C-270/80 *Polydor Limited and RSO Records Inc.* v *Harlequin Records Shops Limited and Simons Records Limited* [1982] *ECR* 329.

C-17/81 *Pabst* [1982] *ECR* 1331.

C-104/81 *Kupferberg* [1982] *ECR* 3641.

Case 174/82 *Officier van Justitie* v *Sandoz* [1983] *ECR* 2445.
C-12/86 *Demirel* v *Stadt Schwäbisch Gmünd* [1987] *ECR* 3719 and Opinion of Advocate General Darmon delivered on 19 May 1987 in 12/86, *Meryem Demirel* v *Stadt Schwäbisch Gmünd* [1987] *ECR* 3719.
C-192/89 *Sevince* [1990] *ECR* I-3461.
C-18/90 *Office National de l'Emploi* v *Bahia Kziber* [1991] *ECR* I-199.
C-312/91 *Metalsa* [1993] *ECR* I-3751.
C-432/92 *Anastasiou* [1994] *ECR* I-3087.
Joined cases C-485/93 and C-486/93, *Maria Simitzi* v *Dimos Kos* [1995] *ECR* I-2655.
C-125/94 *Aprile Srl, in liquidation* v *Amministrazione delle Finanze dello Stato* [1995] *ECR* I-2919.
C-126/95 *A. Hallouzi-Choco* v *Bestuur van de Sociale Verzekeringsbank* [1996] *ECR* I-4807.
C-1/96 *The Queen* v *Minister of Agriculture, Fisheries and Food,* ex parte*: Compassion in World Farming Ltd* [1998] *ECR* I-1251.
C-53/96 *Hermès* [1998] *ECR* I-3603.
C-416/96 *Nour Eddline El-Yassini* v *UK Secretary of State of the Home Department* [1999] *ECR* I-1209.
C-113/97 *Henia Babahenini* v *Belgian State* [1998] *ECR* I-183.
C-350/97 *Monsees* [1999] *ECR* I-2921.
C-179/98 *Mesbah* [1999] *ECR* I-7955.
Joined cases C-300/98 and C-392/98 *Dior and Others* [2000] *ECR* I-11307 et seq.
C-54/99 *Association Eglise de Scientologie de Paris* [2002] *ECR* I-1335.
C-453/99 *Courage Ltd.* v *Bernard Crehan* [2001] *ECR* I-06297.
C-23/02 *Office national de l'emploi* v *Mohamed Alami* [2003] *ECR* I-1399.
C-36/02 *Omega Spielhallen- und Automatenaufstellungs-GmbH* v *Oberburgermeisterin der Bundesstadt Bonn* [2004] *ECR* I-9609.
C-115/02 *Administration des douanes et droit indirects* v *Rioglass SA and Transremar SL* [2003] *ECR* I-12705.
C-97/05 *Mohamed Gattoussi* v *Stadt Rüsselsheim* [2006] *ECR* I-11917.
C-173/05 *Commission* v *Italian Republic* [2007] *ECR* I-4917.
C-336/05 *Ameur Echouikh* v *Secrétaire d'Etat aux anciens combattants* [2006] *ECR* I-5223.
C-276/06 *Mamate El Youssfi* v *Office National des Pensions (ONP)* [2007] *ECR* I-2851.
Opinion of Advocate General Trstenjak delivered on 11 November 2008 in C-62/05 P, *Nordspedizionieri di Danielis Livio & C. Snc in liquidazione, Livio Danielis and Domenico D'Alessandro* v *Commission of the European Communities.*

C. COM documents

White Paper from the Commission to the European Council 'Completing the Internal Market', COM (1985) 310 final.
The Single Act: 'A New Frontier for Europe', COM (1987) 100 final.
Communication of the Commission to the Council and the European Parliament of 3 September 1993 on the future relations and cooperation between the Community and the Middle East, COM (1993) 375 final.
Communication of the Commission to the Council and the European Parliament of 19 October 1994, 'Strengthening the Euro-Mediterranean Policy: Establishing a Euro-Mediterranean Partnership', COM (1994) 427 final.
Communication from the Commission to the Council and the European Parliament of 8 March 1995 'Strengthening the Mediterranean Policy of the European Union: Proposals for Implementing a Euro-Mediterranean Partnership', COM (1995) 72 final.

Communication from the Commission to the European Parliament and Council on the future European Union Economic Assistance to the West Bank and the Gaza Strip of 23 October 1995, COM (1995) 505 final.

Communication from the Commission to the Council and the European Parliament of 19 February 1997, 'Progress Report on the Euro-Mediterranean Partnership and Preparations for the Second Conference of Foreign Affairs Ministers', COM (1997) 68 final.

Communication from the Commission to the European Council and the Council of 6 May 1997, 'Draft Action Plan for a Single Market', COM (1997) 184 final.

Communication of the Commission of 23 September 1998 on the Euro-Mediterranean Partnership and the Single Market, COM (1998) 538 final.

Communication from the Commission to the European Parliament and the Commission of 24 November 1999, 'The Strategy for Europe's Internal Market', COM (1999) 624 final.

Communication from the Commission to the Council and European Parliament of 6 September 2000 to prepare the 4th meeting of the Euro-Mediterranean Foreign Ministers, 'Reinvigorating the Barcelona Process', COM (2000) 497 final.

Communication from the Commission to the Council, the European Parliament, the European Economic and Social Committee and the Committee of the Regions on immigration, integration and employment, COM (2003) 336 final.

Communication from the Commission to the Council and the European Parliament of 11 March 2003, 'Wider Europe – Neighbourhood: A Framework for Relations with our Eastern and Southern Neighbours', COM (2003) 104 final.

Proposal for a Council Regulation on the establishment of a regime of local border traffic at the external land borders of the Member States, COM (2003) 502 final.

Communication from the Commission to the Council and the European Parliament to prepare the 6th Meeting of Euro-Mediterranean Ministers of Foreign Affairs in Naples on 2-3 December 2003 (Barcelona VI), COM (2003) 610 final.

Proposal for a Council Regulation establishing a European Agency for the Management of Operational Cooperation at the External Borders, COM (2003) 687 final.

Proposal for a Council Decision on a Community position in the Association Council on the implementation of Article 36 of the Euro-Mediterranean Agreement establishing an association between the European Communities and their Member States, of the one part, and the Kingdom of Morocco, of the other part, COM (2003) 365 final.

Communication from the Commission, 'Wider Europe – Neighbourhood: A New Framework for Relations with our Eastern and Southern Neighbours', COM (2003) 104 final.

Proposal of the Commission for a Regulation of the European Parliament and of the Council laying down general provisions establishing a European Neighbourhood and Partnership Instrument, COM (2004) 628 final.

Communication from the Commission to the Council and the European Parliament, 'Building our common future – Policy challenged and budgetary means of the Enlarged Union 2007-2013', COM (2004) 101 final/2.

Communication from the Commission, 'European Neighbourhood Policy – Strategy Paper' of 12 May 2004, COM (2004) 373 final.

Commission Staff Working Paper 'European Neighbourhood Policy' Country Report Jordan of 12 May 2004, COM (2004) 373 final.

Commission Staff Working Paper 'European Neighbourhood Policy' Country Report the Palestinian Authority of the West Bank and Gaza Strip of 12 May 2004, COM (2004) 373 final.

Commission Staff Working Paper 'European Neighbourhood Policy' Country Report Israel of 12 May 2004, COM (2004) 373 final.

Commission Staff Working Paper 'European Neighbourhood Policy' Country Report Morocco of 12 May 2004, COM (2004) 373 final.

Commission Staff Working Paper 'European Neighbourhood Policy' Country Report Tunisia of 12 May 2004, COM (2004) 373 final.

Communication from the Commission to the Council of 9 December 2004 on the Commission proposals for Action Plans under the European Neighbourhood Policy, COM (2004) 795 final.

Commission Staff Working Paper 'European Neighbourhood Policy' Country Report Egypt of 2 March 2005, COM (2005) 72 final.

Commission Staff Working Paper 'European Neighbourhood Policy' Country Report Lebanon of 2 March 2005, COM (2005) 72 final.

Communication from the Commission of 16 March 2005, Green Paper 'Confronting Demographic Change: A New Solidarity between the Generations', COM (2005) 94 final.

Communication of the Commission to the Council and the European Parliament of 12 April 2005 'Tenth Anniversary of the Euro-Mediterranean Partnership: A work programme to meet the challenges of the next five years', COM (2005) 139 final.

Communication from the Commission to the Council of 5 July 2006 on the position to be adopted by the European Community and its Member States within the Association Council established by the Euro-Mediterranean Agreement establishing an association between the European Community and its Member States, of the one part, and the Republic of Lebanon, of the other part, with regard to the adoption of a Recommendation on the implementation of the EU-Lebanon Action Plan, COM (2006) 365 final.

Commission Staff Working Document of 4 October 2006, Annex to the Communication from the Commission to the Council, the European Parliament, the European Economic and Social Committee and the Committee of the Regions, 'Global Europe: Competing the World', COM (2006) 1230.

Commission Staff Working Document Accompanying the Communication from the Commission to the Council and the European Parliament on strengthening the European Neighbourhood Policy, ENP Progress Report Israel of 29 November 2006, COM (2006) 726 final.

Commission Staff Working Document Accompanying the Communication from the Commission to the Council and the European Parliament on strengthening the European Neighbourhood Policy, ENP Progress Report Jordan, COM (2006) 726 final.

Commission Staff Working Document Accompanying the Communication from the Commission to the Council and the European Parliament on strengthening the European Neighbourhood Policy, ENP Progress Report PA, COM (2006) 726 final.

Commission Staff Working Document Accompanying the Communication from the Commission to the Council and the European Parliament on strengthening the European Neighbourhood Policy, ENP Progress Report Tunisia, COM (2006) 726 final.

Commission Staff Working Document Accompanying the Communication from the Commission to the Council and the European Parliament on strengthening the European Neighbourhood Policy, ENP Progress Report Morocco, COM (2006) 726 final.

Commission Staff Working Document Accompanying the Communication from the Commission to the Council and the European Parliament on strengthening the European Neighbourhood Policy, Sectoral Progress Report, COM (2006) 726 final.

Commission Staff Working Document Accompanying the Communication from the Commission to the Council and the European Parliament on strengthening the European Neighbourhood Policy, Overall Assessment, COM (2006) 726 final.

Communication of 4 December 2006 from the Commission to the Council and the European Parliament on strengthening the European Neighbourhood Policy, COM (2006) 726 final.

Communication from the Commission to the European Parliament, the Council, the European Economic and Social Committee and the Committee of the Regions of 18 April 2007, 'Global Europe: A Stronger Partnership to Deliver Market Access for European Exporters', COM (2007) 183 final.

Proposal for a Regulation of the European Parliament and of the Council laying down procedures relating to the application of certain national technical rules to products lawfully marketed in another Member State and repealing Decision 3052/95/EC of 14 February 2007, COM (2007) 36 final.

Communication from the Commission to the Council and the European Parliament of 23 October 1995 on Future European proposal for a Council Decision of 15 May 2005 on a Community position in the Association Council on the implementation of Art. 67 and Art. 80 of the Euro-Mediterranean Agreement establishing an association between the EC and their Member States, on one part, and the Arab Republic of Egypt, of the other part, COM (2005) 188 final.

Communication from the Commission to the Council and the European Parliament on Future European Union Economic Assistance to the West Bank and the Gaza Strip, COM (1995) 505 final.

Proposal of the Commission of 11 April 2007 for a Council Decision concerning the Community position within the Association Council on the implementation of Articles 76 and 98 of the Euro-Mediterranean Agreement establishing an Association between the European Community and its Member States, of the one part, and the People's Democratic Republic of Algeria, of the other part, COM (2007) 179 final.

Proposal for a Council Decision on the position to be taken by the Community within the Association Council created by the Euro-Mediterranean Agreement establishing an association between the European Communities and their Member States, of the one part, and the Republic of Tunisia, of the other part, with regard to the adoption of provisions on the co-ordination of the social security systems, COM (2007) 788 final.

Proposal for a Council Decision on the position to be taken by the Community within the Association Council created by the Euro-Mediterranean Agreement establishing an association between the European Community and its Member States, of the one part, and the People's Democratic Republic of Algeria, of the other part, with regard to the adoption of provisions on the co-ordination of the social security systems, COM (2007) 790 final.

Proposal for a Council Decision on the position to be taken by the Community within the Association Council created by the Euro-Mediterranean Agreement establishing an association between the European Communities and their Member States, of the one part, and the Kingdom of Morocco, of the other part, with regard to the adoption of provisions on the co-ordination of the social security systems, COM (2007) 792 final.

Proposal for a Council Decision on the position to be taken by the Community within the Association Council created by the Euro-Mediterranean Agreement establishing an association between the European Communities and their Member States, of the one part, and the State of Israel, of the other part, with regard to the adoption of provisions on the co-ordination of the social security systems, COM (2007) 793 final.

Communication from the Commission of 16 May 2007 to the European Parliament, the Council, the European Economic and Social Committee and the Committee of the Regions: On circular migration and mobility partnerships between the European Union and third countries, COM (2007) 248 final.

Proposal for a Regulation of the European Parliament and the Council laying down procedures relating to the application of certain national technical rules to products lawfully marketed in another Member State and repealing Decision 3052/95/EC of 14 February 2007, COM (2007) 36 final.

Communication from the Commission: A Strong European Neighbourhood Policy, of 5 December 2007, COM (2007) 774 final.
Communication to the European Parliament and the Council of 20 May 2008, 'Barcelona Process: Union for the Mediterranean', COM (2008) 319 final.

D. SEC documents

Commission Staff Working Document Accompanying the Communication from the Commission to the European Parliament and the Council 'Progress Report Israel' of 23 April 2009, SEC (2009) 516/2.
Commission Staff Working Document Accompanying the Communication from the Commission to the European Parliament and the Council 'Progress Report Jordan' of 23 April 2009, SEC (2009) 517/2.
Commission Staff Working Document Accompanying the Communication from the Commission to the European Parliament and the Council 'Progress Report Lebanon' of 23 April 2009, SEC (2009) 518/2.
Commission Staff Working Document Accompanying the Communication from the Commission to the European Parliament and the Council 'Progress Report PA' of 23 April 2009, SEC (2009) 519/2.
Commission Staff Working Document Accompanying the Communication from the Commission to the European Parliament and the Council 'Progress Report Morocco' of 23 April 2009, SEC (2009) 520/2.
Commission Staff Working Document Accompanying the Communication from the Commission to the European Parliament and the Council 'Progress Report Tunisia' of 23 April 2009, SEC (2009) 521/2.
Commission Staff Working Document Accompanying the Communication from the Commission to the European Parliament and the Council 'Progress Report Egypt' of 23 April 2009, SEC (2009) 523/2.
Communication from the Commission to the Council and the European Parliament of 30 April 1992, 'The Future of Relations between the Community and the Maghreb Countries', SEC (1992) 401 final.
Commission Working Document of 17 March 1999 to prepare the 3rd Euro-Mediterranean Conference of Foreign Ministers, SEC (1999) 424 final.
Communication from the Commission to the Council and the European Parliament to prepare the meeting of Euro-Mediterranean Ministers of Foreign Affairs of Valencia on 22-23 April 2002, SEC (2002) 159 final.
Commission Staff Working Document Accompanying the Proposal for a Regulation of the European Parliament and of the Council laying down procedures relating to the application of certain national technical rules to products lawfully marketed in another Member State and repealing Decision 3052/95/EC: Executive summary of the impact assessment, SEC (2007) 113.

E. Literature

1. Books

Barnard, C., *The Substantive Law of the EU: The Four Freedoms* (Oxford, Oxford University Press 2004).
Blockmans, S., and A. Łazowski, eds., *The European Union and Its Neighbours: A Legal Appraisal of the EU's Policies of Stabilisation, Partnership and Integration* (The Hague, T.M.C. Asser Press 2006).

Craig, P., and G. De Burca, *EU Law Text, Cases and Materials Fourth Edition* (Oxford, Oxford Univeristy Press 2008).

Eeckhout, P., *The External Relations of the European Union: Legal and Constitutional Foundations* (Oxford, Oxford University Press 2005).

Greilsammer, I., *Israel et l'Europe: Une histoire des relations entre la Communauté européenne et l'Etat d'Israel* (Lausanne, Fondation Jean Monnet pour l'Europe et Centre de recherches européennes 1981).

Greilsammer, I., and J.H.H. Weiler, eds., *Europe and Israel: Troubled Neighbours* (Berlin, Walter de Gruyter 1998).

Hakura, F.S., *EU-Mediterranean and Gulf Trade Agreements* (Isle of Wight, Palladian Law Publishing 1999).

Keukeleire, S., *Het Buitenlands Beleid van de Europese Unie* (Deventer, Kluwer 1998).

Lenaerts, K., and P. Van Nuffel, *Europees Recht in Hoofdlijnen* (Antwerpen/Apeldoorn, Maklu 2003).

MacLeod, I., I. Hendry and S. Hyett, *The External Relations of the European Communities: A Manual of Law and Practice* (Oxford, Oxford University Press 1996).

Maresceau, M., and E. Lannon, The EU's Enlargement and Mediterranean Strategies: A Comparative Analysis (Basingstoke, Palgrave 2001).

Miralles Sole, D., *An Instrumental Analysis of the European Union's Capability to Act in Conflict Response* (Catalunya, Grup Artyplan-Artympres 2004).

Pomfret, R., and B. Toren, *Israel and the European Common Market: An Appraisal of the 1975 Free Trade Agreement* (Tübingen, J.C.B Mohr 1980).

Shlaim, A., and G.N. Yannopoulos, eds., *The EEC and the Mediterranean Countries* (Cambridge, Cambridge University Press 1978).

Youngs, R., *The European Union and the Promotion of Democracy* (Oxford, Oxford University Press 2002).

Zapater, E., *El Fundamento juridico de la actuación exterior de las Comunidades Europeas en el ámbito de la cooperación energética internacional* (Catalunya, Universidad Autónoma de Barcelona 2000).

2. Articles

Alexander, W., 'Free Movement of Non-EC Nationals. A Review of the Case-Law of the Court of Justice', 3 *EJIL* (1992) pp. 53-64.

Aliboni, R., 'The Geopolitical Implications of the European Neighbourhood Policy', 10 *European Foreign Affairs Review (EFAR)* (2005) pp. 1-16.

Attina, F., 'The Euro-Mediterranean Partnership Assessed: The Realist and Liberal Views', 8 *European Foreign Affairs Review (EFA Rev.)* (2003) pp. 181-199.

Biscop, S., 'Opening up the ESDP to the South: A Comprehensive and Cooperative Approach to Euro-Mediterranean Security', 34 *Security Dialogue* (2003) pp. 183-197.

Calleya, S.C., 'Political and Economic Perceptions in the Euro-Mediterranean Area', *The Southeast European Yearbook: 1997-1998* (Athens, EILIAMEP 1998) pp. 147-148.

Chourou, B., 'Arab Regional Integration As a Prerequisite for a Successful Euro-Mediterranean Partnership', 8/2-3 *Mediterranean Politics* (2003) pp. 194-213.

Del Sarto, R., and T. Schumacher, 'From EMP to ENP: What's at Stake with the European Neighbourhood Policy towards the Southern Mediterranean?', 10/1 *EFA Rev.* (2005) pp. 17-38.

Einhorn, T., 'The Need for a Rule-Oriented Israeli-Palestinian Customs Union: The Role of International Trade Law and Domestic Law', 44/3 *Netherlands International Law Review* (1997) pp. 315-345.

Geradin, D., and N. Petit, 'Competition Policy and the Euro-Mediterranean Partnership', 8 *EFA Rev.* (2003) pp. 153-180.

Geradin, D., and N. Petit, 'Competition Policy in the Southern Mediterranean Countries', 3 *Review of Networks Economics* (2004) pp. 65-82.

Hakura, F.S., 'The Euro-Mediterranean Policy: The Implications of the Barcelona Declaration', 34 *Common Market Law Review (CMLR)* (1997) pp. 337-366.

Hakura, F.S., 'The Extension of E.C. Competition Law to the Mediterranean Region', 19 *European Competition Law Review* (1998) pp. 204-210.

Harpaz, G., 'Enhanced Relations between the European Union and the State of Israel under the European Neighbourhood Policy: Some Legal and Economic Implications', 31/4 *Legal Issues of Economic Integration* (2004) pp. 257-274.

Herman, L., 'An Action Plan or a Plan for Action: Israel and the European Neighbourhood Policy', 1/3 *Mediterranean Politics* (2006) pp. 371-394.

Hufbauer, G., and S. Stephenson, 'Services Trade: Past Liberalization and Future Challenges', 10/3 *Journal of International Economic Law* (2007) pp. 605-630.

Karayigit, M.T., 'Why and To What Extent a Common Interpretative Position for Mixed Agreements?', 11 *EFA Rev.* (2006) pp. 445-469.

Kellermann, A.E., 'The Rights of Non-Member State Nationals under the EU Association Agreement', 10/3 *European Journal of Law Reform* (2008) pp. 340-381.

Kleiman, E., 'The Economic Provisions of the Agreement between Israel and the PLO', 28 *Israel Law Review* (1994) pp. 347-373.

Lannon, E., 'La Déclaration interministérielle de Barcelone, acte fondateur du Partenariat euro-méditerranéen', 398 *Revue du Marché Commun et de l'Union Européenne* (1996) pp. 358-368.

Lannon, E., 'L'accord d'association intérimaire Communauté européenne-O.L.P.: L'institutionnalisation progressive des relations euro-palestiniennes', 2 *Revue des Affaires Européennes* (1997) pp. 169-190.

Leal-Arcas, R., 'The European Community and Mixed Agreements', 6 *EFA Rev.* (2001) pp. 483-513.

Lenaerts, K., and E. De Smijter, 'The European Community's Treaty-Making Competence', 16 *Yearbook of European Law (YEL)* (1996) pp. 1-57.

Maresceau, M., 'Bilateral Agreements Concluded by the European Community', 309 *Recueil des Cours* (2004) pp. 125-451.

Marks, J., 'High Hopes and Low Motives: The New Euro-Mediterranean Partnership Initiative', 1 *Mediterranean Politics* (1996) pp. 1-24.

McMahon, J., 'The Euro-Mediterranean Partnership: Making the Same Mistakes Again?', 6/2 *Irish Journal of European Law* (1997) pp. 203-219.

Pardo, S. and L. Zemer, 'Towards a New Euro-Mediterranean Neighbourhood Space', 10 *EFA Rev.* (2005) pp. 39-77.

Philippart, E., 'The Euro-Mediterranean Partnership: A Critical Evaluation of an Ambitious Scheme', 8 *EFA Rev.* (2003) pp. 201-220.

Sadeh, T., 'The Economic Desirability of the Middle Eastern Monetary Cooperation', 20 *The World Economy* (1997) pp. 809-827.

Smith, M.E., and M. Webber, 'Political Dialogue and Security in the European Neighbourhood: The Virtues and Limits of "New Partnership Perspectives"', 13 *EFA Rev.* (2008) pp. 73-95.

Tovias, A., 'Israeli Policy Perspectives on the Euro-Mediterranean Partnership in the Context of EU Enlargement', 8/2-3 *Mediterranean Politics* (2003) pp. 214-232.

Wessel, R., 'The Inside Looking Out: Consistency and Delimitation in EU External Relations', 37 *CMLR* (2000) pp. 1135-1171.

Wessel, R., 'Revisiting the International Legal Status of the EU', 5 *EFA Rev.* (2000) pp. 507-537.

3. Contributions to books

Biscop, S., 'The EU and Euro-Mediterranean Security: A New Departure?', in N. Casarini and C. Musu, eds., *European Foreign Policy in an Evolving International System. The Road towards Convergence* (Basingstoke, Palgrave Macmillan 2007) pp. 195-208.

Brenton, P., and H. Imagawa, 'Rules of Origin, Trade, and Customs', in L. De Wulf and J.B. Sokol, eds., *Customs Modernization Handbook* (Washington, The International Bank for Reconstruction and Development/The World Bank 2005) pp. 183-214.

Cebeci, M., 'EU Foreign Policy after September 11 and the Significance of the Mediterranean', in P. Xuereb, ed., *The European Union and the Mediterranean: The Mediterranean's European Challenge* (Vol. V) (Malta, European Documentation Centre 2004) pp. 197-213.

Floudas, D., 'The Applicability Framework of European Competition Provisions', in D. Floudas, ed., *The Extraterritorial Application of EU Competition Law: A Contribution to the Study of EU Law in Russia* (Moscow, European Profiles – Business Tezaurus 2007) pp. 21-30.

Galal, A., and B. Hoekman, 'Between Hope and Reality: An Overview of Arab Economic Integration', in A. Galal and B. Hoekman, eds., *Arab Economic Integration: Between Hope and Reality* (Washington D.C., Brookings Institution Press 2003) pp. 1-12.

Ginsberg, R.H., 'The European Community and the Mediterranean', in J. Lodge, ed., *Institutions and Policies of the European Community* (London, Frances Pinter 1994) pp. 154-160.

Hugelin, L., 'L'incidence d'une nouvelle politique communautaire de l'immigration sur le partenariat euro-mediterranéen', in P. Xuereb, ed., *The European Union and the Mediterranean: The Mediterranean's European Challenge*, Vol. V (Malta, European Documentation Centre 2004) pp. 201-232.

Lannon, E., and P. van Elsuwege, 'The EU's Emerging Neighbourhood Policy and Its Potential Impact on the Euro-Mediterranean Partnership', in P. Xuereb, ed., *The European Union and the Mediterranean. The Mediterranean's European Challenge*, Vol. V (Malta, European Documentation Centre 2004) pp. 21-84.

Lannon, E., and P. Van Elsuwege, 'The EU's Northern Dimension and the EMP-ENP: Institutional Frameworks and Decision-Making Processes Compared', in P. Xuereb, ed., *The European Union and the Mediterranean. The Mediterranean's European Challenge* (Vol. V) (Malta, European Documentation Centre 2004) pp. 3-71.

Łazowski, A., and S. Yosifova, 'Bulgaria', in S. Blockmans and A. Łazowski, eds., *The European Union and Its Neighbours: A Legal Appraisal of the EU's Policies of Stabilisation, Partnership and Integration* (The Hague, T.M.C. Asser Press 2006) pp. 207-246.

Malanczuk, P., 'The Legal Framework of the Economic Relations between Israel and the European Union', in A. Kellermann, K. Siehr and T. Einhorn, eds., *Israel among the Nations: International and Comparative Perspectives on Israel's 50th Anniversary* (The Hague, Kluwer Law International 1998) pp. 263-280.

Munin, N., 'Should the High Court Intervene in the Economic Considerations of the Israel Government within the Framework of the Implementation of Israel's Regional Free Trade Agreements?', in A.M. Rabello, ed., *Essays on European Law in Israel* (Israel, Hebrew University of Jerusalem 1996) pp. 1078-1090.

Ott, A., and R. Wessel, 'The EU's External Relations Regime: Multilevel Complexity in an Expanding Union', in A. Łazowski and S. Blockmans, eds., *The European Union and Its Neighbours: A Legal Appraisal of the EU's Policies of Stabilisation, Partnership and Integration* (The Hague, T.M.C. Asser Press 2006) pp. 1-41.

Pace, R., 'Democracy, Economic Development and Regional Stability in the Mediterranean Region', in P. Xuereb, ed., *Euro-Med Integration and the 'Ring of Friends': The Mediterranean's European Challenge* (Vol. IV) (Malta, University of Malta, European Documentation and Research Centre 2003) pp. 101-134.

Philippart, E., 'The MEDA Programme: Evaluation of the New Design of EU Assistance to the Mediterranean', in F. Attina and S. Stavridis, eds., *The Barcelona Process and Euro-Mediterranean Issues from Stuttgart to Marseille* (Milano, Giuffrè 2001) pp. 121-169.

Pieters, K., 'The Mediterranean Countries (Morocco, Algeria, Tunisia, Libya, Egypt, Jordan, Syria and Lebanon)', in S. Blockmans and A. Łazowski, eds., *The European Union and Its Neighbours: A Legal Appraisal of the EU's Policies of Stabilisation, Partnership and Integration* (The Hague, T.M.C. Asser Press 2006) pp. 391-432.

Pomfret, R., 'Main Economic Trends in EC-Israel Economic Relations Since the Creation of the Common Market', in I. Greilsammer and J. Weiler, eds., *Europe and Israel: Troubled Neighbours* (Berlin, Walter de Gruyter, for the European University Institute, 1988) pp. 56-72.

Raya, F.J., 'A Review of the Barcelona Conference and a Summary of Policy Objectives', in C. Cosgrove-Sacks and G. Scappucci, eds., *The EU and Developing Countries: The Challenges of Globalization* (Great Britain, Macmillan Press Ltd. 1999) pp. 193-205.

Salama, C.M., 'The Euro-Mediterranean Partnership: Political and Economic Aspects', in P. Herrmann and A. Tausch, eds., *Dar Al-Islam: The Mediterranean, the World System and the Wider Europe* (New York, Nova Science Publishers 2005) pp. 57-84.

Shachmurove, Y., 'The Integration of the Israeli Economy into the EEC: Recent Trends and a Forecast', in I. Greilsammer and J.H.H. Weiler, eds., *Europe and Israel: Troubled Neighbours* (Berlin, Walter de Gruyter, for the European University Institute 1988) pp. 73-112.

Silber, J., and Z.M. Berrebi, 'The 1975 Free Trade Agreement and Its Impact on Israeli Exports to the EEC', in I. Greilsammer and J.H.H. Weiler, eds., *Europe and Israel: Troubled Neighbours* (Berlin, Walter de Gruyter 1998) pp. 136-155.

Steinberg, G., 'Science and Politics: The Links between Israel and the European Community', in I. Greilsammer and J. Weiler, eds., *Europe and Israel: Troubled Neighbours* (Berlin, Walter de Gruyter, for the European University Institute, 1988) pp. 338-348.

Terracini, S., 'The History of the Israel-EEC Agreement', in A. Rabello, ed., *Essays on European Law and Israel* (Jerusalem, The Harry and Michael Sacher Institute for Legislative Research and Comparative Law 1996) pp. 1063-1074.

Wessel, R., 'Fragmentation in the Governance of EU External Relations: Legal Institutional Dilemmas and the New Constitution for Europe', in J. de Zwaan, J. Jans and F. Nelissen, eds., *The European Union: An Ongoing Process of Integration – Liber Amicorum Alfred E. Kellermann* (The Hague, T.M.C. Asser Press 2004) pp. 123-140.

Yoran, A., 'A Peace-Time Economic Regime for the Middle East – Towards an MEU?', in A.M. Rabello, ed., *Essays on European and Israel Law* (Jerusalem, The Harry and Michael Sacher Institute for Legislative Research and Comparative Law 1996) pp. 1139-1146.

4. Reports and Working Papers

Biscop, S., *The European Security Strategy and the Neighbourhood Policy: A New Starting Point for a Euro-Mediterranean Security Partnership?*, paper presented at the EUSA Ninth Biennial International Conference, Austin, Texas, 31 March-2 April 2005, available at: http://aei.pitt.edu/archive/00002984/01/Paper_EUSA_ESS-EMP.txt.

Breem, Y., and X. Thierry, *Immigration in Europe and Development Levels of the Source Countries: What Are the Associations?* (2004), available at: http://www.irpps.cnr.it/ricmob/web_conf/download/thierry_paper.pdf.

Brenton, P., and M. Manchin, *Trade Policy Issues for the Euro-Med Partnership* (Brussels, Centre for European Policy Studies 2003).

Cremona, M., and C. Hillion, *L'Union Fait la Force? Potential and Limitations of the European Neighbourhood Policy As an Integrated EU Foreign and Security Policy*, EUI Working Paper LAW No. 2006/39.

Dominik, H., and P. Dengler, *Accords d' Association,* Research Paper for the College of Europe (Bruges 2004).

Driss, A., *Putting the Mediterranean Union in Perspective: North-African Perspectives*, Euromesco Paper (2008).

Emerson, M., *Democratisation in the European Neighbourhood* (Brussels, Centre for European Policy Studies 2006).

Geradin, D., *Competition Law and Regional Economic Integration: An Analysis of the Southern Mediterranean Countries*, World Bank Paper No. 35 (Washington, World Bank Publications 2004).

Hirsch, M., *Asymmetric Factor Endowments, Progressive Rules of Origin and Commercial Cooperation in the Middle East*, Working Paper 13/98 for the Hebrew University of Jerusalem (1998).

Hoekman, B., 'A Stake in the Internal Market: Trade in Services As a Partial Substitute for Migration?', paper presented at the Euro-Mediterranean Economic Transition Conference, 6-7 June 2006.

Inbar, E., *An OEEC for the Middle East?*, Working Paper 5/97 for the Hebrew University of Jerusalem (1997).

Jakubiak, M., et al., *Countries Bordering the EU and Enhanced Economic Integration* (Warsaw, Centre for Social and Economic Research 2006).

Melchor, S., *The 1997 Euro-Mediterranean Interim Association Agreement between the European Community and the Palestinian Liberation Organisation*, Working Paper for the College of Europe (Bruges 1998).

Noureddine, F., and J. Quatremer, *The New Euro-Mediterranean Economic Area* (Brussels, Club de Bruxelles 1996).

Radwan, S., and J.-L. Reiffers, *FEMISE Report on the Euro-Mediterranean Partnership 2006: Analysis and Proposals of the Euro-Mediterranean Forum of Economic Institutes* (France, Institut de la Méditerranée 2006).

Schumacher, T., *The Survival of the Fittest: the First Five Years of Euro-Mediterranean Economic Relations*, EUI Working Paper RCSAS No. 2004/13.

Stephens, D., *The European Union and Israel: An Ambiguous Relationship*, Paper for the College of Europe (Bruges 1998).

Togan, S., and J. Michalek, *The Role of the Services As the Factor of Integration of Euromed*, Research Paper for FEMISE (2007).

Tovias, A., *Options for Mashrek-Israeli Regionalism in the Context of the Euro-Mediterranean Partnership*, CEPS Paper No. 67 (Centre for European Policy Studies, Brussels 1997).

UNCTAD Technical Cooperation Project on Trade Relations and Economic Cooperation in the Mediterranean Region, *Anti-Dumping and Safeguards in the Euro-Mediterranean AAs* (INT/93/A34 1998).

Williamson, J., and M. Mahar, *A Survey of Financial Liberalization*, Princeton Essays in International Finance No. 211 (1998).

INDEX

MIX
Papier aus verantwortungsvollen Quellen
Paper from responsible sources
FSC® C105338

If you have any concerns about our products,
you can contact us on
ProductSafety@springernature.com

In case Publisher is established outside the EU,
the EU authorized representative is:
Springer Nature Customer Service Center GmbH
Europaplatz 3, 69115 Heidelberg, Germany

Printed by Libri Plureos GmbH
in Hamburg, Germany

Spin-Stand Microscopy of Hard Disk Data

A Volume in the Elsevier Series in Electromagnetism

Elsevier Science Internet Homepage – http://www.elsevier.com
Consult the Elsevier homepage for full catalogue information on all books, journals and electronic products and services.

Elsevier Series in Electromagnetism

(Series formerly known as Academic Press Series in Electromagnetism)

Edited by

ISAAK MAYERGOYZ, University of Maryland, College Park, USA

Electromagnetism is a classical area of physics and engineering that still plays a very important role in the development of new technology. Electromagnetism often serves as a link between electrical engineers, material scientists, and applied physicists. This series presents volumes on those aspects of applied and theoretical electromagnetism that are becoming increasingly important in modern and rapidly development technology. Its objective is to meet the needs of researchers, students, and practicing engineers.

Books Published in the Series

Giorgio Bertotti, *Hysteresis in Magnetism: For Physicists, Material Scientists, and Engineers*
Scipione Bobbio, *Electrodynamics of Materials: Forces, Stresses, and Energies in Solids and Fluids*
Alain Bossavit, *Computational Electromagnetism: Variational Formulations, Complementarity, Edge Elements*
M.V.K. Chari and S.J. Salon, *Numerical Methods in Electromagnetism*
Goran Engdahl, *Handbook of Giant Magnetostrictive Materials*
Vadim Kuperman, *Magnetic Resonance Imaging: Physical Principles and Applications*
John C. Mallinson, *Magneto-Resistive Heads: Fundamentals and Applications*
Isaak Mayergoyz, *Nonlinear Diffusion of Electromagnetic Fields*
Giovanni Miano and Antonio Maffucci, *Transmission Lines and Lumped Circuits*
Shan X. Wang and Alexander M. Taratorin, *Magnetic Information Storage Technology*
Isaak Mayergoyz, *Mathematical Models of Hysteresis and Their Applications*
Fausto Fiorillo, *Measurements and Characterization of Magentic Materials*

Related Books

John C. Mallinson, *The Foundations of Magnetic Recording, Second Edition*
Reinaldo Perez, *Handbook of Electromagnetic Compatibility*

Related Journals

A sample journal issue is available online by visiting the homepage of the journal (homepage details at the top of this page). Free specimen copy gladly sent on request. Elsevier Science Ltd, The Boulevard, Langford Lane, Kidlington, Oxford, OX5 1GB, UK

Spin-Stand Microscopy of Hard Disk Data

ISAAK MAYERGOYZ

ECE Department
University of Maryland at College Park
University of Maryland Institute for Advanced Computer Studies

CHUN TSE

ECE Department
University of Maryland at College Park

ELSEVIER

AMSTERDAM • BOSTON • HEIDELBERG • LONDON • NEW YORK • OXFORD
PARIS • SAN DIEGO • SAN FRANCISCO • SINGAPORE • SYDNEY • TOKYO

Elsevier
The Boulevard, Langford Lane, Kidlington, Oxford OX5 1GB, UK
Radarweg 29, PO Box 211, 1000 AE Amsterdam, The Netherlands

First edition 2007

British Library Cataloguing in Publication Data
A catalogue record for this book is available from the British Library

Library of Congress Cataloging-in-Publication Data
A catalog record for this book is availabe from the Library of Congress

ISBN–13: 978-0-08-044465-9
ISBN–10: 0-08-044465-2

For information on all Elsevier publications
visit our web site at books.elsevier.com

Printed and bound by CPI Group (UK) Ltd, Croydon, CR0 4YY

Transferred to Digital Print 2011

Contents

Preface

This book is about the science and technology of fast magnetic imaging and analysis of hard disk data, which has been of substantial research interest lately. In 1999, we proposed a high-speed, massive magnetic imaging technique called *spin-stand microscopy*. It is the first magnetic imaging technique where imaging is performed ex-situ on a rotating disk mounted on a spin-stand. This technique is one of the fastest scanning-based microscopy techniques. It is noninvasive and has nano-scale resolution. For these reasons, it provides unique capabilities for the visualization of magnetization patterns recorded on hard disks. This book covers in depth the theory of spin-stand microscopy, its experimental implementation, and its applications in the areas of hard disk recording and beyond.

The ubiquitous use of spin-stands in the research, development, production and testing of hard disk drives makes this book a valuable reference for the hard disk recording community. This book is also of direct relevance to the magnetic microscopy professionals who are always searching for new techniques to perform microscopic imaging on magnetic materials in a rapid and accurate manner. Finally, this book will be beneficial to engineers and scientists involved in computer forensics, commercial data recovery as well as the design of reliable archival data storage systems.

Since the spin-stand microscopy technique is a new technology developed by the authors and their collaborators, this book is the first one on the market on this subject. This book is an outgrowth of the research performed by the authors and their collaborators who, over the last decade, have acquired an extensive knowledge and experience in the fast magnetic imaging and analysis of hard disk data on a spin-stand. In order to make the materials accessible to a broader audience, this book is self-contained with no prior assumptions on readers' familiarity with either magnetic recording or magnetic microscopy. The interdisciplinary nature of spin-stand microscopy is consistently stressed. The outline of the book is as follows.

There are two main parts in the book. Part I deals with the theory of spin-stand microscopy and consists of the first five chapters. Part II focuses on the applications of spin-stand microscopy and consists of the last four chapters.

Chapter 1 is an introductory chapter that covers the necessary background materials. Topics discussed include the technological evolution of hard disk drives; basics of hard disk recording technology; a survey of selected magnetic microscopy techniques; and a brief overview of the spin-stand microscopy technique.

Chapter 2 introduces the hardware of the spin-stand system. The scanning mechanism of the spin-stand microscopy technique is described. This chapter emphasizes the experimental aspects of the imaging technique to obtain two-dimensional "raw" images. Different triggering techniques are considered. The advantages of the spin-stand microscopy technique are listed and compared with other magnetic microscopy techniques.

Chapter 3 presents the theoretical foundation of the image reconstruction technique that is used to retrieve actual magnetization images from raw spin-stand images. This chapter provides a complete description of the image reconstruction algorithm. This algorithm enables the recovery of vectorial magnetization from the scanned 2D "raw" scalar images. The algorithm is based on the notion of the head response function. In order to test the effectiveness of the reconstruction algorithm, the spin-stand microscopy technique is applied to the imaging of overwritten data. The spin-stand images of the overwritten data are then compared with the corresponding ones obtained by using magnetic force microscopy.

Chapter 4 deals with experimental techniques for extraction of the head response function. First, it is demonstrated that the accuracy of the head response function can be substantially enhanced by the method of "spatial averaging." Then, the accuracy of image reconstruction is further improved by the method of scaling which is based on a self-similarity argument.

Chapter 5 presents novel numerical methods for the removal of intersymbol interference (ISI) from spin-stand images. One of the methods is based on the response function characterization of giant-magnetoresistive heads used in microscopy. It is demonstrated that the ISI-free readback image corresponding to the actual underlying magnetization patterns can be extracted from the ISI-distorted readback signal through deconvolution. Another method is based on the Hilbert transform and it is also quite efficient as far as the removal of ISI is concerned. A novel 2D generalization of Hilbert transform for three-dimensional magnetic fields in magnetic recording is presented. This Hilbert transform is of interest in its own right.

The second part of the book deals with the diverse applications of spin-stand microscopy in hard disk recording and data forensics, and it consists of the last four chapters.

In Chapter 6, the spin-stand microscopy technique is applied to the imaging of recorded patterns on disks removed from commercial hard drives. Challenges related to the eccentricity of the disk and the instability of the trigger are examined and solutions are provided. Special techniques of entire-track spin-stand imaging and track centering are discussed in detail. The method of track following using piezo-controlled head movement is thoroughly developed. Spin-stand images of hard disks from drives of different generations are presented as examples.

Chapter 7 presents the procedures and results of using the spin-stand microscopy technique as a tool for data forensics. The conceptual aspects of data detection, decoding and error corrections pertinent to spin-stand data forensics are briefly discussed. Extensive demonstration of spin-stand forensics of hard disk data from drives of different generations is shown via the examples of recovery of JPEG images.

In Chapter 8, the vectorial magnetization of recorded data is investigated. Specifically, the distribution of transverse component of magnetization of recorded tracks is extensively studied for different track widths and various recording frequencies (densities). The fact that only the curl-free component of magnetization can be retrieved using spin-stand imaging is demonstrated.

Chapter 9 deals with the spin-stand study of thermal relaxation (viscosity) of recorded patterns. The distinction between intrinsic thermal relaxations and data-dependent thermal relaxations is emphasized. It is shown that the thermal relaxations of the latter type can be efficiently studied by observing the decay of higher-order harmonics of the recorded patterns. Spin-stand results of thermal relaxation experiments are presented. Finally, the spatial and vectorial characterization of thermal relaxations of recorded patterns is studied via spin-stand microscopy and dynamic images of magnetization relaxations are presented.

During the time of our ongoing research on spin-stand microscopy, magnetic data storage technology has undergone dramatic evolution. This evolution has resulted in drastic reduction of giant magnetoresistive (GMR) head dimensions. The experimental results presented in this book inevitably reflect this evolution. These results correspond to different generations of GMR heads, which were available at the time when the specific experiments were performed.

We want to express our gratitude to Dr. Charles Krafft for the long-standing fruitful collaboration. We are very grateful to our Ph.D. students

Patrick McAvoy, Chun-Yang Tseng, and Sergiy Tkachuk who actively participated in the research on spin-stand microscopy and whose accomplishments are partially reflected in this book.

Part I

Spin-Stand Microscopy: Theory

CHAPTER 1

Introduction

The goal of this introductory chapter is to orient the readers to the status of hard disk data storage and retrieval. It begins by highlighting the technological evolution of hard disk drives. The issues related to data loss are subsequently discussed. This is followed by a survey of selected magnetic microscopy techniques available for the imaging of hard disk data. Finally, the core topic of the book, the spin-stand microscopy technique is introduced along with advanced spin-stand-based data forensic methods.

1.1 TECHNOLOGICAL EVOLUTION OF HARD DISK DRIVES

How much new information is created in a year? That is the question raised and answered by the study [1] conducted by the School of Information Management and Systems at the University of California, Berkeley. According to the study, about 5 exabytes (1 exabyte $= 10^{18}$ bytes) of new information was created in 2002 and 92% of this information is stored in magnetic media. Currently, hard disk drives are the dominant magnetic storage devices because they offer the best overall combination in non-volatility, reliability, large capacity, high data transfer rate, and low production cost. Data from disk drive manufacturers shows that the estimated number of total hard drives sold in 2006 exceeded 400 million units and will exceed 650 million units by 2010, generating worldwide market revenues on the order of tens of billion dollars per year.

Hard disk data storage technology is evolving at a remarkable pace that has few equals. The phenomenal advancement in this technology has been achieved as a result of continuous and coordinated progress in such diverse areas as physics and processing of novel magnetic nano-film structures, mechanics of positioning and flying with extremely small tolerances as well as development of novel techniques for coding, detection and digital signal processing of high-density recorded data. The design of modern disk drives is a fusion of various scientific disciplines entailing magnetics, surface physics, material science, tribology, control theory, information and communication theories. This interdisciplinary nature of disk drive technology is exemplary of the merge between human ingenuity and engineering prowess.

Since the invention of the first hard drive by IBM in 1956, the technological evolution of hard drives has been nothing short of phenomenal. The first commercial hard drive, called the RAMAC (Random Access Method of Accounting and Control), had a total capacity of 5 MB, contained 50 disks each 24 inches in diameter, had an access time of one second and data transfer rate of 0.5 MB per second, and cost \$50 000 [2]. By contrast, today's typical disk drives can hold capacities in excess of 500 GB, use 3.5 inch disks, have an access time of 6 ms and a data transfer rate of 150 MB per second, and cost about \$200. The cost per megabyte—a very important figure of merit for hard drives—has decreased 25 millionfold in half a century!

Perhaps the most significant indicator of the phenomenal progress of disk drive technology is the exponential increase in areal density—the amount of information stored per unit area of disk surface. Areal density, measured in number of bits per square inch, is the product of track density (number of tracks per inch) and linear density (number of bits per inch). From a system perspective, track density is currently limited by the mechanical precision of radial actuators to accurately seek a target track and the ability of the servomechanism to stay on this track. Linear density, on the other hand, depends on head and media properties, the flying height, the disk rotational speed, and the sophistication of the channel to detect and decode the track data.

Over the past years, the rate of increase in track density has been greater than that of linear density, resulting in ever-decreasing bit aspect ratio (BAR or bit width to bit length ratio). In 2005, hard disk drives boast a track density about 150 kilo-track-per-inch (ktpi) and linear density of 800 kilo-bit-per-inch (kbpi), leading to a bit aspect ratio (bit-per-inch/track-per-inch) of about 5:1 and areal density over 100 giga-bit-per-square-inch (Gb/in^2). These numbers are well beyond the limit once thought insurmountable due to the superparamagnetic effect. This effect implies that thermal fluctuations due to ambient temperature are sufficient to spontaneously flip the magnetization orientation of isolated grains inside the bit regions and, when enough of these flippings occur, the recorded information is lost [3–6].

Historically, areal density increased at an annual compound growth rate (CGR) of 25% throughout the 1970s and 1980s. In the early 90's, the growth rate increased to 60% per year. This was due mainly to the development of magnetoresistive (MR) heads to replace the traditional inductive heads for reading. Unlike inductive read heads which detect *temporal* changes of magnetic flux, MR read heads sense *spatial* variations of magnetic fields produced by recorded patterns of magnetization. Toward the late 90's, as a result of the revolutionary development of giant-magnetoresistive (GMR) heads and introduction of advanced read detection channels like PRML (Partial Response Maximum Likelihood), the areal density has been further increased.

This impressive upsurge in data density opens the paths for hard drives to find applications apart from personal computers. Hard disk drives are increasingly being integrated into consumer electronics products. Digital cameras, camcorders, video game consoles, MP3 music players and mobile phones are beginning to embrace hard drives with very small form factors as their storage platforms.

The technological advancement of hard disk drives is the result of extensive multi-disciplinary research in the magnetic recording industry and universities. It is truly a scientific marvel and an engineering feat that hard drives can pack in so much data so fast at so low a cost. Research in magnetic recording is being pursued in the directions of increasing the areal density of storage, increasing the rate of data transfer, decreasing the data access time, and decreasing the cost per megabyte [7]. These are the four figures of merit for hard disk drives, with areal density and cost being the most significant. The higher areal density can directly translate to lower cost and indirectly to higher data transfer rate. Indeed, higher areal density would mean fewer components (platters, heads, and electronics) and thus results in reduced costs. Higher areal density also permits more data to be delivered within a fixed time span, thereby indirectly boosting the data transfer rate. Here, the distinction must be made between two kinds of data transfer rate. The *internal* data transfer rate is the rate at which data is transferred from the disk platter to the head. It is the product of linear density (bit/inch) and linear speed (inch/second). The *external* data transfer rate or the *interface* rate, on the other hand, is the rate at which data are exchanged between the hard drive controller and the host computer. The latter rate is usually the faster of the two. For a more detailed exposition of the components and technology of modern hard disk drives, the reader is referred to Appendix A of this book.

Having reviewed the technological evolution of hard disk drives, the next section deals with the need for advanced hard disk data microscopy methods.

1.2 SURVEY OF SELECTED MAGNETIC MICROSCOPY TECHNIQUES

As the demand for higher data areal density continues to increase, so has the need for advanced scientific instrumentation that can support the corresponding research in high-density magnetic recording. One important aspect of this research is the imaging of the recorded patterns on hard disks. The imaging of these patterns can provide a wealth of information on the overall recording capabilities of the disk drive systems. Insight gained by studying these imaged patterns can then be utilized toward achieving higher areal density and improved performance of the hard drives. Since the magnetization patterns on the hard disks are recorded in ever smaller length scales, magnetic microscopy techniques with ever higher resolution are needed in order to study these patterns.

There are various microscopy techniques for imaging magnetization patterns recorded on hard disks. Most microscopy techniques are indirect and measure only the external fields produced by the magnetization patterns rather than the magnetization itself. These techniques can be further differentiated into two broad categories based on their scanning mechanism.

In the first category, no scanning by a probe is performed on the sample. Rather, outside agents are made to interact or impinge upon the sample surface and the effects of the resultant magnetic interaction are observed via high-resolution microscopes. The Bitter technique, for example, images the patterns coated with a thin film of ferro-fluid [8,9]. The ferro-particles are attracted to the regions of the strong field produced by the pattern magnetization. The resulting patterns of particles (Bitter patterns) are then observed under either an optical microscope or a scanning electron microscope (SEM). In Lorentz microscopy, an electron beam is directed at the sample, deflected by the Lorentz force produced by the pattern magnetization, and the deflections are measured using a SEM or a TEM (transmission electron microscope) [10–12].

In imaging techniques of the second category, commonly called the scanning probe microscopy (SPM), the sample is raster-scanned with an extremely fine (sharp) tip. The tip is mounted on a flexible cantilever, allowing it to follow the surface contour of the sample. In magnetic force microscopy, this tip is coated with a ferromagnetic material such that when it moves in proximity to the sample, forces of interaction between the tip and the sample-magnetization-induced magnetic field influence the movement of the cantilever. These resultant forces are then detected by special sensors. For instance, in magnetic force scanning tunneling microscopy (MFSTM) [13–17], the probe sample separation is recorded by measuring tunneling currents. The magnetic image is obtained by mapping the probe sample displacement as a function of the two-dimensional spatial coordinates.

1.2.1 Magnetic force microscopy (MFM)

Among the great number of SPM techniques, magnetic force microscopy (MFM) is arguably the most widely used in magnetic recording because of its high resolution, advanced development, and relative ease of use [18–26]. In MFM, the spatial variation of the magnetic force between the probe and the sample is recorded. The components of an MFM system include a probe and a cantilever, piezoelectric transducers for positioning the sample, a laser source, and photodetectors. For MFM, the tip of the probe is ferromagnetically coated. The system is operated by detecting changes in the oscillation frequency of the cantilever induced by the magnetic field varying with the position of the tip with respect to the sample.

Principle of operation of MFM

The principle of operation of MFM system is schematically presented in Fig. 1.1. When a time-varying voltage signal is applied to the piezoelectric bimorphs, the cantilever and probe are forced to oscillate around their mechanical resonant frequency. Meanwhile, a laser beam is directed at the back of the probe and reflected onto the photodetector. The scanning is accomplished by the piezoelectric transducers which move the sample beneath the probe in a rastering motion. Because of the magnetostatic interaction between the probe's magnetization and the sample's local magnetic

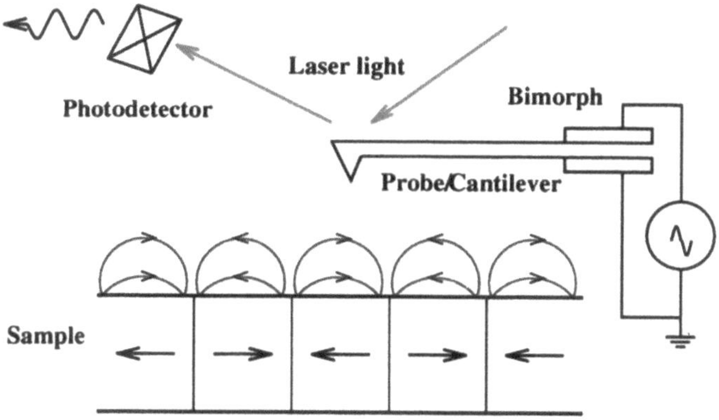

FIGURE 1.1 An MFM imaging system.

field, a magnetic force acts on the probe which modifies the probe oscillations. The derivative of this force is proportional to the phase change of oscillations of the probe with respect to the driving signal. The "raw" scalar MFM image is obtained by displaying this phase change versus the two-dimensional spatial position.

Limitations of MFM

MFM has been routinely used to study magnetization patterns on hard disks. Despite its many advantages over other scanning probe techniques, MFM is known to have some intrinsic limitations.

1. The rate of image acquisition is low. The time to acquire an image spans from dozens of minutes to several hours, depending on the area to be scanned and the desired resolution.
2. Special preparation of the sample is required. Unless the desired magnetization pattern is identically written over a sufficiently large number of neighboring tracks, it is very difficult to locate the particular pattern of interest.
3. It is completely impractical, if not impossible, to accumulate numerous two-dimensional images of the same target area in order to increase the signal-to-noise ratio.
4. The image area of MFM is generally very limited, typically in the range of 100 μm by 100 μm. Even though this may not pose any problem in imaging individual transitions or even sequences of patterns spanning many tracks, this limited scan area is not adequate in applications where massive imaging and forensics study are required. For instance, due to the large capacities of modern hard drives, it is virtually impractical to use the MFM technique to perform massive imaging of hard disk data for the purpose of forensics.
5. The scanning mechanism (rastering motion) of MFM is best defined in Cartesian coordinate systems. Hard disk tracks, however, are naturally defined in polar coordinate systems. MFM is therefore, to say the least, extremely ineffective in imaging whole-tracks of hard disk data.
6. As a result of the nonlinear interaction between the probe's magnetization and the sample's magnetic field, the magnetization of the probe may change. The direction of the magnetization of the tip may flip when the stray field from the media is larger than the coercivity of the magnetic coating of the tip. This may cause distortion in the scanned raw images.

7. Even though an MFM image can provide valuable information about the write head and the media of the hard disk, it contains *no* information on the read head. This is unfortunate because increase in areal density of hard drives is often characterized by the technological breakthroughs of the read heads. Since an MFM imaging system uses an MFM tip as its sensor, an MFM image *cannot* be utilized for read-head characterization.
8. While the areal density of magnetic recording has been increasing at a double-digit compound growth rate, the MFM tip, which acts as the sensor in the MFM technique, has not been miniaturized at the same rate. Unless better tip fabrication technology becomes available, or special efforts are made to trim the MFM tips (e.g. by ion beam milling [27]), the resolution of MFM images may pale in the face of ever increasing areal density. This will ultimately limit the usefulness of the MFM technique in imaging of ultrahigh-density magnetic recording or forensics.

1.3 SPIN-STAND MICROSCOPY

In this book, a novel spin-stand based magnetic microscopy technique which is free from the MFM limitations is described [28–43]. A spin-stand is a sophisticated rigid disk tester designed to simulate an actual hard disk drive. Components and parameters of a hard disk drive such as heads, disks, the particular pattern to be written, the location of the specific sector to be written, the frequency of the writing signal, the speed of the spindle, or even the head skew angle at the time of writing or reading can be freely modified on a spin-stand. The effect of these modifications can subsequently be analyzed, making a spin-stand a very potent tool in the study of high density magnetic recording.

Spin-stands have been commonly used in research environments to study different aspects of magnetic recording [44–52]. They are also routinely used in production environments in the magnetic recording industry to characterize heads, media, and recording channels. It is therefore an issue of great scientific interest and practical significance when one can use spin-stands for the imaging of the magnetization patterns recorded on hard disks.

The proposed technique is the *first* magnetic microscopy technique to perform imaging on a rotating disk mounted on the spindle of a spin-stand. Its novelty comes from using the spin-stand in an unintended way as an imaging device. The technique also derives its novelty from a specially devised image reconstruction algorithm by which vectorial magnetization images can be reconstructed from the scalar "raw" images. It is conceivable that the proposed magnetic microscopy technique is one of the *fastest*, most comprehensive, noninvasive magnetic microscopy techniques available for the imaging of hard disk data. It is the *only* magnetic microscopy technique whose rate of imaging is comparable to the rate of data reading by the magnetic heads in hard drives.

The spin-stand microscopy technique uses a magnetic read head as the sensor for the performance of imaging. Images are acquired by scanning a target area of the rotating disk in the along-track and cross-track directions. Even though other researchers have also used magnetic read heads as sensors to image recorded patterns [53–58], they are all slow imaging (*"static"*) techniques. They are in essence scanning probe microscopy techniques in which the read heads act as the probes for raster scanning across the sample. By contrast, the spin-stand microscopy technique is a fast (*dynamic*) technique where the target area to be imaged is sweeping at high speed relative to the head. Due to the fast (dynamic) scanning mechanism of the spin-stand microscopy technique, it offers the following advantages: a high rate of data acquisition; a large image area; a good signal-to-noise ratio due to rapid accumulation of numerous scanned images; the absence of scanning-induced hysteresis; and imaging under conditions similar to those in actual hard disk drives.

The spin-stand microscopy technique has been extensively tested. As demonstrated in this book, it is capable of producing high-resolution images of magnetization patterns in a rapid and convenient way.

BIBLIOGRAPHY

[1] Available at http://www.sims.berkeley.edu/research/projects/how-much-info-2003.

[2] E. Daniel, C. Mee, and M. Clark, *Magnetic Recording The First 100 Years*, pp. 270–299, IEEE Press, 1999.

[3] W. Hellenthal, "Superparamagnetic effects in thin films," *IEEE Trans. Magn.*, **4**, 11 (1968).

[4] R. Wood, "The feasibility of magnetic recording at 1 terabit per square inch," *IEEE Trans. Magn.*, **36**, 36 (2000).

[5] H.J. Richter and R.M. Brockie, "Measurement of the linear density dependence of thermal decay of square-wave recordings," *IEEE Trans. Magn.*, **37**, 1531 (2001).

[6] H.J. Richter, "Longitudinal recording at 10 to 20 Gbit/in^2 and beyond," *IEEE Trans. Magn.*, **35**, 2790 (1999).

[7] S.X. Wang and A.M. Taratorin, *Magnetic Information Storage Technology*, p. xv, Academic Press, 1999.

[8] F. Bitter, "On inhomogeneities in the magnetization of ferromagnetic materials," *Phys. Rev.*, **38**, 1903 (1931).

[9] T. Linn, J.A. Christner, T.B. Mitchell, J.-S. Gau, and P.K. George, "Effects of current and frequency on write, read, and erase widths for thin-film inductive and magnetoresistive heads," *IEEE Trans. Magn.*, **25**, 710 (1989).

[10] R.F.M. Thornley and J.D. Hutchison, "Magnetic field measurements in the scanning electron microscope," *IEEE Trans. Magn.*, **5**, 271 (1969).

[11] J.B. Elsbrock and L.J. Balk, "Profiling of micromagnetic stray fields in front of magnetic recording media and heads by means of a SEM," *IEEE Trans. Magn.*, **20**, 866 (1984).

[12] C. Denis Mee and Eric D. Daniel, *Magnetic Recording Technology*, Second Edition, Section 9.2.3, McGraw-Hill, 1996.

[13] J. Moreland and P. Rice, "High-resolution tunneling-stabilized magnetic imaging and recording," *Appl. Phys. Lett.*, **57**, 310 (1990).

[14] R.D. Gomez, A.A. Adly, I.D. Mayergoyz, and E.R. Burke, "Magnetic field imaging by using magnetic force scanning tunneling microscopy," *Appl. Phys. Lett.*, **60**, 906 (1992).

[15] R.D. Gomez, A.A. Adly, I.D. Mayergoyz, and E.R. Burke, "Magnetic force scanning tunneling microscope imaging of overwritten data," *IEEE Trans. Magn.*, **28**, 3141 (1992).

[16] R.D. Gomez, E.R. Burke, A.A. Adly, I.D. Mayergoyz, J.A. Gorczyca, and M.H. Kryder, "Magnetic force scanning tunneling microscopy of high density recording," *J. Appl. Phys.*, **73**, 6180 (1993).

[17] R.D. Gomez, E.R. Burke, and I.D. Mayergoyz, "Component-resolved imaging of surface magnetic fields," *J. Appl. Phys.*, **75**, 5910 (1994).

[18] H.J. Mamin, D. Rugar, J.E. Stern, B.D. Terris, and S.E. Lambert, "Force microscopy of magnetization patterns in longitudinal recording media," *Appl. Phys. Lett.*, **53**, 1563 (1988).

[19] D. Rugar, H.J. Mamin, P. Guethner, S.E. Lambert, J.E. Stern, I. McFadyen, and T. Yogi, "Magnetic force microscopy: General principles and application to longitudinal recording media," *J. Appl. Phys.*, **68**, 1169 (1990).

[20] R.D. Gomez, E.R. Burke, and I.D. Mayergoyz, "Magnetic imaging in the presence of external fields: Technique and applications (invited)," *J. Appl. Phys.*, **79**, 6441 (1996).

[21] X. Song, J. Sivertsen, and J. Judy, "Magnetic force microscopy images of ultrahigh-density bit patterns recorded on high-coercivity longitudinal and perpendicular thin-film media," *J. Appl. Phys.*, **79**, 4912 (1996).

[22] M. Schabes, K. Tang, R. Ranjan, N. Yeh, and D. Wachenschwanz, "Magnetic force microscopy study of track edge effects in longitudinal media," *J. Appl. Phys.*, **81**, 3940 (1997).

[23] A. Moser, C.T. Rettner, M.E. Best, E.E. Fullerton, D. Weller, M. Parker, and M.F. Doerner, " Writing and detecting bits at 100 Gbit/in^2 in longitudinal magnetic recording media," *IEEE Trans. Magn.*, **36**, 2137 (2000).

[24] M. Dreyer, R.D. Gomez, and I.D. Mayergoyz, "Resolution enhancement by applying MFM under UHV conditions," *IEEE Trans. Magn.*, **36**, 2975 (2000).

[25] C. Hsu; C.T. Miller, R.S. Indeck, J.A. O'Sullivan, and M.W. Muller, "Magnetization estimation from MFM images," *IEEE Trans. Magn.*, **38**, 2444 (2002).

[26] E. Svedberg, S. Khizroev, and D. Litvinov, "Magnetic force microscopy study of perpendicular media: Signal-to-noise determination and transition noise analysis," *J. Appl. Phys.*, **91**, 5365 (2002).

[27] Z. Liu, Y. Dan, J. Qiu, and Y. Wu, "Magnetic force microscopy using focused ion beam sharpened tip with deposited antiferromagnetic multiple layers," *J. Appl. Phys.*, **91**, 8843 (2002).

[28] I.D. Mayergoyz, C. Serpico, C. Krafft, and C. Tse, "Magnetic imaging on a spin-stand," *J. Appl. Phys.*, **87**, 6824 (2000).

[29] C. Tse, I.D. Mayergoyz, C. Krafft, and A. Adly, "Spin-stand study of data-dependent thermal relaxations of magnetization patterns," *J. Materials Processing & Manufacturing Science*, **9**, 82 (2000).

[30] I.D. Mayergoyz, C. Tse, C. Krafft, and R.D. Gomez, "Spin-stand imaging of overwritten data and its comparison with magnetic force microscopy," *J. Appl. Phys.*, **89**, 6772 (2001).

[31] I.D. Mayergoyz, C. Tse, C. Krafft, and A. Adly, "Spin-stand imaging of transverse magnetization profiles of recorded tracks," *J. Appl. Phys.*, **89**, 6775 (2001).

[32] C. Tse, D.I. Mircea, I.D. Mayergoyz, C. Krafft, and P. Andrei, "Spatial and vectorial characterization of thermal relaxation using the spin-stand imaging technique," *J. Appl. Phys.*, **91**, 8846 (2002).

[33] I.D. Mayergoyz, C. Tse, C. Krafft, D.I. Mircea, and P. Andrei, "Extraction of the response function of GMR head for spin-stand imaging," *IEEE. Trans. Magn.*, **38**, 2453 (2002).

[34] C. Tse, I.D. Mayergoyz, C. Krafft, and D.I. Mircea, "High-speed massive imaging of hard disk data by using the spin-stand imaging technique," *J. Appl. Phys.*, **93**, 6578 (2003).

[35] I.D. Mayergoyz, C. Tse, C. Krafft, and D.I. Mircea, "Scaling of head response function in the spin-stand imaging technique," *J. Appl. Phys.*, **93**, 6581 (2003).

[36] C. Tse, "Magnetic Imaging of Hard Disk Drives on a Spin-Stand," Ph.D. dissertation, May, 2003.

[37] I.D. Mayergoyz, C. Tse, C. Krafft, and P. McAvoy, "A novel approach to removing intersymbol interference from spin-stand images," *IEEE. Trans. Magn.*, **40**, 2197 (2004).

[38] C. Tse, C. Krafft, I. Mayergoyz, P. McAvoy, and C. Tseng, "Forensic recovery of hard disk data by using the spin-stand imaging technique," *Proc. of SPIE*, **5778**, 595 (2005).

[39] C. Tse, C. Tseng, P. McAvoy, C. Krafft, and I. Mayergoyz, "Whole-track imaging and diagnostics of hard disk data using the spin-stand imaging technique," *J. Appl. Phys.*, **97**, 10P104 (2005)

[40] C. Tseng, I. Mayergoyz, C. Tse, P. McAvoy, and C. Krafft, "Dynamic track-following of off-centered hard disks in spin-stand imaging," *J. Appl. Phys.*, **97**, 10R301 (2005).

[41] I.D. Mayergoyz, P. McAvoy, C. Tse, C. Krafft, and C. Tseng, "The 2D Hilbert transform in magnetic recording," *IEEE Trans. Magn.*, **42**, 2282 (2006).

[42] C. Tse, C. Krafft, I.D. Mayergoyz, and D.I. Mircea, "System and Method for High-Speed Massive Magnetic Imaging on a Spin-Stand," US Patent 7,005,849 (2006).

[43] I.D. Mayergoyz, C. Tse, and C. Krafft, "Method for Intersymbol Interference Removal in Data Recovery," US Patent 7,002,762 (2006).

[44] B. Wilson, S. Wang, and A. Taratorin, "Generalized method for measuring read-back nonlinearity using a spin stand," *J. Appl. Phys.*, **81**, 4828 (1997).

[45] J. Himle, R. Bailey, J. Hogue, A. Fishman, R. McKenzie, T. Porter, and W. Boone, "Current transients and the Guzik: A case study and methodology for qualifying a spin stand for GMR testing," *Electrical Overstress/Electrostatic Discharge Symposium Proceedings*, 328 (1998).

[46] P. Dhagat, R.S. Indeck, and M.W. Muller, "Spin-stand measurements of time and temperature dependence of magnetic recordings," *J. Appl. Phys.*, **85**, 4994 (1999).

[47] S.K. Khizroev, M.H. Kryder, Y. Ikeda, K. Rubin, P. Arnett, M. Best, and D.A. Thompson, "Recording heads with track widths suitable for 100 Gbit/in^2 density," *IEEE Trans. Magn.*, **35**, 2544 (1999).

[48] A. Schultz, D. Louder, M. Hansen, C. DeVries, and J. Nathe, "Correlation of magnetoresistive sensitivity mapping (MSM) with spin stand performance," *IEEE Trans. Magn.*, **35**, 2571 (1999).

[49] R.C. Shi, J.G. Zhu, B.B. Lal, S.S. Malhotra, M. Schultz, and M.A. Russak, "Spin-stand characterization of thermal stability in high density disk media," *IEEE Trans. Magn.*, **36**, 2462 (2000).

[50] X. Lin, J. Zhu, and W. Messner, "Spin stand study of density dependence of switching properties in patterned media," *IEEE Trans. Magn.*, **36**, 2999 (2000).

[51] D. Han, M. Hansen, J. Ding, and J. Fernandez-de-Castro, "Study of shield effect on magnetoresistive head performance using magnetoresistive sensitivity map and spin-stand tester," *J. Appl. Phys.*, **87**, 6630 (2000).

[52] P.D. Mathur and W.C. Messner, "Evaluation of test procedures for determining servo compatibility of heads and media in magnetic disk drives," *IEEE Trans. Magn.*, **38**, 1575 (2002).

[53] R. O'Barr, M. Lederman, and S. Schultz, "A scanning microscope using a magnetoresistive head as the sensing element," *J. Appl. Phys.*, **79**, 6067 (1996).

[54] S.Y. Yamamoto and S. Schultz, "Scanning magnetoresistance microscopy," *Appl. Phys. Lett.*, **69**, 3263 (1996).

[55] S.Y. Yamamoto, D.C. Vier, and S. Schultz, "High resolution contact recording and diagnostics with a raster-scanned MR head," *IEEE Trans. Magn.*, **32**, 3410 (1996).

[56] S.Y. Yamamoto, S. Schultz, Y. Zhang, and H.N. Bertram, "Scanning magnetoresistance microscopy (SMRM) as a diagnostic for high density recording," *IEEE Trans. Magn.*, **33**, 891 (1997).

[57] S.Y. Yamamoto and S. Schultz, "Scanning magnetoresistance microscopy (SMRM): Imaging with a MR head," *J. Appl. Phys.*, **81**, 4696 (1997).

[58] D.K. Petrov, A. Gupta, J.R. Kirtley, L. Krusin-Elbaum, and H.S. Gill, "Scanning magnetoresistance microscopy of $La_{0.67}Sr_{0.33}MnO_3$ films," *J. Appl. Phys.*, **83**, 7061 (1998).

CHAPTER 2

Scanning Mechanism of the Spin-Stand Microscopy Technique

Any microscopy technique can be evaluated on the basis of the following features that comprise a generic imaging system: sample preparation, sensor technology, sensing mechanism, scanning mechanism, and signal processing of acquired data. The strength of the spin-stand microscopy technique resides in its scanning mechanism. Since an exposure to the basic components of the spin-stand greatly facilitates the description of the scanning mechanism, this chapter begins with an overview of a generic spin-stand system. This is followed by a description of the scanning mechanism of the spin-stand microscopy technique. Different triggering methods for obtaining the scanned images are then introduced. It is shown that the spin-stand microscopy technique offers many advantages over the conventional magnetic force microscopy technique. A detailed comparison between the main features of the two microscopy techniques is presented as well.

2.1 OVERVIEW OF SPIN-STAND SYSTEM COMPONENTS

A generic spin-stand system is composed of three main functional blocks: a mechanical block for head positioning and disk spinning; an electronics block for signal acquisition and processing; and a software block that provides many built-in signal analysis functions and acts as the user interface for controlling the mechanical and electronics blocks. As an example, a description of a generic Guzik spin-stand system is presented below [1–10]; spin-stand systems produced by other manufacturers by and large operate in similar ways.

2.1.1 The mechanical block

The mechanical block of the spin-stand system, pictorially shown in Fig. 2.1, is the spin-stand itself, which sits on a granite block for stability. It is the central hardware that makes scanning and dynamic imaging possible. It consists of the following components.

- The *Linear Positioning System* provides radial track positioning (*coarse seek*) on the spin-stand by moving the entire *Rotary Housing* in which the head is mounted. The system is driven by a stepper motor inside the spin-stand. The most recent spin-stand model uses an *X* and *Y* coarse positioning stage actuated by linear motors and a micropositioning stage actuated by the piezo element aligned with *X* coordinate axis to place the tested head on the specified track. Software is then used to convert the requested track number and skew angle into *X* and *Y* coordinates.
- The *Micro-Positioning* (MP) *System* uses piezo actuators to perform closed-loop positioning (*fine seek*) once the desired track has been

FIGURE 2.1 Guzik spin-stand system.

reached by the linear positioning system. All modern spin-stands have a closed-loop servo system that reads positional feedback information generated by servo bursts written on the hard disks mounted on the spin-stands. A position error signal is generated based on the relative amplitudes of the servo bursts, which are written with known relative off-track position with respect to the track center. The PES is then fed back to the head positioner for the heads to stay on a track (servo positioning systems are also discussed in some detail in Chapter 6).

- The *Rotary Positioning System* provides skew angle control of the head by rotating the head about the vertical axis defined by the head gap. The skew angle at a particular track is defined as the angle between the head and the tangential to that track. The rotary positioning system is equipped with rotary sensors designed to limit the amount of skew (rotation) that can be performed.
- The *Air Bearing Spindle* uses air pressure to provide a cushion of air for rotation. This minimizes friction of parts and results in very low level of nonrepeatable runout. The spindle requires an air supply from the air box, which is an external box connected to the spin-stand for controlling the air flow to the spindle. The motor of the spindle is a dc brushless (synchronous) motor that spins from 200 RPM to 20 000 RPM, with a RPM jitter of about 0.005%. The spindle should not be rotated without the air supply, which must have a line pressure of at least 90 psi. Rotating the spindle without air will cause the precision surfaces of the spindle to grind one another, leading to irreversible damage.
- The *Head Loading Mechanism and Cartridges* are the devices for mounting the heads and the preamp boards. The head loading mechanism also loads and unloads the heads onto the disk upon start/stop operation of the spindle.

2.1.2 The electronics block

The electronics block of the spin-stand system performs read and write functions and the analysis of the head signals. It is sometimes called the Read Write Analyzer (RWA). It houses numerous printed-circuit boards responsible for signal acquisition and processing, such as PRML (Partial Response Maximum Likelihood). The functions provided by the RWA are necessary for the execution of various built-in engineering tests, both analog and digital. Through the RWA, users can also access a variety of logical signals needed for performing customized tests or diagnostic experiments. One such example of logical signal is the drive index of the spindle, which gives a logical HIGH whenever the spindle completes a full revolution. As will be explained in Chapter 6, this signal can be used as a trigger for performing high-speed massive imaging of hard disk data. The following are the major electronics components that interface with the RWA.

- The *head preamp boards* perform the crucial task of amplifying the weak head signals, which are on the order of hundreds of microvolts. The typical amplification factor of the head preamp boards is several hundreds. These head preamp boards are placed very close to the heads (on the back of the head cartridges) to ensure that the weak head signals may be amplified immediately before other sources of noise are added to the signal. There are connectors on the head preamp boards that allow direct access to the differential signal from the preamp. This signal is useful if one wants to process only the raw head signal before any subsequent filtering and processing by the RWA itself.
- The *universal preamp boards* further amplify the head signals coming out from the head preamp boards. Unlike the head preamp boards, which are designed to work only with particular models of heads, the universal preamp board is not head-specific. In addition to signal amplification, the universal preamp board also controls the Read/Write signals, the write data, the write current, and analog read data. Furthermore, the universal preamp board contains output ports where the amplified head signals may be accessed and displayed on an oscilloscope. This is useful for the purpose of imaging because the signals on the oscilloscope constitute the "raw" signals that have not been subject to excessive filtering and signal processing by the electronics of the RWA.
- The *Analog Channel* (or *Analog Box*) is an external box to the RWA that serves as the channel interface between the RWA and the universal preamp board. With built-in programmable filters and variable attenuator, its main function is to perform all the analog measurements. The analog box , through the use of a digital qualification channel, can also pass qualified digital data to the RWA for digital measurements.

2.1.3 The software block

The software block allows a user to control almost all the functions and capabilities of the spin-stand system. These include monitoring the current

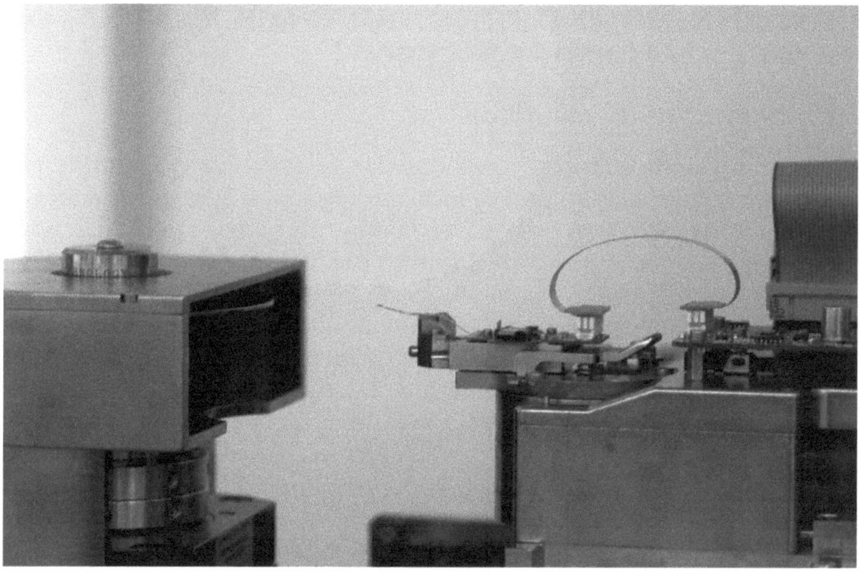

FIGURE 2.2 MicroPhysics spin-stand system.

state of the system, performing write, read, erase operations, and configuring and launching any standard test. Apart from the many dozens of built-in standard tests, the user can also develop customized software modules that interface with the software block, allowing maximal freedom for conducting customized experiments.

As mentioned, other models of commercial spin-stands are available on the market. Figure 2.2 is a picture a spin-stand from MicroPhysics.

The spin-stand system, like an actual hard disk drive, is a sophisticated scientific and engineering device that integrates many branches of knowledge in its design and production. In order to be suitable as a test equipment for the continual technological advancement of hard disk drives, the design of modern spin-stand systems is such that its performance is one or two generations ahead of the current commercial hard disk drives. For example, most spin-stand nowadays support testing of perpendicular recording heads, media, and channel, while hard disk drives employing perpendicular technology are just beginning to enter the market place. In our research on spin-stand magnetic microscopy, we have taken advantage of the flexibility and advanced capabilities afforded by spin-stands for the purpose of developing of novel magnetic microscopy technique of hard disk data.

2.2 SCANNING AND TRIGGERING MECHANISMS OF SPIN-STAND MICROSCOPY

2.2.1 Scanning mechanism

In the spin-stand microscopy technique, raw image acquisition is performed by scanning a target area of a hard disk by a giant-magnetoresistive (GMR) head in two orthogonal (along- and cross-track) directions. Along-track scanning is realized due to the rotation of the disk by the spindle, whereas cross-track scanning is accomplished by using small and precise radial displacements of the head. This cross-track stepping of the head is performed by piezo actuators of the micro-positioning system. While scanning is in process, a digital sampling oscilloscope is used to capture, accumulate and display the raw images in the form of GMR head readback signals. These signals can be accessed through a dedicated output port on the universal preamp board. The sampled waveforms can then be transferred to a computer through a GPIB (General Purpose Interface Board) card or through a network connection. Finally, these raw images are stored in the computer for further signal processing. Figure 2.3 depicts the schematic of the experimental set-up.

Since the target area on the disk is sweeping at high speed relative to the head, spin-stand microscopy is a high speed data acquisition technique. It is therefore necessary to employ special triggering methods in order to always image the same target area on the disk as well as to align circumferentially acquired data corresponding to adjacent radial head positions.

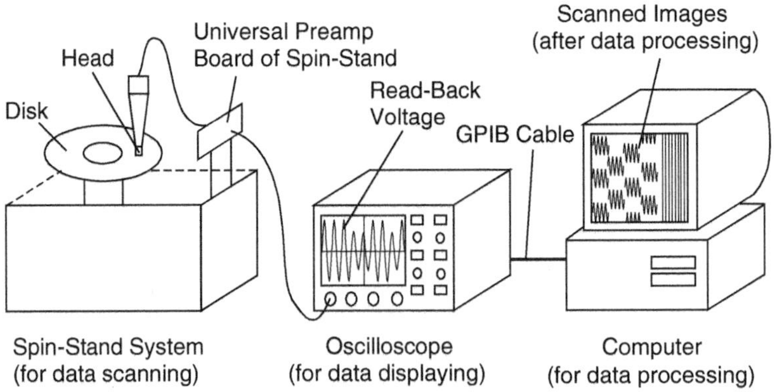

FIGURE 2.3 A schematic of the experimental set-up for magnetic microscopy on a spin-stand.

2.2.2 Triggering methods

There are several ways to achieve triggering. The first method adopts an invasive approach. In this method, square-wave ("all-ones") signals of low frequencies are written onto a portion of the track to be imaged (e.g. one sector). These signals serve as trigger marks which may trigger the oscilloscope for stable waveform acquisition. Because of the relatively gradual spatial exponential fall-off of magnetic fields created by low-frequency magnetization patterns, writing the trigger marks at low frequencies ensures that the peak amplitudes of their readback signals are higher than the rest of the signals on the track. This is an essential criterion for triggering on signal amplitudes. Following the same line of reasoning, it can be inferred that the signal envelope of these low-frequency trigger marks also extends farther in the cross-track direction, allowing a wider triggerable area. In order to image an area that spans n tracks, one trigger mark has to be written on each of these n tracks to be imaged. The advantages of this method are its simplicity and robustness when imaging smaller regions, such as a portion of a track. Due to the high stability of the triggering marks, raw signals obtained at different offset positions across the track are aligned seamlessly. The disadvantages of this method are its invasive nature and the need of writing a large number of trigger marks in the case of massive imaging.

The second method of triggering circumvents the difficulties of the first one. It is a noninvasive method and is especially well suited for imaging data over a vast area, even the whole disk surface. In this method, the triggering signal does not come from the media but from the spindle index of the spin-stand. Since there exists, inevitably, a certain degree of instability in the rotational speed of the motor, the data acquired for different radial head positions will exhibit some shift. It is therefore necessary to devise some alignment algorithm, whether hardware-based or numerical, in order to offset any resultant image distortion. This method of triggering will be described in Chapter 6.

Other methods of triggering can also be used depending on the objectives of imaging and the patterns to be imaged. For example, in the case of imaging "square-wave" periodic ("all ones") patterns, the patterns themselves can be used as triggering marks. This method of triggering is thus nondestructive. In addition, when the oscilloscope is set to the *averaging* mode, this triggering method has the additional advantage of being able to perform *spatial averaging on the fly*. As a result of spatial averaging, noise due to random media fluctuations is largely filtered out and the signal amplitudes are significantly strengthened. The limitation of this method is that it can only be used for imaging "square-wave" periodic patterns.

For patterns with irregular spacing between transitions, triggering on the patterns themselves is still possible if the patterns contain peculiar features (like glitches) that can serve as triggering marks. Depending on the sophistication of the oscilloscope being used, there are also a number of drive-specific triggers that allow the user to trigger on drive signals, such as Sector Pulse, Read Gate, Servo Gate, and Position Error Signal (PES) window [11].

2.3 ADVANTAGES OF SPIN-STAND MICROSCOPY DUE TO ITS SCANNING MECHANISM

Due to the "dynamic" nature of the scanning mechanism of spin-stand microscopy as well as the flexibility of triggering, it is evident that the spin-stand microscopy technique has the following advantages over the conventional MFM technique as far as the imaging of hard disk data is concerned:

1. There is a high rate of image acquisition.
2. The scanning area is large; it can encompass the whole disk surface.
3. Image acquisition is performed under similar conditions as data acquisition in commercial hard disk drives.
4. Numerous images of the same target area can be quickly accumulated in order to increase the signal-to-noise ratio. In other words, *time-averaging* can be performed in order to minimize read and electronic noise.
5. With the appropriate triggering mechanism (e.g. method three in Section 2.2.2 for triggering on periodic signals), one can image weak periodic magnetization patterns that are otherwise buried in noise. In other words, *spatial-averaging* can be performed in order to minimize media noise.
6. There is no scanning-induced hysteresis.
7. The imaging technique is insensitive to particulate contamination due to the high speed rotation of the disk that effectively clears away such contamination.

2.4 ADVANTAGES OF SPIN-STAND MICROSCOPY DUE TO ITS SENSING MECHANISM

Apart from its scanning mechanism, the sensor of the spin-stand microscopy system also plays a central role in making the technique well suited for the microscopy of hard disk data. Since the technological progress in the area of magnetic heads is appreciably faster than that of MFM probes, the resolution and reliability of the spin-stand microscopy technique will be continuously enhanced at a faster pace than in the case of the MFM technique. For example, the availability of smaller (lighter) magnetic heads and smoother disk platters enables the heads to fly closer to the disks, thus improving the spatial resolution of the microscopy technique.

In addition, magnetic heads are easier to model than MFM probes, whose shapes pose many uncertainties for precise characterization. The use of magnetic heads as sensors for spin-stand imaging makes possible the characterization of read heads based on spin-stand images. The interpretation of these images is also very straightforward because the images are proportional to the vertical component of the magnetic field rather than its derivative, as in the case of an MFM image.

Furthermore, since a spin-stand is capable of both reading and writing on a disk using GMR heads, the spin-stand microscopy technique provides an integrated imaging and diagnostic environment that is not available in MFM. Writing and reading can be performed *simultaneously* without the need of moving the disk from one location (for writing) to another (for imaging/reading).

TABLE 2.1 Comparison between MFM and spin-stand

Sample	**MFM**	**Spin-stand**
Contamination	Disk contamination	Little contamination
Target region	Difficult to locate	Easy to locate
Sensor	**MFM**	**Spin-stand**
Improvability	Slow improvement	Fast improvement
Modeling	Hard to model	Easy to model
Sensing mechanism	**MFM**	**Spin-stand**
Sensing	Derivative of field	Vertical magnetic field
Mechanism	Magnetic force	Magnetoresistance
Scanning mechanism	**MFM**	**Spin-stand**
Scanning condition	Unlike hard drive	Similar to hard drive
Scanning rate	Slow	Fast
Scanning range	100×100 µm typical	Tracks and sectors
Scanning mode	Cartesian	Cylindrical
Signal-to-noise ratio	Hard to increase	Easy to increase
Spatial averaging	Practically impossible	Can be done easily
Scanning hysteresis	Raster-scanned hysteresis	No raster-scanned hysteresis
Signal processing	**MFM**	**Spin-stand**
Raw image	Hard to interpret	Easy to interpret

The advantages of the spin-stand microscopy technique are also evident in other features besides its scanning mechanism and sensor. Table 2.1 compares the MFM technique and the spin-stand technique on five criteria that evaluate the performance of any imaging system: sample preparation, sensor technology, sensing mechanism, scanning mechanism, and signal processing of acquired data.

2.5 SUMMARY

In this chapter, we introduced the basic components of the spin-stand microscopy system. The scanning mechanism of the spin-stand imaging technique was then described. The distinct feature of this technique is its high speed of data acquisition. We then discussed the relative merits of different triggering methods suitable for this kind of dynamic imaging. The advantages of the technique are emphasized and its features are compared with that of MFM. It can be concluded that the proposed spin-stand microscopy technique offers many advantages in comparison with existing techniques in magnetic microscopy of hard disk data.

In the next chapter, we present the theoretical foundations of the spin-stand microscopy technique that allows one to retrieve vectorial magnetization from the scalar scanned 2D raw images.

BIBLIOGRAPHY

[1] *Guzik 1701-MP Spin-Stand,* Guzik Technical Enterprises.

[2] W. Ogle and U. Karaaslan, *Spinstand S-1701/S-1701MP User's Manual,* Guzik Technical Enterprises, 1995.

[3] D. Lee and W. Ogle, *Read Write Analyzer User's Manual,* Guzik Technical Enterprises, 1996.

[4] W. Ogle, *Universal Preamplifier Head Adapters,* Guzik Technical Enterprises, 1995.

[5] H. Patland, *WITE Windows Integrated Test Environment User's Guide,* Guzik Technical Enterprises, 1996.

[6] M. Ben-Zeev, *WITE Windows Integrated Test Environment Programmers Reference Guide,* Guzik Technical Enterprises, 1997.

[7] A. Taratorin, *Characterization of Magnetic Recording Systems: A Practical Approach,* Guzik Technical Enterprises, 1996.

[8] *Spinstand S-1701 Users Manual,* Guzik Technical Enterprises, 1999.

[9] *WITE32 System Configuration Users Guide,* Guzik Technical Enterprises, 1999.

[10] *Guzik V2002 Spinstand,* Guzik Technical Enterprises, http://www.guzik.com.

[11] *Disk Drive Analyzer User's Guide,* Lecroy Corporation.

CHAPTER 3

Magnetization Image Reconstruction

If the strength of the spin-stand microscopy technique resides in its scanning mechanism, then the scientific novelty of the technique lies in its image reconstruction algorithm. This chapter introduces this image reconstruction algorithm that allows one to retrieve the vectorial magnetization patterns from the scalar scanned images. It is shown that this image reconstruction technique is based on the response function characterization of the GMR reading element. Experimental methods for determining this response function are then discussed. The effectiveness of the reconstruction algorithm is tested on images of overwritten data. The chapter concludes with a comparison between these images and those obtained by using the magnetic force microscopy technique.

3.1 THE NECESSITY OF IMAGE RECONSTRUCTION

The scanning mechanism of a microscopy technique determines the *speed* of data acquisition and the *range* of the scanned data, while the sensor and the sensing mechanism of a microscopy technique determine the *resolution* and *nature* of the scanned data, respectively. By the word *nature* we mean the physical quantity that is represented by the scanned images. The need of image reconstruction arises because of the distortions introduced by the sensing mechanism and because the nature of the scanned data is not in a desirable form.

Unlike an MFM image, which has a *symmetrical* resolution in the along- and cross-track directions, a scanned image obtained by the spin-stand technique has an *asymmetrical* resolution in the respective directions. This is because the two microscopy techniques employ different sensors. In the case of MFM, image acquisition is performed by a well localized probe. In the spin-stand microscopy technique, however, images are acquired by a giant-magnetoresistive (GMR) head which is appreciably extended in the cross-track direction. Thus, the scanned images can be quite distorted—having asymmetrical resolution—due to the non-localized nature of the GMR head in the cross-track direction. Furthermore, the recorded magnetization and the GMR element also interact in a non-localized manner that contributes to the image distortion. In other words, the signal collected by GMR sensor does not merely come from magnetization directly under the GMR element but also from magnetization in adjacent areas as well. Due to the shielded design of the GMR head in the along-track direction, this distortion may be more pronounced in the cross-track direction.

In addition, since scanned images obtained on a spin-stand are read-back voltages of GMR sensors, they are *scalar* in nature. They reflect changes in magnetization (more precisely, divergence of magnetization, $\nabla \cdot \mathbf{M}$) and not the magnetization itself. However, the physical quantities of interest are the underlying distributions of the magnetization vector, which are *vector* fields. For these reasons, the scanned images must be treated as *raw* images, and image reconstruction is needed. The purpose of the image reconstruction is to remove distortions from these raw images and to retrieve the actual underlying magnetization distributions. Image reconstruction techniques can thus be viewed as transformations of measured physical quantities (scalar GMR read-back signals) into the media magnetization. The image reconstruction technique is based on the response function characterization of the GMR element and is described below.

3.2 THEORETICAL FORMULATION OF THE IMAGE RECONSTRUCTION ALGORITHM

The position of the scanning GMR element can be identified by the x and y coordinates of its center. The recorded magnetization distribution can be characterized by the equivalent distribution of virtual magnetic charges $\sigma_m(x', y')$. The density of these charges is related to the magnetization by the expression:

$$\sigma_m(x', y') = -\mu_0 h \operatorname{div} \mathbf{M} = -\mu_0 h \left(\frac{\partial M_x}{\partial x} + \frac{\partial M_y}{\partial y} \right), \tag{3.1}$$

where h is the thickness of the recording media, and it is tacitly assumed that the recorded magnetization is uniform over the media thickness and, for this reason, $\operatorname{div} \mathbf{M}$ has the meaning of "surface" divergence.

The distribution of virtual magnetic charges is called "equivalent" because it creates the same magnetic field as the actual magnetization distribution. This magnetic field gives rise to the signal collected by the GMR

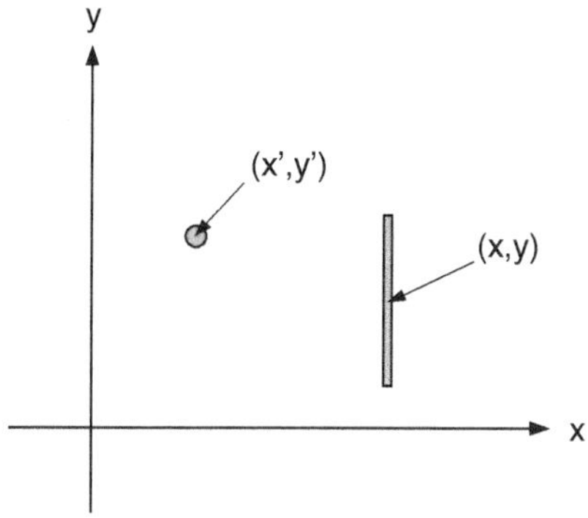

FIGURE 3.1 The physical interpretation of the response function of the GMR element.

element. This signal can be viewed as the superposition of the signals due to the elementary magnetic charges distributed over the disk surface. This superposition can be written as a convolution integral. Mathematically, the last assertion can be expressed as follows:

$$S(x, y) = \iint R(x - x', y - y')\sigma_m(x', y')\,\mathrm{d}x'\,\mathrm{d}y'. \tag{3.2}$$

Here, $S(x, y)$ is the signal of the GMR element, while the kernel $R(x - x', y - y')$ of the above convolution can be physically interpreted as the response function of the GMR element. This function has the physical meaning of the signal induced in the GMR element at position (x, y) by the point unit magnetic charge located at position (x', y') (see Fig. 3.1). Indeed, if $\sigma_m(x', y') = \delta(x', y')$ (where δ is the Dirac function), then from (3.2) we find:

$$R(x - x', y - y') = S(x, y).$$

It is worth stressing that Eq. (3.2) follows from the translational invariance and linearity of the GMR element (in this sense this technique is analogous to the technique used in MFM image reconstruction [1–3]). In other words, Eq. (3.2) suggests that the total readback signal is the weighted superposition of the spatially shifted head response function.

There are several ways to obtain the response function $R(x - x', y - y')$. In our work, we have mainly used two ways to experimentally determine the response function. The first approach is a direct one. In this approach, an isolated sharp transition is first written. This transition is then trimmed

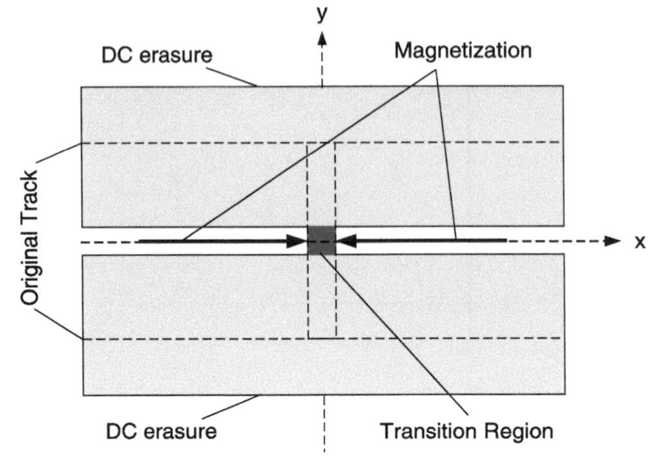

FIGURE 3.2 The dc-erasure process to create a localized magnetic charge distribution.

by using dc erasure on both sides of the same track (see Fig. 3.2). As a result, a "tiny" isolated spot of magnetic charges is recorded that can be viewed as an approximation to a point charge. The GMR reading element can now be used to measure the signal as a function of relative position with respect to the recorded "point" magnetic charge. This signal can be interpreted as an approximate version of the response function $R(x - x', y - y')$.

Another way to determine the response function is to write a well-defined pattern of magnetization (magnetic charge). For this pattern, the GMR element signal $S(x, y)$ is measured as a function of x, y. Then Eq. (3.2) can be interpreted as an integral equation in which $S(x, y)$ and $\sigma_m(x', y')$ are known, while $R(x - x', y - y')$ is unknown. By solving this integral equation, the response function can be determined. It has been our experience that the first approach is easier to implement and it also yields better results.

Having determined the response function, Eq. (3.2) can be viewed as a convolution integral equation that relates the raw image $S(x, y)$ to the distribution of virtual magnetic charges $\sigma_m(x', y')$. This integral equation can be solved by using the two-dimensional Fourier transform:

$$\tilde{f}(k_x, k_y) = \iint_{-\infty}^{\infty} f(x, y) e^{-j(k_x x + k_y y)} \, dx \, dy. \tag{3.3}$$

By using the convolution property of the Fourier transform, we find:

$$\tilde{S}(k_x, k_y) = \tilde{R}(k_x, k_y)\tilde{\sigma}_m(k_x, k_y),$$

where $\tilde{S}$, $\tilde{R}$ and $\tilde{\sigma}_m$ are the Fourier transforms of S, R and σ_m, respectively. Now, the Fourier transform of virtual magnetic charges can be found as follows:

$$\tilde{\sigma}_m(k_x, k_y) = \frac{\tilde{S}(k_x, k_y)}{\tilde{R}(k_x, k_y)}. \tag{3.4}$$

Having found $\tilde{\sigma}_m$, the Fourier transforms of M_x and M_y can be determined. Here, we shall use the known fact [2,4] that only the curl-free component of magnetization can be retrieved from GMR measurements. This is because the curl-free component of magnetization distribution is the field producing part of the total magnetization distribution (extensive discussion of this issue is given in Chapter 8). For this reason, only this component is sensed by the GMR element and only this component is relevant as far as magnetic data storage is concerned. Thus, M_x and M_y in Eq. (3.1) are meant to satisfy the additional equation:

$$\operatorname{curl}_z \mathbf{M} = \frac{\partial M_y}{\partial x} - \frac{\partial M_x}{\partial y} = 0. \tag{3.5}$$

By Fourier transforming equations (3.1) and (3.5), one can derive the following simultaneous equations for $\tilde{M}_x$ and $\tilde{M}_y$:

$$j(k_x\tilde{M}_x + k_y\tilde{M}_y) = -\frac{\tilde{\sigma}_m}{\mu_0 h}, \tag{3.6}$$

$$k_y\tilde{M}_x - k_x\tilde{M}_y = 0. \tag{3.7}$$

By solving Eqs. (3.6) and (3.7), the following equations are readily derived:

$$\tilde{M}_x = \frac{j\tilde{\sigma}_m(k_x, k_y)k_x}{\mu_0 h(k_x^2 + k_y^2)}, \tag{3.8}$$

$$\tilde{M}_y = \frac{j\tilde{\sigma}_m(k_x, k_y)k_y}{\mu_0 h(k_x^2 + k_y^2)}, \tag{3.9}$$

where $\tilde{M}_x$ and $\tilde{M}_y$ stand for Fourier transforms of M_x and M_y, respectively. By performing inverse Fourier transforms on Eqs. (3.8) and (3.9), and by using Eq. (3.4), we arrive at the following explicit formulas for the actual distributions of M_x and M_y:

$$M_x = FT^{-1}\left[\frac{j\tilde{S}(k_x, k_y)k_x}{\mu_0 h\tilde{R}(k_x, k_y)(k_x^2 + k_y^2)}\right], \tag{3.10}$$

$$M_y = FT^{-1}\left[\frac{j\tilde{S}(k_x, k_y)k_y}{\mu_0 h\tilde{R}(k_x, k_y)(k_x^2 + k_y^2)}\right], \tag{3.11}$$

where FT^{-1} is the notation for the inverse Fourier transform.

By computing M_x and M_y, we have circumvented some known challenges involved in solving Eq. (3.2) for σ_m. Equation (3.2) is the integral equation of the first kind and its numerical solution is an ill-posed problem. This means that small perturbations and noise in $S(x, y)$ may cause large errors in σ_m. To demonstrate this, consider a general case of one-dimensional integral equation of the first kind:

$$f(x) = \int_0^{2\pi} H(x, s)\varphi(s)\,\mathrm{d}s \tag{3.12}$$

with sufficiently smooth kernel $H(x, s)$. Let $\varphi_p(s)$ be the perturbation of $\varphi(s)$ by a sinusoidal function $\sin(ms)$:

$$\varphi_p(s) = \varphi(s) + \sin(ms). \tag{3.13}$$

Then by expressing $\varphi(s)$ in Eq. (3.12) in terms of $\varphi_p(s)$ given by formula (3.13), we arrive at the following equation:

$$\int_0^{2\pi} H(x, s)\varphi_p(s)\,\mathrm{d}s = f(x) + 2\pi a_m(x), \tag{3.14}$$

where $a_m(x)$ is the Fourier coefficient of the kernel $H(x, s)$:

$$a_m(x) = \frac{1}{2\pi}\int_0^{2\pi} H(x, s)\sin(ms)\,\mathrm{d}s.$$

Since Fourier coefficient a_m approaches zero as m tends to infinity, from Eqs. (3.12) and (3.13) we conclude that a small noise $2\pi a_m(x)$ in the measured "data" $f(x)$ will cause large and high frequency deviations $\sin(ms)$ in the solution $\varphi(s)$. Indeed, these deviations are characterized by high-frequency oscillations with amplitudes equal to one.

In our image reconstruction technique, however, we do not compute σ_m through numerical solution of integral equation (3.2), rather we solve for $\mathbf{M}$ instead. Since σ_m is the divergence of $\mathbf{M}$, Eq. (3.2) becomes an integral-differential equation with respect to $\mathbf{M}$ which is more stable with respect to small perturbations of the scanned raw image $S(x, y)$. Indeed, by examining Eqs. (3.10) and (3.11), we observe that the factors $\frac{k_x}{k_x^2+k_y^2}$ and $\frac{k_y}{k_x^2+k_y^2}$ behave as low pass filters that effectively filter out the oscillatory high-frequency noise. Therefore, by solving for $\mathbf{M}$ directly, we have achieved two objectives. First, the numerical errors associated with solving an integral equation of the first kind have been avoided. Second, instead of solving for the scalar function σ_m, we have retrieved the underlying vectorial quantity $\mathbf{M}$, which contains more information.

Formulas (3.10) and (3.11) still have one important deficiency related to the fact that multipliers $\frac{k_x}{k_x^2+k_y^2}$ and $\frac{k_y}{k_x^2+k_y^2}$ tend to infinity as k_x and k_y tend to zero. This implies that the following condition must be satisfied:

$$\tilde{S}(0,0) = \iint_{-\infty}^{\infty} S(x, y)\, \mathrm{d}x\, \mathrm{d}y = 0. \tag{3.15}$$

This is indeed the case because

$$\tilde{S}(0,0) = \tilde{R}(0,0)\tilde{\sigma}_m(0,0) \tag{3.16}$$

and

$$\tilde{\sigma}_m(0,0) = \iint_{-\infty}^{\infty} \sigma_m(x, y)\, \mathrm{d}x\, \mathrm{d}y = 0. \tag{3.17}$$

The latter formula follows from the fact that the total virtual magnetic charge is always equal to zero. Although equality (3.15) is theoretically valid, in practical implementation of the described image reconstruction algorithm this equality can be easily violated due to intrinsically noisy measurements and small computational errors. The violations of (3.15) may lead to appreciable "low frequency" distortions. To deal with this complication, the following regularization of formulas (3.10) and (3.11) can be employed:

$$M_x = FT^{-1}\left[\frac{jk_x \tilde{S}(k_x, k_y)\tilde{R}^*(k_x, k_y)}{\mu_0 h(k_x^2 + k_y^2)|\tilde{R}(k_x, k_y)|^2 + \alpha}\right], \tag{3.18}$$

$$M_y = FT^{-1}\left[\frac{jk_y\tilde{S}(k_x, k_y)\tilde{R}^*(k_x, k_y)}{\mu_0 h(k_x^2 + k_y^2)|\tilde{R}(k_x, k_y)|^2 + \alpha}\right], \tag{3.19}$$

where: $\tilde{R}^*(k_x, k_y)$ is a complex conjugate of $\tilde{R}(k_x, k_y)$ and α is a small regularization constant.

It is apparent that the introduction of α suppresses the "low frequency" distortions discussed above. It is also clear that formulas (3.18) and (3.19) are approximate and reduced to formulas (3.10) and (3.11) as α tends to zero. In other words, there is a trade-off between the deliberately introduced small regularization error due to the introduction of α and suppression of appreciable "low frequency" noise. This trade-off is the essence of the regularization procedure. The value of α depends on the level of noise in $S(x, y)$ and it is usually of the same order as this noise. It is worthwhile to mention that other (more sophisticated and complicated) regularization techniques can also be devised.

The image reconstruction requires the evaluation of Fourier transforms of the raw image $S(x, y)$ along with the response function $R(x, y)$ and inverse Fourier transform of expressions (3.18) and (3.19). It can be remarked that the Fourier transforms of $S(x, y)$ and $R(x, y)$ (at least in the along-track direction) can be found experimentally by using a spectrum analyzer in spin-stand measurements.

In summary, the image reconstruction algorithm described above can retrieve the vectorial magnetization pattern from the scalar raw image $S(x, y)$. In the next section, we apply this reconstruction algorithm to the imaging of overwritten data and compare the results with the images obtained by using magnetic force microscopy.

3.3 RECONSTRUCTED IMAGES OF OVERWRITTEN DATA

The first step in the image reconstruction process is to experimentally determine the head response function. Here, we used the method of writing a transition and then trimming it with dc erasure on both sides of the track. It should be noted that we were able to record and measure the response function for such tiny spots of magnetic charges that their counterpart MFM images were found to be elusive and could not be clearly observed.

Having experimentally determined the response function, the image reconstruction technique has been implemented and extensively tested by using a Guzik spin-stand. The main emphasis has been on imaging of edge areas of tracks overwritten with small misregistrations ranging from

0.3 μm to 0.07 μm [5]. On the one hand, this imaging is a stringent test of the image reconstruction technique. On the other hand, this imaging is of interest in its own right because it holds promise for forensics study of overwritten data. In this set of experiments, giant magnetoresistive (GMR) heads were used. First, F6 patterns (hexadecimal F6 = 11110110 in binary notation) were recorded and then they were overwritten by F9 patterns (hexadecimal F9 = 11111001 in binary notation) with controlled misregistrations ranging from 0.3 μm to 0.07 μm. The overwritten tracks were scanned and the collected raw images were reconstructed.

The coding scheme of the write current was NRZI (Non-Return to Zero Inverted). Under this scheme, a "1" signifies a transition while a "0" represents no change in magnetization direction. Therefore, a F9 pattern (in binary 1111100111111001...) has six consecutive changes in magnetization direction separated by two spatial bit periods of no change in magnetization direction. A F6 pattern (in binary 1111011011110110...), on the other hand, has four consecutive changes in magnetization direction, followed by a spatial bit period of no change in magnetization direction, followed by two consecutive changes in magnetization, then followed by a second spatial bit period of no change in magnetization. The sequence then repeats itself.

The middle plots of Figs. 3.3, 3.4 and 3.5 show the reconstructed images of F6 patterns overwritten by F9 patterns with misregistration of 0.15 μm, 0.09 μm, and 0.07 μm, respectively. The top and bottom plots of these figures are, respectively, the reconstructed images of the F9 and F6 patterns. It is apparent that remnants of F6 patterns can be clearly seen and identified on the edges of the overwritten track (see middle plots). These figures reflect only the M_x (along-track) component of magnetizations. In order to emphasize the binary nature of the patterns, the shade contrast of the images of M_x has been deliberately saturated. The artifact of this saturation is that noise has also been magnified.

To assess the accuracy and the resolution of the described spin-stand imaging technique, extensive comparison of this technique with MFM imaging has been carried out. The sample results of this comparison are shown in Figs. 3.6 and 3.7 for misregistrations of 0.3 μm and 0.15 μm, respectively. Any such comparison, however, should be carried out in the context that MFM images represent magnetic charges of the patterns while the reconstructed spin-stand images are the magnetization distributions of the patterns. Still, it remains apparent from Fig. 3.7 that remnants of the overwritten F6 patterns are barely visible on the MFM image, while on the spin-stand image (see Fig. 3.3) these remnants are well pronounced with many interesting details. This comparison suggests that the developed spin-stand microscopy technique has at least the same level of res-

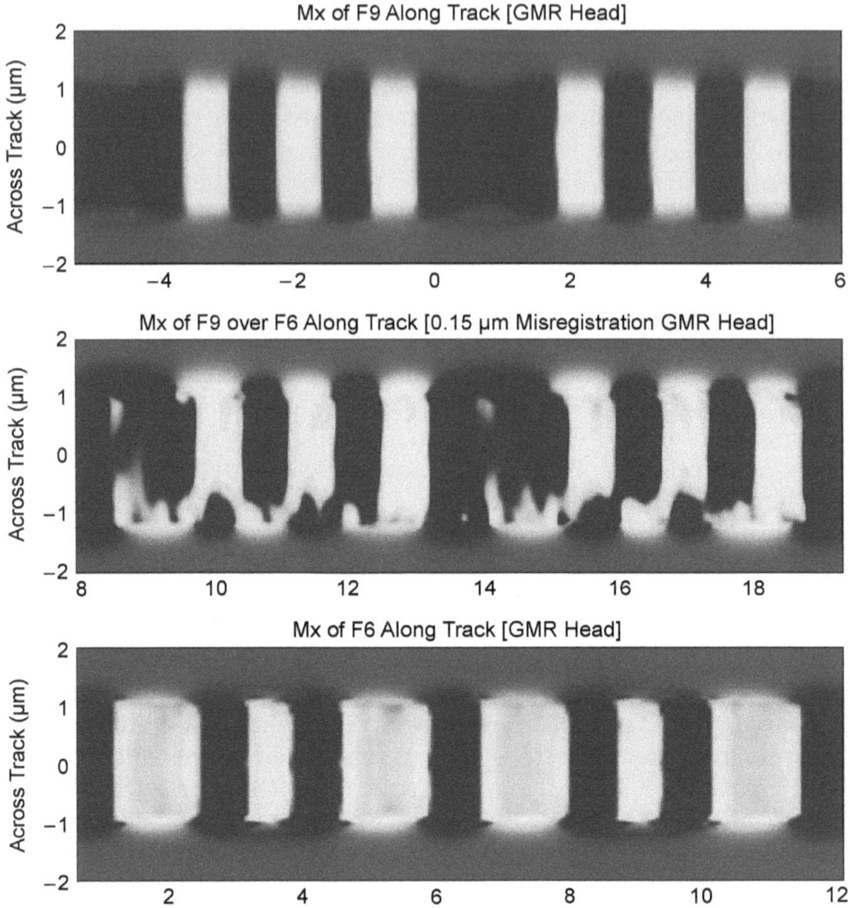

FIGURE 3.3 A reconstructed image of F6 overwritten by F9: 0.15 μm misregistration.

olution and accuracy as the MFM technique and it is clearly superior to the latter as far as the rate and conditions of image acquisition are concerned.

3.4 SUMMARY

In this chapter, we have presented the theoretical formulation of the image reconstruction technique. This technique allows one to remove the distortions of the scanned raw images due to the nonlocal nature of sensing and

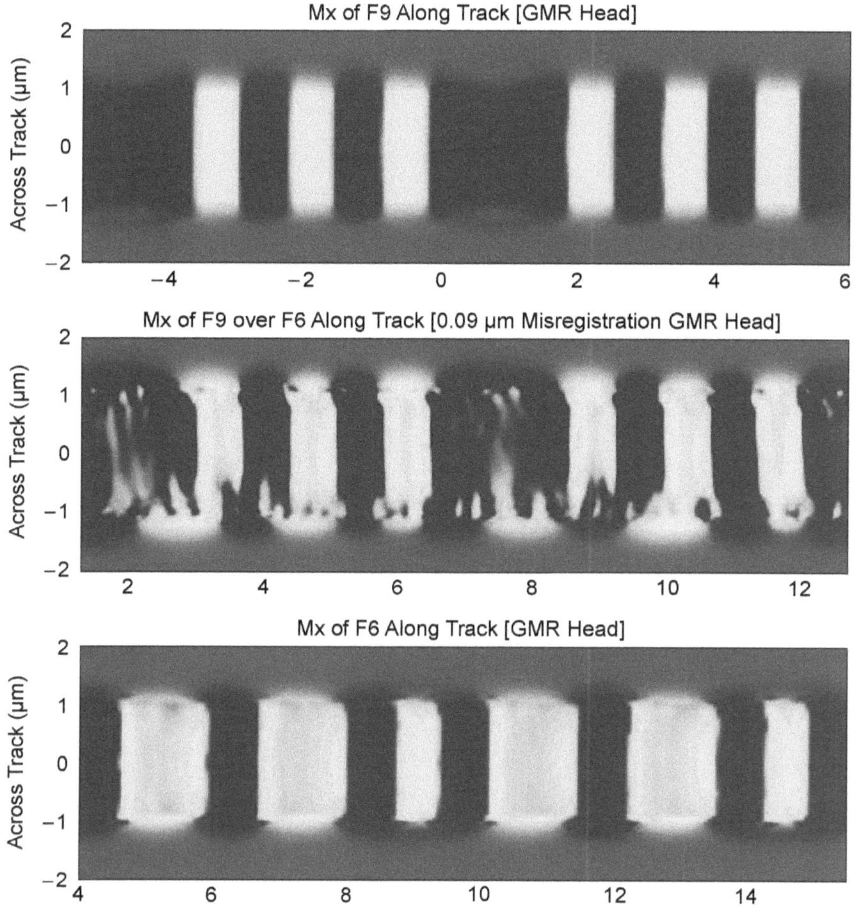

FIGURE 3.4 A reconstructed image of F6 overwritten by F9: 0.09 µm misregistration.

the extended nature of the GMR element in the cross-track direction. It also makes possible the retrieval of the vectorial patterns of magnetization from the initially collected scalar raw images. The effectiveness of the technique has been demonstrated by reconstructing images of overwritten data.

For any new microscopy technique, the important figures of merit are imaging resolution (accuracy), its actual comparison with the well-established microscopy technique such as MFM, its repeatability and possible limitations. To compare the resolutions of the spin-stand microscopy

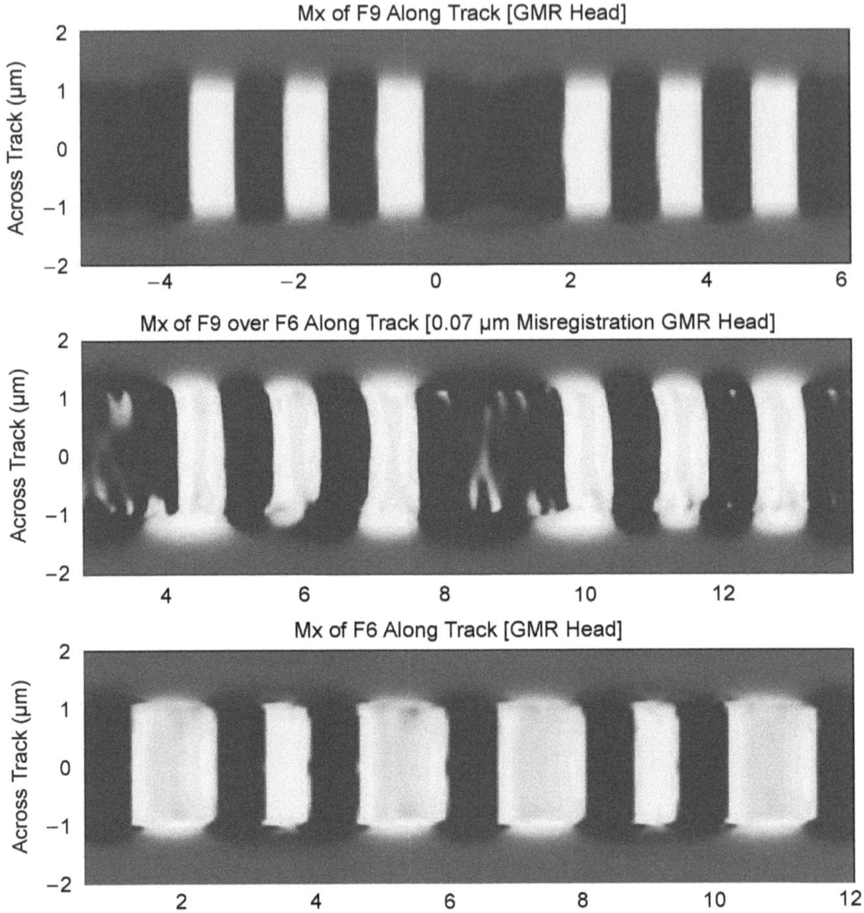

FIGURE 3.5 A reconstructed image of F6 overwritten by F9: 0.07 μm misregistration.

technique and MFM, trimmed (partially dc erased on both sides of a track) isolated transitions were imaged by using both techniques. Such trimmed transitions can be viewed as tiny isolated spots of magnetic charges. We were able to obtain clear spin-stand images of such tiny spots of magnetic charges, while their counterpart MFM images proved to be elusive and could not be clearly observed. This can be attributed to the ability of spin-stand microscopy technique to accumulate (in a timely fashion) numerous images of the same target area and, in this way, appreciably increase the signal to noise ratio.

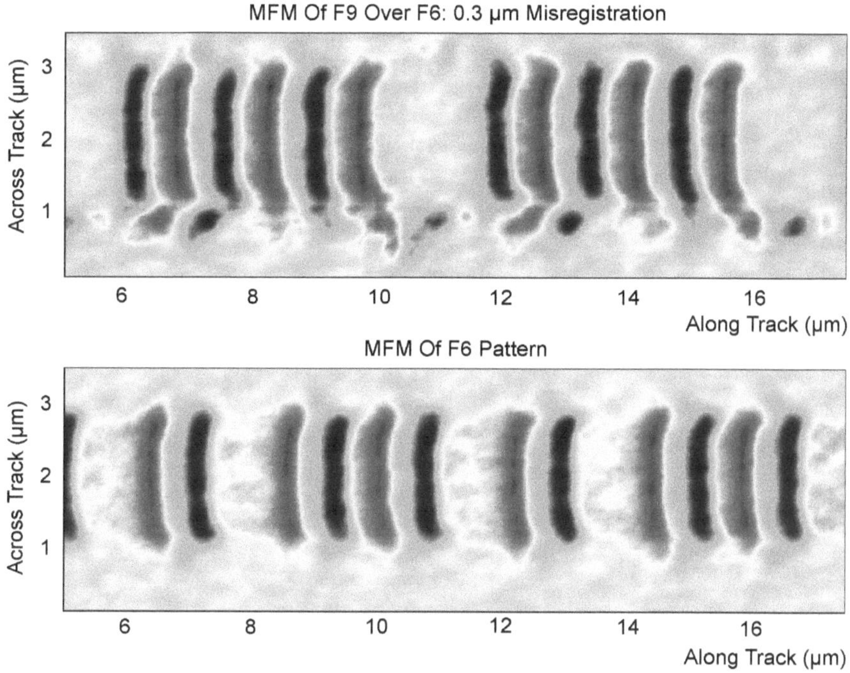

FIGURE 3.6 An MFM image of F6 overwritten by F9: 0.3 µm misregistration.

A comparison of spin-stand images with those obtained from MFM shows that the spin-stand microscopy technique has at least the same level of resolution and accuracy as MFM. The same conclusion was independently reached in [6] where it is also stated that by using the spin-stand microscopy technique "one can readily obtain two-dimensional images with 30 nm resolution."

Currently, the most serious limitation of the spin-stand microscopy technique is the non-localized (extended in the cross-track direction) structure of GMR reading elements. The ability to circumvent this limitation by using response function characterization of GMR elements is important for the progress in the spin-stand imaging technique. In this respect, it is worthwhile to stress that the resolution and reliability of the spin-stand microscopy technique will be further improved by the progress in magnetic recording, which proceeds along the lines of increasing reading capabilities of GMR heads and reduction of their geometric dimensions.

In the next chapter, we introduce two experimental techniques that greatly increase the clarity and accuracy of the experimentally obtained

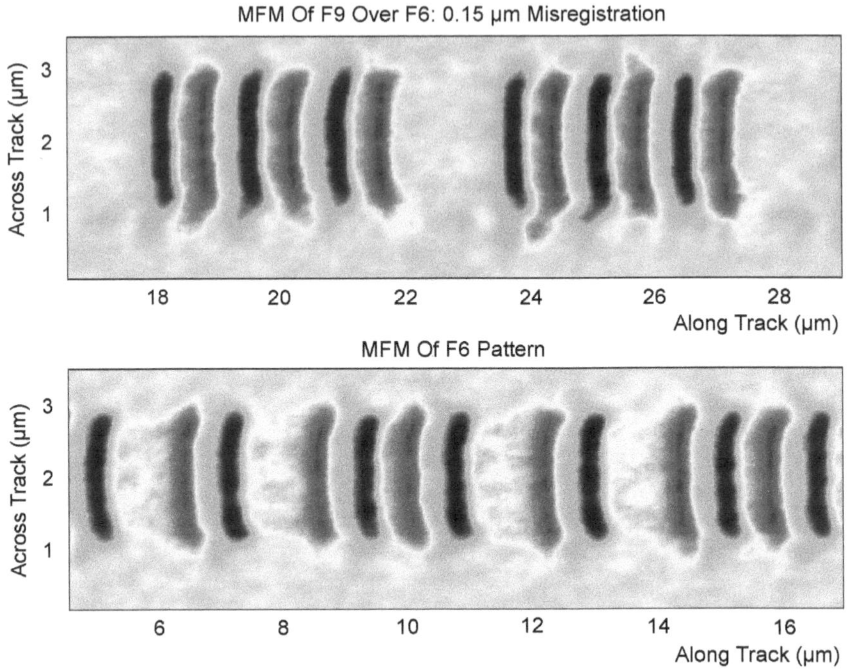

FIGURE 3.7 An MFM image of F6 overwritten by F9: 0.15 μm misregistration.

head response function. These techniques enable one to obtain spin-stand images of overwritten data with even higher resolution.

BIBLIOGRAPHY

[1] R. Madabhushi, R.D. Gomez, E.R. Burke, and I.D. Mayergoyz, "Magnetic biasing and MFM image reconstruction," *IEEE Trans. Magn.*, **32**, 4147 (1996).

[2] R. Madabhushi, "The Reconstruction of Magnetic Force Microscopy Images and its Application to High Density Magnetic Recording," Ph.D. dissertation, University of Maryland, 1996.

[3] I.D. Mayergoyz, A.A. Adly, R.D. Gomez, and E.R. Burke, "Magnetization image reconstruction from magnetic force scanning microscopy images," *J. Appl. Phys.*, **73**, 5799 (1993).

[4] I.A. Beardsley, "Reconstruction of the magnetization in a thin film by a combination of Lorentz microscopy and external field measurements," *IEEE Trans. Magn.*, **25**, 671 (1989).

[5] I.D. Mayergoyz, C. Tse, C. Krafft, and R.D. Gomez, "Spin-stand imaging of overwritten data and its comparison with magnetic force microscopy," *J. Appl. Phys.*, **89**, 6772 (2001).

[6] A.A. Companieh, R. Eaton, R. Indeck, and M. Moser, "In situ ultra-high resolution magnetic imaging," *IEEE Trans. Magn.*, **37**, 1257 (2001).

CHAPTER 4

Extraction and Scaling of the Head Response Function

In the last chapter, we stressed that the image reconstruction is required in order to remove the distortion of the scanned images and to extract the vectorial magnetization from the scalar "raw" images. At the heart of this image reconstruction technique is the experimental determination of the head response function. In this chapter, we introduce two techniques: averaging and scaling that can significantly improve the accuracy of the extraction of the response function.

4.1 EXTRACTION OF THE HEAD RESPONSE FUNCTION

4.1.1 The necessity of extraction

In order to experimentally determine the head response function, an isolated transition is written. This transition is then trimmed by dc-erasure on both sides of the track. As a result, a tiny isolated spot of magnetic charge is created and it can be viewed as an approximation to a point charge. The response function is then obtained by scanning this "point" charge in the along-track and cross-track directions. However, experiments show that the response function thus determined is very noisy, which happens for the following reasons.

First, the trimmed isolated transition is very small and the level of the corresponding readback signal is very low. This signal is buried in signals produced by random magnetic charges that are inevitably present due to the fluctuations of magnetic medium properties. Consequently, the response function is severely contaminated with the noise produced by random magnetic charges and the task of filtering out this noise presents itself.

Second, undesirable "fringe" magnetic charges are written during the dc-trimming procedure. These "fringe" magnetic charges create constant magnetic fields that result in an asymmetrical response [1].

Below, we detail an advanced extraction technique that overcomes the difficulties described above and produces a "clean" response function [2]. By using the extracted head response function, we were able to reconstruct magnetization images of overwritten data with high spatial resolution and accuracy.

4.1.2 Extraction algorithm and results

In determining the head response function experimentally, a spatially periodic low frequency signal was first written on an entire track such that successive peaks and troughs were sufficiently spaced (isolated). Then, both edges of this track were dc-erased. As a result, a sequence of equally spaced isolated spots of magnetic charges with alternate polarity was created. The readback voltage corresponding to this sequence of "point-like" charges was subsequently captured by the oscilloscope after many time averages in order to remove the read noise and electronic noise.

Because the trimming action results in very small spots of magnetic charges, the voltage levels due to these "point-like" magnetic charges are comparable to those produced by the surrounding random magnetic charges created by random fluctuations of medium magnetic properties. As a result, signals produced by "point-like" charges are buried in media noise and are visibly unintelligible. In order to extract from these noise-contaminated readback voltages the signals corresponding to the isolated dc-trimmed transitions, the following algorithm has been employed.

First, we divided the waveforms of this sequence of "point-like" charges into many spatial periods. Specifically, knowing the frequency f of the written transitions and the linear speed of rotation v corresponding to the track location, each spatial period length can be found as v/f. Second, the readback signals were numerically averaged over these spatial periods.

As a result of this spatial averaging, the noise generated by random fluctuations of medium properties is greatly suppressed, while the peaks and troughs corresponding to the isolated transitions are appreciably enhanced. Fig. 4.1(a) shows three samples of the "raw" readback waveforms before spatial averaging. As can be seen, before spatial averaging, the signals due to isolated dc-trimmed transitions are unintelligible. Fig. 4.1(b) shows the effect of spatial averaging over 10, 40, and 400 such spatial periods. After spatial averaging, the quality of the waveforms is improved dramatically: both the locations and shapes of the isolated transitions are

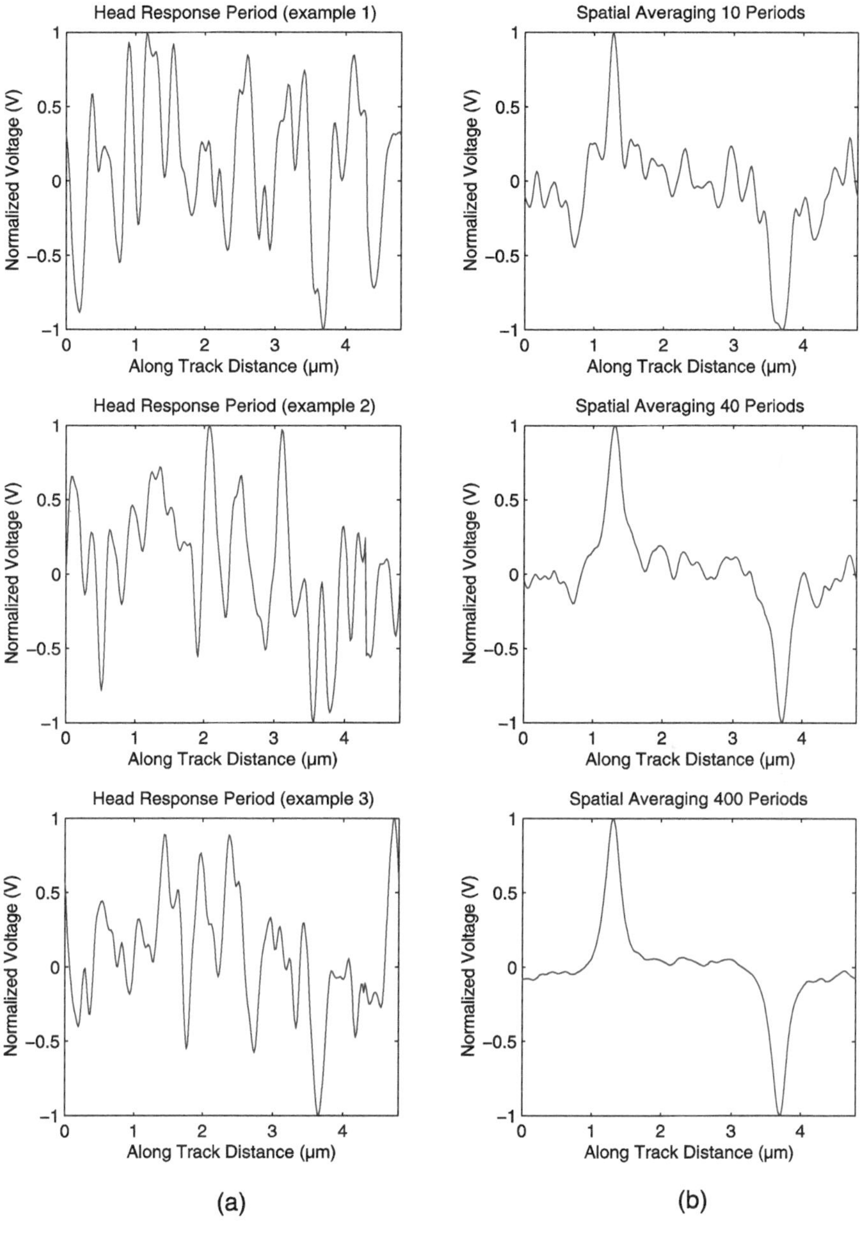

FIGURE 4.1 (a) Three "raw" samples of readback signals; (b) effects of spatial averaging over 10, 40, 400 "raw" periods.

clearly identifiable and free of excessive noise. This occurs because, as a result of averaging, the deterministic components of signals (due to "point-like" charges) accumulate, while random components of signals due to uncorrelated (or weakly correlated) media noise are canceled out.

A special technique has also been developed for the elimination of the peak asymmetry of the head response function. This peak asymmetry appears because the dc-trimming results in undesirable side magnetic charges which in turn lead to baseline shifts [1] of the readback voltage. In particular, dc-trimming of the isolated transitions with the same polarity on both sides of the track would result in uneven baseline shift of the readback waveform, which in turn would accentuate the asymmetry of the head response function. It was observed that dc-trimming of the isolated transitions with *opposite* polarity on both sides of the track minimizes the baseline shift and reduces the response function asymmetry.

However, due to tolerances in geometrical dimensions of the pole tip widths and the finite head positioning accuracy during the erasure procedure, some asymmetry still remains. This asymmetry can further be minimized by properly adjusting the read current of the GMR head. A comparison between the extracted head response function for the cases before and after adjusting the biasing of the read element is shown in Fig. 4.2. As can be seen, after properly adjusting the read current, the head response function is almost symmetrical.

In order to assess the accuracy of our extraction technique, the normalized readback waveform of the original untrimmed isolated transitions is compared with the corresponding extracted waveform in Fig. 4.3. It can be observed that both the width and the spatial period of the transitions are essentially the same. The apparent higher level of noise in the baseline of the extracted waveform can be attributed to the normalization process.

Figure 4.4 shows the image of the extracted head response function. It can be concluded that the dc-trimmed isolated transition is a good approximation to a magnetic "point" charge.

In order to demonstrate that by using narrower and narrower magnetic heads one can indeed obtain a response function closely corresponding to a "point" charge, Fig. 4.5 is presented. This figure shows an image of an extracted head response function using a GMR head with read width which is more than two times narrower than the one used in Fig. 4.4. As can be seen, the aspect ratio of this extracted head response function is closer to 1, suggesting a more accurate head response function.

By using the extracted head response function, we were able to reconstruct magnetization images with high spatial resolution. As in Section 3.3, the main emphasis was on imaging track edges where data were deliberately overwritten with a small misregistration. In our experiment, F6 pat-

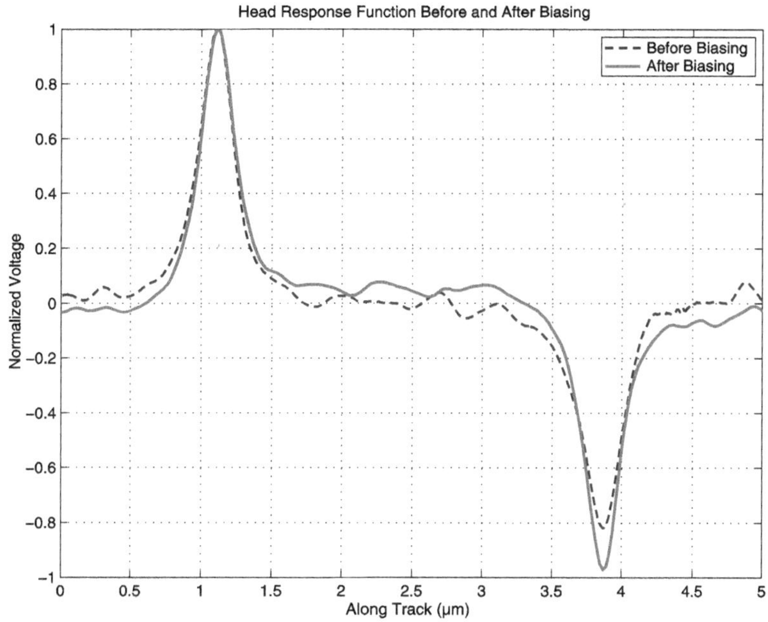

FIGURE 4.2 The extracted head response function before and after adjusting the read bias.

terns (hexadecimal F6 = 11110110 in binary notation) were recorded and then they were overwritten by F9 patterns (hexadecimal F9 = 11111001 in binary notation) with misregistrations as small as 50 nm. The overwritten tracks were scanned and the collected raw images were reconstructed by using the image reconstruction technique described in the previous chapter. Figure 4.6 shows the reconstructed image of the along-track component of magnetization (M_x) for F6 patterns overwritten by F9 patterns with a misregistration of 50 nm.

4.2 SCALING OF THE HEAD RESPONSE FUNCTION

As mentioned, the head response function is determined by imaging an isolated transition substantially dc-trimmed in the cross-track direction. As a result of this trimming, a tiny isolated spot of magnetic charge is created (see Figs. 3.2 and 4.4). This trimmed spot of magnetic charge can be viewed as an approximation to a "point" charge. However, since the "point" charge has finite dimensions, the measured response function is distorted. This is detrimental to the accuracy of the imaging technique.

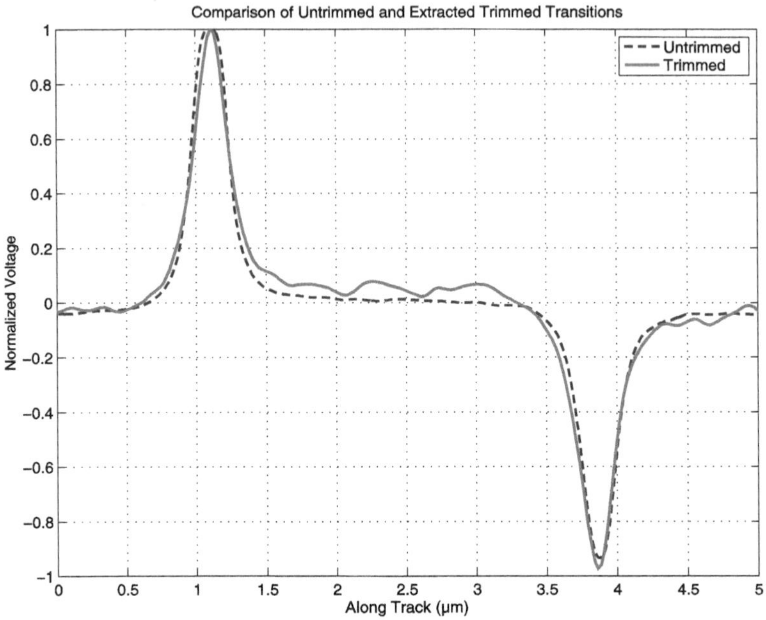

FIGURE 4.3 Comparison of untrimmed and trimmed isolated transitions.

In this section, we described a scaling of the measured head response function that has by and large circumvented this difficulty and significantly improved the accuracy of the measured head response function [3]. The theoretical justification for the scaling is the "nearly self-similar" nature of the measured response function with respect to the cross-track dimension of the charged spot. We have tested this scaling technique experimentally. It is demonstrated that the scaling of head response function allows one to reconstruct magnetization images of overwritten data that cannot be discerned otherwise.

The scaling of the head response function is illustrated by Fig. 4.7. Consider first the case when the charged spot is an infinitely thin line strip of finite cross-track width which is substantially smaller than the cross-track width of the read head (Fig. 4.7(a)). Then the cross-track read head width (as compared with the width of the charged line strip) can be viewed as infinite (Fig. 4.7(b)). The geometric configurations shown in Fig. 4.7(b) can be transformed into geometric configurations shown in Fig. 4.7(c) by the appropriate scaling in the cross-track direction. This suggests that the corresponding response functions for configurations Fig. 4.7(b) and 4.7(c) can also be scaled into each other.

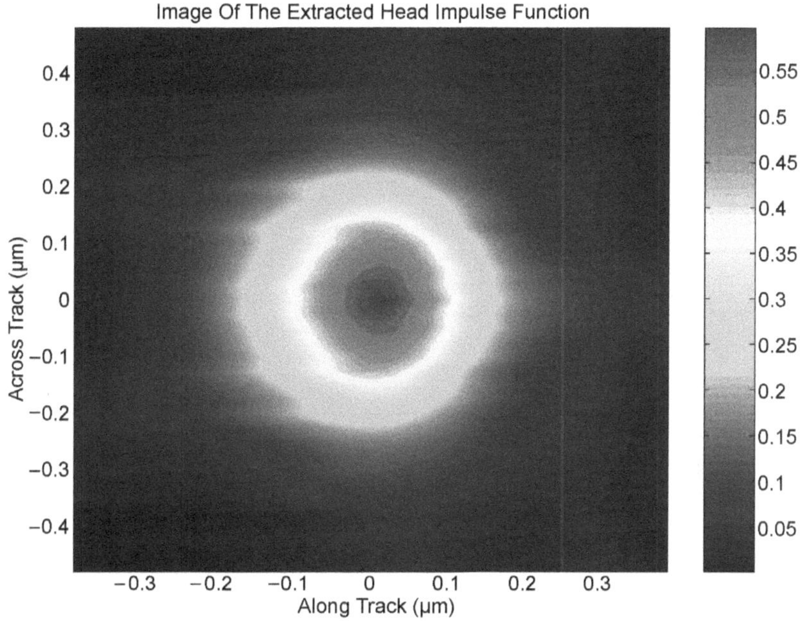

FIGURE 4.4 An image of the extracted head response function. (See color plate 1.)

An actual charged spot has finite thickness, and it can be represented as a superposition of many charged line strips. As a result, the measured response function can be viewed as a superposition of line strip response functions, which can be scaled along the cross-track direction as well. The above self-similarity argument justifies the scaling procedure of measured response functions.

4.3 EXPERIMENTS AND RESULTS

The scaling procedure described above has been experimentally tested. In our experiments, all measurements were performed by using a Guzik spin-stand and readback voltages were acquired with an oscilloscope. In determining the head response function experimentally, we used the extraction technique outlined in the first part of this chapter.

In order to investigate the relationship between the quality of the reconstructed image and the scaling factor, the following experiments were performed. F6 patterns (hexadecimal F6 = 11110110 in binary no-

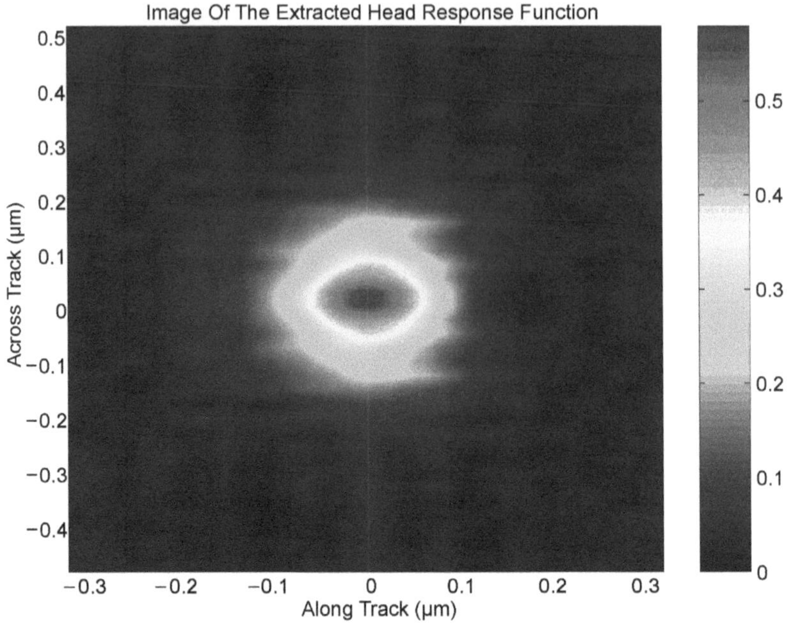

FIGURE 4.5 An image of the extracted head response function (using narrower GMR head). (See color plate 2.)

tation) were recorded and then they were overwritten by F9 patterns (hexadecimal F9 = 11110110 in binary notation). The overwritten tracks were scanned and the magnetization distributions were reconstructed by using the deconvolution algorithm described in Chapter 3. This reconstruction was then performed by utilizing the measured head response function scaled in the cross-track direction by using different scaling factors.

Figure 4.8 shows the reconstructed images of F9 pattern (top plot) and F6 pattern (bottom plot). Figure 4.9 presents images of the reconstructed magnetization obtained by scaling the measured response function by a factor of 1 (i.e. no scaling), 8, and 50, respectively. As can be seen, the quality and accuracy of the image reconstruction vary appreciably with the scaling factor. In the absence of scaling, no overwritten pattern of F6 can be discerned, as is evident from the top plot of the figure. When the response function is scaled down by a factor of 8, remnants of the old data (F6) can be clearly seen on the edge of the newly written pattern (F9). In view of the bottom plot of Fig. 4.9, further scaling of the response func-

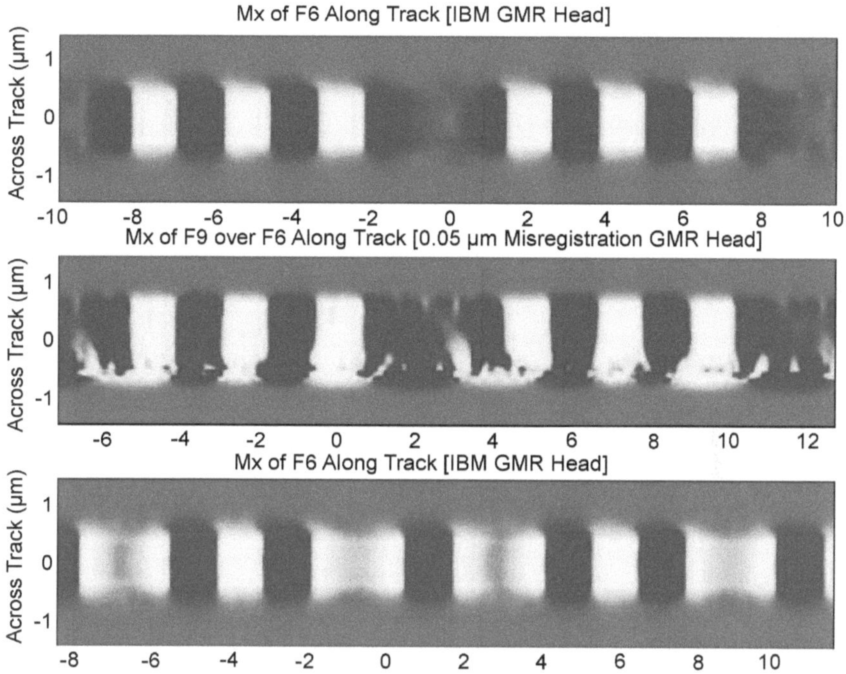

FIGURE 4.6 A reconstructed image of F6 patterns overwritten by F9 patterns with a misregistration of 50 nm.

tion has not improved the quality of the reconstructed image, but rather somewhat degrades it.

In order to investigate the relationship between the value of the scaling factor and the quality of the reconstructed image, the least mean squared measure of fitting to "test" images has been used. A test image of the overwritten pattern was created numerically to be compared with the actual reconstructed image of the scanned overwritten data. The test image is a simple concatenation of the F6 and F9 patterns, taking into account the fact that the former pattern is overwritten by the latter with a specific misregistration.

The next step is to compute the mean squared measures between the test image and the corresponding reconstructed images of the experimentally overwritten data obtained by using various scaling of the response function. The mean squared measures as the sum of the squares of the differences between the values of the corresponding points of the test image and the reconstructed overwritten data were calculated. The smaller

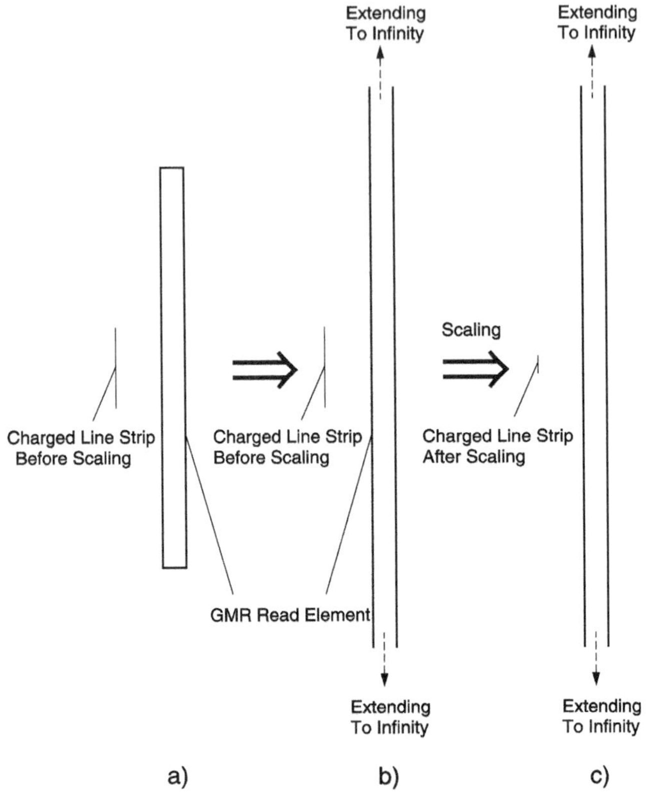

FIGURE 4.7 A schematic of the scaling of the response function.

the mean squared measure, the larger the degree of resemblance of the reconstructed images with the test image.

It was found that the quality of the reconstructed image improves dramatically with the scaling factor until the mean squared measure achieves its minimum. Further scaling down of the measured head response function gradually degrades the quality of the reconstructed image. This gradual degradation can be attributed to the fact that geometric dimensions of scaled down "point" charge become much smaller than the dimension of discretization (scanning step size). Another reason for the image degradation is that deeply scaled down charged spot will be more extended in the along-track direction and will no longer geometrically resemble an ideal point charge.

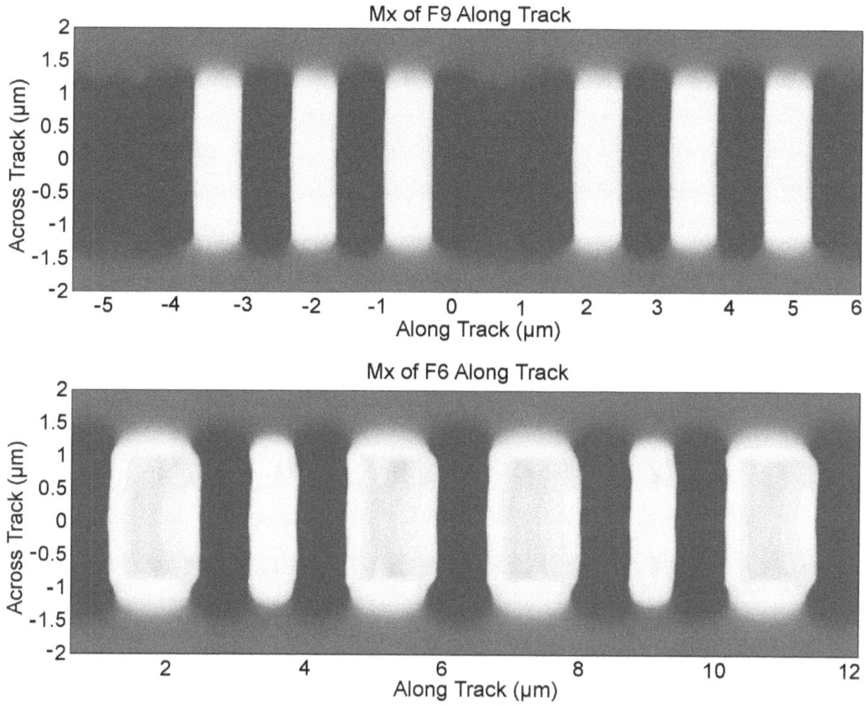

FIGURE 4.8 A reconstructed image of F9 (top plot); Reconstructed image of F6 (bottom plot).

4.4 SUMMARY

In this chapter, we introduced two techniques that significantly improve the accuracy of the head response function extraction. These techniques are very important and are at the heart of the image reconstruction algorithm.

First, we developed a spatial averaging technique to retrieve the response function of GMR read elements. The essence of this extraction technique is the spatial averaging of the readback signals over many identically dc-trimmed isolated transitions. This averaging effectively suppresses the noise due to random magnetic charges caused by spatial fluctuations of media properties and dramatically increases the accuracy of the recovering of the underlying response function. A unique feature of this technique is the dc-trimming of the track with opposite polarity in order to minimize the effect of fringe writing. The same procedures of spatial averaging and dc-trimming with opposite polarity can find applica-

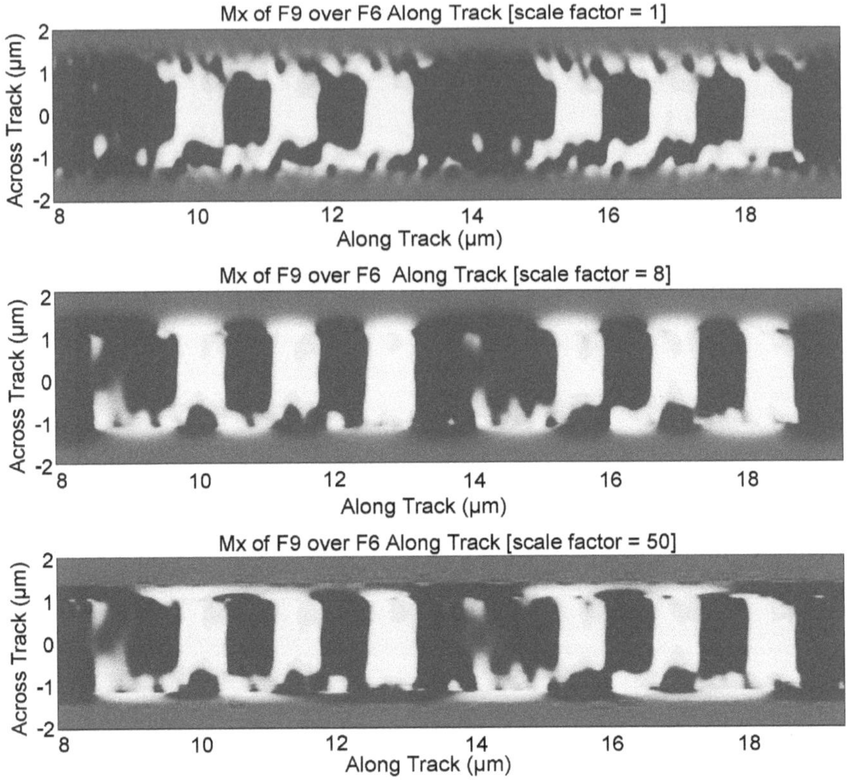

FIGURE 4.9 Images of reconstructed magnetization scaled by different scale factors: (top plot): scale factor = 1 (no scaling); (middle plot): scale factor = 8; (bottom plot): scale factor = 50.

tions in other areas of magnetic recording. For example, spatial averaging has been employed to image the thermal relaxations of periodic magnetization patterns at track edges [4] where the magnitude of media noise is comparable to that of the thermal relaxation effects. Also, the method of dc-trimming with opposite polarity can be used to generate "microtracks" [1] that are less contaminated by side writing.

Second, we devised a technique for the scaling of the measured head response function. This technique is justified on the basis of the self-similarity argument. By using the scaled response function, we were able to capture the image of an overwritten pattern on the edge of a newly written pattern that cannot be discerned otherwise. The appreciable improvement of the reconstructed images has been demonstrated.

In the following chapter, we employ the techniques developed in this chapter and the previous one for the removal of intersymbol interference from spin-stand images of hard disk data.

BIBLIOGRAPHY

[1] S.X. Wang and A.M. Taratorin, *Magnetic Information Storage Technology*, pp. 155–156, Academic Press, 1999.

[2] I.D. Mayergoyz, C. Tse, C. Krafft, D.I. Mircea, and P. Andrei, "Extraction of the response function of GMR head for spin-stand imaging," *IEEE. Trans. Magn.*, **38**, 2453 (2002).

[3] I.D. Mayergoyz, C. Tse, C. Krafft, and D.I. Mircea, "Scaling of head response function in the spin-stand imaging technique," *J. Appl. Phys.*, **93**, 6581 (2003).

[4] C. Tse, D.I. Mircea, I.D. Mayergoyz, C. Krafft, and P. Andrei, "Spatial and vectorial characterization of thermal relaxation using the spin-stand imaging technique," *J. Appl. Phys.*, **91**, 8846 (2002).

CHAPTER 5

Intersymbol Interference Removal

In this chapter, only "along-track" images are discussed and novel ISI-removal techniques based on the "response function" characterization of giant-magnetoresistive (GMR) heads and Hilbert transforms are presented [1–3]. It is demonstrated that the ISI-free readback along-track images that correspond to the actual underlying magnetization patterns can be efficiently extracted from the ISI-distorted readback signals.

5.1 THE NECESSITY OF INTERSYMBOL INTERFERENCE REMOVAL

In many data storage related applications, only along-track images are of interest. However, along-track raw spin-stand images obtained in the form of head readback signals are contaminated by intersymbol interference (ISI). This interference is caused by the superposition in time of pulses of opposite polarities generated by adjacent transitions (bits) recorded on hard disks. ISI chiefly manifests itself as a shift in time in the locations of the adjacent peaks as well as a decrease in the readback signal amplitude. It is important to note that ISI is a result of the very nature of the readback process of high-density data, while there is no ISI in the actual magnetization patterns recorded on the hard disk media.

To counteract ISI, the partial response maximum likelihood (PRML) channel is often used in the hard drive industry to detect the written data. The PRML channel is based on the linearity assumption and prior knowledge of the shape of the ideal readback signal from an isolated transition. By using superposition of properly equalized and time-shifted ideal readback signals of isolated transitions, all possible readback signals can be constructed and subsequently compared with the actual equalized readback signal by using maximum likelihood detection criteria.

While PRML has been a very successful read channel detection scheme that *deals with* ISI, it does not *remove* ISI. Rather, it purposely introduces it into the detection process. Furthermore, PRML deliberately changes, during the process of equalization, the very physical signatures of the magnetization patterns to be imaged. The *digital* output sequences of the PRML channel have little resemblance to the *analog* magnetization patterns physically written on the media. Thus, for the purpose of magnetic microscopy, PRML cannot recover the underlying media magnetization of spin-stand images. In addition, as far as recovering the written binary sequences from spin-stand images is concerned, PRML will only work if the proper time shifts of superimposed ideal transitions are known on the basis of *a priori* information of the write channel characteristics. However, this information about the write channel of the native drive, such as the bit cell period, is not available in the reading environment on a spin-stand. In view of the above facts, novel ISI-removal techniques that are insensitive to the specifications of the write channel are needed. Such techniques are discussed in this chapter. These techniques are based on the response function characterization of the GMR element and Hilbert transforms.

5.2 ISI REMOVAL ALGORITHM

In the case of "along-track" images, the position of the scanning GMR element can be identified by the x coordinate of its center. As before, recorded magnetization distributions can be characterized by equivalent distributions of virtual magnetic charges $\sigma_m(x')$. The density of these charges is related to the magnetization by the expression

$$\sigma_m(x') = -\mu_0 h \nabla \cdot \mathbf{M} = -\mu_0 h \left(\frac{\partial M_x}{\partial x} + \frac{\partial M_y}{\partial y} \right), \tag{5.1}$$

where h is the thickness of the recording media, and it is tacitly assumed that the recorded magnetization is uniform over the media thickness and, for this reason, $\nabla \cdot \mathbf{M}$ has the meaning of "surface" divergence.

For the purpose of removing ISI from readback signals obtained at the track center, one can assume that the magnetization is uniform over the width of the track. Under this assumption, Eq. (5.1) can be simplified as follows:

$$\sigma_m(x') = -\mu_0 h \nabla \cdot \mathbf{M} = -\mu_0 h \frac{\partial M_x}{\partial x}. \tag{5.2}$$

The above one-dimensional treatment of the magnetization is possible only for along-track images when readback signals at the track center are all that is relevant. This is in contrast with the case of removing ISI at the track edges. The latter case by its very nature is a 2D ISI-removal problem, and it requires a two-dimensional treatment of magnetization patterns.

The previously-used term "equivalent distribution of virtual magnetic charges" comes from the fact that this distribution creates the same magnetic field as the actual magnetization distribution. This magnetic field gives rise to the signal collected by the GMR element. This signal can be viewed as the superposition of the signals due to the elementary magnetic charges distributed over the disk surface. This superposition can be written as a convolution integral whose kernel has the physical meaning of the 1D response function of the GMR element. Mathematically, the last assertion can be expressed as follows:

$$S(x) = \int R(x - x')\sigma_m(x')\,\mathrm{d}x'. \tag{5.3}$$

Here, $S(x)$ is the ISI-distorted signal of the GMR element, while $R(x - x')$ can be interpreted as the 1D response function of the GMR element. This function has the physical meaning of the signal induced in the GMR element at position x by the line of unit magnetic charge located at position x'. It is worth stressing that Eq. (5.3) follows from the translational invariance of the readback process. In other words, the readback signal is the weighted superposition of spatially-shifted head response function.

There are various ways to obtain this 1D response function $R(x - x')$. The most attractive approach is a direct one. In this approach, an isolated and very sharp transition is first written. As a result, a "thin" isolated stripe of magnetic charges is created that can be viewed as an approximation to an ideal line charge (see Fig. 5.1). The GMR reading element can now be used to measure the signal as a function of relative position with respect to the recorded "line" magnetic charge. This signal can be interpreted as an approximate version of $R(x - x')$: the sharper the transition, the more accurate it will be to the actual response function.

Another way to determine the 1D response function is to write a well-defined pattern of magnetization (magnetic charge). For this pattern, the GMR element signal $S(x)$ is measured as a function of x. Then Eq. (5.3) can be interpreted as an integral equation in which $S(x)$ and $\sigma_m(x')$ are known, while $R(x - x')$ is unknown. By solving this integral equation, the 1D response function can be determined.

Having determined the response function, Eq. (5.3) can be viewed as a convolution integral equation that relates the raw, ISI-distorted signal $S(x)$ to the distribution of virtual, ISI-free magnetic charges $\sigma_m(x')$. This

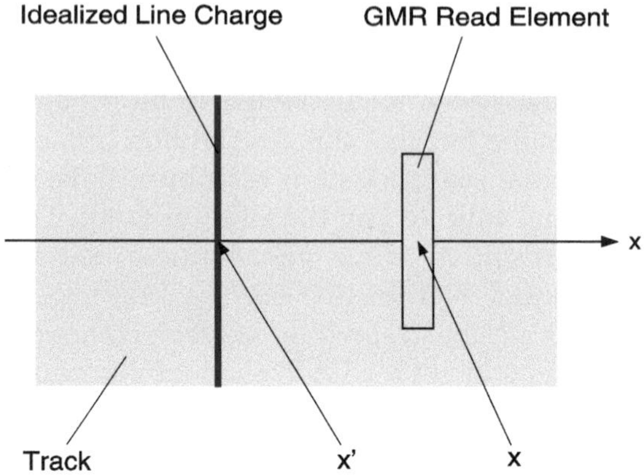

FIGURE 5.1 Geometry of the idealized line charge and the GMR element.

integral equation can be solved by using a 1D Fourier transform:

$$\tilde{f}(k_x) = \int_{-\infty}^{\infty} f(x)\mathrm{e}^{-jk_x x}\,\mathrm{d}x. \tag{5.4}$$

By using the convolution property of the Fourier transform, the solution can be written as follows:

$$\tilde{\sigma}_m(k_x) = \frac{\tilde{S}(k_x)}{\tilde{R}(k_x)}, \tag{5.5}$$

where $\tilde{S}$, $\tilde{R}$ and $\tilde{\sigma}_m$ are the Fourier transforms of S, R and σ_m, respectively. Having found the solution for $\tilde{\sigma}_m$, the Fourier transform of M_x can be determined. By Fourier transforming equation (5.2), one can derive the following relation:

$$jk_x\tilde{M}_x = -\frac{\tilde{\sigma}_m}{\mu_0 h}, \tag{5.6}$$

where $\tilde{M}_x$ is the Fourier transform of M_x. By performing inverse Fourier transform of Eq. (5.6), and by using Eq. (5.5), the following explicit formula for the actual distributions of $M_x(x)$ is derived:

$$M_x(x) = FT^{-1}\left[\frac{j\tilde{S}(k_x)}{\mu_0 h k_x \tilde{R}(k_x)}\right], \tag{5.7}$$

where, as before, FT^{-1} is the notation for the inverse Fourier transform. Thus, the reconstructed M_x is free from any ISI distortions.

As mentioned, the above 1D treatment of the magnetization is naturally suitable for the recovery of hard disk data where the relevant information is sought only along the center of the track. For magnetization patterns at the track edges, however, a 2D treatment of the ISI-removal problem is needed. In this respect, while PRML does not have an easy generalization to the 2D case, the described ISI-removal technique has a straightforward extension to combat 2D ISI. The algorithm of this 2D ISI-removal is the image reconstruction technique that has been presented in Chapter 3. Here, we only reproduce the formula for the reconstructed, ISI-free $M_x(x, y)$:

$$M_x(x, y) = FT^{-1}\left[\frac{j\tilde{S}(k_x, k_y)k_x}{\mu_0 h\tilde{R}(k_x, k_y)(k_x^2 + k_y^2)}\right]. \tag{5.8}$$

The numerical aspects of implementation of the ISI-removal algorithm are similar to those discussed in Chapter 3 and rely on regularization of formulas (5.7) and (5.8) in order to suppress "low frequency" noise. It is worthwhile to note again that only the curl-free component of the magnetization is recoverable. The divergence-free component of the magnetization is not field-producing and thus cannot be recovered through spin-stand images. This issue is discussed in detail in Chapter 8.

5.3 EXPERIMENTS AND RESULTS

The development and extensive testing of the proposed ISI-removal technique was carried out in several stages. First, using computer simulations, different data patterns with different degrees of ISI corruption were created and the ISI-free patterns were reconstructed using Eq. (5.7). In the second stage of testing, controlled experiments were performed in which known magnetization patterns (with varying degree of ISI in readback signals) were written using a spin-stand and the corresponding ISI-free patterns were recovered by using the proposed algorithm. The third stage of testing involved the capturing of ISI-corrupted 1D readback signals and 2D images from actual commercial hard drives and the subsequent recovery of the ISI-free signals and images by using Eqs. (5.7) and (5.8), respectively.

In the first stage of computer simulation based testing, the head response function was obtained by assuming that the media magnetization has an arctangent transition. The subsequent differentiation of the arctan-

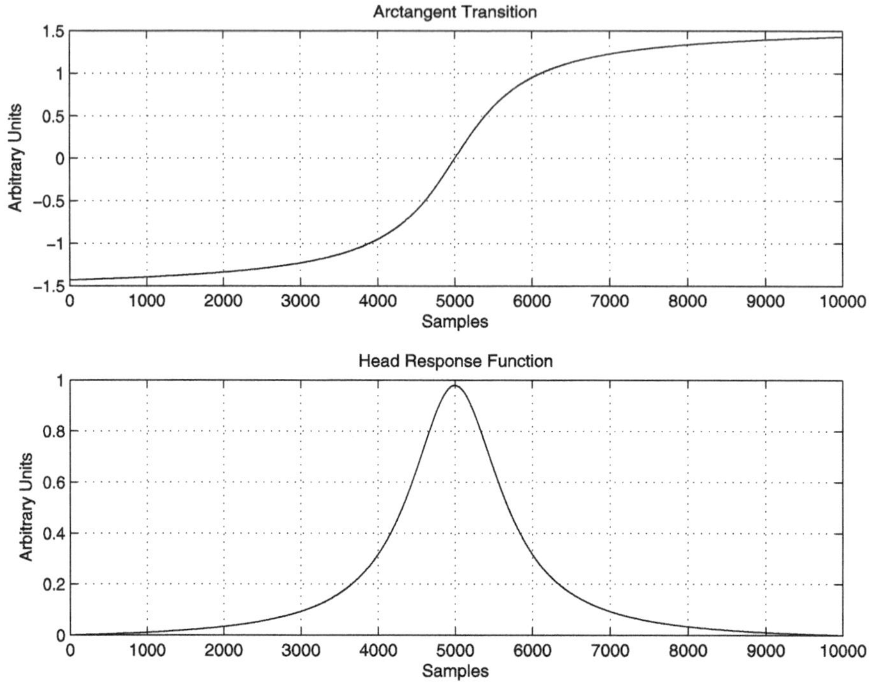

FIGURE 5.2 Arctangent function (top) and simulated head response function (bottom).

gent transition was performed to produce an isolated pulse, which was used in simulations as the head response function. The top and bottom plots of Fig. 5.2 show the arctangent transition and the simulated head response function.

After choosing the simulated head response function, some simulated data patterns with ISI were created by using Eq. (5.3). Then, Eq. (5.7) was employed to recover the ISI-free patterns. In the numerical simulations, tribit patterns with increasing degree of ISI corruption were first studied. A tribit pattern is one that has three consecutive transitions. In the presence of ISI, the middle transition in the readback signal will be increasingly corrupted with the increase in linear data density. With a high enough data density, the middle transition will not be "legible" (discernible) due to ISI. The amount of ISI corruption was simulated using the parameter PW50/T where PW50 is the pulse width at 50% of the pulse amplitude (also known as full width at half maximum) and T is the sampling clock period. The parameter PW50/T is an effective measure of the density of the channel, D_{ch}, where a high D_{ch} value would also mean that ISI would be more pronounced. In the simulation, T was 512 samples and D_{ch} had values of 1.68, 2.26, and 3.43. Figure 5.3 presents the raw, ISI-corrupted signal (thicker lines) and the recovered, ISI-free signal (thinner lines). As is clearly seen, even for the severe ISI-corrupted case of D_{ch}=3.43, the middle peaks of the tribit patterns which were lost had been recovered using the ISI-removal algorithm.

The next set of simulated patterns were F9F9, corresponding to "1111100111111001." This pattern essentially has six consecutive transitions instead of three. Figure 5.4 shows the ISI-corrupted F9F9 patterns and the recovered ISI-free patterns.

The third set of numerical experiments was the recovery of an ISI-corrupted 57-bit pseudo-random binary sequence (PRBS):

000010110111001111001010100111101100111011100000000101000,

which was extracted from the output of a 10th order scrambler, $1 + x^7 + x^{10}$, when the input to the scrambler was all zeros. Figure 5.5 shows the ISI-corrupted PRBS and the recovered ISI-free PRBS.

Moving beyond computer simulations, in the second stage of testing of the ISI-removal algorithm, a series of experiments had been performed to remove ISI from deliberately written spin-stand patterns by using the response function of GMR read head. In the first experiment, tribit patterns with different degrees of ISI, with D_{ch} values of 1.7, 2, and 3.25, were written and read back. These different D_{ch} values were created by first writing the tribit patterns at a fixed 1500 RPM, and then reading back the data at 2700, 3600, and 4500 RPM, respectively. Figure 5.6 shows the reconstructed readback signals (thinner lines) superimposed on the ISI-distorted readback signals (thicker lines) of tribit patterns with increasing densities (from the top plot to the bottom plot). It is clear that the middle transitions of the tribit patterns, which were not discernible due to varying degrees of ISI, had been successfully reconstructed.

In the second experiment, hexadecimal F9F9 patterns ("1111100111111001" in binary) were written with increasing data density (D_{ch} values). Figure 5.7 shows the reconstructed readback signals (thinner lines) superimposed on the ISI-distorted readback signals (thicker lines) of the F9F9 patterns. As can be seen, the specific transitions associated with the F9F9 patterns have been recovered after the ISI has been removed from the original raw readback F9F9 signals.

In the third stage of testing of the ISI-removal algorithm, the reconstruction of the actual recorded magnetization patterns (both 1D and 2D) from ISI-ridden readback signals by using the response function charac-

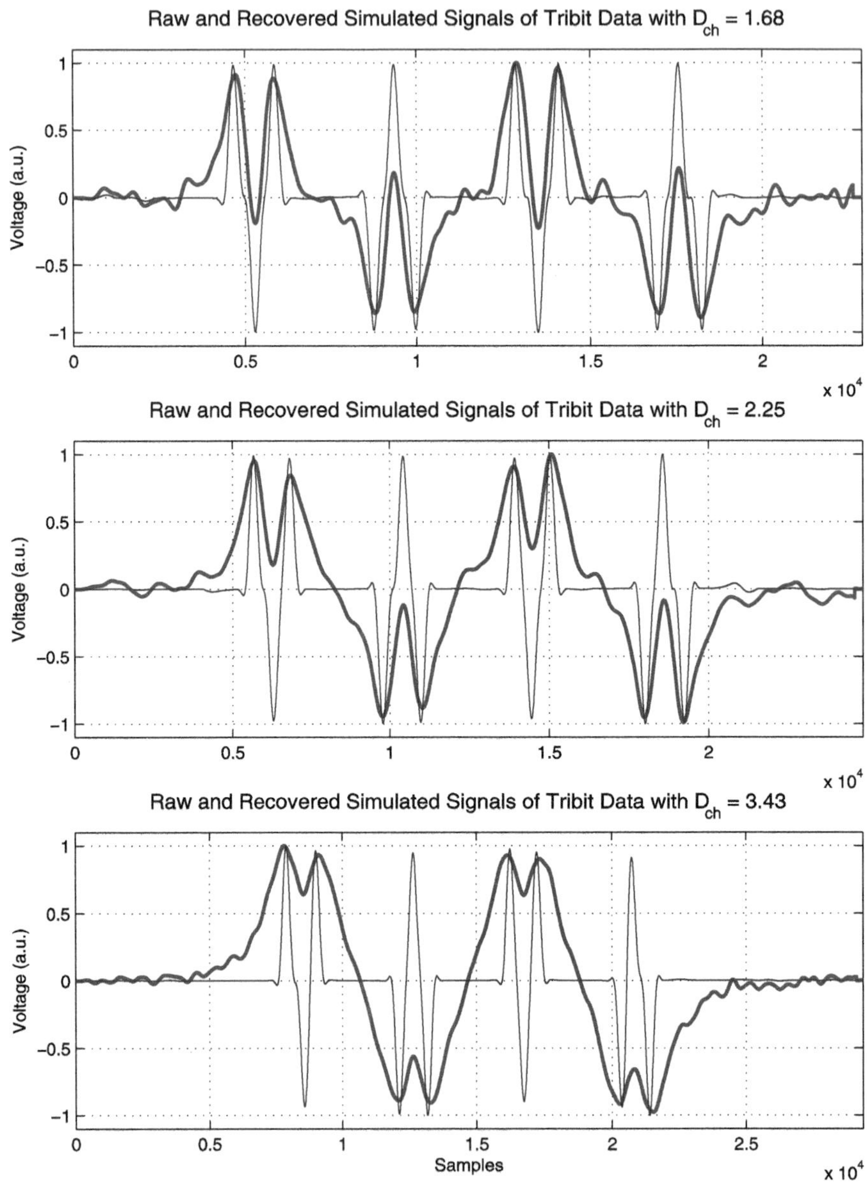

FIGURE 5.3 Raw and recovered tribit patterns.

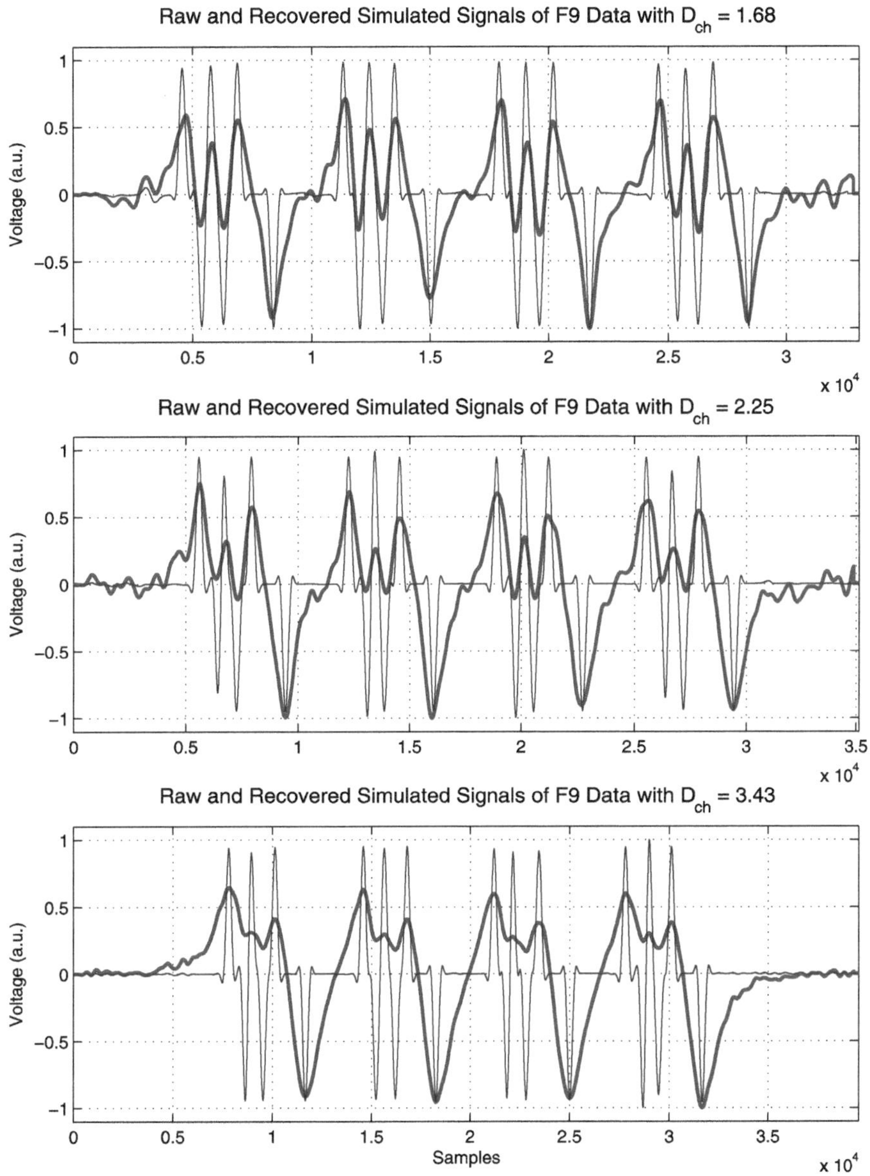

FIGURE 5.4 Raw and recovered F9F9 patterns.

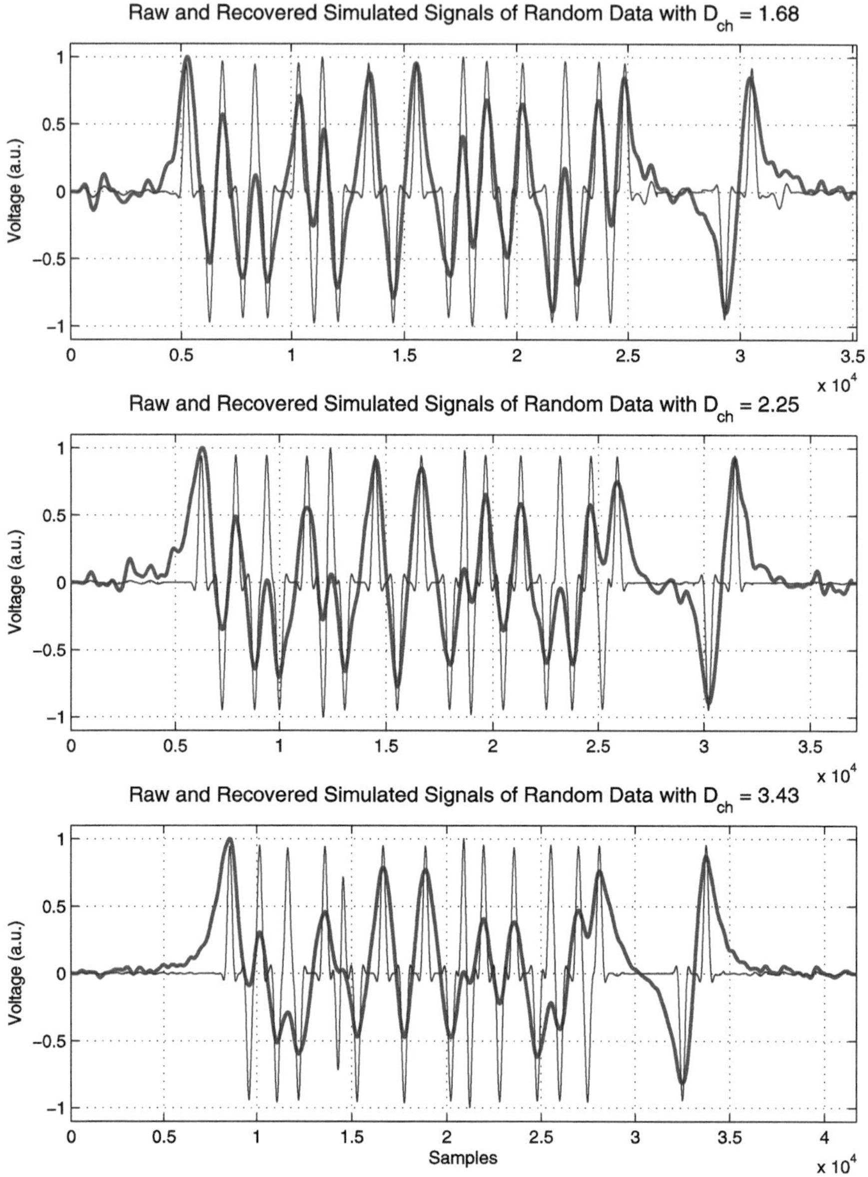

FIGURE 5.5 Raw and recovered PRBS patterns.

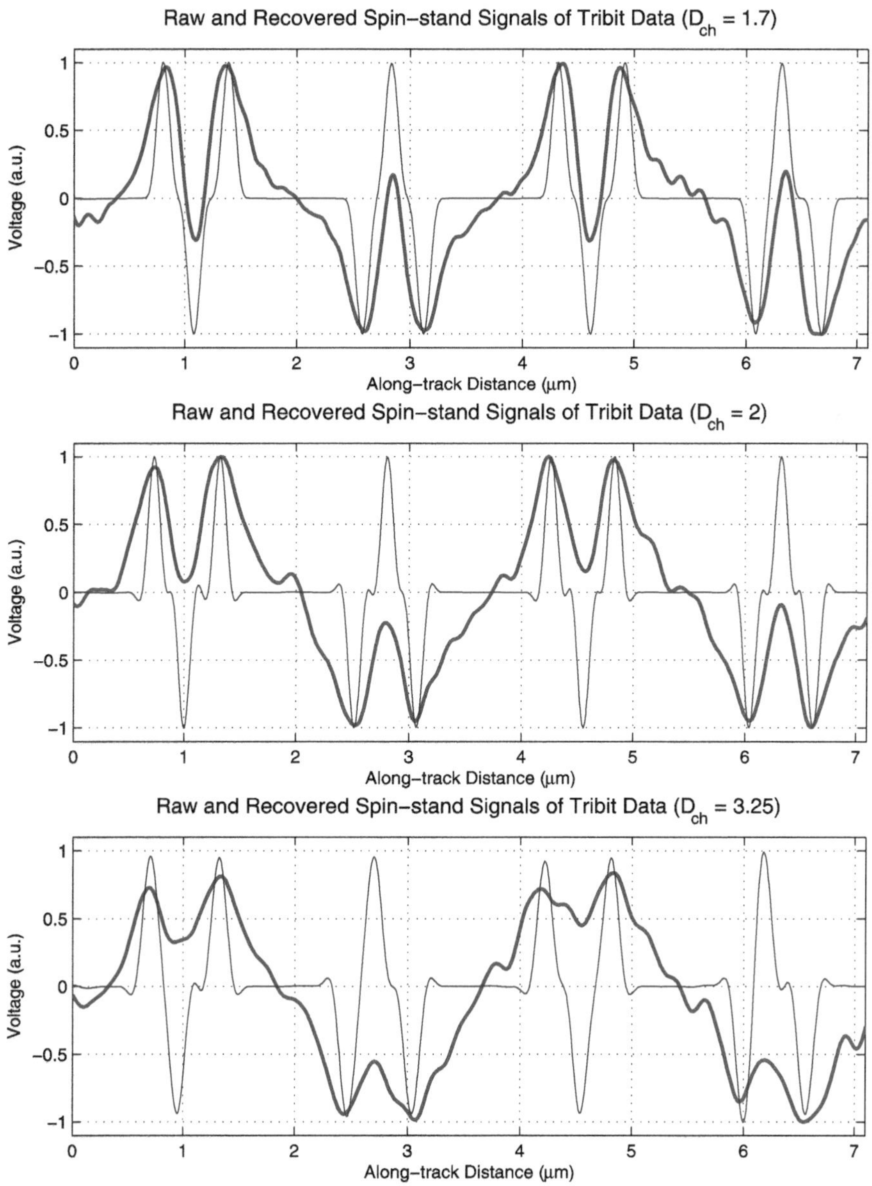

FIGURE 5.6 Raw and recovered tribit patterns on a spin-stand.

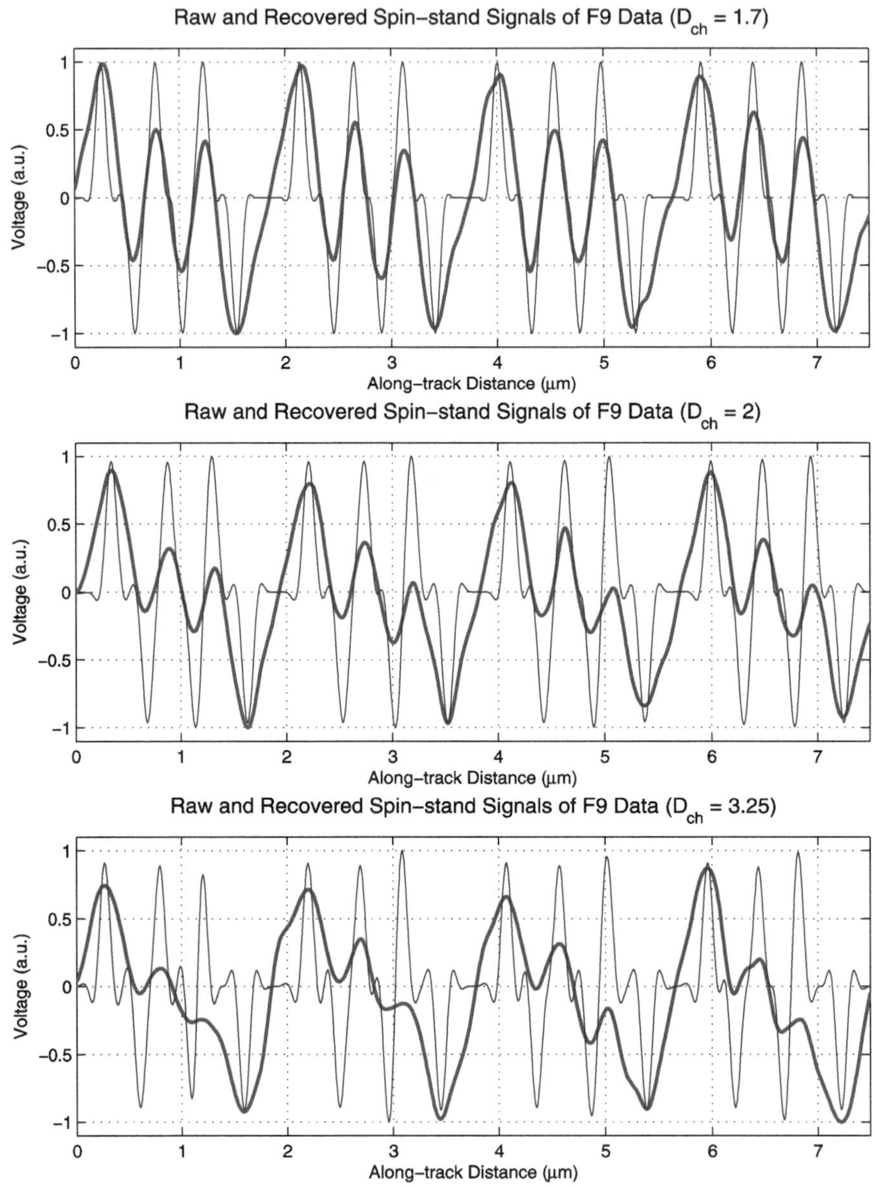

FIGURE 5.7 Raw and recovered F9 patterns on a spin-stand.

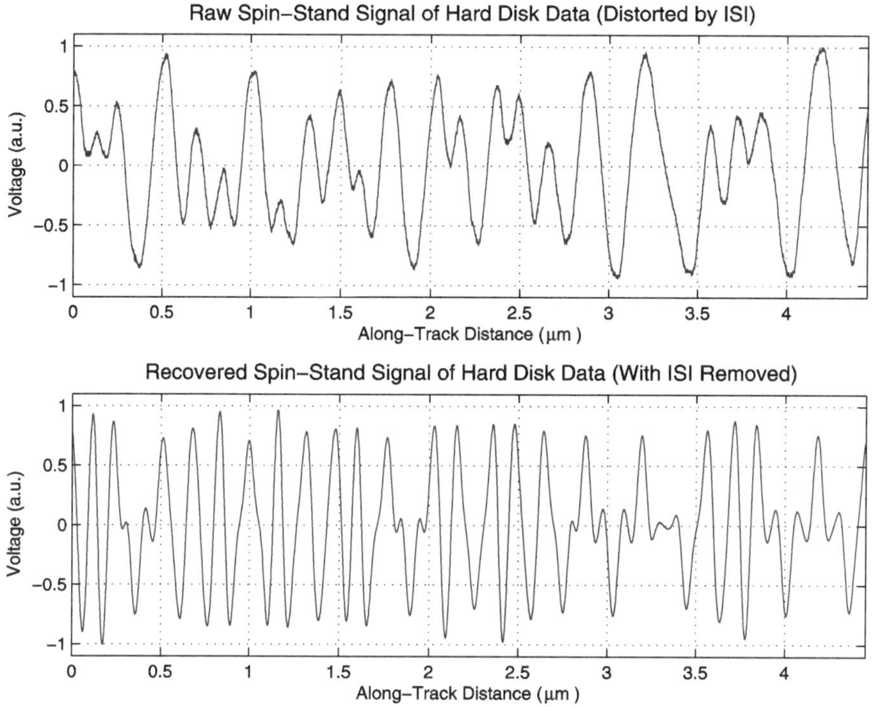

FIGURE 5.8 Raw and recovered hard disk patterns (40 GB/platter disk).

terization of GMR heads was performed. In the experiment, a disk taken from a commercial hard drive (40 GB/platter, year 2002) with track density of 55 ktpi (kilo track per inch) and bit density of 570 kbpi (kilo bit per inch) was mounted on the spin-stand. A GMR head with read width of 0.19 μm was used to capture the raw readback signals and the described ISI-removal technique was applied to the raw signals. Figure 5.8 compares the raw, ISI-distorted readback signal (top plot) with the reconstructed, ISI-free signal (bottom plot). Clearly, all the peaks in the raw readback signals have been restored to their correct amplitude and locations after using the ISI-removal algorithm. Figure 5.9 presents the raw spin-stand image of hard disk data of the same disk (top plot) and the reconstructed image (bottom plot). The raw image was obtained using a cross-track step size of 1 microinch. The distortions caused by ISI in the raw image were manifested as consecutive peaks of the same polarity. In comparison, consecutive peaks in the reconstructed image all had different polarities, indicating that the ISI distortions were removed.

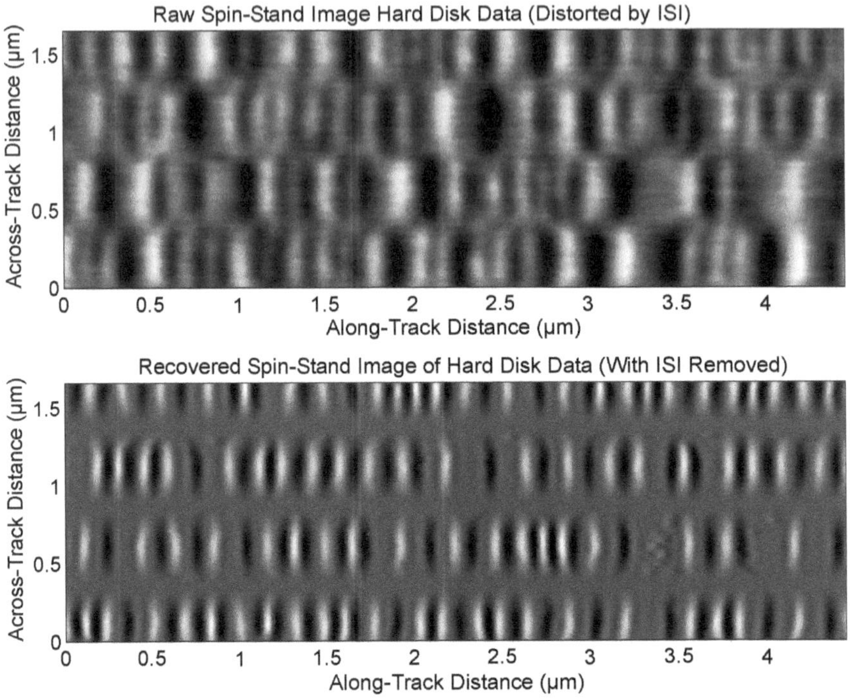

FIGURE 5.9 Raw and recovered hard disk images (40 GB/platter disk).

We next used a GMR head with a read width of 0.13 μm to read the signal from a commercial hard drive (80 GB/platter, year 2003) with track density of 89 ktpi and bit density ranging from 615–770 kbpi. Figures 5.10 and 5.11 show the ISI-corrupted signal and image and the recovered ISI-free signal and image, respectively. Since the track density of this 80 GB/platter hard drive was about 50% higher than that of the 40 GB/platter disk, a cross-track step size below one microinch was required to scan the raw hard disk image. However, due to the instrumentation limitations (nonrepeatable runout), a cross-track step size below one microinch was not readily attainable. As a result, compared to Fig. 5.9, the recovered image of Fig. 5.11 contains some errors at the track edges.

Apart from the ability to remove ISI distortions, the developed technique has an additional advantage in that it is not sensitive (unlike PRML) to hard, soft, and nonlinear transition shifts in the media. This is because the technique is based on the response function characterization of GMR heads and the fact that actual readback signals are convolutions of the underlying magnetization patterns and the head response function.

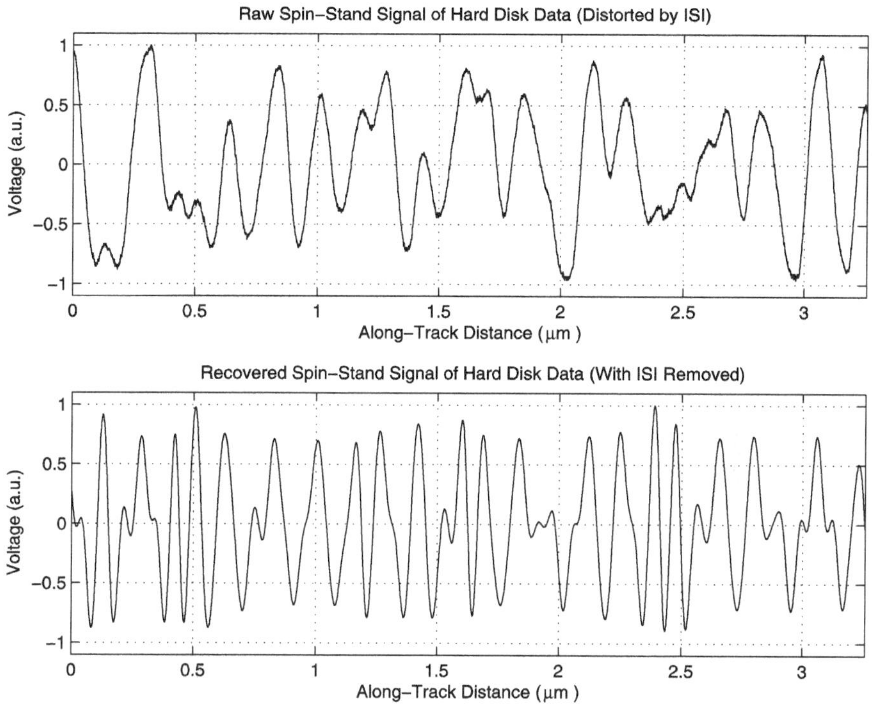

FIGURE 5.10 Raw and recovered hard disk patterns (80 GB/platter disk).

Thus, the underlying magnetization patterns can be recovered by using response function characterization of heads and deconvolution of the ISI-distorted readback signal.

5.4 ANOTHER METHOD FOR OBTAINING THE HEAD RESPONSE FUNCTION

In this section, another method of obtaining the head response function based on spin-stand measurements is discussed. The central idea of this method is based on the fact that the readback signal is a convolution of the head response function and the actual magnetic charge distribution on the media. For this reason, it is apparent that for a single isolated transition the readback signal will emulate the response function when the width of the isolated transition becomes much narrower than the width of the response function itself and the corresponding charge distribution can be modeled by Dirac δ-function. This implies that as the isolated tran-

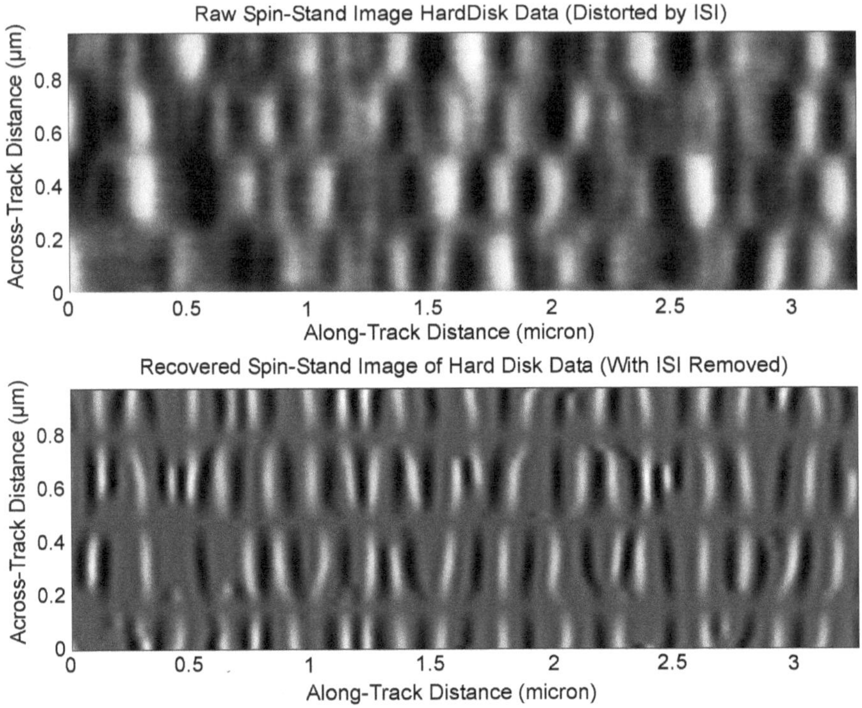

FIGURE 5.11 Raw and recovered hard disk images (80 GB/platter disk).

sition is progressively narrowed, the readback signal should converge to the actual head response function. This has been confirmed by numerical simulations as well as by experimental studies that are presented below.

Figure 5.12 demonstrates the numerically computed readback signals for several progressively narrowed isolated transitions. It is clear from this figure that the readback signals shown by the dashed lines indeed converge to the head response function as shown by the solid line. We have also performed the experiments in which isolated transitions of progressively narrower widths were written on a spin-stand and subsequently read back with the same read head. It was found that there existed a limit at which the readback signal became insensitive to the further narrowing of the width of the written transitions. At this limit, the readback signal corresponding to an isolated transition replicates the head response function. To illustrate the above reasonings, Fig. 5.13 shows the convergence of readback pulse to progressively narrower isolated transitions written on increasingly higher coercivity disks.

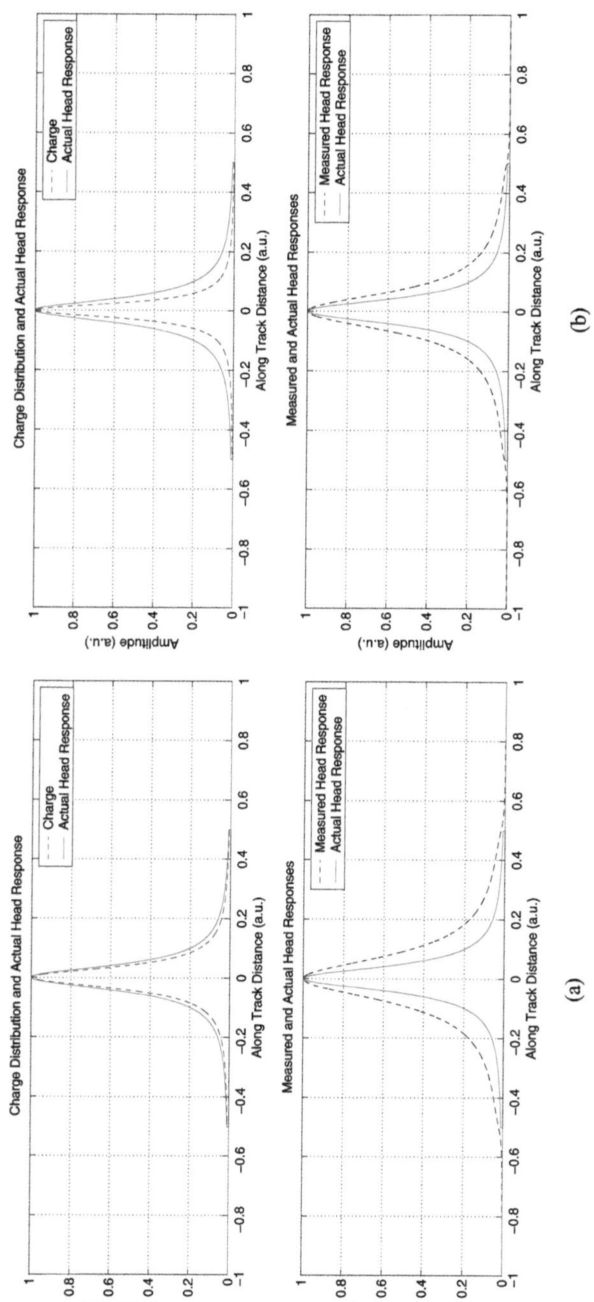

FIGURE 5.12 Convergence of measured head response to the actual head response.

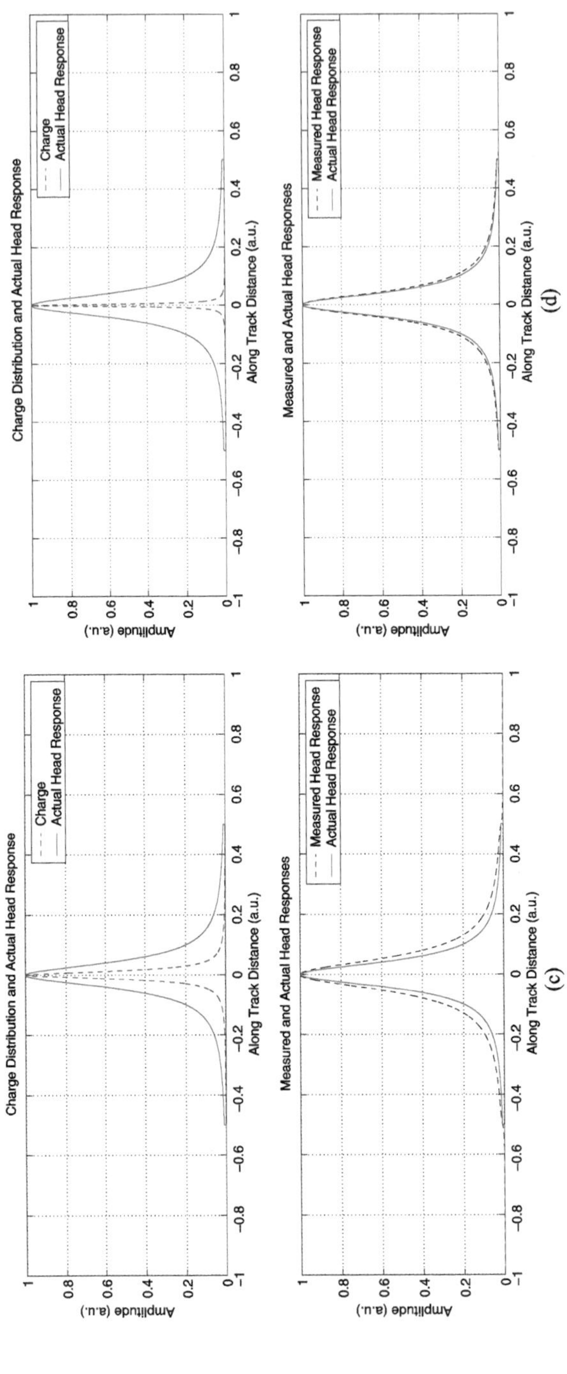

FIGURE 5.12 Continued.

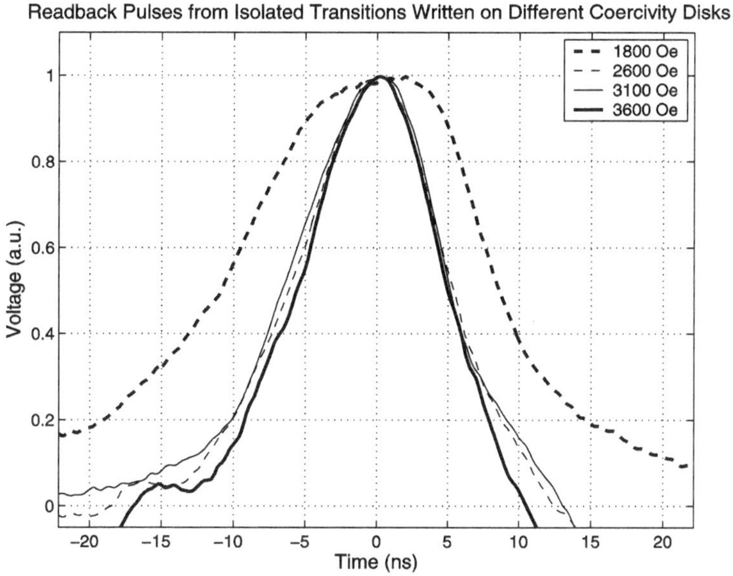

FIGURE 5.13 Extraction of head response function.

5.5 ISI-REMOVAL USING HILBERT TRANSFORM

In this section, another ISI-removal method based on the Hilbert transform is discussed. As described in the literature [4], the two-dimensional longitudinal and transverse (vertical to media) magnetic fields form a Hilbert transform pair. This fact is mathematically expressed by the following formulas:

$$H_x(x) = \frac{1}{\pi}\int_{-\infty}^{\infty} \frac{H_y(x')\,\mathrm{d}x'}{x - x'}, \tag{5.9}$$

$$H_y(x) = \frac{1}{\pi}\int_{-\infty}^{\infty} \frac{H_x(x')\,\mathrm{d}x'}{x - x'}, \tag{5.10}$$

where H_x and H_y are the longitudinal and transverse components of magnetic field on the media surface, respectively. The integrals in (5.9) and (5.10) are singular and they exist in the sense of Cauchy principal value. The Fourier transform representation of 1D Hilbert transform is given by the formulas:

$$\tilde{H}_x(k_x) = -j\frac{k_x}{|k_x|}\tilde{H}_y(k_x),$$

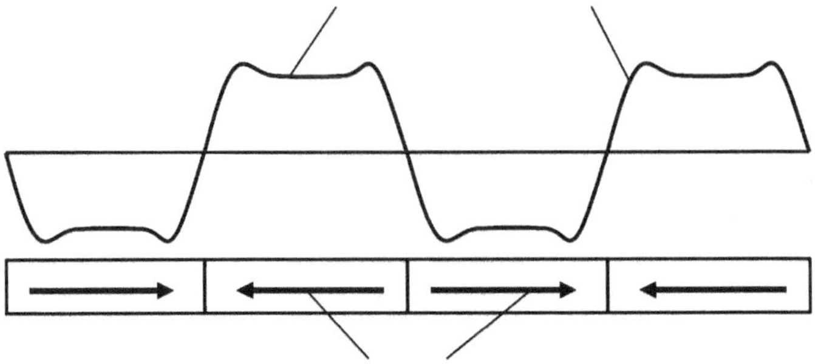

FIGURE 5.14 Longitudinal (demagnetizing) magnetic field H_x.

$$\tilde{H}_y(k_x) = -j\frac{k_x}{|k_x|}\tilde{H}_x(k_x).$$

Readback signals $S(x)$ mimic (with some accuracy) the transverse component H_y of magnetic field:

$$S(x) \sim H_y(x). \tag{5.11}$$

For this reason, the Hilbert transform of readback signals approximate the longitudinal components H_x of magnetic field. As is evident from Fig. 5.14, the longitudinal (demagnetizing) magnetic field H_x closely resembles (up to a sign) the written magnetization patterns:

$$M_x(x) \sim -H_x(x). \tag{5.12}$$

Therefore, up to a sign, the Hilbert transform of the head readback signals emulates the longitudinal remanent magnetization (M_x) in the media which represents the recorded data. Then, the M_x-representation of recorded data can be transformed into a "magnetic charge" representation of the same data (see Appendix on the implementation of ISI-removal algorithm). To demonstrate the effectiveness of this approach, consider the following two examples. The top plot of Fig. 5.15 shows an ISI-distorted readback signal of tribit data (thick line) deliberately written on a spin-stand. On the same figure, the ISI-free signal recovered by using the Hilbert transform is represented by the thin line. This thin line has been arrived at by using the sequence of the following steps. First, the Hilbert transform (5.9) and formula (5.12) were used to compute the longitudi-

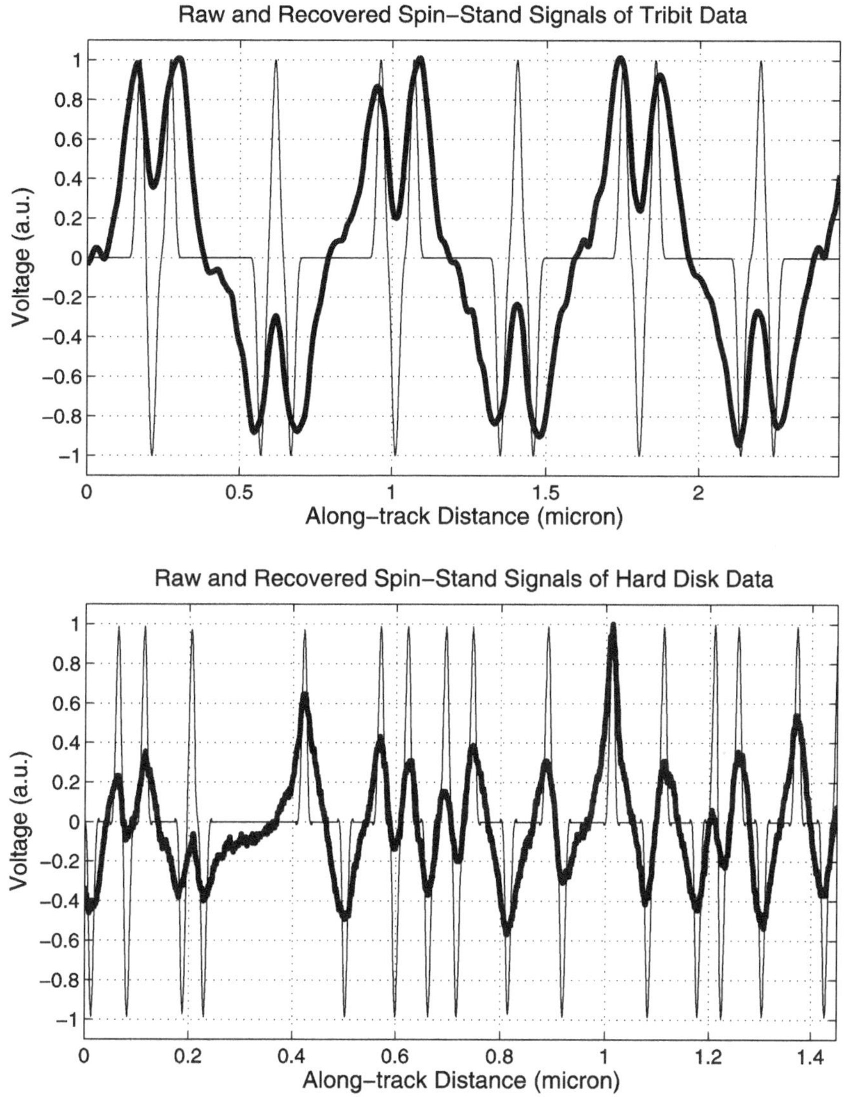

FIGURE 5.15 ISI-corrupted signals and recovered ISI-free signals via Hilbert transform.

nal magnetization M_x (see Fig. 5.16). Then, the "arctangent smoothing" (see Appendix B) was used, which transformed Fig. 5.16 into Fig. 5.17. Finally, the differentiation of the "smoothed" M_x and subsequent low-pass

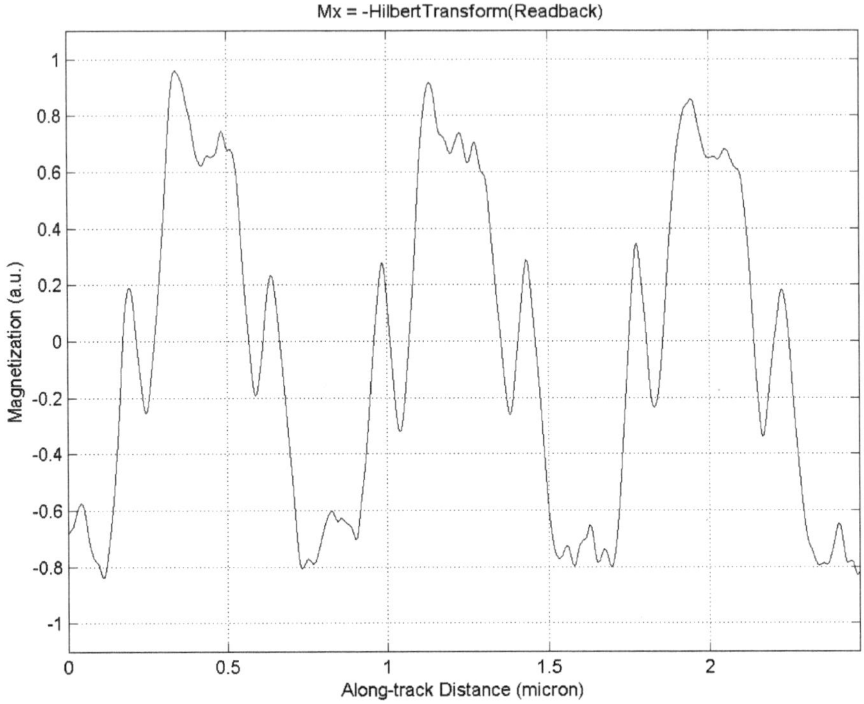

FIGURE 5.16 Hilbert transform of a tribit pattern.

filtering result in the ISI removed signal shown by the thin line on the top portion of Fig. 5.15.

The bottom plot of Fig. 5.15 shows a raw ISI-distorted readback signal of hard disk data from a commercial hard drive (thick line) and the recovered ISI-free signal (thin line) found by using the Hilbert transform. The sequence of ISI removal steps was the same as for the top plot and the results of intermediate steps are illustrated by Figs. 5.18 and 5.19, respectively.

It is remarkable that the Hilbert transform is endowed with ISI-removal capabilities. One possible explanation of this phenomenon can be the fact that the direction of the demagnetizing field H_x is more or less stable with respect to the ISI induced distortions of magnetic transitions, if these distortions are not appreciably pronounced. Indeed, we have found that for strongly pronounced ISI typical for very high density recording, the Hilbert transform approach may fail. In this respect, the ISI removal algorithm based on the head response function has clear advantages.

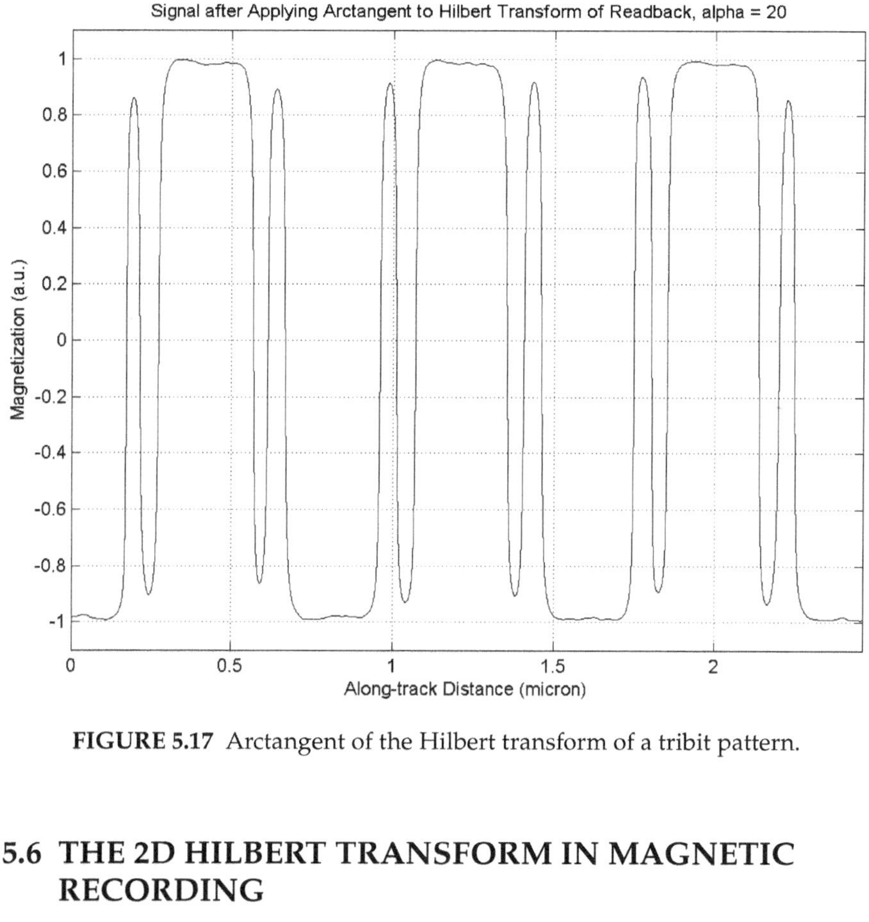

FIGURE 5.17 Arctangent of the Hilbert transform of a tribit pattern.

5.6 THE 2D HILBERT TRANSFORM IN MAGNETIC RECORDING

The importance of the Hilbert transform (5.9)–(5.10) in magnetic recording has been long understood [4–8]. However, the classical one-dimensional Hilbert transform relates the longitudinal and transverse magnetic fields on the magnetic media surface only under the assumption of the two-dimensional nature of the magnetic fields. Due to the dramatic increase in track density in hard disk drives, the 2D approximation of the magnetic fields emanating from the recording media has become exceedingly inaccurate. This prompted our efforts to find a 2D generalization of the Hilbert transform for three-dimensional magnetic fields in magnetic recording. The derivation of such a generalization is presented below. This derivation is conceptually based on the simultaneous use of "magnetic charge" and "electric current" models of the recording media. It is apparent that this 2D generalization of the Hilbert transform is of interest in its own

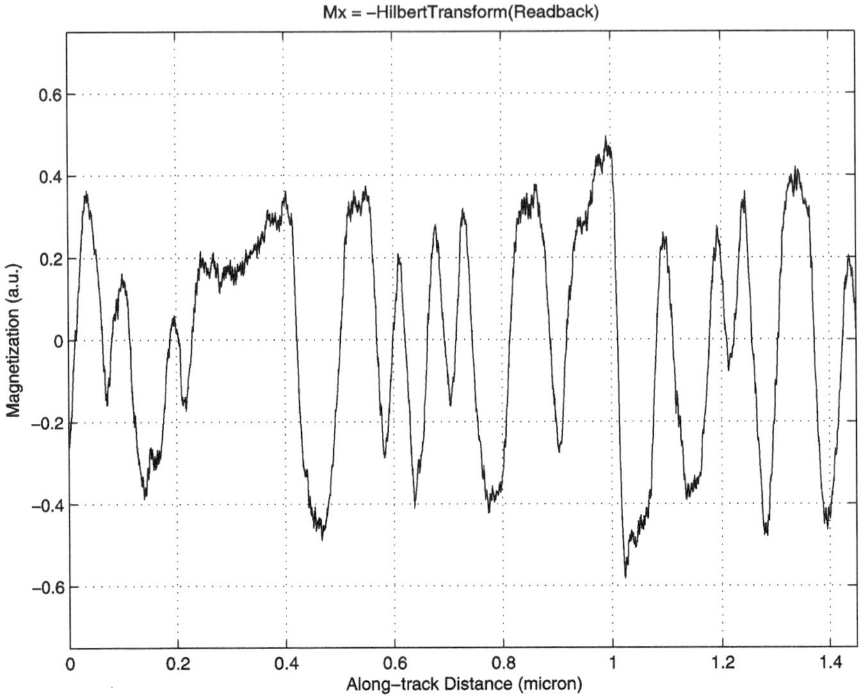

FIGURE 5.18 Hilbert transform of a hard disk signal.

right. It must be mentioned that several attempts have been made in the past in the area of signal processing to generalize the Hilbert transform to higher dimensions [9,10]. These generalizations are mostly mathematical in nature and deal with scalar (analytic) signals defined on multidimensional spaces. In contrast, our approach is physically motivated and closely connects the generalization of the 2D Hilbert transform with three-dimensional magnetic fields emanating from recording media. For this reason, this generalization is vectorial in nature. It also preserves the unique scaling properties of the classical Hilbert transform.

We shall proceed to the derivation of a 2D generalization of the Hilbert transform [2]. This 2D generalization will be understood as the integral transforms that relate the normal (transverse) component H_z of the magnetic field to the tangential (longitudinal) components H_x and H_y of the same field on the flat surface of infinitely thin magnetic media; and vice versa. The conceptual basis for the derivation of the above 2D Hilbert transform is the equivalent representation of the magnetic media by virtual magnetic charges or by virtual electrical currents. According to the

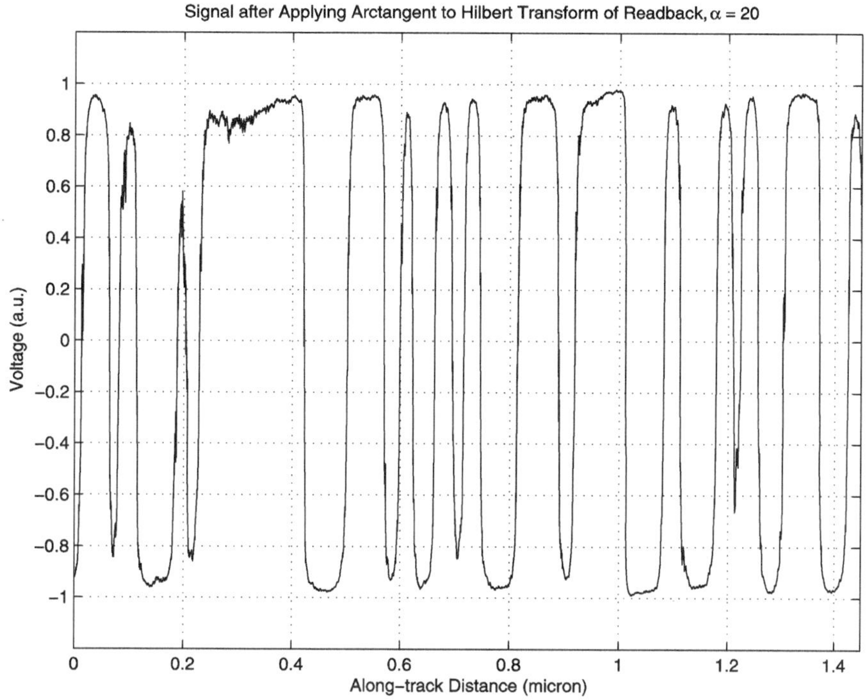

FIGURE 5.19 Arctangent of the Hilbert transform of a hard disk signal.

"magnetic charge representation" (Fig. 5.20), the actual magnetic media is replaced by a surface layer of magnetic charges σ_m that create in homogeneous space the same magnetic field as that created by the actual media. The normal components of the magnetic field created by the surface magnetic charges are related by the formula:

$$H_z^- - H_z^+ = \frac{\sigma_m}{\mu_0}. \tag{5.13}$$

On the other hand, the "plane symmetry" implies that

$$H_z^- = -H_z^+, \tag{5.14}$$

which in combination with (5.13) leads to the following expression:

$$H_z^- = \frac{\sigma_m}{2\mu_0}. \tag{5.15}$$

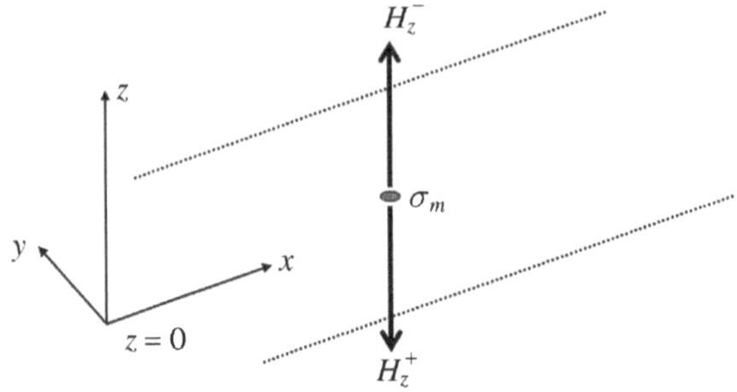

FIGURE 5.20 The "magnetic charge representation" of the magnetic media.

On the other hand, the scalar magnetic potential of the field created by the magnetic charges is given by the formula

$$\phi_m(x, y, z) = \frac{1}{4\pi\mu_0} \int_{-\infty}^{\infty} \int_{-\infty}^{\infty} \frac{\sigma_m(x', y')\, dx'\, dy'}{[(x-x')^2 + (y-y')^2 + z^2]^{1/2}}. \tag{5.16}$$

This potential is related to the magnetic field $\vec{H}$ by the standard expression:

$$\vec{H} = -\nabla\phi_m. \tag{5.17}$$

By substituting formula (5.15) into (5.16) and taking into account formula (5.17), we arrive after simple transformations at the following 2D Hilbert transform:

$$H_x(x, y, 0) = \frac{1}{2\pi} \int_{-\infty}^{\infty} \int_{-\infty}^{\infty} \frac{H_z(x', y') \cdot (x - x')}{[(x-x')^2 + (y-y')^2]^{3/2}}\, dx'\, dy', \tag{5.18}$$

$$H_y(x, y, 0) = \frac{1}{2\pi} \int_{-\infty}^{\infty} \int_{-\infty}^{\infty} \frac{H_z(x', y') \cdot (y - y')}{[(x-x')^2 + (y-y')^2]^{3/2}}\, dx'\, dy'. \tag{5.19}$$

To derive the "inverse" 2D Hilbert transform, the "electric current representation" of the magnetic recording media is used. According to this representation (see Fig. 5.21), the actual magnetic media is replaced by a surface layer of electric currents, which create in the homogeneous upper half-space the same magnetic field as that created by the actual magnetic media.

The tangential components of the magnetic field created by the surface distribution of electric currents are related by the formula:

$$\vec{e}_z \times (\vec{H}^- - \vec{H}^+) = \vec{i}, \tag{5.20}$$

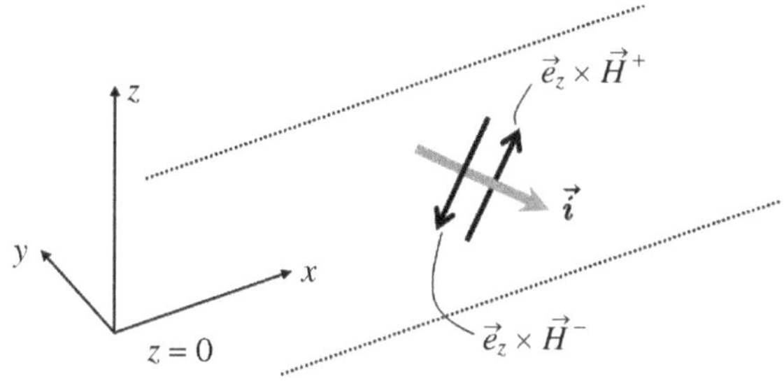

FIGURE 5.21 The "electric current representation" of the magnetic media.

where $\vec{e}_z$ is the unit vector along the z-axis normal to the recording media.

On the other hand, the "plane symmetry" implies that

$$\vec{e}_z \times \vec{H}^- = -\vec{e}_z \times \vec{H}^+, \tag{5.21}$$

which in combination with (5.10) leads to the following expression:

$$\vec{e}_z \times \vec{H}^- = \frac{\vec{i}}{2}. \tag{5.22}$$

By expressing the magnetic field in terms of the electric currents by means of the Biot–Savart law and using straightforward (but somewhat lengthy) transformations, we arrive at the following inverse 2D Hilbert transform:

$$H_z(x, y, 0) = -\frac{1}{2\pi} \int_{-\infty}^{\infty} \int_{-\infty}^{\infty} \frac{H_x(x', y') \cdot (x - x') + H_y(x', y') \cdot (y - y')}{[(x - x')^2 + (y - y')^2]^{3/2}} \, dx' \, dy'. \tag{5.23}$$

The integrals involved in the 2D Hilbert transforms (5.18), (5.19), and (5.23) are singular and they exist in the sense of Cauchy principal value.

It is useful to find a Fourier transform representation of the 2D Hilbert transforms (5.18), (5.19), and (5.23). To this end, consider the following boundary value problem for the scalar magnetic potential $\phi_m(x, y, z)$ in the region above the magnetic medium ($z > 0$):

$$\frac{\partial^2 \phi_m}{\partial x^2} + \frac{\partial^2 \phi_m}{\partial y^2} + \frac{\partial^2 \phi_m}{\partial z^2} = 0, \tag{5.24}$$

$$\frac{\partial \phi_m}{\partial z}(x, y, 0) = -H_z(x, y, 0), \tag{5.25}$$

$$\phi_m(x, y, \infty) = 0. \tag{5.26}$$

By using the Fourier transform

$$\tilde{\phi}_m(k_x, k_y, z) = \frac{1}{2\pi} \int_{-\infty}^{\infty} \int_{-\infty}^{\infty} \phi_m(x, y, z) \mathrm{e}^{j(k_x x + k_y y)} \, \mathrm{d}x \, \mathrm{d}y, \tag{5.27}$$

the boundary value problem (5.24)–(5.26) can be reduced to the form:

$$\frac{\mathrm{d}^2 \tilde{\phi}_m}{\mathrm{d}z^2} = -(k_x^2 + k_y^2)\tilde{\phi}_m = 0, \tag{5.28}$$

$$\left.\frac{\mathrm{d}\tilde{\phi}_m}{\mathrm{d}z}\right|_{z=0} = -\tilde{H}_z, \tag{5.29}$$

$$\tilde{\phi}_m(k_x, k_y, \infty) = 0. \tag{5.30}$$

The solution of the boundary value problem (5.28)–(5.30) is given by the formula:

$$\tilde{\phi}_m(k_x, k_y, z) = \tilde{H}_z \frac{\mathrm{e}^{-\sqrt{k_x^2 + k_y^2} z}}{\sqrt{k_x^2 + k_y^2}}. \tag{5.31}$$

From (5.31), we easily derive:

$$\tilde{H}_x(k_x, k_y, 0) = -\tilde{H}_z \frac{j k_x}{|\vec{k}|}, \tag{5.32}$$

$$\tilde{H}_y(k_x, k_y, 0) = -\tilde{H}_z \frac{j k_y}{|\vec{k}|}, \tag{5.33}$$

which can be combined into one formula:

$$\vec{e}_x \tilde{H}_x + \vec{e}_y \tilde{H}_y = -\frac{j\vec{k}}{|\vec{k}|} \tilde{H}_z. \tag{5.34}$$

By "dot" multiplying both sides of (5.34) by $\vec{k}$, we obtain:

$$\tilde{H}_z = \frac{j(\tilde{H}_x k_x + \tilde{H}_y k_y)}{|\vec{k}|}. \tag{5.35}$$

Formulas (5.34) and (5.35) are Fourier representations of the 2D Hilbert transforms (5.18), (5.19), and (5.23). The similarity between formulas (5.34) and (5.35) and the well-known Fourier representation of the classical Hilbert transform (5.9)–(5.10) (see the previous section) is easily recognizable. Formulas (5.32) and (5.33) and Parseval's relation give the following remarkable equality:

$$\int_{-\infty}^{\infty}\int_{-\infty}^{\infty}\left[H_x^2(x,y)+H_y^2(x,y)\right]\mathrm{d}x\,\mathrm{d}y=\int_{-\infty}^{\infty}\int_{-\infty}^{\infty}H_z^2(x,y)\,\mathrm{d}x\,\mathrm{d}y. \quad (5.36)$$

By using formulas (5.15) and (5.21), this last equality can be transformed into the following relation between virtual surface magnetic charges and surface electric currents:

$$\int_{-\infty}^{\infty}\int_{-\infty}^{\infty}\left|\vec{i}(x,y)\right|^2\mathrm{d}x\,\mathrm{d}y=\frac{1}{\mu_0}\int_{-\infty}^{\infty}\int_{-\infty}^{\infty}\sigma_m^2(x,y)\,\mathrm{d}x\,\mathrm{d}y. \quad (5.37)$$

By using formula (5.35) and the scaling property of the Fourier transform, the following unique scaling property of the Hilbert transform can be deduced. The scaling

$$H_x(x,y)\longrightarrow H_x(\alpha x,\alpha y), \quad (5.38)$$

$$H_y(x,y)\longrightarrow H_y(\alpha x,\alpha y) \quad (5.39)$$

results in the scaling

$$H_z(x,y)\longrightarrow H_z(\alpha x,\alpha y). \quad (5.40)$$

This scaling property implies that readback signals cleared from ISI and corresponding to different recording densities are self-similar, i.e., they are connected through scaling transformations (provided that the media coercivity is sufficiently high and the increase in recording densities does not result in appreciable reduction in magnetization).

Figure 5.22 presents an example of a two-dimensional H_z-image cleaned from ISI by using 2D Hilbert transforms. This image corresponds to the spin-stand readback data from a platter extracted from a commercial hard drive with track density of 60 kilo-track per inch.

It can be remarked that the 2D Hilbert transforms (5.18), (5.19) and (5.23) can be formally extended to n dimensions. In this n-dimensional extension, the Hilbert transform will be understood as an integral trans-

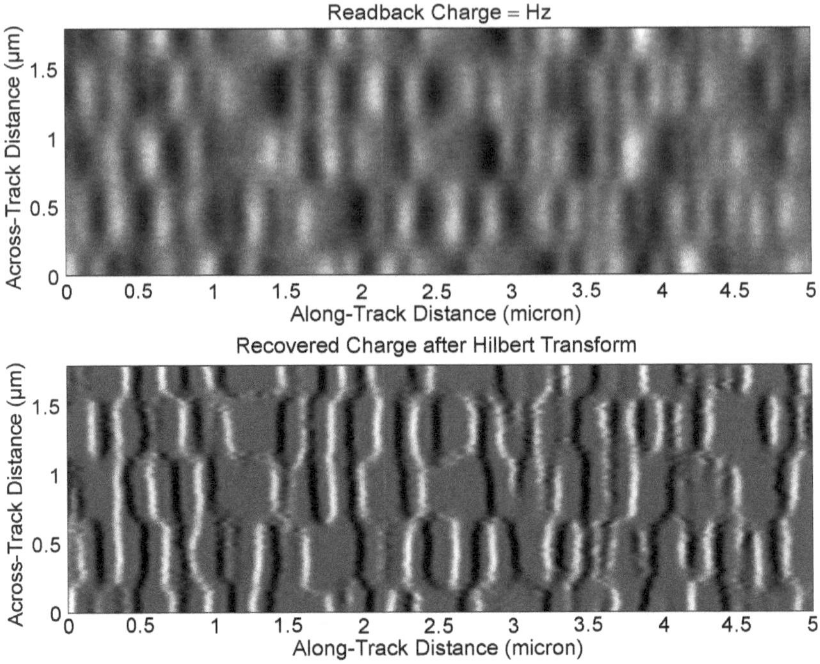

FIGURE 5.22 ISI-removed spin-stand image of hard disk data.

form that relates the normal derivative of a harmonic function to the components of the tangential derivative of the same harmonic function on the flat boundary of an n-dimensional half-plane; and vice versa.

5.7 SUMMARY

Two novel techniques for ISI-removal from spin-stand images have been developed. These techniques are based on the response function characterization of GMR heads and the Hilbert transforms, respectively, and they can recover hard disk data independent of the native write channel. They have applications in the magnetic microscopy and imaging of hard disk data. The 2D generalization of the Hilbert transform is introduced as the integral transform connecting the normal and tangential components of the magnetic field on the flat surface of an infinitely thin magnetic medium. The Fourier transform representation of this 2D Hilbert transform is derived. The unique scaling properties of the 2D Hilbert transform are emphasized.

BIBLIOGRAPHY

[1] I. Mayergoyz, C. Tse, C. Krafft, and P. McAvoy, "A Novel approach to removing intersymbol interference from spin-stand images," *IEEE Trans. Magn.*, **40**, 2197 (2004).

[2] I.D. Mayergoyz, P. McAvoy, C. Tse, C. Krafft, and C. Tseng, "The 2D Hilbert transform in magnetic recording," *IEEE Trans. Magn.* **42**, 2282 (2006).

[3] I.D. Mayergoyz, C. Tse, and C. Krafft, "Method for intersymbol interference removal in data recovery," US Patent 7,002,762 (2006).

[4] H. Bertram, *Theory of Magnetic Recording*, Cambridge University Press, 1994.

[5] J.C. Mallinson, "One-sided fluxes—a magnetic curiosity?," *IEEE Trans. Magn.*, **9**, 678 (1973).

[6] V.B. Minuhin, "Hilbert transform and phase distortions of signals," *Radio Eng. Electron. Phys.*, **18**, 1189 (1973).

[7] V.B. Minuhin, "Phase distortions of signals in magnetic recording equipment," *Telecom. Radio Eng.*, **29/30**, no. 1, 1975.

[8] J.C. Mallinson, "On the properties of two-dimensional dipoles and magnetized bodies," *IEEE Trans. Magn.*, **17**, 2453 (1981).

[9] H. Stark, "An extension of the Hilbert transform product theorem," *Proc. IEEE*, **59**, 1359 (1971).

[10] S. Hahn, "Multidimensional complex signals with single-orthant spectra," *Proc. IEEE*, **80**, 1287 (1992).

Part II

Spin-Stand Microscopy: Applications

CHAPTER 6

High-Speed Ex-Situ Spin-Stand Microscopy of Hard Disk Data

In this chapter, we apply the spin-stand imaging technique to the high-speed massive (entire-track) imaging of hard disk data from commercial hard disk drives. In high-speed massive imaging, hard disks are removed from their native drives and mounted onto a spin-stand. It is shown that, because the hard disks are off-centered with respect to the spin-stand spindle, the tracks are (almost sinusoidally) modulated in the circumferential direction due to eccentricity. Special algorithms for "disk-centering" and "open-loop track-following" are devised. In addition, a "closed-loop track-following" technique has been developed. This technique makes use of preexisting servo marks on the hard disks to generate feedback signals for precise positioning of the magnetic heads over the center of the data tracks. The developed methods have been used to successfully demodulate the imaged tracks. Techniques of triggering, data capturing, and image aligning have also been developed. By using the developed techniques, disk data with track densities as high as 90 000 tracks per inch have been imaged. It is demonstrated that with a specially designed automated algorithm, the developed technique can be fully programmed to image the drive data of the whole disk surface with high resolution and speed.

The results of this chapter have been obtained in cooperation with our Ph.D. student C. Tseng.

6.1 THE NEED FOR HIGH-SPEED DATA MICROSCOPY

It is known that a great number of hard drive failures are hardware in nature. Either the heads have crashed onto the disks or the disks simply do not spin for a variety of reasons. In these situations, forensic studies of data cannot be performed even through the means of special data recovery software. For this reason, there has been a great interest in techniques that can enable the forensic studies of data from hard drives experiencing various hardware failures.

One approach to these forensic studies is through entire-track magnetic imaging of hard disk data on a spin-stand (which is covered in this chapter) and the subsequent decoding of the imaged data (which is discussed in the next chapter). Existing microscopy techniques are too slow to cope with the vast amount of data in modern hard drives. As an illustration, let us assume that we want to image an entire 160 gigabyte hard drive. Let us further assume that it only takes one second to image the data in a sector (this imaging rate is by far higher than any existing microscopy technique except for spin-stand imaging). Since each sector contains 512 bytes, a 160 GB drive contains 335 544 320 sectors (160 gigabytes $\times 2^{30}$ bytes/gigabytes $\div$ 512 bytes/sector). This translates into an imaging time of more than ten years! The need of high-speed massive data imaging becomes fairly obvious.

It is also desirable in many applications that entire tracks, not merely sectors, of the hard disk be imaged. These whole-track images are instrumental for diagnostics of hard disk data and for characterizing the uniformity and integrity of track and servo writing. Whole-track imaging is also important in the evaluation of commercial hard drives when the hard disk platters must be removed from their native drives and mounted on a new (foreign) spindle. It is evident that in these situations the hard disk tracks will be off-centered. The purpose of this chapter is to detail the techniques of whole-track spin-stand microscopy of hard disk data from off-centered disks.

To perform high-speed magnetic microscopy of hard disk data removed from its native drive and mounted on a spin-stand, the following issues have to be addressed. First, the problem of eccentricity of hard disks needs to be dealt with. Second, a special method of triggering must be employed because it is not possible in this case to write trigger marks on the disk. Writing such trigger marks would overwrite the recorded patterns to be imaged. Third, even when a reasonably stable trigger is available, a mechanical or numerical aligning scheme must be devised in order to compensate for the imperfection of the trigger. In addition, all the above procedures must be performed in an automatic and efficient way so that the task of massive data microscopy of hard disk data can be performed at high speed. We will address these challenges in the following sections.

6.2 ECCENTRICITY PROBLEM

The spin-stand microscopy involves the removing of a hard disk from its native drive and mounting it on a spin-stand. Due to the mechanical clearance tolerance between the spindle of the spin-stand and the inner rim of the hard disk platter, the disk once mounted on the spin-stand will not be centered with respect to the rotational center of the spindle. In order to facilitate subsequent discussion, it would be expedient at this point to introduce some "centering" terminology. The *geometrical center* (*GC*) is the physical center of the hard disk platter being imaged. The *read center* (*RC*) is defined to be the center of any circular path traced by the read head on the spin-stand (*RC* is the same as the rotational center of the spin-stand spindle). The *write center* (*WC*) is defined as the center of the concentric tracks that have been written on the hard disk in its native drive. Since the *GC* might not coincide with the rotational center of the spindle of the native drive, the *WC* is usually different from the *GC* and should be distinguished as such. The essence of disk centering is the positioning of the disk platter in such a way that RC and WC coincide.

The placement of an off-centered disk on a spin-stand is depicted in Fig. 6.1, where the spindle center is chosen to be the origin of the Cartesian coordinate system. In this figure, δ is the distance between the *RC* and the *WC*; R is the radius of the circular trajectory of the read head; r_1 is the radius of the first track being crossed; r_i is the radius of the ith track being crossed; and r_n is the radius of the nth track being crossed (i.e. the last crossed track). It should be noted that any track with radius smaller than r_1 or larger than r_n will not be crossed. It is easy to observe that the total number, n, of tracks being crossed is equal to the product of L and the *track density (TD)*, where L is $r_n - r_1$. Furthermore, the expression for L can be obtained by solving the following two simultaneous equations obtained through simple geometrical observations:

$$R = \delta + r_1, \tag{6.1}$$

$$r_n = \delta + R, \tag{6.2}$$

from which we find:

$$L = r_n - r_1 = 2\delta. \tag{6.3}$$

Therefore, except in the direct proximity to the innermost and the outermost track, the total number of tracks being crossed is independent of the radius of the read head trajectory and is a function of only two variables,

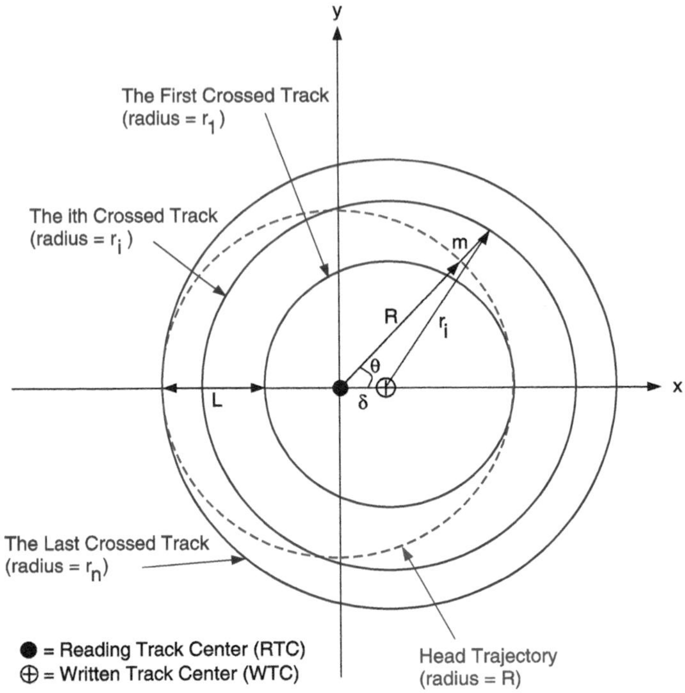

FIGURE 6.1 The geometry of an off-centered disk.

δ and the track density TD. Specifically,

$$n = L \cdot TD = 2\delta \cdot TD. \tag{6.4}$$

Due to the continuous variation of the head skew angle across the disk platter, the value of TD is not constant. For this reason, the value of TD in (6.4) is meant to be the *local* track density between the radii r_1 and r_n, which are usually sufficiently close to one another.

In order to image an entire track of the hard disk data, for instance the track with radius r_i, it is first necessary to determine the trajectory of this track in the presence of eccentricity. Assuming that the tracks are *perfectly* circular and, taking into account that $\delta \ll r_i$, the equation for radial difference $m(\theta)$ between the ith track and the head trajectory in RC frame of references can be derived. Indeed, from Fig. 6.1 we observe:

$$(R+m)^2 = \delta^2 + r_i^2 + 2r_i\delta\cos\phi, \tag{6.5}$$

where ϕ is the angle opposite to the $(R+m)$-side. Taking into account the smallness of δ, we find that $\phi \approx \theta$ and the last equation can be written as follows:

$$R + m \approx \sqrt{r_i^2 + 2r_i\delta\cos\theta + (\delta\cos\theta)^2}. \tag{6.6}$$

Thus, from formula (6.6), we obtain:

$$R + m \approx r_i + \delta\cos\theta, \tag{6.7}$$

which leads to:

$$m(\theta) \approx r_i - R + \delta\cos\theta. \tag{6.8}$$

It is apparent that $\delta\cos\theta$ can be construed as the modulation of m. In other words, the imaged track when observed in the *RC* frame of reference is modulated in the circumferential direction as a sinusoidal function with an amplitude of δ and an angular frequency defined by the rotational speed of the spindle. In the sections below, three approaches to dealing with off-centered modulated tracks are discussed. These approaches are:

- Mechanical track-centering,
- Dynamic track-following,
- Servo feedback control based track-following.

Mechanical track-centering is used to compensate the eccentricity when it is more than 3 µm, while dynamic track-following is used to compensate the eccentricity below 3 µm. The purpose of servo feedback control based track-following is to compensate for any residual eccentricity and to deal with repeatable runout (RRO) and non-repeatable runout (NRRO) smaller than the width of the servo patterns. The RRO is mainly due to disk eccentricity and the fact that the data tracks are not perfectly circular. The NRRO is caused by thermal drift and the vibration from the spindle motor bearing.

6.2.1 Mechanical track-centering

The goal of mechanical track-centering [1] is to micro-position the disk in such a way that its *WC* coincides with the *RC* of the spin-stand (or equivalently the spindle center). This is different from "disk-centering" where the goal is to match the *GC* with the *RC*. The disk positioning is accomplished by using a dial-gauge as a calibrating device to find where to move the disk platter mounted on the spin-stand. This movement of the disk can be controlled within 3 µm. The feedback of the effects of these disk position adjustments during mechanical centering is provided by

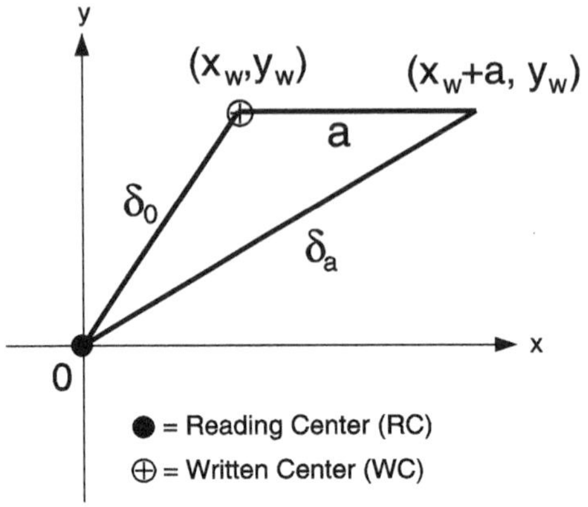

FIGURE 6.2 The geometry for centering an off-centered disk.

the oscilloscope whose time-base is set large enough to include the data of the entire track.

The central issue of the disk centering is to determine the direction in which the disk must be moved in order to close the gap between the *WC* and the *RC*. Clearly, a reliable algorithm rather than a "trial and error" method is needed in order to center the disk platter in a fast and accurate manner. We have devised such an effective disk centering algorithm, which is presented below. This algorithm is based on the appropriate movements of the disk in two orthogonal directions. Figure 6.2 depicts an off-centered disk with its *WC* at an initial distance δ_0 from the *RC* of the spindle, which is chosen as the origin of the x–y coordinate system. By using Eq. (6.4) and Fig. 6.2, δ_0 can be expressed as follows:

$$\delta_0 = \frac{n_0}{2 \cdot TD} = \sqrt{x_w^2 + y_w^2}, \tag{6.9}$$

where n_0 is the number of tracks being crossed in the case of an initial eccentricity of δ_0. It is evident that any eccentricity can be reduced to zero if the position of *WC*, (x_w, y_w), is known with respect to the coordinates of *RC*. To find x_w and y_w, the disk is displaced in the positive x-direction by a distance a, with the new position of *WC* being at $(x_w + a, y_w)$. By using Eq. (6.4) and Fig. 6.2, the following equation can be established:

$$\delta_a = \frac{n_a}{2 \cdot TD} = \sqrt{(x_w + a)^2 + y_w^2}, \tag{6.10}$$

where n_a is the number of tracks being crossed for the new eccentricity of δ_a.

Solving Eqs. (6.9) and (6.10) for (x_w, y_w), one obtains:

$$x_w = \frac{\delta_a^2 - \delta_0^2 - a^2}{2a}, \qquad y_w = \pm\frac{\sqrt{4a^2\delta_0^2 - (\delta_a^2 - \delta_0^2 - a^2)^2}}{2a}. \tag{6.11}$$

Since TD, n_0 and n_a can be determined from the oscilloscope, the values of δ_0 and δ_a in Eq. (6.11) can be deduced from (6.9) and (6.10), respectively. It is apparent that in the geometrical configuration shown in Fig. 6.2 (i.e. when y_w is positive), the track eccentricity can be reduced to zero if the disk is first moved in the negative x-direction by $x_w + a$ and then moved in the negative y-direction by y_w. However, if an appreciable eccentricity still remains (i.e. when y_w was actually negative), then the disk should be moved in the positive y-direction by $2y_w$. In this way, the disk platter can be centered.

Experimental results

In our experiments, track imaging is performed during the mechanical centering by scanning the hard disk in the along- and cross-track directions. While scanning is in process, a digital sampling oscilloscope is used to capture and display the raw images in the form of GMR head readback signals. These signals can be accessed at the output of the read head preamplifier on the spin-stand. The sampled waveforms can then be transferred to a computer through a network connection. Finally, these raw images are stored in a computer for further signal processing. In our experiments, GMR heads with read widths of 0.24 μm, 0.19 μm, and 0.13 μm were employed as the sensing elements. In the example presented below, the particular hard disk being scanned was from a commercial drive with an average track pitch of 1.22 μm.

The imaging of the entire track data was readily accomplished by triggering on the drive index of the spin-stand spindle. This drive index pulse was generated for each complete revolution of the spindle. As such, it can be used as an external trigger to the oscilloscope for whole-track data triggering. Due to the slight variations of the rotational speed of the spindle, trigger-induced shifts were exhibited in the captured data corresponding to different radial positions of the read head. These shifts can be compensated by a numerical aligning technique to be described later in the chapter. The essence of this technique is the shifting of circumferentially acquired data to achieve maximization of the inner (dot) products between the vectors representing circumferentially acquired data for adjacent radial positions.

Figure 6.3 is a spin-stand image showing the track hard disk data (from 25 mm to 275 mm in the along-track direction) for the off-centered

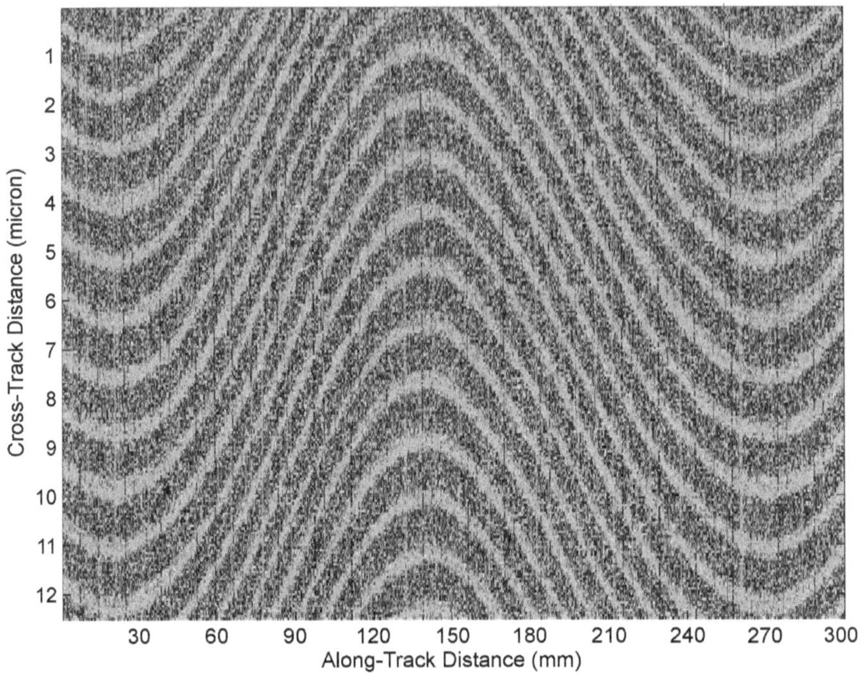

FIGURE 6.3 Spin-stand image of track hard disk data before track demodulation.

disk. For the purpose of clarity of image displaying, the image has been down-sampled in the along-track direction. As is evident, the bands of the track data are sinusoidally modulated in the circumferential direction due to track eccentricity. The δ, defined as one half of the peak-to-peak amplitude (in distance) of the modulated track, is calculated from the figure to be about 4.5 µm (the reader can verify the validity of Eq. (6.4) from the value of δ and the local averaged track density). When no efforts are made to center the disk, the value of δ could be quite high (tens of microns or more).

Figure 6.4 shows the spin-stand image of the track hard disk data of the same disk after it has been properly centered. It is apparent from the figure that the tracks still contain some residual modulation because the written tracks were not *perfectly* circular in the first place. This small degree of residual modulation, however, does not impede the utility of the track imaging technique for the analysis of track and servo writing. Different data regions along the tracks, such as the preamble fields, the servo fields, and the track-id fields can be readily extracted from these track im-

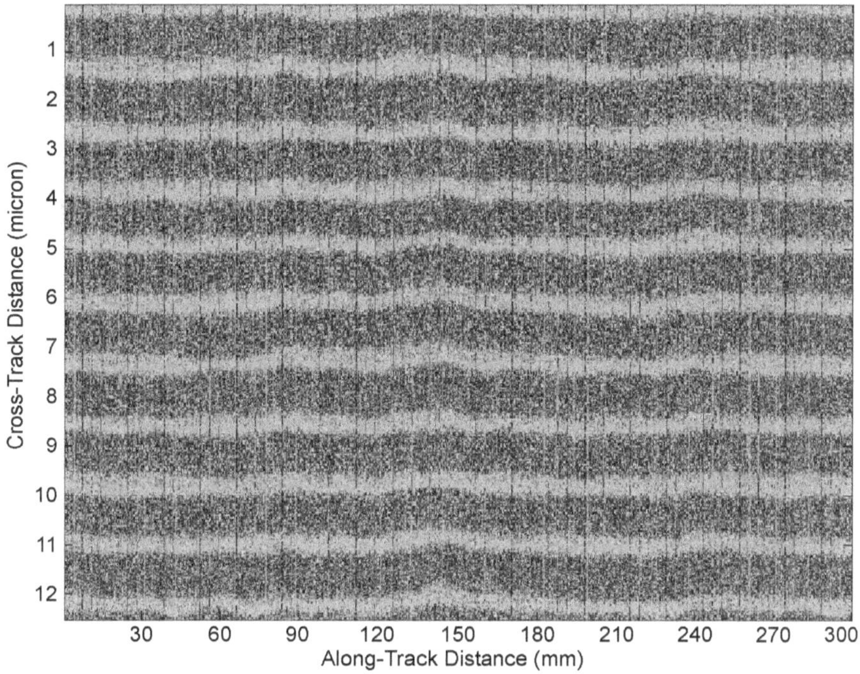

FIGURE 6.4 Spin-stand image of track hard disk data after track demodulation.

ages for evaluation and analysis. Any defects along the tracks and across the disk surface can also be quickly spotted by using this technique. The technique itself can be programmed to expedite a surface scan.

Figure 6.5 shows the image of the system area of the same hard disk obtained by using the described technique. The firmware information (such as channel and controller parameters) is stored in this system area. The figure also shows 16 *maintenance tracks* (top) and 4 *data tracks* (bottom) with the first of these tracks containing the Master Boot Record and the partition information on the drive.

The same mechanical track centering technique was used for a hard disk with an average track pitch of 0.43 μm. Figures 6.6 and 6.7 show the spin-stand track images before and after track centering, respectively. In Fig. 6.6, one of the data tracks was highlighted and the peak-to-peak amplitude of the modulated track was calculated to be about 32 μm. There were 77 tracks crossed in one revolution. Even after proper mechanical track centering, the amount of residual modulation was still quite large and comparable to the track pitch, as it is clear from Fig. 6.7. It is apparent

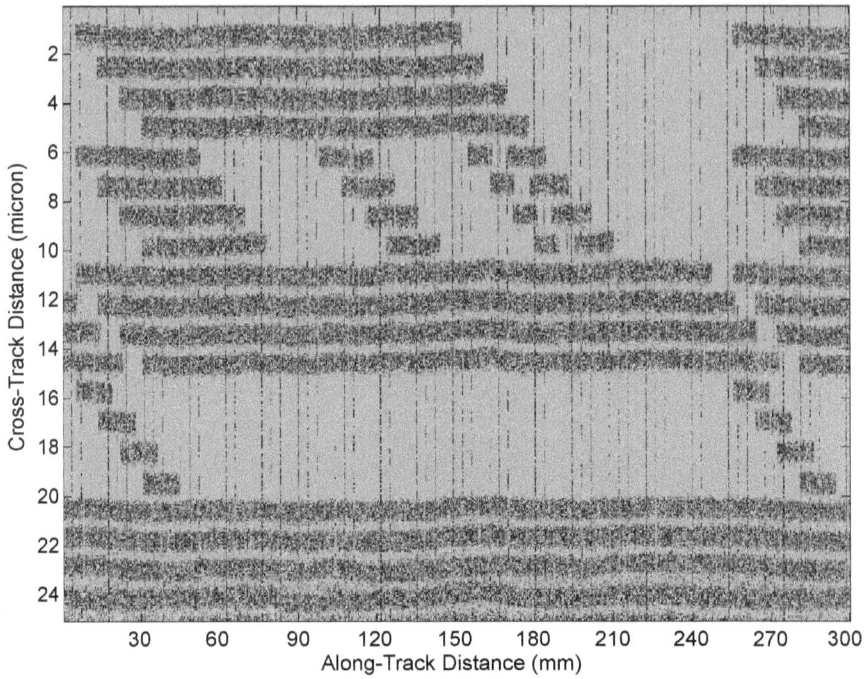

FIGURE 6.5 Spin-stand image of hard disk track data in the system area.

that the read head was not at track centers during a complete revolution. This example highlights the need for the techniques of dynamic track following and servo feedback control track following, which are discussed in the next two sections.

6.2.2 Dynamic track-following

This technique [2] is extremely useful in retrieving the on-track hard disk data in real time for data forensics applications. It is needed because the written magnetic tracks on hard disk drives are not *perfectly* circular due to repeatable and nonrepeatable runouts (RRO/NRRO) caused by small imperfections of spindles, bearings, disks, actuators, and windage (turbulent wind flow generated by the rotating disks). Several approaches have been reported in the literature to improve the accuracy and capability of existing servo and track-following systems to follow hard disk tracks (see, for instance, [3,4]). The emphasis there has been on compensating for *small* geometrical deviations from the track center caused by RRO/NRRO and thermal drift. The main emphasis in our research has

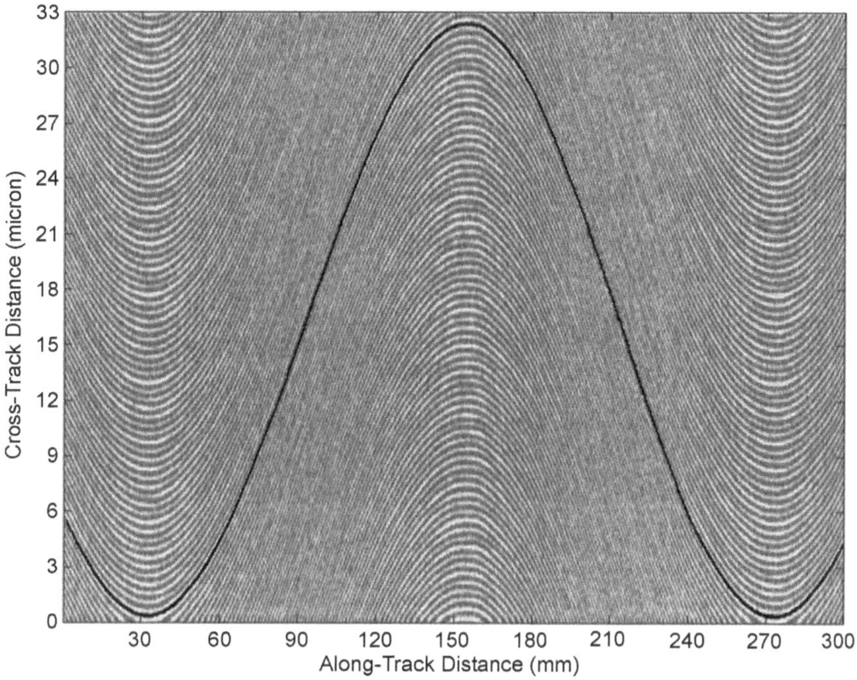

FIGURE 6.6 Spin-stand image of hard disk track data before track centering.

been on track-following that can compensate for relatively *large* deviations of the magnetic head from the track center in order to follow *inherently off-centered* hard disk tracks caused by eccentricity residual after mechanical centering.

Track-following is accomplished by using piezo-actuators to move the magnetic head mounted on the spin-stand to follow the curve of the modulated track in the radial direction. According to Eq. (6.8), the curve describing the modulated track can be rewritten as follows:

$$m(t) = r_i - R + \delta \cos(\omega t + \psi_0), \tag{6.12}$$

where ω is the angular frequency defined by the spindle rotation and ψ_0 is the initial phase of the modulated track. In order to accomplish the dynamic following of off-centered hard disk tracks, the trajectories that the read head traverses must coincide with the trajectories of the written tracks on the disk. To achieve this, a small piezoelectric transducer (PZT) has been attached to the head cartridge of the spin-stand as a micropositioning device. In using a PZT for dynamic track-following, three issues

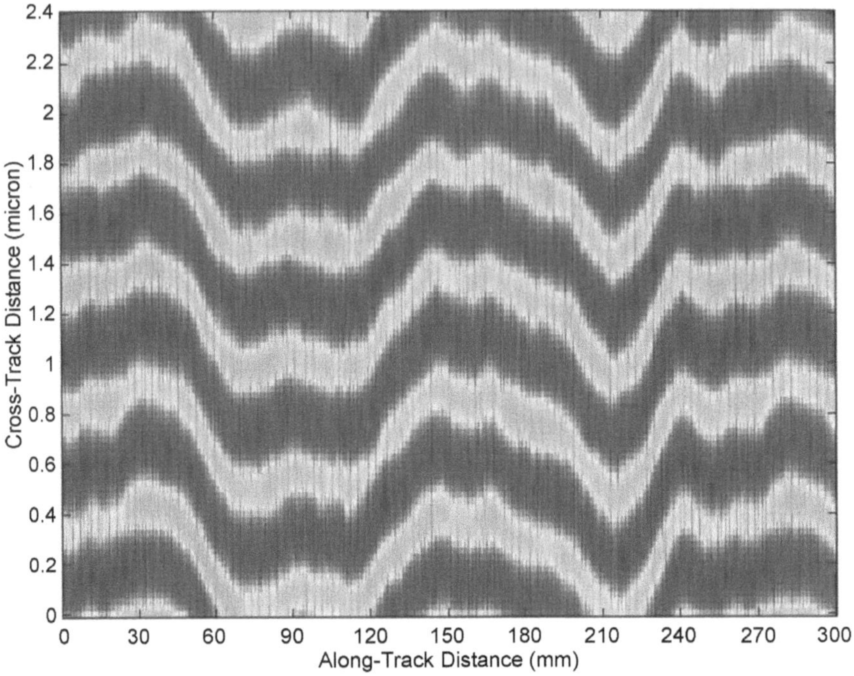

FIGURE 6.7 Spin-stand image of hard disk track data after track centering.

need to be addressed. First, the trajectories of the written tracks need to be extracted. Second, since input voltage vs displacement characteristics of PZT exhibit hysteresis, the required input signal to the PZT should be different from the otherwise applied signal had there been no hysteretic effects. Therefore, an algorithm has to be developed to generate modified input signals to the PZT that account for hysteresis. Third, the input signal to the PZT is required to be injected at the appropriate initial phase and the phase needs to be locked thereafter.

The setup for the dynamic track-following system is based on a Guzik spin-stand that is used to obtain images of actual off-centered hard disk tracks in the manner described above. The track-following system consists of a digital oscilloscope for signal capturing, a personal computer (PC) for performing extraction of track trajectories and for implementing the algorithm of hysteresis compensation, a waveform generator for generating the desired input signal to the PZT, and a signal amplifier for amplifying the PZT input signal. The spin-stand head cartridge that houses the GMR head has been modified to make it compatible with a PZT as the micropo-

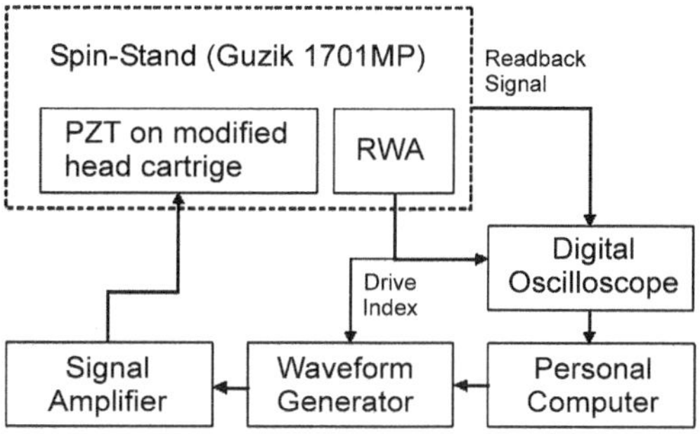

FIGURE 6.8 Block diagram of the track-following set-up.

sitioning device. Figure 6.8 shows the block diagram of the experimental setup.

The algorithm for extraction of actual off-centered track trajectories is illustrated by Fig. 6.9. The first step is to obtain the raw image of hard disk tracks through spin-stand microscopy (Fig. 6.9(a)). As expected, the magnetic tracks of off-centered hard disks are modulated in the circumferential direction due to eccentricity. The along-track distance between two consecutive troughs corresponds to one period of revolution of the spin-stand spindle. It is evident that the read head senses stronger signal at the center of the data tracks than at off-track regions. To ensure that the signal amplitude of the on-track data is made significantly much stronger than that of the off-track region, the track image is enhanced by a 2D averaging filter with constant averaging kernel. The enhanced track image is shown in Fig. 6.9(b). The off-centered trajectory of the tracks can then be extracted by locating the points with maximum signal value within the track region in the radial direction, as shown in Fig. 6.9(c). However, there can still be some noise in the extracted raw trajectories due to high-frequency user data and the existence of preamble patterns (whose signal amplitudes remain the same both in the on-track and off-track regions). While these preamble patterns are of lower and fixed frequency compared to the user data, their frequency is much higher than that of the extracted whole-track trajectory, as one period of the track trajectory contains hundreds of periods of preamble patterns. Therefore, a 1D low-pass filter is employed to extract the track trajectory and to filter out any high-frequency noise caused by the user data and the preamble patterns. In Fig. 6.9(d), the acquired extracted trajectory is shown and over-plotted on the raw image of hard disk tracks. This trajectory must be used for PZT control.

The two prevalent ways for controlling the PZT are the voltage control method and the current control method. The voltage control method is

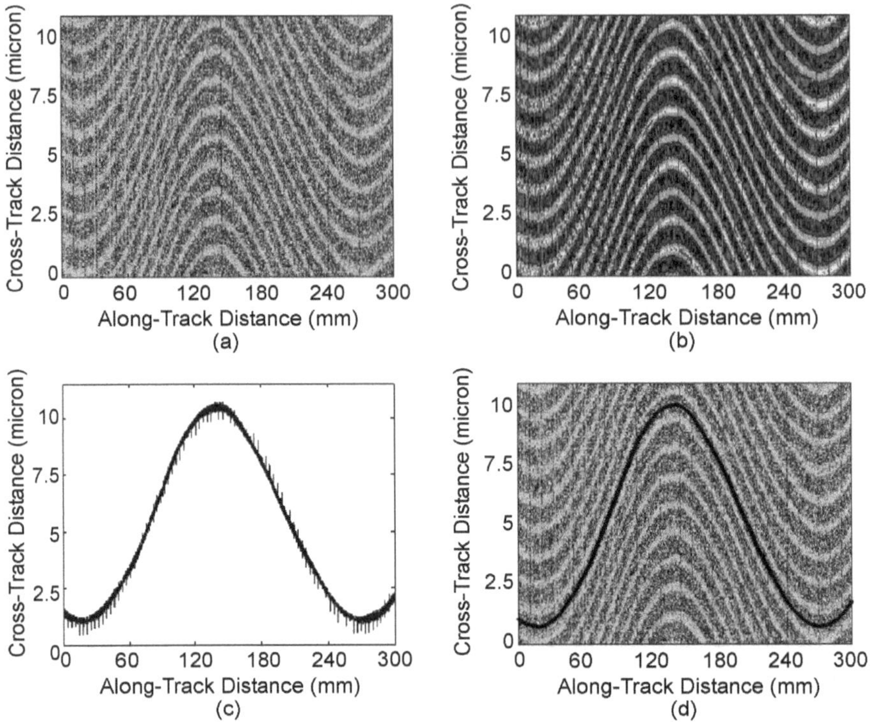

FIGURE 6.9 Extraction of track trajectory.

stable and has high degree and ease of controllability. However, the hysteresis effects between the applied voltage and the PZT's displacement are quite pronounced. On the other hand, the current control method can achieve an almost linear relation between the current through the PZT and the corresponding displacement. Nevertheless, there is still some residual hysteresis which may not be totally negligible. In addition, the amplitude of the current applied to the PZT is only a few mA and such small current requires additional and more elaborate equipment for control realization. For this reason, the voltage control method is preferable and has been used in our research.

Figure 6.10(a) presents a typical hysteresis loop between the displacement of the PZT and the input voltage. This loop was obtained experimentally through the characterization of the PZT. The PZT hysteresis can be represented by the Preisach model [5], which can be written as follows:

$$v(t) = \iint \mu(\alpha, \beta)\hat{\gamma}_{\alpha\beta}u(t)\,\mathrm{d}\alpha\,\mathrm{d}\beta, \tag{6.13}$$

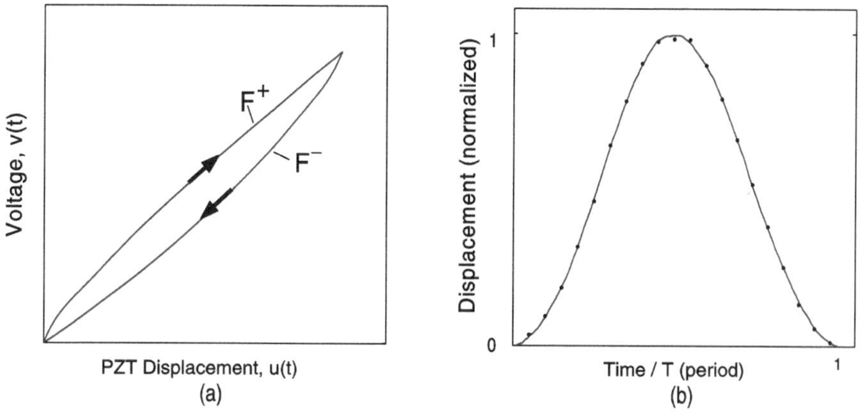

FIGURE 6.10 (a) Hysteresis loop. (b) Curves of PZT input signal and extracted trajectory.

where $v(t)$ is the voltage applied to the PZT, $\mu(\alpha, \beta)$ is the weight function that can be fully characterized by using "first-order reversal curves," $\hat{\gamma}_{\alpha\beta}$ are rectangular loop operators with α and β as "up" and "down" switching thresholds, respectively, and $u(t)$ is the input (desired) displacement. However, in the particular case when a track trajectory consists of two monotonic sections, the equation for controlling voltage signal can be simplified and represented in the form:

$$v(t) = F^{\pm}\big(u(t)\big), \tag{6.14}$$

where $v(t) = F^{+}(u(t))$ when the PZT displacement corresponds to the ascending branch and $v(t) = F^{-}(u(t))$ when the PZT displacement follows the descending branch of PZT hysteresis loop (Fig. 6.10(a)). The Preisach approach is especially instrumental for highly irregular tracks where the PZT must trace numerous minor hysteresis loops in order to follow these tracks.

The accuracy of voltage control of the PZT and its immunity to hysteresis effects has been tested. The results of this testing is demonstrated by Fig. 6.10(b), where the actual extracted trajectory (solid line) is overplotted with the trajectory of the properly controlled PZT-driven head (dots).

Before the signal from the output of the waveform generator is sent to the amplifier, a phase-locking system is activated to locate the initial phase of the input signal to the PZT and lock the phase thereafter. As shown in Fig. 6.8, both the waveform generator and the digital oscilloscope are triggered by the same drive index of the spin-stand spindle, which is generated for each complete spindle revolution. From the captured track image, the initial phase is determined as the time offset between the first data point of the image and the data point corresponding to the first trough. Although the phase is already locked by the triggering, this phase is adjustable by the waveform generator. By using the phase-locking system, the driving signal for the PZT and the off-centered trajectory are kept in phase. This driving signal is then amplified and sent to the PZT, which is attached to the modified head cartridge of the spin-stand. Our experiments showed that the motion of the head assembly followed the motion of the PZT practically without any delay.

Experimental results

In our experiments, the imaged hard disk drives had track density of 60 and 90 ktpi and capacity of 40 GB per platter and 80 GB per platter, respectively. GMR heads with read widths of 0.15 μm have been used. To demonstrate the robustness of the dynamic track following technique, the hard disks were preliminarily mechanically centered with different residual eccentricities. Depending on the residual eccentricity remained after mechanical centering, a PZT with the appropriate dimensions whose displacement range covers the range of track eccentricity was chosen. Then, dynamic track-following was performed on hard disks spinning at 7200 RPM.

The top and bottom plots of Fig. 6.11 show the images of a hard disk (with capacity of 40 GB per platter and track density of 60 ktpi) without and with track-following, respectively. It can be seen that five hard disk tracks were being crossed before track-following due to eccentricity, while after track-following the read head was able to stay on the tracks.

Figure 6.12 shows the track image of a hard disk (with capacity of 80 GB per platter and track density of 90 ktpi) without and with track-following. The top plot of Fig. 6.12 shows a spin-stand image of a few data tracks (with track widths of about 0.2 μm). As illustrated in the image, the read head crossed six tracks due to eccentricity. The cross-track distance between the trough and the peak of the trajectory is about 1.5 μm. The width of the data tracks is about 75% of the track pitch with the remaining 25% accounting for the guard bands. The bottom plot of Fig. 6.12 shows the image of the same region after the tracks have been dynamically followed by using the described dynamic track-following technique. The read head is now able to dynamically follow any particular track in its entirety without crossing any adjacent tracks. The amplitude of residual variations is found from the figure to be about 50 nm.

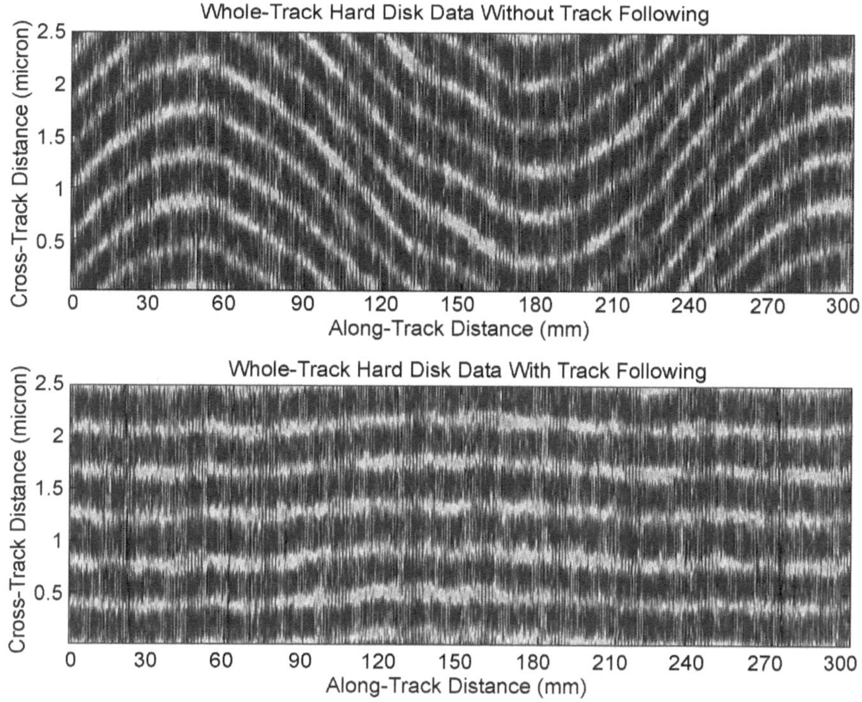

FIGURE 6.11 Spin-stand image of track hard disk data (40 GB per platter) without and with track-following.

The top plot of Fig. 6.13 is a spin-stand image of the same disk after it has been centered to the extent where the read head crossed only two tracks per revolution. Note that in this case the tracks are irregularly modulated rather than monotonically ascending and descending. This phenomenon becomes evident only if the eccentricity is below 0.5 μm. This suggests that the written tracks are not *ideally* circular in the first place. In this case, even if the tracks are perfectly centered, the head is still not able to follow the specific track without crossing adjacent tracks. As shown in the bottom plot of Fig. 6.13, the eccentricity as well as the track irregularity is substantially reduced after employing the described track-following technique. The residual irregularity visible on the bottom plot of Fig. 6.13 can be attributed to some dynamic effects related to head cartridge inertia.

In order to further reduce the amplitude of the residual variations to about one tenth of the write track width and to obtain on-track data for irregular track, a more sophisticated track-following technique is needed.

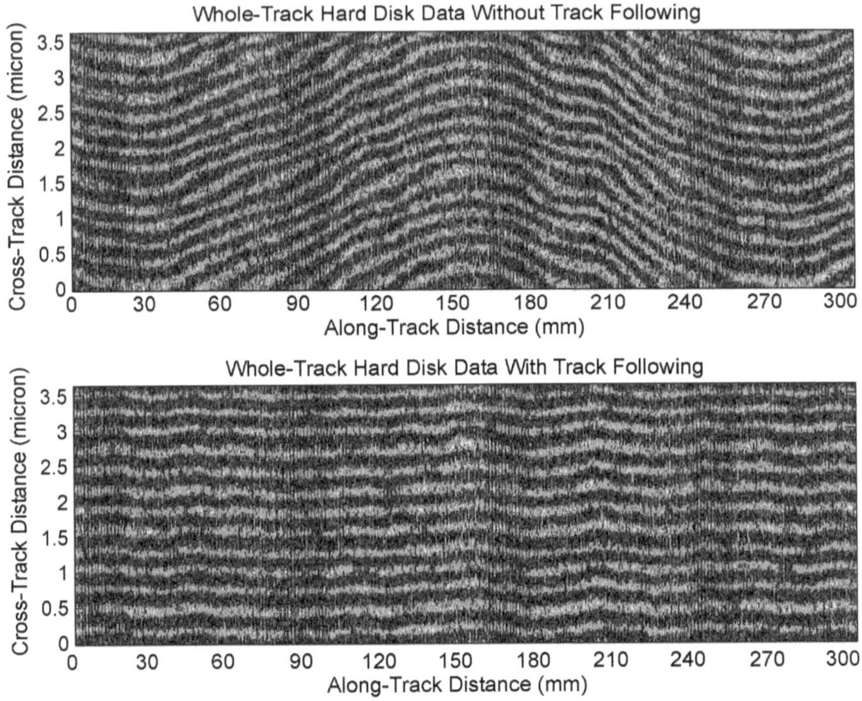

FIGURE 6.12 Spin-stand image of track hard disk data (80 GB per platter) without and with track-following.

Specifically, the described open-loop technique of track-following of *off-centered* hard disk tracks must be complemented by a (close loop) track-following technique that makes use of the existing servo patterns for a feedback signal generation This technique is discussed in the next section.

6.2.3 Servo feedback control based track following

In order to position a read head with an accuracy of one-tenth of the track width, a close-loop method of track-following must be used. This method is based on the feedback from the preexisting servo bursts in the hard disk platters whose data is to be imaged or subject to forensic study. A close-loop approach of track following based on the feedback from the servo bursts deliberately written by the spin-stand itself has previously been studied in [3,4]. The novelty of our approach is the track following of off-centered disks by using preexisting servo marks written on the hard disks by manufacturers.

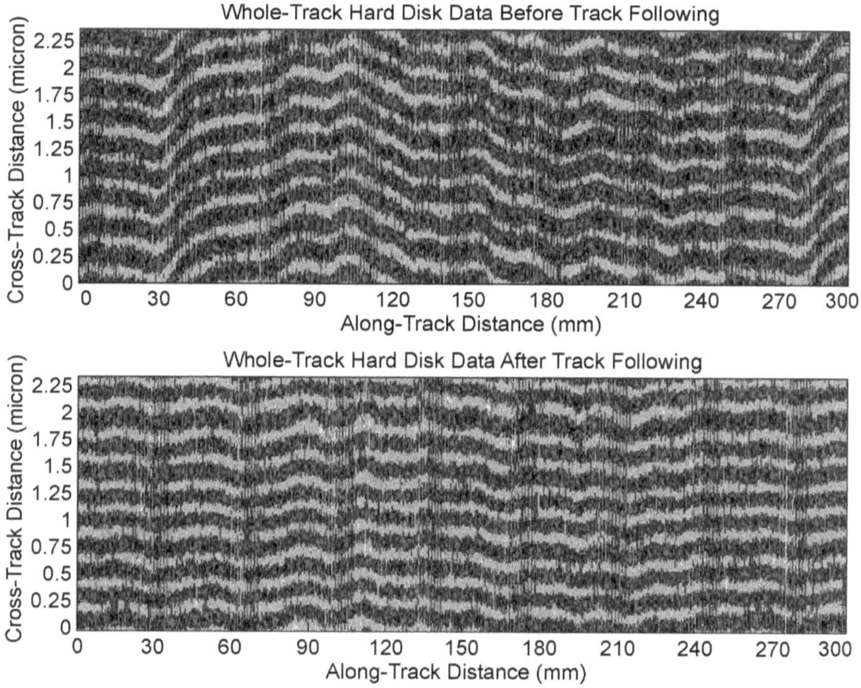

FIGURE 6.13 Spin-stand image of irregular track hard disk data (80 GB per platter) before and after track-following.

As in the case of the open-loop track following approach described in the last section, the servo positioning system also utilizes a small PZT to control the displacement of the read head. In other words, two PZT actuators are used in the servo positioning system. The first PZT uses an open-loop approach to compensate for large deviations (several microns) of systematic repeatable runout due to eccentricity. The second PZT compensates for small deviations (hundreds of nanometers) of both repeatable and nonrepeatable runout by utilizing the position error signal (PES) generated by the prewritten servo marks on the hard disk. This dual-stage positioning system is controlled by a PC by using an integral controller.

The feedback signal is extracted from signal generated by the servo marks. The servo marks are mainly composed of track ID and servo bursts. The track ID encoded in Gray code indicates the track number. The servo bursts are special magnetization patterns written on the disk to generate signals used to encode displacement of the read heads from the center of the data tracks. The off-track displacement information generated by the servo patterns can be used to create position error signals

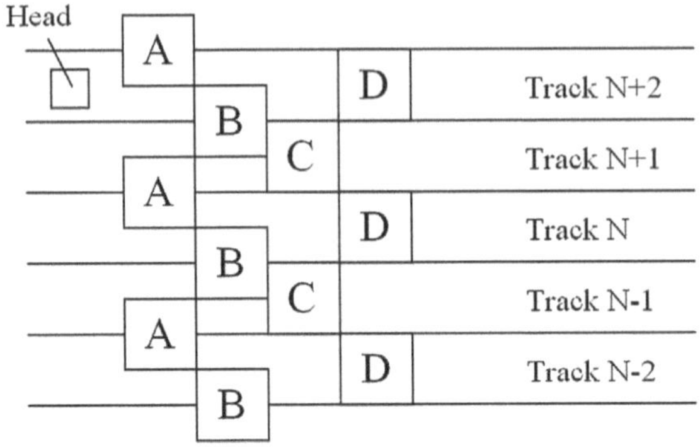

FIGURE 6.14 A typical 4-burst servo pattern.

(PES) [6]. An ideal PES is proportional to the distance between the center of the read head and the center of the track.

Figure 6.14 illustrates a servo pattern of a servo sector that is commonly used in modern hard disk drives. This servo pattern consists of four bursts of single frequency magnetization patterns written sequentially in the along-track direction and placed with known offset with respect to each other in the cross-track direction. The PES is determined by the amplitude difference of the signals generated by adjacent servo bursts. Indeed, if the read head is flying exactly at the center of the track, the amplitudes of signals generated by burst A and burst B are equal. When the head drifts away from the track center, the amplitude of the signal generated by one burst increases in comparison with the signal generated by the other burst. The difference in amplitude between signals generated by burst A and burst B is known as *in-phase PES*, and the difference in amplitude between signals generated by burst C and burst D is known as *quadrature PES*. The in-phase PES (PES_{ip}) and quadrature PES (PES_{qu}) are usually expressed as follows:

$$PES_{\text{ip}} = \frac{\bar{A} - \bar{B}}{\bar{A} + \bar{B}}, \tag{6.15}$$

$$PES_{\text{qu}} = \frac{\bar{C} - \bar{D}}{\bar{C} + \bar{D}}, \tag{6.16}$$

where $\bar{A}$, $\bar{B}$, $\bar{C}$, and $\bar{D}$ are signal amplitudes generated by respective bursts.

When the position of the head is close to the center of the track, PES_{ip} is linearly proportional to the difference between the location of the read

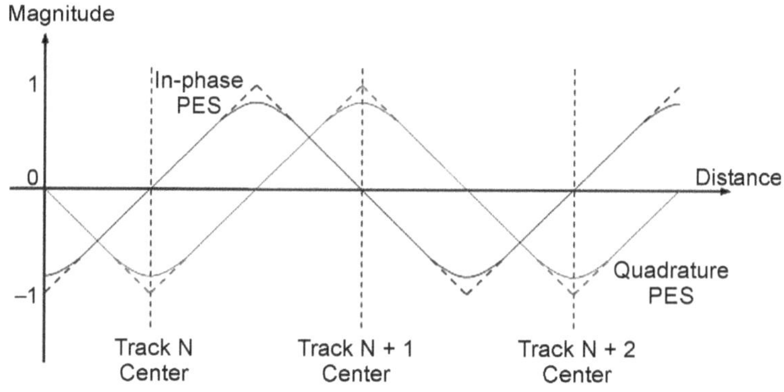

FIGURE 6.15 Typical PES_{ip} and PES_{qu} signals.

head center and the center of the track. However, since the read width of the head is usually narrower than the track width, PES_{ip} will saturate when the head drifts to the off-track region. Likewise, PES_{qu} becomes non-linear when the read head center is near the center of the track. Figure 6.15 shows the relation between the magnitudes of PES_{ip} and PES_{qu} versus the read head center displacement in the cross-track direction. It can be seen that the saturation phenomenon occurs at the edges of the tracks for PES_{ip} and at the center of the tracks for PES_{qu}.

The problem of nonlinearity is overcome by combining the linear regions of PES_{ip} and PES_{qu}. It is apparent that the absolute value of PES_{ip} is less than that of PES_{qu} when the read head center is closer to the center of the track than to the edge. Therefore, PES_{ip} is used as the position error signal whenever the absolute value of PES_{ip} is less than that of PES_{qu}. Similarly, PES_{qu} is used for the position error signal whenever the absolute value of PES_{ip} is larger than that of PES_{qu}. In addition, the sign of the position error signal indicates on which side of the track (above or below the track center) the read head is located. The equation for calculating position error signal can be summarized as follows:

$$PES = \begin{cases} PES_{\text{ip}}, & \text{when } |PES_{\text{ip}}| < |PES_{\text{qu}}| \text{ and } PES_{\text{qu}} < 0, \\ -PES_{\text{ip}}, & \text{when } |PES_{\text{ip}}| < |PES_{\text{qu}}| \text{ and } PES_{\text{qu}} > 0, \\ -PES_{\text{qu}} - 1, & \text{when } |PES_{\text{ip}}| \geqslant |PES_{\text{qu}}|,\ PES_{\text{ip}} < 0 \text{ and } PES_{\text{qu}} < 0, \\ -PES_{\text{qu}} + 1, & \text{when } |PES_{\text{ip}}| \geqslant |PES_{\text{qu}}|,\ PES_{\text{ip}} < 0 \text{ and } PES_{\text{qu}} \geqslant 0, \\ PES_{\text{qu}} + 1, & \text{when } |PES_{\text{ip}}| \geqslant |PES_{\text{qu}}|,\ PES_{\text{ip}} > 0 \text{ and } PES_{\text{qu}} < 0, \\ PES_{\text{qu}} - 1, & \text{when } |PES_{\text{ip}}| \geqslant |PES_{\text{qu}}|,\ PES_{\text{ip}} > 0 \text{ and } PES_{\text{qu}} \geqslant 0. \end{cases} \tag{6.17}$$

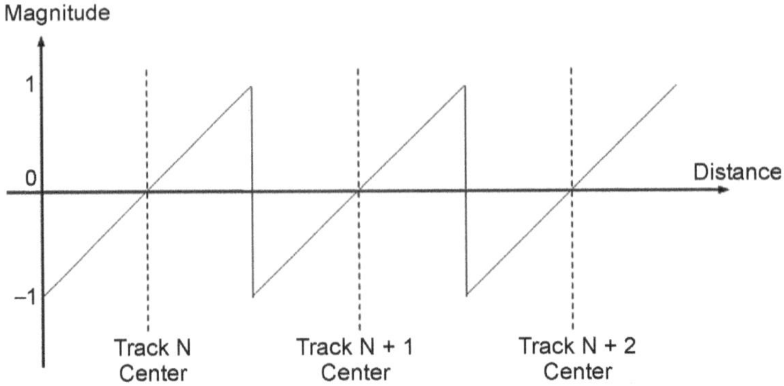

FIGURE 6.16 Ideal position error signal.

An ideal PES computed according to Eq. (6.17) is shown in Fig. 6.16. It can be seen that the magnitude of PES is proportional to the distance between the read head center and the center of the track. PES is positive when the read head is above the center of the track and is negative when the read head is below the center of the track.

Figure 6.17 shows the waveform of the readback signal generated by a typical servo data region, which includes the gain, track ID, servo bursts and part of the user data.

The PES generation algorithm is composed of three parts: the triggering scheme, the burst signal amplitude measurement, and the PES calculation. The triggering scheme is used to locate the exact position of the four servo bursts. It utilizes the gain as the trigger pattern and obtains a reference point with respect to the servo bursts. The starting and ending point of each of the four servo bursts can be found by knowing the distance from the reference point to the beginning of the first burst and the length of each burst, which are measured by counting the number of sampled points from Fig. 6.17. The amplitudes of the four servo burst signals are obtained by summing the sample signal values for all sampled points for each burst. Since the sampling rate can be set high enough to have at least ten samples for each pulse, the summing of sample values is approximately equal to the result of integration. When the amplitudes of the four servo burst signals are found, the PES can be calculated by using Eq. (6.17).

The PES generation algorithm has been programmed to ensure that the PES can be generated on-the-fly. The relation between PES magnitude and cross-track read head displacement can be obtained by microstepping the head in the cross-track direction. The top plot of Fig. 6.18 presents the examples of the in-phase and quadrature PES signals, while the bottom

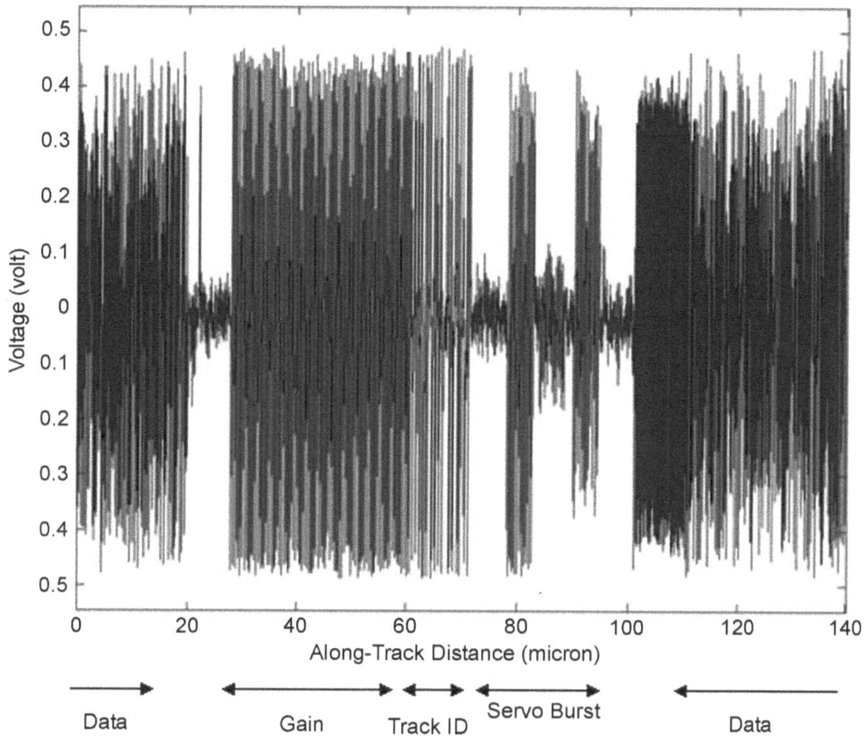

FIGURE 6.17 Waveform of the readback signal from a typical servo region.

plot illustrates the corresponding position error signal. The experimental data was acquired from a commercial hard disk with track pitch of 2.15 μm.

The experimental setup of servo positioning system is very similar to that of the dynamical track following system. The only difference is that the waveform generator in Fig. 6.8 is replaced by a multi-function card (NI PCI-6070E) as shown in Fig. 6.19. The PES generation algorithm is realized by a personal computer (PC). After the servo data is processed by the PC, a voltage signal proportional to the magnitude of the PES is generated by the multi-function card. This voltage signal is then amplified by the signal amplifier and sent to the PZT as the servo control signal. Due to the hysteretic effect of the PZT, several iterations might be needed in order to correct the position of the read head at each servo sector. Once the read head reaches the center of the track within one servo sector, user data in this servo sector is read, and then the servo system starts to adjust the position of the head at the next servo sector. Since the servo data

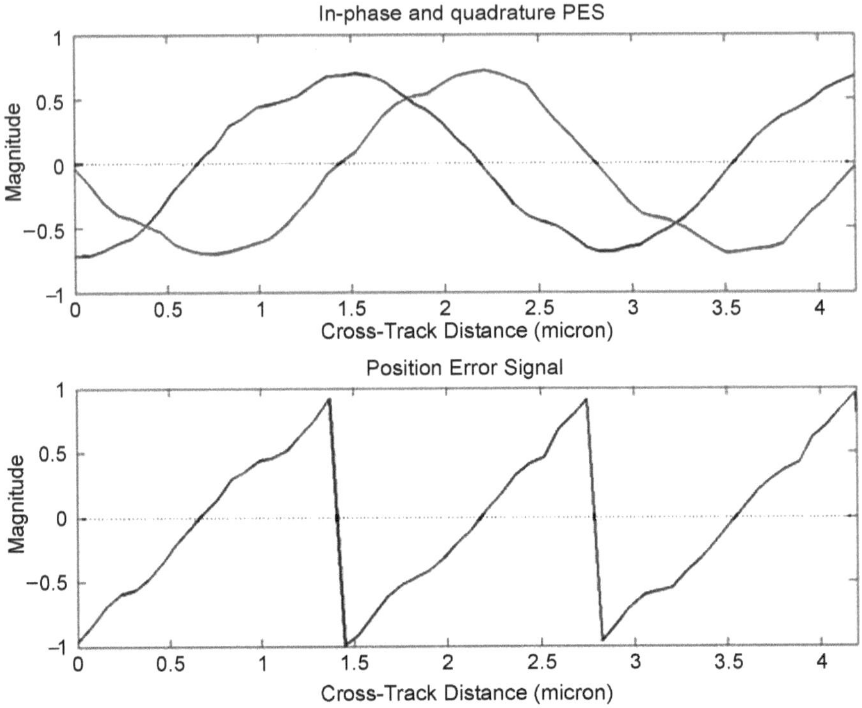

FIGURE 6.18 Experimental PES_{ip}, PES_{qu} and PES.

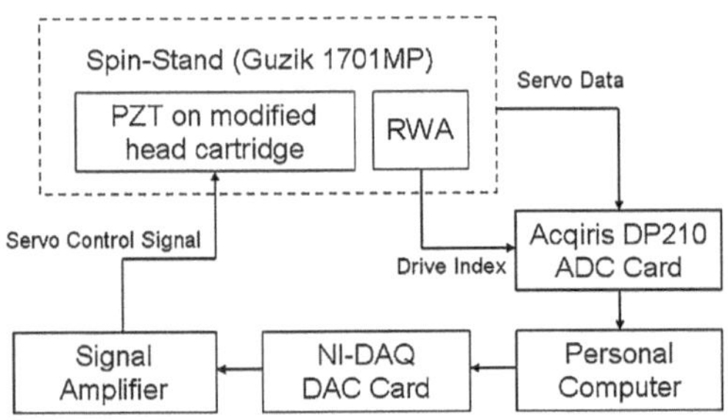

FIGURE 6.19 Block diagram of the servo control system.

in one particular servo sector can only be read once per spindle revolution, the time taken for head position adjustment is equal to the period of spindle revolution.

Figure 6.20 presents the block diagram of the servo control system. The "Plant" is the read head to be controlled. The block "A/D" repre-

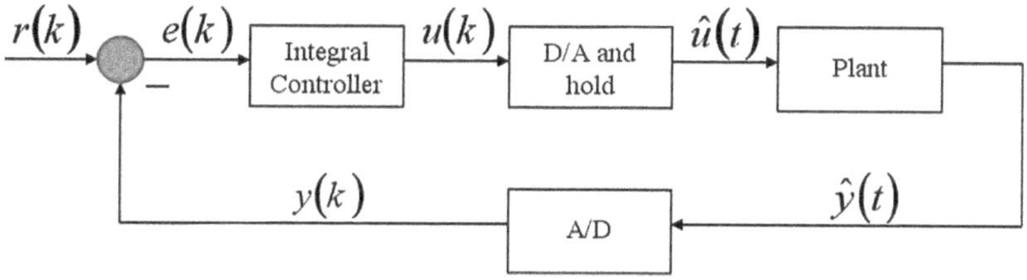

FIGURE 6.20 Block diagram of the servo mechanism.

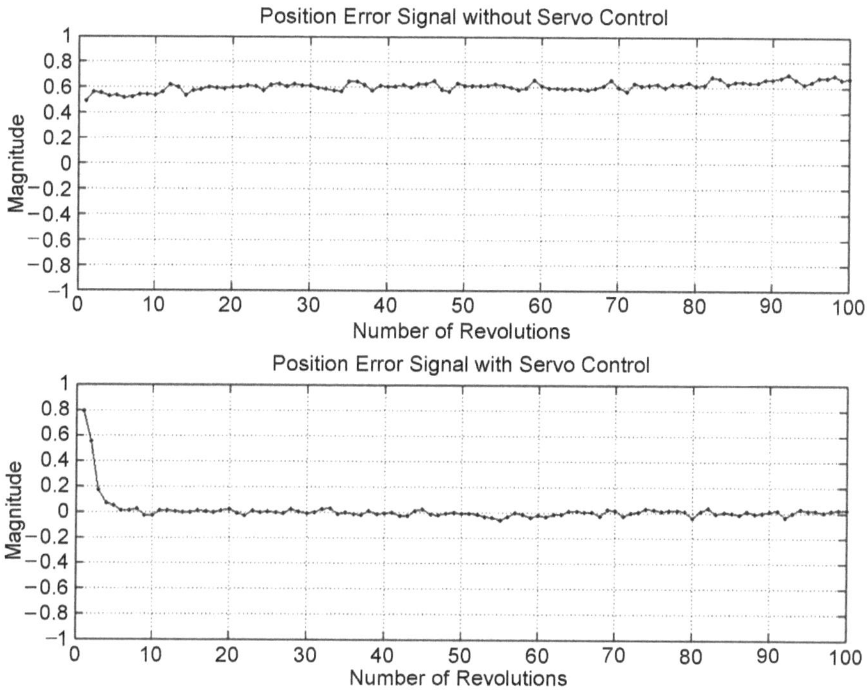

FIGURE 6.21 Position error signal with and without servo control.

sents the analog-to-digital converter. The true PES $\hat{y}(t)$ is converted to $y(k)$ through the A/D, while $r(k)$ corresponds to the reference position. The tracking error $e(k)$ is equal to the difference between $r(k)$ and $y(k)$. The error signal is sent to the integral controller, and the controller computes the controlling signal according to the following equations:

$$u(k) = K_I a(k), \tag{6.18}$$

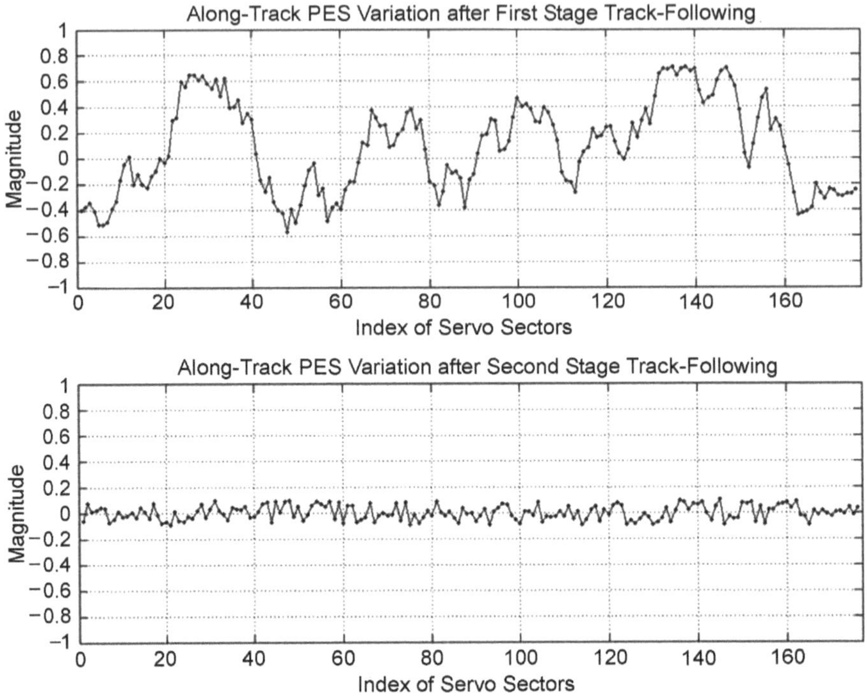

FIGURE 6.22 Along-track PES variations after first and second steps of track following, respectively.

$$a(k) = a(k-1) + e(k), \tag{6.19}$$

where K_I is the integral gain.

The signal $u(k)$ represents samples of the input signal to the head. The block "D/A and hold" holds each sample of $u(k)$ for T seconds to produce a continuous controlling signal $\hat{u}(t)$ to the head. If the spindle of the spin-stand rotates at 3600 revolutions per minute (RPM), T is equal 0.016667 since each revolution takes 16.667 milliseconds. The integral gain K_I depends on the track pitch of the hard disk and the size of the PZT. K_I has to be chosen properly so that the read head will be moved to the center of the track as quickly as possible.

Experimental results

The described servo control system has been implemented and extensively tested. Two examples are presented below to illustrate the effectiveness of this control system. The first example deals with a commercial

TABLE 6.1 Parameters of hard disks used in the spin-stand microscopy

Disk	Year	Media	Areal density ($Gbit/in^2$)	Track density (ktpi)	Track pitch (μm)
A	1998	Longitudinal	1.6	9.2	2.76
B	2000	Longitudinal	5.0	17.3	1.47
C	2002	Longitudinal	34.1	60.0	0.42
D	2004	Longitudinal	54.8	91.0	0.28
E	2006	Perpendicular	132.0	145.0	0.18

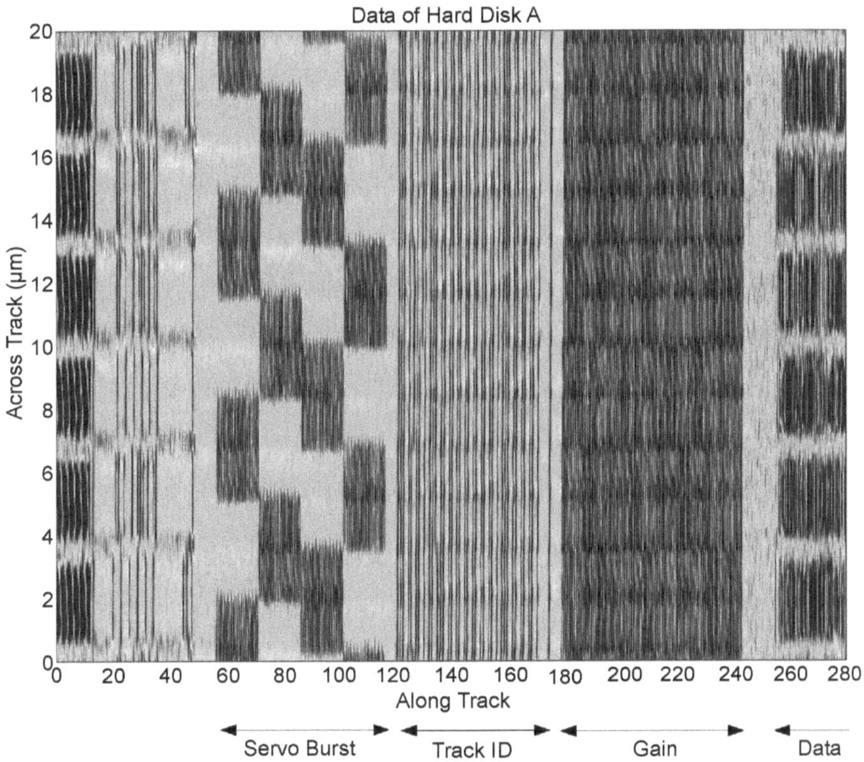

FIGURE 6.23 A spin-stand image of hard disk A.

hard disk whose track pitch is 1.22 μm. A PZT with a length of 5 mm was used for servo control purposes. The integral gain K_I was set to be 1.0. Figure 6.21 shows the position error signal in the time domain for one particular sector of a track. The top plot of Fig. 6.21 indicates that initially the read head was off-track by about 50 to 70 percent of the track width.

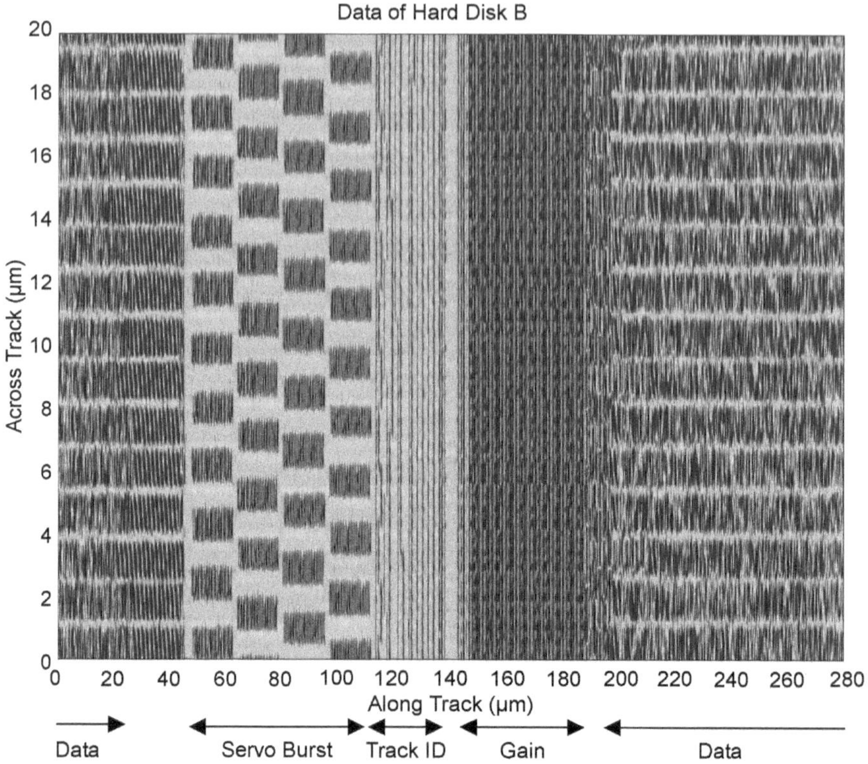

FIGURE 6.24 A spin-stand image of hard disk B. (See color plate 3.)

However, the read head was moved to the center of the track (within 10 percent of the track width) after three iterations in the servo control loop, as shown in the bottom plot of Fig. 6.21.

Figure 6.22 is related to the second example and it illustrates the results of the first and second steps of track-following. The first-step of track-following is the open-loop approach discussed in the last section, while the second step of track-following is the close-loop servo feedback control based track following. The track pitch of the hard disk was 0.43 μm. A GMR head with a read width of 0.15 μm was used as the reading element. After mechanical centering, the distance between the read center and the write center was about 1.5 μm. Seven tracks were crossed before the implementation of the first step of track-following. The top plot of Fig. 6.22 shows the PES for all 176 servo sectors along the data track after the first step track-following. It can be seen that the read head center was displaced of track center by more than 60 percent of the track

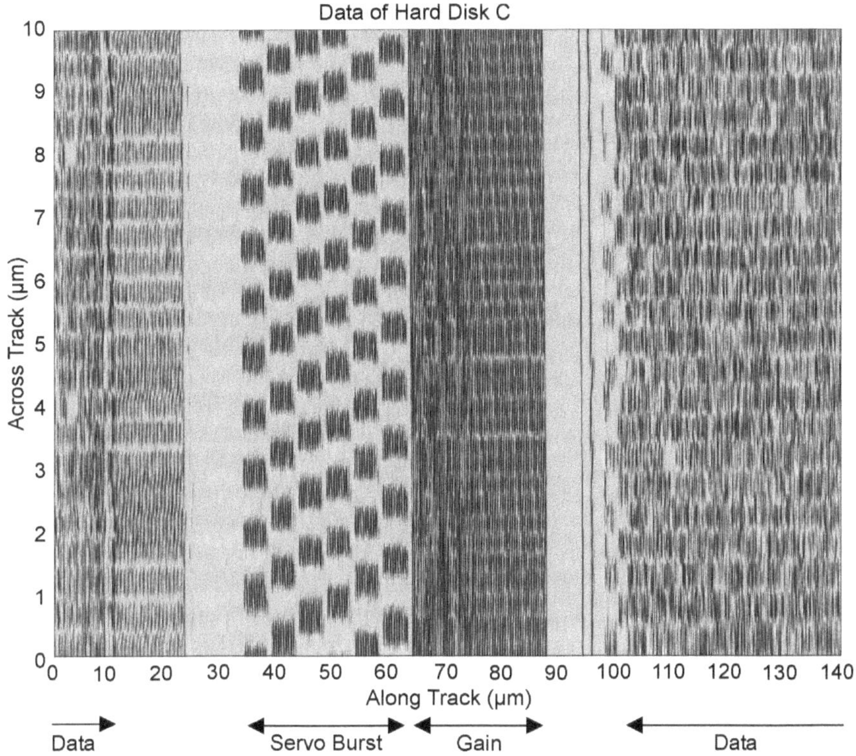

FIGURE 6.25 A spin-stand image of hard disk C. (See color plate 4.)

width at some of the servo sectors. However, after the second step of track-following, the PES error was reduced by 84.3% as compared with the first step of track-following.

The best result in reading of off-centered tracks is obtained when all three approaches to the disk centering are combined. Mechanical disk centering is used first to reduce the value of δ, then the head actuator is programmed for dynamic track-following of the imaged track, and finally servo feedback control is used to precisely stay on the center of the track. This multi-step data acquisition system can dynamically follow off-centered hard disk tracks with large initial eccentricity to within 10% of the track width. In order to utilize the resultant on-track readback signals for forensic data studies, these signals need to undergo several steps of processing including the removal of intersymbol interference (ISI), the precoding, the run-length-limited (RLL) encoding, and the encoding introduced by scramblers [7,8].

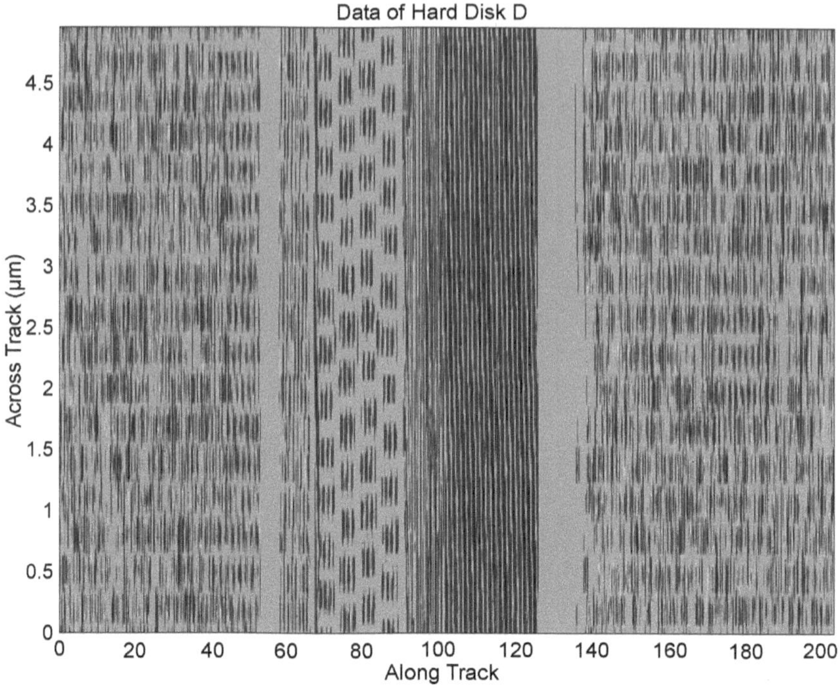

FIGURE 6.26 A spin-stand image of hard disk D.

6.3 TRIGGERING AND ALIGNING

The main challenge in massive data microscopy is to capture the disk data nondestructively. This is accomplished by providing a reasonably stable trigger in order to always image the same target area on the disk. To this end, the *drive index* of the spindle was used in our studies as an *external trigger* to the scope. This drive index of the spindle is generated by the drive electronics of the spin-stand for each complete revolution of the spindle. However, due to the random fluctuations of the rotational speed of the spindle motor, this drive index is not sufficiently stable or accurate and, as a result, circumferentially acquired data for different radial positions of read head exhibit some shifts.

The challenge is thus to devise a numerical aligning algorithm in order to remove any trigger-induced shifts. In the alignment algorithm, successive circumferential (along-track) voltage measurements are compared with adjacent (in the cross-track direction) circumferential voltage measurements. Specifically, cross correlations between adjacent circumferen-

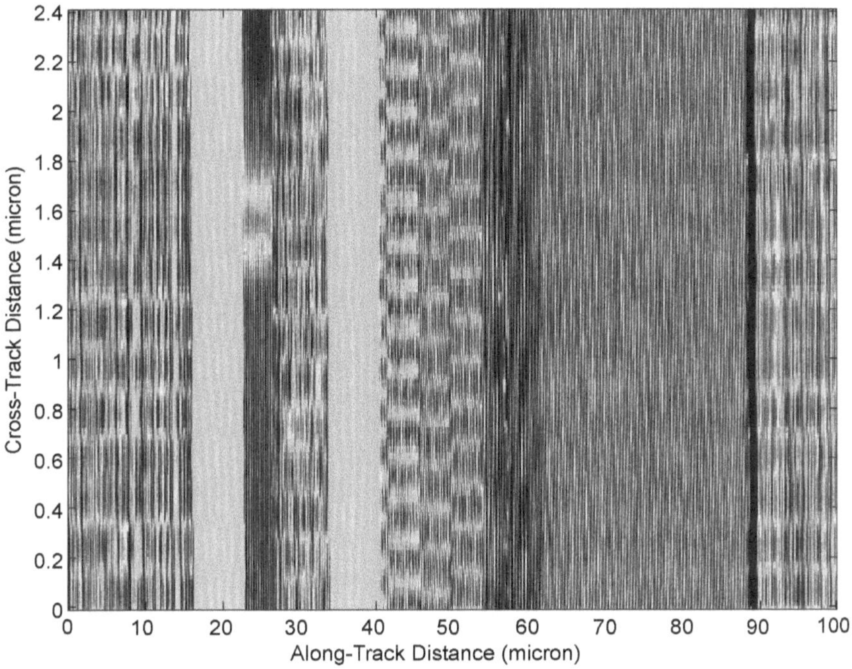

FIGURE 6.27 A spin-stand image of hard disk E.

tially acquired data are computed. The along-track data are then shifted in the along-track direction such that the cross correlation between successive along-track data achieves its maximum. The inner (dot) product between data vectors representing two radially adjacent track reading can be used as a good cross correlation measure.

As an illustration of the above alignment procedure, let us assume that a total of N radially adjacent track readings are collected. If line number 1 represents the first track reading, then line number 2 (which corresponds to the radially adjacent track reading) is shifted with respect to line number 1 such that their cross-correlation (inner product) is maximal. Next, line number 3 (which is the track reading one radial step from line number 2) is shifted with respect to line number 2 such that their cross-correlation is also maximal. The process continues until all the lines have been shifted, i.e. line number N has been shifted with respect to line number $N - 1$. The reader is advised to consult Appendix C for the details of numerical implementation of the above algorithm.

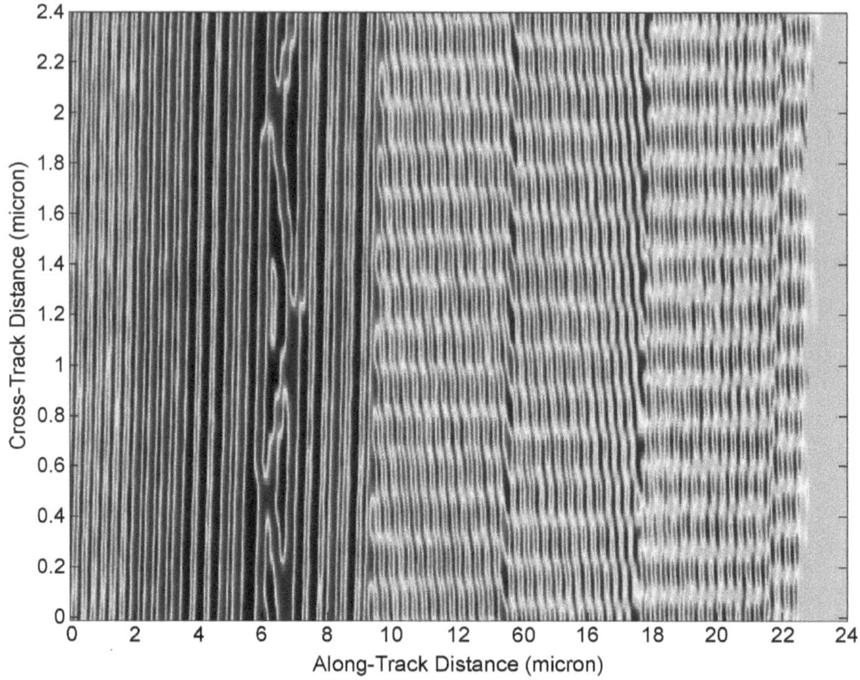

FIGURE 6.28 Servo bursts (zoomed) on hard disk E (laptop perpendicular drive).

6.4 SAMPLE HARD DISK IMAGES

By using the techniques described above, many hard disks have been successfully imaged. Below, we present some sample images of five hard disks taken from commercial hard drives whose parameters are shown in Table 6.1.

In this set of experiments, GMR heads with read widths of 0.24 and 0.13 μm were used. All measurements were performed by using a Guzik spin-stand and read-back voltages were acquired by a digital oscilloscope. The scan range is determined by the number of scanning steps in the cross-track direction and the time base of the scope. The scope has enough memory and a high sampling rate such that the entire track can be captured with high resolution. When the full-range timebase is set to $2\pi/\omega$ (where ω is the angular velocity of the spindle rotation), the whole track can be captured at once. The schematic of the experimental set-up is shown in Fig. 2.3.

Figures 6.23, 6.24, 6.25, and 6.26 show the images of data recorded on longitudinal disks A, B, C and D, respectively (note that the scan area

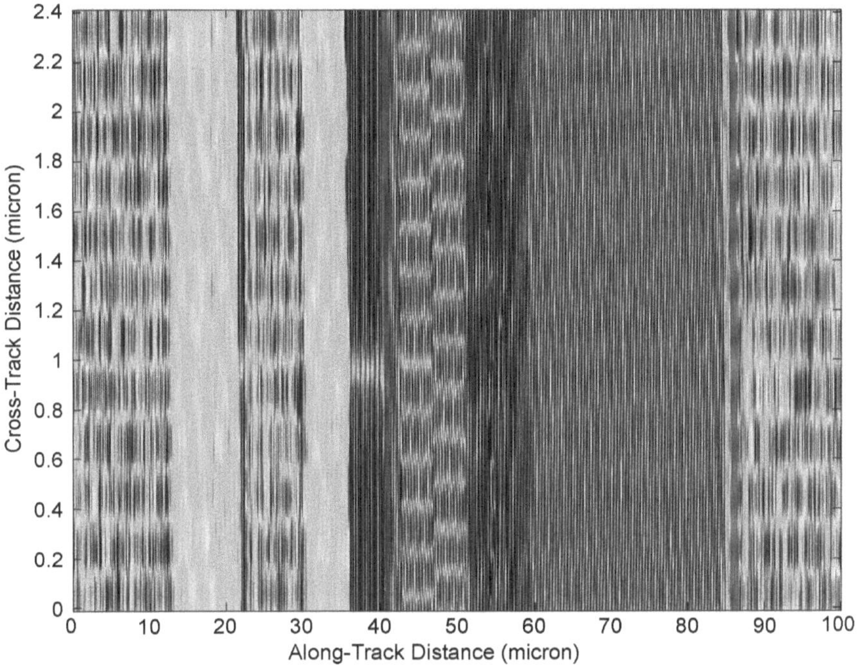

FIGURE 6.29 A different servo bursts arrangement (desktop perpendicular drive).

of Figs. 6.25 (year 2002) and 6.26 (year 2004) is only one-fourth and one-eighth of that of Figs. 6.23 (year 1998) and 6.24 (year 2000), respectively. Figure 6.27 presents the servo data region on a commercial laptop hard drive with perpendicular recording technology and Fig. 6.28 shows an amplified view on the servo burst region of this disk. It can be seen that this disk also has four servo bursts with the area of the fourth burst much smaller than that of the other three bursts. However, other arrangements for burst distribution are possible. Figure 6.29, for example, shows the servo burst region of a desktop hard drive with perpendicular recording technology. In these figures, the dark area represents changes in magnetization directions (i.e. virtual magnetic charges of opposite polarities), while the light area represents the regions where there is zero magnetization or no change in magnetization at all. It should be noted that the aspect ratio of these images are somewhat distorted because the horizontal axis is in millimeters scale while the vertical axis is measured in microns. These images, being only a very small portion of much larger images, show the servo burst region, the track-id region, the gain region, and

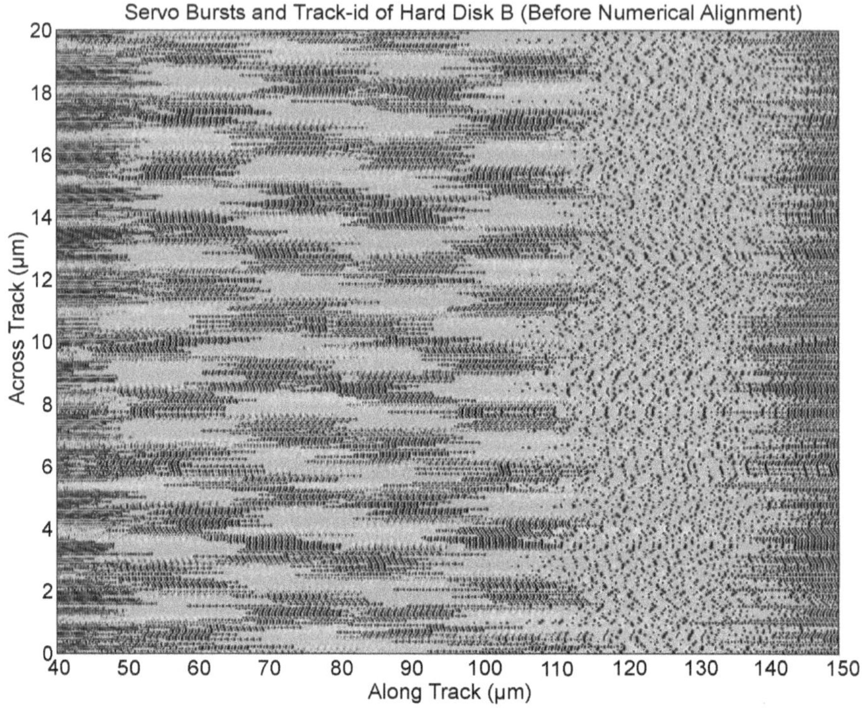

FIGURE 6.30 Servo bursts and track-id of hard disk B (before alignment).

part of the user-data region. From these images, it can be seen that the effects of increasing the data areal densities are clearly more pronounced in the cross-track direction than in the along-track direction.

As a demonstration of the effectiveness of the numerical alignment procedure, Figs. 6.30 and 6.31 show the zoomed servo region of disk B before and after alignment, respectively. Figure 6.31 clearly shows the high-frequency burst marks and the details of the track-id written in Gray code, which are not legible at all in the unaligned image of Fig. 6.30.

In order to give the idea of the resolution of the massive magnetic microscopy technique, Fig. 6.32 presents the user data region of disk A. The resolution of the spin-stand microscopy technique is determined by both intrinsic and extrinsic factors. The along-track resolution is intrinsically limited by the finite thickness of the read element and extrinsically limited by the sampling rate of the oscilloscope. The cross-track resolution is intrinsically limited by the width of the read element and extrinsically limited by the minimum radial step size and positional repeatability allowable by the spin-stand. Besides, the resolution in both directions is de-

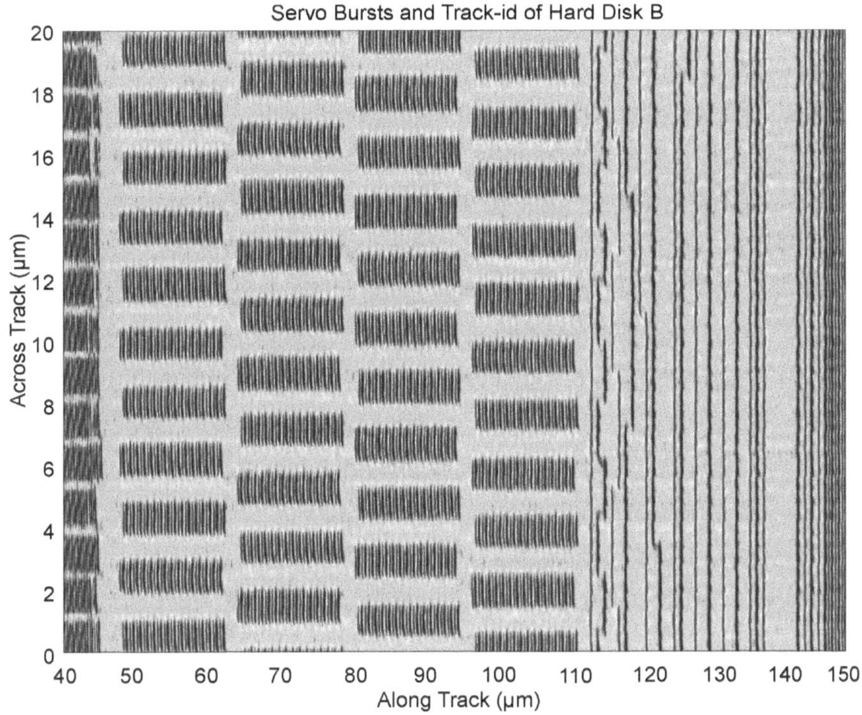

FIGURE 6.31 Servo bursts and track-id of hard disk B (after alignment). (See color plate 5.)

pendent on the flying height of the read head. The closer the head to the surface, the higher the resultant resolution. The cost of a low flying height, however, is the susceptibility to lubricant pick-up and head wear, which in time will degrade the performance of the head.

In order to remove the limitation of the cross-track resolution due to the finite read width of the head, image reconstruction can be performed. This reconstruction is accomplished by deconvolving the voltage wave forms of the scanned image using a specially designed algorithm based on the GMR head response function (see Chapter 3).

It can be seen from Fig. 6.32 that edges of the tracks contain remnant data of previous recordings. This is because exact overwriting will almost never occur due to track misregistration. This suggests that the forensics of overwritten data is possible and it is facilitated by the industry practice of write-wide-read-narrow. This is the practice where the write head writes a track wider than the read head width. This will minimize track interference during the readback process. In addition, as disks in the fu-

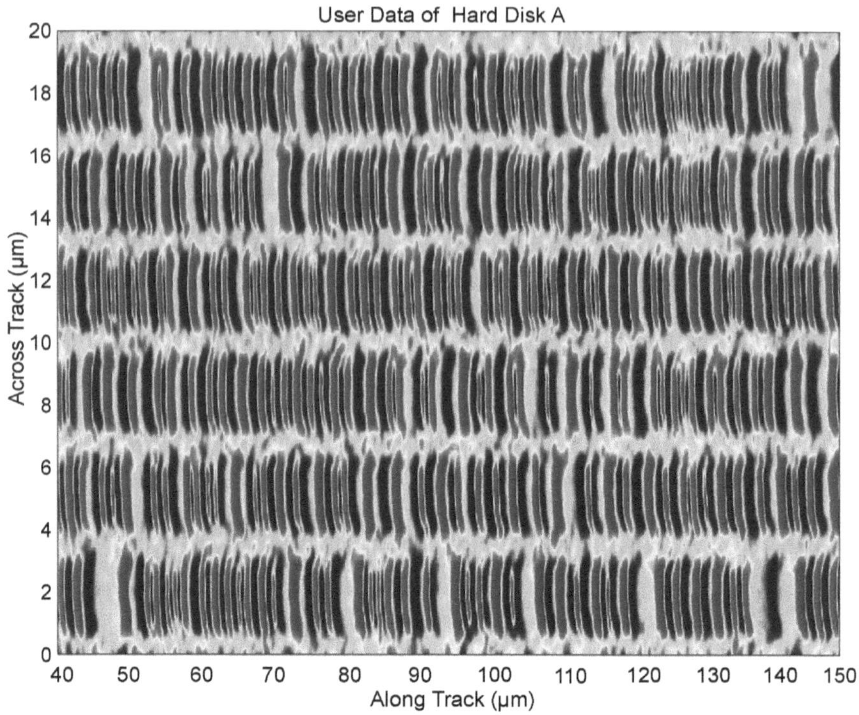

FIGURE 6.32 User data of hard disk A. (See color plate 6.)

ture will have even higher coercivity, the fringe field of the write head may not be sufficient to overwrite the data at the track edges, leaving the regions there with rich preserved information. User data is especially susceptible to recovery if newer generation heads that have narrower read widths are used to read hard disk data recorded with older technologies. For the purpose of comparison, Fig. 6.33 is a spin-stand image of the data on a virgin disk (from year 1998) with no underlying previous recordings.

One of the unique features of the developed spin-stand magnetic microscopy technique is that all the procedures can be easily programmed such that the entire disk surface can be imaged. This automatic image acquisition is not possible with MFM imaging because of its limited scan range and slow rate of data acquisition. In addition, while hard disk images obtained by the MFM technique do not contain any information regarding the read head, the images obtained by using spin-stands provide crucial information on the performance of the read head. This is because the read head acts as the sensor of the spin-stand microscopy tech-

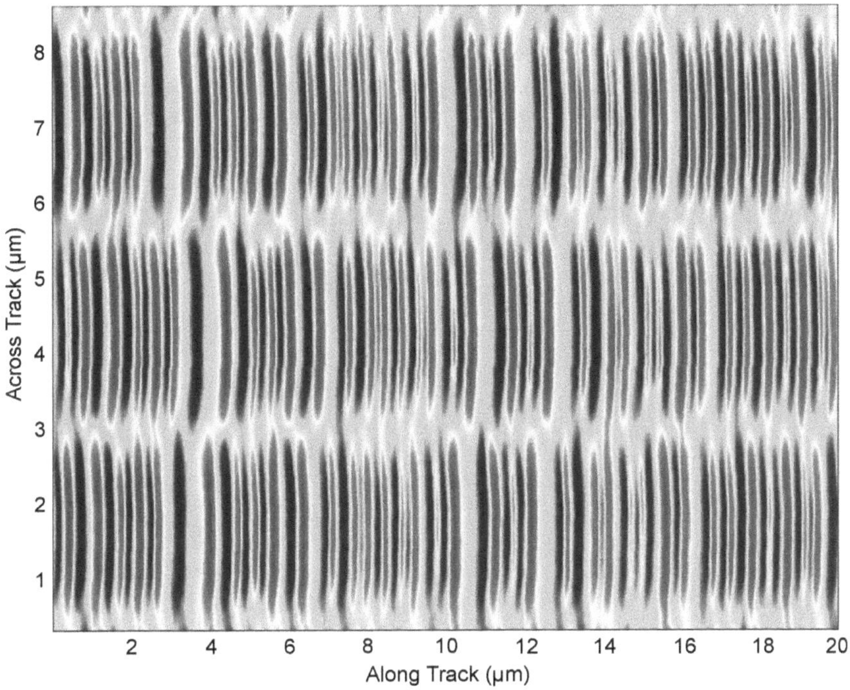

FIGURE 6.33 User data written on a virgin disk. (See color plate 7.)

nique. As such, a spin-stand image can be used for read head characterization.

6.5 SUMMARY

The technique of entire-track spin-stand microscopy of hard disk data from off-centered disks has been developed and presented. The related challenges of track-centering and track-following have been addressed. This technique allows for rapid analysis of track and servo writing. It is also promising for forensics of hard disk data in situations when the hard disk platters are removed from native drives and are inevitably off-centered during the readback process.

Data from commercial hard drives of different generations have been scanned and sample spin-stand images are presented. From these images, the width and spacing of the tracks, the spatial distribution of the servo bursts, the correct combination of the track-ids, and the details of the encoded user patterns became readily available.

The technique of entire-track spin-stand microscopy and diagnostics of hard disk data from off-centered disks also opens the path for *in-situ* drive centering and imaging. This has significant implications for hard disk data forensics in situations when, for example, the hard drive spindle suffers from irreparable damage that deems a replacement necessary. Through suitable modifications of the technique described in this chapter, the magnetization patterns on any off-centered disk mounted on the new spindle can be read back after the proper track demodulation. The developed technique is a potent tool for analyzing hard disk drives including read head characterization.

BIBLIOGRAPHY

[1] C. Tse, C. Tseng, P. McAvoy, C. Krafft, and I. Mayergoyz, "Whole-track imaging and diagnostics of hard disk data using the spin-stand imaging technique," *J. Appl. Phys.*, **97**, 10P104 (2005).

[2] C. Tseng, I. Mayergoyz, C. Tse, P. McAvoy, and C. Krafft, "Dynamic track-following of off-centered hard disks in spin-stand imaging," *J. Appl. Phys.*, **97**, 10R301 (2005).

[3] W.E. Wong, L. Feng, G. Guo, W. Ye, and A. Al-Mamun, *Proc. 29th Annual Conf. of the IEEE Industrial Electronics Society*, 2114 (2003).

[4] S. Mori, T. Hoshino, H. Tada, G. Obinata, and K. Ouchi, *The 2003 JSME-IIP/ASME-ISPS Joint Conf. on Micromechatronics for Information and Precision Equipment*, June 16–18, 2003, Yokahama, Japan.

[5] I.D. Mayergoyz, *Mathematical Models of Hysteresis and Their Applications*, Elsevier Press, 2003.

[6] A.H. Sacks, "Position signal generation in magnetic disk drives," Ph.D. Thesis, Carnegie Mellon University, 1995.

[7] S. Wang and A. Taratorin, *Magnetic Information Storage Technology*, Academic Press, 1999.

[8] C. Mee and E. Daniel, *Magnetic Storage Handbook*, McGraw-Hill, 1996.

CHAPTER 7

Spin-Stand Based Forensic Studies of Hard Disk Data

In this chapter, we report on an ex-situ technique for the microscopy of hard disk data [1]. For drives which have suffered damage from a head crash or other mechanical problems and cannot be accessed by using standard software, firmware, or part-replacement techniques, there is currently no viable means to analyze the data, even though the files are still stored on the magnetic disks. Here, we report on the results of spin-stand based data microscopy, where the failed disk is removed from its native drive, placed on a spin-stand, and scanned with a giant magnetoresistive head. After disk centering and track following (see the previous chapter), data decoding, error correction, and sector mapping must be performed to make sure that the user data can be retrieved to the computer operating system. This chapter deals with those data decoding issues within the framework of spin-stand microscopy. As a result, it is demonstrated that spin-stand based data microscopy may have the potential for forensics at data rates approaching those in native drives.

The results of this chapter have been obtained in cooperation with our Ph.D. student P. McAvoy.

7.1 INTRODUCTION

Hard disk drives are used to store the majority of digitally-created information due to their large capacity, fast access time and data transfer rate, and low cost. From personal data in desktop and notebook computers, to databases in educational and research institutions, to large servers in corporate enterprises and federal agencies, more and more mission-critical data is being stored and backed up on hard disk drives. Despite the extreme sophistication of modern hard disk technology, hard disk drives have been and will be the weakest links in computer systems because they are electro-mechanical devices in otherwise predominantly-electronic systems. The question is not whether a hard drive will fail but when it will fail and what to do when it fails. A head on a hard drive may crash onto the magnetic platter. An electronic chip on the drive controller may malfunction due to an electrical shock. A computer virus might attack the information residing in the boot sector or file record of the hard disk. A user may intentionally abuse and sabotage a computer system containing digital traces of criminal activities. No matter what the causes of the failure might be, the data stored in the hard drive is often worth far more than the value of the drive itself. As such, the need for data forensics presents itself. The rapid forensic study of hard disk data is especially critical in security and law enforcement communities where the retrieved data may serve as digital evidence for criminal and terrorist prosecution, thus promoting homeland security.

As hard disk technology increases in sophistication, so does the corresponding need for more advanced data forensics technology and tools. Unlike a decade ago, a substantial percentage of failed, modern hard disk drives can no longer be forensically studied by employing standard hard drive forensic techniques. These standard techniques encompass software programs to retrieve files or directories that have been deleted, formatted, or corrupted; firmware restoration practices including the repair of printed circuit boards of hard drives and the reproduction of critical operational data. Current magnetic imaging techniques, like magnetic force microscopy, are too slow for forensic purposes.

As mentioned, among all the possible forensic scenarios, retrieval of lost data from hard disks that have experienced mechanical damage is the most challenging. The spin-stand forensic technology is the most promising in this situation to retrieve the lost data. This technology has a promise for high-speed, massive, ex-situ hard disk data retrieval which is currently regarded as unreadable due to a variety of mechanical, electrical, or logical causes. In addition, the spin-stand based forensics provides the examination of hard disk data on the most fundamental level, at the disk media surface, before the data have any chance to be misrepresented or concealed by malicious hardware and software schemes inside the drive.

7.2 PROCEDURES FOR SPIN-STAND BASED FORENSIC STUDIES OF HARD DISK DATA

In spin-stand based forensics, a magnetic head is used to scan the data of a hard disk mounted on a spin-stand. The images thus obtained represent raw images of the head readback signals. In order to retrieve the data, these analog readback signals must be converted into the decoded binary data that the operating system recognizes. Given the large data capacities

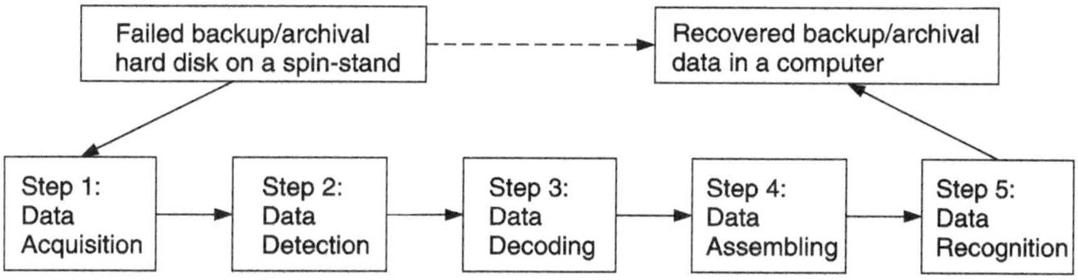

FIGURE 7.1 Steps of drive-independent spin-stand data recovery.

of modern hard drives, this process is not simple. It consists of five steps that deal with the acquisition, detection, decoding, assembling, and the recognition of spin-stand hard disk data (see Fig. 7.1).

Data acquisition

The central issue of data acquisition is track-centering and track-following, which are discussed in detail in the previous chapter. Since a hard disk once removed from its native drive and mounted on a spin-stand will become off-centered, the hard disk must be centered in the same way as it was centered when the data was recorded. In other words, the write track center must coincide with the read track center. Without proper centering, a read head will cross many tracks in one revolution of reading. In order to accommodate the deep submicron track widths of modern and future drives, this track-centering technique must be accompanied by a dynamic track-following technique and the ability to utilize preexisting servo marks on the hard disks as feedback for precise following of the hard disk tracks in real time.

Data detection

Data detection [2–4] must be performed on the track data in order to remove the distortions of the signals due to intersymbol interference (ISI) and noise. The readback signals before data detection represent the signals as seen by the heads. The signals after data detection represent the encoded magnetization patterns physically written on the disk. Accurate data detection is a precondition for correct decoding of the data. In addition, timing information that corresponds to the write clock must be extracted and determined from the acquired track data in order to convert them into raw binary bit streams for data decoding.

Most hard drives use some form of a partial response maximum likelihood (PRML) scheme. This is a detection technique in which the analog head readback voltage is first equalized (transformed) to specific desired form and then sampled. A timing recovery circuit synchronizes samples. These synchronized and equalized samples are passed through a Viterbi detector, which outputs an estimated data sequence by selecting the sequence with the maximum-likelihood path through the corresponding trellis. In modern hard drives, the Viterbi detection process incorporates noise prediction and post-processing to compensate for the increased media noise seen at very high bit densities.

Data decoding

The process of decoding requires intimate familiarity with various layers of encoding schemes, which at the minimum include error correction codes [5], scramblers, and run-length-limited codes. Different disk drive manufacturers employ different encoding schemes in different drive models in different years. These various encoding schemes involve proprietary information that cannot be directly obtained from drive manufacturers. Therefore, successful decoding involves a sophisticated process of identification and uncoupling of the different layers of encoding in order to arrive at the user data.

The decoding process is essentially the reverse sequence of steps in which the user data was encoded in the write channel. Before the data is written to the disk, it is divided into blocks of data of size ranging from 512 bytes to 4096 bytes. The block data plus the cyclic redundancy check (CRC) bytes are then encoded by using error correction codes (ECC) of the Reed–Solomon type. These are systematic codes in which ECC bytes are usually appended at the end of the sector following the user data. The ECC encoded data is then scrambled by a scrambler (or data randomizer) to break up repetitive patterns, e.g., long strings of zeros. This scrambled data is then further modified by a run-length limited (RLL) code to constrain the maximum and minimum number of zeros between successive ones. Together, the scramblers and RLL codes transform data sequences which are difficult to detect into more tractable sequences. Without scrambling and RLL, certain data sequences will cause the timing, gain, and adaptive equalization circuits of the read channel to lose synchronization with the readback. Before being written to the disk, the RLL-encoded data is passed through a write precompensation circuit to adjust for the timing of the write signals to account for nonlinear effects (shifts) in the write process. Accordingly, in the read channel, the readback data first goes through a detection process to remove distortions due to noise and intersymbol interference (ISI). The detected data sequence then successively goes through the RLL decoder, descrambler, and ECC decoder. Some of

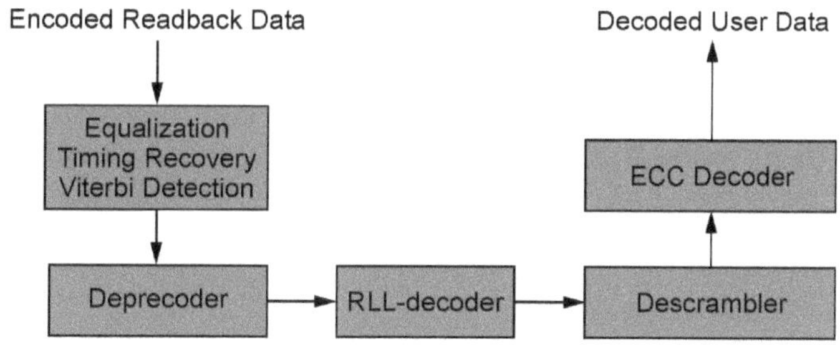

FIGURE 7.2 Generic decoding steps.

the more recent hard drives have eliminated RLL codes altogether and they rely solely on the scramblers and the deliberate flipping of bits which are later corrected by ECC. The ECC decreases the bit error rate from about 10^{-6} at the output of the detector to smaller than 10^{-13} for the delivered user data. Figure 7.2 shows the generic decoding steps described above.

The three most important decoding layers are the decoding of run-length-limited (RLL) codes, the decoding of the scramblers, and the decoding of ECCs. The possible technical approaches to these three types of decoding are described below.

Identification of RLL codes

The purpose of RLL codes is to improve the performance of magnetic recording systems by matching the properties of RLL encoded signals to those of the recording channel. There are three characteristics of the RLL codes: the *constraint*, the *code rate*, and the *encoding scheme*. The constraint of RLL specifies the minimum and maximum number of zeroes between successive ones. For example, 16/17 $(0, 6/8)$ RLL codes have a minimum of zero zeroes between successive ones (i.e. consecutive ones are allowed), a maximum of six zeroes between successive ones in the encoded data, and a maximum of eight zeroes in the odd and even interleave subsequences on which encoded data is subdivided. By running statistics on the ISI-removed binary data, one can identify the constraints of the RLL codes. The code rate of RLL specifies the ratio of the input and output bits of the RLL encoder. In our example 16 input bits are encoded into 17 output bits by the RLL encoder. The code rate can also be identified by having some educated assumption on the number of total bits in the sector ((data pads + sync bytes + user bytes + CRC bytes + ECC bytes) $\times$ 8 bits/byte) and multiply by the inverse of the assumed code rate and compare the result to the total number of bits per sector obtained experimentally. The assumed code rate that gives the closest match to the number of bits per sector obtained experimentally will be the true code rate. RLL codes are nonlinear, for this reason, one has to rely on a combination of look-up tables and equations found in different publications for the identification of encoding schemes. But once the constraint and the code rate are found, the number of possible encoding schemes is significantly reduced.

Identification of scramblers

In a hard disk channel the scrambler/descrambler circuit is used to reduce undesirable (e.g., many consecutive zeroes) data pattern effects on the channel's performance. In the write mode, the scrambler circuit randomizes the 8-bit internal NRZ data before passing it to the encoder. This randomization is done by using specific finite difference equations which generate pseudo-random binary sequences (PRBS), and, in this way, eliminating many consecutive zeros and other repeatable patterns in recorded data. One typical example of such a finite difference equation is given below:

$$x(n) = y(n) + x(n-7) + x(n-10), \tag{7.1}$$

where $x(n)$ is the scrambled sequence and $y(n)$ is the sequence of data being scrambled. The PRBS generated by Eq. (1) can be descrambled by using the following equation:

$$y(n) = x(n) + x(n-7) + x(n-10). \tag{7.2}$$

By using Z-transform, the above descrambler can be fully characterized by the transfer function polynomial: $H(z) = 1 + z^7 + z^{10}$. It is important to keep in mind that in magnetic recording practice the scrambling data can be byte-interleaved and, in addition, multi-layer scrambling can be employed. Furthermore, it is clear from Eq. (7.1) that the scrambling data are dependent on initial conditions of the scrambler. All these make the identification of scrambling a very involved process. The central idea of the scrambler identification is to utilize the linearity of scrambler finite difference equations and to use proper "interrogation" of disk drives of the same model. This interrogation will lead to linear binary equations used for the determination of nonzero coefficients in the finite difference scrambler equations. This approach has been tested in our studies and the proper scrambler identification for some models of hard disk drives has been demonstrated.

Identification of ECCs

In modern hard disk drives, sophisticated error correction codes (ECCs) are used to substantially decrease the bit error rate (BER) of detection of readback signals. Special attention is paid to the detection and correction of burst errors which are typical for magnetic recording systems. The central idea of ECCs is to introduce rigid structures in the recorded patterns by appending the recorded data by additional error correction bytes (these are so-called systematic error correction codes). Whenever an error occurs, it may violate these rigid structures and these violations can be utilized for error detection as well as error correction. In the widely-used cyclic error correction codes, the rigid structures are introduced by using specific polynomial algebra in generating ECC bytes. The center piece of this algebra is the generating polynomial of the cyclic ECC code. In other words, the encoded data is represented by the binary data polynomial and the ECC bytes are obtained as the binary coefficients of the remainder polynomial resulted in the division of the data polynomial by the generating polynomial. To enhance the burst error detection and correction capabilities, the interleaved Reed–Solomon codes are widely used in magnetic recording systems. In the Reed–Solomon codes, polynomials whose coefficients are the elements of finite Galois fields are systematically employed. Most of the error correction codes (including Reed–Solomon codes) used in magnetic recording systems are linear codes and this linearity property opens the opportunity for their identification by the appropriate "interrogation" of disk drives of the same models. This interrogation is based on recording of specific (known) data patterns and extracting the ECC bytes corresponding to these patterns. By using these extracted ECC bytes, the interleaved structure as well as the finite Galois field coefficients of the generating polynomial of specific Reed–Solomon codes can be determined. As soon as the generating polynomial is found, it can then be used for error detection and correction of the spin-stand (drive-independent) readback data by employing well-known techniques from the coding theory. In our studies, successful Reed–Solomon ECC code identification for certain models of hard disk drives have been demonstrated. The error detection and correction capabilities can be integrated into a data forensics system based on raw data acquisition from platters removed from native drives and mounted on a spin-stand. This will result in the decrease in the bit error rate of spin-stand based data forensics to the same level as in the native hard disk read channels.

Data assembling

In order to retrieve computer files, different decoded sectors must be correctly assembled. This is necessary as most files span multiple sectors that may reside on different tracks or surfaces. This involves knowledge of file systems and operating systems under which the data is organized [6]. Extensive knowledge in software and computer engineering is also required in order to assemble the good sectors and filter out the bad ones based on the primary defective sector list (P-list) or the grown defective sector list (G-list) stored on the firmware in the hard disks. Different hard drives have different ways of handling the so-called sector slipping due to the existence of bad sectors.

Data recognition

The available standard and custom-designed software programs are used to recognize the assembled, decoded files. Additional work on decryption is needed if the users encrypts their hard disk data.

The successful implementation of the above five steps is the key for high-speed, massive, ex-situ, spin-stand based data forensics.

7.3 DEMONSTRATION OF SPIN-STAND BASED FORENSIC STUDIES OF HARD DISK DATA

In this section, we present several examples of spin-stand based data forensics. First, we illustrate the decoding process for a single-platter commercial hard drive manufactured in 1997 with a capacity of about 3 gigabytes. This particular hard drive uses a RLL encoded scheme with PRML detection. The RLL code imposes limitations on the length of a "run" (uninterrupted series of zero bits) between successive one bits. The particular encoding scheme is 8/9 (0, 4/4) RLL. In this scheme, 8 bits of user data are encoded into 9 bits of channel data. "0" means that the minimum number of 0's between successive 1's (magnetic transitions) is zero. In other words, sequences of successive 1's are allowed in the encoded data. The first "4", called the global run length constraint, indicates that the maximum number of consecutive 0's between successive 1's in the encoded data is equal to 4. The second "4", called the interleave run length constraint, requires that the maximum number of consecutive 0's between successive 1's in the odd and even interleave subsequence is also 4. In this hard disk, each servo sector contains three to five data sectors, depending on the recording zone (see Fig. 7.3).

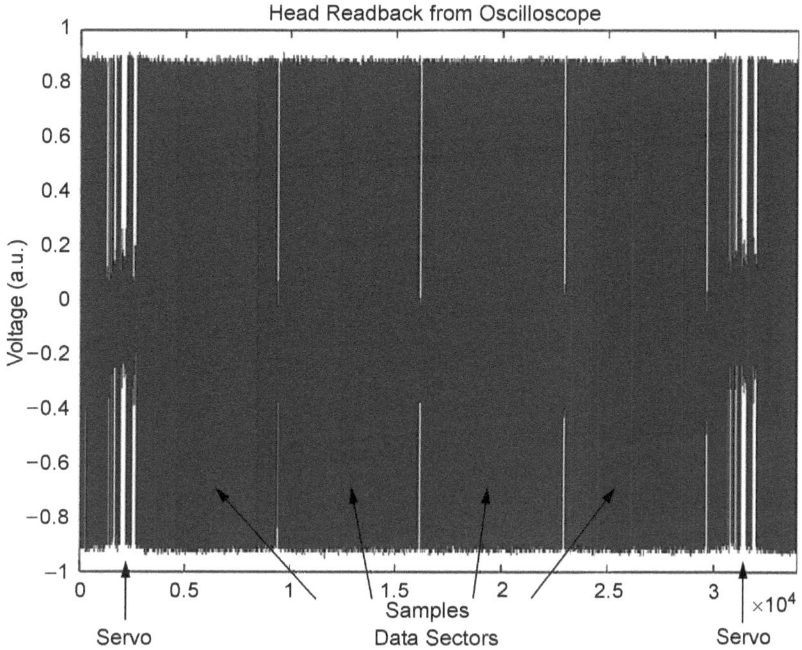

FIGURE 7.3 One servo sector.

Figure 7.4 shows the beginning of a data sector. The top plot of Fig. 7.4 is the raw head readback signal with inherent ISI distortions. The middle plot of Fig. 7.4 shows the head readback signal with the ISI removed through the ISI-removal algorithm. The bottom plot of Fig. 7.4 is the ISI-removed readback signal after passing through a low-pass filter in order to facilitate further signal processing to convert from digital samples to actual binary sequences. In this particular hard disk, each data sector begins with a fixed-frequency preamble pattern for gain and timing recovery purposes, followed by five bytes of training sequence, followed by one to two sync bytes, and, finally, followed by the user data. The training bytes are used to set the correct parameters for the digital adaptive filters in the equalization process in the native read channel. The sync byte signifies the end of the preamble pattern and the beginning of the user-data portion of the sector.

Since the distortions of the ISI are sufficiently removed as seen in the bottom plot of Fig. 7.4, the ISI-removed readback data can simply pass through a peak detector in order to convert from samples to actual binary bits, as shown in Fig. 7.5(a). Figure 7.5(b) shows the detected bits

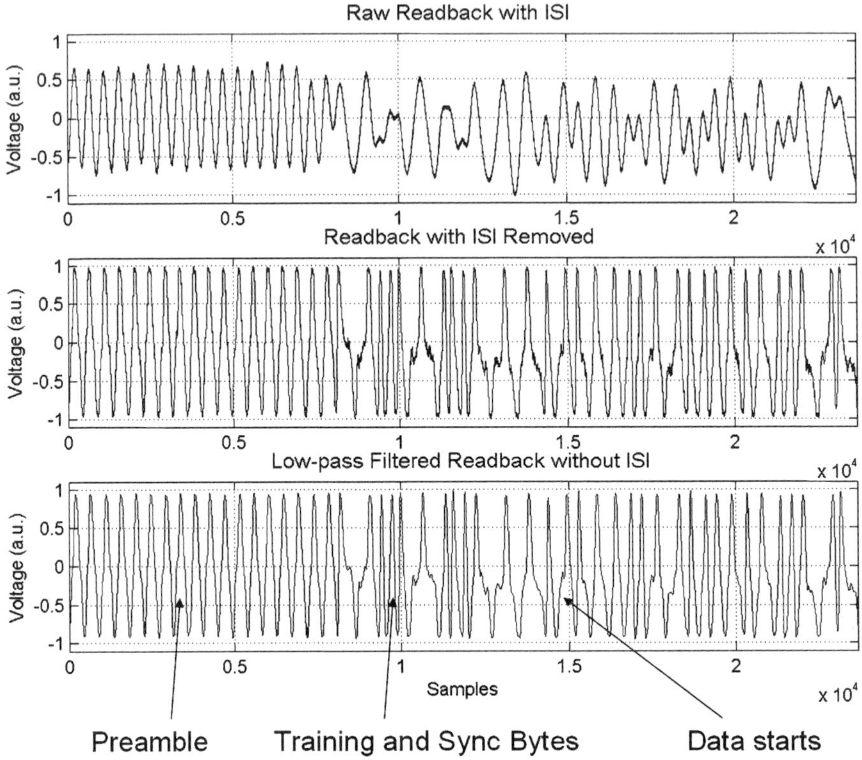

FIGURE 7.4 Beginning of a data sector.

after the precoding was removed. The deprecoded data was obtained by reversing the precoding operation of $\frac{1}{(1+D)^2}$, where "D" is a bit delay operator and "+" is in modulo-2 addition. The next step in the decoding process was to pass the deprecoded data through the RLL-decoder of the 8/9 (0, 4/4) type. Figure 7.5(c) shows the output bits from the RLL decoder. Next, after passing the RLL decoded data through the descrambler, the user data is shown in Fig. 7.5(d). Finally, to increase the reliability of the recovered user data, ECC can be applied to detect and possibly correct any errors occurred during data detection.

Experiments were performed to demonstrate the application of the above process of ex-situ spin-stand based data forensics to the retrieval of computer files. Specifically, JPEG image files were written to the hard disk. JPEG stands for *Joint Photographic Experts Group*, which is a standardization committee that invented compression algorithm used in JPEG files.

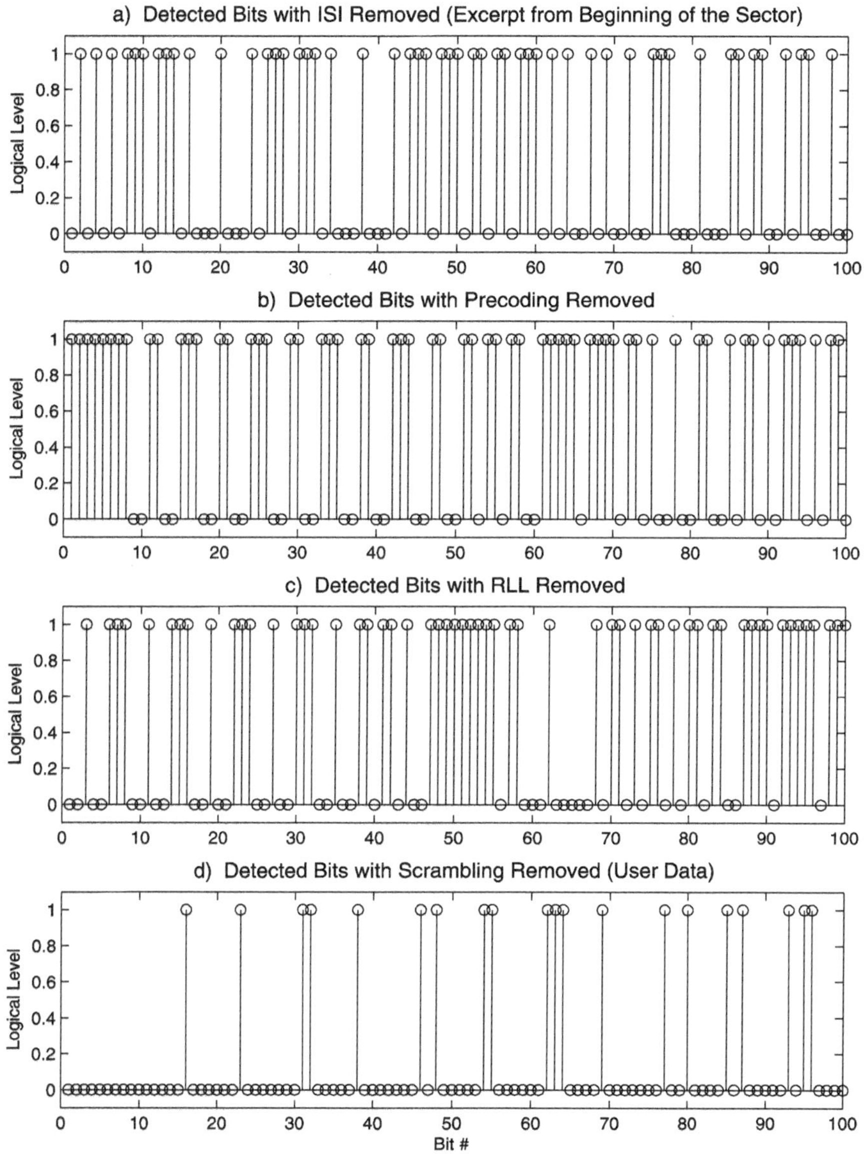

FIGURE 7.5 Detected bits at different stages of decoding.

The reasons JPEG files were chosen are the following: (1) JPEG image files are often the files of interest in criminal prosecution cases; (2) the successful recovery of JPEG files are immediately verifiable in the final resultant

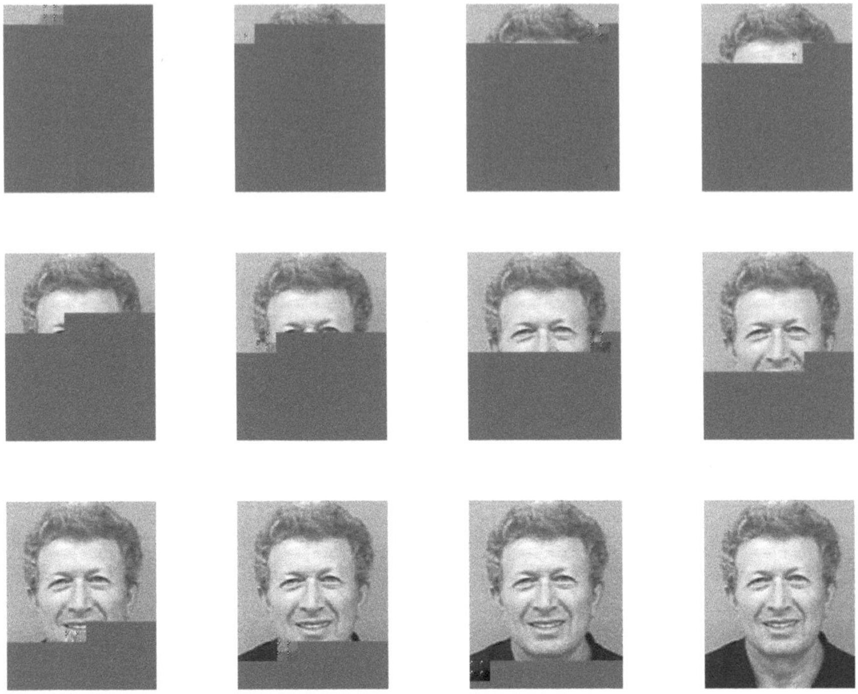

FIGURE 7.6 JPEG file retrieved sector by sector.

image; (3) JPEG files are binary files so it is not possible to modify the raw binary data to produce the desired JPEG image; and (4) JPEG files have stringent format such that any false bit detection in the raw data may cause the whole JPEG image to be nondisplayable.

In one of the experiments, a JPEG file of a human face was written to the described hard disk. The hard disk was then removed from its native drive and mounted on a spin-stand. The JPEG file written was 6 kB and consisted of 12 sectors. Using the detection steps shown in Fig. 7.2, the JPEG image was retrieved sector by sector, as shown in Fig. 7.6. It is evident from the figure that sector 1 contains much less graphical information than other sectors. This is because the file header information is contained in this sector so less space is available for graphical information. Figure 7.7 is a comparison between the original image written to the hard disk and the image retrieved via spin-stand microscopy. There

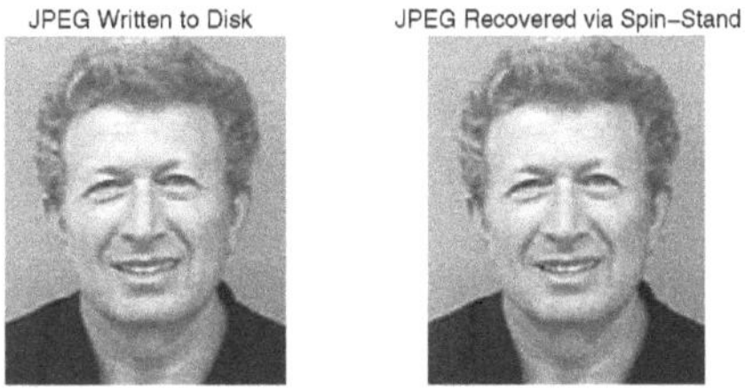

FIGURE 7.7 Comparison of the retrieved file with the original.

is no difference either at the bit level or in the final visual image. The error-free JPEG image file is completely retrieved through spin-stand microscopy.

In another experiment, a known JPEG file of 64 kB and 129 sectors was written on a year 2000 hard disk with a capacity of 27 GB (Fig. 7.8(A)). This hard disk was then removed from its original drive, mounted on a spin-stand, properly centered, track-followed, bit-detected, and read back. Decoding was performed and the written JPEG image was retrieved sector-by-sector (Fig. 7.8(C)), indicating an error-free recovery (Fig. 7.8(B)).

We have also made use of the knowledge we gained from ECC in the detection and correction of actual recovered data from spin-stand. In this experiment, we wrote a JPEG image (file size 120 kB, Fig. 7.9 left plot) on the hard disk, removed the disk platter and mounted it on a spin-stand. After disk-centering, track-following, data detection, data decoding (de-RLL, descrambler), we obtained the recovered JPEG image (Fig. 7.9 right plot). It can be seen that one error occurred (it is circled), corresponding to a bit error rate of about 1×10^{-6} (which is consistent with the bit error rate of the native read channel before applying the ECCs). This error was then easily corrected by using the identified ECCs.

One of the key steps in the retrieval process is the identification of the scrambler used to randomize the user data. To illustrate the effect of the scrambler, Fig. 7.10 presents two columns of user data at successive levels of decoding. The left column contains a section of a JPEG sector while the right column contains a section of data with all ones (i.e. data consisting of 1111111...). The first and second rows of Fig. 7.10 show the input bits and output bits to the RLL decoder, respectively. It can be seen that the two columns of data are very similar at this point, before the data is descrambled. After the data is descrambled, as shown in the third row of Fig. 7.10, the clear distinction between the original data patterns has emerged.

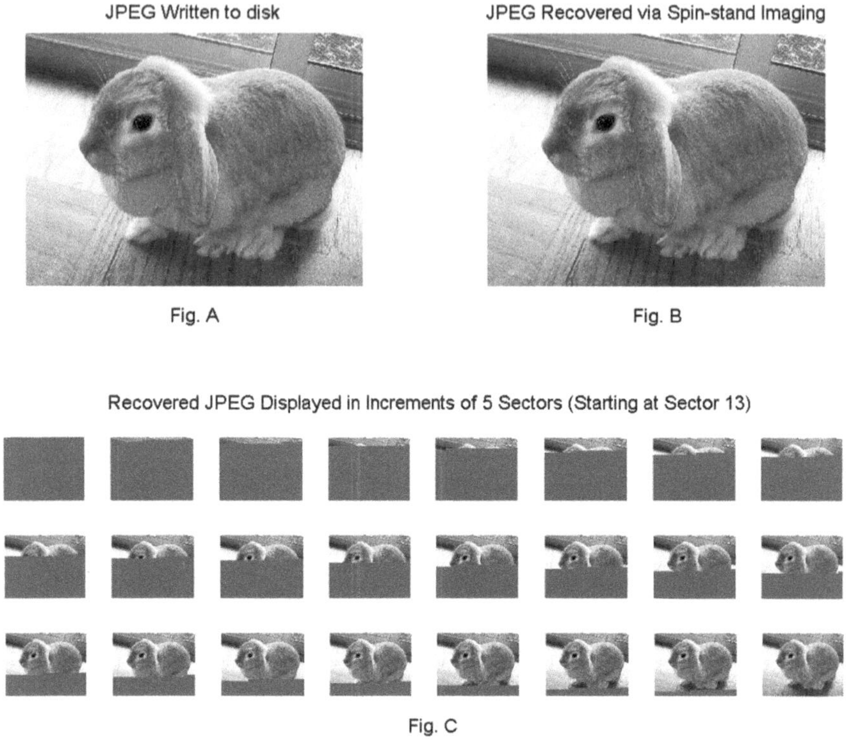

FIGURE 7.8 JPEG file of a rabbit recovered via spin-stand microscopy.

FIGURE 7.9 JPEG file of a cactus recovered via spin-stand microscopy. (See color plate 8.)

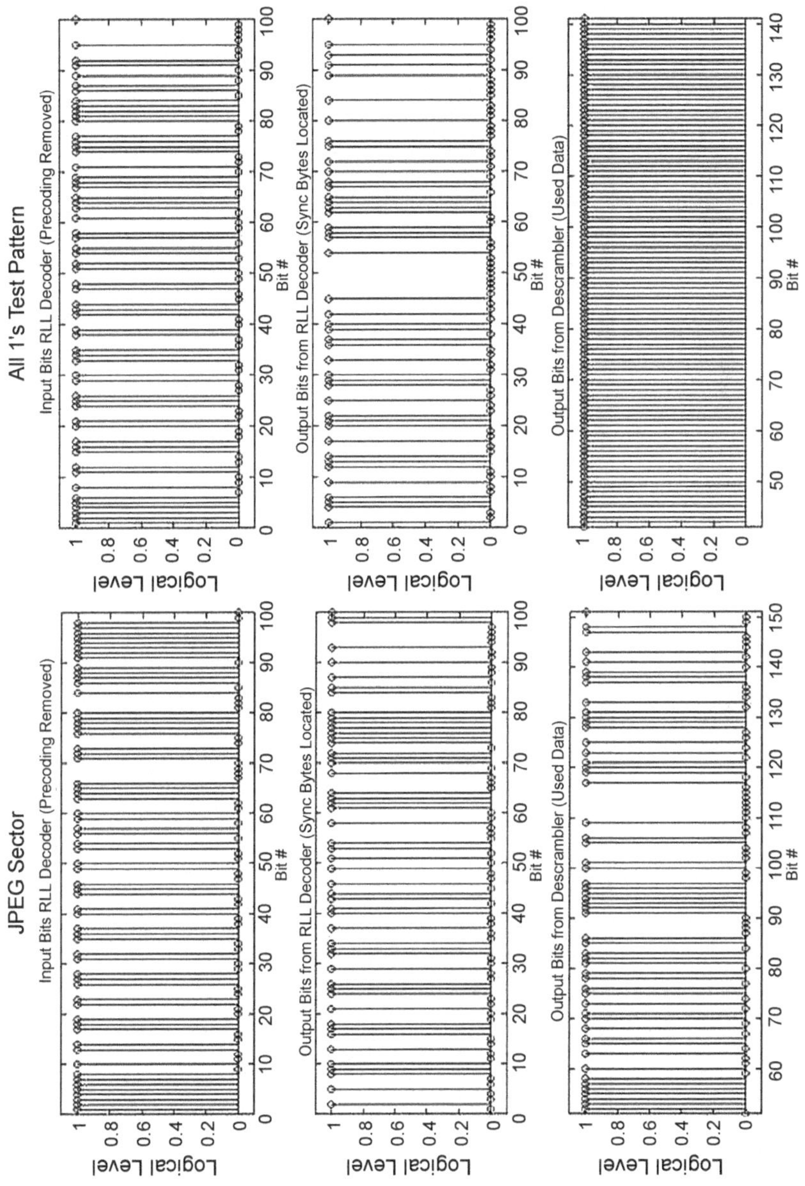

FIGURE 7.10 The effect of the scrambler.

7.4 SELECTIVE DATA RETRIEVAL

There has been an exponential growth in the number of files stored in modern hard disk drives. Factors contributing to this trend include the dramatic increase in the storage capacity of hard disk drives, the acceleration in the migration from paper-based to electronics-based storage by businesses, the increasing popularity of e-commerce and the use of broadband technology for downloading content from the Internet onto hard drives. However, not every file on the hard disks is equally valuable. Some files are more important than others. For example, a graduate student's dissertation file stored in Microsoft Word format is much more valuable than the Microsoft Word software itself because the latter is easily replaceable or can be reinstalled. From a practical perspective it is very important to allocate the time and resources to the retrieval of particular files that are of most significance to the users. It is thus very important to have the capability to selectively retrieve particular desirable files on hard disks mounted on a spin-stand by recovering the file directories first. In this way, one does not need to scan the whole disk surface just to recover one file. Instead, the particular files to be recovered can be selected from the recovered directory structures for recovery.

We have performed experiments on selective data retrieval by recovering the directory listings of a hard disk. In one particular experiment, a hard disk was first formatted in FAT32 format where each logical address is represented by 32 bits. Then four directories were created in the root directory: *DOCUMENT*, *Patent*, *Piezo*, and *PUBLIC*. Different subdirectories were then created and files were written to those subdirectories. Then the hard disk was removed from its native drive and mounted on the spin-stand. Using the decoding algorithm described above, we first went to the first sector of the first track to decode the master boot record (MBR). The decoded MBR gave us the information about the location and size of the boot sector of the partition of this drive. Next, we went to the boot sector of the partition to decode the information there, which in turn told us where the two copies of the file allocation tables (FATs) were. From the FAT, after decoding its entries, we were able to know the location of the root directory. Then we went to the root directory to decode the entries there and we obtained *DOCUMENT*, *Patent*, *Piezo*, and *PUBLIC*, exactly as we wrote them. The root directory also contains information on subdirectories and files and, in this way, the complete directory structure of the whole disk can be mapped. Figure 7.11 shows the recovered root directory, the subdirectories under *DOCUMENT*, and the file names under the subdirectory *device manuals*.

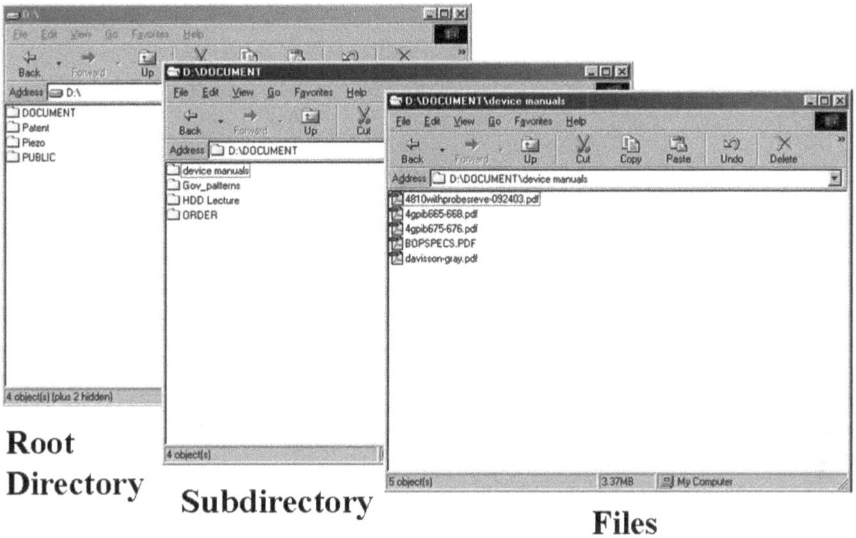

FIGURE 7.11 Recovered directory listings.

7.5 SUMMARY

Ex-situ spin-stand based data forensics has been demonstrated. Techniques of track-centering, track-following, ISI-removal, data detection, and data decoding have been developed and illustrated. It is conceivable that the proposed spin-stand based forensic technology is the most comprehensive noninvasive data technique available for the imaging and analysis of hard disk data. This technique can image and analyze data from drives not accessible by current standard practices. In addition, since the developed techniques are repeatable, reproducible, and verifiable, they afford unique capabilities in computer forensic applications for the acquisition, authentication, and analysis of the seized data for which the results are admissible to courts.

BIBLIOGRAPHY

[1] C. Tse, C. Krafft, I. Mayergoyz, P. McAvoy, C. Tseng, "Forensic recovery of hard disk data by using the spin-stand imaging technique," *Proc. of SPIE*, **5778**, 595 (2005).

[2] J. Bergmans, *Digital Baseband Transmission and Recording*, Kluwer Academic Publishing, 1996.

[3] S.X. Wang and A.M. Taratorin, *Magnetic Information Storage Technology*, p. xv, Academic Press, 1999.

[4] Z. Wu, *Coding and Iterative Detection for Magnetic Recording Channels*, Kluwer Academic Publishers, 2000.

[5] W. Peterson and E. Weldon, *Error-Correcting Codes*, Second Edition, MIT Press, 1972.

[6] B. Carrier, *File System Forensic Analysis*, Addison-Wesley, 2005.

CHAPTER 8

Spin-Stand Microscopy of Transverse Magnetization

In magnetic recording, the dramatic increase in areal density is being achieved by increasing track densities. This leads to much narrower tracks and smaller bit aspect ratios than in the past. In narrow tracks, end (fringe) effects are strongly pronounced and this results in appreciable transverse components of magnetization. In this chapter, the spin-stand microscopy technique is used to study the transverse magnetization profiles of recorded tracks. These profiles are investigated for different track widths and various recording frequencies. It is demonstrated that for narrow tracks the transverse magnetization component can be quite substantial and it significantly protrudes (extends) toward the track center. The conclusion is reached that the spin-stand microscopy technique can provide more comprehensive information concerning magnetization distributions on recorded tracks than is possible to obtain by using standard cross-profiling spin-stand routines.

8.1 VECTORIAL IMAGES OF MAGNETIZATION

In Chapter 3, we detailed the image reconstruction algorithm by which vectorial magnetization can be retrieved from the scanned scalar raw images. Here, we shall stress the important fact that the total (complete) magnetization distribution cannot in principle be retrieved from GMR readback signals (or MFM images). This is because the GMR measurements (or MFM images) are based on sensing the magnetic field produced by the magnetization distribution. However, this magnetic field is produced not by the total magnetization distribution but only by its curl-free component. In other words, the total magnetization can be decomposed into two parts: a curl-free part $\mathbf{M}_{\parallel}$ and a div-free part $\mathbf{M}_{\perp}$ [1–4]. This means that:

$$\mathbf{M} = \mathbf{M}_{\parallel} + \mathbf{M}_{\perp}, \tag{8.1}$$

where, respectively,

$$\nabla \times \mathbf{M}_{\|} = 0, \tag{8.2}$$

$$\nabla \cdot \mathbf{M}_{\perp} = 0. \tag{8.3}$$

By using Eqs. (8.1)–(8.3), the following boundary value problems for $\mathbf{M}_{\|}$ and $\mathbf{M}_{\perp}$ can be derived.

Vector field $\mathbf{M}_{\|}$ satisfies the equations:

$$\nabla \cdot \mathbf{M}_{\|} = \nabla \cdot \mathbf{M}, \tag{8.4}$$

$$\nabla \times \mathbf{M}_{\|} = 0 \tag{8.5}$$

inside the magnetic media and the following boundary condition

$$\mathbf{n} \cdot \mathbf{M}_{\|} = \mathbf{n} \cdot \mathbf{M} \tag{8.6}$$

on its boundary S.

Vector field $\mathbf{M}_{\perp}$ satisfies the equations:

$$\nabla \cdot \mathbf{M}_{\perp} = 0, \tag{8.7}$$

$$\nabla \times \mathbf{M}_{\perp} = \nabla \times \mathbf{M}, \tag{8.8}$$

inside magnetic media and the following boundary condition on its boundary

$$\mathbf{n} \times \mathbf{M}_{\perp} = \mathbf{n} \times (\mathbf{M} - \mathbf{M}_{\|}), \tag{8.9}$$

where $\mathbf{n}$ stands for a unit outward normal to S.

In order to establish the relationship between $\mathbf{M}_{\|}$ and $\mathbf{M}_{\perp}$, the three-dimensional spatial Fourier transform

$$\tilde{\mathbf{M}}(\mathbf{k}) = \iiint_{-\infty}^{\infty} \mathbf{M}(\mathbf{r}) e^{-i\mathbf{k}\cdot\mathbf{r}}\, d^3 r \tag{8.10}$$

can be used. Here, $\tilde{\mathbf{M}}$ is the Fourier transform of $\mathbf{M}$, $\mathbf{k}$ is the wavevector, and $\mathbf{r}$ and r are the position vector and its magnitude, respectively.

By applying the Fourier transform to Eqs. (8.2) and (8.3), we find:

$$\mathbf{k} \times \tilde{\mathbf{M}}_{\|} = 0, \tag{8.11}$$

and

$$\mathbf{k} \cdot \tilde{\mathbf{M}}_{\perp} = 0. \tag{8.12}$$

Therefore, the Fourier transforms of $\mathbf{M}_{\|}$ and $\mathbf{M}_{\perp}$ are, respectively, parallel and orthogonal to the wave vector $\mathbf{k}$. This motivates the choice of the subscripts $\|$ and $\perp$ in the notations of the curl-free and the div-free components of magnetization, respectively. From Eqs. (8.11) and (8.12), one can readily establish the local orthogonality condition for the curl-free and div-free components of magnetization in $\mathbf{k}$ space:

$$\tilde{\mathbf{M}}_{\|} \cdot \tilde{\mathbf{M}}_{\perp} = 0. \tag{8.13}$$

It can be shown that these two components of magnetization are orthogonal in an integral sense in the real space as well. The latter means that:

$$\iiint_V \mathbf{M}_{\|} \cdot \mathbf{M}_{\perp} \, dv = 0, \tag{8.14}$$

where V represents the finite volume of the magnetic media. The above formula can be proved by using Eqs. (8.2), (8.3), and (8.6). Since $\mathbf{M}_{\|}$ is curl-free, it can be expressed as the gradient of a scalar function:

$$\mathbf{M}_{\|} = \nabla \phi. \tag{8.15}$$

Substituting (8.15) into (8.14) yields:

$$\begin{aligned} &\iiint_V (\nabla \phi) \cdot \mathbf{M}_{\perp} \, dv \\ &= \iiint_V \nabla \cdot (\phi \mathbf{M}_{\perp}) \, dv - \iiint_V \phi (\nabla \cdot \mathbf{M}_{\perp}) \, dv. \end{aligned} \tag{8.16}$$

According to Eq. (8.3), the second term on the right side of Eq. (8.16) is equal to zero. By using the divergence theorem, the first term on the right hand side can be written as follows:

$$\iiint_V \nabla \cdot (\phi \mathbf{M}_{\perp}) \, dv = \oint_S \phi (\mathbf{n} \cdot \mathbf{M}_{\perp}) \, ds. \tag{8.17}$$

From Eqs. (8.1) and (8.6) it follows that:

$$\mathbf{n} \cdot \mathbf{M}_{\perp} = 0. \tag{8.18}$$

This implies that the volume integral in (7.17) is equal to zero, and this concludes the proof of orthogonality property (8.14).

It can be demonstrated [1–3] that only the curl-free part $\mathbf{M}_{\parallel}$ creates the magnetic field and, consequently, only this part can be sensed through MR measurement (or MFM imaging for that matter). Indeed, the magnetic field $\mathbf{H}$ and magnetic flux density $\mathbf{B}$ created by a magnetized object V^{+} satisfy the following equations:

$$\nabla \times \mathbf{H}^{\pm} = 0, \tag{8.19}$$

$$\nabla \cdot \mathbf{B}^{\pm} = 0 \tag{8.20}$$

and boundary conditions

$$\mathbf{n} \times \left(\mathbf{H}^{+} - \mathbf{H}^{-}\right) = 0, \tag{8.21}$$

$$\mathbf{n} \cdot \left(\mathbf{B}^{+} - \mathbf{B}^{-}\right) = 0, \tag{8.22}$$

where, as before, $\mathbf{n}$ is the vector of unit outward normal to the boundary S of V^{+}.

In the above formulas, superscripts "+" and "−" refer to the physical quantities inside and outside V^{+}, respectively. Thus, the constitutive equations for $\mathbf{B}^{+}$ and $\mathbf{B}^{-}$ are as follows:

$$\mathbf{B}^{+} = \mu_0\left(\mathbf{H}^{+} + \mathbf{M}\right), \tag{8.23}$$

$$\mathbf{B}^{-} = \mu_0 \mathbf{H}^{-}. \tag{8.24}$$

Now, let us assume that there exists only divergence-free component of magnetization:

$$\mathbf{M} = \mathbf{M}_{\perp} \quad \text{and} \quad \mathbf{M}_{\parallel} = 0. \tag{8.25}$$

Then, according to Eq. (8.4) and boundary condition (8.6), we find:

$$\nabla \cdot \mathbf{M} = 0, \tag{8.26}$$

$$\mathbf{n} \times \mathbf{M} = 0. \tag{8.27}$$

Next, by substituting the constitutive relations (8.23) and (8.24) into Eqs. (8.20) and boundary condition (8.22) and taking into account formulas (8.26) and (8.27), the boundary value problem (8.19)–(8.22) can be easily transformed to the following form:

$$\nabla \times \mathbf{H}^{\pm} = 0, \tag{8.28}$$

$$\nabla \cdot \mathbf{H}^{\pm} = 0, \tag{8.29}$$

$$\mathbf{n} \times \left(\mathbf{H}^{+} - \mathbf{H}^{-}\right) = 0, \tag{8.30}$$

$$\mathbf{n} \cdot \left(\mathbf{H}^{+} - \mathbf{H}^{-}\right) = 0. \tag{8.31}$$

The last boundary value problem is homogeneous (i.e. there are no sources) and, for this reason, it can be concluded that

$$\mathbf{H}^{-} \equiv 0 \tag{8.32}$$

in the entire space.

The rigorous mathematical proof that formula (8.32) follows from Eqs. (8.28)–(8.31) completely parallels the proof of the uniqueness theorem in electrostatics and, for this reason, it is omitted here.

Thus, it is demonstrated that only the curl-free part $\mathbf{M}_{\parallel}$ creates the magnetic field. The part $\mathbf{M}_{\parallel}$ is the only relevant one as far as magnetic recording is concerned. This is because the curl-free part, $\mathbf{M}_{\parallel}$, stores the information that can be read back by sensing magnetic fields. The last statement can be illustrated by an example of a dc erased track (see Fig. 8.1). In this example, there exists nonzero magnetization within the track. This track, however, does not produce any external magnetic field. That is because the magnetization within the track is divergence free (but not curl free). In other words, during the dc erasure procedure, the curl-free magnetization on the track is transformed into the div-free magnetization.

It is interesting to note that the div-free part, $\mathbf{M}_{\perp}$, can be imaged by using the Lorentz transmission microscopy [2,4], which is sensitive to $\mathbf{M}_{\perp}$ rather than to $\mathbf{M}_{\parallel}$. In this sense, the Lorentz transmission microscopy is complementary to imaging techniques based on the sensing of magnetic fields. To demonstrate this, consider an electron moving in the z direction, perpendicular to a thin magnetized film. Newton's equation of electron motion within the magnetized film can be written as follows:

$$\frac{d\mathbf{p}}{dt} = q\mathbf{v} \times \mathbf{B}, \tag{8.33}$$

where $\mathbf{p}$ is an electron momentum, while q is the electron charge.

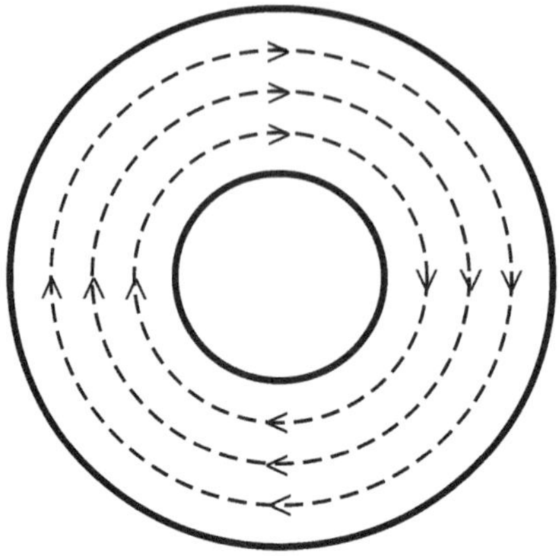

FIGURE 8.1 An example of a dc erased track.

The transverse component $\mathbf{p}_\perp$ of momentum is of interest in the Lorentz transmission microscopy. Equation (8.33) for this component is reduced to the form:

$$\frac{\mathrm{d}\mathbf{p}_\perp}{\mathrm{d}t} = q v_z \, \mathbf{e_z} \times \mathbf{B}, \tag{8.34}$$

where $\mathbf{e_z}$ is the unit vector along the z-axis. Since the film is thin, it can be assumed that the tangential (in-plane) components of **B**, **M** and **H** are uniform across the film thickness, i.e. they do not depend on z. For this reason, the transverse component of momentum acquired during the time T of the electron motion through the magnetized film can be derived as follows:

$$\mathbf{p}_\perp = \int_0^T \frac{\mathrm{d}\mathbf{p}_\perp}{\mathrm{d}t} = q(\mathbf{e_z} \times \mathbf{B}) \int_0^T v_z \, \mathrm{d}t = qh(\mathbf{e_z} \times \mathbf{B}), \tag{8.35}$$

$$\mathbf{p}_\perp = qh(\mathbf{e_z} \times \mathbf{B}) = \mu_0 qh \, \mathbf{e_z} \times (\mathbf{H} + \mathbf{M}), \tag{8.36}$$

where h is the film thickness.

Now, it is easy to find that

$$\nabla \times \mathbf{p}_\perp = qh \, \mathbf{e_z} \nabla \cdot \mathbf{B} = 0, \tag{8.37}$$

while

$$\nabla \cdot \mathbf{p}_\perp = -\mu_0 qh \, \mathbf{e_z} \cdot \nabla \times \mathbf{M} = -\mu_0 qh \, \mathbf{e_z} \cdot \nabla \times \mathbf{M}_\perp. \tag{8.38}$$

Thus, the vector field $\mathbf{p}_\perp$ is fully controlled by $\mathbf{M}_\perp$. For this reason, the Lorentz transmission microscopy, which is based on $\mathbf{p}_\perp$ measurements, may reveal only the divergence-free component $\mathbf{M}_{\perp}$ of the film magnetization.

It is apparent from the above discussion that the spin-stand microscopy technique has the ability to produce vectorial images of the curl-free (field producing) part of magnetization. In this way, the quantitative information on transverse and longitudinal components of $\mathbf{M}_{\parallel}$ can be obtained.

8.2 EXPERIMENTAL RESULTS

In our experiments, the distribution of the transverse component of magnetization has been examined for different track widths and various recording frequencies (densities). Specifically, in order to examine the effect of track width on the transverse magnetization, write heads produced by TDK (AMR heads) were used to write relatively wide tracks, while the heads produced by ALPS (GMR heads) were used to write relatively narrow tracks. Furthermore, in order to investigate the effect of linear density on the transverse magnetization, both of these heads were used to write periodic magnetization patterns of frequencies ranging from 2 MHz to 8 MHz.

Figure 8.2 shows the (reconstructed) images of M_x and M_y, as well as the vectorial plot of $\mathbf{M}_{\parallel}$ for a 2 MHz F6 pattern written by a TDK head. The shade contrast of the reconstructed images of M_x has been deliberately saturated in order to make the binary nature of the pattern apparent. It is apparent from Fig. 8.2 that $\mathbf{M}_{\parallel}$ is fairly strong along the length of the bit and is predominantly longitudinal except at the track edges where the strong presence of M_y bends the field lines of magnetization outward and makes them cease to be longitudinal. Since the magnetization lines are exactly parallel to the along-track direction at the track center, M_x is strongest at the track center, while M_y is zero there due to the odd symmetry.

Figure 8.3 presents the (reconstructed) images of the magnetization for a 2 MHz F6 pattern written by using a GMR head. Figure 8.3 shows that the magnetization lines begin to curve outward at a distance closer to the track center than in the previous case. In other words, the relative value of M_y with respect to M_x is increased with decreasing track width. This increase in M_y can be explained qualitatively by using an electrostatic analogy. The virtual magnetic charges located at transitions of digital patterns can (roughly speaking) be likened to electric charges at the surfaces of a parallel plate capacitor. When the track width is reduced while the frequency of the signal remains the same, the bit aspect ratio is de-

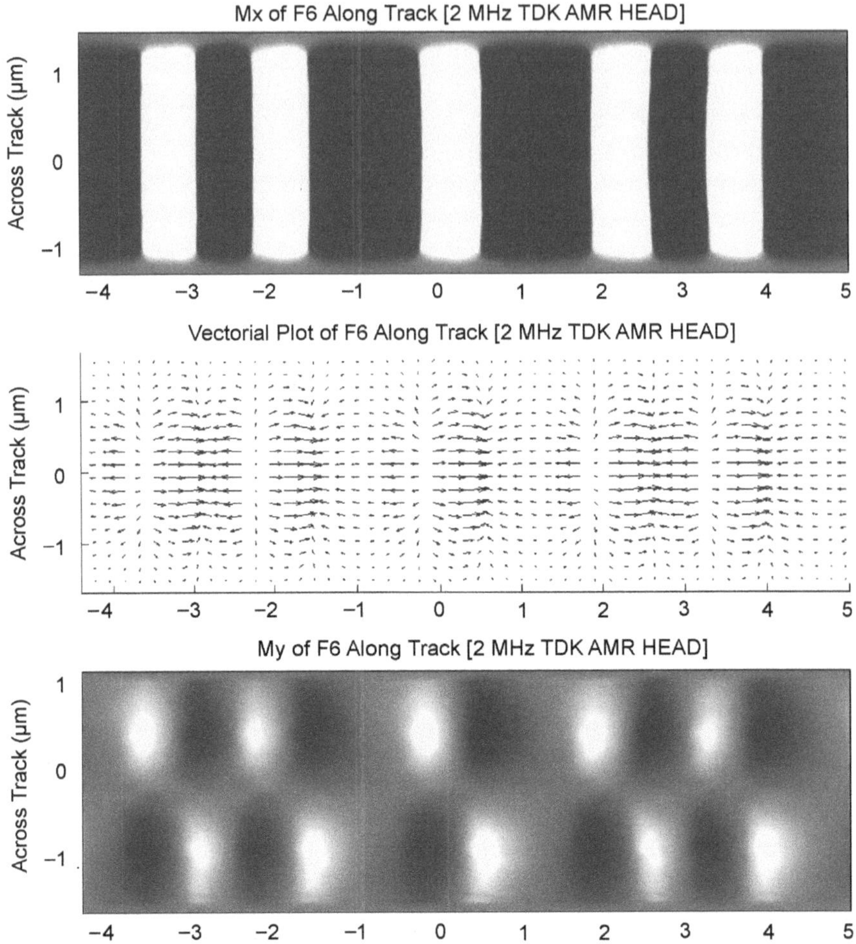

FIGURE 8.2 The magnetization distribution of a pattern signal written by a TDK head (wide track).

creased. This produces the equivalent effect of reducing the geometric dimensions of the plates of the parallel-plate capacitor while maintaining the same separation between the plates. As a result, the electric field lines are not curved only over a small region around the center of the plates, and large fringing fields are formed and extended away from the edges. A similar phenomenon occurs when the track width is reduced. For an easy comparison between Figs. 8.2 and 8.3, the vectorial magnetization of the wider and narrower track has been superimposed onto the corre-

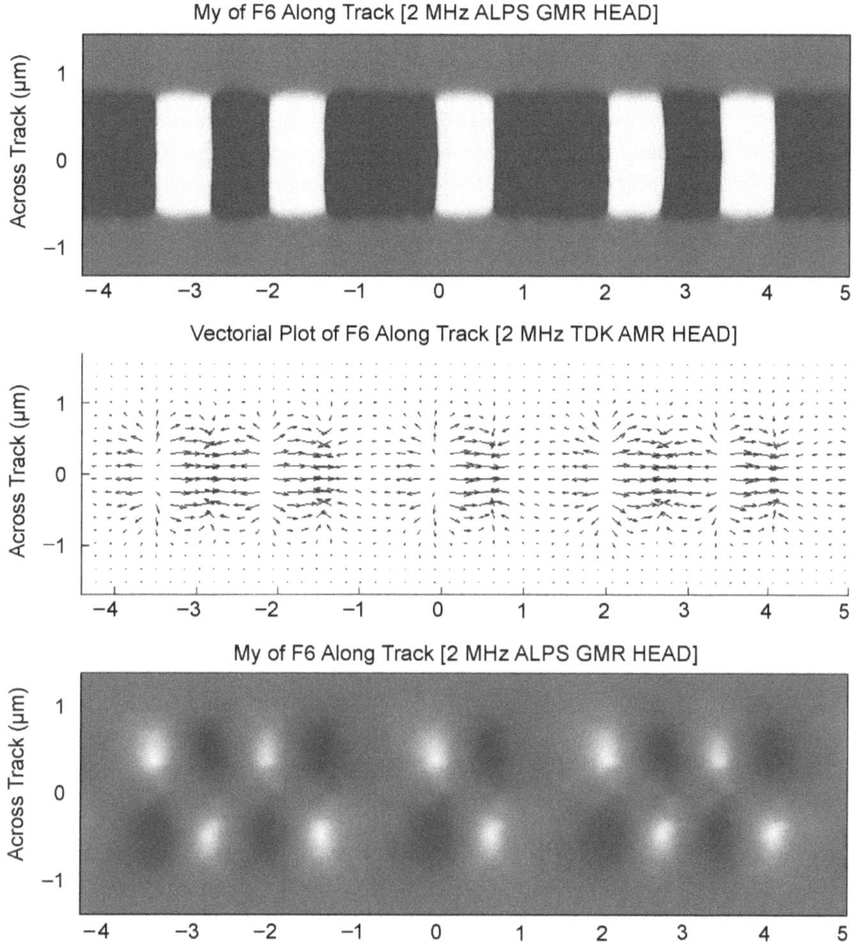

FIGURE 8.3 The magnetization distribution of a pattern signal written by an ALPS head (narrower track).

sponding reconstructed images of M_x of the F6 pattern, which is shown in the top and bottom plot of Fig. 8.4, respectively.

In order to obtain quantitative information about the transverse magnetization component for different track widths and various recording frequencies, it is instructive to consider the "line" plots of M_x and M_y across the tracks. Figure 8.5 presents such plots that give the relative magnitudes of M_y with respect to M_x for different track widths written with signal frequencies of 2 MHz, 4 MHz, and 8 MHz. Several observations are

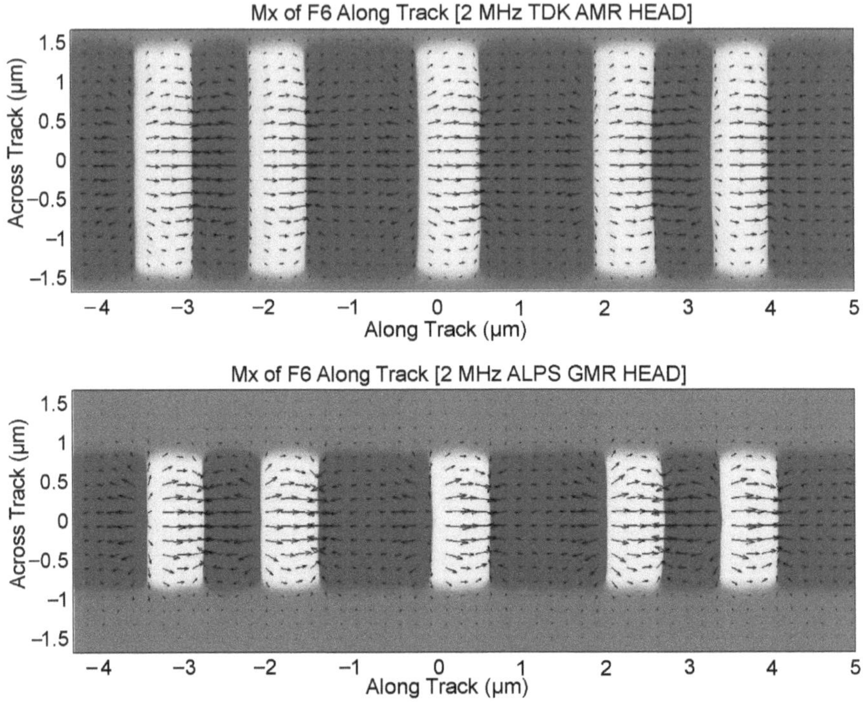

FIGURE 8.4 The vectorial magnetization superimposed onto the reconstructed images of M_x of F6 pattern.

deemed noteworthy concerning Fig. 8.5. First, the relative magnitude of M_y is higher for the narrower tracks, as explained previously. Second, for the same track width, the relative magnitude of M_y is lower with increasing frequencies. This again can be explained by using the parallel-plate capacitor analogy that suggests that as the spacing between the plates is decreased, the field lines are more parallel and fringing is less. Finally, in the case of narrower tracks, M_y significantly protrudes toward the center of the tracks, as opposed to the case where M_y is concentrated at the edges when the track widths are larger. The line plots of M_y may provide an alternative way of determining the track width of written tracks. While the interval of the cross-track profile subtended at full width at half maximum (FWHM) is a common way of approximating the width of a written track, it is apparent from Fig. 8.5 that the effective track width may also be deduced by measuring the distance between the peak and trough of M_y. The track width measured by this alternative method is slightly smaller than that measured at FWHM.

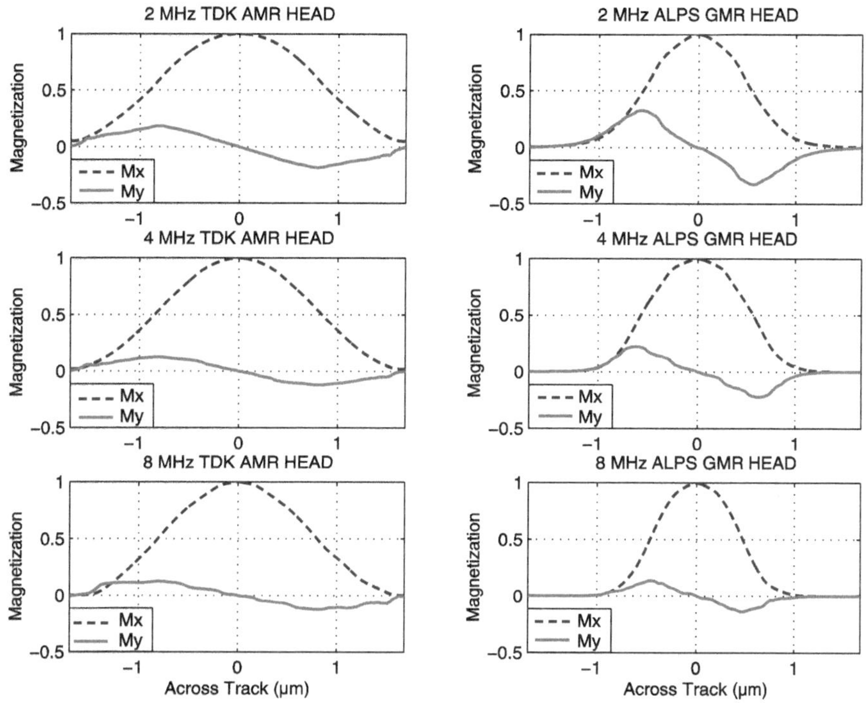

FIGURE 8.5 Line plots of M_x and M_y across tracks for different track widths and various recording frequencies.

In order to show how the transverse component of the magnetization behaves in even narrower tracks, we performed additional experiments and used an advanced GMR head with read and write width 50% smaller than the one used in Fig. 8.3. The same F6 pattern was written and the reconstructed images of the magnetization for this pattern is shown in Fig. 8.6. It is clearly seen from the middle plot of Fig. 8.6 that except at the track center, the magnitude of the transverse component of the magnetization is substantial.

8.3 SUMMARY

We have successfully imaged the transverse magnetization components of recorded tracks. The ability of the spin-stand microscopy technique to extract the transverse component of magnetization may find interesting applications in magnetic recording. For example, the imaging of M_y can

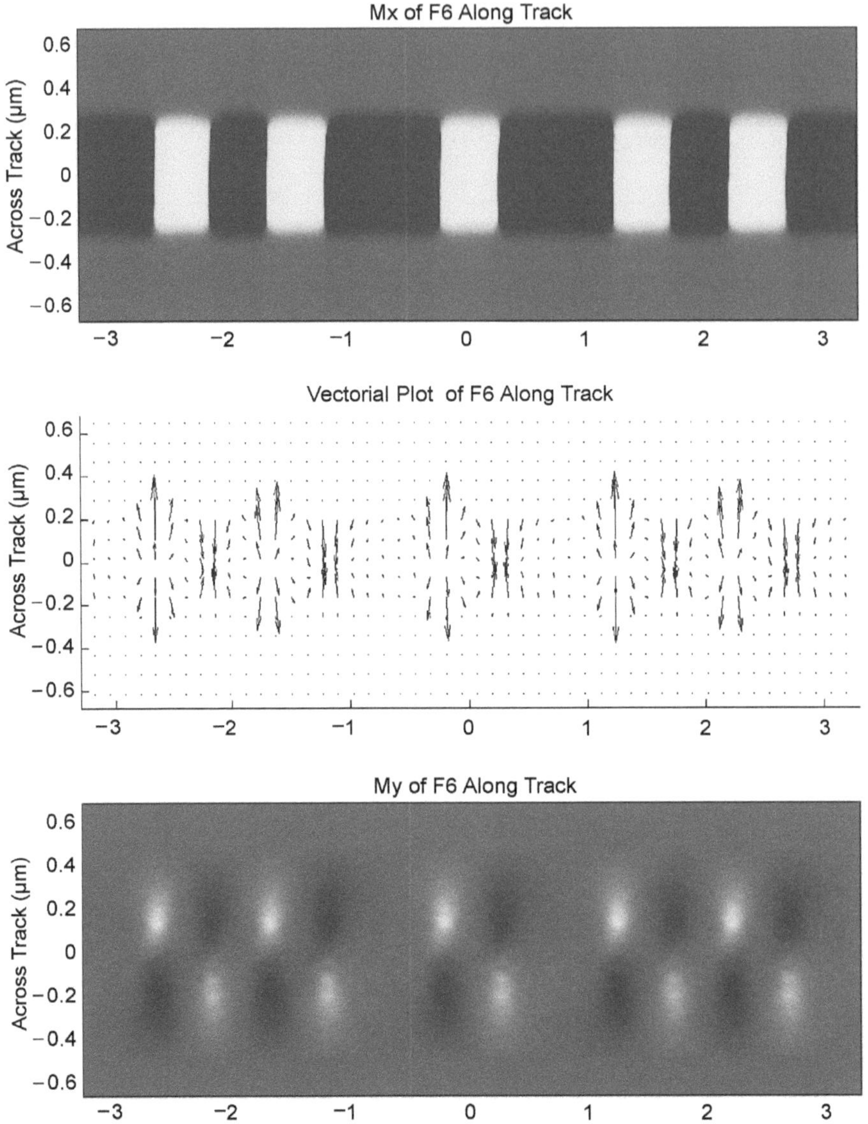

FIGURE 8.6 The magnetization distribution of F6 pattern written by an advanced GMR head.

help study the phenomenon of "cross-talk" between tracks that has become a challenge to high density magnetic recording as the inter-track spacing is increasingly reduced. Also, by studying the fringing distribution produced by M_y, head design engineers may design better heads that write data with less fringing. In conclusion, the spin-stand microscopy technique can provide both qualitative and quantitative information on magnetization distributions on recorded tracks that is not readily derivable from currently available standard cross-profiling spin-stand routines.

BIBLIOGRAPHY

[1] R. Madabhushi, "The Reconstruction of Magnetic Force Microscopy Images and its Application to High Density Magnetic Recording," Ph.D. dissertation, University of Maryland, 1996.

[2] I.A. Beardsley, "Reconstruction of the magnetization in a thin film by a combination of Lorentz microscopy and external field measurements," *IEEE Trans. Magn.*, **25**, 671 (1989).

[3] I.D. Mayergoyz, A.A. Adly, R.D. Gomez, and E.R. Burke, "Magnetization image reconstruction from magnetic force scanning microscopy images," *J. Appl. Phys.*, **73**, 5799 (1993).

[4] D.R. Fredkin and S. Shtrikman, "Magnetostatic analog for the calculation of phase contours in electron holography of magnetic films," *IEEE Trans. Magn.*, **24**, 2105 (1988).

CHAPTER 9

Spin-Stand Study of Data-Dependent Thermal Relaxations

Thermal magnetic relaxations of recorded data (magnetic viscosity) have been the focus of considerable experimental research lately [1–11]. In this chapter, we report on thermal relaxations of magnetization patterns observed for over 40 hours for magnetic media with different coercivities. Special averaging techniques are presented to counteract the temporal sensitivity variations of the read heads. Thermal relaxation measurements were performed on first and third spatial harmonics of magnetization patterns for different recording densities. It was observed (as expected) that the third spatial harmonics exhibits steeper decay than the first harmonics. In this chapter, we also report on the spatial and vectorial characterization of thermal relaxations of recorded magnetization patterns by using the spin-stand microscopy technique. It is demonstrated that the spatially inhomogeneous and vectorial nature of thermal relaxations of recorded patterns may result in temporal track broadening. It is found that this temporal track broadening is more pronounced for disks with higher coercivities.

9.1 SIGNIFICANCE OF THERMAL RELAXATIONS

It is widely known that the data stored in magnetic hard disk drives gradually deteriorate with time. This deterioration of stored data may result in the gradual loss of the recorded information, although the disk drive system as a whole appears fully functional. This time deterioration of stored information may reveal itself in the appearance of bad sectors on the drives. These bad sectors grow in numbers over time and are updated by the so called *G-lists* (or *grown defect lists*) in the disk firmware. Sectors are marked as bad when the sector error correction codes (ECCs) are overwhelmed and cannot adequately correct read data errors. The appearance of bad sectors can be especially devastating when those sectors contain critical operational information such as the master boot record, file allocation table, master file table, or firmware information such as G-lists. Thus, the time deterioration of stored information severely compromises the integrity of the storage systems and it negatively affects both the original data and its backup.

It is also known that the four key figures of merit of modern magnetic disk drives are data density, data access time, data transfer rate, and cost, while reliability is of secondary concern in the *cut-throat* market competition between hard drive manufacturers. This is consistent with the fact that magnetic disk drives are considered as commodity products and disk drive manufacturers expect users either to replace or upgrade their storage systems every two to three years. Since the time deterioration of stored information is a long-term phenomenon, and it is only one of the reliability issues of hard disk drives, it is usually not thoroughly tested during the relatively short product development and manufacturing phase of hard disk drives due to cost concerns. This is reflected in the manufacturers' warranty of magnetic disk drives, which can be as short as one year and never exceeds five years. This generic issue of insufficient reliability of modern hard drives has long been recognized and expensive backup systems have been developed. These backup systems utilize error correction codes, backup software, and sophisticated hardware configuration of several levels of RAID (Redundant Array of Independent Disks). However, existing backup systems are primarily designed to protect data against logical, electrical, or mechanical failures of the disk constituents, while the temporal degradation of stored information is usually not adequately addressed for similar reasons as in the case of hard disk drive manufacturing. In addition, these backup systems rely heavily on ECCs and various schemes of data replication and redundancy to protect the data. Nevertheless, these approaches are not completely foolproof. For instance, not all errors can be detected by ECCs and not all detected errors can be corrected. All the facts presented above clearly highlight the intrinsic risks involved in using disk-based storage/backup systems as massive and archival storage devices. They point to the importance of research and development efforts to counteract the long-term degradation of recorded data in magnetic storage systems.

9.2 INTRINSIC MAGNETIC THERMAL RELAXATIONS

The main reason for deterioration of stored information is magnetic thermal relaxations. The essence of these relaxations is gradual temporal variations of magnetization in magnetic media in spite of temporally permanent external conditions. These temporal variations are caused by the multiplicity of metastable states and the presence of intrinsic thermal noise in magnetic materials. On the one hand, the multiplicity of metastable states is at the very foundation of magnetic data storage where specific metastable states are used to store different digital information. On the other hand, this multiplicity makes the stored data vulnerable to intrinsic thermal noise. Indeed, at temporally permanent external conditions, random thermal perturbations cause the magnetization in storage media to move from one metastable state to another. This phenomenon is especially pronounced for high density recording where demagnetizing fields approach the coercivity of the magnetic materials. These temporal variations of magnetization driven by the internal thermal perturbations are the essence of thermal relaxations and they compromise the long-term reliability and integrity of stored data.

Experimental studies of thermal relaxations reported in the literature are mostly performed for magnetic samples subject to external magnetic fields that are constant in time and spatially uniform. In these experiments, the applied fields and sample magnetization are usually aligned, while demagnetizing fields are negligible. These experimental studies are usually carried out by using magnetometers [1–3] and they reveal the *intrinsic* thermal relaxation properties of magnetic materials that are scalar in nature.

As previously mentioned, at temporally permanent external conditions, large deviations of internal random (thermal) perturbations cause the magnetization in the storage media to move from one metastable state to another. This results in slow time variations of magnetization, which are the essence of thermal relaxations. These temporal variations of magnetization are usually characterized by the following *intermediate* "$\ln t$" asymptotics:

$$M(t) \sim M_0 - S(H, T) \ln t, \tag{9.1}$$

where $M(t)$ is the magnetization at time t, M_0 is the initial magnetization, $S(H, T)$ is the viscosity coefficient which depends on the magnetic field H, temperature T, and the history of magnetic field variations. The viscosity coefficient $S(H, T)$ can be construed as the (logarithmic) rate of thermal relaxations of magnetization. The term "intermediate" asymptotics means that formula (9.1) describes fairly well the long-time behavior of magnetization, but it does not describe satisfactorily the ultimate (at $t \to \infty$) value of magnetization. In other words, the asymptotic behavior (9.1) breaks down in *very* long time, at which $\ln t$ diverges.

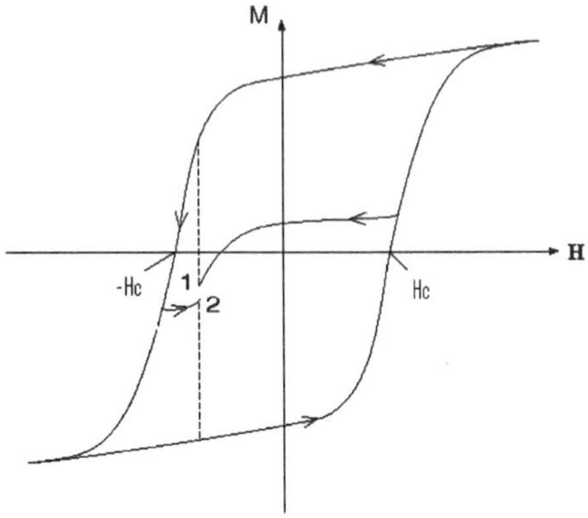

FIGURE 9.1

Next, we shall report on the study of intrinsic thermal relaxations of magnetization for high-coercivity thin-film CoCrPt recording media by using a vibrating sample magnetometer (VSM) with a temperature-controlled furnace (model Micro Mag 3900 of Princeton Measurements Corporation). First, experiments were performed to clearly demonstrate that thermal relaxations and the viscosity coefficient strongly depend on the past history of magnetic-field variations. To this end, the thermal relaxation measurements were conducted for two distinct states of magnetic material, which had almost the same values of initial magnetization achieved at the same value of the external magnetic field but correspond to two different past histories of magnetic-field variations. These two distinct states and their histories are shown in Fig. 9.1. Figure 9.2 presents the observed time variations of magnetization for the above two states plotted on $\ln t$ scale. It is apparent from Fig. 9.2 that the above two magnetization variations have different (in magnitude and sign) viscosity coefficients. This clearly reveals the strong dependence of the viscosity coefficients on the past history.

In subsequent experiments, the viscosity coefficients were measured as a function of magnetic field H for various temperatures T for the same past histories. Namely, specimens were first driven into the state of positive saturation by applying sufficiently strong external magnetic fields and then the magnetic field was gradually decreased to a desired value at which thermal relaxation measurements were performed. Thus, the thermal relaxation measurements were performed for the states corresponding to the points on the descending branch of the major hysteresis loops. For various fixed values of T, viscosity coefficients $S(H, T)$ are "bell-shaped" functions of H with the maximum near (but not necessary

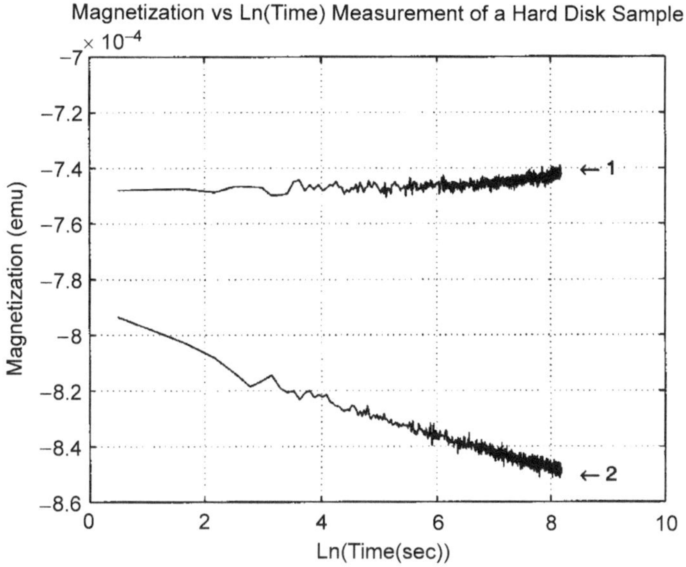

FIGURE 9.2

equal to) the coercivity. These bell-shaped curves measured for two different samples are shown in Figs. 9.3 and 9.4. The samples had coercivities of about 1600 and 2600 Oe at temperature of 25 °C, respectively. The material of the second sample (with higher coercivity) had a small value of remanence ($M_r t \approx 0.85 \times 10^3$ emu/cm^2). For this reason and in order to increase the signal level, the second sample was formed by stacking several layers of the same material.

By using the experimental data shown in Figs. 9.3 and 9.4, the hypothesis that $S(H, T)$ admits the following scaling:

$$S(H, T) = S_{\max}(T) f\left(\frac{H}{H^*(T)}\right) \tag{9.2}$$

was tested. In the above formula, $S_{\max}(T)$ is the maximum of the viscosity coefficient as a function of T, while $H^*(T)$ is the value of the magnetic field at which $S_{\max}$ is achieved. The last formula suggests that S vs H curves experimentally measured for different temperatures must collapse onto one universal curve when plotted in coordinates:

$$s = \frac{S}{S_{\max}(T)}, \qquad h = \frac{H}{H^*(T)}. \tag{9.3}$$

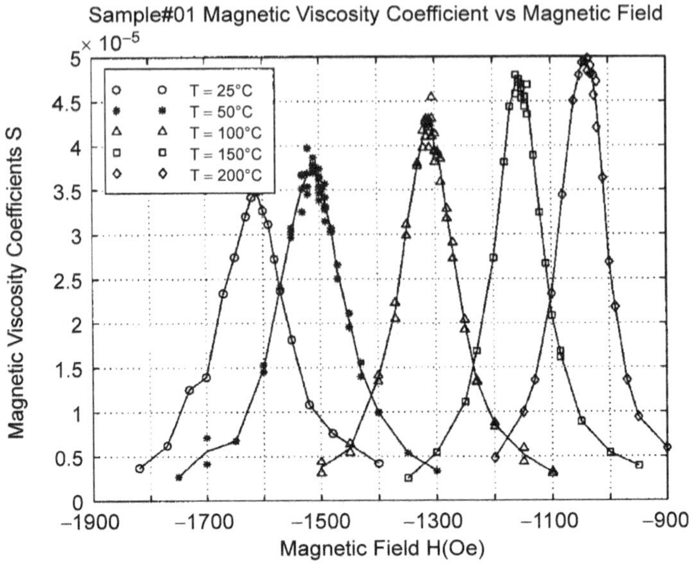

FIGURE 9.3

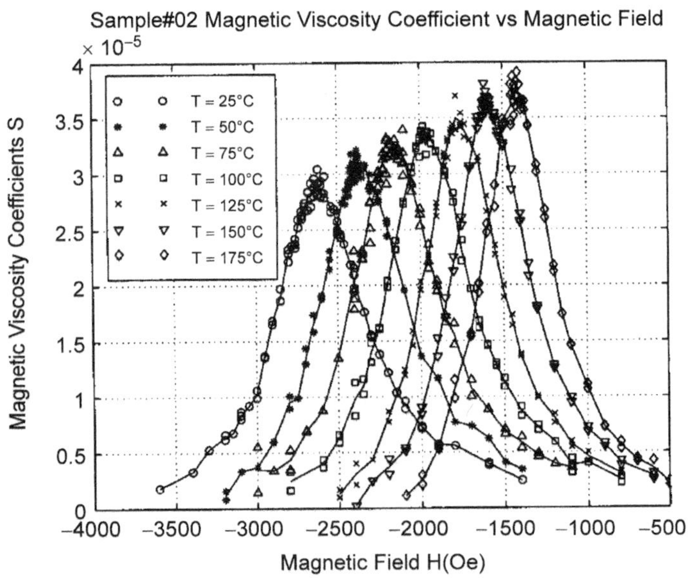

FIGURE 9.4

This phenomenon of data collapse is the principal significance of scaling and its occurrence was observed for the collected experimental data.

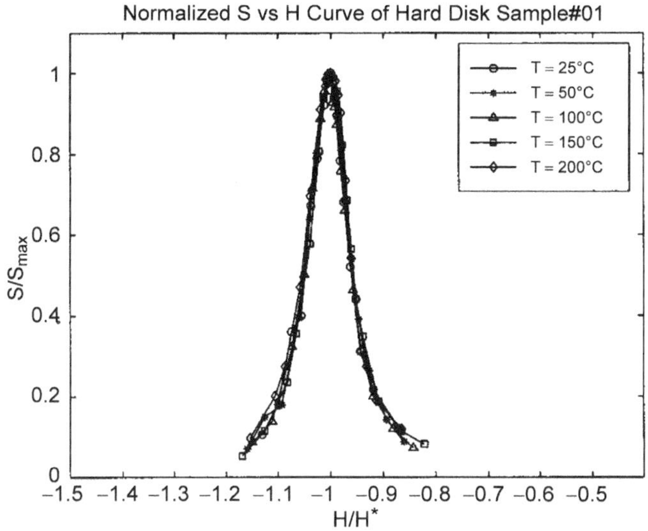

FIGURE 9.5

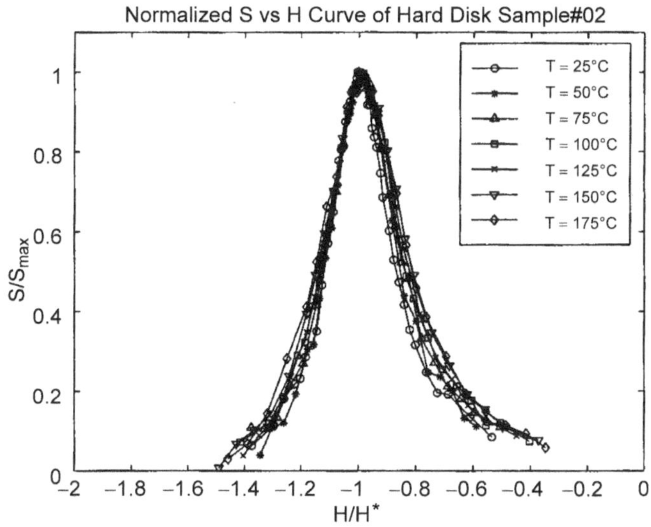

FIGURE 9.6

Namely, by performing the scaling described above, it was found that the curves shown in Figs. 9.3 and 9.4 practically collapsed onto the single curves shown in Figs. 9.5 and 9.6, respectively.

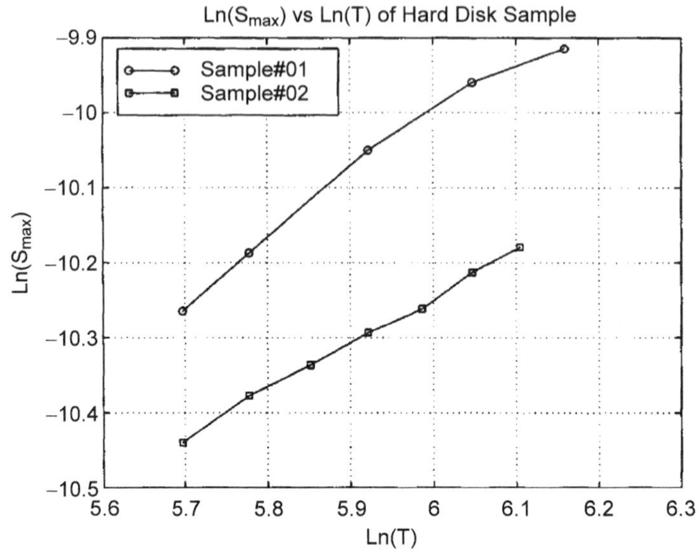

FIGURE 9.7

In addition, the following scaling hypotheses:

$$S_{\max}(T) = aT^{\alpha}, \tag{9.4}$$

$$H^{*}(T) = bT^{\beta}, \tag{9.5}$$

were also experimentally tested and verified with sufficient accuracy. The results of this testing for samples 1 and 2 are shown in Figs. 9.7 and 9.8, respectively. It was found that, for thin-film recording media with coercivity below 2000 Oe, the exponent β was fairly close to -1. For recording media with coercivity above 2000 Oe, deviations from the above value of β were observed.

Hypotheses (9.4) and (9.5) along with the formula (9.2) lead to the following *self-similar* expression for the viscosity coefficient

$$S(H, T) = aT^{\alpha} f\left(\frac{H}{bT^{\beta}}\right). \tag{9.6}$$

The last formula (as well as formula (9.3)) reveals an interesting and peculiar mathematical structure of the viscosity coefficient as the function of two variables: H and T. The essence of this structure is that the normalized viscosity coefficient $S/S_{\max}$ is a function of one variable $h = H/H^{*}(T)$.

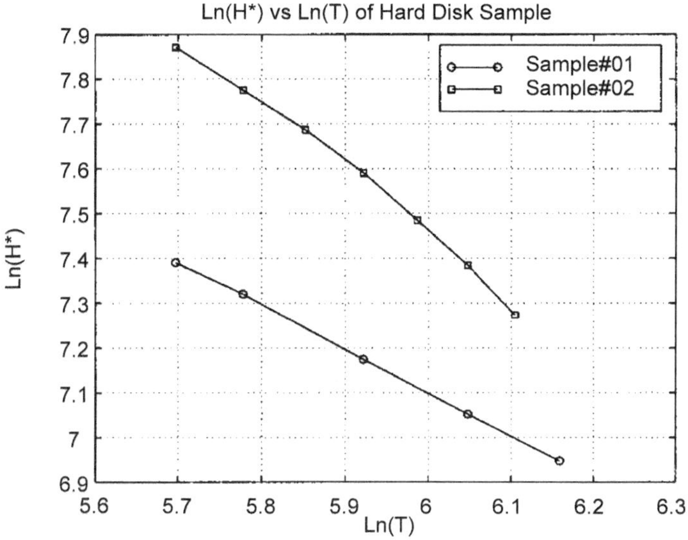

FIGURE 9.8

This structure is quite different from the traditional representation of $S(H, T)$ in terms of irreversible differentiable susceptibility; the representation that is mostly analyzed and discussed in the existing literature. The structure of $S(H, T)$ expressed by formula (9.6) is a direct and concise reflection of experimental observations and it is not based on any *ad hoc* assumptions.

The experimental evidence of scaling of $S(H, T)$ and data collapse has been presented here only for two samples. However, the described scaling and data collapse were observed for many samples as well.

Since thermal relaxations of magnetization are long-term phenomena at disk operating temperatures (usually between 35–40 °C), it is desirable to study these relaxations at elevated temperatures when the time rate of these relaxations is substantially increased. The immediate and crucial question is how to use the experimental data obtained at elevated temperatures for the prediction of long-term thermal relaxations at disk operating temperatures. It is clear that the experimentally observed phenomena of data collapse can be used for temperature scaling of thermal relaxation rates measured at elevated temperatures to predict the long-term thermal relaxations at normal temperatures.

The experimental results presented above reveal the *intrinsic* scalar thermal relaxations properties of magnetic materials. In storage applications, thermal relaxations of magnetization patterns recorded on hard disks are of interest. These are *data-dependent* thermal relaxations (DDTR) and they occur under quite different conditions than in the case of *intrinsic* thermal relaxations. First, the recording media are subject to strong local demagnetizing fields. These fields depend on recorded patterns and they vary with time due to the temporal deterioration of these patterns. Second, the demagnetizing fields are spatially nonuniform. As a result, DDTR occur with different local rates. Third, the local demagnetizing fields and magnetization are not aligned. Therefore, DDTR are inherently vectorial. Finally, DDTR are measured by using giant magneto-resistive (GMR) head. Signals in these heads are generated by magnetic fields produced by virtual magnetic charges that are proportional to the divergence of magnetization ($\nabla \cdot \vec{M}$). It is quite possible that, due to spatially inhomogeneous and vectorial nature of thermal relaxations, very small temporal changes in local magnetization may result in appreciable magnetic charges and substantial changes in GMR head readback signals. Indeed, on a magnetic media with recorded patterns, the demagnetizing field is significantly higher near the transitions of the recorded patterns and it decreases with distance from the transitions, as shown in Fig. 9.9. Being subject to a higher demagnetizing field than the *average* demagnetizing field along the bit, the transitions will exhibit faster thermal decay than other regions of the track. This *local* thermal viscosity around the transitions will in time broaden the width of the transitions, which has the effect of lowering the values of the higher order harmonics of the signal. This suggests that local thermal viscosity can be more efficiently observed by studying the decay of higher order harmonics. Since the read-back signal is roughly proportional to magnetic charges which are determined by the derivatives

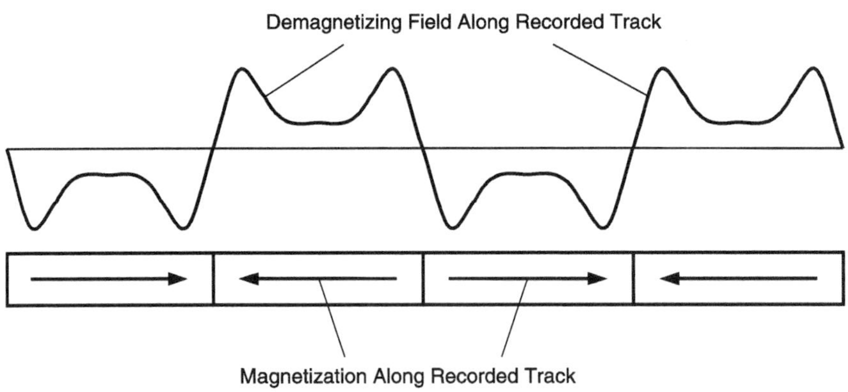

FIGURE 9.9 A schematic of spatial variations of demagnetizing field along recorded track.

of the magnetization, the broadening of the transitions due to local thermal viscosity leads to the reduction of the signal sensed by the read head, which in turn limits the achievable recording densities and affects the long term stability of recorded data.

9.3 EXPERIMENTAL STUDY OF DATA-DEPENDENT THERMAL RELAXATIONS

The main challenge faced in the GMR measurements of data-dependent viscosity is the problem of decoupling the temporal variations of sensitivity of giant-magnetoresistive (GMR) read heads from the magnetization relaxations being measured. This difficulty is further compounded when thermal relaxations (which are inherently analog phenomena) are observed for long time durations by using a spin-stand, a device mostly designed for short term digital characterizations of media and heads.

This explains why very few publications to date have reported spin-stand studies of thermal relaxations of recorded data for very long duration (24 hours and beyond). In the publications that did report long duration measurements, either the data points were widely spread out (see, for example, [5]) or there were only very few data points reported (see, for example, [6]) to ascertain conclusively the actual trend of decay. Furthermore, with an effort to accelerate the thermal decay rate and heighten the viscosity effects, many researchers have resorted to artificially thinning the magnetic layer of low coercivity disks in order to lower the remanence-thickness product ($M_r t$). In these experiments, magnetic media of very low coercivities (in the range of 500 Oe to 1500 Oe) were used. These coercivity values, however, are far removed from those of commercial hard drive disks (over 3000 Oe), thus calling into question the pertinence of the obtained results to thermal stability of recorded data in real-life situations.

In order to cope with the difficulties mentioned above, a number of experimental schemes have been developed in the literature to counteract the temporal sensitivity variations of GMR heads. In [8], for example, in order to calibrate the thermal relaxation measurements against the temporal sensitivity variations of the read head, a reference track that contained the same data to be observed was freshly written each time thermal relaxation measurements were taken. In order to calibrate the thermal relaxation measurements on the decaying track, which contained the data to be observed for thermal decay, the change in the magnitudes of the data on the reference track was subtracted from the magnitudes of the data on the decaying track. Rewriting reference tracks, however, may bring about write-head induced fluctuations to the read signals, which are not properly accounted for in the method. In addition, while the inductive write head is quite robust and does not suffer from the same degree of sensitivity variations as the read head, we have observed that small variations of the write field do exist. These performance variations of the write head, however small, may cause experimental errors since the magnitudes of these variations may be comparable with small thermal relaxation variations being measured.

Another experimental approach to calibrate the thermal relaxation measurements against temporal head sensitivity variations is through the use of "aged" reference tracks [4]. Instead of rewriting reference tracks each time thermal relaxation measurements were taken, these "aged" reference tracks were written tens of hours prior to the measurements on the decaying tracks so that the decay of the data on the reference tracks became negligible by the time measurements on the decaying tracks were started. Therefore, the data on the reference tracks can serve as monitors of the temporal head sensitivity variations and can be used to calibrate the thermal relaxation measurements. Calibration in this sense means that the calibrated signals are obtained by subtracting the change in the signals on the reference tracks from the signals on the decaying tracks. However, since some time elapsed between taking measurements on the reference tracks and the decaying tracks, this method cannot account for the short time scale read head sensitivity variations due to noise and temperature fluctuations.

Our approach to counteract the temporal head sensitivity variations is to use averaging of many consecutive thermal relaxation measurements performed immediately one after another (a variant of this approach has been reported in [9]). Our averaging method has the obvious advantage that short time scale read head sensitivity variations due to noise and temperature fluctuations can be greatly reduced. This is because the accumulated deterministic component of the signal is proportional to the number N of measurements taken, while the accumulated noise component of the signal is only proportional to $\sqrt{N}$. As a result, the act of signal averaging can significantly improve the signal to noise ratio (SNR).

In order to assess the relative merits of using "aged" reference tracks and using the averaging technique as viable means of calibration against head sensitivity variations, we performed the following experiment. Periodic square wave signals ("all ones" patterns) of density 0.4 kfc/mm (kilo flux change per millimeter) were written on a 1400 Oe disk (see Table 9.1 for disk parameters) using a GMR head. These square wave signals were used as reference tracks and were written 24 hours prior to the writing of the data on the "decaying" tracks. The decaying tracks contained the same

TABLE 9.1 Media parameters used in the data-dependent thermal relaxations measurements

Disk	Company	Coercivity H_c (Oe)	Remanence-thickness product $M_r t$ (memu/cm^2)
1	Komag	1400	1.58
2	Komag	2600	0.85
3	Komag	3100	0.71

data as on the reference tracks and were written minutes before the actual thermal relaxation measurements were started. Measurements were then made at different time instants such that the time intervals between these instants generally followed a logarithmic scale. In this experiment, there were 11 time intervals and the sum of these intervals spanned a duration of 53.6 hours.

At each instant of these measurements, data from both the reference tracks and decaying tracks were read back. Specifically, three types of measurements were made. The first type of measurement was made by using one-shot read-back signals from the decaying tracks; no averaging of any kind was performed. The second type of measurement was the averaging of many consecutive thermal relaxation read-back signals collected immediately one after another from the decaying tracks. The third type of measurement was the same as the second type except that the averaging was performed on the read-back signals from the reference tracks.

After all measurements were taken, the fundamental harmonics of the square wave patterns were processed in four different ways and the results are depicted in Fig. 9.10. Figure 9.10(a) shows the thermal relaxation data from the first type of measurement where no averaging was performed and the data were not calibrated by using the "aged" reference tracks. As mentioned before, the calibration means to subtract the change in the signals on the reference tracks from the signals on the decaying tracks. Figure 9.10(b) presents the averaged thermal relaxation data from the second type of measurements, but no calibration using the reference tracks was performed. Figure 9.10(c) presents the case when the reference track data from the third type of measurement were used to calibrate the thermal relaxation data from the first type of measurement. Figure 9.10(d) corresponds to the case when the reference track data from the third type of measurement were used to calibrate the thermal relaxation data from the second type of measurement.

From Fig. 9.10(a) and 9.10(c) we can see that when no averaging of the signals on the decaying tracks was performed, the thermal relaxation

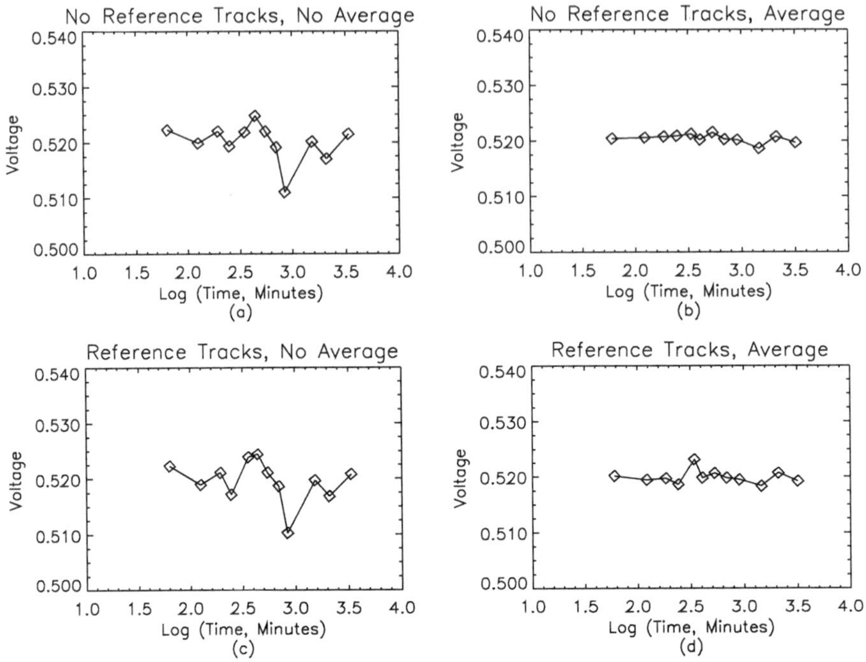

FIGURE 9.10 Comparison of read-back signals: averaging versus reference tracks.

read-back signals were almost identical whether or not calibration using reference tracks was employed. Similarly, when averaging the signals on the decaying tracks had been performed in Fig. 9.10(b) and 9.10(d), the thermal relaxation read-back signals were almost identical regardless of the use of reference tracks for calibration. Furthermore, by comparing the two columns in Fig. 9.10, it is clear that averaging significantly reduces the amplitude of the fluctuations of the read-back signals. In other words, the key to stable, reliable reading of the GMR heads lies in employing averaging of the signals measured on the decaying tracks, rather than in calibration based on reference tracks. While Fig. 9.10 only presents the results for the case of using a GMR head on disk 1, we reached the same conclusion when other combinations of heads and disks were used.

It should be noted that the square wave signals in this experiment were deliberately chosen to have very low densities so that thermal relaxations of the signals were very small and any fluctuation in the read-back signals could be attributed chiefly to noise and the head sensitivity variations. Moreover, the choice of the 1400 Oe disk used in this experiment was motivated by the fact that such a low coercivity disk has a higher degree of surface roughness. This high surface roughness can accentuate the noise in the read-back signals and allows efficient testing of the effectiveness of the averaging algorithm.

After a reliable method for counteracting read head sensitivity variations was determined, we performed the following experiments to quantitatively study data-dependent thermal relaxations. In these experiments, periodic square wave signals of different recording densities were written on disk 2 and disk 3 by using a GMR head whose write and read widths were 50% narrower.

Before taking each measurement, a track profile plot was taken to determine the track center. This procedure is necessary in order to offset any mechanical drift of the head from the center of the track. After the track center was located, the head was used to perform averaging on the thermal relaxation time signals. As illustrated, this averaging significantly boosted the signal-to-noise ratio of the measurements and our results showed that it reduced the measurement errors to approximately 0.5%.

After the averaging was completed, the first and third harmonics of the signals were then numerically computed through the application of the Fourier transform. The timebase of the scope was set sufficiently large to include an adequate number of sampling points so that the resolution of the resulting Fourier transform was not compromised. For all the measurements in this chapter, a Guzik spin-stand was used along with a Lecroy oscilloscope. All measurements were performed on magnetic media with parameters shown in Table 9.1.

9.4 RESULTS AND DISCUSSION

Figure 9.11 shows the thermal relaxation measurements of first and third harmonics for recording densities of 6.6 kfc/mm, 7.7 kfc/mm, and 8.8 kfc/mm written on a 2600 Oe disk. The data were under observation of thermal relaxations during 46.8 hours. The decay rate is the slope of the linear best fit through the data points. The absence of wide-spread data points in Fig. 9.11 reflects the effectiveness of the averaging procedure.

It can be seen from the data shown in Fig. 9.11 that as the recording densities were increased, the relative decay rate of the first harmonics of the signals increased due to the higher ratio of *average* demagnetizing field to coercivity at higher recording densities. For the same reason, the absolute amplitudes of the first harmonics also decreased with increasing recording densities. It is also apparent from Fig. 9.11 that the third harmonics of the signals decay at a higher rate than the first harmonics due to the stronger *local* demagnetizing fields around the transitions of

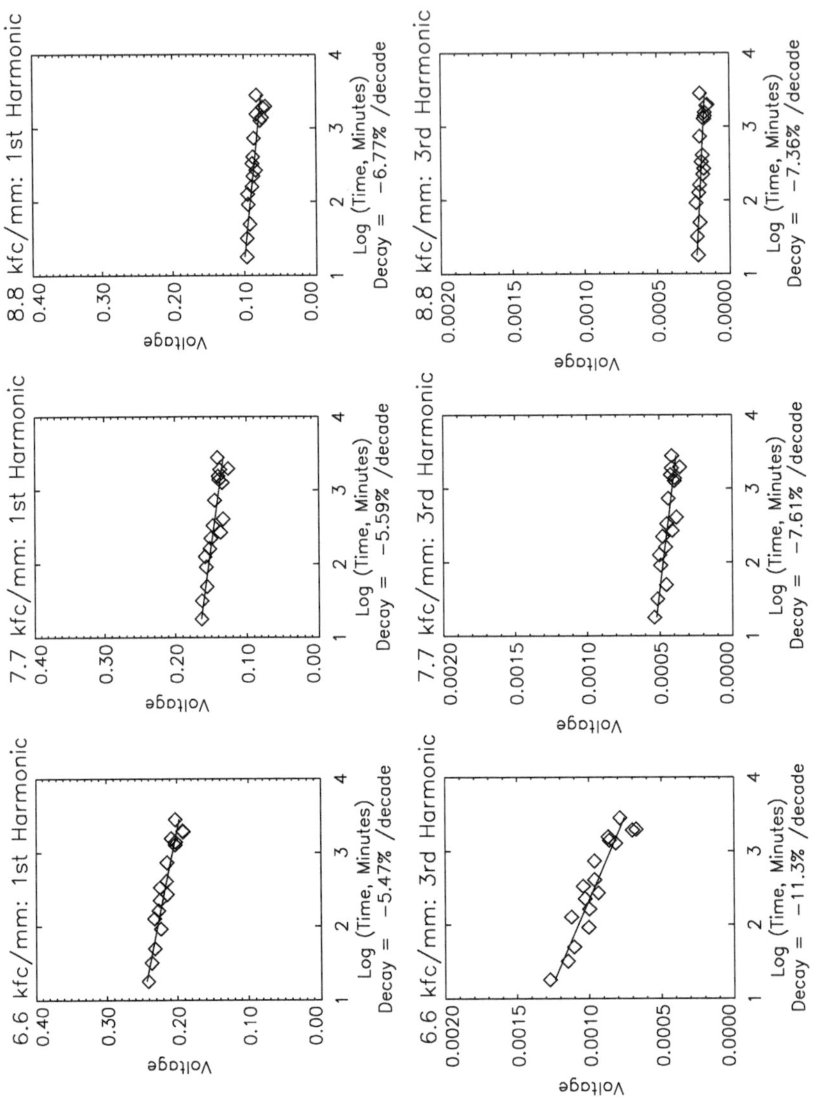

FIGURE 9.11 Spin-stand thermal relaxation measurements on 2600 Oe disk.

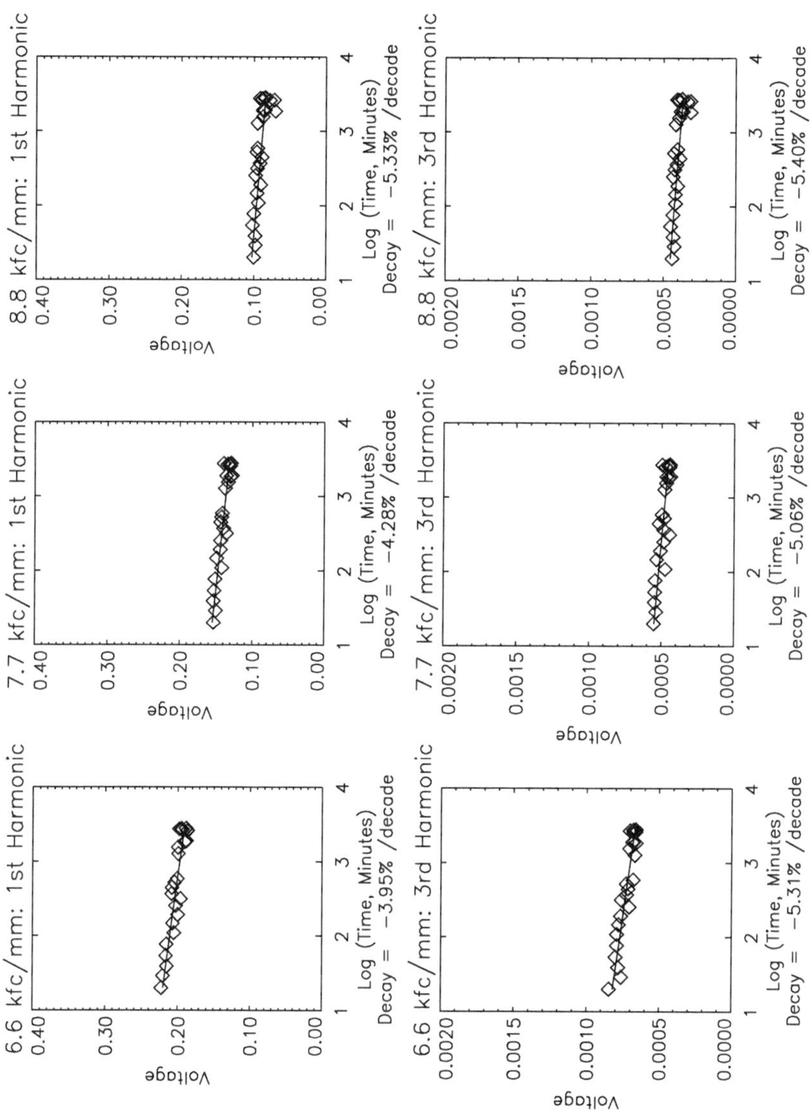

FIGURE 9.12 Spin-stand thermal relaxation measurements on 3100 Oe disk.

the recorded patterns, which in time broadened the width of the transitions and effectively reduced the values of the third (and higher) harmonics.

Figure 9.12 shows the thermal relaxation measurements for recording densities of 6.6 kfc/mm, 7.7 kfc/mm, and 8.8 kfc/mm written on a 3100 Oe disk. The data were under observation of thermal relaxations for 46.5 hours. Comparing Fig. 9.12 with Fig. 9.11, it can be seen that the relative decay rates of the signals written on the 3100 Oe disk were lower than the corresponding decay rates on the 2600 Oe disk. This is because the 3100 Oe disk, having a thinner magnetic layer and a smaller value of magnetization-thickness product ($M_r t$), has a lower ratio of *average* demagnetizing field to coercivity than the 2600 Oe disk.

9.5 SPATIAL AND VECTORIAL CHARACTERIZATION OF THERMAL RELAXATIONS

In this section, we report on the spatial and vectorial characterization of thermal relaxations of recorded magnetization patterns by using the spin-stand microscopy technique. It is demonstrated that the spatially inhomogeneous and vectorial nature of thermal relaxations of recorded patterns may result in temporal track broadening. It is found that this temporal track broadening is more pronounced for disks with higher coercivities.

9.5.1 Vectorial thermal relaxations

Data-dependent thermal relaxations have usually been studied by using spin-stands. However, traditional spin-stand studies have only examined the harmonic content (mostly the fundamental harmonic) of recorded patterns [12–17]. For this reason, the spatially inhomogeneous and vectorial nature of data-dependent thermal relaxations has not been captured. The purpose of this section is to report on the spatial and vectorial characterization of data-dependent thermal relaxations. This characterization is performed by using the developed spin-stand imaging technique.

In our experiments, all measurements were performed by using a Guzik spin-stand and read-back voltages were acquired by a digital oscilloscope. Giant-magnetoresistive (GMR) heads were used to write and read signals. In order to examine the data-dependent thermal relaxations of recorded magnetization, "all-ones" patterns with density of 220 kfci (kilo flux conversion per inch) were written. The parameters of the disks used in the study are shown in Table 9.2.

In order to obtain the spatial distributions of the read-back voltages of recorded data, tracks were scanned successively over 70 hours. The scanning in the along-track direction was realized due to the rotation

TABLE 9.2 Media parameters used in the measurements of spatial and vectorial characterization of thermal relaxations

Disk	Coercivity H_c (Oe)	Remanence-thickness product $M_r t$ (memu/cm^2)
A	2600	0.85
B	3100	0.71
C	3600	0.50

of the disk, while scanning in the cross-track direction was performed at discrete steps by using small controlled radial displacements of the head. In order to avoid mechanical hysteresis resulting from moving the head in opposite radial directions, the scanning in the cross-track direction was always performed unidirectionally by stepping the head from one side of the track to the other without back-stepping. The signal waveforms at each offset position across the track were then captured by the digital oscilloscope after 1000 sweeps of averaging (over identically written patterns) in order to minimize the read noise and the electronic noise. It is worthwhile to mention that the described scanning mechanism is superior to that used in magnetic force microscopy (MFM) as far as the rate and conditions of data acquisition are concerned. Without this efficient scanning mechanism, the imaging of thermal relaxations of recorded patterns would be virtually impossible.

By using the above experimental procedures, the spatial distributions of the read-back voltages that constitute the raw images of the track were obtained. These are raw images because they are distorted due to the nonlocalized nature of the GMR head response. In addition, these images are scalar in nature, while magnetization distributions are vector fields. Therefore, image reconstruction was required in order to remove these distortions and to retrieve the vectorial images of the magnetization patterns. This reconstruction was performed by deconvolving the measured voltage distributions using the algorithm described in Chapter 3. In this way, the images of curl-free (field-producing) component of the magnetization patterns were reconstructed.

By using the retrieved magnetization images, relaxation rates of different magnetization components were computed at each point of the scanning mesh. The relaxation rate was defined as the slope of the best fit of the local magnetization with respect to a logarithmic time scale (see Eq. (9.1)). As a result, data-dependent thermal relaxations of recorded magnetization patterns were characterized spatially and vectorially. It was observed that a good logarithmic fit of the relaxation data can be obtained in the time interval from a few hours to about 70 hours. At the early and very late stages of thermal relaxations, these rates deviate appreciably from the logarithmic law (9.1). This once again suggests that this law represents an *intermediate* asymptotics of actual relaxation rates.

9.5.2 Results and discussion

In Fig. 9.13, the along-track component of magnetization (M_x) and its corresponding relaxation rate are shown for the case of disk A (see Table 9.2). Figure 9.13(a) depicts the image of M_x at the beginning of relaxation process, while Fig. 9.13(b) is the image of the corresponding local relaxation rate evaluated over a period of 70 hours. As can be seen, the M_x relaxation rates are spatially inhomogeneous. Across the track, the steepest decay of M_x occurred at the central region of the track. It can also be observed that the locations of maximum M_x decay rates along the track do not coincide with the centers of the magnetic transitions but are slightly shifted. These findings are consistent with the spatial distribution of the demagnetizing fields [18].

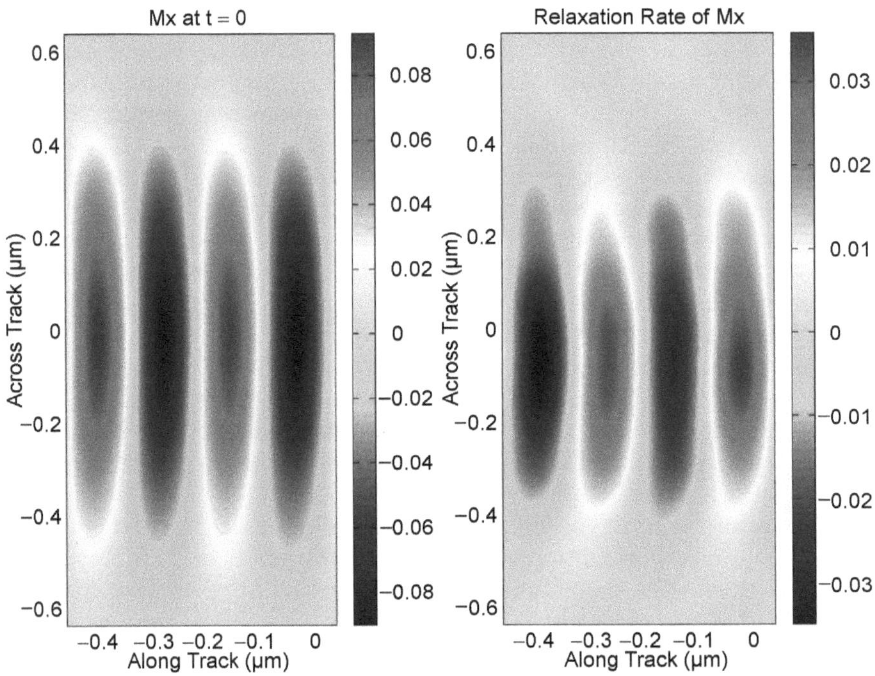

FIGURE 9.13 (a) Spatial distribution of along-track magnetization component (M_x) for disk A; (b) spatial distribution of relaxation rates of M_x for disk A. (See color plate 9.)

Figure 9.14 presents the images of relaxation rates of M_x for disks A, B, and C. It can be observed from this figure that for disks B and C the relaxation rates at the track center and at the track edges have opposite signs. For the case of positive values of M_x (see the shading bar in Fig. 9.14), the corresponding relaxation rates change gradually from negative to positive values as one moves across the track from the center toward the edges. Similarly, the relaxation rates corresponding to negative values of M_x (see the shading bar in Fig. 9.14) change gradually from positive to negative values. This results in the increase in M_x at track edges over time, which manifests itself as a temporal broadening of the track. It can be observed that the local relaxation rates in the central portion of the track decrease as the disk coercivity is increased. However, the local relaxation rates at track edges have the opposite tendency, i.e. disks with higher coercivity exhibit more pronounced track broadening.

This temporal track broadening is evident from Fig. 9.15 where the cross-track profiles of read-back voltage at two different time instants ($t = 3$ hours and $t = 70$ hours) are plotted. In other words, the observed temporal track broadening is consistent with collected raw data at the above-mentioned time instants.

Figure 9.16 depicts the distribution of magnetization vectors at $t = 0$ and $t = 30$ hours. Only the region around a track edge is represented in order to emphasize the viscosity effects near edges.

It has also been observed that thermal relaxations led to the symmetry restoration of the magnetization distributions as revealed by Fig. 9.16. It is obvious from Fig. 9.16(a) that asymmetry of magnetization distribution existed in the track edge region at the initial time instant. The cause of this asymmetry can be attributed to the media's past "magnetizing" history that could not be completely wiped out by the weak fringing write fields at the track edges. However, due to thermal relaxations, this asymmetry was removed after 30 hours, as can be seen in Fig. 9.16(b).

The temporal track broadening is an unexpected and puzzling result of our experiments. It may also be attributed to local thermal deformation of the track which in time may lead to track eccentricity. Special efforts have been made to exclude this explanation of track broadening. Namely, the same portion of the track was imaged consecutively (over 70 hours) and no "skewness" of the track was observed with respect to the fixed frame of reference. From a theoretical point of view, the temporal track broadening is puzzling because it occurred in the region of low demagnetizing fields where thermal relaxations of magnetization are allegedly not strongly pronounced. One plausible explanation for the temporal track broadening can be based on the fact that GMR head signals are generated by magnetic fields produced by virtual magnetic charges that are pro-

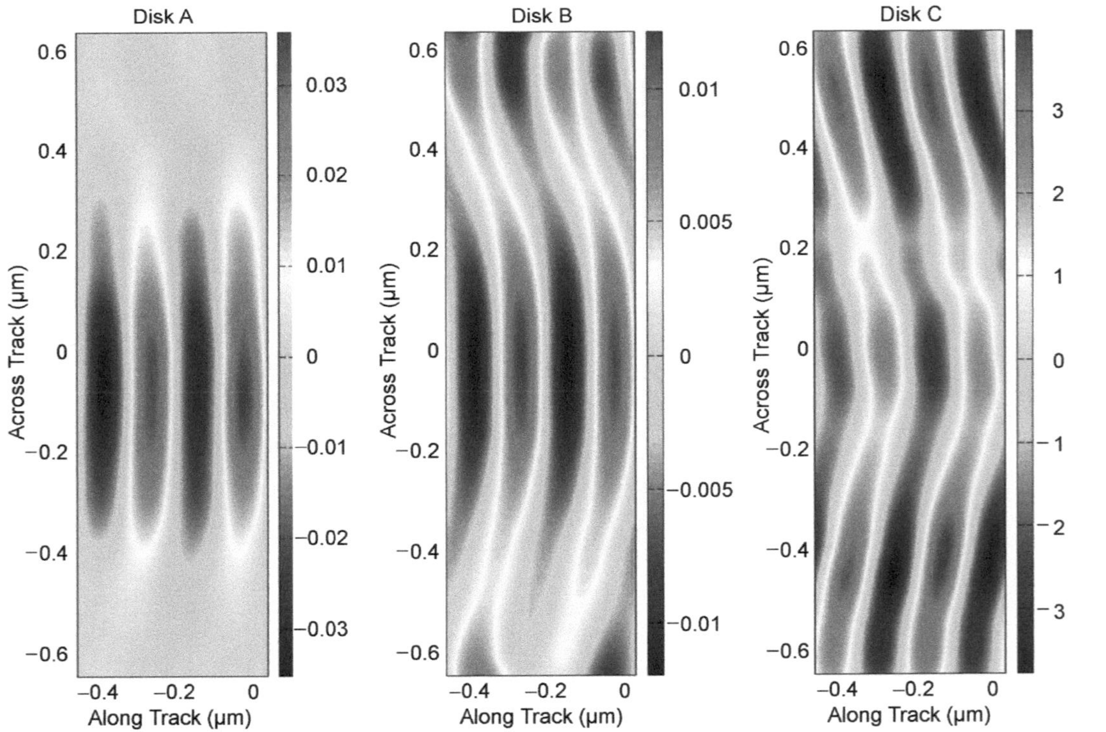

FIGURE 9.14 (a) Spatial distribution of relaxation rates for disk A; (b) spatial distribution of relaxation rates for disk B; (c) spatial distribution of relaxation rates for disk C. (See color plate 10.)

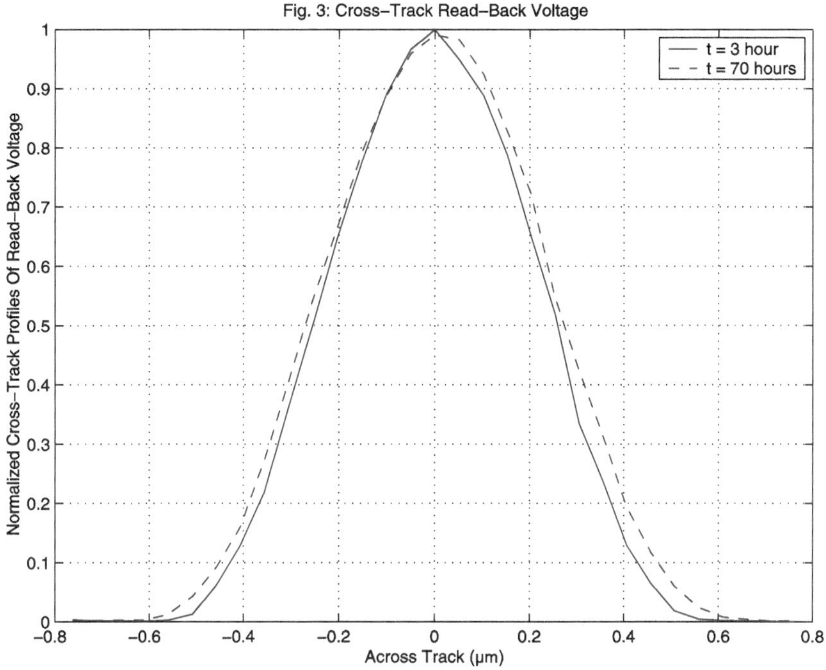

FIGURE 9.15 Normalized cross-track profiles of read-back voltage at two instants of time ($t = 3$ hours and $t = 70$ hours) for disk C.

portional to divergence of magnetization. It is quite possible that due to spatially inhomogeneous and vectorial nature of thermal relaxations very small temporal changes in local magnetization may result in appreciable magnetic charges and GMR head signals.

9.6 SUMMARY

Data-dependent thermal relaxations of magnetization patterns of thin film media negatively affect the long term thermal stability of recorded information. In this chapter, we experimentally studied data-dependent thermal relaxations of periodic square wave signals of densities 6.6 kfc/mm, 7.7 kfc/mm, and 8.8 kfc/mm written on magnetic media with coercivities of 2600 Oe and 3100 Oe. The duration of study extended over 40 hours. Thermal relaxations were studied by using special averaging to neutralize head sensitivity variations. We found that averaging of the thermal relaxation measurements is more effective in decoupling the variations of

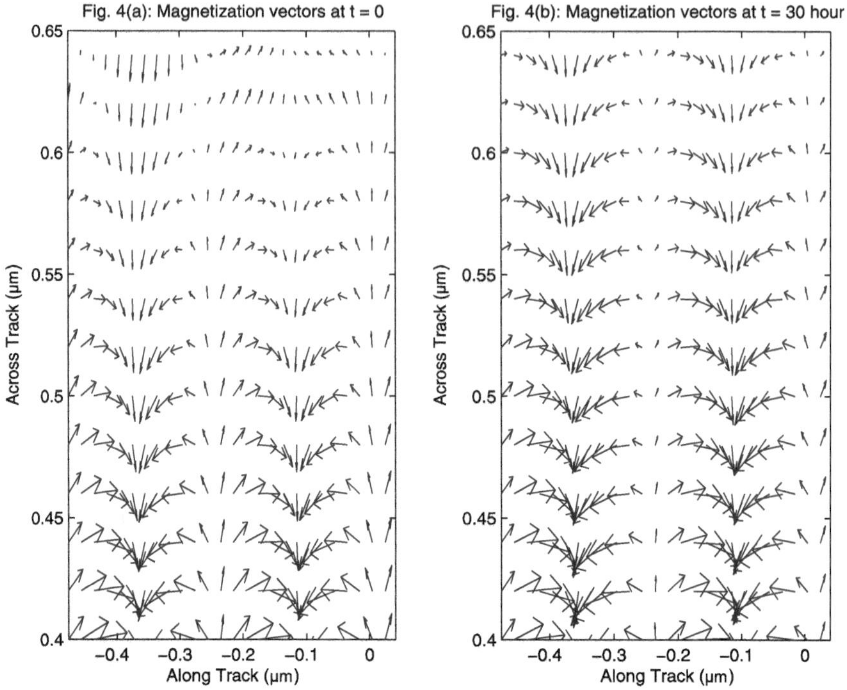

FIGURE 9.16 (a) Spatial distribution of vectorial magnetization at $t = 0$ for disk B; (b) spatial distribution of vectorial magnetization at $t = 30$ hours for disk B.

read head sensitivity from the magnetization relaxations than other experimental schemes suggested in the literature. It is obvious from the results of this chapter that the decay of the third harmonics is faster than the decay of the fundamentals. The steeper decay of the third harmonics clearly reveals the local thermal viscosity near the transitions, which works to broaden the transition width, thus lowering the values of the third harmonics.

The efficient scanning mechanism and the magnetization reconstruction algorithm provided by the spin-stand microscopy technique also make possible the spatial and vectorial characterization of data-dependent thermal relaxations. It was found that the relaxation rates of magnetization patterns are spatially inhomogeneous. The highest decay rates occurred at the central region of the track close to the magnetic transitions. These results are consistent with our previous findings that the transitions, being subject to a higher demagnetizing field than the average demagnetizing field along the bit, exhibited faster thermal relaxations than regions of the track away from the transitions. Moreover, an increase in magnetization at track edges was observed which in turn led to track broadening. The obtained results demonstrate that the spin-stand microscopy technique is a valuable tool for the spatial and vectorial characterization of data-dependent thermal relaxations.

BIBLIOGRAPHY

[1] I.D. Mayergoyz, A. Adly, C. Korman, M. Huang, and C. Krafft, "Scaling and data collapse in magnetic viscosity," *J. Appl. Phys.*, **85**, 4358 (1999).

[2] I.D. Mayergoyz, A.A. Adly, M.W. Huang, and C. Krafft, "Scaling and data collapse in magnetic viscosity (creep) of superconductors," *IEEE Trans. Magn.*, **36**, 3208 (2000).

[3] I.D. Mayergoyz, *Mathematical Models of Hysteresis and Their Applications*, Elsevier Press, New York, 2003.

[4] Y. Zhang and H.N. Bertram, "Thermal decay in high density disk media," *IEEE Trans. Magn.*, **34**, 3786 (1998).

[5] J. Chen, J.H. Judy, and T.M. Coughlin, "Comparison of time-decay of readback signals in keepered and non-keepered media," *IEEE Trans. Magn.*, **34**, 1624 (1998).

[6] Y. Hosoe, I. Tamai, K. Tanahashi, Y. Takahashi, T. Yamamoto, T. Kanbe, and Y. Yajima, "Experimental study of thermal decay in high-density magnetic recording media," *IEEE Trans. Magn.*, **33**, 3028 (1997).

[7] P. Dhagat, R.S. Indeck, and M.W. Muller, "Spin-stand measurements of time and temperature dependence of magnetic recordings," *J. Appl. Phys.*, **85**, 4994 (1998).

[8] M. Alex and D. Wachenschwanz, "Thermal effects and recording performance at high recording densities," *IEEE Trans. Magn.*, **35**, 2796 (1999).

[9] P. Dhagat, A. Jander, R.S. Indeck, M.W. Muller, and H.J. Richter, "Submillisecond spin-stand measurements of thermal decay in magnetic recordings," *IEEE Trans. Magn.*, **36**, 528 (2000).

[10] M. Madison, T. Arnoldussen, M. Pinarbasi, M. Parker, M. Doerner, C. Singh Bhatia, D. Call, J. Li, L. Dorius, K. Tang, L. Ingall, E. Lee, S. Yuan, R. Schwenker, J. Tabib, L. Lauchlan, J. Raniseski, R. Smith, W. Hsiao, T. Lin, D. Mauri, and H. Zolla, "Design tradeoffs for beyond 20 Gb/in^2: Using a merged notched head on advanced low noise media (invited)," *J. Appl. Phys.*, **87**, 4996 (2000).

[11] A. Taratorin, D. Cheng, and E. Marinero, "Experimental study of nonlinear transition shift and error rate degradation caused by thermal decay," *J. Appl. Phys.*, **85**, 5309 (1999).

[12] Y. Zhang and H.N. Bertram, "Thermal decay in high density disk media," *IEEE Trans. Magn.*, **34**, 3786 (1998).

[13] Y. Hosoe, I. Tamai, K. Tanahashi, Y. Takahashi, T. Yamamoto, T. Kanbe, and Y. Yajima, "Experimental study of thermal decay in high-density magnetic recording media," *IEEE Trans. Magn.*, **33**, 3028 (1997).

[14] P. Dhagat, R.S. Indeck, and M.W. Muller, "Spin-stand measurements of time and temperature dependence of magnetic recordings," *J. Appl. Phys.*, **85**, 4994 (1998).

[15] M. Alex and D. Wachenschwanz, "Thermal effects and recording performance at high recording densities," *IEEE Trans. Magn.*, **35**, 2796 (1999).

[16] P. Dhagat, A. Jander, R.S. Indeck, M.W. Muller, and H.J. Richter, "Submillisecond spin-stand measurements of thermal decay in magnetic recordings," *IEEE Trans. Magn.*, **36**, 528 (2000).

[17] A. Taratorin, D. Cheng, and E. Marinero, "Experimental study of nonlinear transition shift and error rate degradation caused by thermal decay," *J. Appl. Phys.*, **85**, 5309 (1999).

[18] H.N. Bertram, *Theory of Magnetic Recording*, Cambridge University Press, Cambridge, England, 1994.

APPENDIX A

Overview of Hard Disk Drive Components and Technology

In this appendix, a brief review of basic facts and ideas related to hard disk data storage technology is presented. This review is not complete by any standards and is presented here to make this book more or less self-contained. The detailed discussion of many modern aspects of magnetic data storage technology can be found in Refs. [1,2].

A.1 CHANNEL

Before user data from a host computer is written onto the hard disk platter, it is divided into data blocks. Each of these data blocks must then go through a series of processing steps in the `write channel` (`or recording channel`) in order to facilitate their subsequent retrieval in the `read channel` (`or reproduction channel`). The goal of hard disk channels is to maximize the linear storage density and data transfer rate and minimize the channel bit error rate (BER). The channels are implemented by the electronics on printed circuit boards (PCB) of disk drives. Figure A.1 shows a generic block diagram of a portion of the hard disk write and read channels.

A.1.1 Write channel

The first processing step in the write channel is the error correction code (ECC) encoding. The `ECC encoder` calculates special redundant data bits containing content-dependent information about the data block and appends them at the end of the block. Error correction codes are used during data retrieval to detect and possibly correct a variety of single-burst or multiple-burst reading errors. These errors may be caused by electronic noise, media noise, sporadic media defects, or thermal asperity (as when a head encounters a sizable dust particle on the disk). The most common ECC codes in use today belong to the *Reed–Solomon* class. It is particularly

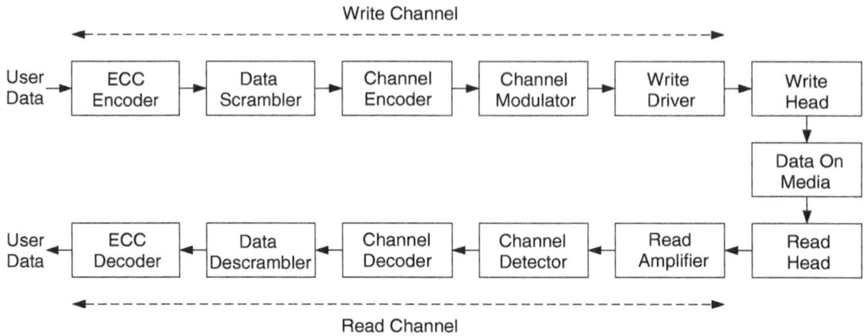

FIGURE A.1 A block diagram of a portion of hard disk write and read channels.

effective for correcting bursts of errors while minimizing the total number of redundant ECC bytes required.

After the data is ECC encoded, a `data scrambler` is used to randomize the content of the data. This randomization process is the transformation of the data block into a pseudo-random data sequence. This reduces the fixed-pattern effects caused by long strings of identical patterns. These long strings of identical patterns create uncompensated DC offset which lead to undesirable baseline shift of the readback signals. The scrambling of the data also decreases jitter accumulation and in general permits more effective use of the channel bandwidth.

The next step in the processing sequence is channel encoding. A `channel encoder` encodes the now randomized data with *run-length-limited (RLL) codes* or *modulation codes*. These codes, usually specified as RLL $(m/n)(d,k)$, map m incoming bits into n encoded bits (where $m < n$). The codes also have at least d zeroes (the *run length*) and at most k zeroes (the *run limit*) between two consecutive transitions. The (d,k) constraint in channel encoding essentially prevents transitions from being written too close together or too far apart. Closely spaced transitions may result in reduced amplitudes and bit shifts in the readback signals due to intersymbol interference (ISI). In addition, when transitions are written too close together, non-linear transition shift (NLTS) and partial erasure may occur, which contribute to false detections. However, it is not desirable to have transitions too far apart, either. This may cause the read data to be out of synchronization with the channel clock data. The *out-of-sync* condition has its root in the (inevitable) fluctuations of the spindle rotational speed. These fluctuations in turn cause transitions to occur earlier (for a faster rotation) or later (for a slower rotation) than they should. By limiting the maximum number of allowable zeros between ones, the RLL scheme ensures the periodic generation of the timing signal for adjustment of the clock frequency. This is usually realized by a phase locked loop (PLL) in a clock recovery circuit where the clock frequency is synchronized to the current variation of the spindle speed. The subsequently recovered timing information then allows the read data to be sampled at the proper time.

The data, which until now are still in the digital format, must then be transformed into voltage levels by a `channel modulator`. This transformation is usually based on the non-return-to-zero inverted (NRZI) representation of recorded data where a one represents a change in magnetization (i.e. voltage level) and a zero represents no change in magnetization (or voltage level). At this point, some data-dependent analog adjustment must be made to separate the timing between write pulses. This is done to precompensate for nonlinear effects during the write operation, a process known as *write precompensation*. The output of the `channel modulator` is then passed through a `write driver` which changes the direction of electric current based on the voltage levels. Finally, a write head produces a change in magnetization in the media every time its write current direction is reversed.

A.1.2 Read channel

The processing steps in the write channel are essentially reversed in the read channel during data retrieval. First, a read head senses local magnetic fields produced by the divergence of the magnetization (or by virtual magnetic charges) in the media. A `read amplifier` subsequently amplifies the readback voltage signals. These amplified readback signals, however, are heavily distorted by intersymbol interference (ISI) and contaminated by noise originated from the media, the read head, and the electronics. The readback signals must therefore pass through the `channel detector` for detection of the timings of the magnetization transitions. Before signals are sent for detection, their amplitudes are modified by a variable gain amplifier (VGA) to have a constant value.

The prevalent read detection channel used in modern disk drives is the partial response maximum likelihood (PRML) channel [1]. PRML channel is based on the linearity assumption and prior knowledge of the shape of the ideal readback signal from an isolated transition. By using superposition of properly time-shifted ideal readback signals of isolated transitions, all possible readback signals can be reconstructed and subsequently compared with the equalized readback signal by using maximum likelihood sequence detection criteria. The maximum likelihood detection can be implemented effectively by using the Viterbi algorithm.

Upon data detection, a `channel decoder` is used to decode the scrambled RLL encoded data. A `data descrambler` is then employed to derandomize the scrambled RLL decoded data. Finally, the `ECC decoder` calculates anew the error correction bytes of the retrieved data block and compares them with the readback ECC bytes appended at the end of the block. If the ECC bytes match, a successful read operation occurs and the data are sent to the host computer. If there is a mismatch between these bytes, the ECC bytes are used to locate and possibly correct the errors. If the errors cannot be corrected, the data is usually read again.

A.2 MEDIA

Magnetic disks are multi-layer structures sputter deposited on top of a substrate usually made of aluminum alloy (such as Al–Mg) or glass (see Fig. A.2). The substrate provides the necessary rigidity for the hard disk platter spinning at high speed. Once the substrate is machined to the appropriate thickness, an undercoat layer of amorphous nickel–phosphorus (NiP) is electroplated onto it. This undercoat layer provides a smooth and nonmagnetic deposition surface which further enhances rigidity. Above the NiP undercoat a chromium (Cr) underlayer is deposited for enriching the initial growth. The underlayer also controls the microstructure properties of the magnetic recording layer. The recording layer itself, which is

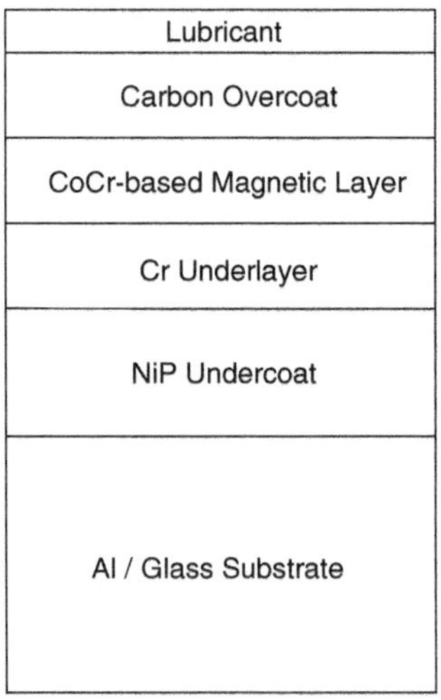

FIGURE A.2 The structure of a multilayer magnetic media.

made of polycrystalline cobalt-based alloys such as CoCrTa and CoCrPt, is only about 20–50 nm thick. These Co-based alloys have a hexagonal crystalline structure allowing a high coercivity to be attained through a large uniaxial magnetocrystalline anisotropy. A carbon overcoat layer subsequently covers the recording layer for tribological reasons and for reducing media wear. The carbon in the overcoat (with thickness ranging from a few to a few tens of nanometers) can be either hydrogenated or nitrogenated carbon. The former provides wear protection and the latter better bonding between the lubricant layer and the surface. Unlike other layers which are sputter deposited onto the substrate, the lubricant layer is dip-coated after the platter is removed from the deposition chamber. The lubricant layer is only a few nanometers thick. It is used for the durability of the head disk interface and the protection of the magnetic layer.

Magnetic layers of modern thin film disk have granular structures. The magnetic recording layer is polycrystalline and the grains are continuous throughout the film thickness. The grains interact with one another via both long-range and short-range forces. The long-range forces are mainly of magnetostatic nature, while the short-range forces are due to intergranular exchange coupling. Since Co-based alloys possess uniaxial crystalline anisotropy, it is crucial for longitudinal media to align the easy axes of the grains in the film plane in order to increase the remanent magnetization and coercivity of the media. For perpendicular recording media, the crystalline easy axes are aligned perpendicular to the film plane.

Longitudinal media can be either *isotropic* or *oriented*. For isotropic media, the crystalline easy axes do not have a preferred direction and are randomly oriented. For oriented media, the crystalline easy axes are mostly aligned in circumferential (or along-track) directions. This alignment is established by using special techniques to texture the media substrate circumferentially before film deposition. The orientation ratio is then defined as the ratio of the remanence magnetization in the along-track direction to that of the across-track (radial) direction.

Increase in areal density requires a decrease in the average grain size in order to maintain a sufficient signal-to-noise ratio. Ever-decreasing grain size, however, will eventually lead to the situation where the recorded bits are no longer thermally stable. It is widely believed that the degree of thermal stability is determined by the ratio of the anisotropy energy $K_u V$ (where K_u is the uniaxial anisotropy energy density and V the volume of each grain) to the thermal energy $k_B T$ (where k_B is the Boltzmann constant and T the absolute temperature). To prevent the onset of thermal instability, $K_u V$ must be an order of magnitude greater than $k_B T$. To increase thermal stability of the recorded bits while shrinking the volume of individual grain, K_u must be increased to increase the magnetocrystalline anisotropy energy.

Different solutions have been proposed to tackle the challenge of thermal stability. In patterned media, for example, the recording media film is patterned into quantized regions (islands) and each bit is stored in a single magnetic island. Perpendicular media presents another very promising direction to deal with thermal stability. The perpendicular write process requires a pole probe write head design and a media with soft underlayer (SUL) to increase the head write field. This in turn allows a higher coercivity media to be used for more thermally stable recorded bits. Antiferromagnetically coupled (AFC) media and heat assisted magnetic recording (HAMR) have also been considered as ways to counteract thermal instability. For AFC media, the top recording layer (with thickness t_1) is anti-ferromagnetically coupled to the bottom layer (with thickness t_2) through a thin layer of ruthenium (Ru). The anti-ferromagnetic coupling increases the energy barrier against magnetization reversal. It has been shown that the effective $M_r t$ for an AFC media is $M_r(t_1 - t_2)$. This enhances thermal stability by allowing individually larger t_1 and t_2 but an effectively smaller value of $M_r t$. Heat assisted magnetic recording works by using heat (e.g. generated by a laser beam) during the write process to temporarily reduce the coercivity of a localized write spot on a media with otherwise very high coercivity. In this way, once the heat is removed, the recorded bit becomes thermally stable on this high-coercivity media.

A.3 HEADS

The technology for controlling thin film growth at the nano-level has been adapted in the manufacturing of thin film magnetic recording heads. A magnetic hard disk head consists of a thin film inductive write head and a giant magnetoresistive (GMR) read head. The write head and the read head are fabricated as a single device usually with a common soft magnetic pole. The magnetic read–write element is mounted on the trailing edge of the slider. The air bearing surface (ABS) of the slider is precision machined to contain special patterns to guide the air flow created by the rotating disk. These patterns are designed by using aerodynamics and tribological principles for flying with low height and high stability on a thin cushion of air above the disk surface. When the disk is not spinning, the head, being of the contact start/stop (CSS) type, is parked at a designated region (usually at the inner circumference) of the disk. The head will be lifted off automatically before the disk starts spinning.

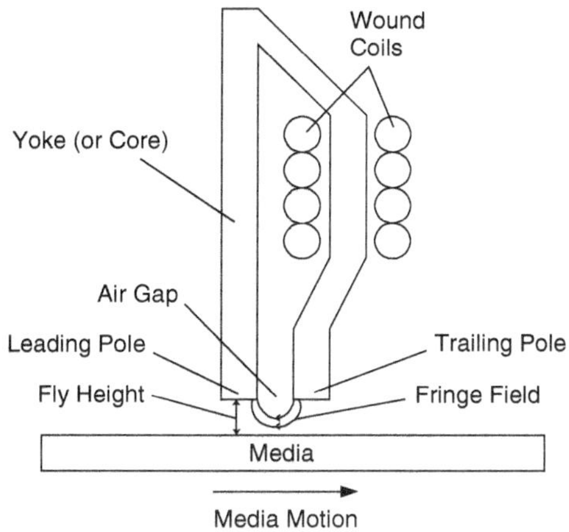

FIGURE A.3 A schematic of a write head.

A.3.1 Write head

The inductive write head consists of a yoke (or core) with coils wound around it (see Fig. A.3). At the end of the yoke are two pole tips with a small air gap between them. The yoke is made from high permeability, soft magnetic material such as permalloy (19% Fe, 81% Ni) or AlFeSil (a metal alloy). During the write process, the write current applied through the coil generates magnetic field which is channeled through the high permeability yoke and the air gap. The fringe field near the write head gap switches and aligns the magnetization of the media according to the polarity of the write current. Since the bit length of the recorded magnetization is determined by the sharpness of the head write field, a shorter bit length can be achieved by flying the write head closer to the disk surface.

A.3.2 Read head

Modern disk drives use giant-magnetoresistive (GMR) heads to read data. These heads belong to the class of *spintronic devices*. Unlike conventional devices where only the electric charge of the transport electrons is important, spintronic devices exploit the electron spin as well. Figure A.4 depicts the structure of the most simple GMR head, called a spin-valve head.

A spin-valve head consists of four layers. The first layer is the sensing layer. It is also called the *free* layer because the magnetization in this layer is free to rotate under the influence of external magnetic fields. Next to the free layer is a thin non-magnetic metal spacer usually made of copper. This

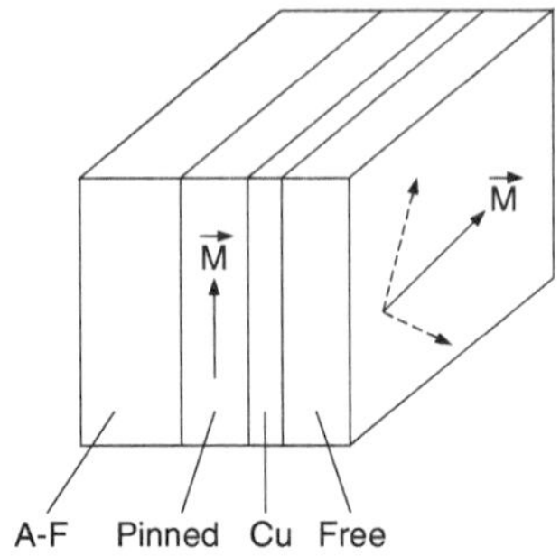

FIGURE A.4 A schematic of the structure of a spin-valve head.

spacer separates the free layer from the *pinned* layer whose magnetization direction is pinned (fixed) by the exchange coupling forces provided by the antiferromagnetic (AF) layer next to it. Exchange coupling is a quantum mechanical phenomenon by which an antiferromagnetic layer causes an adjacent ferromagnetic layer to establish a certain and correlated direction of magnetization. The antiferromagnetic layer is usually made of MnFe or CoO, the free layer and the pinned layer are usually permalloy or CoFe. Permalloy has been the head material of choice because of its extremely low value of magnetostriction. Spin-valve heads are created by using photolithography and microfabrication techniques similar to those employed in the semiconductor industry.

It has been found that the magnetic coupling between the free layer and the pinned layer changes from ferromagnetic to antiferromagnetic (and vice versa) as one varies the thickness of the spacer [2]. In fact, the magnetic coupling between the free layer and the pinned layer is a periodic function of the thickness of the spacer. This thickness is chosen to guarantee that the coupling is practically zero and in the absence of external magnetic fields the direction of the magnetization of the free layer and the pinned layer are not correlated and made orthogonal by the appropriate anisotropy of the free layer (as shown in Fig. A.4.) Under these conditions, the magnetization of the free layer is free to rotate under the influence of magnetic fields emanating from transitions recorded on disk platters.

The GMR effect arises from the spin-dependent scattering of electrons. When the magnetizations of both layers are aligned, the resistance is low. When the magnetizations have opposite directions, the resistance is high. In this manner, a magnetoresistive readback voltage will be produced when a current is passed through the spin-valve head. The magnitude of this voltage is proportional to the sensing current and the resistance

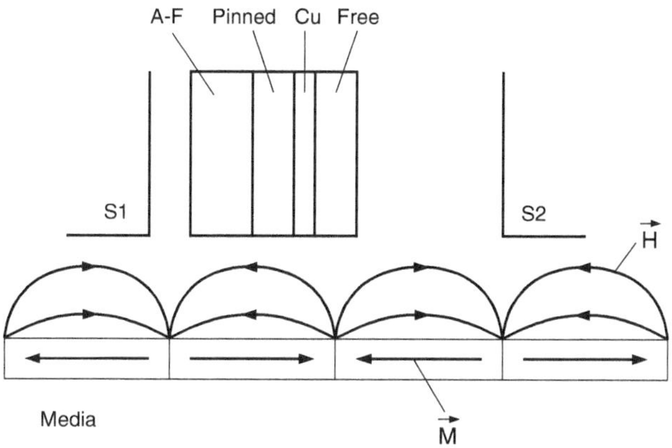

FIGURE A.5 A schematic of a spin-valve head with medium underneath.

of the spin-valve structure. This readback voltage will exhibit maximum and minimum values when the magnetization in the free layer is parallel or antiparallel to the magnetization in the pinned layer, respectively. These extremum values signify recorded transitions.

The sensing mechanism of the spin-valve head can be described as follows. Consider the schematic shown in Fig. A.5 which depicts a spin-valve head placed between two high-permeability shields (S1 and S2) with the magnetized media underneath. In this configuration, the vertical magnetic fields emanated from the written transitions point upward toward the free layer. The cross product of the effective magnetic field with the magnetization in the free layer ($\mathbf{H}_{\text{eff}} \times \mathbf{M}_{\text{free}}$) produces a torque which tilts the magnetization out of the plane of the free layer. As soon as this happens, a large demagnetizing field in the free layer is generated and produces precessional torque ($\mathbf{H}_{\text{demag}} \times \mathbf{M}_{\text{free}}$). It is this torque that facilitates the switching of the magnetization direction of the free layer. By the same line of reasoning, a downward magnetic field emanating from the sample magnetization causes the magnetization direction of the free layer to switch downward.

The dynamics of the magnetization switching is governed by the Landau–Lifshitz equation:

$$\frac{\mathrm{d}\mathbf{M}}{\mathrm{d}t} = -\gamma(\mathbf{M} \times \mathbf{H}_{\text{eff}}) + \alpha\left[\mathbf{M} \times (\mathbf{M} \times \mathbf{H}_{\text{eff}})\right], \tag{A.1}$$

where $\mathbf{M}$ is the magnetization, $\mathbf{H}_{\text{eff}}$ is the effective magnetic field, γ is the gyromagnetic ratio, and α is the damping constant. The first term on the right of equation (A.1) is the precession term, the second term represents the damping term. The effective magnetic field $\mathbf{H}_{\text{eff}}$ includes the applied field, the anisotropy field, the exchange field, and the demagnetizing field produced by the magnetization distribution.

In Fig. A.5, the spin-valve structure is placed between two high-permeability shields, S1 and S2, for shielding the free layer from sensing magnetic fields coming from transitions not immediately underneath the free layer. The purpose of these shields is to ensure a sharp read-back voltage corresponding to the transition directly underneath the free layer.

Spin-valve heads are highly susceptible to damage caused by electrostatic discharge (ESD) [3–6]. A transient ESD current often results in physical melting of the GMR element and renders the head unusable. Even the very act of testing a spin-valve head by a voltmeter may damage the head magnetically, causing the pinned layer to become unpinned.

ESD can be avoided by properly handling the heads. Effective measures include using conductive tweezers, gloves, clothing, table benches, chairs, and floor mats. Whenever possible, spin-valve heads should be operated inside a clean room with high relative humidity. The use of ionized air blowers also significantly reduces the risk of ESD damages.

A.3.3 Perpendicular recording

Figure A.6 illustrates the designs of the perpendicular media and write head, which reveal the main differences between perpendicular and longitudinal recording. In longitudinal recording the magnetization is written parallel to the media surface, while in perpendicular recording the magnetization is oriented normally. Furthermore, perpendicular recording media employ a soft magnetic underlayer to facilitate the return of the write magnetic flux. Matched to this perpendicular recording media is a write head with two poles, one narrow for concentrating flux in the gap during writing, and another wide to receive the return flux. This return pole is constructed wide so as to complete the magnetic circuit during writing in such a way that does not disturb appreciably the previously written bits. An important modification of this write head design was proposed by M. Mallary [7,8], which incorporates high-permeability side shields to divert the undesirable fringing components of the write field to the return pole, as shown in Fig. A.7. This shielded design has the effect of increasing the magnetic field gradient at the sides of the write head, thereby enabling higher recording densities.

The advantage of perpendicular recording is twofold. First, the magnetic fields in the head gaps are used for writing rather than fring-

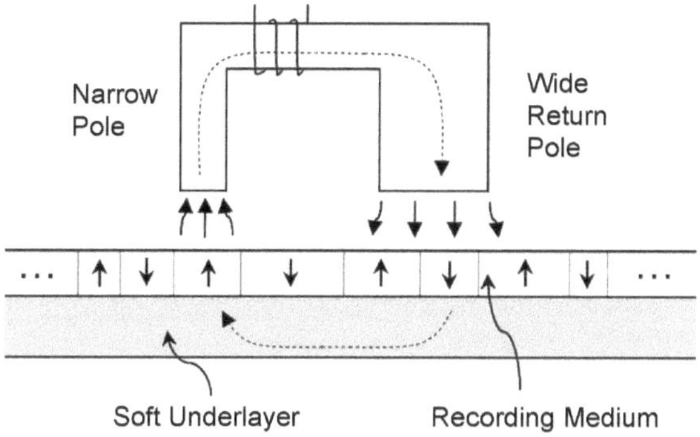

FIGURE A.6 A schematic of perpendicular recording.

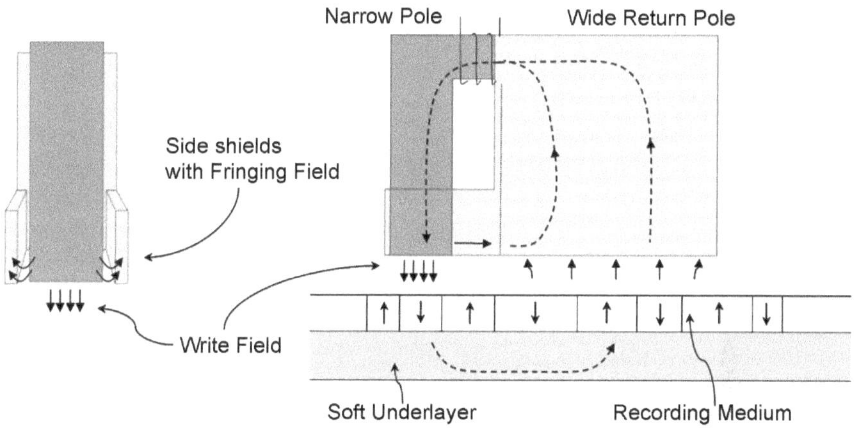

FIGURE A.7 A schematic of side-shielded write head.

ing fields, as in the case of longitudinal recording. Using the gap fields leads to the increase in the write field to be produced for a given write current and, more importantly, allows for recording on higher coercivity media than would be possible in the case of smaller magnitude fringing write fields. Second, with the magnetization oriented normal to the media surface, the demagnetizing field is controlled not by the recording density (bit size), but by the media thickness. Compared to longitudinal recording, these two factors imply a reduced impact of thermal relaxation (superparamagnetic) effects and thus lead to a higher fundamental recording density for perpendicular recording.

A.4 MOTION CONTROL SYSTEM

The mechanical motion control system of a hard drive includes a spindle, a radial actuator, head suspensions, and servomechanism. The spindle motor is usually a DC brushless (permanent magnet synchronous) motor. The radial actuator is a voice coil motor (VCM) which rotationally moves the head in the radial direction to access data tracks. It is the control of this radial motion that makes possible the fast and accurate random access of data.

A.4.1 Head suspensions

The head suspension assembly, also called a head gimbal assembly (HGA), consists of a stainless steel suspension and a gimbal located at the end of the suspension to hold the head slider. The suspension itself is mounted on a carriage called an *E-block* because it has an E-shaped side view. The combined heads, suspensions, and the E-block are called the head stack assembly (HSA).

A good suspension is designed to be hard and rigid in the in-plane direction but soft and flexible in the out-of-plane direction. The rigidity in the in-plane (or horizontal) direction minimizes tracking errors whereas the softness in the vertical direction allows the slider to follow the curve of the air flow above the spinning disk. In order to achieve a low flying height, sliders have been made smaller and smaller in dimensions, thereby reducing the force exerted by the flow of air on the sliders. Because of the *negative pressure* design of modern sliders, the flying height no longer increases with higher spindle velocity as was the case in the old *positive pressure* design. These newer sliders therefore are less sensitive to the spindle rotational speed. Consequently, the fly height is also less sensitive to the disk linear velocity variations caused by different head skew angles as the head moves across the disk surface.

A.4.2 Servomechanism

The hard disk's servomechanism is used to control the spindle servo and actuator servo systems. The goal of the spindle servo system is to maintain a constant disk rotational speed. This is realized by the spindle motor control circuit which periodically generates signals within a revolution to detect the rotational speed of the spindle motor. The detected speed is then compared with the target rotational speed and an electric signal based on the difference is sent to the frequency speed control circuit for speed adjustment.

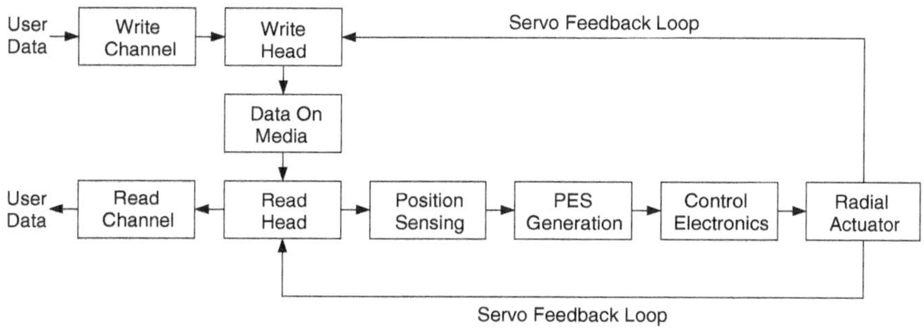

FIGURE A.8 A block diagram of the actuator servo feedback loop.

The objective of the actuator servo system is to perform *track seek* and *track follow* operations. The essence of track seek is to go to the desired track location in *a minimum time*. Once the desired track is reached, the track follow operation positions the head at *a minimum distance* from the center of this track. Since the track seek and track follow operations are quite distinct, they are handled by different control circuits. Track follow is achieved through a negative feedback loop featured in Fig. A.8.

In the figure, the PES (positional error signal) indicates the deviation between the desired head location and the current head location. It is generated by the servo electronics in response to the head position signal. This signal is in turn obtained through demodulation of the relative signal amplitudes generated by the servo bursts that are preliminarily and deliberately written in special servo sectors of the disks. These servo bursts (usually called A, B, C, and D bursts) are prewritten using high-precision *servo writers*.

The servo sectors are equally spaced in a hard disk platter with data sectors in between. Figure A.9 schematically illustrates the concept of data and servo sectors and details a generic embedded servo format used in many hard disk drives [9]. The various fields (regions) in the servo sectors contain information used by the servo electronics to correctly generate the PES. Their functions are listed in Table A.1 [9].

The following observations can be made concerning Fig. A.9. First, as one moves from the inner diameter to the outer diameter of the disk, more data sectors are present. This is called *zone-bit recording* where the disk is divided into different zones with respect to a radial position where each zone having a different number of data sectors per track. This geometrical arrangement permits the hard disk to have a uniform data density. This kind of recording is also called *variable-rate recording* because the outer tracks of the disk have a higher data rate than the inner tracks. Sec-

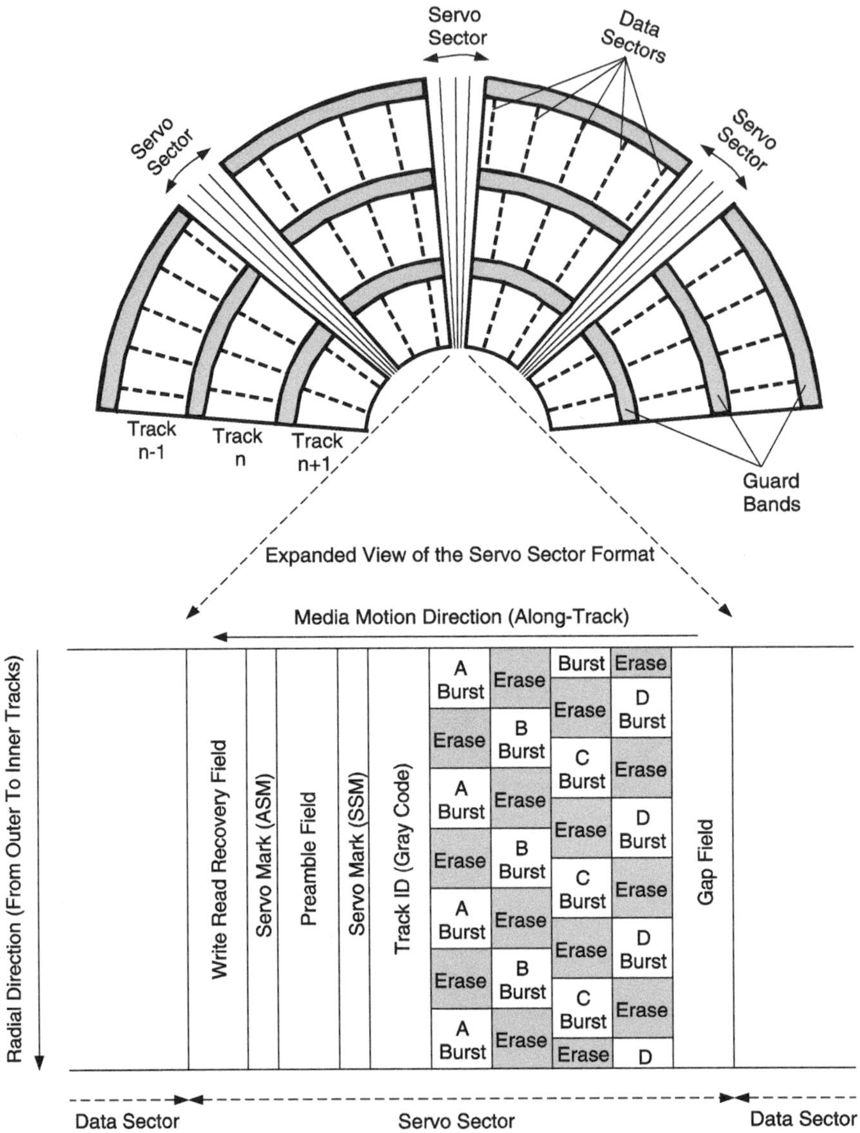

FIGURE A.9 A typical servo sector format.

ond, even though the outer tracks have more data sectors than the inner tracks, the number of servo sectors are the same for each track. Third, some data sectors are split between servo sectors. Fourth, while there are

TABLE A.1 Servo fields and their functions

Servo fields	Functions
Write read recovery	Absorb transient and stabilize the AGC
Servo mark ASM	Generate a timing for demodulating the gray code
Preamble	Synchronize the phase locked loop
Servo mark SSM	Generate a timing for demodulating the gray code
Track ID (gray code)	Contain cylinder (track) address
A, B, C, D Bursts	Used as positional signals for position demodulation
Gap	Used as a gap buffer region between servo and data

guard bands (regions with zero magnetization) between the data sectors, there are no guard bands between the servo sectors.

BIBLIOGRAPHY

[1] S.X. Wang and A.M. Taratorin, *Magnetic Information Storage Technology*, p. xv, Academic Press, 1999.

[2] J.C. Mallinson, *Magneto-Resistive and Spin Valve Heads*, Second Edition, Academic Press, 2002.

[3] J. Himle, R. Bailey, J. Hogue, A. Fishman, R. McKenzie, T. Porter, and W. Boone, "Current transients and the Guzik: A case study and methodology for qualifying a spin stand for GMR testing," *EOS/ESD Symposium*, 328 (1998).

[4] A. Wallash and Y. Kim, "Magnetic changes in GMR heads caused by electrostatic discharge," *IEEE Trans. Magn.*, **34**, 1519 (1998).

[5] M. Takahashi, T. Maeda, K. Inage, M. Sakai, H. Morita, and M. Matsuzaki, "ESD induced pinned layer reversal in spin-valve GMR heads," *IEEE Trans. Magn.*, **34**, 1522 (1998).

[6] A. Wallash, "In-situ spin stand ESD testing of giant magnetoresistive (GMR) recording heads," *EOS/ESD Symposium*, 349 (2000).

[7] M. Mallary, A. Torabi, and M. Benakli, "One terabit per square inch perpendicular recording conceptual design," *IEEE Trans. Magn.*, **38**, 1719 (2002).

[8] M. Mallary, "Vertical Magnetic Recording Arrangement," US Patent 4,656,546 (1987).

[9] *Fujitsu MPF3xxxAH Disk Drives Product Manual.*

APPENDIX B

Implementation of ISI-Removal Algorithm

In this appendix, we detail two numerical techniques that have proven to have significantly reduced the noise and improved the accuracy of the image reconstruction. The noise reduction and signal smoothing is accomplished through the exploiting of the arctangent function. The accuracy of the reconstruction is improved by using the scaling of the experimentally obtained head response function. At the end of this section, we present flow charts of the complete 1D and 2D ISI-removal algorithms.

B.1 NOISE REDUCTION BY USING THE ARCTANGENT FUNCTION

There are two potential sources of numerical errors. First, small values of $\tilde{R}(k_x)$ in Eq. (5.7) and $\tilde{R}(k_x, k_y)$ in Eq. (5.8) may amplify the noise level. Second, since differentiation of the reconstructed magnetization is needed in order to obtain the readback signal, changes in magnetization might create undesirable noise after differentiation. Due to the above reasons, some special scheme is required to suppress and remove this noise.

To this end, it has been demonstrated that the noise can be appreciably reduced by properly exploiting the properties of the arctangent function. The most salient properties of the arctangent function are that: (1) it accentuates its argument when there is a change in sign (switching) of the argument; and (2) it is grossly insensitive to changes in its argument when these changes occur outside the "switching region." Therefore, the arctangent function is a natural and effective tool for filtering of noise in the computation of the reconstructed images. It is a natural choice because magnetization patterns themselves are often modeled as the arctangent transition.

Specifically, noise can be significantly reduced if, instead of differentiating the magnetization directly, the arctangent of the magnetization is differentiated. In this way, the level of noise reduction can also be controlled by multiplying the x-component of the magnetization by a scalable number. The equation below describes this arctangent operation:

$$S_{\text{recovered}}(x) = \frac{\mathrm{d}}{\mathrm{d}x}\left[\arctan\left(\alpha M_x(x)\right)\right], \tag{B.1}$$

where α is a scalable factor that controls the level of noise reduction.

As an illustration of this approach, Fig. B.1 demonstrates the effect of the arctangent operation in reducing the noise level of the recovered readback signal of tribit patterns. Here, the thinner lines represent the readback signals of tribit patterns while the thicker lines are the recovered patterns. In the figure, the values of α go from 1 (i.e. no amplification in arctangent smoothing) in Fig. B.1(a) to some optimum value in Fig. B.1(c). As is evident, the arctangent smoothing has effectively suppressed the noise in the reconstructed readback signals.

Similar improvement in the reconstructed readback signals has also been observed in experiments on a spin-stand. In Fig. B.2 the dashed lines represent the measured patterns while the solid lines are the recovered patterns. In the figure, the values of α go from 1 (i.e. no amplification in arctangent operation) in Fig. B.2(a) to some optimum value in Fig. B.2(d). Clearly, the arctangent operation has suppressed the noise.

B.2 SCALING OF THE HEAD RESPONSE FUNCTION

It is shown in Chapter 4 that the scaling of the head response function can greatly improve the accuracy of the vectorial magnetization reconstruction. Below, similar improvement is demonstrated for scalar 1D images.

Figure B.3 demonstrates the improvement in the accuracy of the recovered tribit signals by scaling the 1D head response function (the thinner and thicker lines assume their previous meanings). When no scaling was performed (Fig. B.3(a)), the middle peaks of the tribit patterns could not be clearly discerned. However, as the head response function is gradually scaled (Fig. B.3(b) and B.3(c)), all the peaks of the tribit patterns become clearly pronounced.

Figure B.4 shows the improvement in the accuracy of the recovered tribit signals by scaling the 1D head response function in the experiments performed on a spin-stand (the dashed and solid lines assume their previous meanings). When no scaling is performed (Fig. B.4(a)), the two peaks at locations 1.2 μm and 1.27 μm cannot be clearly discerned. However, after scaling of the head response function (Fig. B.4(b) and B.4(d)), all the peaks of the tribit patterns are eventually clearly revealed.

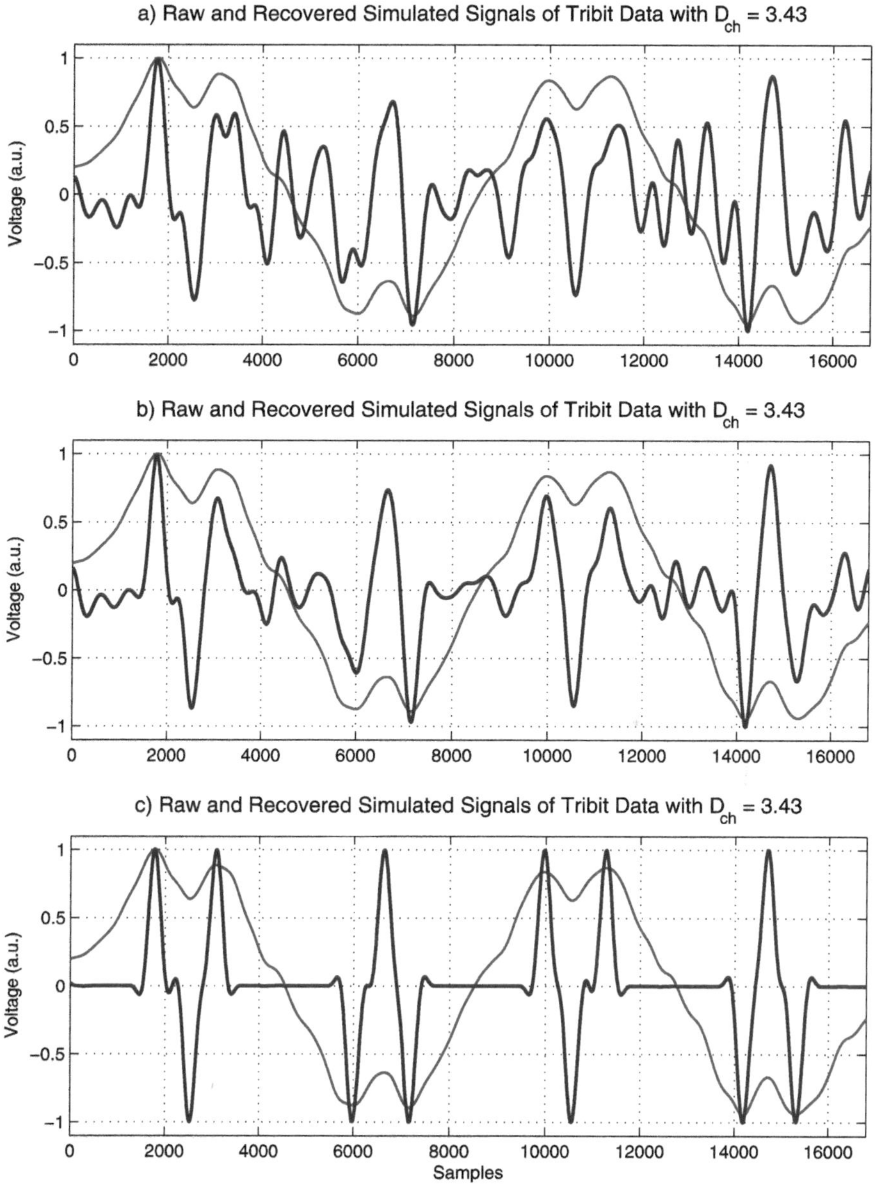

FIGURE B.1 Raw and recovered hard disk tribit patterns: with different values of α.

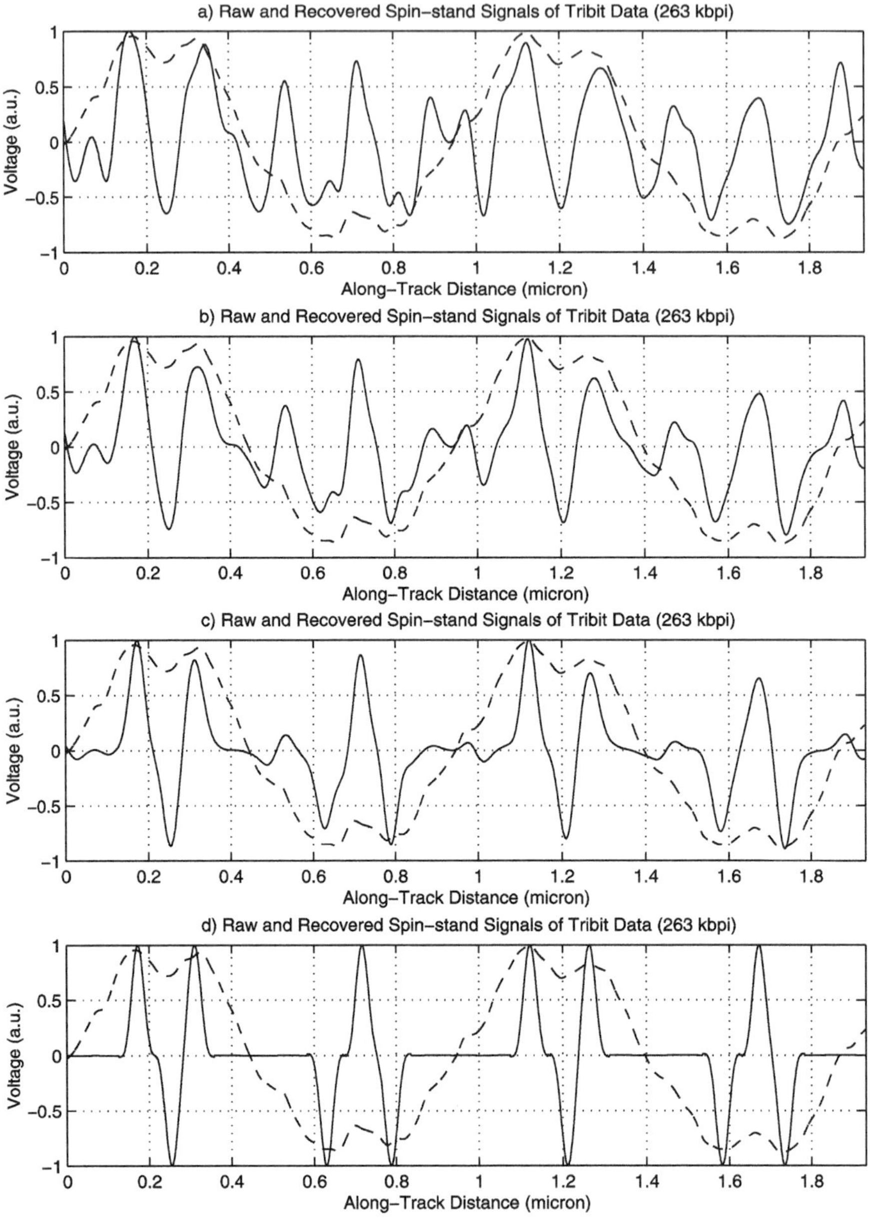

FIGURE B.2 Raw and recovered hard disk tribit patterns: with different values of α.

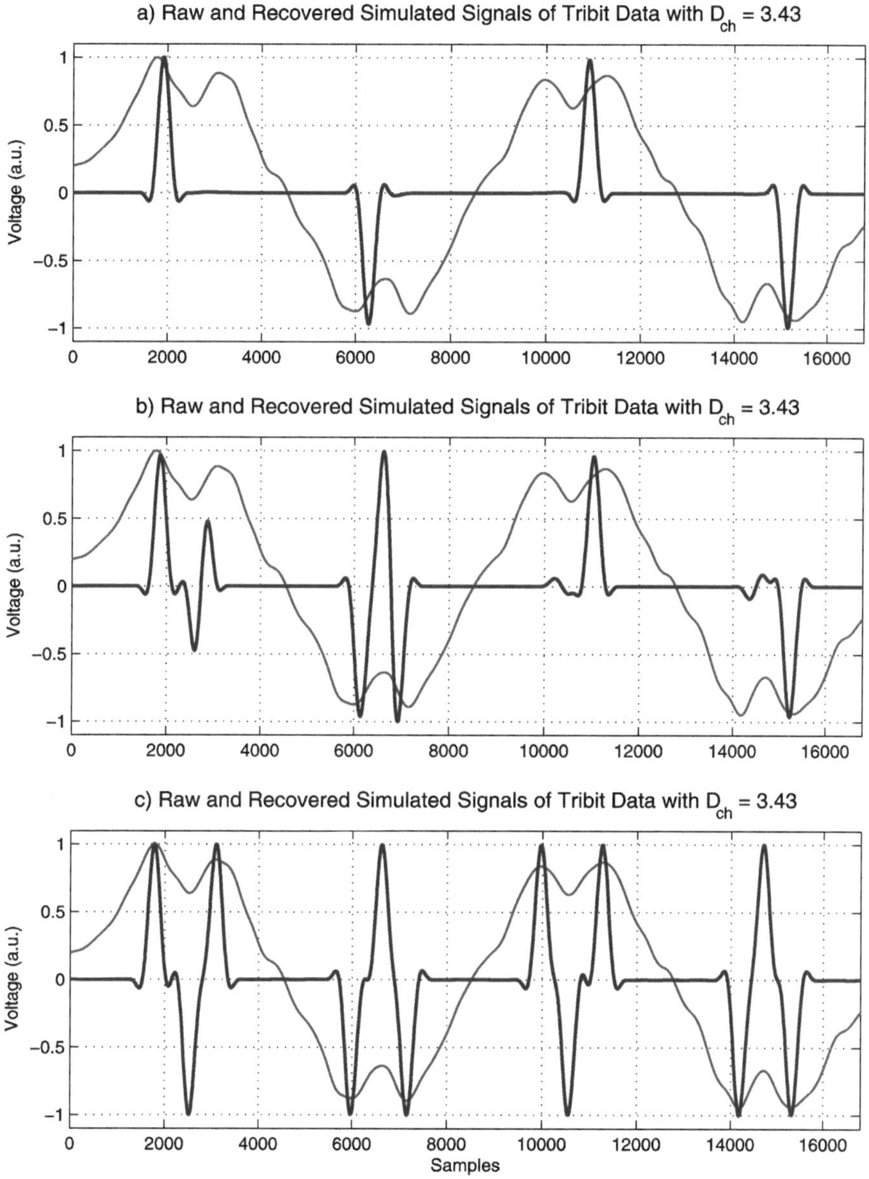

FIGURE B.3 Raw and recovered hard disk tribit patterns: with different scaling factors.

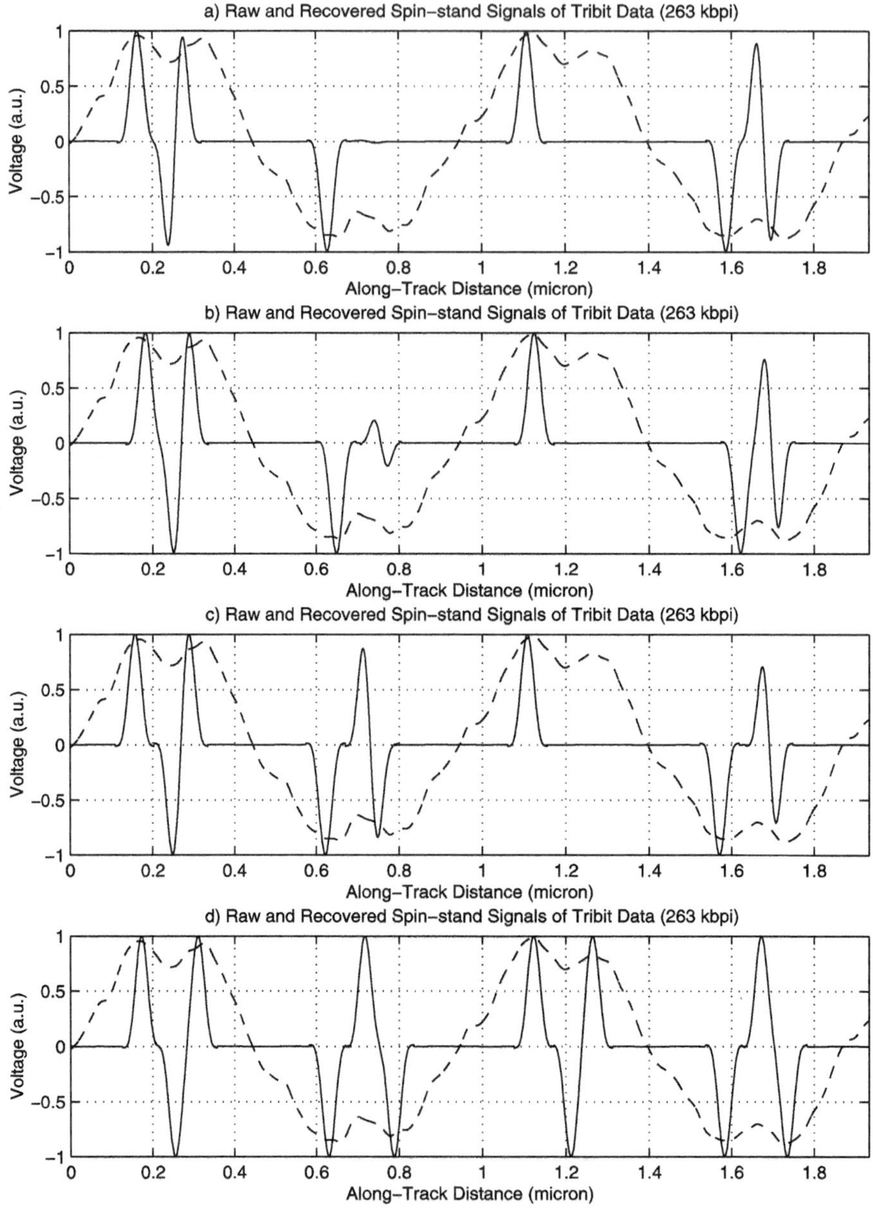

FIGURE B.4 Raw and recovered hard disk tribit patterns: with different scaling factors.

The use of the arctangent smoothing and the suitable scaling of the head response function are very instrumental in the practical implementation of the ISI-removal algorithm.

B.3 FLOW CHARTS OF THE ISI-REMOVAL ALGORITHM

Figure B.5 depicts the flow chart for the 1D ISI-removal algorithm.

First, as is indicated at block 100, the raw ISI-distorted readback signal $S(x)$ is acquired from the spin-stand imaging system. From the readback signal $S(x)$, the length of the signal, N_x, is determined, where N_x is the number of taken samples of signal $S(x)$. Next, as shown at block 300, a spatial mesh X is defined as:

$$X = \mathrm{d}x[-N_x/2 + 0.5, \ldots, N_x/2 - 0.5], \tag{B.2}$$

where $\mathrm{d}x = L_x/(N_x - 1)$ and L_x is the along-track distance over which the readback signal $S(x)$ has been acquired.

As shown in block 400, a similar mesh is defined for the frequency domain, where the frequency mesh is designated K_x. K_x is defined as:

$$K_x = (1/L_x)/X, \tag{B.3}$$

where k_x are the elements of K_x.

In Fig. B.5, it is assumed that the head response function $R(x)$ has been determined in accordance with the procedures outlined in Chapter 5. Then, as is shown at block 500, the response function $R(x)$ is scaled according to the formula:

$$R'(x) = R(\beta x), \quad \beta \in (0, 1). \tag{B.4}$$

The scaled response function $R'(x)$ is then normalized in amplitude as follows:

$$R''(x) = R'(x)/\max\left(\left|R'(x)\right|\right) \tag{B.5}$$

as is shown at block 600. At block 700, the normalized response function $R''(x)$ is centered at the origin by either delaying or advancing in space the response function $R''(x)$.

After the raw data has been acquired, and the response function scaled, normalized and centered, flow is transferred to block 800 where the Fourier transform of $R''(x)$ and $S(x)$ is performed to produce $R_{\mathrm{ft}}(k_x)$ and

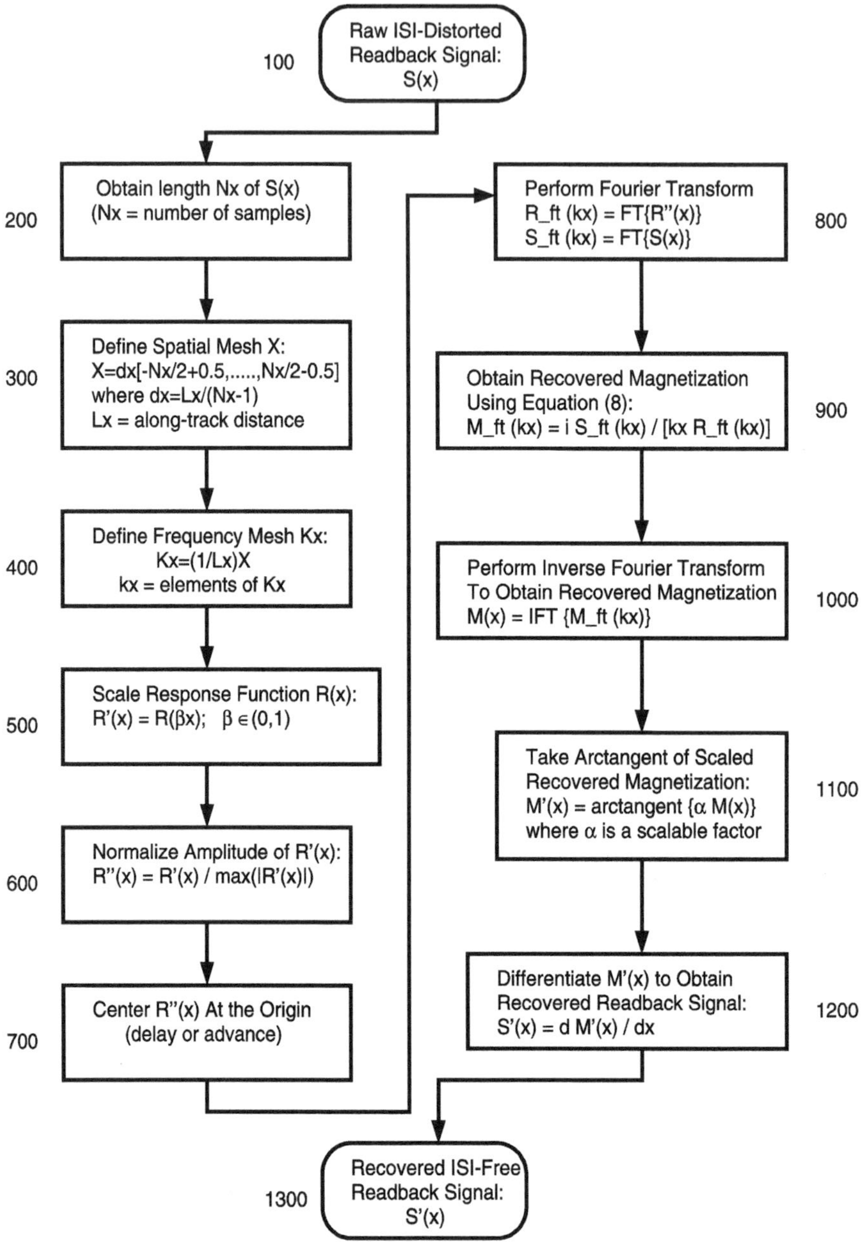

FIGURE B.5 Flow chart of the ISI-removal algorithm for the 1D case.

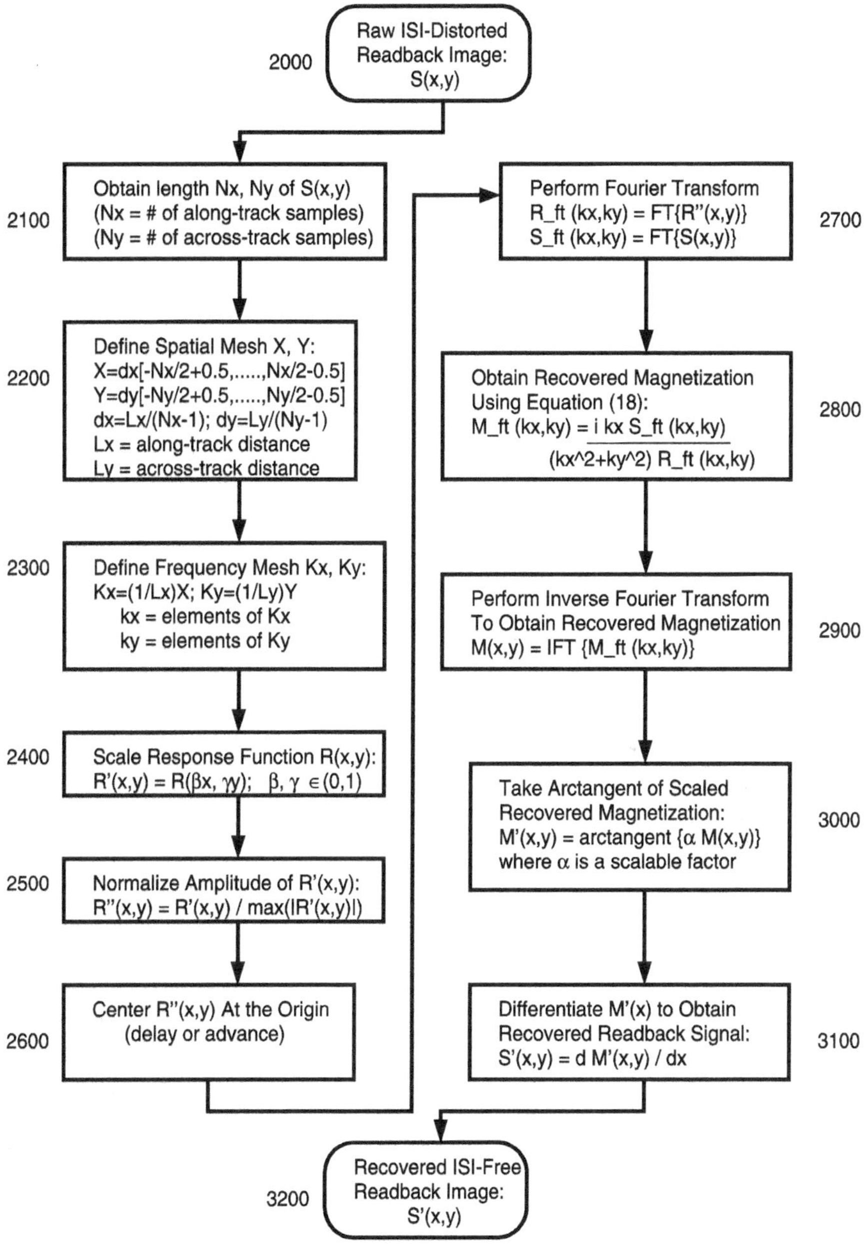

FIGURE B.6 Flow chart of the ISI-removal algorithm for the 2D case.

$S_{\text{ft}}(k_x)$, respectively. Then, as is indicated at block 900, the Fourier transform of the recovered magnetization is obtained according to the equation:

$$M_{\text{ft}}(k_x) = \frac{i\,S_{\text{ft}}(k_x)}{k_x\,R_{\text{ft}}(k_x)}. \tag{B.6}$$

The recovered magnetization in the spatial domain is then obtained by taking the inverse Fourier transform of $M_{\text{ft}}(k_x)$ as shown at block 1000.

When recovered magnetization $M(x)$ has been obtained, a noise reduction technique such as the application of the arctangent smoothing as discussed above, is applied to produce

$$M'(x) = \arctan\big(\alpha M(x)\big), \tag{B.7}$$

where α is a user-scalable factor. The smoothed signal $M'(x)$ is differentiated to produce the ISI-free readback signal according to:

$$S'(x) = \frac{\mathrm{d}}{\mathrm{d}x} M'(x) \tag{B.8}$$

as shown at block 1200. The ISI-free readback signal thus recovered is then output as $S'(x)$ as shown at block 1300.

Figure B.6 is a flow chart of the two-dimensional version of the ISI-removal algorithm. The process steps are self-explanatory in view of the previous discussion of Fig. B.5 with the obvious modifications relevant to the two-dimensional case.

APPENDIX C

Aligning Algorithm

The essence of the aligning algorithm is the shifting of the circumferentially acquired data based on the successive maximization of the inner dot products between the vectors representing circumferential data for radially adjacent tracks. The explicit algorithm of the alignment procedure for compensating the imperfection of the trigger is as follows. Assume that the scanned data is already put into a 2D-array called *scan_data*, with N_x rows and N_y columns, where N_x and N_y are the number of points in the along- and cross-track direction, respectively. Assume also that the aligned data is to be put into a 2D-array called *align_data*. In the following, "*" represents all the points in a particular dimension of an array. Then the alignment algorithm can be implemented by the software coding on the next page.

For $j = 1$ to $N_y - 1$:

Begin

- Compute the cross-correlation of $scan\_data(*, j)$ and $scan\_data(*, j + 1)$
- Find the position shift required (in terms of the number of points) in the along-track direction that corresponds to the maximum value of the computed cross-correlation
- Put the found position shift into a 1D-array called *scan_shift*, i.e. $scan\_shift(j) =$ the found position

End

- Compute cut where cut is the maximum value of the 1D-array *scan_shift*
- Initialize the 2D-array *align_data* where $align\_data = scan\_data(cut + 1 : N_x - cut, *)$

For $j = 2$ to N_y:

Begin

- $align\_data(*, j) = scan\_data(cut + 1 + scan\_shift(j) : Nx - cut + scan\_shift(j), j)$

End.

C.1 FLOW CHART OF THE ALIGNING ALGORITHM

As shown in the flow diagram of Fig. C.1, at step 120, the algorithm begins with j set to 1. At step 130, the cross-correlation between $scan\_data(*, j)$ and $scan\_data(*, j + 1)$ is computed. At step 140, the position shift re-

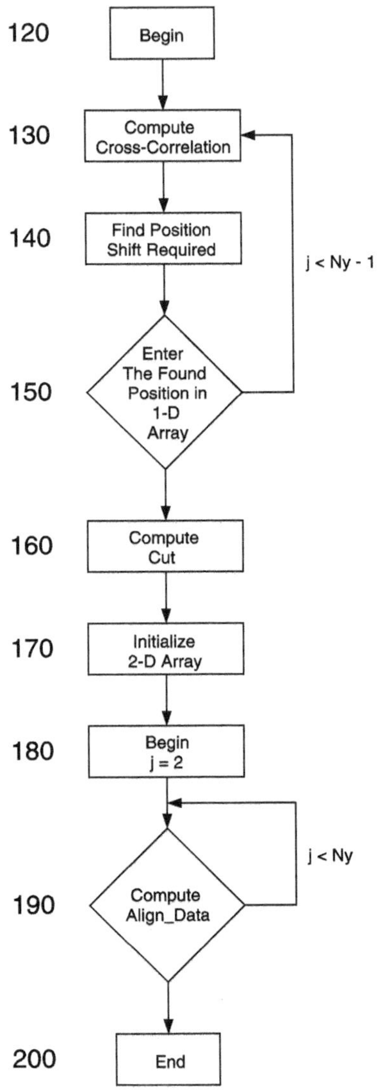

FIGURE C.1 Flow chart of alignment algorithm.

quired (in terms of the number of points) is found in the along-track direction. This corresponds to the maximum value of the computed cross-correlation, found in step 130. At step 150, the found position is placed into a one-dimensional array called *scan_shift*. For j, *scan_shift*(j) is equal to the found position. If $j = N_y - 1$, then the algorithm passes to step 160. If, however, $j < N_y - 1$, then the algorithm passes back to step 130 to repeat.

At step 160, *cut* is computed, where *cut* is the maximum value of the one-dimensional array *scan_shift*. At step 170, a two-dimensional array is initialized. This array is called *align_data* where *align_data* = *scan_data* $(cut + 1 : N_x - cut, *)$.

Following the initialization in step 170, the value of j is then set equal to 2 at step 180. At step 190, the value of *align_data*$(*, j)$ is computed. If $j = N_y$, then the array is completely filled and at step 200, the algorithm ends. However, if $j < N_y$, then the algorithm stays on step 190 to repeat.

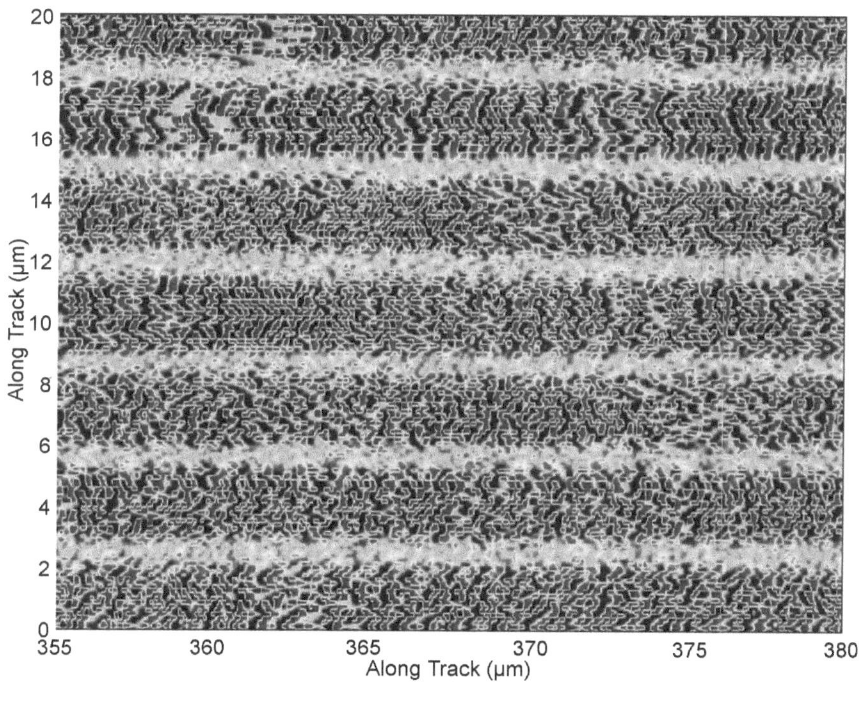

FIGURE C.2 User data before aligning.

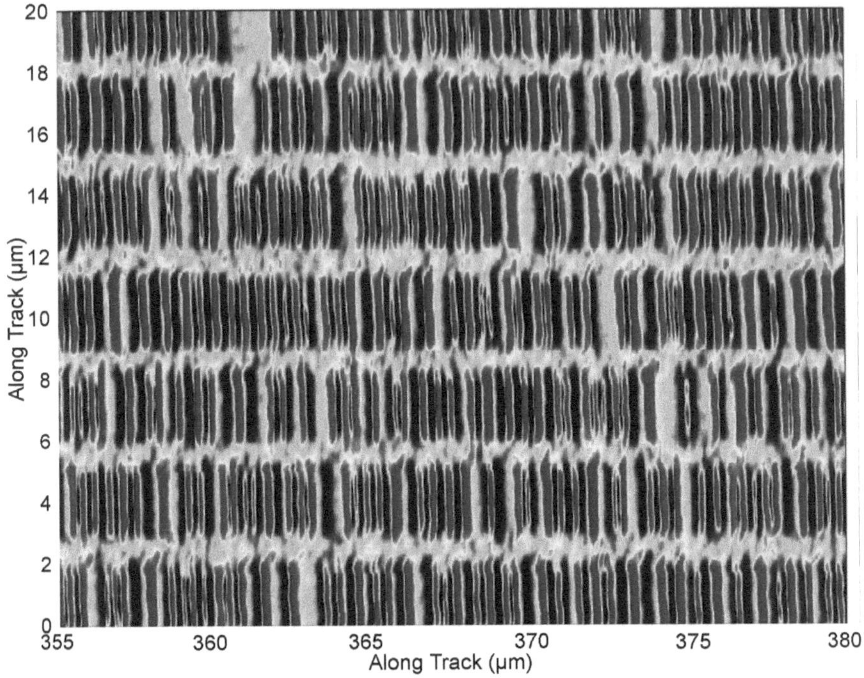

FIGURE C.3 User data after aligning.

Figures C.2 and C.3 are raw images of the user data region of a 1998 hard disk before and after alignment, respectively. The effectiveness of the alignment algorithm is clearly demonstrated.

Subject Index

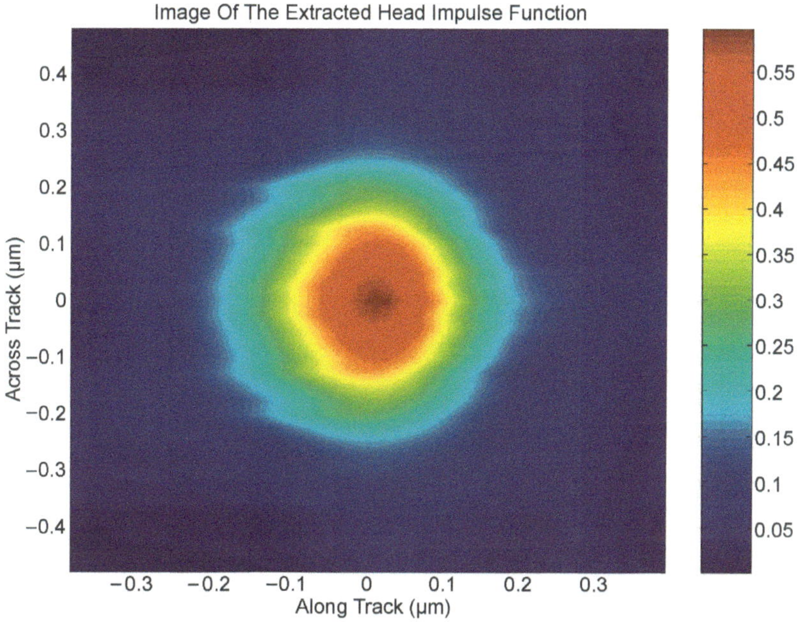

PLATE 1 See B/W figure plus complete legend on p. 47.

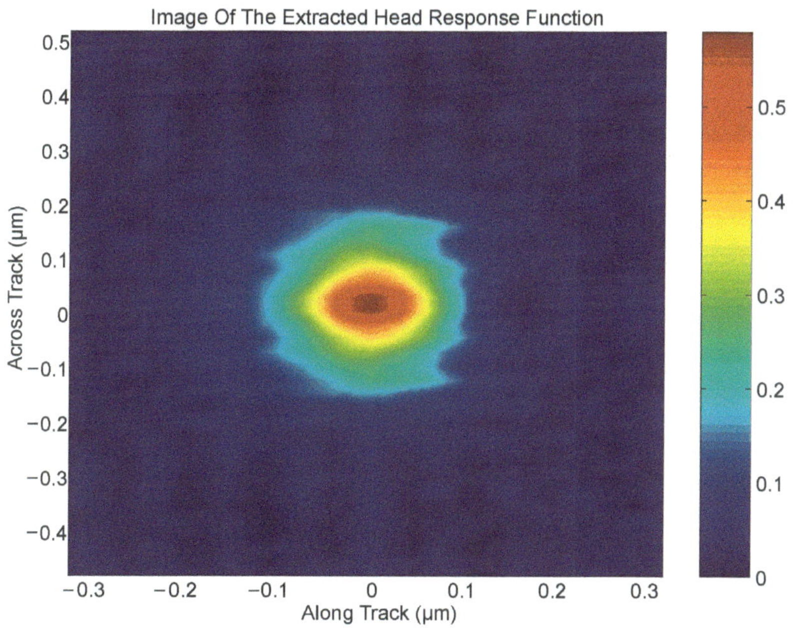

PLATE 2 See B/W figure plus complete legend on p. 48.

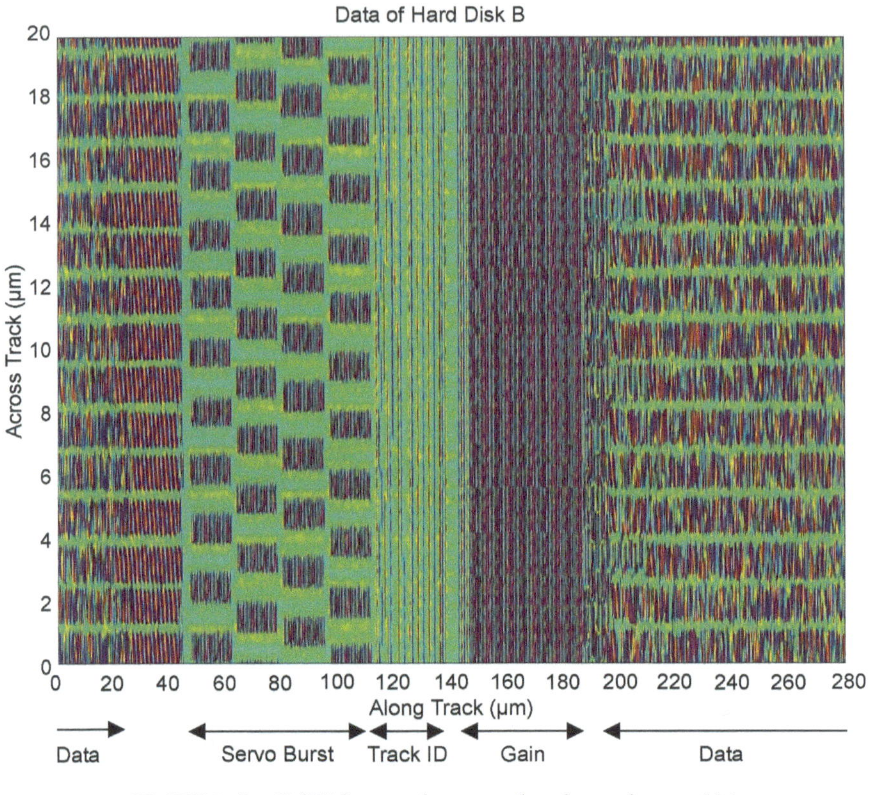

PLATE 3 See B/W figure plus complete legend on p. 116.

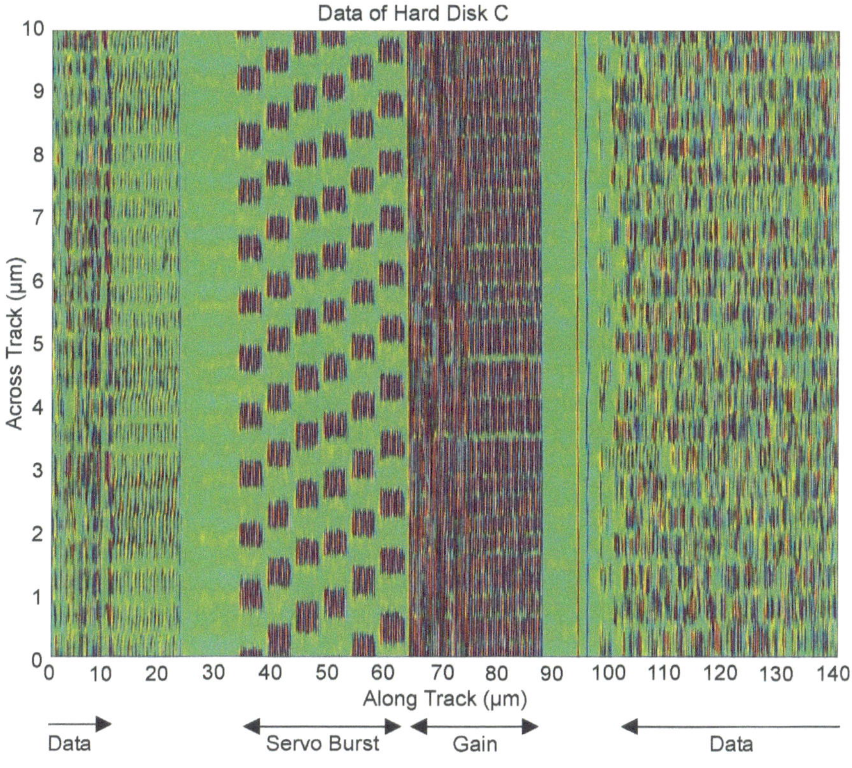

PLATE 4 See B/W figure plus complete legend on p. 117.

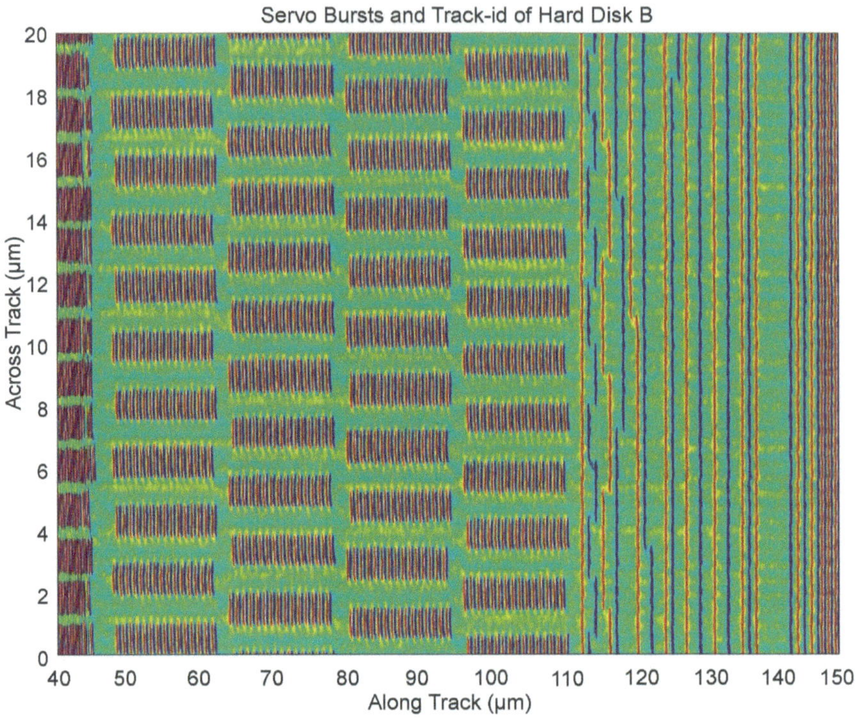

PLATE 5 See B/W figure plus complete legend on p. 123.

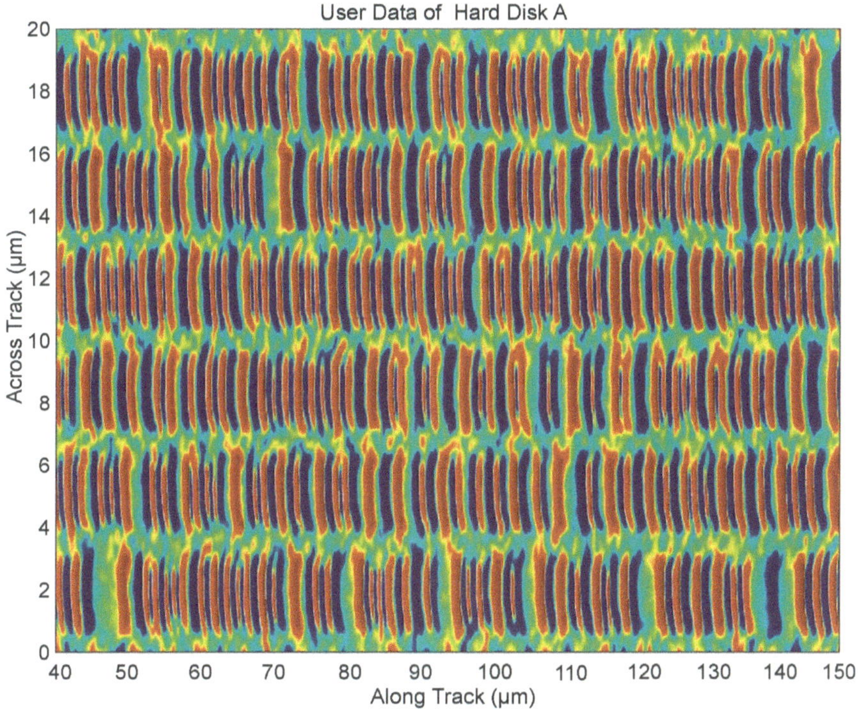

PLATE 6 See B/W figure plus complete legend on p. 124.

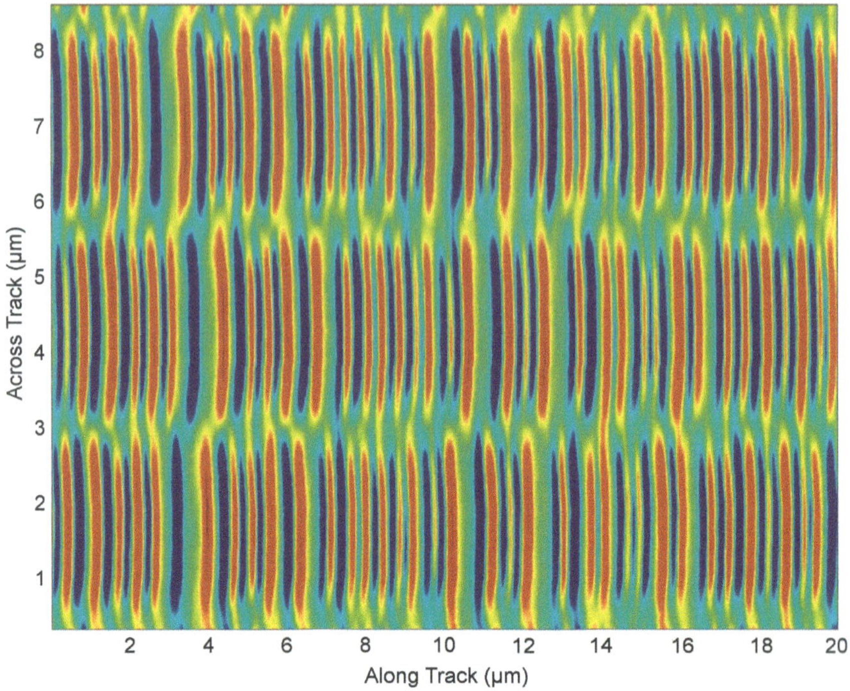

PLATE 7 See B/W figure plus complete legend on p. 125.

PLATE 8 See B/W figure plus complete legend on p. 140.

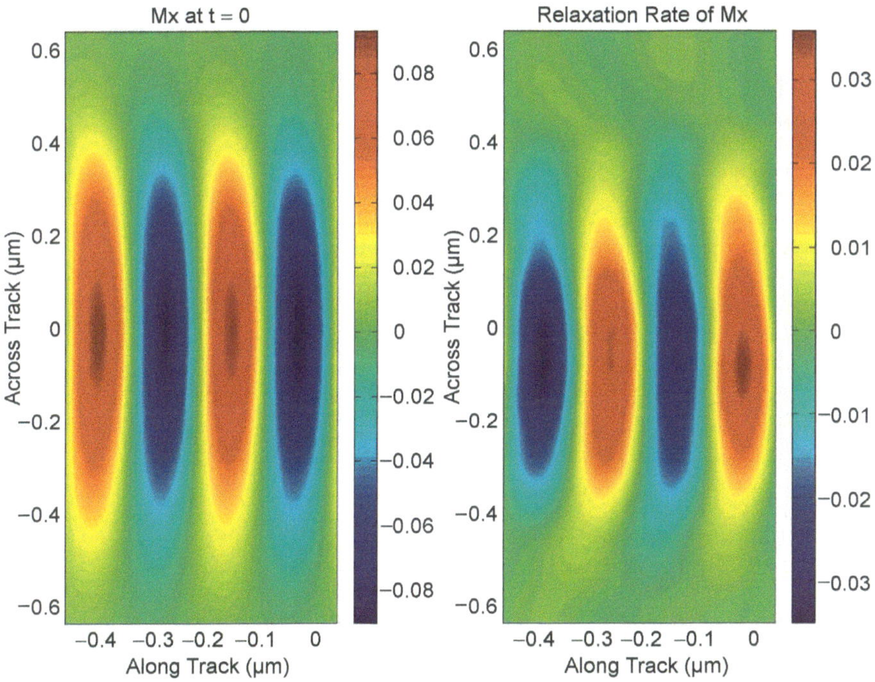

PLATE 9 See B/W figure plus complete legend on p. 178.

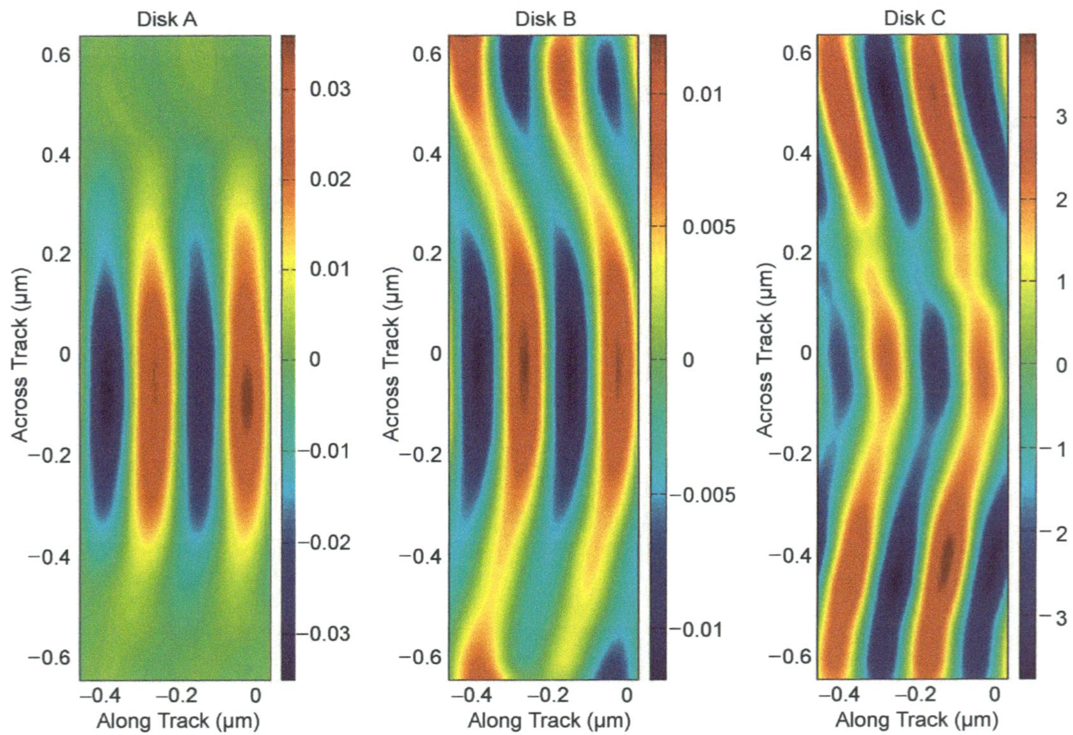

PLATE 10 See B/W figure plus complete legend on p. 180.

FSC
www.fsc.org
MIX
Papier | Fördert
gute Waldnutzung
FSC® C083411

Kolibri 360 GmbH
Ferdinand-Jühlke-Straße 7
99095 Erfurt, Deutschland
produktsicherheit@kolibri360.de